Social Problems

Social Problems
Globalization in the Twenty-First Century

R. Dean Peterson
Delores F. Wunder
Harlan L. Mueller

College of DuPage

Prentice Hall, Upper Saddle River, New Jersey 07458

Library of Congress Cataloging-in-Publication Data
Peterson, Robert Dean.
Social problems : globalization in the twenty-first century / Robert Dean Peterson, Delores F. Wunder, Harlan L. Mueller.
p. cm.
Includes bibliographical references and index.
ISBN 0-13-146895-2
1. Social problems—Cross-cultural studies. 2. Social problems—United States. 3. International cooperation. I. Wunder, Delores F. II. Mueller, Harlan L. III. Title.
HN17.5.P49 1999
361.1—dc21 98-40360
CIP

Editorial Director: Charlyce Jones Owen
Editor-in-Chief: Nancy Roberts
Senior Acquisitions Editor: John Chillingworth
Editorial Assistant: Allison Westlake
Development Editor-in-Chief: Susanna Lesan
Development Editor: Marilyn Miller
AVP, Director of Production and Manufacturing: Barbara Kittle
Managing Editor: Ann Marie McCarthy
Production Liaison: Fran Russello
Project Manager: Linda B. Pawelchak
Manufacturing Manager: Nick Sklitsis
Prepress and Manufacturing Buyer: Mary Ann Gloriande
Creative Design Director: Leslie Osher
Art Director: Nancy Camuso-Wells
Interior Designer: Carmela Pereira
Cover Designer: Ximena P. Tamvakopoulos
Cover Art: Nicholas Wilton/SIS Inc.
Director of Marketing: Gina Sluss
Marketing Manager: Christopher DeJohn
Line Art Coordinator: Guy Ruggiero
Electronic Art Creation: Asterisk Group, Inc.
Director, Image Resource Center: Lori Morris-Nantz
Photo Research Supervisor: Melinda Lee Reo
Image Permission Supervisor: Kay Dellosa
Photo Research: Karen Pugliano
Copy Editor: Kathleen Babbitt
Proofreader: Nancy Menges

This book was set in 10/12 Meridien
by Publications Development Company of Texas
and was printed and bound by Banta Company.
The cover was printed by Banta Company.

Credits may be found on page 445, which constitutes an extension of the copyright page.

Printed in the United States of America
10 9 8 7 6 5 4 3

ISBN 0-13-146895-2

Prentice-Hall International (UK) Limited, London
Prentice-Hall of Australia Pty. Limited, Sydney
Prentice-Hall Canada Inc., Toronto
Prentice-Hall Hispanoamericana, S.A., Mexico
Prentice-Hall of India Private Limited, New Delhi
Prentice-Hall of Japan, Inc., Tokyo
Prentice-Hall of Asia Pte. Ltd., Singapore
Editora Prentice-Hall do Brasil, Ltda., Rio de Janeiro

Brief Contents

CONTENTS

PART THREE GLOBALIZATION, VICTIMIZATION, AND EMPOWERMENT

Boxes

CHAPTER 8

CHAPTER 9

CHAPTER 10

CHAPTER 11

CHAPTER 12

PREFACE

THEMES AND RATIONALE

Several years ago, our college set forth to "internationalize the curriculum." As part of this new emphasis, we changed our traditional Social Problems course to a class called "Issues of Contemporary Societies." The idea was to teach social problems from a crosscultural perspective. The new course was designed not only to help students understand issues in our own society, but also to enable them to see how similar issues played out in other societies.

This text grows out of the search for an appropriate book for the "Issues of Contemporary Societies" class. At the time, the available options were texts in anthropology, international politics, geography, and the like. We soon concluded that there was a real need for a sociologically based book focusing on the interplay between global issues and U.S. social problems.

As we began researching and writing this text, we became convinced that something radically new is occurring on the world scene. We are at one of those moments in history when we are in the midst of a major paradigm shift. Literally, a new age is emerging to replace the age of modernism that has dominated global ideological, social, economic, and political structures over the last 500 years. This new age is variously called postmodernism, the information age, the postindustrial era, and the global village. However, *globalization* is the term that best encapsulates the diverse, and frequently conflicting, trends recognized all across the intellectual spectrum of academic disciplines.

Globalization is a process that goes far beyond objective worldwide connections, such as increased international travel, rapid and dependable global communications, and the emergence of supranational organizations like the United Nations, the World Bank, the World Trade Organization, and Human Rights Watch International. The globalization process also restructures our socially constructed worlds and, at the most basic subjective level, changes our self-identity. As a result, we believe it is imperative that we help students achieve a fundamental understanding of globalization. Such an understanding is not only essential to assessing and addressing worldwide problems; it is also the key to alleviating detrimental situations in our own society. Our main goal in writing this book has been to create a text that would not simply tack on international connections to U.S. social problems but would be constructed from the premise that most, if not all, of the social problems we face are immersed in a global context. Since we began this project, other texts in the field have examined similar social problems in other societies from a historical perspective and from the macrolevel, as we do. But we believe that what makes this text unique is that we have started from the premise that to understand and deal with contemporary social problems in our society and those we expect to encounter in the next century, we must put the globalization process in its rightful place at the center of today's world and then rigorously assess each problem from that perspective. It is for this reason that we have titled this book *Social Problems: Globalization in the Twenty-First Century.*

Although basic social problems texts often emphasize comparative theory, our experience in teaching confirms students' need for a thorough grounding in the day-to-day events of social life, the forces that influence them, and the historical matrix out of which today's news grows. This is especially the case when dealing with the unfamiliar but important events and organizations shaping global social interaction. We make a concerted effort in this book to describe and delineate many of these interactions. We also take seriously the fact that present social and cultural processes can be understood only when we have a grasp of their historical roots. We present material on antecedents of contemporary occurrences and issues as appropriate.

The specific issues addressed in this book were chosen in an informed fashion. Each issue is part of an interrelated set of problems that form key pieces of the larger puzzle of globalization, social problems, and human survival. Although for the sake of analysis, issues are treated in more or less discrete chapters; in real life they must be dealt with as a unified whole. For this reason, this book proposes much more than a piecemeal, "Band-Aid" approach to assessing and possibly solving social problems. It argues that the globalization process, with its attendant difficulties, demands a rethinking of politics, religion, gender relations, economics, and, indeed, the relation of the human sociosphere to the ecological biosphere. Fortunately, our analysis reveals that such a rethinking is occurring. Although we would like to say that the twenty-first century offers a bright future, we cannot. We do conclude, however, that there is reason for hope.

Structure of This Text

With these thoughts in mind, we use the first chapter to present the themes necessary to form a viable frame of reference for analyzing global issues and national problems. Chapter 1 begins with a brief overview of basic sociological concepts, such as the sociological imagination. We then turn our attention to the nature of social problems. We next address the question, "What makes an issue a *global* problem?" We find a solution to this enigma in a fundamental conflict between the sociosphere (the realm of human activity) and the biosphere (the ecological support systems that maintain all life on this planet, including human existence).

A discussion of the emergence of modernism in Chapter 1 also provides the background for understanding the sweeping changes produced by globalization. We summarize the complexity of the globalization process by focusing on five themes illuminating the impact of globalization. The need for an ecological sociology and the significance of the emergence of global civil society are introduced. We deal with difficulties associated with pluralism by presenting the United Nations Universal Declaration of Human Rights as a minimal standard to be used in determining the "desired state" and in defining the outcomes to be sought when dealing with global and national social problems.

Chapters 2 through 4, which compose Part One, "Negotiating the New Global Culture," discuss in a historical context three aspects of our world today where this new interconnectedness has affected social problems: human rights, religion, and science and technology. In each of these arenas, globalization has impacted old social problems, created new problems, posed new dilemmas, and suggested new solutions for our generation and future generations. On completing Part One, students should have a wider appreciation for the interconnectedness of societal problems and how profoundly the emergence of globalization has influenced not only social problems, but even the way that we view them and our relation to the world itself.

Chapters 5, 6, 7, and 8 compose Part Two, "Globalization and Changing Institutions." These chapters explore the basic idea of the global commons—that we are all citizens of the earth, sharing its resources and its problems. It follows that nations must act in concert with each other to protect the global commons. From this perspective, we show how the population rises and how the urbanization process has influenced population shifts, leading to the endangerment of the global commons by producing a world with too many people and too few resources (5). We next examine, from the same crosscultural perspective, how we are depleting the global commons through destruction of our environment (6). Globalization has also been a powerful factor in creating power shifts and possibly a new world order, with their accompanying social problems (7). In the economic arena, the effects of globalization are widespread, ranging from widening gaps between rich and poor to the changing nature of work (8).

Part Three, "Globalization, Victimization, and Empowerment," first looks at the effects of globalization on women, children, and the family in our own society and the rest of the world (9). We next explore globalization's influence on health and education (10) and on minorities (11). Part Three ends with an exploration of violence in today's global society (12). The Epilogue draws together theoretical, human rights, and practical threads. Here readers are challenged to imagine the future, seeing it as the breeding ground for an innovative "culture" for the twenty-first century, a culture in which the pressing needs of humankind can possibly be effectively addressed.

Features

A major feature of this book is that we carry the underlying constructs introduced in the first chapter throughout the text. We further develop relevant theoretical concepts in the three part introductions.

At the end of each chapter, we again return to the key themes presented in Chapter 1 to assess the situation and explore the options available for dealing with social issues. Options are assessed for their practical strengths and weaknesses, their human rights implications, and how they interact with the theoretical themes introduced in the first chapter.

To help students more easily grasp the themes of this text and come away with a deeper understanding of the true nature of contemporary social problems, we have included a number of instructional tools. Our book includes pictures, maps, and graphs offering visually attractive means of reinforcing key information. Scenarios that humanize the large issues brought up open each chapter. We also have included several types of boxes throughout the text. "Human Faces of . . ." boxes provide students with opportunities to see real-life consequences of the social forces and issues being discussed. "Contemporary Dialogue" boxes afford students opportunities to see contrasting views on issues. At the end of each dialogue box, we have introduced questions to encourage students to use critical thinking to explore options other than the ones presented in the dialogue. "FYI" boxes give readers the opportunity to review materials that furnish more in-depth analysis of ideas presented in the main text or to learn about significant side issues related to the conditions detailed in each chapter. At the end of each chapter, chapter summaries briefly highlight all the main points and "Thinking Critically" questions encourage students to apply their new understandings. Finally, every chapter enumerates books and web sites that provide students with resources for further study.

We have designed *Social Problems: Globalization in the Twenty-First Century* to be cutting-edge enough to communicate a new matrix for teaching and understanding social issues. At the same time, we have tried to make our book always stimulating and accessible to students. We have tried to keep this text closely enough related to more traditional approaches to social problems to make it an evolution of, not a radical break from, more standard texts. Although we make appropriate use of materials from the natural sciences, other social sciences, and the humanities, this text is thoroughly rooted in the sociological perspective and sociological theory. We trust that students and teachers alike will find *Social Problems: Globalization in the Twenty-First Century* to be a powerful tool for preparing for the global society of the future.

Supplements for Students

STUDY GUIDE (0-13-643172-0). This carefully written guide helps students better understand the material presented in the text. Each chapter consists of chapter summaries, definitions of key terms/concepts, critical thinking exercises geared to the questions in the text, and self-test questions that are page referenced to the text.

SOCIOLOGY ON THE INTERNET (0-13-096274-0). This brief guide introduces students to the origin and innovations behind the Internet and provides clear strategies for navigating the complexity of the Internet and World Wide Web. Exercises within and at the end of the chapters allow students to practice searching for the myriad of resources available to the student of sociology. This supplementary book is free to students when packaged with Peterson, Wunder, and Mueller's *Social Problems: Globalization in the Twenty-First Century.* Please see your Prentice Hall sales representative for shrink-wrap options.

THE NEW YORK TIMES/PRENTICE HALL THEMES OF THE TIMES, Social Problems. This student newspaper features recent clippings from the *New York Times* that relate to topics discussed in the text. Supplied to each student free, it is updated once a year. It can also be packaged with the text at no additional charge.

Supplements for Instructors

INSTRUCTOR'S RESOURCE MANUAL (0-13-642844-4). This essential instructor's tool includes detailed chapter outlines, teaching objectives, discussion questions, classroom activities, and additional resources.

TEST ITEM FILE (0-13-642919-X). This carefully prepared manual consists of over 1,000 questions (multiple-choice, true/false, fill-in, and essay). Each question is page referenced to the text.

PRENTICE HALL CUSTOM TEST. This computerized test item file allows you to create your own personalized exams. You can create alternate versions of the same test, add your own questions and instructions, as well as print out an answer key.

DOS PH Custom Test: (0-13-642968-8)

WIN PH Custom Test: (0-13-643024-4)

MAC PH Custom Test (0-13-642984-X)

PRENTICE HALL COLOR TRANSPARENCIES SOCIAL PROBLEMS (0-13-619800-7). Full-color illustrations, charts, and other visual materials have been selected to make up this useful lecture tool.

ABCNEWS ABC NEWS/PRENTICE HALL VIDEO LIBRARY. Selected video segments from award-winning ABC News programs such as *Nightline, ABC World News Tonight/American Agenda,* and *20/20* accompany topics featured in the text. Please contact your local Prentice Hall sales representative for more details.

Volume V: Social Problems I (0-13-437823-7)

Volume IX: Social Problems II (0-13-095774-7)

Acknowledgments

We are indebted to the following reviewers who offered their time, insight, and suggestions, many of which have been incorporated into the final manuscript:

Brian Aldrich
Winona State University

Thomas Arcaro
Elon College

Patricia Atchison
Colorado State University

Chet Ballard
Valdosta State University

Arturo Biblarz
Pacific Lutheran University

Carole A. Campbell
California State University

Phillip Davis
Georgia State University

Margaret Ksander
Onondaga Community College

David Olday
Moorhead State University

Robert Perry
Johnson Community College

Edward Ponczek
Harper College

Rita Sakitt
Suffolk Community College

We would also like to thank the following people at Prentice Hall, each of whom has made significant contributions toward the preparation of this book: Editorial Director, Charlyce Jones Owen; Editor-in-Chief, Nancy Roberts; Senior Acquisitions Editor, John Chillingworth; Development Editor-in-Chief: Susanna Lesan; Editorial Assistant, Allison Westlake; Development Editor, Marilyn Miller; Editor, Leslie Carr; Project Manager, Linda B. Pawelchak; Art Director, Nancy Camuso-Wells; Interior Designer, Carmela Pereira; Cover Designer, Ximena P. Tamvakopoulos, Line Art Coordinator, Guy Ruggiero; Photo Research, Karen Pugliano, Electronic Art Creation, Asterisk Group, Inc.; Copy Editor, Kathleen Babbitt; and Proofreader, Nancy Menges.

R. Dean Peterson
Delores F. Wunder
Harlan L. Mueller

College of DuPage
Glen Ellyn, IL

About the Authors

Photo by Gene Sladek, College of DuPage

R. Dean Peterson was born and raised in East Texas. He received a bachelor's and two master's degrees from Baylor University and earned his Ph.D. from St. Louis University. He has more than 20 years of teaching experience at the college and university levels. Courses that he has frequently taught include Sociology, Marriage and the Family, and Issues of Contemporary Societies (Social Problems). Dr. Peterson came to the College of DuPage as the associate dean of the Social and Behavioral Sciences. After several years in that position, he returned to his first love—the classroom. He is currently professor of sociology and religious studies at the College of DuPage. Among other works, Dr. Peterson has published *A Concise History of Christianity.* Dr. Peterson and his wife Connie have two grown children, both of whom majored in sociology in college.

Delores F. Wunder has nearly 20 years of teaching experience, primarily at church-affiliated four-year colleges. She is currently associate professor at the College of DuPage in suburban Chicago. Dr. Wunder earned her doctorate in sociology from Michigan State University. Her areas of interest include inequality, gender, minorities, and world systems.

Harlan L. Mueller was raised as an Air Force brat and did tours of duty in the territory of Alaska, in Florida, and in West Germany. He spent his first two years of college at the University of Maryland in Munich, Germany. Then he attended the University of Illinois in Urbana, where, in the 1960s, he got involved in the antiwar movement. He went on to receive his bachelor's and master's degrees in sociology from the University of Illinois in Urbana. Since 1970, he has taught sociology at the College of DuPage. Professor Mueller pursues a wide range of interests, including science and spirituality, Hindu and Buddhist thought, consciousness studies, near-death experiences, and interfaith dialogue. At present, he lives with his wife and her two children and their dog Lucas.

Social Problems

CHAPTER ■ ONE

The Sociological Perspective, Global Problems, and Globalization

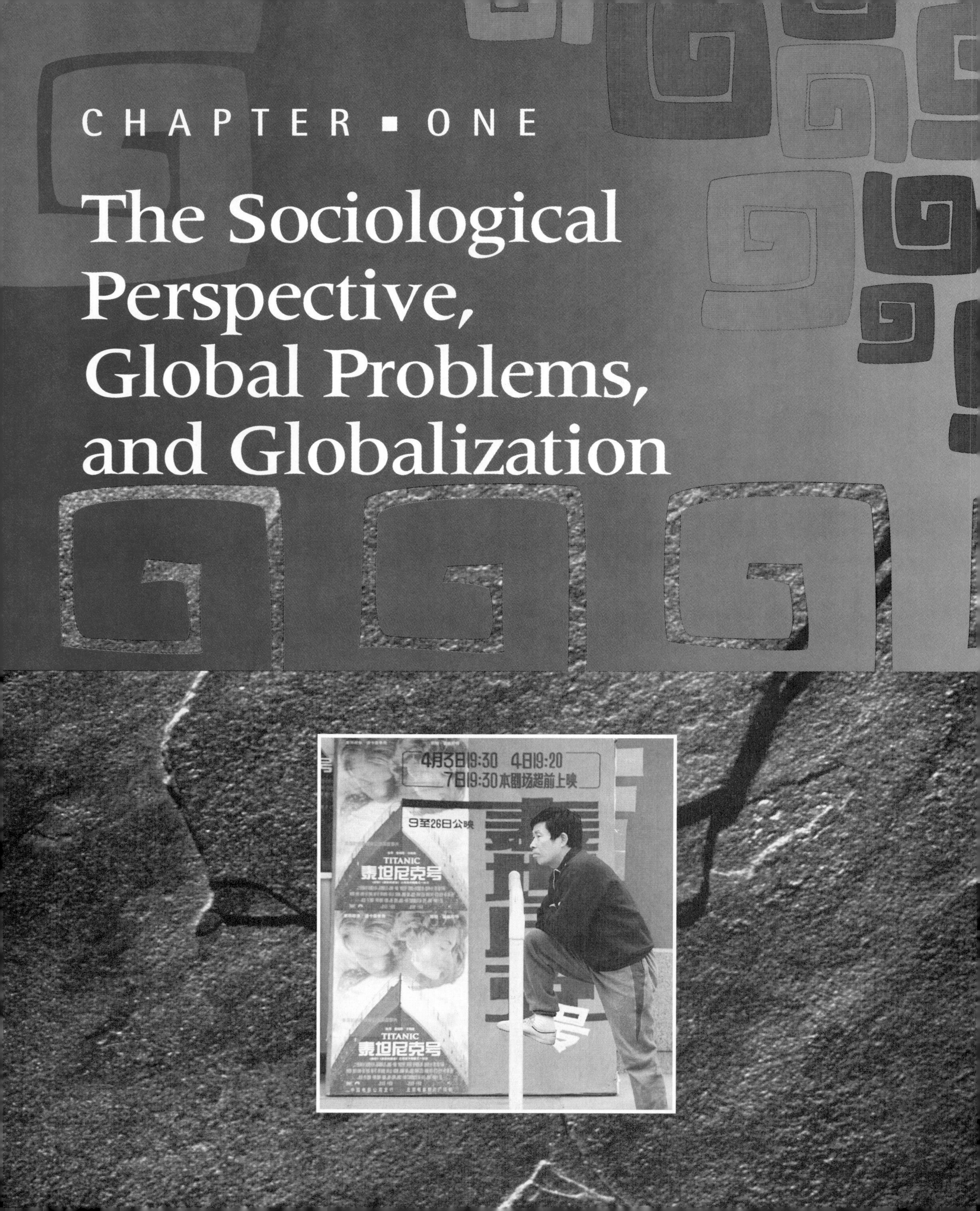

"Español. The company-sponsored course promises I am going to learn Español. In just 12 weeks I will be able to speak Spanish well enough to negotiate a business meeting in Peru.

I'm game for learning new lingo. Latin American work assignments could be in my future. However, the promise of knowing more than how to order a cold beer after just 24 lessons reminds me of the claim, 'Flat abs in 30 days.'

Steve, the English-speaking Berlitz instructor, tells the class we will succeed if we follow the program. I knew there was a catch. The program. Total immersion, repetition, tapes and picture books. No written words allowed in this learning process.

Jose, the real instructor, stands silently to the side. Steve says Jose may only speak in the target language. Jose will teach us words for images and actions using oversized picture books. We will listen, repeat, respond and role play. No one mentioned role playing before. I'll do it to be fluent, but I start to sweat.

Jose introduces himself—I think. His words are to our ears what headlights are to a deer crossing the road.

Decisive managers turn into startled students in face of Jose's Spanish. Who cares about fluency, just tell me how to yell 'help!' He indicates he wants a response by waving his arm as if he could pull the right words out of us. He waves and pulls until we finally understand it's our time to speak, 'Mi nombre es Julia.'

'Bueno,' he responds. Great. I made it through my name.

Next comes counting. 'Uno, dos, trrray,' I say. He waves his hands and says something like 'traysss.'

'TRRRAY,' I repeat.

'Traysss,' he waves again. I realize instead of saying three I'm saying 'very' with a very nice French accent. Who would have thought I could remember how to trill my r's like the French? Certainly not my French teacher.

Jose tries to show me where my r's should be originating—somewhere between throaty French and mouthy English. I count again with mixed results. Uno, dos, tres (YEAH!), quatro, cinco, six, seven, ocho, something that sounds like nuevo but with more of a "b" sound than a "v" and ten.

We move to the picture book family—Miguel, Ana, Lucia, and Alberto. 'Es este Miguel?' Jose asks, pointing to Alberto. I want to say, 'No, that's not Miguel,' but cannot find the Spanish words.

'How do you say "confused?"' I ask in English, only to be reminded no English is allowed.

Jose moves to a map of Latin America and points to unmarked land masses. With time I am sure I will be able to discern Cuba from Puerto Rico. Once again my French trill interferes. Let's just say I shouldn't ask for directions to Peru and expect to get there.

Then Jose asks, 'Is Buenos Aires the capital of Chile?' Of course not, I think.

But then I wonder. Thinking in Spanish makes me wonder about everything. I wonder if mistaking Ecuador for Venezuela would derail my career or just my luggage.

Will I ruin business deals by speaking Spanish with a French accent or just sound multilingual? Will I ever learn Spanish or should I ask for a domestic assignment now?

I leave class with many tapes and a couple of revelations: (1) Teaching this old dog a new trick is going to take longer than a short course; and (2) I really need a course for the geographically disadvantaged.

Oh well, as they say in French 'que sera, sera.' Or is that Italian?"

Source: Julie Davis. "To Learn the Lingo, You Gotta Get with *el programa. Chicago Tribune,* May 31, 1998: 6.1.

American Problems and the Global Community

This vignette illustrates a major theme of this book: Although Americans often choose to remain ignorant of the fact, we are living in a progressively global community. That is, many lifestyle choices, concerns, and problems we see as uniquely "ours" are actually immersed in an international context. Consequently, U.S. problems are not only often "caused by" conditions abroad—or at the very least have parallels in other countries—but are frequently aggravated by planetwide forces. Conversely, problems in other parts of the world are often related to the political and economic policies of the United States and the lifestyle choices of ordinary American citizens. Whether we like it or not, the nations of the world are both interrelated (connected to one another) and interdependent (rely on one another).

This fact is recognized in the popular media by phrases like "the global village," which refers to the perception that modern communications technology has brought people in widely separated places so close together that the entire planet seems like one village, or common community. That we are now a global community explains why when we watch them on television or read about them in newspapers and magazines, or access them through the Internet, events occurring in distant lands—like a rebellion in Latin America, the coronation of a queen in Europe, a famine in Africa, or the Winter Olympics in Japan—seem as if they are happening in our own backyard. Instant communications integrate people around the globe into a common community.

The effects of this integration are felt by ordinary Americans on a variety of different levels. For example, it is amazing to realize how many of our Christmas gifts are produced in China, Thailand, or Sri Lanka, despite campaigns by American labor unions to persuade consumers to "buy American." In fact, buying American has become very difficult, not only because of competition from foreign manufacturers but also because it is almost impossible to tell what is really made in this country. As economist Robert Reich notes, "One of the ironies of our age is that an American who buys a Ford automobile or an RCA television is likely to get less American workmanship than if he bought a Honda or a Matsushita TV" (1988: 78). Today it is hard to really "buy American," according to Reich, because many American brands are produced outside of the United States or foreign manufacturers often have facilities here that employ American workers.

Not only are large corporations going international, even medium-sized to small companies are moving into the global marketplace. One effect on American employment is that jobs may now be won or lost at the local level depending on how well smaller companies compete in South America, Mexico, or Singapore. Another effect is that American employees—from company presidents to telephone switchboard operators—frequently find themselves frustrated in dealing with customers and other businesspersons who do not speak their language or share their customs or who operate their firms differently than do Americans.

Although a majority of American business is still conducted within the United States, an increasing share of our trade is international. The largest markets with potential for growth are not in this country or even in the industrialized world, but are in developing regions like Mexico, Central and South America, Asia's Pacific Rim, and Africa. Free trade among nations in the decades since World War II has put the American economy in a strange position. The U.S. economy is by far the most powerful economy in the world and the economy to which other nations' economies tend to be linked. Yet although the United States is the largest exporter nation, it is also the world's largest importing nation. Because our imports outpace our exports, overall we have a *trade deficit;* that is, more international trade dollars are flowing out of this country than into it. This outflow of wealth means that American business has less money available to invest in new plants, create new jobs, and improve American workers' wages. Chapter 8 discusses these issues in greater detail.

Besides influencing our economy in this way, globalization also has affected Americans socially and politically. For example, the United States is the last surviving military superpower. From the end of World War II until the early 1990s, we invested billions of dollars in maintaining a massive military presence and engaging in nonmilitary actions to "defeat communism," especially as manifested by the former Soviet Union. Shortly after the Berlin Wall separating the "communist" East from the "free" West was torn down in 1989, the entire Soviet empire and then the Soviet Union itself unraveled. An immediate effect of this collapse was to leave U.S. foreign policy in disarray; for the first time in nearly 50 years, the United States had no significant international foe to confront. On the domestic front, the long struggle with the Soviet Union pushed this country deeply in debt, causing us to have difficulty funding necessary programs at home such as new housing for the poor, health care reform, and improved public education. The downsizing, conversion to other uses, or closing of military bases and defense plants as world events moved our economy to a "peacetime footing" has directly affected thousands of defense industry workers and many communities and states. For many former defense industry employees, the immediate job future is at best uncertain, at worst bleak.

We can also see the cultural effects of globalization. American movies, television shows, books, and popular music reach a world audience, while foreign books, movies, and popular music are absorbed into our society. Fashion too has become international. Women in the United States wear clothes created by designers not only from Europe but also from Japan, while American jeans are among the most sought-after items in markets as far-flung as Cairo, Moscow, and Buenos Aires. Similarly, scientific knowledge and technological innovation are shared internationally. For example, the global scientific research establishment is working together to solve a variety of problems, from dealing with the dangers of environmental waste to curing and treating Acquired Immune Deficiency Syndrome (AIDS). In sports too we see many examples of our being part of a global community. For example, American basketball players play in the European league, whereas Europeans play in the National Basketball Association (NBA) or on U.S. college teams. None of these exchanges, even the most popular and positive, are typically without attendant problems, as we note throughout this book.

THE SOCIOLOGICAL PERSPECTIVE

One of the criticisms of the U.S. education system is that it does not adequately prepare young people to participate in the global village. Increased awareness has caused educators to begin to correct this lack of attention by insisting on globalizing the curriculum. By bringing the unique perspective of sociology to bear on the study of global issues, this book is part of that trend. To assist students in understanding this new perspective, we define sociology, present the concept of social construction of reality, and discuss the sociological imagination.

Sociology Defined

Sociology is the disciplined study of patterns of human social interaction and their effects on human thought and conduct. Most sociologists, including the authors, believe that sociology is a science because it applies the scientific method to the study of human behavior. Not only does being scientific require careful, disciplined study, it also requires subscribing to the standards of science when conducting research. These standards include (1) trying not to let biases influence conclusions, (2) systematically collecting evidence to support conclusions, (3) committing to the unfettered search for truth, (4) submitting research findings to the larger scientific community for review, and (5) constantly questioning and revising what is accepted as "truth."

The main goal of sociology is to understand human behavior. Many sociologists argue that sociology is a pure science because it seeks knowledge for its own sake—the knowledge obtained does not have to have practical application. We agree with this view but also agree that much knowledge obtained by pure research turns out to have practical applications. For example, the information sociologists acquire by studying mass behavior simply to learn more about it may have a practical use in controlling urban riots. Or, perhaps more obviously, research into the causes of crime may turn out to be employed by police to devise more effective crime prevention. In this book we go one step further by suggesting that the methods and findings of sociological research not only can, but should be, used to improve the conditions underlying global problems.

Human Beings as Social Creatures

The focus of sociology on understanding the social influences on behavior is vital because human beings are social creatures. We are born because two people mated, usually after courtship rituals and customs prescribed by their social group. We develop our identities as individuals, gendered people, members of families and social classes, citizens of countries, and believers of religious faiths as we interact with others. We learn to speak the language of our families, friends, and peers. We receive our education, choose our mates, give birth to our children, make our living, grow old, die, and are carried to our graves (or launched to sea in a burning Viking ship!) according to the prescriptions of our particular society.

In sum, we are immersed in the **social web**—the complex net of social relations stemming from the interlocking relationships among various groups to which we belong—at almost every moment from birth to death. Within this social web our personalities develop, we learn what is supposed to make us happy, or we experience frustrations that cause our lives to be nearly unbearable.

Within, and by means of, this web we create the meanings, structures, and patterns that enable us to live in what often appears to be a chaotic universe. Yet because human beings cannot live in a disorderly and unpredictable world, we engage in a process that allows us to impose order on our environment. The process of interaction that creates a shared reality is known as the **social construction of reality** (Berger and Luckmann, 1967). This reality includes everything from entire **cosmologies** (complex sets of ideas about how the universe was formed and functions) to shared definitions of how people are to behave in given situations (see the box, "The Human Face of the Social Construction of Reality: Urban Myths").

This socially constructed reality is often the basis for cultures. A **culture** is the way of life shared by a group of people. Every culture is quite intricate, consisting of thousands of **norms** (behavioral expectations), **values** (defensible criteria for determining what is desirable or undesirable, good or bad, beautiful or ugly), **beliefs** (understandings about the universe and its component parts, including human beings), **symbols** (objects, actions, or sounds given specific meanings by social definition), technology, and material creations. Culture is transmitted to children

THE HUMAN FACE OF THE SOCIAL CONSTRUCTION OF REALITY

Urban Myths

You may have heard the story about a woman who wanted the cookie recipe from a famous cookie maker. On calling the head office of the company, the woman was told that she could have a copy of the recipe for "two-fifty." Thinking this a very reasonable price, she gave the customer assistance representative her credit card number. Later, when she received her credit card bill, the woman was very surprised to find that the recipe had cost $250 rather than $2.50. Extremely annoyed, she paid that amount but then proceeded to share the recipe with everyone she could, thereby reducing the company's profit because now the recipe-holders didn't have to buy the cookies but could make them on their own. There's only one problem with this story: It isn't true.

This story (and an accompanying recipe) has been posted on college bulletin boards, passed around among friends, circulated on the Internet, and has even appeared in newspapers. Yet no one can identify the angry woman or even the company in question. (Several major department stores and shopping mall cookie shops have been implicated in this story.) This story is a modern-day legend called an *urban myth.* Urban myths may or may not have a factual basis. Their significance to sociologists is that they are feasible and indirectly tell some important truth. The morals of this urban myth are (1) don't reveal your credit card number to a retailer without being really sure how much something costs and (2) if a bargain seems to be too good to be true, then something is probably wrong.

Perhaps the most interesting thing to sociologists about this story (and many other urban myths) is that it does not need to be true to have a real effect on people's behavior. After hearing the story of the cookie recipe fiasco, people tend to become more cautious of advertising and other marketing ploys. Such responses represent a real-life application of the *Thomas Theorem* (named after sociologist W. I. Thomas): "If people define situations as real, they are real in their consequences" (Thomas and Thomas, 1928:592). Urban myths are a powerful example of how reality is constructed from our social environment.

The process of constructing reality is described by sociologists Peter Berger and Thomas Luckmann (1967) as one in which people start by creating a material or nonmaterial cultural product, such as an automobile or a theory of capitalism. After a while people forget that the society created these objects or ideas, and only subsequently did the objects become a part of the reality in and of themselves. Then, large numbers of people in a society eventually accept this new reality as "just the way it is." For example, horseback riding used to be a common mode of transportation. Now when we think about transportation—of visiting a friend 20 miles away, for example, we would never consider riding on horseback; rather, we immediately think of a different kind of horsepower that is dependent on the internal combustion engine. We have thus replaced what our ancestors saw as a real mode of transportation with forms of transportation powered by the internal combustion engine. A faster paced life has been a real consequence of this constructed reality.

Source: Shelley Kilpatrick, University of North Carolina, Chapel Hill. Personal communication to authors.

and other new members of society and serves as a blueprint by which members of society construct their lives.

In addition, culture provides the symbols, shared understandings, and structures that make communication possible. Suppose, for example, you are at a ball game sitting several seats from the aisle. As a hot dog vendor passes, she yells, "Hot dogs! Hot dogs! Get your dogs here!" You raise your hand. She stops and asks, "How many?" You raise your index finger. She passes down a "dog," then raises two fingers. People in the row between you and her pass the "dog" until it reaches you. You then pass back a "five." Upon receiving it, she sends over three "ones." You start to eat your treat while she continues down the aisle in pursuit of the next sale.

A thorough analysis of all of the ways culture makes this small transaction possible would take several pages. We describe only several to stimulate your thinking. Our mention of a ball game, an aisle, and a hot dog vendor immediately establishes a particular context for your understanding of the symbols, meanings, and normative patterns attached to this anecdote. First, let us look at the sounds uttered. If we had placed you at a dog race on a torrid summer day rather than at a ball game, this change of setting would cause you to assign an entirely different meaning to "hot dogs" and "eating a dog"! The fact that you and the other people present at the ball game share a particular understanding of "hot dogs" and the other words spoken shows that there is social agreement on the meaning of the sounds uttered. Next, consider the various hand gestures employed. Raising your hand in a classroom usually means you want to ask or answer a question. But within the context of a ball game, raising your hand in a carefully prescribed manner means you want to purchase one or more hot dogs.

In addition, your raising your hand and the vendor's response of stopping placed you both within the context of a commercial transaction. It also defined your role as the buyer and her role as the seller. To perform these roles in a transaction that lasted only a minute or two, both of you had to depend on a very complex systems of norms, values, and assumptions you share as Americans. In this context, raising your index figure (a symbol) indicated to her that you wanted to buy one hot dog. Lifting another finger (another symbol) could have had an entirely different shared meaning. But in your encounter when the vendor raised two fingers (still another symbol), you rightly assumed that the cost was two dollars.

A complex system of norms also came into play during this exchange. When the vendor passed one hot dog to you, you knew you were expected to pass in return at least two dollars to her. When she received a five-dollar bill from you, she knew not to simply pocket the money and leave but to return to you three dollars in change. Moreover, the spectators

Culture provides the symbols, shared understandings, and structures that make communication possible. The interactions between you and a vendor at a baseball game, as you signal what you want, pay for it, and get change and your purchase back, all depend on basic understandings between you, the vendor, and the crowd that are part of our culture.

sitting in the seats between you and her assumed they were expected to pass the dog to you, the five to her, and the change to you. They understood they were not at liberty to eat the dog nor to take the money you and she exchanged, no matter how hungry they were or how much they needed the cash.

From this example, you can easily see that in our society we engage in literally thousands of such complex interactions daily, as do people in every society. In addition, most societies organize themselves in clusters of norms, values, statuses, symbols, and beliefs centered on major human activities known as *institutions.* Industrialized societies have five basic institutions—the family, the economy, the government, education, and religion. These institutions also serve as complex systems of communication that allow people to meet their needs.

But the ways in which a particular culture may build lives for its members to meet their needs can be incompatible with the ways of life in other cultures. This understanding has led sociologists to believe the only way to understand people from other societies is to employ **cultural relativism,** the practice of judging a culture by its own standards. Indeed, most people actually employ **ethnocentrism,** the practice of using the standards of their own culture to judge other cultures. Ethnocentrism has historically often been the source of confusion and conflict among different cultures, as we note throughout this book.

The Sociological Imagination

The key insight of sociology is how our lives and personal biographies are intertwined with other people with whom we interact, groups to which we belong, social structures in which we are immersed, and the social world in which we live. Additionally, sociologists are keenly aware of the *transformative powers of history,* or how significant historical events have affected dramatically the ways people feel, think, and behave (Ferrante, 1992). Sociologist C. Wright Mills (1959) calls the ability to place our personal biographies in the larger social and historical context the **sociological imagination.** The sociological imagination involves the ability to distinguish personal troubles from public issues. **Personal troubles** are private matters that affect mainly individuals and their immediate circle of family, friends, or coworkers. Individuals can usually deal with personal troubles by making some change in themselves ("I'll try to control my temper because it's causing me to lose friends"), or by making changes within their immediate circle of acquaintances ("We can't be friends anymore because you lied to me"). **Public issues** are matters that transcend the immediate lives of individuals. These problems can be dealt with only by more sweeping changes in societies or social systems ("Without health care reform, we can't pay for medical coverage for our family").

Often, individuals cannot see that their problems are really part of larger issues that cannot be changed by persons acting alone. In effect, they confuse issues with troubles; or conversely, they don't see their troubles are really issues. In such instances some people may feel personally inadequate ("After my company downsized and I was laid off as a telephone repairman, the only job I could find didn't pay enough to support our family, so my wife now has to work full-time; I feel like such a loser") rather than realizing that their self-labeled personal failure stems from changes or shortcomings in a social system like the economy (e.g., the downsizing of American industry) and that changes in the social structure can create a solution to their problem (e.g., federal or state job retraining programs).

In contrast, some people project private troubles into the public realm; that is, they believe that something that is actually a personal failure results from a shortcoming in a social system such as the family or education ("I can't keep up with my class work because my school demands too much"). Part of the reason for the confusion is that public issues do affect our personal lives. For example, a city's rising crime rates make many people feel insecure and unsafe ("I don't like to go out alone because of the drug dealers in the neighborhood; even in my house it's like I'm under siege"). Such feelings when multiplied within a city may in turn create or escalate an atmosphere of fear, leading people to purchase weapons for self-protection and to demand that politicians "do something" about the crime problem.

This book uses the sociological perspective to analyze global problems. We realize that some of the personal frustrations people experience stem from individual difficulty. But many of our problems have their roots in overarching historical trends and the national and global systems that these trends generate. Our goal is to enable you to develop your own sociological imagination so that you can begin to distinguish between private troubles and public issues. To this end we next describe the nature of social problems and demonstrate how they are similar to and different from global problems. Then we develop theoretical concepts to encourage your understanding of social problems within the context of globalization.

Social Problems and Global Problems

So far we have provided some background by discussing the reality of globalization and reviewing the sociological perspective. We now come directly to the focus of this book by examining issues related to the nature of global problems. We first discuss a widely used definition of social problems and show some implications of this definition for studying global problems. We next ask whether global problems are qualitatively different from traditional social problems. Finally, we present our own definition of global problems.

Global Problems as an Extension of Social Problems

A traditional area of sociological investigation has been the study of national social problems. For example, many books have been written and courses taught about such problems as racism, poverty, sexism, and unemployment in the United States. We may, to some degree, see global social problems as a quantitative extension of this national-oriented approach. That is, it is possible to view global problems as social problems that are bigger than national problems. As such, global problems affect not only social systems, but also massive numbers of people. From such a perspective it is obvious that many of the same dynamics operating in national social problems are present in global problems. We illustrate this conclusion by examining a widely used definition of social problems. Sociologists Paul Horton, Gerald Leslie, Richard Larson, and Robert Horton define a **social problem** as "a condition affecting a significant number of people in a way considered adverse about which it is thought something can be done through collective social action" (1994:2). Let us look more carefully at the implications of this definition.

Objective Condition and Subjective Definition. One implication is that social problems involve objective (real) conditions affecting significant numbers of people. If some condition is not present, then it would be nearly impossible to convince people that a problem exists. We agree, but caution that the relationship between what is real and what is perceived to be real can be complex. Indeed, sometimes people define conditions in ways that do not "square" with the facts, often with disastrous consequences. For example, during the 1950s Wisconsin Senator Joseph McCarthy instituted a widespread persecution, alleging that many Americans were involved with communist plots to overthrow the U.S. government. Artists, actors, directors, authors, educators, homosexuals, persons who opposed McCarthy, "strange" individuals, and ordinary citizens accused of leftist sympathies were ordered to testify about their communist leanings at Senate hearings, were publicly humiliated, and suffered ruined careers. Despite the reality that most of the accused individuals had no involvement with communism and that communism itself has never posed a serious threat to this country, McCarthyism was, nevertheless, a response to an objective set of conditions. That is, it arose during the Cold War (1950–1991) between the Soviet Union and its allies and the United States and its allies.

During this era both sides possessed nuclear weapons that they threatened to use to obliterate each other. Both sides also angrily confronted each other in such international forums as the United Nations and used or allied with surrogates in "hot" wars around the world. For example, U.S. soldiers fought with South Korean soldiers against North (Communist) Korea in the Korean War, 1950–1953. During the Cold War some external threat to the United States from the Soviet Union may have existed, although its likelihood was probably exaggerated. As for the internal threat to the United States, historians generally agree that it came more from fear of communism than from communism itself. It was, however, this condition of fear that led many Americans to perceive a communist menace from within. And it was the same fear that also led to McCarthyite attacks on loyal citizens.

The same types of dynamics used during the McCarthy witchhunt years apply to global problems. Obviously, global problems are conditions that affect massive numbers of persons in different parts of the world. But how many people must be affected for the problem to be seen as global remains unclear. We may say that it is not necessary that everyone in the world be affected for a condition to be viewed as a global problem. Still, enough persons must adversely experience some condition so that a large number will become concerned and demand action to alleviate it. But even here we need to be cautious, for although large numbers of people in a nation may be affected by a situation or condition, this by itself does not necessarily mean that the condition or situation will be defined as a global problem. For example, because about 20 percent of the world's population lives in China, numerous conditions there affect a large segment of humanity. But whereas some of these conditions are considered to affect global problems (overpopulation, which the Chinese government attempts to control), others simply affect the Chinese (residents of some rural areas are hindered from harvesting crops because of inefficient policies created by urban bureaucrats). Likewise, a condition that affects significant numbers of people in several nations (e.g., famine in southern African countries) does not necessarily ensure that this condition will come to be seen as presenting a global problem. Conditions must generate debate in international organizations, controversy in scholarly journals concerned with global issues, attention from the international media, and growing public awareness in numerous countries before they come to be seen as global problems.

In addition, conditions alone do not constitute social problems. Large groups of people must come to define the effect of these conditions as adverse. In fact, this subjective element—defining conditions as adverse—is so crucial that social problems as such do not exist without it (Mauss, 1976; Tallman, 1976). On a regional, national, or international scale, many conditions are viewed positively. When people are well fed, adequately educated, and experience a reasonable degree of justice, none of these conditions are likely to be viewed as social problems. Even when negative conditions are present, they may or may not be understood as problems. For example, most Americans today are very concerned about crime, but the types of activity they define as crime are in those categories that are often associated with the lower classes, such as burglary, robbery, or murder. Americans tend to ignore **white-collar crime** (crimes committed by professionals, managers, and businesspeople in the course of their professional lives), although this type of criminal activity appears to be widespread and probably costs the country more than all "lower-class" crimes combined.

Moreover, particular conditions may be defined as social problems at one time in history, only to be ignored at other times. This shift in view occurs despite the fact that the basic conditions themselves have been largely unchanged (Mauss,1976; Erikson, 1966; Durkheim, 1950). For example, the violation of minorities' civil rights, racial segregation, poverty, and the unequal treatment of women have always existed in U.S. society. But the view that these conditions are social problems has ebbed and flowed with the times. In the 1960s and early 1970s, a variety of forces brought these issues to the forefront. As a result, a series of laws and social programs were enacted to improve conditions for women and minorities. But despite some improvement, the basic conditions leading to the activism of this period remain largely unaltered. Yet public interest in most of these subjects has waned partly because many Americans think that the problems were "fixed" by the passage of laws and partly because they cannot see how these issues affect them personally.

The way that a society defines social problems also has significant implications for their solutions (Gusfield, 1989; Woolgar and Pawluch, 1985; Spector and Kitsuse, 1974; Kitsuse and Spector, 1973). Sociologist Helena Lopata (1984) demonstrates this principle by showing how the "problem" with newcomers (children and immigrants) has been constantly defined and redefined in the course of history. For example, Lopata notes that in nineteenth-century America poverty was blamed on the moral depravity of the immigrant poor. A common consequence of this "definition" was to take children from such households whenever middle-class public officials and volunteer workers judged the parents to be unfit. These unfortunate children were then placed in almshouses or workhouses or were shipped from big cities to rural areas, where they presumably would be reared in a suitable environment. But by the early part of the twentieth century, reform movements led to new definitions of the problems of poor children that stressed the importance of maintaining the family without undue governmental interference. One result was that many states started providing "mother's pensions" to enable destitute women to keep their children in their homes. As society changed its definitions of the problems of poor children, the types of solutions that were proposed changed too.

The way problems are defined may also inhibit viable solutions (see the box, "FYI: Don't Believe

The way society defines social problems has implications for their solution. For example, in the nineteenth century, poverty was looked on as a moral weakness on the part of poor immigrant families such as these, and as a result their children were often removed from the parents and placed in workhouses or shipped to the country to be reared in a suitable environment. By the early part of the twentieth century, states started providing "mother's pensions" to enable destitute women to keep their children with them in their homes.

Everything You Read"). For example, it is common to define conflicts centering on social issues as a **zero-sum game,** a process by which the gains of some groups must be subtracted from the assets of other groups. By pitting groups against each another, we therefore discourage the compromises necessary for finding workable resolutions. Although situations do exist in which the gains of some must come at the cost of others, this is not always the case. In fact, the improvement of conditions associated with social problems frequently benefit all concerned. For instance, the business community often argues that the passage of laws requiring safer work conditions for workers will drive up costs and perhaps will force the closing of entire industries. Yet, not only do workers benefit from safer working conditions, but businesses also gain because of fewer injuries to workers, which results in fewer absences from work, lower premiums on insurance, fewer law suits for injury, and better worker morale.

Value Conflicts. Defining conditions as affecting people in a way considered undesirable implies a **value judgment,** an assessment of conditions or situations based on deeply held values. Sociologists have traditionally contended that values and value judgments are intimately involved in social problems (Fuller and Meyer, 1941a, 1941b; Waller, 1936). In fact, **value conflicts**—disagreements between groups over which set of values should dominate—are influential in generating social problems as well as in preventing resolution of these issues. An example is the lengthy and continuing debate in the United States over abortion, in which people who want to limit abortion call themselves "pro-life," whereas those who want women to continue to have comparatively easy access to abortion call themselves "pro-choice." The key to the debate between the two factions is whose rights should dominate. "Pro-lifers" hold that the unborn infant's "right to life" must be protected at all costs; "pro-choicers" contend that the mother's right of choice in controlling her own body is primary. As the abortion debate shows, many values cannot be "proven" as superior to other values by methods upon which all parties can agree. Because it is not possible to demonstrate conclusively which side is "correct," the abortion controversy will probably rage indefinitely.

Sociologists have been reluctant to try to settle value disputes because values appear to vary so widely among groups in a given society, as well as among the many cultures in the world, and because of the lack of a means to objectively decide which values should dominate. Frequently, sociologists

Don't Believe Everything You Read

Every day on the television, in the newspapers, and in innumerable magazines and professional journals some new and exciting "scientific" findings are published. Inevitably, you will read or hear, "researchers at university X have discovered . . ." Each page of these reports should be stamped "caveat emptor" (let the buyer beware). Although some of the reports are the product of years of high-quality research, they may still present preliminary findings that will be revised later. Other reports may simply be the ideas of one person without legitimate supporting data, or they may be the result of poor or incomplete research.

Many unsupportable, unfounded ideas find their way into print or are released over the airways. This problem is compounded when one is reading sources on the Internet. One of the joys as well as terrors of this technology is that anyone can put anything on the Internet. They can publish on the World Wide Web whether their material is valid or invalid. How are you to know what information to trust?

As you review material, ask yourself several questions:

1. *Consider the source of your information.* Are you reading from a reputable journal, such as the *American Sociological Review,* or are you reading from a newsstand tabloid? What kind of credentials does the author have to give him or her the right to publish on the topic? For instance, if the topic is a sociological issue such as sex and gender problems, is the person a sociologist or other social scientist associated with a college or university, or is the author simply a "person on the street" offering an opinion?
2. *Identify the main point of the article.* Does the author describe some phenomenon? Does the author suggest a relationship between two or more variables? Does the author suggest a cause-and-effect relationship between these variables?
3. *Evaluate the evidence the author uses to support the main point.* Does the author present evidence? Is the evidence the thoughts or opinions of someone else? If so, is that person a recognized authority on the topic? Does the evidence include statistics? If so, do the statistics seem to support the author's contention? How adequate are the methods used to collect and analyze the statistics?
4. *Identify the perspective of the author.* For example, is the author speaking from a liberal or a conservative position? Is the author's perspective related to one of the theories you find in this book or have encountered in other studies? The perspective of the author often colors how he or she views an issue as well as the research outcome.
5. *Think about the practical implications of the author's contentions.* How would the author's contentions change society or the world? What are the benefits of the knowledge presented? What are the drawbacks if the author is correct? If you take the author's arguments to the extreme, what are the consequences?

These questions are not intended to provide you with comprehensive tools for assessing information. Rather, they are a starting point for viewing more critically the materials you may encounter.

Source: Benjamin Kilpatrick, University of North Carolina, Chapel Hill. Personal communication to authors.

have suggested that their task in dealing with values is to use their expertise to point out the consequences of the value judgments held by the various contending groups.

Although this position has merits, in this book we take a more proactive stance. We argue that most sociologists who claim to take a value-neutral posture in relation to social problems actually operate from a covert system of values by which they implicitly judge various situations. That is, they customarily impose their values on their supposedly unbiased assessments simply because, like everyone else, they are products of their time and place—in other words, products of their culture. Many sociologists do make strong efforts to identify their positions and assumptions and to limit explicitly the interpretation of their findings within this position. Still, we need to recognize it is impossible for them (or for anybody else) to be truly value-free and objective when dealing with social problems. Even so, as sociologists we must strive to base our conclusions on well-founded and, in so far as possible, unbiased evidence.

In addition, the ultimate goal of sociology, we suggest, is not merely to analyze problems but to help create better societies and a better global community. In taking this position, we are following what sociologist Sal Restivo calls the "high tradition" in sociology: "The high tradition in sociology and in the world of learning in general has always been directed simultaneously toward learning about the world and making it more livable" (Restivo, 1991:193).

The same dynamic also applies on a global scale to social problems. Like conditions on the national scale, global conditions must still be brought to the public awareness, at which point they can be defined as adverse. The way conditions are understood affects the type of solutions proposed. If competing values make the resolution of national problems difficult, we can easily see that different value orientations can create a quagmire on the global scene. Nevertheless, sociologists can and, we believe, should make value judgments, deciding which conditions—even global ones—are "desirable."

Doing Something through Collective Action. Even when people do define conditions as negative, corrective action is not the inevitable consequence. One factor inhibiting such action is a widely held perception among people that they can do nothing to change things. People simply suffer difficult situations when they believe that change is impossible. The responses to the possibility of—and the reality of—many natural disasters underline this phenomenon. For example, people living in areas subject to hurricanes typically believe that little can be done to prevent these storms. Therefore, what they usually do when a hurricane approaches is prepare their property to withstand nature's onslaught, ride out the storm, and pick up the pieces when it is over. Yet when people believe they can prevent a natural disaster, the belief itself encourages them to take positive actions. For example, a growing belief in the United States during the 1930s that the periodic and devastating flooding around most major riverways could be controlled resulted in massive public works programs to build dams, levies, floodgates, and reservoirs. It is important to recognize then that people must *believe* something can be done to prevent, improve, correct, or eliminate a negative condition before action will occur to improve the condition. It is not necessary that something be done to prevent or completely fix it. For example, flood control methods seem to be relatively effective in ordinary years. But in the summer of 1993 prodigious rains in the Midwest overloaded the river system. The resulting massive flooding may have been more disastrous than it would have been if nature had been left alone. Certainly, the human costs were higher because people had been encouraged by the relative protection of the flood control measures to move into areas vulnerable to flooding.

What can be said of natural disasters can also be said of various human issues. People have to believe that something can be done before they are likely to become involved in efforts to improve or solve social problems. People who believe that "you can't fight city hall" or that a given set of conditions are too overwhelming ("poverty will always exist") are unlikely to take action. This attitude explains why resignation is a common reaction to national, much less global, social problems.

Another attribute of social problems is relevant to their study and solution: People must understand that *collective social action* is necessary to alleviate the particular adverse condition. Numerous problems exist that do not require collective action to solve ("I missed class all week because I overslept and am now in danger of failing, so I'm buying an alarm clock"). None of these types of problems could be termed social problems because the very nature of social problems generates group involvement. Sociologist Irvin Tallman (1976) contends that the value conflicts apparent in social problems stir strong feelings that stimulate people to act together to produce change or to resist it. Without the passions generated by value conflicts, people are unlikely to act on something; in such a situation, we can say that no social problem exists.

Finally, the strong passions associated with social problems frequently generate social movements (Mauss, 1976). **Social movements** are organized collective behaviors aimed at producing or preventing change in existing social structures. Participants in social movements attempt to create pressure on political bodies, the media, and public opinion to gain advantages for their positions. Social movement participants frequently create organizations to further their interests. Numerous instances of the creation of social movements in response to adverse conditions may be found in this nation's history. One example is the American labor movement, which arose after the Civil War (1861–1865) in response to rapid industrialization. The labor movement so effectively employed organizations called unions as instruments to further its aims of protecting workers that working situations substantially improved in many industries.

The same dynamic also applies on a global scale to global problems. Negative situations often spark social movements whose participants seek to further their interests through organizations. For example, a host of groups such as **Greenpeace,** which focuses on ways to stop the deterioration of our natural habitat, have emerged to combat global environmental problems. These movements, and the organizations they create, exert their influence from outside of normal (formal) governmental and economic structures, although social movement organizations may at times work together with more formal social institutions. We discuss their impact throughout this book.

Greenpeace, a social movement that focuses on ways to stop the deterioration of our natural habitat, exerts its influence from outside the formal governmental and economic structures. Here Greenpeace protesters demonstrate against a Norwegian whaling boat.

Global Problems as Qualitatively Different

Although global problems exhibit many of the characteristics of social problems, they are qualitatively different. Global problems are effects of the globalization process that threaten human well-being or undermine efforts to achieve valued states such as economic security or health. These undesired effects are produced by human activities that are organized in ways that distort the balance between legitimate needs of human beings in relation to others and/or in relation to their shared life-sustaining biophysical systems. In labeling something a global problem, we acknowledge that the dominant cultural, economic, and political systems that have evolved over the last five hundred years jeopardize continued human survival in the face of social and ecological limits.

This idea may be illustrated by looking at some of the implications of the definition of the term *global problem.* We define a **global problem** as an identifiable subset of interrelated conditions resulting from negative effects of relations, both within the **sociosphere** (the social systems, including such elements as the economy and technology, by which humans organize their lives and sustain themselves) and between the sociosphere and the **biosphere** (the delicate set of natural ecological systems necessary to sustain life on this planet), which threaten a significant portion of humankind and relief from which requires coordinated multinational action. We next review briefly the elements of this definition.

Subset of Interrelated Conditions. Any global problem is but one part of an intertwined set of conditions. Conditions are so interlocked that they cannot in the real world be separated from each other, although we attempt such a separation for the purposes of analysis. The indivisibility of global problems should be apparent in later sections of this book; for although each chapter focuses on a different problem, some overlap exists between chapters. Thus we see that population pressures (Chapter 5) are related to environmental problems (Chapter 6), which in turn are interlinked with political (Chapter 7) and economic (Chapter 8) systems, and so forth.

Similarly, dealing with global problems involves cutting across a range of disciplines—from the social sciences to the biological sciences. Traditional approaches that work from within the framework of a single discipline cannot encompass the complexities of contemporary global problems. For example, because environmental problems (ecology) have their roots (history) in population growth (sociology, technology, and medicine), capitalism (economics and sociology), and industrialization (technology, economics, sociology, and anthropology), to study them from the point of view of ecology alone would be short-sighted. Many different fields of study must be consulted about any particular issue. No one can be an expert in all the areas of study necessary to understand global problems, but we can draw as needed on the expertise of people from a variety of relevant disciplines. We can insist on a comprehensive approach that takes into account the complexity of global problems rather than merely seeing them from the narrow confines of a single discipline.

Negative Effects Threatening Humankind. Global problems are the consequence of negative effects of relations within the sociosphere and the biosphere. The sociosphere and biosphere are both essential for human survival. Traditionally, many of the conditions identified as social problems focused solely on relations within the sociosphere, such as economic or racial exploitation. Although these interactions still occur, we are more aware that destructive social systems also negatively affect ecological systems. Many of the issues commonly identified as global problems were created because the social systems human beings have created in the modern era are often in direct conflict with the ecological systems necessary to maintain life. For example, we are now more aware that warring societies may, besides killing each other in direct combat, pollute ecological systems such as lakes, their fish, and the birds that eat the fish. We discuss in detail the nature of these negative interactions at a number of points throughout this book.

Another key factor in the dynamics of global problems is the threat they pose to large segments (if not all) of humanity. Although we recognize that the subjective element operates in defining global problems as it does with social problems, widespread agreement exists among physical and social scientists, as well as governmental and business leaders, that many of the conditions we address in this text represent a grave threat to the well-being and, perhaps, the continued existence of humans (Barney, 1980). Perhaps nowhere is this more obvious than in warfare and environmental conditions. Human beings have always had a remarkable propensity for violence. War is one way this tendency expresses itself. Whereas war itself is not new, modern technology has made us much more efficient killers.

This efficiency has reached its apex with the invention of nuclear weapons, which give humans the capacity to annihilate their enemies. For more than forty years—from the development of nuclear weapons by the former Soviet Union to compete with the United States' arsenal until the dissolution of European communism—the world lived under the military/political doctrine known as MAD (Mutually Assured Destruction). Since then, however, the world is not necessarily a safer place. Some argue that the possible nuclear proliferation into the hands of non-developed nations and/or terrorists may actually make the current situation more dangerous than things were at the height of Cold War competition. Chapter 7 discusses these issues.

The testing of ecological limits brought about by the combined workings of industrial society and population growth represents another agreed on threat to human existence. This is apparent in a host of problems such as the depletion of natural resources, pollution, the destruction of rain forests, and global warming, as discussed in Chapter 6. Possibly less obvious is the seriousness of the threat to humankind caused by economic exploitation (see Chapter 8) combined with violations of human rights reviewed in Chapter 2. We term this a threat to humankind because it affects directly the welfare of a significant portion of the world's peoples. The same social, economic, and political systems causing exploitation and rights violations also create the conditions for warfare, ecological disaster, and depletion of natural resources that may additionally menace human survival on this planet.

Relief Requires Coordinated Multinational Action. The final characteristic of a global problem is that its resolution depends on coordinated multinational action. No one government or even an alliance of governments can unilaterally resolve these conditions. Many of them literally demand global changes (Barney, 1980). Two additional points need to be made at this juncture.

First, multinational efforts are not likely because governments generally put their national interests ahead of global interests. For example, during the Cold War pressing global issues were often neglected because each side believed that addressing them would help the other side. The numerous "civil wars" that erupted throughout the Cold War prove this point. Many of these civil wars were created by the Cold War itself, or the participants were used as pawns of the two superpowers. (Both of these scenarios operated throughout the conflict between North and South Vietnam called the Vietnam War, 1954–1975). Efforts to relieve the suffering caused in these wars were frequently blocked by the United States or the Soviet Union. But since the collapse of the Soviet Union, hopeful signs have emerged such as the humanitarian missions of the United Nations (UN) in Somalia and Bosnia. There, UN troops were sent into wars with a charge to create and enforce peace. In each of these situations, the peace missions were supported by the two former enemies, the United States and Russia.

Another positive sign is a growing awareness of global threats by ordinary people in many parts of the world. This awareness has led to attempts by some to take meaningful action to counteract such global threats despite governmental intransigence. Such grassroots movements are usually accompanied by the creation of global networks and/or organizations for coordinating international endeavors to solve the problem. Organizations not representing governments that speak for various causes at sessions of the UN General Assembly, the UN Economic and Social Council, the U.S. Congress, or other governmental meetings are called **nongovernmental organizations (NGOs).** Some NGOs have become quite influential and offer the possibility of generating meaningful change. One NGO you may have heard of or even joined is **Amnesty International,** a privately funded organization that works to improve human rights around the world.

Nevertheless, such efforts are frequently ineffective because most of them are directed toward attacking different aspects of complex problems. Without coordination, large numbers of governmental and nongovernmental agencies and organizations tend to work at cross-purposes, at times even counteracting the efforts of other groups focusing on the issue from another perspective. The lack of effective coordination between NGOs and governments does not diminish the need for international cooperation.

GLOBALIZATION

Earlier we discussed a definition of global problems as negative consequences of globalization. In this section we develop the concept of globalization, encompassing both its objective and subjective forms. In the definition we use in this text, **globalization** is the growing interconnectedness of the sociosphere on a worldwide scale. Viewed from this perspective, globalization has a long history, going back to the time of ancient empire building. It includes the spread of religions with universal messages such as Buddhism, Christianity, and Islam (see the box, "FYI: The Historical Phases of Modern Globalization"). But our focus here is on the more recent phase of that process that began with the expansion of Western European civilization and the spread of modern culture, spanning approximately the last five centuries. We refer to this as the modern phase of globalization.

Globalization has, as we suggested, both objective and subjective aspects (Robertson, 1992). **Objective globalization** is the increasing planetary interconnectedness of human social activity and the worldwide effects or repercussions of that activity. This increasing interconnectedness significantly alters the context of ideas, values, expectations, and identities with which all human beings must view their world and themselves. **Subjective globalization** involves the social redefinition of identities and worldviews that emerges from the human confrontation and dialogue caused by objective globalization itself.

Interactions Driving Objective Globalization

Objective globalization is a complex and as yet poorly understood process. It is beyond the scope of this text to attempt to describe it completely. Rather, we look at patterns of interaction that are driving the process. Some key patterns include the following:

- *Economic growth:* Global economic growth includes the competitive struggle for markets, labor, jobs, technology, and resources. It is of course affected by the growth of population that stems from the world's poor families investing in having more children. At this level, the reality of globalization is widely acknowledged by many authorities.

The Historical Phases of Modern Globalization

In his book *Globalization: Social Theory and Global Culture* (1992), Roland Robertson, a leading thinker in this area, says that the modern globalization process has gone through five phases. Each phase has produced sweeping political, social, economic, and ideological changes. And each in turn has made a significant contribution to the globalization process.

Phase I: The Germinal Phase—Phase I, or the *Germinal Phase,* lasted from the early fifteenth to the mid-eighteenth centuries. During this time nations began to form as the "internationalism" of the medieval period waned. What we conceive of as nations did not exist during the medieval period. People had ethnic loyalty but came to see themselves as a larger Europa (Europe) held together by loyalty to a common faith, Christianity. Toward the end of the fifteenth century, Spain and Portugal began to emerge as nations under a united monarchy. England and France, among others, followed, organizing themselves into nation-states in the sixteenth century. In addition, new concepts of the individual and of humanity were formed. The heliocentric (sun-centered) model of the solar system came to dominate, and the Gregorian calendar, still our way of reckoning dates, was developed.

Phase II: The Incipient Phase—Phase II, or the *Incipient Phase,* extended from the mid-eighteenth century to 1870. During this period the concept of a homogeneous, unified national government (or "state") was formed. The concepts of formalized relationships between nations and of the individual as a citizen of a nation were crystallized. These new concepts gave rise to a new sense of identity based on membership in the nation. The problem of whether or not non-European nations should be admitted to "international society" became important, as did the issue of nationalism (primary commitment to one's own nation) versus internationalism (primary commitment to the larger society of nations).

Phase III: The Takeoff Phase—Phase III, or the *Takeoff Phase,* lasted from 1870 to the mid-1920s. Tendencies that were more submerged in previous eras formed a more coherent and unified pattern of globalization. There was a new focus on the entity of the nation-state, an increasing focus on the "generic" human individual (with an emphasis on the masculine gender), a drive toward forming an international society, and a further development of the concept of "humanity." The "problems" of the modern period became a topic of discussion. Issues of national and personal identity become important themes. Asian and other non-European societies were "recognized" by Europeans if they met a code of "civilization," based on Western values. Although the code of civilization was an imposition of foreign standards on Asian cultures, it involved a recognition of the possibility of a universal standard of conduct and of citizen rights. The variety, speed, and means of global communication also increased during this era. World time zones were established, and the Gregorian calendar became almost universally used. International competitions such as the Nobel Prize and the modern Olympic Games were established. World War I was waged.

Phase IV: The Struggle-for-Hegemony Phase—Phase IV, or the *Struggle-for-Hegemony Phase,* extended from the 1920s to the late 1960s. According to Robertson, the wars and political struggles of this phase, including the Cold War and the anticolonial wars, were struggles over the terms of the globalization process itself. There was resistance to *modernism* (defined by Robertson as an orientation toward the rational manipulation of nature and society in the interests of progress) in the form of Fascist and Nazi regimes. After their defeat in World War II, the struggle became one between different versions of modernism, the Soviet (or socialist) version and the American/Western European version (or capitalism). During this time the League of Nations was formed as the first international political institution and, after it failed, the United Nations was established. The Nazi-engineered Holocaust and the invention of nuclear weapons focused increased concern on the nature of humanity and the question of its ultimate survival. The concept of the "Third World," referring to poor societies of the southern hemisphere with only limited industrialization, was invented.

(continued)

Phase V: The Uncertainty Phase—Phase V, or the *Uncertainty Phase,* which began in the late 1960s and continues today, entered a crisis period in 1990. The end of the Cold War, signaled by the collapse of the Soviet Union, has created a fluid international structure, a proliferation of nuclear weapons, and an expanded concern over human rights. Identities of individuals, groups, and entire societies have become more complex and problematic as societies become increasingly multicultural and multiethnic. Gender, race, sexual preference, and other factors also add to the complexity of issues of identities and rights. Global consciousness has also increased since the 1960s, aided by space exploration. Environmental issues and the spread of new and revived diseases raise more urgently the problem of humanity, its survival, and its role on this planet. The number of global institutions and groups has also expanded dramatically. Global civil society and global citizenship are increasingly discussed, despite a heightened sense of ethnicity. Global mass media are firmly established. World conferences on environmental, religious, scientific, and other dialogues are occurring at an increasing rate. Postmodern culture, a critique of the modern Western worldview (e.g., the idea that all the great literature is Western, written mainly by white males, is under attack) is proliferating. Islam (and Confucianism) now plays a more significant role in that critique, and proposes alternatives to Western modernism.

Source: Adapted from Robertson, Roland. 1992. *Globalization: Social Theory and Global Culture.* Newberry Park, CA: Sage.

- *Ecological effects:* Economic expansion has placed a burden on the planetary life-support system because of escalating rates of consumption and production. Such expansion promotes the recognition of global environmental concerns. For example, it has inspired what is perhaps the first truly global social movement—environmentalism.

- *Information technology:* The technology of communication and information, including computers and satellite television, is increasing the frequency of human interactions at an exponential rate. The speed of social change is itself partly a function of the speed and ease of these interactions. Therefore, the present technology is hastening social change.

- *Social movements and organizations:* Today thousands of organizations are working to promote or prevent change; still other organizations are concerned simply with sharing knowledge and ideas among people with related interests or common problems in a global forum. This proliferation of groups with various agendas—from radical environmentalism to Christian evangelism—is greatly facilitated by communication technology.

- *Concern for equal rights:* In many ways the processes we have described contribute to a growing awareness among people throughout the world of the living conditions of each other. Women and repressed minorities have come to see that the exploitation they have taken for granted is not experienced to the same degree in some other societies. Many national and international groups actively work for the equal treatment of persons around the globe.

- *Global recognition:* From its beginning in the fifteenth century, the system of nation-states was based on principles of mutual recognition. Today cultural groups, leaders of nations, oppressed minorities, athletes, artists, scientists, and others seek the recognition and acknowledgment of global audiences. Global recognition gives legitimacy to groups seeking power. Such recognition provides a world forum for groups seeking justice to air their grievances while offering them leverage against what may be otherwise overwhelming opposition. For scientists, artists, athletes, and entertainers, global recognition represents the ultimate confirmation of the worth of their talents.

- *Quest for breakthrough ideas:* In many areas—from interfaith dialogue to scientific discovery to the issue of universal human rights—there is a search for deeper global understanding. Modern communication and transportation have made available the teachings of the world's cultures to

The technology of communication and information, including computers and satellite television, is increasing the frequency of human interactions at an exponential rate. The speed of social change is itself partly a function of the speed and ease of these interactions.

everyone today, a new development in human history. The depth of inquiry and the scope of dialogue now possible are unprecedented, as is the perceived need for shared answers to contemporary issues. Because this quest for shared understanding is engaging some of the best and most creative minds, its results may prove to be among the most enduring contributions of globalization.

Discourse, Culture, and Subjective Globalization

According to anthropologist Kay Milton (1996), we need to modify the picture we have of a humanity divided by invisible walls made up of cultural differences. Rather, we should view human culture today as consisting of numerous "discourses." *Discourse* refers to the way knowledge (our sense of what is real) is formed and supported in the activity of communication. In today's world, cultural elements—ideas, values, worldviews, practices, beliefs—cross boundaries previously thought to be impenetrable barriers to communication. These cultural "objects," or elements, are part of the ongoing discourse—international conferences, books, televised events, and conversations on the Internet, as well as other patterns of interaction—comprising much of the globalization process. Such cultural interactions are too numerous and too elusive to be directly observed. Therefore, we must attempt, Milton contends, to understand the perspectives of the participants in cultural interactions by examining the many written and spoken statements and actions they generate. These discourses naturally focus on various themes. And it is these themes that make up the core of subjective globalization.

Identity as a Theme of Subjective Globalization

One of the most fundamental themes of subjective globalization concerns changing or forming new identities and boundaries. The processes of objective globalization have brought about conditions in which many persons are asked to reexamine their senses of self, of group membership, and of their place in the larger world. In our definition, **identities** are individuals' sense of what or who they are in relationship to the surrounding world in which they perceive themselves to live. **Boundaries** are symbolic limits that separate one person, group, or species from other people, groups, or species. These identities and boundaries emerge out of interaction between the individual and the various groups to which she or he may belong and among groups themselves. Identities and boundaries are rather arbitrary and require social recognition and support if they are to be effective. During today's ongoing process of globalization, identities and boundaries are being redefined at three levels: (1) self and group, (2) the intergroup level (i.e., the global community), and (3) our identity as a species.

At the first, or self and group level, the person may, as a result of globalization, begin to question his or her responsibilities to the group and its traditions. A person might feel compelled to ask, "Am I first and foremost a part of the group, and, if so, do I owe it my full allegiance? Or am I primarily a distinct psychological being, a self, with special rights apart from the group? For example, if my group imposes on me a set of duties that I find burdensome, painful, or inconvenient, am I obliged to bear them?"

A brief discussion of the rite of female genital mutilation practiced in certain societies illustrates the usefulness of our redefining our notions of identities and boundaries. If a female does not wish to suffer this ordeal, has she the right to refuse, although her culture gives her no such right? Traditionally, a female's pleas that she does not want to submit to genital mutilation because of her personal feelings or desires have been ignored by societies practicing this ritual. But such a refusal may carry some weight within her own nation if she appeals for intervention or support from the global community, basing her resistance on the principle that the practice is a violation of universal human rights. In couching her appeal this way, she could be said to be claiming a more inclusive identity—not as a single person, but as a member of the human species, or of the larger global community. Increasingly, group boundaries have become permeable to these more inclusive identity claims. Like all human boundaries, all claims to identity are workable only when they receive sufficient social support and acknowledgment. In this example of female genital mutilation, the value of individualism may be too extreme a notion for non-European cultures to assimilate. But the concept of universal human rights is a potent force throughout the world today. As such, a non-European culture practicing female genital mutilation may listen to pleas that the ritual violates human rights.

At the second, or intergroup level of redefining identities and boundaries, the group is viewed as a *collectivity,* or whole. Globalization seriously challenges groups' understanding of themselves and their relationship to other collectivities within the global context. This uncertainty may be illustrated by looking at the role of ethnic groups within nations. Members of ethnic groups frequently question whether their primary identity is as a part of their ethnic group or as citizens of the nations. People of one ethnic background may also question the identity of ethnic groups different from their own. For example, as Mexican Americans do we primarily see ourselves as Mexicans or as Americans? Further, how do Anglo Americans see us, as Mexicans or as Americans? If we decide to emphasize our ethnicity (i.e., we are *Mexican* Americans), how do we relate to the dominant group (Anglo Americans)? Do we recognize and submit to the dominant group? Do we violently or otherwise oppose the dominant group? Do we isolate ourselves from the dominant group? Do we assimilate into the dominant group?

We also are confronted with the boundary issue of who belongs to our group. Do we have to be born in Mexico to be considered a Mexican American? Or are children born to Mexican parents in the United States also Mexican Americans even though these children are themselves citizens of the United States? Should intermarriage with other ethnic groups be permitted? If intermarriage with other ethnic groups occurs, are the children of these marriages true Mexican Americans? If so, how Mexican do they have to be to be considered Mexican Americans? Do they have to be ¾, ½, ¼, or ⅛ Mexican?

Questions of citizenship or ancestry are not the only ones involved in establishing boundaries. For example, religious or secular ideologies and moral or normative behaviors may also be involved. Continuing our example, are those persons of Mexican ancestry who believe in assimilation true Mexican Americans? Or, are only those who advocate the strong assertion of their ethnic identity the true Mexican Americans? Behaviorally, just how "Mexican" does one have to "act" in order to be a true Mexican American?

Whereas these issues have been part of the dynamics of nations, which bring together many different religious, ethnic, class, and interest groups within their boundaries, such questions of identities and boundaries are further complicated by globalization. The globalization process enhances these questions by bringing more and more groups into contact with each other. With each new contact we have to answer questions about who we are, how the groups to which we belong see us in relationship to this new group, and what this new contact means to our personal identity. Is this new group within the boundary of some group or groups to which we belong, or is it outside of these groups? What happens if this group is included within the boundaries of some groups to which we belong and outside the boundaries of other groups to which we belong?

Globalization further aggravates identity/boundary issues by calling on people to identify with ever larger collectivities and to adopt universal norms. For example, members of certain groups may claim that their groups are distinct entities whose customs and practices cannot be questioned or interfered with by "outsiders." Yet some members within those groups may identify with more universal norms and

International disaster relief is an example of the cooperation of diverse groups across national boundaries.

claim the right to challenge practices of their group on the basis of universal expectations. An illustration of this basic conflict is found in the previously discussed practice of female genital mutilation. Those societies practicing female genital mutilation may claim that their way of life must not be challenged, but it may be challenged from within by activists emphasizing universal standards. Such societies also might listen to arguments based on membership in the inclusive community of many groups (nations) and traditions that comprise the global community. These issues are further complicated by the fact that the values and norms that currently are dominant in the global community are those derived from Western Europe. Many persons reared in societies with, for example, a Confucian or Islamic base question whether European values and norms should be used to judge behaviors in their non-European cultures. Chapter 9 discusses female genital mutilation in more detail.

The third, or species level, of redefining identities and boundaries involves our seeing ourselves as a species (the human species) among other species. In other words, it brings to our attention our relationship with something that we call "nature." The idea of what it means to be human and how this relates to the rest of the world varies tremendously from culture to culture. The modern Western world believes that human beings are distinct from the rest of nature. From this belief it follows that we must (and can) control and dominate nature. The awesome power of modern technology has made this approach to nature a problem, not only for European-based societies like our own, but also for all of humanity, perhaps for all forms of life on this planet. Yet many other cultures do not share this view that humans are distinct from the rest of nature. That is, they do not recognize what we call "nature," the "environment," or the "ecology" as different from human beings and their sociosphere. This situation is changing, however, as the rest of the world's cultures are becoming caught up in our definition of human identity and our perception of its effects. Thus, they are also becoming influenced by our need to redefine our relationship to the planet. It may turn out that the contribution of other cultures to our search for a global understanding on this issue will be immensely significant.

Social Perspective Taking and Globalization

Underlying the process of discourse (or dialogue) is **social perspective taking,** the process of taking into account the point of view of others. When we learn to take into account other perspectives, we extend our own mental and social boundaries and expand our views of the world and ourselves. In this interaction each participant's separate view becomes more inclusive through understanding the perspectives of others. In attempting to gain deeper mutual understanding, we usually seek common ground, to find the more general or basic things we share in common. Thus dialogue tends to generate more universal ideas, values, and principles. This search for universals does not involve simply seeking the lowest common denominator (e.g., we all must eat). It involves the search for ideas, principles, and values that permit those with diverse perspectives to make sense to one another (e.g., we all have human dignity). Continuing communication is supported by values of inclusiveness and universalism that are generated by genuine and open social perspective taking. It has been noted that social perspective taking drives the process of psychological (intellectual, social, moral) development, suggesting that this process may be basic to human growth (White, 1995; Basseches, 1984; Kohlberg, 1981; Selman, 1971; Mead, 1934).

Both inclusiveness, which honors and preserves important differences, and universalism, which acknowledges and promotes what is shared, are essential aspects of subjective globalization. Cooperation among diverse groups—both within the same nation and across national boundaries—requires skills based on these values. Business deals, negotiations between governments, dialogue among religious groups, exchanges of ideas among scientists, democratic governance in an increasingly pluralistic world all require social perspective taking and the values it generates.

But inclusiveness and universalism are often perceived as threats. In the process of becoming a member of any group, we internalize that group's way of life. Its culture gives our life meaning and purpose. We come to cherish the beliefs of the group and those who represent those beliefs and impart them to us, including our parents, teachers, and cultural heroes. Taking the perspectives of other groups challenges our beliefs and questions the authority of those from whom we learned them. This is especially true when the past relationship to these groups has been one of hostility, dominance, or submission (e.g., in the United States, an ardent Democrat may find it more difficult than a new voter who is less partisan to vote for a Republican). Indeed, it may be easier for many members of any group to rely on set group beliefs and ways of life than to trust the process of intergroup dialogue and social perspective taking. Examples of such resistance to change include paramilitary groups within the United States that oppose U.S. involvement in the UN, which they see as the tool of an international plot to overturn "Christian" civilization. Paramilitary group members and their sympathizers are so resistant to outside views that they are often ready to back up their opinions with acts of violence, as shown in the 1995 bombing of the federal building in Oklahoma City. Subjective globalization can generate greater inclusiveness and universalism and at the same time expand conflict and resistance to the globalization process.

Specific Value Themes in Subjective Globalization

A variety of specific themes arise in the subjective globalization process that involve values and perspectives, many of which stem from modern European cultural dominance. But other themes are far older in origin. Briefly, some of these are

- *Andocentrism:* The tendency to view the world from a culturally masculine point of view is called **andocentrism.** Someone who is andocentric assumes that those attitudes, actions, and ideas commonly perceived as traditionally characteristic of males represent the norm for both genders (e.g., "to get ahead in business, you have to be aggressive"). It is now often said, mainly in Western societies, that what have been socially marginal and denigrated "feminine" values and perspectives are necessary to deal with the complexity of contemporary issues (e.g., "To recognize that land mines are even an issue, you need compassion"). Accepting the female point of view (or voice) is a particularly important step in the direction of inclusiveness and universality.

- *Eurocentrism:* The assumption that European culture (also commonly referred to as Western culture, which includes the culture of the United States) and European experience are the norm for the world is called **Eurocentrism.** European culture and power have played a very influential role in the total globalization process. But European ideas, values, and social institutions are only part of the ongoing discourse that constitutes global cultural processes today. They are likely to become less important and less persuasive as globalization progresses. For example, the Western idea of separation of church and state has been increasingly challenged by Islamic ideas of the intertwining of church and state.

- *Homocentrism:* The practice of placing the interests and well-being of the human species before that of any other species or the biosphere itself is called **homocentrism.** We discussed earlier the notion of treating nature and culture (human beings) as distinct and separate and as such to assume that human beings need to control and master nature. This perspective derives from modern European thought, in which human culture is seen as purposive and, when led by modern science and technology, rational. Nature, in contrast, is viewed as without purpose or meaning, indifferent to human life and values. Although homocentrism remains a powerful influence within the global community, other ideas are challenging it. One such opposing idea is that if humans are to survive they will have to be more nurturing of the environment (e.g., the movement to save the Brazilian rain forest).

- *Dominance hierarchies and empowerment:* The centralized, top-down control structures characteristic of androcentric or patriarchal culture are called **dominance hierarchies.** Government bureaucracies and corporations have adopted these methods of organization and control throughout much of the modern period. They are very much the types of structure used in mass production and industrialization until fairly recent decades. Today's information technology, trends in networking and cooperative organization, and our growing understanding of the way ecosystems are organized may continue to contribute to the global erosion of hierarchical structures.

- *Mechanistic worldview:* The view that the world (and ourselves) can best be viewed as complex machines that are essentially lifeless, purposeless, and unconnected with human values and goals is called the **mechanistic worldview.** This view, mainly the product of Western science, has been extremely influential, leading to among other things the dependence on machines ("Without a car, I don't know how we'd survive"). Today many of the most powerful challenges to this view have come from within the sciences themselves. Modern quantum physics undermines the idea that a material universe exists apart from the conscious observer. The development and spread of the global environmental movement increasingly challenges the machine model, substituting a view of the universe based on the model of living organisms and conscious interaction among these living organisms (see Chapter 5 for a more detailed discussion of these concepts). Consciousness itself plays a key role in defining and creating the "material world."

Many of the specific themes we have touched on are developed throughout this book. For now it is important to understand what an all-inclusive process globalization is. In this discussion we simply suggest the acceleration of social interdependence across the cultural and political boundaries and the increasing recognition that all of humanity is affected by the same general forces. Globalization is a multifaceted process; it is not limited to economic and trade relations or to war and diplomacy. For the last five hundred years, modern Western European civilization has significantly influenced globalization in both its objective and subjective aspects.

Defining the Desired State

The ongoing evolution of the emerging world culture (or the ways in which it is being negotiated) forms the context in which national issues and global problems must be addressed. To deal effectively with global problems, we must have some common concept of a desired state. By **desired state** we mean that condition or situation to which a society or the planet should be aspiring. The desired state also may be used as a norm by which contemporary conditions are judged. For example, when dealing with racial discrimination, many experts at least implicitly advocate the desirability of a society without discrimination. Thus, they may judge current situations on the basis of the degree of racial discrimination compared to the desired state of no discrimination or advocate steps to take in moving society toward the sought-after goal of no discrimination.

We textbook authors do not always specify what we mean by the desired state (e.g., in discussing a free society, many of us simply assume this means a democracy but do not explicitly reveal this assumption to the reader). Moreover, criteria for assessing controversial positions and moving society toward some desired state are not frequently presented in sociology texts. We believe, however, that it is useful to the reader for us to state up front the basic assumptions that underlie our assessment of the various issues discussed in this book.

Dealing with the Real

One criteria we apply is taking a "realistic" approach to reform, whether on the local or global level. Some people believe that we can obtain the perfect world in which all want, hunger, and pain are eliminated; all people live in harmony; everyone is happy; and all human rights are secure. This state of society is not attainable, as desirable as it may be. The real world offers a limited amount of the things people want, such as power or wealth. The earth itself has biological and ecological limits and a finite quantity of resources. People simply cannot have everything they desire (see the box "FYI: Classifying Global Inequality"). Furthermore, situations in which everyone gains in the short term are not always possible. At times, the gains of one group come at the expense of at least one other group. This seems especially true when economic issues are in dispute. For example, in January 1994, a peasants' revolt broke out among desperately poor Indians in southern Mexico. Their basic demand was for land reform to permit them a greater share of the nation's wealth and a better chance at self-sufficiency. But the region's wealthy landowners saw the land as theirs. If they gave in to the peasants, they would, they believed, be depriving themselves of their property and their livelihood. The landowners were so resistant to the peasants' demands that they even threatened to use their own private armies to crush the revolt if the government was unwilling to do so. Frequently, hard decisions must be made between conflicting interests to settle problems at the national or the international level.

The difficulty of resolving conflicting interests and needs is intensified when global issues are involved. Here the short-term interests of entire nations may conflict with those of other countries. So it is that residents of First World countries maintain their lifestyles at the expense of residents of Third World countries. Third World countries in turn generally assert that they cannot curb destruction of the environment because they cannot afford to do so. Therefore, if they want the environment protected, First World societies should pay for that protection. Traditionally, First World nations have refused to do this, insisting that the country in which the destruction is occurring should be responsible. For example, the United States and other First World countries have often called on Brazil, a Third World country, to halt development in, and destruction of, its Amazonian rain forests, but they have been unwilling to provide funds to Brazil to develop means for supporting the mostly poor people whose livelihood would be destroyed if development of the rain forests were to be stopped.

Although we will demonstrate that some of these supposed conflicts are resolvable, nevertheless, at times choices must be made among seemingly irreconcilable alternatives. The conflict between Mexican peasants and wealthy landowners described earlier provides a good illustration. If the landowners keep their lands, the peasants will remain poor. If the peasants improve their lot by taking land for themselves, landowners will lose their property.

Defining the Ideal

Given that real-life situations demand making tough choices, some sort of standards in choosing among conflicting interests and needs must be provided for society. Many sociologists hesitate to select among competing interests because of their awareness of cultural relativity. This concern is even greater when value judgments about the desirability of certain conditions or decisions about whose interests should dominate are made. Especially when faced with such issues, sociologists commonly contend that science demands objectivity and that value judgments require subjective decisions. An additional difficulty for sociologists in deciding among competing interests is how to sift among the many criteria used by the groups involved in an issue.

Deciding the ideal becomes even more unwieldy for sociologists when entire cultures or groups of cultures disagree over the desirability of certain situations. For example, the United States and other societies in which Western values dominate usually

Classifying Global Inequality

A number of schemes have been proposed to define the categories for discussion of solutions to global inequities. Although they are commonly used, all of these schemes have some defects. One frequently used concept is the idea of "three worlds." The **First World** is comprised of the capitalistic, industrialized, Western nations of the Cold War period. The **Second World** is comprised of the Commonwealth of Independent States (the former Soviet Union) and its East European allies. The **Third World** consists of those nations—in Asia, Africa, and Latin America—that are not yet industrialized or are in the process of industrializing. This division remains the most widely used scheme, but it has serious drawbacks.

One difficulty with this typology is that it is a relic of the Cold War. In describing the First World this typology is obsolete in one major way: The Soviet bloc it describes no longer exists. Nevertheless, the economies that make up the former Soviet bloc do share common dilemmas. For example, many of these nations have terrible environmental problems that were compounded under socialist regimes. Additionally, many of their industrial plants are obsolete and cannot compete effectively in the global marketplace. Most of these nations also face the specter of mass unemployment as inefficient state-supported industries lose their subsidies, close, or are forced to streamline their workforce to become competitive.

Another problem with this typology is that a wide diversity of conditions is found among Third World countries. Some of these countries are rapidly improving their lot, while others are slipping into an ever deepening quagmire. Possibly for this reason some observers now speak of the **Fourth World,** made up of those nations whose economies are in such disarray that they have little hope of participating in the global trading system, let alone of dealing with the myriad of social and political problems plaguing them. Ethiopia and Bangladesh are examples of Fourth World countries.

Another scheme distinguishes among advanced industrial, industrial, industrializing, and nonindustrial nations. **Advanced industrial nations** (also called postindustrial nations) are those countries that have been industrialized the longest but are shifting the preponderance of their workforces from manufacturing sectors to service and information sectors. By *service sector* we mean those jobs providing some service to other people. Included in this category are salesclerks, teachers, lawyers, social workers, counselors, financial planners, and medical personnel. The information sector consists of companies and organizations that engage largely in creating, gathering, or distributing various kinds of data. These include enterprises focusing on researching and developing, but not manufacturing, new products. Other organizations in the information sector generate, collect, and distribute scientific, financial, and governmental information.

Industrialized nations are those in which the heaviest portion of their workforce is engaged in manufacturing some type of goods. **Industrializing nations** have begun a movement of their workforces from agricultural work and other occupations that meet the basic needs of their populations to industrial manufacturing. In contrast, the workforces of **nonindustrialized nations** have yet to make any movement from work that meets basic needs to the manufacture of goods.

support (at least nominally) the idea of the equality of men and women. In contrast, societies dominated by traditional values originating, for example, in many African cultures or in Islamic fundamentalism, consider male dominance to be the norm. When looking at such examples, it is not difficult to see that the cultures of the world are very different.

The great differences among cultures, then, is another reason that some sociologists argue that it is impossible to objectively choose between competing values, norms, and interests on both the global and national scale. According to this viewpoint, it is difficult to decide which set of standards should dominate in determining "desirable" outcomes in social

In contrast to Western values, societies dominated by traditional values originating in Islamic fundamentalism consider male dominance to be the norm.

conflicts. Moreover, sociologists are well aware of the problems inherent in ethnocentrism. We realize, as discussed earlier, that like other humans we judge others' values and behaviors from our own narrow perspective. For some sociologists these considerations cause them to argue that we must not impose our values on others or take sides in situations involving national and global social conflicts or problems.

But it seems to us that realistically most sociologists do take sides on social problems, at least implicitly, despite protestations of objectivity. Additionally, we suggested earlier that the effort to improve society is part of the "high tradition" in sociology to which sociologists should aspire. Yet some still argue that the diversity of world cultures may cause sociologists to arbitrarily choose normative (ethnocentric) standards and then to impose these standards on people not sharing them, as they choose the means and goals of efforts to solve global problems. For example, Western sociologists often impose their standard of equality between the sexes in assessing African or Southeast Asian cultures that are based on the assumption of inherent inequality between the sexes. When these "unequal" societies are found wanting by Western sociologists and others, programs for correcting the situation by moving the sexes toward equality may be set in motion.

World Cultures and Common Standards

We are certainly sympathetic to the concerns raised by ethnocentrism, cultural relativity, and cultural diversity. We believe, nevertheless, that it is demonstrable that for some time there has been emerging a "world culture" already operating according to certain standards that are being applied in the assessment of social issues by the international community. True, some societies reject these standards, the international community cannot always enforce them, and international norms continue to be debated and refined. Yet, a widely held, relatively clear set of criteria does exist by which we can begin to judge issues and establish goals for a desirable world order.

Even though these standards provide common ground for cross-cultural intercourse, the divergent cultures themselves do not necessarily become uniform. Rather, widely held norms, values, and beliefs often find unique expression at the local level. Thus, some departure from international norms may be acceptable within the international community. Such deviation by a given society may also be subject for debate with representatives of the larger community or may precipitate extranational intervention. Even within global systems, tensions continue to exist among nations, as well as among **ethnic groups**—people sharing a culture within contemporary nation-states.

The major social transformation in Western society associated with the rise of **modernism** has informed the emerging global culture. The values and standards of Western Europe have spread worldwide through exploration, colonization, commerce, and intellectual dialogue. Conversely, Western ideas have undergone modification as they interacted with non-Western traditions.

Out of this interchange certain acceptable standards have emerged by which we may establish desirable conditions in the global community as well as in individual nations. One of these standards is quite simple—situations or actions must be judged by their contribution to the long-term survival of the human race. Driven by population pressures and the ecological limits of the earth, people around the world are starting to examine the long-range impact of contemporary actions. For example, in the short run, industries that pollute the environment may be beneficial, providing jobs and improving the economic status of workers. Historically, people have accepted pollution as a tolerable side effect of the prosperity industry can bring. But now people often question whether the short-term gains associated with polluting industries outweigh the long-term risks to the health of employees and their families and whether the short-term benefits outweigh the long-term risks of destroying the biosphere that supports us all. The question of whether a given action or policy contributes to long-term human survival is increasingly becoming a factor in national decisions. Some even argue that the current generation must make sacrifices for future generations. This so-called *fourth-generation of human rights* is discussed in greater length in Chapter 2.

Restivo (1991) argues that science itself has provided significant mechanisms for the emergence of a common world culture. The norms of science such as (1) striving for objectivity; (2) eliminating bias in assessing objectives (or situations) studied; (3) presenting logical, tangible evidence for conclusions drawn; (4) conducting open inquiry; and (5) questioning everything, including authorities, traditions, and previously accepted scientific propositions are widely accepted as "proper" rules for determining truth. Societies that operate according to scientific principles have come to be increasingly seen by most social scientists and social critics as "desirable," whereas those that operate on unscientific principles are increasingly considered "undesirable."

Universal Declaration of Rights. The United Nations' **Universal Declaration of Human Rights** (see Appendix A) is an extremely significant document for establishing the standards of the "desirable state" in the global community. The Universal Declaration was written in 1948 for the United Nations by an international committee chaired by U.S. delegate to the UN Eleanor Roosevelt (1884–1962). The declaration was a response to the Nazi atrocities of World War II, which resulted in the perceived need for acceptable standards of behavior in the world community. But the declaration, a resolution of the UN, did not bind member states to obey its articles. This situation was corrected in 1966 by the **International Human Rights Covenants** (treaties), which were considered binding on those nations ratifying them. Most of the nations of the world have subsequently signed the covenants. The covenants are used by the international community to judge situations in nation-states whether they have ratified the covenants or not. The Universal Declaration and the covenants implementing it are generally called the **International Bill of Rights** (see Chapter 2 for more discussion of these documents).

The Universal Declaration is by far the most significant human rights standard in modern history, and the Human Rights Covenants represent elaborations on its basic tenets. Most of the subsequent major presentations of rights such as various UN resolutions, the European Convention for the Protection of Human Rights and Fundamental Freedoms, and the Charter of the Organization of African Unity (OAU) are based on the Universal Declaration. Moreover, numerous other attempts to protect rights of minorities, women, children, and other exploited groups worldwide represent an extension of the declaration's articles to specific populations. Finally, the Universal Declaration has been the foundation for most of the constitutions of the new nations that have been formed since the end of World War II in 1945.

Political and Social Rights. Most Americans are likely to think of human rights in terms of political rights. However, one of the remarkable features of the Universal Declaration is that it contends that both political/civil and social/economic rights are fundamental and universal. Through the Universal Declaration of Human Rights, the General Assembly of the UN proclaimed

> a common standard of achievement for all peoples and all nations, to the end that every individual and organ of society keeping this Declaration constantly in mind, shall strive by teaching and education to promote respect for these rights and freedoms and by progressive measures, national and international, to secure their universal and effective recognition and observance. (Universal Declaration, Preamble)

After holding that all people are born "free and equal" and are entitled to the rights and freedoms spelled out "without distinction of any kind, such as race, color, sex, language, religion political or other opinion, national or social origin, property, birth or other status" (Universal Declaration, Articles 1 and 2), the declaration sets out a series of basic rights and freedoms (see the box "FYI: Universal Human Rights" for a list of some of the important rights recognized by the global community).

The political and civil rights recognized by the global community may be seen as protections, whereas those recognized as social and economic rights may be viewed as aspirations or goals for the various nations of the world. In essence these interrelated sets of rights represent a "preferred state," or "utopia," toward which humankind should strive (De Kadt, 1980).

A Word of Caution. It is beyond the scope of this chapter to look at the theoretical debates and practical obstacles to efforts to implement the political and social rights presented in the Universal Declaration

Universal Human Rights

Universal Human Rights

Although the Universal Declaration ensures a number of rights, those that are most important for the purposes of this book are summarized here.

Political and Civil Rights—Universal Declaration Articles 3–21

1. life, liberty, and security of person (Article 3)
2. freedom from slavery (Article 4)
3. freedom from torture and inhumane treatment (Article 5)
4. equality before the law (Article 7)
5. freedom from arbitrary arrest (Article 9)
6. presumption of innocence (Article 11)
7. the right to privacy (Article 12)
8. marriage based on consent (Article 13)
9. the right to own property (Article 17)
10. freedom of religion and belief (Article 18)
11. freedom of association (Article 20)
12. the right to free and fair elections (Article 21)

Economic and Social Rights—Universal Declaration Articles 22–30

1. the right to social security and those resources of each state necessary for the realization of economic, social and cultural rights indispensable for personal dignity (Article 22)
2. the right to work and the right to compensation necessary to ensure that the worker and the worker's family can maintain a dignified existence (Article 23)
3. the right to health care, food, clothing, housing, medical care, and social services as well as security in case of unemployment (Article 25)
4. the right to education that prepares for careers and that promotes understanding, tolerance, and friendship (Article 26)

and the Human Rights Covenant. Chapter 2 describes these obstacles in detail. A few words about some of these issues should suffice here.

First, despite the objections of numerous groups that argue that these standards should not be applied to them, these rights criteria are being employed throughout the global community to define "civilized behavior." Nations or groups not conforming to these standards are frequently labeled "outlaws" by the international community through such organizations as the United Nations, human rights NGOs, the news media, and even global sports organizations such as the International Olympic Committee. Such labeling frequently has negative moral, economic, political, and/or military ramifications. For example, for more than a decade South Africa was isolated by most of the global community because of its racially discriminatory policies. News media brought international moral pressure to bear on South Africa's government to change its discriminatory practices. Trade with the country was severely limited. South Africa could not fully participate in international organizations like the UN. Its athletes were barred from participation in international sports. Exports of military goods to South Africa were restricted. This pressure helped to peacefully end the racist white government and replace it with a democratic government that better represented the interests of white and black South Africans alike.

Second, despite the international community's frequent difficulty in ensuring a nation's compliance with them, these rights still have a moral impact worldwide and remain the sought-after "desired state" for assessing the way countries handle internal problems. Finally, we are not claiming these rights are ultimate—either in the sense that they reflect cosmic values or in the sense that they cannot be questioned. We are suggesting, however, that they are a readily available tool for assessing and dealing with conflicts concerning the various global and U.S. problems studied in this book.

SUMMARY

1. Increasingly, we are living in a global community. A consequence is that many problems we perceive as uniquely "ours" are actually embedded in an international context.
2. **Sociology** is the study of social influences on human behavior. Humans are embedded in a **social web** (a complex net of social relations) from birth to death. By forming a **social construction of reality,** people develop explanations of reality and definitions of appropriate behavior.
3. While most sociologists teach **cultural relativism** (judging a culture by its own standards), most people practice **ethnocentrism** (judging other cultures by the standards of their own).
4. Having the **sociological imagination** (the ability to place our own biographies in historical context) involves awareness of the *transformative powers of history,* or history's impact on individuals.
5. A **social problem** is a condition adversely affecting a significant number of people. Defining a social problem implies a **value judgment,** an assessment based on values. A **global problem** consists of identifiable conditions threatening a significant number of people, resulting from negative effects of relations with the **sociosphere** and the **biosphere,** relief from which requires coordinated multinational action.
6. **Objective globalization** is the growing planetary interconnectedness of human social activity. **Subjective globalization,** or the shared meaning people assign to themselves and to others as a result of the globalization process, involves the redefinition of **identities** and **boundaries** on three levels: (1) self and group, (2) intergroup, and (3) our identity as a species.
7. **Social perspective taking,** taking into account others' points of view, extends our mental and social boundaries and expands our views of the world and self. The tendency to view the world from a culturally masculine point of view is called **andocentrism. Eurocentrism** is the assumption that European culture is the norm for the world. **Homocentrism** places the interests of the human species before that of any other.

8. A "world culture" may be emerging involving some shared standards and values. Within global systems, tensions continue to exist among **ethnic groups,** people who share a given culture within contemporary nation-states.
9. **Modernism** is the spread of European values and standards worldwide through exploration, colonization, commerce, and intellectual dialogue. One standard for desirable conditions in the global community as well as in individual nations is that situations or actions must be judged by their contribution to the survival of the human race.
10. The **International Bill of Rights** implements the **Universal Declaration of Human Rights** and the **International Human Rights Covenants,** treaties that set standards for acceptable behavior in the world community. These documents contend that both political/civil and social/economic rights are fundamental and universal.

Thinking Critically

1. The social construction of reality is one of the key concepts in sociology. Potentially, there are as many "realities" as there are groups to construct them. Does this mean that there are no common features in the constructed reality? If commonality does occur, what is its source? Is there any "reality" besides those realities we socially construct?
2. How are the failures in economic, social, political, and ecological systems the result of modernism reaching its limits? How are these failures being propelled by globalization? In what sense could these failures be considered the birth pangs of a new stage of social organization that goes beyond modernism?
3. This text argues that we should avoid Eurocentrism but also acknowledges the importance of European influences and values (such as human rights) in the globalization process. Why does this apparent contradiction occur? In the future, will non-European values and ideas (such as those of Confucian Asia and Islam) come to play a large role? Discuss your answers.

Suggested Readings

Berger, Peter. 1963. *Invitation to Sociology: A Humanistic Perspective.* New York: Doubleday.

Boulding, Elise. 1990. *Building a Global Civic Culture.* Syracuse, NY: Syracuse University Press.

Collins, Randall and Michael Makowsky. 1984. *The Discovery of Society.* New York: Random House.

Fitzpatrick, Ellen. 1990. *The Endless Crusade: Women Social Scientists and Progressive Reform.* New York: Oxford University Press.

Gouldner, Alvin W. 1962. "Anti-Minotaur: The Myth of Value Free Sociology." *Social Problems.* 9:199–213.

Horton, Paul B. and Donald H. Bouma. 1971. "The Sociological Reformation: Immolation or Rebirth." *Sociological Focus.* 4:24–41.

Magaziner, Ira C. and Mark Patinkin. 1989. *The Silent War: Inside the Global Business Battles Shaping America's Future.* New York: Random House.

Mills, C. Wright. 1959. *The Sociological Imagination.* New York: Oxford University Press.

Restivo, Sal. 1991. *The Sociological Worldview.* Cambridge, MA: Basil Blackwell, Inc.

Rifkin, Jeremy. 1980. *Entropy: A New World View.* New York: Viking.

Robertson, Roland. 1992. *Globalization: Social Theory and Global Culture.* Newberry Park, CA: Sage.

Spector, Malcolm and John I. Kitsuse. 1987. *Constructing Social Problems.* Hawthorne, NY: Aldine.

Wapner, Paul. 1996. *Environmental Activism and World Civil Politics.* Albany, NY: State University of New York Press.

Wilber, Ken. 1996. *A Brief History of Everything.* Boston: Shambala.

Worsley, Peter. 1984. *Three Worlds: Culture and World Development.* Chicago: University of Chicago Press.

Web Sites

United Nations Development Program (UNDP)

URL: http://www.undp.org

At this site an abundance of information about UN agencies can be found, especially the UNDP. The UNDP statement of purpose and governing structure are available, as are copies of current press releases and current information about UN conferences. The site also provides links to other UN organizations as well as to related organizations.

World Bank

URL: http://www.worldbank.org/html/extdr/country.htm

This site contains reports presenting a number of statistics on global poverty, financial assistance, and standard of living measures. A good source on problems of development.

PART ▪ ONE

Negotiating a Global Civil Society

We tend to think of governance as being the sole business and privilege of the government (or the state), but we shall see that this is not the case. The state *is that organization within a society that makes binding decisions regarding the collective actions of its citizens and enforces these decisions by means of its monopoly over the legitimate use of force, including the police and the military. But traditionally the state has been contrasted with a more encompassing and more fundamental aspect of collective governance called the civil society.*

Civil society *consists of all nonstate social processes that have an impact on how people collectively behave, including those forms of empowerment that rest on norms, values, and communication processes rather than on law and the use of or threat of force. Civil society, then, represents a more subtle form of power than that exercised by the state, in that it actually shapes people's perceptions of themselves and their world. By influencing people's tastes and desires, the civil society provides extremely effective constraints over their actions. Such constraints are less likely to lead to resistance and resentment than are law and its enforcement. Building a degree of consensus among the world's peoples based on developments such as emerging value systems and identities, which require ongoing dialogue, is what we mean by* negotiating a global civil society.

Traditionally, discussions that have sought to build consensus have included economic activity in the concept of what is a civil society. This is still technically *accurate. However, both the state (the government) and the economy have long since become dominant institutions of modern societies and of the global arena. Consequently, much of the economic activity in the world today is orchestrated by powerful groups and their leaders. Because of this fact, economic activity represents a form of power and influence that needs to be kept conceptually separate from our discussion of civil society. Therefore, in this book we have chosen to consider the dominant spheres of economic activity and governments as distinct from global civil society and to deal with their contributions separately. Moreover, political and economic actions are influenced by the normative and affective (emotional) commitments that make up the civil society. It is this broader cultural context that forms the matrix in which government, economy, and, indeed, all types of social life occur. We focus on that context in this section.*

Civil Society and Global Culture

The negotiation of civil society is a very complex process that is only beginning to take shape on a global level. In the following three chapters, we examine changes in global culture, concentrating on the processes of interaction in which ideas, information, symbols, and concepts are shared among the people of the world. In these processes of interaction, concepts of reality, of personal and group identity, and of the global community itself are created and modified. Because of these processes of interaction, deep changes are taking place in the fundamental assumptions and ideas that shape contemporary life. In the three chapters of this section, we examine several aspects of globalization in light of changes described by anthropologist Kay Milton. Milton (1996) describes these as changes within contemporary social science. As such, they represent challenges to the assumptions of modernism. The same patterns, we believe, are applicable to the larger arena of globalization.

Culture as Process

Today we see an increasingly global culture emerging that is caused by a process of interaction in which elements of many distinct cultures, scientific ideas, health practices, art, music, values, and religious beliefs are now communicated across social boundaries that were previously thought to be barriers to communication. Indeed, contemporary global culture is not a single coherent system of shared beliefs but is a web of interactions. It is a dynamic process of change, in which identities, values, beliefs, and experiences are continuously being negotiated. Naturally, during this process ideas and values will converge and diverge. The passionate struggle to find universals and to achieve agreement will continue to compete with equally passionate struggles to define what is unique and different in each group. Efforts to come together will compete with efforts to remain apart. Culture as process encompasses all of these options.

Critique of Cultural Relativism

Another important trend is the questioning of extreme cultural relativism. Cultural relativism has reigned supreme in intercultural discussions and in the social sciences for some time. The fact that we can communicate across cultural lines to some extent, that we can appreciate one another's unique cultural creativity and then find a degree of convergence among diverse cultures about many basic values, suggests that we human beings share more in common than we may have previously imagined. In the discussion in this section of human rights and interfaith dialogue, we show that although deep differences remain among the world's people, groups are still able to find similar ideas and values and ways of coming together in order to cooperate on basic issues. A new understanding of what is universal may be coming about.

These developments create questions about two divergent assumptions of the modern outlook. One is that there is a single universal point of view represented by the dominant modern culture which, as the result of progress, will supersede traditional and primitive views. The other is that, apart from science, with its universal method of objective observation, human judgments are relative matters of opinion about which there can be no consensus. Today both the notions of the progress of culture and the objectivity of science are under challenge. The possibility that judgments of value and meaning in areas of morality and human rights may converge is now being acknowledged.

Dualism Challenged

Dualism, *long a hallmark of modern thinking, is the belief that a wall of separation exists between mind and body, culture and nature, male and female, self and others, and so forth. The way to dualism was led by twentieth-century scientists who showed that the act of observation changed the object observed, which made the idea of objective reality and of complete prediction and control impossible. But now scientists are gradually showing that dualism is only a concept and not an explanation of the way things really are. More and more we see that we cannot separate human beings (and society) from nature or nature from ourselves. Nor can we as people of diverse cultures define and understand ourselves without also understanding other cultures. Today we are coming to understand that the world's cultures have never been as isolated as we sometimes like to think. All of today's supposedly unique cultures, religions, or worldviews are really the outcomes of countless influences. The processes of interaction and cultural change we address in the following chapters are simply the contemporary experience of the interpenetration and mutual enrichment of cultures.*

The elements of culture, beliefs, values, norms, and practices are not simply fixed components that affect our actions and interactions in specific ways. They are variable factors that are also affected by our actions and interactions. Awareness of this fact amounts to the recognition that the dualism perceived between culture (mind) and nature (body) is a fallacy. A similar insight is applicable to our social, and even our species, identities. Believing that their group, its beliefs and its way of life, is alone good and true sometimes sets one group of people against other groups. Yet social identities change; in fact, even the process of opposing other groups changes identities. The challenge to dualism may be most significant in the area of ecology. Our sense that we are a unique species separate from nature not only causes us to believe we can exploit nature for our use; it may also deprive us of a sense of being a meaningful part of the world in which we live.

Globalization

A final set of changing assumptions has to do with the recognition of the globalization process itself. Everything we have said in this introduction contributes to this recognition. However, globalization itself rests on the possibility that out of today's interactions a new global civil society is arising. The new civil society consists of a web of relationships that give rise to informal norms and values that direct collective action in certain directions.

Social movements are especially important in the formation of a global civil society. Social movements *are more or less large-scale collective activities that operate outside the institutionalized (i.e., socially established) order and arise in response to what are widely perceived as social issues. Today social movements have been spawning groups referred to as nongovernmental organizations (NGOs), of which there are some 100,000 in existence. Many of these are international or even global in scope. Of interest to us in the following chapters are groups dedicated to human rights, groups dedicated to interfaith dialogue, and groups dedicated to environmental and ecological issues.*

In his book Environmental Activism and Global Civil Society *(1996), Paul Wapner describes the role of environmentally oriented NGOs. The recent growth of these organizations, he says, parallels the emergence of a new type of social movement (called, simply, new social movements) that differs from previous ones in the following ways:*

1. *They are less focused on narrowly defined economic issues and are more oriented toward quality of life issues.*
2. *Their organizational structures emphasize participation in decision making and decentralization of power.*
3. *They are formed in response to postindustrial problems, such as the inability of governments to deal with total environmental collapse or the invasion of governments into private spheres.*
4. *They hold conferences, give nature walks, create citizen's tribunals, and so forth, with the goal of getting*

"people" to change rather than getting governments (states) to act. This is in contrast to previous movements that sought to influence state actions by petitioning government agents, trying to win elections, and similar methods.

Cultural Change and Consciousness

Social change is generally gradual and tends to emerge from minor adjustments or variations in the patterns of human action and interaction. Of course, social change is occasionally dramatic and results in a transformation of nearly all aspects of society. These changes often involve a shift in the resource base on which a society draws. (We will look into these kinds of change in Part Two.) There is also another variety of deep change that has occurred at times in human history. This kind of change involves a transformation in consciousness that alters the way people experience themselves and their world. You may believe that how you experience yourself and the world is a given fact and that it could not be different. But actually consciousness of self and consciousness of the world are themselves variable. As sociologist Peter Berger says, "History brings forth and dissolves one structure of consciousness after another" (Berger, 1979:120).

In this book we at times refer to structures of consciousness called modernism and postmodernism, as well as other such structures. We explore these further in the following chapters but let us offer a brief explanation of them here. **Modernism** *is a set of assumptions and orientations to the world that holds that progress in all aspects of human life can be achieved by the application of reason to nature and to society. It supports science, technology, and what we view as rational social institutions such as democracy and capitalism (or socialism, depending on which version of modernism is involved). Modernism engaged in an all-out skeptical attack on traditional culture based on modernism's own version of rationality.*

Postmodernism *is the phase of contemporary culture that recognizes the failure of modernism to achieve progress after centuries of effort. This failure is especially apparent for situations in which modernism equated material growth (which has occurred) with social and moral progress (which is highly doubtful). Postmodernism applies an advanced version of rational skepticism to modernism, much in the manner that modernism was and is skeptical of traditional cultures. Postmodernism questions progress and science and believes that worldviews serve political ends. Any attempt to arrive at a single worldview is, according to this view, an act of political domination. We explore whether other possibilities for contemporary cultures exist today. For example, can we find signs of any way out of the dilemmas of relativism and skepticism with which postmodernism presents us?*

In this unit we examine the division between values and meaning (human rights and religion), on the one hand, and the realm of objective fact (science and technology), on the other hand. This split is a characteristic of modernism as it developed over time. Postmodernism tends to view even science as a product of social and political forces rather than as a purely objective and value-free enterprise. Again, we ask whether there is a possible way of thought and culture that might bring these opposing tendencies together. We look at elements of this process of convergence in the following chapters and review the concept of integral culture in greater detail in the Epilogue.

CHAPTER ▪ TWO

Human Rights

Negotiating the New Civil Order

In 1995, Guadalupe Montenegro arrived by bus in Longview, Texas, with two small children and two suitcases. She had graduated from college and was a registered nurse in her native El Salvador. Her saga of repression, torture, and killings in her homeland puts a human face on the tragedy of political violence still existing in many places around the globe, as shown in the following excerpts from an interview she gave in the United States.

> My country has a long history of killing, torture and repression. My grandmother told me of terrible things which happened when she was small. We have no bill of rights, but have come to realize we have the responsibility to struggle for our freedom and rights. . . .
>
> I went to the university to study to be a medical doctor. About 1968, a "student revolt" broke out at the university against the U.S. and the Salvadoran regime. It was popular to hate the US and our government because we realized the money sent by the US didn't help the people. It was used to support the corrupt government. . . .
>
> We were not taught about rights at the university. We learned about rights from the followers of Fidel Castro (1926–) and Che Guevara (1928–1967). Most of us were not communists, but anyone who spoke out against the government was called "communist" by the government. This gave the authorities a reason for attacking opponents. . . .
>
> When my mother heard of the disturbances at the university, she came and dragged me home. She took away my clothes and locked me in my room in my underwear so I couldn't leave. I was very angry at the time, but later I was glad. Most of my friends demonstrating at the university were killed. Mother probably saved my life. . . .
>
> At first, the National Guard was not too harsh. . . . Later they became more repressive. They started abducting people—mostly men. They disappeared and their families never saw them again. The lucky ones came back after light torture like beatings. . . . The National Guard became the real power. They were like Nazis in my country. . . .
>
> One of my friends . . . disappeared because he came from a "communist family." They, the National Guard, were tracking him and he disappeared. . . . His uncle was the Minister of Defense and Security. Even he could do nothing to save his nephew. . . . They found him dead with many signs of torture. . . .
>
> My best friend, a psychologist, got killed. . . . She was married to a left-wing architect. Her husband was forced to leave the country. . . . My friend stayed in the country, but the death squads were active. . . . They couldn't get her husband, so they got her. . . . She was taken by the right wing. . . . [Her family] found her hanging on a bridge. . . . They had cut off her breasts, pulled out her fingernails, and burned her with cigarettes. Only her family, my husband, and I went to the funeral. Everyone else was afraid. . . .
>
> Women were subjected to torture and rape. If they had babies, the National Guard would take the babies and sell them. . . . They placed welding rods [electric probes] in the men's rectums and women's vaginas to make them confess. I don't know what they wanted the prisoners to confess. . . .
>
> Left-wing guerrillas became stronger, but they were no good either. They took what they wanted, including young girls. . . . The left wing talked about justice, food, and equal distribution of land and goods, but these [ideas] were used by the real communists to mask their purposes. We were afraid of the real communists. . . .
>
> Things are better now [in El Salvador]. There is healing produced by a new government and activities of the Christian church. I am not afraid to go back any more.

Printed by permission of Guadalupe Montenegro.
Personal communication to the authors.

Most Americans would recognize the conditions Guadalupe Montenegro described as human rights violations. Unfortunately, her story is not unique, neither in this century nor in any other. People have always had to flee from war and brutal repressions of their human rights. Many Americans, however, would probably fail to recognize that human rights are also violated when people work in unsafe work environments or are inadequately compensated by their employers. Even fewer would probably understand that forcing a single mother and her children into the streets because she has lost her job and cannot pay her rent also represents a violation of human rights. Yet, according to the UN Universal Declaration of Human Rights and numerous subsequent international agreements, they are indeed human rights violations. For, according to these documents, all people not only have basic rights to political freedom, but to safety and dignity at work, health care, shelter, and education. We agree with such standards and in this book we agree with sociologist John Humphrey's definition of **human rights** as all of "those individual rights and freedoms that pertain to the human person by reason of his [her] humanity, whether they are civil and political or economic, social and cultural rights" (1989:21).

In Chapter 1 we discussed the necessity of defining a "desired state" before global problems can be addressed. We also indicated that the human rights situation within nations provides a widely recognized standard for assessing even diverse conditions and for choosing among conflicting interests when seeking solutions to global problems. But to understand adequately the role of human rights in the global civil order, we need to be aware of the history and development of human rights, the nature of these rights, and the current debates about them.

In this chapter we also examine human rights as a pivotal force in the contemporary world in which a new global civil order is emerging. To set the proper context, we explain why the human rights theme runs throughout this book and review the history of such rights before, during, and immediately after World War II. We look at issues associated with the expansion of human rights in the last half of our century, then discuss some additional contemporary issues revolving around human rights. Next, we review some of the worst examples of civil and political rights violations in the twentieth century. Finally, we assess the international and domestic human rights record of the United States.

Why Emphasize Human Rights?

When understood in the broad sense outlined in the UN Universal Declaration, human rights are key components of the emerging civil society for several reasons. First, a close relationship exists between human rights and dignity. As human rights expert John Humphrey argues, "human rights are those without which there can be no human dignity" (1989:21). What is this connection? Noted writer on human rights David Forsythe explains:

> If one has a human right, one is entitled to make a fundamental claim that an authority, or some other part of society, do—or refrain from doing—something that affects significantly one's human dignity. Human rights [are not] property, something possessed, but a social and behavioral process. Human rights constitutes a fundamental means to the end of basic human dignity.
>
> Human dignity . . . has never been precisely defined . . . but it accords roughly with justice or the good society. (Forsythe, 1991:1)

Human rights, then, focus on people's relation to power structures and society. Because they believe they have certain rights, individuals and groups can have certain expectations of their communities and their nations. Let us look at this connection more closely. Human rights frequently are said to reflect human needs. It has been commonly agreed that people have basic needs for food, clothing, and shelter. In the emerging civil society, in many nations these basic needs have also been extended to include the need for a societal life-support system. By *societal life-support system* we mean that society has the obligation to provide people with the means necessary for survival such as food, shelter, job security, health care, and education. Many members of modern western societies also believe that people need civil rights and the right to democratic participation in order to lead lives of dignity.

This expansion of needs suggests the importance of the social context in defining "basic rights." That is, human rights do not simply exist in some unchanging form; human beings define what are and what are not human rights. Throughout the twentieth century the modern social community (or the societies of the world) has continually extended human rights to additional groups while identifying new rights. Indeed, numerous social issues worldwide pivot around the question of what is and what is not a basic human right. For example, some people contend that human rights should encompass not only the satisfaction of physical needs and the protection of political freedoms but also people's desires and aspirations.

Second, human rights are a driving force in globalization because they provide universal standards that transcend national boundaries and interests by undermining the sovereignty of nation-states. That is, human rights require people to identify with global standards that erode their connection to particularisms such as nation-states or ethnic groups. Human rights also are based on widely held values, and as such, set limits to actions originating from narrowly defined political and economic interests. Partly for these reasons, in the international community, "human rights" is already used as a convenient umbrella term for standards applied in judging a multitude of situations in all societies, including the United States. In other words, although human rights conventions are constantly evolving, a relatively clear set of widely accepted international norms is now in place which can "help achieve a match between human needs and available resources" (Wronka, 1992:3). Said differently, when the goal of society is to extend basic human political, social, and economic rights to everyone, allocating scarce resources will present little difficulty; for all people are entitled by birthright not only to political and civil freedoms but also to social and economic conditions that allow them to maintain a dignified standard of living. The use of such a standard immediately clarifies many situations. More specifically, by applying the standard of human rights to situations in which portions of the population do not have access to the economic or social resources to live decently, it becomes clear that sufficient assets must be reallocated to those in need.

Finally, human rights are a pivotal aspect of a larger global dynamic—the renegotiation of the global civil order. Globalization has recently passed from one phase, which lasted for the 40 years of the Cold War and was characterized by the struggle of the two superpowers for domination of the globalization process itself, and has moved into a new phase characterized by uncertainty. This new phase was ushered in by the collapse in the early 1990s of the former Soviet Union, and with it the end of the Cold War. No comparable set of issues and international relations has since emerged to direct global politics.

The end of the Cold War is not the only cause for the uncertainty that marks the decade. Another is the widespread perception that the world is at a turning point (the literal meaning of "crisis") and that the present generation may determine whether we continue to experience a rapid breakdown of the old social order, or an equally rapid breakthrough to some kind of new order. The phrase "new order" raises justified fears in some people's minds, but it does not necessarily signify a single world government or a top-down planetary management system. Rather, what is more likely to emerge is the renegotiation of principles and procedures that may possibly permit the earth's diverse human groups, cultures, nations, and religions to live together with a degree of peace and harmony rooted in mutual respect and a shared sense that we exist for the common good both of humanity as a whole and of the planet itself. This new order, which will include the constant renegotiation of issues of identities, values, social organization, and modes of involvement in the world, will eventually become a tentative global civil culture. Such a culture will help guide behavior in the **global civil society,** or "that slice of collective activity that takes place above the individual and below the state yet across state [national] boundaries" (Wappner, 1996:150). The continuing controversies and intercultural dialogues we now see that focus on issues of rights (and duties) really are about discovering the shared higher principles to govern the ever growing networks of human relationships extending beyond the boundaries of nation-states—in other words, the burgeoning global civil society.

A Brief History of Human Rights

To understand the significance of human rights in the new global civil society, we first must examine their long evolution. The historical development of human rights contains many twists and turns but generally has revolved around questions related to people's obligations toward one another and their relation to the state. In this evolution people's duties and privileges usually rested upon changing religious and philosophical precepts. For our purposes we divide the history of human rights into three periods: (1) before World War II, (2) during the period encompassing World War II and the founding of the United Nations, and (3) after the establishment of the United Nations.

Human Rights prior to World War II

The term "human rights" is a relatively new creation, rarely used before World War II. Although the focus on human rights originated in Western culture, other societies, including those in the East, also have used and continue to use the concept. The foundations for both Eastern and Western thought (including ideas underlying the notion of human rights) lie in their respective religious traditions. It is beyond the scope of this text to explore these traditions in depth. Rather, we briefly discuss some key notions leading to the modern idea of human rights.

Greek and Roman Origins of Western Tradition. Among the most significant contributions Greek culture made to the notion of human rights were those of the philosopher Aristotle (384–322 B.C.E. or Before the Common Era, i.e., before the era shared by Christians and Jews). Like all ancient philosophers, Aristotle stressed the importance of cultivating human nature by acquiring virtuous attitudes and character. He believed that humans are rational, political animals; that is, they are members of a *polis* (a social-political order). Our rationality and our sense of justice are rooted in our social context (MacIntyre, 1988). Society is necessary to the development of higher-level aspects of the person. Duty, as well as rights, exist as part of our human nature.

Justice, which entails equality before the law, is central to Aristotle's thinking. These realities of moral and social life are embedded in some fashion in our essence, or human nature, or as German political philosopher Karl Marx (1818–1883) would later suggest, our "species being." Aristotle's concept of rights, as such, involves freedom from coercion, a freedom necessary to the fair and equal participation of the citizen in the life of the polis.

After the Romans conquered the Mediterranean basin, wresting power from the Greeks (146 B.C.E.), they also took over much of Greek culture. The Romans further developed the concept of the duties and rights of citizens. The privileges of full Roman citizenship were highly coveted. Roman concepts of citizenship and law had a tremendous impact on the development of Western civilization.

A school of Roman philosophy known as Stoicism also was very influential in developing notions about human rights. Like the Greek philosophers, the Stoics emphasized the cultivation of personal virtue. But the Stoics also were concerned about the social or political order. Although they believed a person could still be virtuous in a corrupt society, the Stoics recognized the social, or political, nature of human beings and the need for a just society. Indeed, "equality" of all classes of people before the law is a central Stoic concept. The notion of a "brotherhood of man" represents a key idea in later Stoic thinking. The Stoics also believed that international law is rooted in nature and so transcends the norms of specific societies.

The ancient Romans also recognized many negative freedoms or negative rights. They recognized that people should be free from external forces imposing on them. Coercion, intimidation, lies, and bribery were viewed as depriving people of their just due in a court and were therefore recognized as social ills.

The Judeo-Christian Origins of Western Tradition. The Hebrew scriptures (Old Testament) trace the origins of the Jewish religion, nation, institutions, and philosophy from the Exodus, or the escape from Egypt (ca. thirteenth century B.C.E.), until roughly the lifetime of Jesus of Nazareth. Several human rights concepts emerged in ancient Judaism. One concept is that a person's relationship to God is expressed by the ethical treatment of fellow Jews. Thus, the first four of the Ten Commandments have to do with the Hebrews' (early Jews) relation to God, whereas the last six commandments concern human-to-human affairs, such as not stealing from or killing other Hebrews. Moreover, Jews saw themselves as equal before the biblical Law and God's judgment regardless of their social status.

The prophets introduced another significant element into Jewish thought: The true way to worship God and be obedient to his Law is to practice justice. At the minimum justice entails fair treatment for all. The king has a special obligation to see that justice is done in his land. The true measure of a society, according to the Hebrew scriptures, is how it treats its "weakest links" (usually expressed as the poor, widows, and orphans). Eventually, these principles were applied to all people, not just to Jews. This approach has been encapsulated in the phrase the "Fatherhood of God and the brotherhood of man."

Like the Hebrew texts, the Christian scriptures (New Testament) say little specifically about what we now call human rights. Jesus continued the basic teachings of his Jewish heritage about the Fatherhood of God, the ethical nature of true religion, and the equality of everyone before God and spent much of his ministry among outcasts. Jesus challenged his listeners to recognize the presence of God's Kingdom and live according to its ethics, which granted special favor to the poor and the meek. The early Christian church dealt little with issues of human rights; however, it did emphasize assisting fellow Christians in need. It taught an ethic of basic equality among its members (including men and women as well as masters and slaves) but did not try to change the injustices of societies in which it was embedded.

Human Rights in the Middle Ages in Europe. During the Middle Ages (roughly from the fifth to the fifteenth centuries C.E.), the Church faced a number of difficult questions, including the relationship between church and state—the obligation of Christians to the state and the duty of the state toward its citizens, especially Christians. Much of Western Europe's understanding of the role of the state during the Middle Ages originated in two documents: *City of God* by Augustine of Hippo (354–430 C.E.) and *Pastoral Rule* by Pope Gregory I, who was pope from 590 to 604 C.E., or Christian Era. Augustine and Gregory introduced the concept that the bishop and the king must rule according to the principles of Christ or be subject to deposition. Although ruling "according to the principles of Christ" had considerable possibilities for advancing human rights, the medieval Church mainly focused on protecting the "faith" (i.e., its authority) against "heretics" and secular rulers. Personal duty consisted of obeying authority and carrying out obligations to religious and secular rulers. Little concern was shown for safeguarding individual rights.

In the later Middle Ages, theologians developed a powerful doctrine of natural law, according to which the universe is infused by principles laid down by God. These principles are observable in the laws of nature, but appear also in social relations and human nature, where they demand moral behavior and justice. Natural law was to become a basis for later assertions of human rights (Wronka, 1992). For example, during the eighteenth century, European thinkers translated natural law into the "self-evident truths" that informed such documents as the Declaration of Independence (1776) and the U.S. Constitution (1788).

The Middle Ages were brought to an end by the Protestant Reformation, a series of complex social, cultural, political, religious, and intellectual changes occurring from the fifteenth to the seventeenth centuries that set the stage for the modern world. During the Reformation, theologians such as Martin Luther (1483–1546) asserted the freedom of individual conscience while various groups such as Anabaptists, Baptists, and Puritans fanned the flames of religious liberty. Eventually, the dynamics begun in the Reformation resulted in religious freedom becoming the first human right to be recognized in international law (Humphrey, 1989).

Human Rights in England. Three developments in England deserve special attention for their influence on the development of our notions of human rights. In 1215 English nobles defeated the tyrant King John (ruled 1199–1216), forcing him to sign the Magna Carta, a landmark document in the development of human rights. The Magna Carta limited the power of the king by placing him under the rule of law while granting citizens minimal protections against unreasonable arrest and trials without proper legal processes. The subsequent prolonged struggles between the English people and their kings resulted in the expansion of these rights, documented in the Petition of Right (1628) and the English Bill of Rights (1689). Together these two documents further restricted the king's ability to act arbitrarily, limited taxation without approval from the people's representatives, defined legal protections of a fair trial, helped ensure free speech, and assured fair and open elections. Although these documents did not claim universal rights (but were limited to privileges won by Englishmen), their effects were wide-ranging. For example, the ideas in these two documents helped inspire the American Revolutionary War (1775–1783) and the French Revolution (1789); in addition, many nations have subsequently included a bill of rights in their constitutions.

The Enlightenment and Human Rights. The Petition of Right and the English Bill of Rights were drawn up during the Enlightenment, a new school of thought that continued throughout the eighteenth century, emphasizing rational, liberal, and scientific ideas. During the Enlightenment (also called the Age of Reason), thinkers asserted the existence of individual, natural, self-evident rights and the powers of human reason. The Enlightenment culminated in the American and French Revolutions, in which people attempted to form governments based on what they saw as the inalienable rights due to all citizens. Several important documents that have immensely influenced world opinion came out of these revolutions. The American Revolution created the Declaration of Independence (1776), the U.S. Constitution (1788), and the Bill of Rights (1791). The French Revolution produced the Declaration of the

Rights of Man and Citizen (1791). For the next two centuries, these three documents underpinned much of political thought.

Despite the significance of these three documents, they enunciated a limited number of human rights, mainly political and civil rights (whose implementation was often impeded). This focus largely explains why most Americans today do not identify social, economic, and cultural issues as human rights problems. Thus, although these documents protect citizens against the tyranny of government (which was the major concern of their drafters), they do not require the government to provide for the welfare of its citizens. For example, freedom of speech and religion are protected, but the government is not required to educate or give economic security to its citizens. It is only during the twentieth century that economic, social, and cultural issues have become human rights concerns.

Another limitation of these documents is that they do not specify who is entitled to these rights. For example, they contain the statement that "all men" are endowed by their Creator with inalienable rights. But originally the protections of the Constitution and the Bill of Rights were extended solely to white property-holding male citizens. Women, slaves, and non-property owners were excluded. Many of the civil rights battles of the nineteenth and twentieth centuries have centered on extending constitutional protections to these groups.

Additionally, the "inalienable rights" in these documents applied only to citizens of the nation that produced the document. Aliens residing within these nations or people who lived in, or were citizens of, other countries were not protected. This convenient exclusion allowed the United States and European nations (those adopting constitutions based on these models) to exploit minorities within their boundaries and to develop colonies abroad that enslaved native peoples.

This exclusion had devastating import. For example, because of little concern for the rights of native peoples, the "Indian problem" in the United States was not "solved" until the 1890s, after Native Americans had been killed or deprived of their ancestral lands and herded onto reservations. The United States also joined the major European nations in establishing colonies abroad. Most European nations did not divest themselves of their colonies until after World War II. The problems produced for many native peoples affected by colonization have yet to be fully addressed. Issues of minorities, native peoples, and colonization are discussed at greater length in Chapters 7, 8, and 11.

Human Rights in the Nineteenth and Early Twentieth Centuries. The nineteenth and twentieth centuries witnessed progress on some human rights fronts. Most notably, slavery and the slave trade were ended. Other slave-like practices such as trade in women and children also have been limited or outlawed by the international community. In addition, the Geneva Conventions (1864–1949), a series of treaties signed by nations, attempted to ensure that the human rights of combatants during wartime were not violated.

World War I (1914–1918) marked a significant turning point in human history. The terrible destruction wrought by increasingly advanced weapons produced through modern science and technology made future war seem unthinkable to survivors. In the war's aftermath, the victors created the first modern international peace organization, the League of Nations, to provide mechanisms other than armed conflict to resolve disputes between nations. The league proved generally ineffective for a number of reasons. Probably the most important was that the United States retreated into **isolationism**—a policy of nonparticipation in international political and economic affairs—and refused to join the league. The league, weakened by its ineffectiveness in preventing World War II, dissolved itself in 1946.

The Impact of World War II and the Holocaust

The period after World War I was a turbulent time. Political instability and worldwide depression led to the domination of fascist parties in Italy and Germany. **Fascism** is a system of government led by a dictator holding complete power who crushes the opposition, espouses extreme nationalism, and often employs racism in pursuit of state ends. The same internal conditions strengthened a powerful military dictatorship in Japan. Eventually, the dictatorships in Germany, Italy, and Japan formed the Fascist, or Axis powers, whose military aggression was opposed by the Allies—England, the Soviet Union, the United States, free France, free portions of China, and a host of other smaller nations.

Before and during World War II (1939–1945), Germany and Italy occupied or dominated almost all of western Europe, eastern Europe, the western Soviet

Union, and much of North Africa. The Japanese empire incorporated much of the western Pacific, Korea, eastern China, small parts of the eastern Soviet Union, the Philippines, southeast Asia, Indonesia, and eastern Burma (see Map 2–1 and Map 2–2). The process of recovering these conquered territories from the Axis powers was long and costly. At the war's end large sections of Europe and the Soviet Union were devastated. Much of southeast Asia, China, Korea, and Japan was decimated. The war itself directly resulted in the deaths of some 15 million combatants and at least as many civilian casualties (Kagan, Ozment, and Turner, 1987:994). The property damage was uncountable. However, these represented only a portion of the horrors this conflict inflicted.

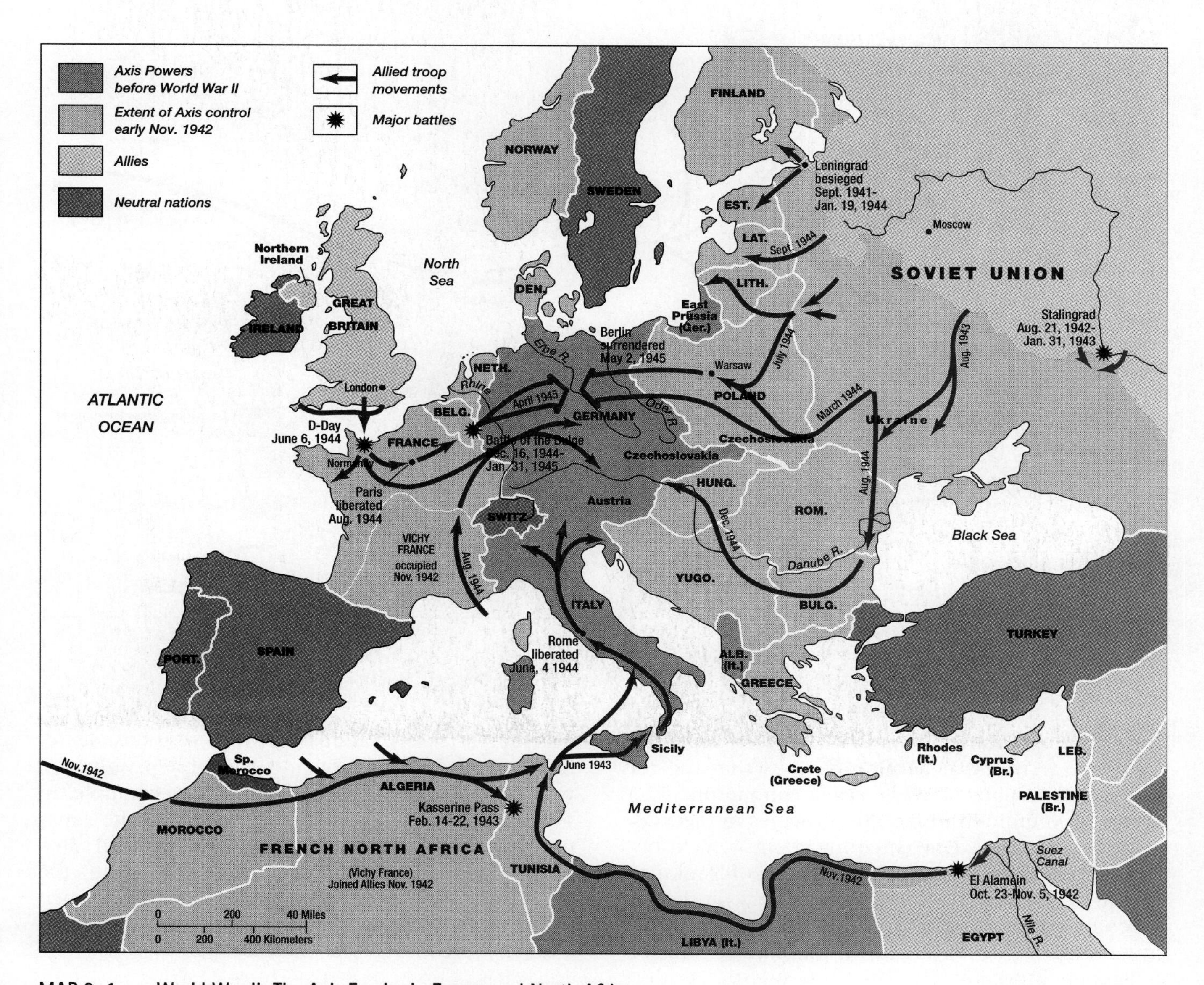

MAP 2–1 World War II: The Axis Empire in Europe and North Africa
During World War II the Axis empires extended over large portions of the world. Throughout these regions, the civil populations were enslaved, tortured, and killed in huge numbers. These experiences became a springboard for the founding of the United Nations, the writing of the Universal Declaration of Human Rights, and subsequent global efforts to protect human rights.

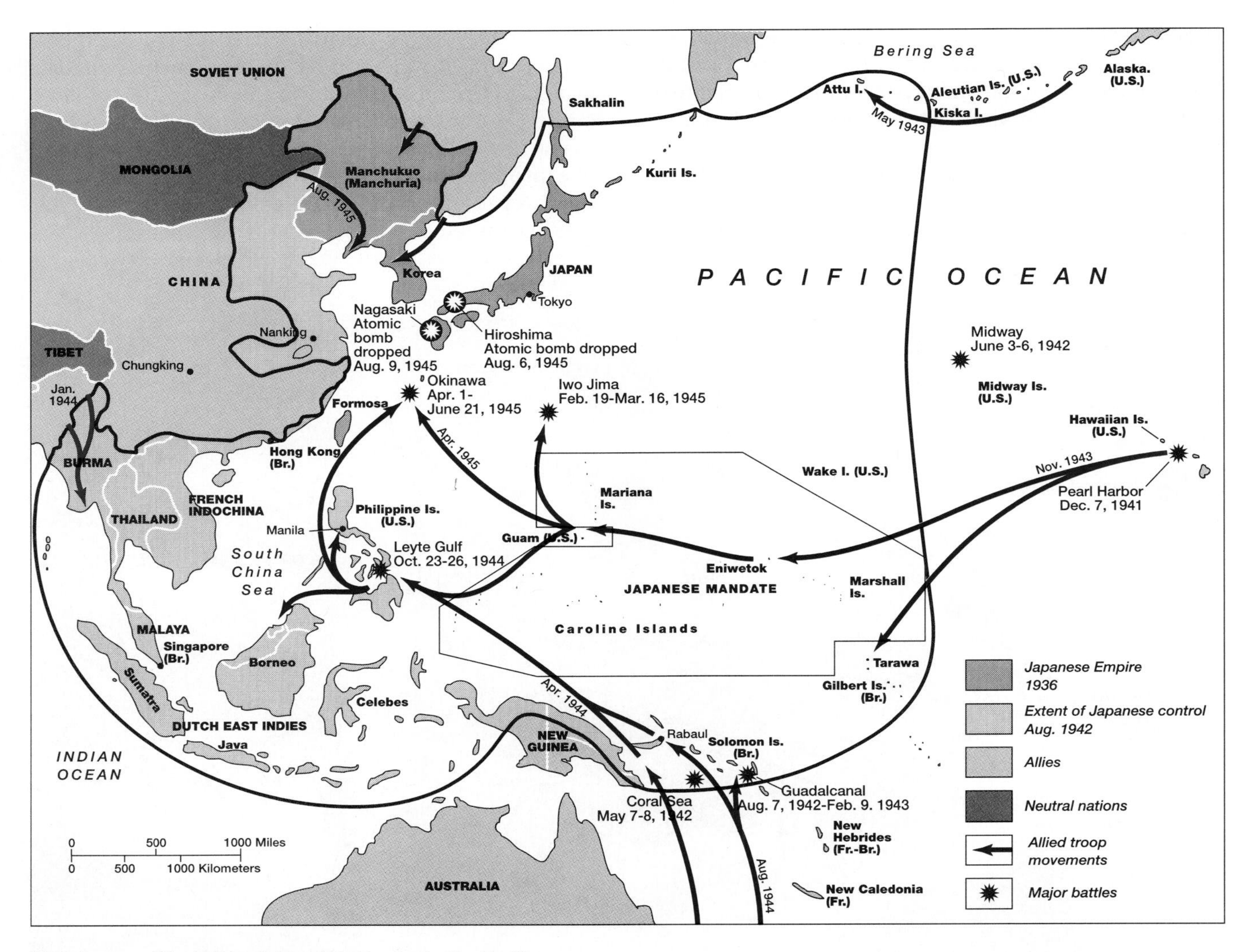

MAP 2–2 World War II: The Axis Empire in the Pacific

Japanese Atrocities. As Allied forces began to recapture territory, it became obvious that the retreating Axis powers were cruel conquerors. The Japanese committed numerous atrocities in their occupied territories. One such incident, which occurred in 1937, was the so-called "Rape of Nanking" (Nanjing). Driven by racism and angry at heavy losses in earlier combat, Japanese soldiers took the city, raping, pillaging, torturing, and killing Chinese civilians indiscriminately. The Chinese estimate that at least 100,000 Chinese died in this incident alone (Borthwick, 1992). In addition, throughout Indonesia the Japanese forced civilians to work on construction projects, treated them inhumanely, and distributed so few rations that tens of thousands of Indonesians died of starvation. Japanese prisoners of war were also treated inhumanely. For example, in 1942 thousands of prisoners captured by the Japanese on the Philippine peninsula of Bataan died during a forced march to prison. In addition, the Japanese forced hundreds of thousands of women from conquered countries to serve as "comfort women" (prostitutes) for their troops.

The Final Solution and the Holocaust. But the acts that most aroused the world's conscience were committed by German Nazis and their sympathizers. The **Nazis,** or the National Socialist German Workers'

Party, were fascists who ruled Germany from 1933 to 1945 under the leadership of Adolf Hitler (1889–1945). Like the Japanese, the Germans acted ruthlessly in dealing with conquered peoples. But the Nazis are especially infamous for their attempts at genocide. **Genocide** is the deliberate and systematic killing of people from racial, religious, ethnic, or political groups deemed to have common undesirable characteristics. A less severe form of genocide involves the contrived destruction of a people's culture. The Nazis came to power preaching a doctrine of racial purity and blaming Germany's economic and political woes on conspiracies by various "inferior races," particularly Jews. In blaming the Jews, the Nazis were building upon a long tradition of **anti-Semitism** (prejudice against Semitic peoples, especially Jews). As the Germans consolidated their power in conquered Europe, they began a systematic persecution of Jews and other groups in their disfavor such as Gypsies, Soviets, Slavic peoples,

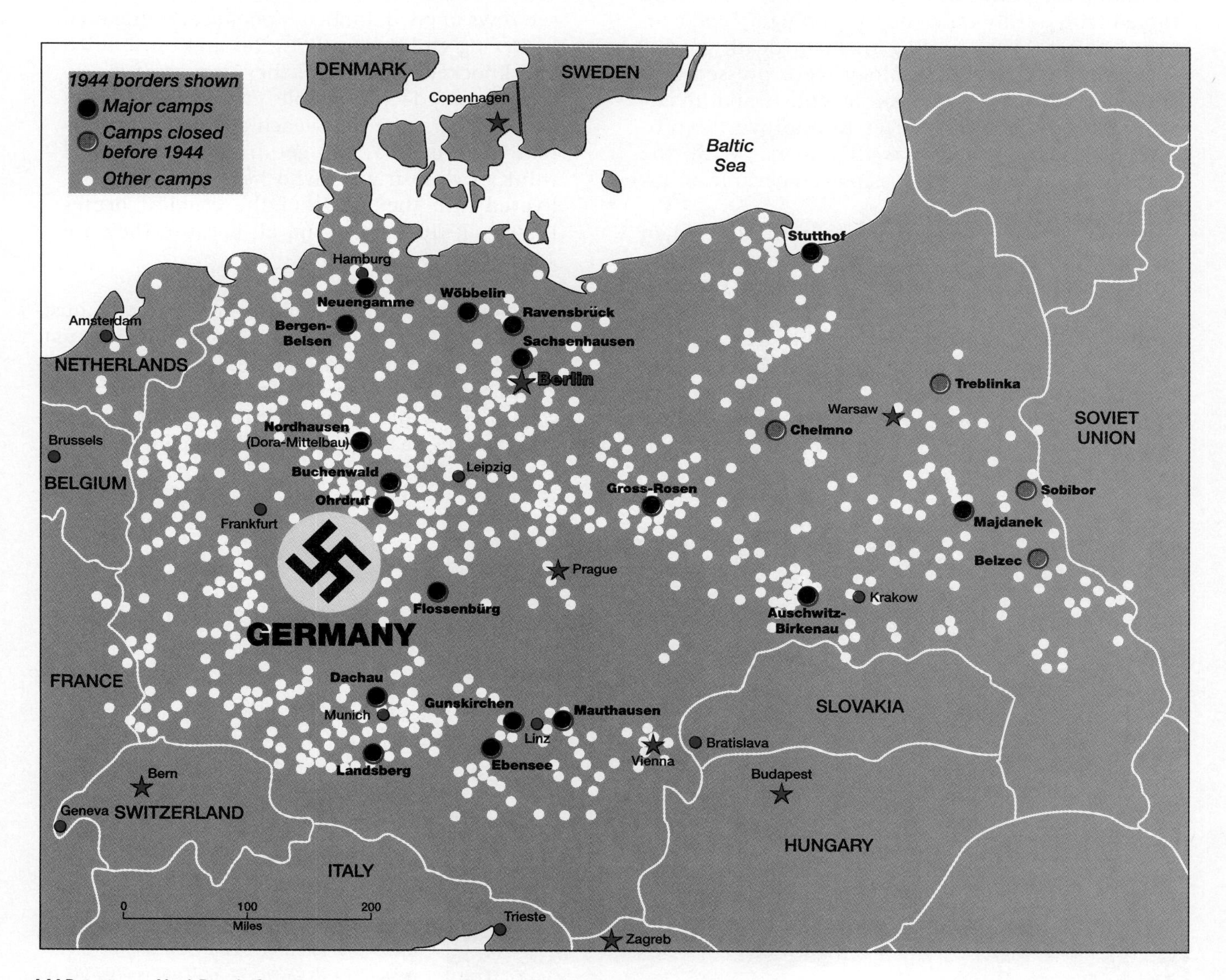

MAP 2–3 Nazi Death Camps
Here we see the extent of the Nazi death industry. When the Nazis realized they were losing World War II, they redoubled their efforts to kill as many inmates as possible. Money, resources, and human power desperately needed on the military fronts continued to be diverted to the death industry at home.

homosexuals, mental patients, and political dissidents. As early as 1933 the Nazis sent opponents, without any legal process, to concentration camps. Inmates were abused, tortured, killed, or used for grotesque medical experiments. Many died from malnutrition, mistreatment, and disease.

Late in 1941 Nazi officials began implementing their "final solution" to the "Jewish problem," although numerous other undesirable groups also were included. The **final solution** was an extensive, systematic program to kill "undesirables." The Nazis worked with deadly efficiency, rounding up and executing their prey or putting them in death camps. German science and technology were pressed into service for the gruesome task. Scientists and inventors created numerous devices to improve the process, such as portable gas chambers. With the creation of the death camps, genocide became an industry (see Map 2–3).

Anne Frank was a young Jewish girl in Amsterdam hidden with her family and several other persons by Christians after the German invasion of Holland. Shortly before the Allies liberated the city, the Nazis discovered their hiding place. Anne was sent to Auschwitz, one of the most notorious Polish death camps, where she died (see the box, "The Human Face of Evil: Auschwitz"). She left behind in the hiding place a remarkable diary of her experience that was published in many languages after the war. In her diary she described the horrors of witnessing innocents being arrested.

> Countless friends and acquaintances have gone to a terrible fate. Evening after evening the green and gray army lorries trundle past. The Germans ring at every house . . . to inquire if there are any Jews living in the house. If there are, then the whole family has to go at once. . . . In the evenings when it's dark, I often see rows of good, innocent people accompanied by crying children walking on and on, bullied and knocked about until they almost drop. No one is spared—old people and babies, expectant mothers, the sick—each and all join in the march of death. . . . I get frightened when I think of close friends who have now been delivered into the hands of the cruelest brutes that walk the earth. And all because they are Jews! (Frank, 1952:48)

This period of hitherto-unknown systematic, businesslike slaughter is referred to as the **Holocaust.** Approximately 6 million Jews and 400,000 Gypsies were murdered. They were joined by countless Poles, Slavs, Russians, and others. The final toll of the Holocaust may range as high as 26 million people.

Late in 1941, the Nazis began implementing their "final solution" to the "Jewish problem," which was an extensive, systematic program to kill "undesirables." These men were inmates of the Buchenwald concentration camp; many were dying of malnutrition when U.S. troops liberated the camp in 1945.

THE HUMAN FACE OF EVIL

Auschwitz

It is difficult to grasp the magnitude of the crime committed in the Holocaust and its impact upon the last half of the twentieth century. Perhaps some words from liberators, reporters, and survivors of the notorious Auschwitz-Birkenau camp recorded 50 years after Soviet troops liberated the camp in January 1945 will help:

> It is 50 years since Soviet soldiers entered the gate marked ARBEIT MACHT FREI [Work Makes Free] and found some 7,000 starving, sick, pitiful survivors of Auschwitz. Young and gaunt then, aging and gray now, some of them returned last week to remember and to grieve. They walked, once again, down the street of death from the rail spur to the ramps where they saw the last of mothers, fathers, brothers, sisters. They shuddered before the gas chambers, peered into the wooden barracks, stood in silence amid the ruins of crematoria dynamited by the Nazis in a failed attempt to hide the evidence of the greatest crime. They saw, they remembered, they mourned—and they wondered if the world would ever learn the lessons of Auschwitz and the Holocaust. (Jackson, 1995:1)

> Retired Lt. Gen Vasily Petrenko, the only surviving commander among the four Red Army divisions that encircled and liberated the camp, was a hardened veteran of some of the worst fighting of the war. "I had seen many people killed," Petrenko says. "I had seen hanged people and burned people. But still I was unprepared for Auschwitz." What astonished him especially were the children, some mere infants, who had been left behind in the hasty evacuation. They were the survivors of the medical experiments perpetrated by the Auschwitz camp doctor, Josef Mengele, or the children of Polish political prisoners rounded up after the ill-fated revolt in Warsaw. . . . But Petrenko didn't yet know that. "I thought: we're in a war. We've been fighting for four years. Million-strong armies are battling on both sides—and suddenly you have children. How did they find themselves there? I just couldn't digest it." Only later did Petrenko realize that this was a place were children were brought to be killed. By the hundreds of thousands they had vanished into thin air, and Petrenko's troops marched by the ashes of their bones. (Adler, 1995:47–48)

> "Although we know that God is merciful, please, God, have no mercy on those who have created this place," prayed Elie Wiesel, the Nobel Peace prize laureate. . . . "God of forgiveness, do not forgive those murderers of Jewish children here. Remember the nocturnal processions of children and more children and more children, frightened, quiet, so quiet and so beautiful. If we could simply look at one, our hearts would break." Wiesel knows. He was 14 when he entered Auschwitz in 1942. (Jackson, 1995:2)

> Perhaps Auschwitz is simply too monstrous for passions to cool. . . . Auschwitz was by far the worst of the Nazi concentration camps, containing the bones and ashes of the estimated 1.5 million of Hitler's victims who died there. . . . The camp is at once the world's largest cemetery and most gruesome industrial artifact. (Jackson, 1995:2)

> History has dripped with blood. Some argue that humans will never change. But Auschwitz was something new on the earth. Its elaborate mechanisms for transporting, selecting, murdering and incinerating thousands of people a day constituted a kind of industrialization of death. It raised the terrifying possibility that with the advent of modern technology human nature really had changed. . . . At Auschwitz . . . the 20th century saw itself in the mirror, and turned away in horror. (Adler, 1995:49)

Source: From Jerry Adler, "The Last Days of Auschwitz." *Newsweek,* January 16, 1995.

Nuremberg War Crimes Trial. After the war the Allies conducted war crimes trials in Japan and Europe of high enemy officials and lower-ranking persons who had committed particularly heinous acts. The most influential for the cause of human rights was the 10-month mass trial of 22 top Nazi officials in Nuremberg, Germany (1945–1946). The Allies, who carefully conducted the trial according to all of the conventions of international law, sentenced some to death, imprisoned others, and acquitted only three.

The Nuremberg tribunal became somewhat controversial for its handling of one crucial point of law. The German officials had clearly violated international conventions for the treatment of prisoners of war. But it was less clear whether their treatment of civilians had also been illegal. Defense lawyers argued that barbaric and genocidal treatment of civilians, however reprehensible, was not illegal because no international conventions against such actions existed. This issue was critical because a basic point of law is that a person cannot be tried for acts that were not illegal when committed. After much deliberation the Nuremberg judges justified the convictions for "crimes against humanity" by holding that "international law" does not consist solely of treaties and statutes but "is also generated by the customary usage and beliefs of the civilized people of the world" (Frankel, 1989:37). The treatment of civilians by the Nazis, then, was criminal because it violated what civilized people everywhere defined as acceptable conduct.

The "customary usage" tenet first applied at Nuremberg subsequently became crucial to human rights law. This tenet still functions as a strong doctrine that justifies holding nations that have not signed various agreements such as the International Bill of Rights or the international accords of the rights of children responsible for abiding by the requirements of those treaties. But even though justice was most probably served by the application of the customary usage principle at Nuremberg, the trial did indicate the need for a clear global definition of human rights. The fledgling United Nations soon addressed this issue.

The Universal Declaration of Human Rights

Before the end of World War II, the Allies met in a series of conferences to determine the structure of the postwar world. The victors faced monumental practical problems, including dealing with enormous numbers of refugees; restoring civil order in places left without effective government by the collapse of Axis powers; and reconstructing Europe, Japan, and other areas devastated by the war. In addition the Allies realized that it was necessary to prevent the conditions that had led to two world wars in the twentieth century. They sought, therefore, to create economic and political structures that would ensure a more peaceful and stable future.

The primary economic structures were developed at a conference in Bretton Woods, New Hampshire, in 1944. The aim of the conference was to institute an "international monetary regime characterized by stability, predictability, and orderly growth" (Kegley and Wittkopf, 1995:209). Chapter 8 describes the Bretton Woods economic system. After World War II, the United Nations was created to ensure political stability. In this chapter we limit our discussion to the UN's role in human rights. Chapter 7 discusses its role in the larger global political system.

Human Rights and the Founding of the United Nations

Even before World War II, it was generally recognized that the League of Nations was too weak to cope effectively with global political problems. The Allies sought to learn from the past and make the proposed United Nations a more effective instrument to peacefully handle world political situations. They also perceived that world peace would be impossible if basic human rights were ignored around the globe.

From its inception, therefore, the UN became more than a forum for defusing political crises. Its mandate contained a strong human rights component. The UN Charter, signed June 26, 1946, in San Francisco, commits the organization to affirming human rights, the worth of the human person, the equality of men and women, and the parity of large and small nations. These key elements are found in Articles 1, 55, and 56 of the charter (Frankel, 1989). Article I states that the UN's main purpose is to achieve international cooperation on international problems and "[to encourage] respect for human rights and for fundamental freedoms for all without distinction as to race, sex, language, or religion." Article 55 binds the UN to promote human rights and fundamental freedoms. Article 56 pledges all members to take action jointly and separately with the organization to achieve the goals set out in Article 55. Although one of the key goals of the UN was to promote "human rights and fundamental freedoms," the charter does not define the nature of those rights and freedoms. But the UN soon dealt with this omission.

The Universal Declaration of Human Rights

The organization gave the newly formed UN Commission on Human Rights the task of drafting a nonbinding international covenant (treaty) on human rights. A committee of three, chaired by Eleanor Roosevelt, was charged with writing the actual covenant and began working on it in January 1947. Nearly two years later, in December 1948, the UN General Assembly approved the document the committee produced—the Universal Declaration of Human Rights (for more about the Universal Declaration, see Chapter 1). In defining the rights and freedoms to which people everywhere are entitled, the Universal Declaration provided positive goals for nations to pursue in treating their citizens. In addition the Universal Declaration solved the Nuremberg dilemma by implicitly presenting guidelines for defining "crimes against humanity." In the more than 50 years of its existence, the Universal Declaration has become the basis for all subsequent human rights efforts and the cornerstone of international law on the subject. For these reasons it is the greatest human rights document of this century and one of the most significant in history.

The Universal Declaration reflects a strong U.S. influence. It draws on the famous Four Freedoms Speech delivered by President Roosevelt at the onset of World War II. In this address he outlined the four freedoms—freedom of speech, freedom of worship, freedom from want, and freedom from fear—for which the Allies were fighting (Humphrey, 1989). The document also relies heavily on three other American documents—the Declaration of Independence, the Constitution, and the Bill of Rights—as well as on the French Declaration of the Rights of Man and Citizen. Another shaping influence was the former Soviet Union, which led the drive to include articles on social and economic rights.

What is the Universal Declaration's significance to the international legal community? Some see the declaration as the source on which to base an authoritative interpretation of human rights sections of the UN Charter. Others maintain that it has been raised to the status of "customary international law" because it is routinely consulted by rights organizations, governments, the World Court (at the Hague, the Netherlands), and regional organizations in dealing with legal matters around the world.

Still, perhaps we need to be cautious about the declaration's importance to the international legal community. The declaration is universal in the sense that it has "formal acceptance by governments" and is generally acknowledged as a "control standard" against which to judge the appropriateness of governments' actions. Nevertheless, not all provisions of the Universal Declaration, in terms of philosophy or understandings of human society, are universally accepted (Alston, 1990). For example, in Asia, the government of Singapore recently rejected international pressure to stop the caning of a young American man living there who had been convicted of defacing property. Such international pressure was based largely on the declaration's opposition to harsh forms of punishment. But the government of Singapore protested that the notion that the rights of the individual were more important than or equal to the rights of society as a whole was a Western value. In the East, the rights of society as a whole were of greater value, hence the severity of the punishment.

International Bill of Human Rights. The declaration itself was a nonbinding resolution of the UN; that is, it did not bind member states to obey its articles. In 1966 two International Human Rights Covenants that *were* considered binding on those nations ratifying them corrected this situation. The Covenant on Civil and Political Rights and the Covenant on Economic, Social, and Cultural Rights went into effect in 1976, ten years after they were drafted. (They had to be formally signed by a majority of the world's nations before they could become international law.) Both documents contain language similar to the Universal Declaration but spell out in more detail what does and does not constitute human rights violations. Moreover, these two agreements incorporate tools for rights implementation and enforcement absent from the declaration (Wronka, 1992).

The Universal Declaration and the two Covenants on Human Rights are known as the International Bill of Human Rights. Although many nations have officially accepted the covenants, roughly 40 percent, including the United States, China, and some Islamic countries, have yet to sign them. Nevertheless, the international community uses the covenants and the Universal Declaration to judge human rights situations in countries even if these countries have not ratified the International Bill of Human Rights. Still, the failure by powerful countries to ratify these agreements and thus fully support them on the international stage remains a major block to the most forceful international implementation of human rights.

The Indivisibility of Rights. In his Four Freedoms Speech, President Roosevelt linked together individual freedom, economic security, and freedom from fear, which not only includes fear of injustice, but also the fear of war itself. Such a connection illustrates a key concept for understanding human rights—their indivisibility. The **indivisibility of human rights** is the understanding that in the quest for justice, security, and peace, political and civil rights cannot be separated from economic, social, and cultural rights.

Individuals or governments, according to this precept, are not allowed to "pick and choose" which rights to implement and which to ignore. Nor can they rank some rights as more important than others or employ "time ordering" of rights, that is, act under the assumption they can implement some rights before others. Nor, according to this precept, can a nation decide to sacrifice one set of rights to protect other rights. To deny one human right is to impinge on all rights.

Indeed, human rights "constitute . . . an indivisible whole and are a reflection of the fundamental unity and uniqueness of the human being" (Theo van Boven quoted in De Kadt, 1980:102). The Human Rights Commission and the General Assembly of the United Nations have consistently supported this view, insisting that

> All human rights and fundamental freedoms are indivisible and interdependent; equal attention and urgent consideration should be given to the implementation, promotion and protection of both civil and political, and economic, social, and cultural rights. (General Assembly Resolution 32/130 adopted 1977. Quoted in Eide, 1986:382)

In today's world, however, this ideal situation is far from being realized, as we see throughout this book.

Issues Involving Human Rights

The Universal Declaration of Human Rights was the starting point for an explosion of activities by the United Nations, nation-states, and nongovernmental organizations (NGOs). Human rights have never received the attention that they have in the last half of the twentieth century, although much remains to be done. But increasingly human rights have begun to be recognized as key tools in negotiating the global civil order. This section reviews some of the major contemporary theoretical and practical human rights issues. We first look at the expansion of human rights to include an increasing number of categories. We next describe groups responsible for establishing human rights. Finally, we discuss some problems concerning human rights enforcement.

The Expansion of Human Rights: What Are Human Rights and Who Should Have Them?

Although human rights has been a major theme in national and global affairs for the last 50 years, our thinking about them is paradoxical. We view human rights, on the one hand, as indivisible and unchanging because they reflect inalienable privileges that people possess by virtue of being human. Yet the list of "fundamental" rights, on the other hand, is continually expanding, as is the array of groups who claim such rights for themselves.

This paradox perhaps is explained by looking at how human rights function in sociopolitical settings. In such settings, when a group makes demands on power structures, it usually invokes its members' human rights. For example, if a minority group is not allowed to vote, group members may demand that the courts intervene to ensure their human right to vote. Because human rights are understood as "fundamental," "inalienable," and "indivisible," the group is in a position to demand and receive legal support for its position. Rights, then, are created in the cauldron of society. They "are created . . . by those who actively shape and live them in the thick of personal and social struggles . . . rights are not static concepts but dynamic moral forces—'grounds for action' that do not exist apart from cultural, economic, and political environments" (Burns and Burns, 1991:13).

Even so, from a practical point of view, there seems to be a "core" of human rights, such as those found in the International Bill of Human Rights, about which there is little debate within the global community. Whatever debate exists usually does not focus on whether these are fundamental rights, but on whether to apply them to certain populations. For example, in this country homosexuals in the military do not have the same protections against being fired as do other military personnel. That is, if a homosexual reveals that he or she is gay, this can be cause for dismissal. A second major source of debate is about how to implement human rights in specific situations. For instance, people have a right to expect reasonable job security. This means that they have the right to be laid off for legitimate reasons only. But what constitutes a legitimate reason? Illness that prevents the worker's ability to perform the job? The company's desire to increase profits? Downsizing? There remains much confusion about these issues.

Four Generations of Human Rights. One useful way to look at the evolution of human rights is to see the process as occurring in four generations. The **first generation of human rights** concerns political and civil rights, the long history of which we outlined earlier in this chapter. Political and civil rights are presented in articles 3 to 21 of the Universal Declaration and in the Covenant on Political and Civil Rights. This generation of rights is probably the most established and least debatable. The international community views them as safeguards for individuals—protecting against unjustified intrusion by government, ensuring a fair judiciary, and allowing for the free exercise of democratic citizenship. This first generation of rights has received the most attention by the international community and NGOs and has been strongly promoted by First World industrial democracies (De Kadt, 1980:98).

The **second generation of human rights** involves economic, social, and cultural rights. Both the Universal Declaration and the Covenant on Economic, Social, and Cultural Rights recognize these rights as indivisibly linked to the first generation of rights. Second generation rights may be described as "aspirations" for nations to provide a dignified life for their citizens (De Kadt, 1980). As **decolonization** (the process of colonial powers freeing their colonies) sped up after World War II, Third World nations and their needs became more prominent in discussions of human rights. The countries of the Third World often grudgingly won recognition of their economic and social needs from First World nations, leading international forums and organizations such as the World Bank to also recognize these needs. Yet developed countries have made only limited commitments of resources to deal with the problems of developing nations. At present First World nations appear unwilling to jeopardize their high standards of living for Third World progress.

Both the first generation and second generations of human rights are well established partly because they operate on the level of the individual. That is, they are protections or assurances that the individual may claim as a member of a group (Mayor, 1990). The third and fourth generations, in contrast, are far from universally accepted. The **third generation of human rights,** or "solidarity" or "collective" rights, refers to those privileges that collectivities—often defined loosely as "peoples"—may claim. Today peoples are claiming such diverse privileges as the rights to self-determination, economic development, environmental quality, and peace. As an emerging area of human rights philosophy and law, solidarity rights remain highly controversial.

Most human rights thinkers do not deny that people live in groups and that positive conditions in those groups are necessary for dignified human life. But whether collectivities, as opposed to individuals, possess rights is being argued. And if collectives do have rights, can we call these human rights or does such an identification muddy the definition of human rights and diminish the moral force that, associated with the term human rights, protects individuals (see the box "Contemporary Discussion: Have Rights Gone Too Far?")?

If, moreover, we admit to people's or collectivities' rights, how are these groupings to be defined? Are "peoples" nations, ethnic groups within nations, religious groups, states or provinces, cities, neighborhoods, or social classes? Or are they all of these categories? We may in some circumstances legitimately classify any of these entities as a collectivity or "people." But if we decide, therefore, to accept that they have human rights as a collectivity, how are we to deal with situations in which the rights of one collectivity, such as a nation-state, conflict with those of other collectivities living within its borders, such as ethnic or religious groups?

For example, many ethnic and religious groups are claiming rights to some measure of self-

CONTEMPORARY DISCUSSION

Have Rights Gone Too Far?

We have shown the key role of human rights in the second half of the twentieth century. Human rights, it is almost universally agreed, serve as a powerful moral and legal force. But their extensive application to a multitude of different groups and an ever widening array of situations raises a number of questions. Some of these questions center on a basic issue: Have human rights gone too far? That is, can the application of human rights sometimes actually hinder justice? Does the application of human rights to a situation reinforce democracy or interfere with democratic deliberation?

Critics of the Extensive Application of Human Rights

Some critics argue that the extensive application of human rights, along with the tendency to claim special rights by more and more vulnerable groups, actually undermines the quest for justice and impedes the democratic process. First, they contend that the desire to protect human rights frequently results in the passage of numerous laws attempting to define in minute detail exactly what does and does not protect those fundamental rights. Such laws cause the legal system to focus on the details of law rather than on its intent. These laws also build a rigidity into the system, which often prevents public officials and ordinary citizens from acting sensibly because to conform to the law, they must take actions that defy common sense. For example, in New York City, an order of nuns recently sought to rehabilitate an abandoned building for use as a homeless shelter. The nuns made a deal with city officials for transferring ownership of the building to them. But before they could proceed further, the nuns learned that the federal Citizens with Disabilities Act required that the building be retrofitted for handicapped access. Although it was estimated that relatively few disabled homeless persons were likely to use the building, the renovation for handicapped access escalated costs so much that the nuns had to abandon their efforts to provide shelter for the homeless.

Second, the use of rights as a tool for addressing the ills of society may encourage subverting democratic processes on several levels. Whereas laws can be frivolous and overly rigid, one of the functions of government is to pass laws that serve the common good. Determining the common good in a democracy tends to be a long, difficult, messy process involving competition, debate, and compromise. Claiming the moral authority of undeniable human rights encourages people to use the legal system to secure these rights rather than resort to the more difficult legislative process. Moreover, because human rights are considered moral absolutes protecting our basic freedoms, they contradict the true spirit of

determination in the nation-states in which they live. In such situations it becomes appropriate to ask: Does the nation-state or any other collectivity have the right to assert its rights at the cost of the rights of a collectivity? In addition, such situations may also cause us to ask whether the rights of the individual are more important than the rights of a collectivity or vice versa (Baehr and VanderWal, 1990; Mayor, 1990; De Kadt, 1980). We discuss in detail many of these issues throughout this book.

The **fourth generation of human rights** comprises intergenerational rights, or those rights presumed to exist between generations. Intergenerational rights have gained prominence as ecological problems mount and resource bases dwindle. Few would oppose the need of contemporary global society to develop a long-range perspective about our impact on the world and then to plan for the future as well as for the present. But whether intergenerational rights is the proper mechanism to accomplish democracy, which involves compromise—the positions of competing groups cannot be considered absolute. Finally, admitting special rights to numerous vulnerable groups encourages casting social issues as zero-sum games—pitting the interests of groups against one another and so denying the possibility of a common good.

Supporters of Extensive Application of Human Rights

Other human rights thinkers disagree with this viewpoint. Rather, they believe that the notion of human rights is the most powerful tool yet developed to oppose oppression and unequal treatment and to assure the full democratic participation of all members of contemporary societies. Although some rights may seem frivolous to the dominant or majority groups in a society, the needs and perspectives of diverse groups within society differ considerably. Moreover, the needs of disadvantaged sectors of society especially call for the spelling out of human rights. Such rights may seem extensive and unessential to those who do not share the same disadvantages or needs. Society cannot compensate people for all the vagaries of nature and accident or the disfavors of historical circumstances. But society has the obligation to provide the conditions necessary for the full participation of each of its members, not simply those who do not have to overcome societal obstacles to achieve this goal. If dominant or majority groups readily extended full participation to everyone, and were always willing to make concessions to disadvantaged minorities, these groups would probably not need to fight for rights. But such a situation is not typical; this is why nations and localities write rights into law—in order to secure them.

When the founders of this country fought for basic civil rights, they fought for those rights that served the interests of white, male, able-bodied property owners. Like any other dominant groups that secured their power, the founding fathers generally opposed or ignored the demands of other groups—working men, slaves, free blacks, and women—that they receive the same rights. These nondominant groups, consequently, had to wage long and bitter struggles to gain the same rights as the dominant group.

But the nature of American society has changed. The diversity of groups that now can claim legitimate rights of full social participation has increased, as has our understanding of the factors limiting access to the advantages of societal life. Full participation is an absolute requirement if a society is to remain a democracy. Similarly, full participation requires a legal, and therefore, a detailed enactment of rights. That such detail is necessary owes much to the attitudes and behaviors of dominant or majority groups.

◇ **For Critical Thought:** (1) What are the assumptions of each side in this discussion? (2) How do these assumptions relate to major theoretical themes in this book? (3) What are the human rights implications of the position of each side? (4) What problems would be created if the position of each side was taken to its logical conclusions? (5) Are there possibilities other than those presented by each side in this discussion?

this long-range task is problematic because a fundamental question has been unanswered, namely, "Do future generations have rights?" If they do, how should we divide the world's scarce resources between our generation and future generations?

Human Rights and Vulnerable Groups. Since the founding of the UN, efforts have been made to extend specific protections to a growing list of vulnerable groups. By **vulnerable groups** we mean identifiable categories of people who are especially open to abuse and exploitation. Because of their relative powerlessness, these categories are seen by rights activists as first needing identification and then special mechanisms beyond ordinary human rights machinery to protect them. For example, many rights activists believe that women are a vulnerable group because in most societies they are relatively powerless. Therefore, many activists argue that special laws protecting them have to be written

The United Nations has been behind a series of international accords to protect specific threatened categories of people, such as migrant workers. Here Latino migrant workers harvest red peppers in Texas.

into international treaties and national legal codes. In addition, activists believe that ordinary court procedures intended to ensure rights for everyone may need to be supplemented by national and international commissions dedicated to enforcing these special laws.

Internationally, efforts to secure the rights of vulnerable groups have taken several forms. For example, the UN has led a series of international accords to protect specific threatened categories of people. A few of these agreements include the Convention Relating to the Status of Refugees (1951), the Convention Concerning Migration in Abusive Conditions and the Promotion of Equality of Opportunity and Treatment of Migrant Workers (1975), the International Convention on the Elimination of All Forms of Racial Discrimination (1966), the Convention on the Elimination of All Forms of Discrimination against Women (1979), and the Convention on the Rights of the Child (1989).

In addition, a host of special commissions or agencies dedicated to vulnerable groups has sprung up. A partial listing includes the Commission on the Status of Women, the Advancement of Women Branch of the Center for Social Development and Humanitarian Affairs, the Subcommission on the Prevention of Discrimination and the Protection of Minorities, and the International Children's Emergency Fund (UNICEF).

Finally, the United Nations sponsors "special occasions" to form policy, to educate the public, and to raise awareness of the problems of vulnerable groups. For example, it proclaimed 1975 as International Women's Year, holding a women's world conference in Mexico City that year, which produced the Declaration of Mexico on the Equality of Women and a World Plan of Action for advancing women's causes. This plan led to the declaration of 1976 to 1985 as the United Nations Decade for Women. Subsequent international conferences on women's issues were held in Copenhagen (1980), Nairobi (1985), and Beijing (1995). Women's issues also were a major focus of the world population conference held in Cairo (1994). But despite the focus on their problems and repeated declarations of their equality, "for women, international human rights presents the biggest gap between principle and practice known in the legal world" (MacKinnon, 1993:96). We discuss some of the major women's rights issues in detail in Chapter 9.

The Implementation and Protection of Human Rights

A great deal of machinery has been created during the latter half of the twentieth century to implement and protect human rights. Historically, the nation-state has held the primary responsibility for observing or not observing human rights within its own borders. This responsibility operated under the more general principle of national sovereignty, a basis of international law for the last five hundred years. **National sovereignty** means that a nation-state has absolute control of its own territory and that other nations cannot interfere with its internal affairs. In response to the global emphasis on human rights, many, if not most, countries have set up human rights commissions on the local and national levels, have passed rights laws, and have actively pursued human rights violations through their judiciary systems.

Although nation-states still have principal responsibility for human rights implementation, the "global village" has been much more active since World War II. There has been a strong tendency for nations acting individually, or in conjunction with multinational organizations, to become involved when human rights violations come to the attention of the international community. The nations of the world have formally or informally condemned offenders; have brought rogue countries before existing international courts or special tribunals; have pressured offenders via diplomatic, economic, or military channels; and have intervened directly by military force.

One relatively effective tool indicates the key position of human rights in global civil society. This tool is the judging of scofflaws in the "court of world opinion," that is, bringing the situation to the attention of the people of the world and then allowing their condemnation to exert moral force for the restoration of rights. Such a process often involves the media and NGOs exposing human rights violations and bringing them to public attention. Education of populations experiencing violations also has proven formidable. Once people become aware of the denial of their civil/political rights or become aware of their economic deprivation relative to other peoples of the world, they tend to become more active in agitating for improvement. More often than not, a combination of several of these tools or mechanisms is used to secure the acquiescence of an offending nation-state.

Admittedly, there are serious limitations in the global community's ability to correct human rights abuses. Still, there has been a dramatic change since World War II from a complete rejection of international society's competency to judge a government's treatment of its own citizens to a "situation in which it is almost routine for respondent states to explain and defend themselves before international agencies" (Eide, 1986:389). Moreover, nations that criticize other countries' human rights records now find that they must submit to international standards in relation to their own performance. In addition to nation-states, three other actors significantly impact global human rights: the UN, regional associations, and NGOs. We examine each of these briefly in the following sections.

The United Nations and Human Rights. We have already noted a number of international accords sponsored by the UN that serve as worldwide standards for assessing political, economic, and social conditions. In addition to agencies focusing on vulnerable groups, the UN also includes a number of specialized organizations that concentrate on specific problems, such as the World Health Organization (WHO), the Food and Agricultural Organization (FAO), and the Educational, Scientific, and Cultural Organization (UNESCO). These and other special organizations educate, gather data, sponsor conferences, bring problems to the attention of the UN General Assembly, and implement plans to solve problems in their respective jurisdictions.

The structure of the UN has become increasingly complex through the years, with human rights issues distributed among an array of committees and commissions (see Figure 2–1). Nevertheless, the main responsibilities for overseeing human rights work of the organization falls to a few divisions. The UN contains two central branches—the Security Council and the General Assembly. The Security Council is composed of five permanent members (the United States, Russia, the United Kingdom, France, and China) and ten members elected for two-year terms by the General Assembly. The Security Council is the only organ of the UN with the power to compel nations to behave in specified fashions and to be able to move forcefully (sanctions, military involvement, and the like) against noncompliant states. Each of the five permanent members can veto any proposed action of the UN. The Security Council has the primary responsibility for peacemaking and peacekeeping (Frankel, 1989).

The General Assembly is composed of all the member nation-states. Each state has one vote. The Assembly debates issues and recommends actions to the Security Council and to various UN agencies. The General Assembly's third committee (Social,

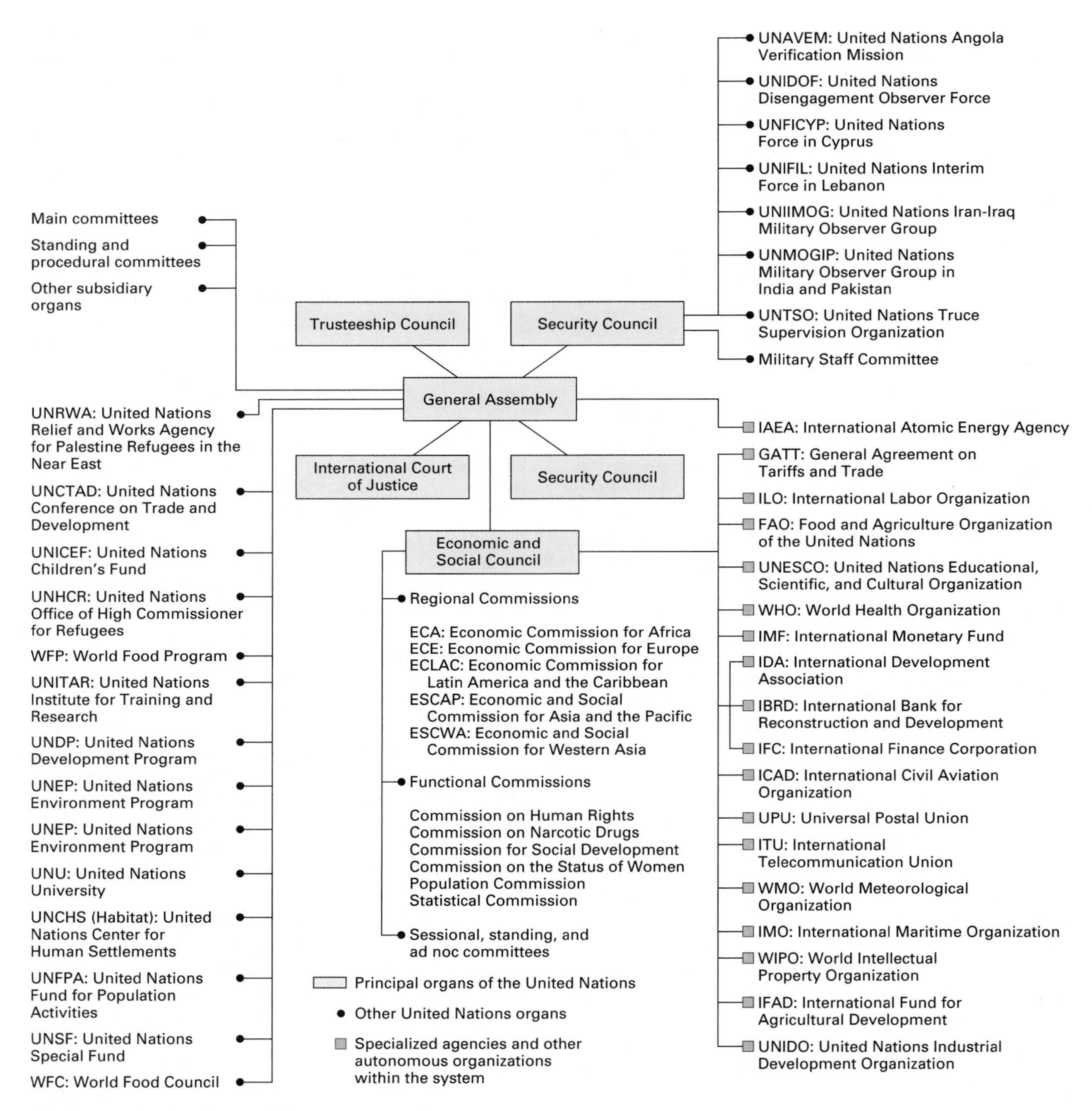

FIGURE 2–1 Organizational Chart of the United Nations
As this chart indicates, the UN has committees and commissions to address nearly all of the problems we discuss in this text. (Adapted from Charles W. Kegyley, Jr., and Eugene R. Wittkopf, *World Politics: Trend and Transformation*, 5th ed. New York: St. Martin's, 1995, p. 159.)

Humanitarian, and Cultural) prepares recommendations on human rights for approval by the full assembly. The Economic and Social Council plays a powerful role through its specialized agencies as well as its standing Commissions on Human Rights, the Status of Women, and Social Development.

The UN's effectiveness in dealing with civil or economic rights violations is somewhat limited. A main reason is that the organization relies on contributions from member nations, which may or may not be forthcoming. For instance, early in 1995, the UN war crimes tribunal charged several Bosnian Serbs with genocide and other related atrocities during the ongoing Bosnian war. However, fears immediately arose over whether the international community would provide the tribunal with the necessary funds to prosecute the criminals (Neuffer, 1995). Although donor nations contributed some funds, these were inadequate for investigating and prosecuting all those suspected of war crimes at the camp.

Similarly, the UN does not have its own military force; rather, the organization depends on member states to supply troops for its operations. Frequently, some members object to the use of military force by the body. UN military personnel, consequently, have usually been employed as unarmed or lightly armed "peacekeepers" inserted into situations only after the warring parties have made a cease-fire agreement. For example, the UN sent peacekeeping forces into southern Lebanon in 1978 after Israel had agreed to withdraw forces from that region. UN troops are still in southern Lebanon, keeping the peace. Far more rarely, the UN has involved itself in "peacemaking" operations in which its forces were inserted to establish a truce between warring groups. For example, since 1993 UN forces have been in Somalia trying to effect peace between warring factions, but the conflict continues.

Another limitation on the UN's effectiveness in dealing with human rights issues stems from the fact that its moves are often subject to international politics. For example, during the Cold War the UN's every move was reviewed by both superpowers for the possible effect on the struggle between capitalist and communist nations. Each side used vetoes liberally to prevent the other side from obtaining some kind of advantage. The United States and its allies frequently used the UN as a forum to charge communist countries with violations of civil and political rights. The Soviet Union and its allies often did the same, accusing the capitalist nations of violations of economic and social rights. The real goal of these accusations was not to correct violations, but to embarrass the opponent.

But the superpowers were not the only ones to use the UN as a political football. For example, the UN has frequently condemned Israel for violating the rights of Palestinians in its occupied territories, but it has seldom condemned the poor human rights records of a number of other nations in the Middle East, mainly because these countries had more allies in the UN than did Israel.

In addition, domestic politics often play a larger role in UN actions than do global politics. For example, in 1995, the United States cut its world food aid in half from the level it had maintained for 20 years, despite a growing need for food worldwide. The decision was partly the response of the Democratic President Bill Clinton (who cut international food aid in his budget) to pressure from the Republican-controlled Congress for reductions in foreign aid ("U.S. Halves Pledge," 1995).

Despite these limitations, UN commissions and agencies have implemented strategies to deal with many serious human rights problems. For instance, in Bosnia prior to the U.S.-brokered peace treaty, UN peacekeepers tried unsuccessfully to enforce numerous cease-fires negotiated by the belligerents. But at many other places in the war-torn region, peacekeepers kept the combatants separated, thereby saving many lives, both civilian and military. Free elections were held under UN supervision in Cambodia in 1993 for the first time in decades, although the democratically elected government later developed into a dictatorship. A successful operation to oust a bloody military dictatorship from Haiti was conducted by UN forces under United States leadership in 1994.

Undoubtedly, the greatest success of the United Nations in the cause of human rights was its decades-old boycott of South Africa. In South Africa, a white minority government ruled a heavily black majority, enforcing a system of segregation known as **apartheid.** In 1994 the UN-sponsored boycott—along with other international and internal pressures—forced the installation of a new government elected by the vote of all South Africans under the leadership of former political prisoner Nelson Mandela.

With the end of the Cold War, there is greater hope that the UN can function even more effectively without the hindrance of **bipolar politics** (politics driven by the two-sided conflict between capitalist

New South African President Nelson Mandela takes the oath of office during his inauguration ceremony in Pretoria in 1994. Undoubtedly, the greatest success of the United Nations in the cause of human rights was its decades-old boycott of South Africa for its enforced system of segregation known as apartheid.

and communist countries). Still, we must recognize that much remains to be done, as human rights abuses are rising to unprecedented levels ("UN Agency Meets," 1995).

Regional Governmental Alliances and NGOs. Nation-states and the UN are not the only organizations associated with implementing human rights. A significant portion of human rights work worldwide is carried out by regional governmental alliances. These include the Council of Europe (with its European Commission on Human Rights), the European Court of Human Rights (with its machinery for implementing its Social Charter), the Organization of American States (OAS), the Organization of African Unity (OAU), the League of Arab States, and the Association of Southeast Asian Nations, Peoples, and Governments (ASEAN). The charters of these organizations generally reflect the Universal Declaration. However, the African Charter on Human and People's Rights (or Banjul Charter) includes recognition of third generation rights as well as citizen responsibilities not included in other similar charters (Eide, 1989). The regional alliances work alone or with other international bodies to address human rights problems in their respective regions.

International nongovernmental organizations (INGOs) have become major players on the global human rights scene and, thus, in global civil society. Most of these organizations focus on special functions. The International Red Cross distributes aid to victims of natural and human-made disasters and aids prisoners of war in securing their rights under international agreements. Amnesty International deals with a limited range of human rights abuses, especially those associated with the conditions of prisoners. They are most effective in working for the release of **prisoners of conscience** (people imprisoned for expressing their views, usually in opposition to an authoritarian regime). Other NGOs, such as the various Human Rights Watches, monitor a range of violations, bringing them to governmental and public attention.

NGOs frequently combine forces with professional-oriented groups, such as the International Commission of Jurists, the Committee of Concerned Scientists, and Doctors Without Borders, that have become involved in segments of human rights problems. Often INGOs have regional, national, and local chapters. They also work with national NGOs, like the American Civil Liberties Union (ACLU) and the National Association for the Advancement of Colored People (NAACP), on specific concerns. Many INGOs have gained such respect that their reports are viewed by the UN and other governmental organizations as reliable presentations of conditions.

However, INGOs frequently lack power to affect conditions in areas where they work. Their singular focus on a limited range of human rights violations often means that other problems go unnoticed even where a given INGO has strong representation. In this sense, the success of the human rights INGOs has accentuated the division of political and civil rights from social and economic rights. Whereas the INGOs have made the world aware of certain political and civil rights abuses, this focus has left sometimes more pressing social and economic problems without representation.

Cultural Imperialism, Cultural Relativity, and Human Rights

A number of ongoing controversies center on the impact of human rights on the emerging civil order. Some we have mentioned; others we describe in more detail later in this chapter. At this point, however, we believe it is necessary to address the connections among cultural imperialism, cultural relativity, and human rights.

Non-Western governments at times charge the West and/or the UN with *cultural imperialism,* or the imposition of outside values and practices on their cultures. Documents such as the Universal Declaration of Human Rights, they argue, reflect an individualistic, Judeo-Christian Western tradition that is foreign to their own heritage. As a result, their governments cannot and indeed should not be judged by standards that are being forced upon them. Generally, this claim is advanced to avoid sanctions from the global community for human rights violations. Despite the fact that such claims are routinely ignored in international forums, they merit discussion (Alston, 1990).

Cultural Relativity and Universal Standards. A rather simplistic cultural relativity argument underlies the cultural imperialism charge. Namely, the assumption is made that cultures are so different that they have nothing in common. Or, to take this line of reasoning further, cultures are so different that there can be no common basis for morality within the human community. We concur with sociologist Philip Selznick when he argues that such an understanding was not implied by those founders of anthropology who developed the concept of cultural relativity. Behind the thinking of early cultural relativists "lies a conception of what it is like to live in a well-integrated community where there is a basic harmony of self and society" (Selznick, 1992:95). Moreover, the diversity that is often recognized by social scientists and others has its limits. Rather, we may draw up a long list of "moral universals," including

- the fact of morality itself, which involves subordination of individual inclination to the perceived welfare of the group;
- the idea of preserving human life;
- concern for the well-being of close relatives;
- the prohibition of murder and theft;
- the valuing of affection and companionship;
- reciprocity in helping and being helped, hospitality.

According to Selznick, "The existence of 'strange practices' does not undermine the continuity of human culture. [I]t is just as easy to be impressed by the uniformity as by the variation" (1992:96).

Such a convergence is possible because human beings share a common humanity. That is, human beings everywhere are a single kind of animal, one that is physiologically and psychologically adaptable to a wide range of cultural patterns. But adaptability is not unlimited; rather, it occurs within a relatively narrow set of limits. For instance, the human infant is dependent for an incredibly long period of time, which necessitates that we protect and provide for neophytes. The human body cannot survive in extreme temperatures; cooling or warmth must be provided and food and water obtained regularly. But not all cultural requirements are imposed by the human body's physical limits. As Selznick argues, "to be counted as part of 'humanity' is to show evidence of participation in complex forms of social, moral, and aesthetic experience" (Selznick, 1992:100). Such distinctively human concerns entail a group life that meets requirements that permit people to flourish. Moreover, it is this necessity of meeting human needs and allowing humanity its expression that underlies universal morality.

Human Rights in Islam and Confucianism. Support for universal morality comes from what may be to some a surprising source—religion. Students of comparative religion have long noted similarities in a number of religious motifs, including basic ethical constructs. In 1993 religious and spiritual leaders representing all the world's major faiths gathered in Chicago for the second Parliament of the World's Religions. As part of this gathering, many of these leaders signed Towards A Global Ethic (An Initial Declaration) as "an initial statement of those rules for living on which the world's religions agree" (Council for a Parliament, 1993:Preface). Most, if not all, of the principles expressed in the Ethic are compatible with the Universal Declaration and its derivatives.

At this juncture, we examine the roots of human rights in Islam and Confucianism. It is important that we look at these religious traditions for three reasons. First, these great religions provide the ideological underpinning of the belief systems of large sections of the world. Islam has sway from North Africa through the Middle East into northern India and Pakistan, through much of southern Asia, and into parts of Southeast Asia, Indonesia, and the Philippine Islands. Confucianism originated in China, then spread into southeast Asia, Korea, and (to a lesser degree) Japan. Much of Eastern culture is strongly influenced by Confucian teachings.

Second, the argument is sometimes made that the teachings of Islam and Confucianism are incompatible with Western individualistic human rights. At times Islamic countries have contended that the individualistic tendencies of the West have led to its decadence and conflict with the Qur'an (or Koran). Similarly, at times Asian nations such as China have contended that international rights standards cannot be applied to them because these norms approach the "good society" from an individualistic viewpoint and as such undermine the "collective" ideology taught in Confucianism.

Finally, because of their different orientations and the vast numbers of people under their sway, Islamic and Confucian civilizations often are proposed as offering viable challenges to Western hegemony. Indeed, Islam and Confucianism, experts predict, will probably provide alternatives to Western views for negotiating the new global order.

Islam, which like Judaism and Christianity, originated in the Middle East, sees itself as the fulfillment of these two earlier faiths. Jewish and Christian scriptures also are its holy writ. But the Islamic religion believes these traditions were corrupted by human sin. Therefore, Allah (God) sent the angel Gabriel to the prophet Muhammad (570–632 C.E.) with his complete and final revelation, which was written down by Muhammad's followers in the Qur'an. As Islam shares so much with Judaism and Christianity, it is not surprising that its views on God, human beings, God's Law, our human responsibility to one another, and our duty to God are also very similar to those religions. But is Islam, with its stress on human duties to God, society, and other people, really compatible with the Western ideas of individualistic human rights?

The Qur'an holds human life as sacred. It compels Muslims (followers of Islam) to adhere to the law of Allah and seek justice in this world. Islam strives to free people from "'the chains which bind them—traditionalism, authoritarianism (religious, political, economic), tribalism, racism, sexism, and slavery.' [It also] attempts to free the individual from the abuse of political authority" (Wronka, 1992:40).

Charity, or love, is a driving force in Islam. Muslims are supposed to act in charity to those around them. Such charity is to be expressed in actively seeking and assisting those less fortunate than themselves. Muslims are constantly reminded that no matter how poor they themselves are, there are always others with less. The Qur'an expresses great empathy for the unfortunate, downtrodden, oppressed, and weak, who are seen to deserve assistance in attaining a dignified standard of living (Wronka, 1992:40). This emphasis on human dignity and social justice, as indicated, also underpins Western human rights thought.

Confucianism was born in China in the sixth century B.C.E. during a period of social unrest and feudal warfare. In many ways Confucianism appears to be the antithesis of Western individual rights and political democracy. Confucius (or Kong Fuzi) was a wandering scholar who traveled among various royal courts proclaiming how rulers could create orderly societies. After his death his followers gathered the master's teachings together into a volume called the Analects. In this form Confucius's ideas have had tremendous impact on all Eastern societies. To Westerners, Confucianism does not seem to be a religion at all. Although the assumption underlying much Chinese political thought is that the emperor is the "son of heaven," Confucianism is not concerned with the supernatural but with human conduct. It may best be described as a system of ethics or even manners.

Confucius envisioned societies as run by "sage kings" who wisely and justly administered the affairs of their realms. In return for the stability, protection, and care supplied by such rulers, subjects were expected to render their respect and loyalty.

This rendering of respect entailed following carefully defined forms of traditional behavior entailing submissiveness to those higher in the social hierarchy. The ethical behavior of the ruler determined the moral and spiritual health of the entire society. The ruler was to be sensitive to and provide for the needs of his people. In sum, in the good society morality prevailed, people recognized their duties to one another, and high and low alike had the means for a dignified life. These values are not unlike many Western values (Bothwick, 1992).

From this discussion we do not want you to conclude that there are no differences among the religions of the world in their respective worldviews, understandings of society, or interpretations of proper treatment of individuals. Rather, we are suggesting that the emphasis on differences can cause us to overlook similarities. The conclusions of numerous philosophers, religious thinkers, and social scientists in vastly different cultures and historical circumstances about the nature of the good society (and human rights within it) suggest that there actually exists a fair degree of consistency (Wronka, 1992).

Twentieth-Century Political and Civil Rights Violations

The record on political and civil rights has improved considerably by the latter half of the twentieth century, partly because of a noticeable shift in the global matrix of civil culture. Actions and practices formerly viewed as acceptable by some (if not all) segments of the global community now often draw a swift negative response. These include slavery, torture to exhort confessions, treatment of women and children as second-class citizens, warfare against civilians, denial of democratic participation to minorities, and the absence of **due process** (the act of conducting trials according to legal norms designed to protect the accused from abusive governmental practices). Among the most pressing issues the international community has had to deal with have been genocide and disappearances.

Genocide and Disappearances

In 1951 the UN Convention on the Prevention and Punishment of the Crime of Genocide met for the first time. The convention defined genocide as any act committed with the intent to destroy partly or totally any "national, ethnic, racial, or religious group." Actions constituting genocide included (1) killing of group members; (2) causing serious bodily or mental harm to group members; (3) deliberately inflicting on the group conditions of life intended to physically destroy it; (4) imposing measures to prevent births within the group; or (5) forcibly transferring children from one group to another. Publicly inciting people to commit any of these five types of behavior also constitutes an act of genocide (Hampton, 1995).

Instances of Genocide. The 1951 UN convention represented a direct response to the Holocaust. Unfortunately, the Holocaust was not the only instance of genocide in this century. Indeed, some argue that the twentieth century has been the bloodiest in history because of the sheer number of persons slaughtered in genocidal attacks. For example, one of the World War II Allies—Joseph Stalin (1879–1953), dictator of the Soviet Union—murdered or imprisoned vast numbers of individuals whom he saw as his domestic opponents from the time he came to power in 1924 until his death. The year he came to power, he began a campaign to force landowning peasants to give up their land in favor of state-operated collective farms. It is estimated that 10 million peasants died during collectivization. Millions more died in the human-made famine that resulted from it. But Stalin did not stop here. The period from 1936 to 1938 saw the Great Purges, during which he attacked perceived enemies in the government, the Communist Party, and the army. Besides those executed outright, millions more died from harsh conditions in gulags (Soviet political prisoner camps) and from exile in such foreboding places as Siberia. The full extent of Stalin's slaughter may never be realized, but estimates run as high as 20 million (Frankel, 1989). Moreover, the political repression he raised to new levels did not end until the demise of the Soviet Union, nearly 40 years after his death. The plight of Soviet prisoners of conscience is graphically detailed in Russian novelist Aleksandr Solzhenitsyn's nonfiction account, *The Gulag Archipelago* (1975).

Despite the UN convention, efforts like Hitler's and Stalin's to eradicate entire groups of people have not ceased. Major instances of genocide since World War II include the following: in Asia, Cambodia under Pol Pot and the Khmer Rouge (more than 1 million dead); in Africa, Rwanda by the Hutu majority against the Tutsi minority (500,000), and in Uganda under Idi Amin (300,000). Less extensive genocidal campaigns have been conducted in such diverse places as China, India, Sri Lanka, Iran, Iraq, Turkey, Israel, Bosnia, Chechnya, Somalia, Sudan, Haiti, Guatemala, Honduras, El Salvador, Nicaragua, Argentina, Brazil, Colombia, Chile, and Peru. This partial list demonstrates how prevalent genocidal attacks continue to be.

The Disappearances. The term **disappearances** denotes the practice, usually employed by totalitarian regimes, of making perceived opponents vanish without ever acknowledging their apprehension or detention. The practice, begun by the Nazis in France during World War II, has spread worldwide (Staunton and Fenn, 1991). The initial abduction is generally carried out by the government or security forces, but sometimes death squads or "unknown" assailants representing the government or its opposition seize victims. The captives are detained, tortured, raped, and frequently killed. Sometimes they mysteriously "reappear," but typically they are never heard from again. The stress on families and friends waiting—sometimes for years—to learn about their fate is obviously enormous.

The United Nations Working Group on Enforced and Involuntary Disappearances investigated more than 15,000 cases in 40 countries between 1980 and 1988 (Staunton and Fenn, 1991). The practice was so widespread in South and Central American countries during the 1970s and 1980s that *desaparecido* (a "disappeared one") became a noun in the Spanish language (Frankel, 1989). Disappearances number 10,000 in Argentina, 2,000 in Brazil, 2,700 in Chile, 2,000 in Colombia, 5,000 in El Salvador, and more than 2,000 in Peru (Luft and Goering, 1995). Numerous other individuals in these countries have been murdered or forced to flee because of the threat of violence.

War Crimes

One of the more significant human rights concerns in the last two centuries has been to find ways to limit or prevent the suffering incurred by civilians caught up in conflict. International accords such as the Geneva Conventions specifically prohibit the direct targeting of civilian populations for campaigns of violence and intimidation. They also forbid torture, mutilation, cruelty, taking of hostages, and any degrading treatment (Whalen, 1989). Still, civilians frequently have been, and continue to be, the direct targets of aggression during war. Just prior to World War II, modern weapons of mass destruction were turned to the task of terrorizing civilian populations during Italy's invasion of Ethiopia (1935) and the Spanish Civil War (1936–1939). In the war itself the Nazis used their powerful air force to bomb civilians in Poland, Russia, and Britain. The Allies, in turn, employed their air forces to demoralize Axis civilians. For example, on February 13 and 14, 1945, waves of British and American bombers dropped tons of high explosives and incendiary devices on Dresden, Germany, a city of little or no military value. Those not killed directly by the bombs faced another peril. A huge firestorm was created that literally sucked the air out of the surrounding area: "At least 39,733 people died in what Britain's wartime Prime Minister Winston Churchill [in office 1940–1945] later acknowledged was an act of terror" (Moseley, 1995:1.21).

Tokyo was firebombed in similar fashion by the American air force toward the end of the war. Then, on August 6, 1945, an American B-29 dropped an atomic bomb on the Japanese city of Hiroshima. Three days later a second atom bomb devastated the Japanese city of Nagasaki. Neither Hiroshima nor Nagasaki was of any particular military value. The sole purpose of the bombing was to inflict such damage and high casualties that Japan would be forced to surrender. About 70,000 were killed outright in Hiroshima and approximately 75,000 in Nagasaki. Tens of thousands died later of wounds or radiation sickness, multitudes were maimed, and many children born to survivors suffered birth defects caused by radiation-induced genetic damage to their parents. The United States is still the only country to have used nuclear weapons against its enemies.

Since World War II opposition to attacks on civilian populations has grown significantly. Western military forces now claim to take careful precautions in order to limit *collateral damage,* or injury or death to civilians not directly involved in fighting. Even so, civilians remain targeted by some military forces. During the war in Bosnia, Serbs conducted a policy of ethnic cleansing, reminiscent of the Nazi final solution, against Croatians and Muslims. **Ethnic cleansing** is a program of genocide and intimidation intended to drive Croatian and Muslim civilians out of sections of the former Yugoslavia occupied by Serbian forces. Other war crimes the Serbians are accused of include torture, politically motivated rape,

THE HUMAN FACE OF RIGHTS VIOLATIONS

Child of War

Ten-year-old Zlata Filipovic of Sarajevo in the former Yugoslavia began keeping a diary late in 1991. Her diary soon became the chronicle of an eyewitness to the horrors of war, much of which is directed against civilians. In the diary Zlata compares herself to Anne Frank, whose diary we described earlier in this chapter. The following excerpts are from Zlata's diary, which she calls "Mimmy."

Thursday, 3/5/92.

OH GOD! THINGS ARE HEATING UP IN SARAJEVO. On Sunday a small group of armed civilians (as they say on TV) killed a Serbian wedding guest and wounded the priest. On March 2 (Monday) the whole city was full of barricades. There were "1,000" barricades. We didn't even have bread. At 6:00 people got fed up and went out into the streets. The procession set out from the cathedral and made its way through the entire city. Several people were wounded at the Marshal Tito [deceased former communist dictator of Yugoslavia] army barracks. People sang and cried "Bosnia, Bosnia," "Sarajevo, Sarajevo," "We'll live together" and "Come Outside."

Tuesday, 4/28/92. Dear Mimmy,

SNIFFLE! MARTINA, *SNIFFLE,* AND TATEA, *SNIFFLE,* left YESTERDAAAY! They left by bus for Krsko [a town in Slovenia]. Oga has gone too, so has Dejan. Mirna will be leaving tomorrow or the next day, and soon Marijana will be going too.

SNIFFLE!

Everybody has gone. I'm left with no friends.

Saturday, 5/2/92. Dear Mimmy,

TODAY WAS TRULY, ABSOLUTELY THE WORST DAY ever in Sarajevo. The shooting started around noon. Mommy and I moved into the hall. Daddy was in his office, under our apartment, at the time. We told him on the intercom to run quickly to the downstairs lobby where we'd meet him. We brought Cicko [the canary] with us. The gunfire was getting worse, and we couldn't get over the wall to the Bobars', so we ran down to our own cellar.

The cellar is ugly, dark, smelly. Mommy, who's terrified of mice, had two fears to cope with. The three of us were in the same corner as the other day. We listened to the pounding shells, the shooting, the thundering noise overhead. We even heard planes. At one moment I realized that this awful cellar was the only place that could save our lives. Suddenly, it started to look almost warm and nice. It was the only way we could defend ourselves against all this terrible shooting. We heard glass shattering in our street. Horrible. I put my fingers in my ears to block out the terrible sounds.

Monday, 6/29/92. Dear Mimmy,

BOREDOM!!! SHOOTING!!! SHELLING!!! PEOPLE BEING KILLED!!! DESPAIR!!! HUNGER!!! MISERY!!! FEAR!!!

That's my life! The life of an innocent 11-year-old schoolgirl!! A schoolgirl without a school, without the fun and excitement of school. A child without games, without friends, without the sun, without birds, without nature, without fruit, without chocolate or sweets, with just a little powdered milk. In short, a child without a childhood.

Source: From *Zlata's Diary* by Zlata Filopovic. Translation copyright © 1994 Editions Robert Laffont/Fixot. Used by permission of Viking Penguin, a division of Penguin Putnam, Inc. [Capitalization and boldfacing in original.]

the establishment of concentration camps for prisoners that are more like death camps, the seizure and/or destruction of noncombatants' property, and the driving of civilians from their homes and from occupied territories (Beaubien, 1995; "21 Serbs Indicted," 1995; Jackson, 1994; MacKinnon, 1993).

The UN has established a war tribunal to deal with crimes committed in the Bosnian War, but it may never be able to bring the violators to justice. Because many of these war criminals live in areas still controlled by the Serbs, they are protected from arrest and trial. See the box "The Human Face of Rights Violations: Child of War" for a description of the other effects of this war on civilian populations.

The ethnic cleansing in Bosnia is not the only example of war crimes committed against contemporary civilian populations. Recently, for example, Russian troops brutalized and massacred civilians in the rebelling province of Chechnya. Turks assaulted the Kurdish minority in Iraq, Indian forces used terror to control the northern state of Kashmir, and China abused civilians in Tibet.

Around the world women and children are routinely arrested, harassed, and killed for their ethnic origins or their beliefs. Moreover, children are not immune from being imprisoned and tortured by brutal governments as a means of pressuring dissident parents.

Prisoners of Conscience and Lack of Freedom

Other abuses of civil and political rights continue to abound. Amnesty International estimates that "over half of the UN's member countries are currently holding prisoners of conscience" (Staunton and Fenn, 1991:16). The use of the death penalty is on the rise in countries around the world, although there is no evidence that it serves as a deterrent to crime or political violence. In fact, ample evidence demonstrates that the death penalty is used disproportionately against the poor and against racial, religious, and ethnic minorities (Staunton and Fenn, 1991).

In addition, crimes against vulnerable groups are unabated. Around the world women and children are routinely arrested, harassed, and killed because of their ethnic origins or their beliefs. Moreover, children are not immune from being imprisoned and tortured by brutal governments as a means of pressuring dissident parents. And millions of people live in societies where there are no fair trials and they do not have access to lawyers. The list of abuses of even the most fundamental rights is long indeed.

Freedom House is a nonprofit human rights organization that each year since the early 1960s has conducted the *Comparative Survey of Freedom* of the world's nations. The survey divides countries into three categories: free (those nations exhibiting a high degree of political and civil rights); partially free (those nations exhibiting some realization of political and civil rights, but with considerable room for improvement); and not free (those nations whose citizens enjoy almost no political and civil rights). The 1994 survey found 40 percent of the world's people living in partially free countries and another 40 percent residing in not free societies. Only 20 percent of our globe's inhabitants live in countries where they experience a high degree of respect for their political and civil rights. The list of the worst political and civil rights offenders include Afghanistan, Algeria, Angola, Bhutan, Burma, China, Cuba, Guinea, Iraq, Libya, Mauretania, North Korea, Rwanda, Saudi Arabia, Somalia, Sudan, Syria, Tajikistan, Turkmenistan, Uzbekistan, and Vietnam. Freedom House designated Sudan as the worse offender, followed closely by Iraq, then North Korea ("Democracies Double," 1994).

The United States and Human Rights

We already have noted the direct contribution of the U.S. Declaration of Independence, Constitution, and Bill of Rights to the UN Charter and the Universal Declaration. In this section, we discuss in more detail the involvement of the United States in international human rights and outline some major human rights problems at home.

The United States and Global Human Rights

The Puritans were some of the earliest and most influential European settlers in what is now the United States. A group of Puritans departed from Plymouth, England, on September 20, 1620, aboard the sailing ship the *Mayflower* on what historian Perry Miller (1956) called an "errand into the wilderness." The goal of these pilgrims was to create a model *theocracy* (a society ruled by God and religious principles) in New England. This godly society was to be a "shining light upon a hill" for the world to see and emulate. Many argue that this tenet of Puritanism formed the core of the Great American Myth.

By myth we mean a story a people use to define themselves and their relation to other people and to the universe. The **Great American Myth,** originating in Puritan New England, sees the United States as a "righteous nation" endowed by God for the special mission of being a "light in the world." Although through the years the myth lost much of its religious significance, it underpinned, to a degree, the role of the United States in World War II, the founding of the UN, the Bretton Woods conference, and the Cold War. Today, Americans still tend to view their country as a "special nation" with the mission of spreading the blessings of democratic freedom and economic capitalism around the globe. Millions living in oppressive political and economic conditions around the world still see the United States as the great land of freedom and opportunity.

The reality, however, is different from these perceptions when we view the record of the United States on international human rights since the creation of the UN. Human rights has not been a major concern of U.S. foreign policy; Congress is generally more active about such issues than American presidents. For example, in 1986, over President Ronald Reagan's veto, Congress took strong action against apartheid when it placed an embargo on almost every type of goods that could be sold to South Africa and threatened to move against other nations that violated the military portions of the embargo. President Jimmy Carter (president 1977–1981) was the only president to focus on human rights. For example, when the communist government in Poland declared martial law in 1981 in an effort to break the Solidarity labor union, he imposed trade sanctions on that country (Frankel, 1989).

The occasions on which America has acted on the global scene for purely humanitarian reasons are also rare. Rather, the human rights concerns of this country usually have been subordinated to other foreign policy goals. For example, the United States used human rights as a weapon in the Cold War. After Cuba drifted into the communist camp following Fidel Castro's 1959 revolution, the U.S. government consistently criticized Cuba's violations of political and civil rights while ignoring infractions by many of our noncommunist Latin American supporters. Meanwhile, during the Cold War the United States frequently supported dictatorial, brutally abusive anticommunist regimes such as those of Ferdinand Marcos in the Philippines (president 1966–1986), Augusto Pinochet in Chile (president 1973–1990), and General Mohammad Zia ul-Haq in Pakistan (president 1978–1988) (Frankel, 1989) in the name of "saving the world for democracy!"

In the aftermath of the Cold War, the United States still does not have a clear and consistent human rights policy. For example, beginning in 1994, the government deviated from its traditional position of linking human rights improvements in a nation to trade agreements with it and opted for keeping China's *most favored nation* status (a status that entitles a nation to receive the best trading conditions with the United States) despite China's consistent refusal to even discuss improving its dismal human rights record (Schmetzer, 1994). President Bill Clinton announced that trade was the primary goal of our foreign policy, thereby implying that human rights are to take a backseat (Zimmerman, 1995). By separating foreign policy from human rights, the United States is not exercising leadership in an area of growing concern to the global community (Forsythe, 1991). Other nations or regional groupings such as the European Union or the Organization of American States continue to fill the gap left by the sporadic human rights performance of the United States.

The United States and Human Rights at Home

On the domestic front our human rights record is also mixed. Almost 30 years after the signing of these agreements, the government still has not ratified the

Covenant on Political and Civil Rights or the Covenant on Social, Economic, and Cultural Rights, nor has it formally approved numerous other international rights accords. America's failure to commit to global norms may be traced mainly to fears that it may be held to international standards in its domestic affairs. At home many Americans even refuse to recognize that basic rights extend to *entitlements* to social and economic security. These omissions have resulted in one of the worse social and economic rights resumes in the First World, as we discuss throughout this book.

The domestic record of the United States is better on political and civil rights. Most Americans enjoy freedom of speech, religion, and association. They can form labor unions with little interference. Their rights before the law are respected. There are, however, notable exceptions. Minorities, the poor, and immigrants often have difficulties in obtaining even the most fundamental rights enjoyed by most Americans (see Chapter 11).

There are other areas of serious concern. For example, fear of crime has led to erosions of American's civil and political rights. Many people seem willing to give up bits of their constitutional protections against unwarranted government intrusion in order for more criminals to be convicted. The main solution to the perception of a crime wave in this country offered by politicians and many citizens is to "get tough" on lawbreakers. This attitude has resulted in rising conviction rates; longer prison terms; and overcrowded, unsafe prisons. Another way officials have "gotten tough" on lawlessness has been to increase the use of the death penalty. In 1995, the UN censured the United States for deplorable conditions in its maximum security prisons and for executing persons under 18 in violation of international law.

Assessing the Situation

Since the end of World War II, human rights has been an especially powerful tool for social and political change. But controversy continues to rage about global civil rights. Questions range from how effective civil rights are to protect individuals and vulnerable groups to whether they are an appropriate vehicle for determining the nature of the good society. In this section we assess the position of human rights on the world scene and discuss some theoretical issues concerning the interaction of globalization and human rights.

Human Rights in Today's World

Though human rights are technically recognized by most of the world's nations, no individual country has a perfect record in this area. At one end of the spectrum, some nations like Iraq merely pay lip service to the cause of human rights. But even in most of the industrial democracies of the First World, which boast fairly good records in assuring human rights, room for improvement exists. The world community has intervened successfully in some countries with particularly brutal violations of human rights. But such intervention is sporadic, and many difficult human rights situations remain unaddressed. Several factors account for this failure. First, powerful nations can afford to resist global pressure for change. For example, UN condemnations of the application of the death penalty to minors has not stopped this practice within the United States.

Second, failures to stop global human rights abuses also stem from the ways that social and political energy are mobilized for addressing these issues. National or international political organs too often respond only to public pressure. Such pressure is generated when NGOs or the media bring outrages to public attention. For example, in 1998 China released some prodemocracy activists from prison only after prolonged worldwide media attention. Although this interaction indicates the power of the civil society, it also suggests that the approach to addressing human rights abuses will remain piecemeal for the foreseeable future.

One other impediment to global human rights enforcement needs to be mentioned. Human rights represents an understanding of human worth that emerged out of the Enlightenment. Yet another, conflicting, value, which also originated in the Enlightenment, has often negatively impacted on the human rights situation. According to the notion of *materialism,* human good is measured by material well-being. At the end of the twentieth century, materialism is a main force underlying the increasingly powerful assumption that the good society is determined solely in terms of ever higher levels of consumption. Constantly expanding consumption is the essence of the *market economy,* a term used to describe a capitalistic economy driven by consumer choices of goods.

This ever increasing consumption will actually undermine the very biosphere upon which all life depends. The focus on consumption also discourages our seeing human beings as having undeniable rights that define them and their relation to each other, to their governments, and to the economy.

From this materialistic perspective, people are identified as consumers rather than as fully functioning, loving, caring, and moral human beings. Anything or anybody interfering with consumption and the spread of the market economy is often condemned, further undermining efforts to deal with even severe violations of human rights. In sum, current forms of materialistic thought trivialize human rights and orient government policy away from protecting the vulnerable and toward assuring the spread of the market economy. Protecting and increasing the market economy seems to be a key goal of many nations, including the United States.

In addition, within the United States, and possibly within other industrialized nations, the strong emphasis on human rights combined with individualism may be producing some undesirable consequences. Some critics argue that the strong individualism of twentieth-century America is undermining the nation's social and political life. Human rights is part and parcel of that individualism because it stresses the privileges of individuals more than their duties to society and other collectives like the family. Human rights then leads to the tendency to assert freedom. For these reasons, the industrialized nations may, such critics contend, need to return to teaching the virtues and duties of citizenship.

Theoretical Concerns

Human rights play major roles in redefining the global scene. To explore these roles, we examine them in the context of the globalization process.

Human Rights and the Globalization Process

Human rights have been a powerful tool in redefining the identity of every living person because human rights are attached to each of us, regardless of the traditional ways of defining identity, such as by gender, race, religion, or birth status. Many societies have historically considered large segments of their people as second-class citizens, or even less than human, because of these traditional identifications. But in recent times more and more disadvantaged groups have used human rights to redefine themselves as human beings with legitimate claims to honorable treatment. For example, liberation movements throughout the world have begun with a sense of outrage that a people's human rights have been violated.

Human rights have also provided a potent value system from which to define the nature of the good society. Such a value system is now used as a standard for assessing political, economic, and environmental concerns worldwide. In this way human rights have helped break down traditional boundaries among cultural and national groups. Today, the cultural practices of such groups are increasingly evaluated by universal standards. The idea of human rights—with its emphasis on the rights of each person—has aided this process by empowering individuals to question their treatment by a group or collectivity.

The assertion of human rights does not automatically result, however, in the spread of Western, individualistic modernism. Rather, various ethnic groups are employing the third generation of human rights to demand the privilege of maintaining their distinct way of life. This reality illustrates the emerging approach to inclusiveness we discussed in Chapter 1. The new inclusiveness recognizes universal principles while allowing for cultural distinctiveness.

Whereas the idea of human rights has been a mechanism for changing the sociosphere, it seems to be spreading to engage the biosphere. That is, people are now arguing that stable civil, political, social, and cultural rights cannot be maintained when the biological basis for life is destroyed. The fourth generation of human rights, if it matures, has the potential to provide a tool for determining the allocation of resources necessary for a sustainable future.

Human rights have also resulted in changed or new social structures by creating different relationships, groups, and social organizations, all working to effect a global community that recognizes the rights of its citizens everywhere. For example, people around the world concerned with human rights routinely communicate with one another about rights issues and conditions. Social organizations have been formed within governmental bodies as well as outside government to promote human rights. Not only have human rights provided new forms of engagement and social agency, but they also have redefined how governments, business, and other collectivities relate to the individual. Since human rights are viewed as absolutes, they must be considered whenever a collectivity interacts with the individual.

Human Rights and the Future of Civil Society. Theologian and expert on interfaith dialogue Raimundo Panikkar (1995) has suggested that the notion of human rights is not universal but is based on modern Western assumptions. These assumptions include such beliefs as the idea that human nature can be understood or grasped by reason, and that the human individual is a reality separable from society and the cosmos of which he or she is an integral part. Many, if not most, cultures do not share these assumptions. Not all Western philosophies and religions in fact share these assumptions either. In many other cultures it is not the human individual who comes first but the entire cosmic order. That order must be upheld, a responsibility that human beings must share with one another. All living creatures, not simply human beings, have a place within this world. Such factors as social position, age, gender, and ritual duties define each person's place in the cosmos. In the end, most human cultures share some concern for human dignity and the well-being of their weakest members.

Many of the world's cultures do not even have words corresponding literally to our term "human rights." Yet although cultures have differed in the past, the forces of modernization and globalization may sweep these differences aside, leading to the emergence of a homogenized global culture that includes the Western understanding of rights. Some experts like Panikkar believe we cannot know in what direction societies are heading. But the authors of this text believe that we can be relatively certain of one thing—that all human societies are in the process of passing from traditional communities to modern, contract-based societies (that is, societies based on legal agreements). Moreover, when such modernization occurs, it will probably mean the adoption of Western-style identities and values such as human rights, as these too are part of modern notions about the world.

Meanwhile, many indigenous peoples invoke human rights concepts in defense of maintaining their traditional ways of life. This appeal to human rights has often been effective in dealing with Western powers. But in general those waving the banner of human rights to defend themselves, their dignity, and their particular cause are participating in the dynamic of globalization, helping to drive the process while also benefiting from it. The claim that one's rights are being violated by political forces attempting to crush a social cause becomes effective when supporters appeal successfully to the "court of world opinion." Such appeals via the media will probably become more frequent, especially insofar as they continue to prove effective. Probably those subjected to the effects of modernization and Westernization will make such appeals the most frequently, but of course others will too. Even antimodern and anti-Western groups will at times possibly find rights-oriented rhetoric and the force of world opinion to their advantage. Whatever their origin, such appeals will be effective mainly because of the continued hegemony of the West, its ideas, and its institutions. But as the unquestioned domination of the West declines and other cultures find their voice, especially Islamic, Indian, and Confucian-based cultures (possibly indigenous tribal peoples too), the entire basis for global civil society will be renegotiated, including the Western concept of rights.

SUMMARY

1. Humphrey defines **human rights** as "those individual rights and freedoms that pertain to the human person by reason of his [or her] humanity, whether they are civil and political or economic, social and cultural rights." Human rights are a driving force in globalization because they provide universal standards that transcend national boundaries and interests by undermining the sovereignty of nation-states.

2. Following the atrocities of two world wars, the UN Charter, signed June 26, 1946, commits the organization to affirming human rights, the worth of the human person, the equality of men and women, and the parity of large and small nations. The Universal Declaration of Human Rights and the two Covenants on Human Rights implementing it are known as the **International Bill of Human Rights.** The failure by

powerful countries, including the United States and China, to ratify these agreements remains a major block to the international implementation of human rights.

3. The **indivisibility of human rights** is the understanding that in the quest for justice, security, and peace, political and civil rights can not be separated from economic, social, and cultural rights. Within the global community, debate over human rights usually focuses not on the definition of basic human rights but on whether to apply them to certain populations.
4. The UN tries to extend specific protections to **vulnerable groups,** categories of people who are especially susceptible to abuse and exploitation, through international accords and with special commissions and agencies.
5. Critics argue that the extensive application of human rights undermines the quest for justice and impedes the democratic process. Others believe that human rights is a powerful tool to oppose oppression and unequal treatment and to assure the democratic participation of everyone.
6. Non-Western governments have charged the West and the UN with **cultural imperialism,** or the imposition of outside values on their cultures. Others argue that it is possible to draw up a list of moral universals to be applied to all humanity, regardless of culture, a position that is supported by principles common to diverse religions.
7. Among the most pressing issues for the international community have been **genocide** (acts committed to destroy a national, ethnic, racial or religious group) and **disappearance** (the practice of making perceived opponents of a regime vanish without ever acknowledging their apprehension or detention).

Thinking Critically

1. We have stated several times throughout this chapter that the emphasis on rights may have gone too far. It has been suggested that if such a situation exists, it may partly be addressed by reestablishing the sense of responsibility. Would an emphasis on responsibility make a difference in how we define and address social problems? Would such an emphasis cause new and unexpected problems? Explain your answer.
2. The ancient Greeks and Romans were concerned with the relationship between personal virtue and the development and maintenance of a just society. Many conservatives believe that the loss of the sense of virtue or good character may lie at the root of many problems in contemporary society. How would a social order based on perfecting one's character by developing virtues (e.g., self-control, honesty, service to others, loyalty, courage) differ from a social order based on conformity to our society's social norms? How can our families, churches, and schools be oriented to building character? Do human beings possess a higher nature that needs to be cultivated, or are we simply what society and its norms make us?
3. Feminist psychologist Carol Gilligan asserts that female moral reasoning focuses on caring for others with whom we have actual relationships, whereas male moral reasoning deals with abstract principles of justice. As women play an increasingly significant role in global culture, will a distinctly feminine orientation to issues of right and wrong in human social conduct emerge? If so, how would it differ from our present orientation? How would our approach to global social issues be different? How would our relationship with nature and other living things be different?
4. Where will the issue of human rights on a global scale lead us? Will the entire world adopt Western views? Will the present relative decline of the West lead to the emergence of a non-Western global culture? Do leaders in other societies resist human rights because they sincerely believe in their own cultural values, or are they simply trying to justify their power and domination?

Suggested Readings

Berting, Jan, Peter R. Baehr, J. Herman Burgers, Cees Flinterman, Barbara de Klerk, Rob Kroes, Cornelis A. van Minnen, and Koo Vander Wal, eds. 1990. *Human Rights in a Pluralist World: Individuals and Collectivities.* Westport, CT: Meckler Corporation.

Eide, Asbjorn. 1986. "The Human Rights Movement and the Transformation of the International Order." *Alternatives.* II: 365–402, 535–38.

Filipovic, Zlata. 1994. *Zlata's Diary: A Child's Life in Sarajevo.* New York: Viking Penguin.

Fitzpatrick, Joan. 1994. *Human Rights in Crisis: The International System for Protecting Rights During States of Emergency.* Procedural Aspects of International Law Series, vol. 19. Philadelphia: University of Pennsylvania.

Forsythe, David P. 1991. *The Internationalization of Human Rights.* Lexington, MA: Lexington.

Frank, Anne. 1952. *The Diary of a Young Girl.* New York: Pocket Books.

Humphrey, John. 1989. *No Distant Millennium: The International Law of Human Rights.* Paris: United Nations Educational, Scientific and Cultural Organization (UNESCO).

Kaufman, Natalie H. 1990. *Human Rights Treaties and the Senate: A History of Opposition.* Chapel Hill: University of North Carolina Press.

Küng, Hans. 1998. *A Global Ethic for Global Politics and Economics.* New York: Oxford University Press.

Randall, Kenneth C. 1990. *Federal Courts and the International Human Rights Paradigm.* London: Duke University Press.

Selznick, Philip. 1992. *The Moral Commonwealth: Social Theory and the Promise of Community.* Berkeley: University of California Press.

Shute, Stephen and Susan Hurley, eds. 1993. *On Human Rights: The Oxford Amnesty Lectures 1993.* New York: Basic Books.

Solzhenitsyn, Aleksandr. 1975. *The Gulag Archipelago.* New York: Harper & Row.

Staunton, Marie, Sally Fenn, and Amnesty International, eds. 1991. *The Amnesty International Handbook.* Claremont, CA: Hunter House.

Timerman, Jacobo. 1981. *Prisoner Without a Name, Cell Without a Number.* New York: Knopf.

Web Sites

The following web sites function mainly as directories or resource pages. At them you can find many links to a wealth of human rights Internet sites. These sites contain names of human rights organizations, resources (such as libraries and databases), and links to other sites that provide documents, as well as links to newsgroups. Many also provide a brief summary of each link.

Human Rights (Internet Links)
http://www.gn.apc.org/peopleinaction/rights.html

United Nations
www.un.org

IGC: Human Rights: Internet—Resources Collection
http://www.igc.org/igc/issues/hr

People in Action for a Better World
http://www.geocities.com/RainForest/1980/

Some independent sites found in these directories are

Amnesty International

http://www.amnesty.org/

The official web site for Amnesty International, it contains a wealth of information, including publications, documents, searchable databases, press releases, links to all other Amnesty web pages (i.e., Amnesty International USA), and other sites related to human rights.

Human Rights Internet

http://www.hri.ca

This site, an international network of human rights organizations, contains publications, documents, resource guides, and United Nations information.

Human Rights Watch

http://www.hrw.org/

This site supplies information about Human Rights Watch and data on human rights conditions sorted by country and region.

One World Online

http:/www.oneworld.org

This site is both a meeting place for people concerned about the world and its people and an information resource center about issues of global justice and sustainable human development.

CHAPTER ■ THREE

Religion

Negotiating the Cosmological Order

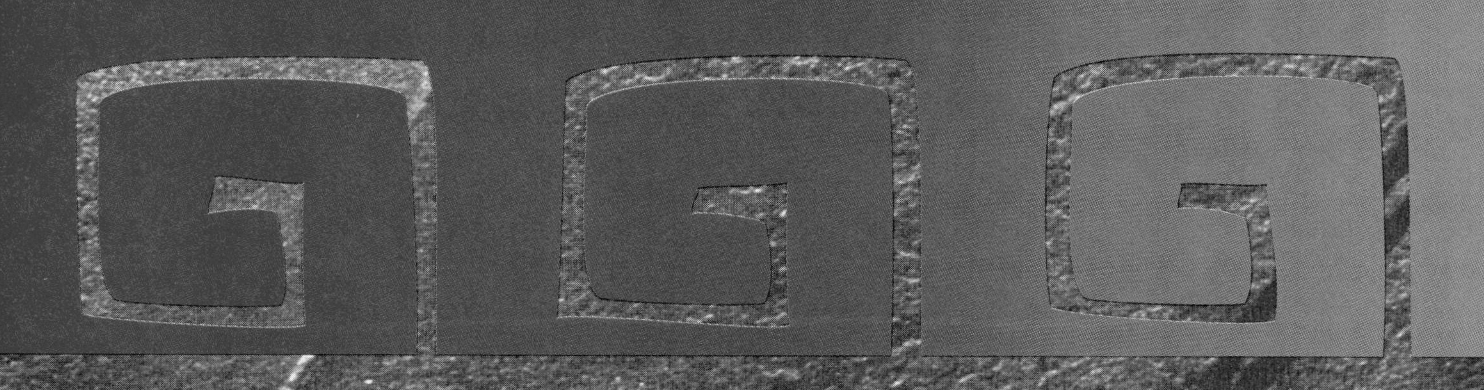

One of the most remarkable leaders the world has ever known was born in the small village of Taktser, Tibet, in 1935. Two years after his birth, Tenzin Gyatso was recognized as the reincarnation of the thirteenth Dalai Lama, or the incarnation of Avaloketishvara, the Buddha of Compassion. The Dalai Lama looks rather exotic to Western eyes in his maroon and yellow monk's robes, yet he is a humble and kind man who calls himself simply a "Buddhist monk." Jovial and down-to-earth, the Dalai Lama manifests many of the best Buddhist virtues: simplicity, nonattachment to ego, and forgiveness. It is this last quality that has been sorely tested—since the 1950s the Chinese government has attempted to wipe out Tibetan Buddhism and dominate Tibet by the most brutal of means.

Although it might not fit your image of what a "living Buddha" might be like, the fourteenth Dalai Lama has been deeply interested in modern science and technology (and material progress) since he was a boy. For many years he carried on long conversations about science—one of his favorite topics—with the eminent physicist David Bohm. As this is being written, he is taking part in discussions and experiments in mind-body medicine with medical experts at some of the leading hospitals in New York City. While still a young boy in Tibet, he indulged his interest in technology by repairing the only automobile to be found at that time in his somewhat technologically backward country. Once he got the car running he proceeded to have an accident. After all, there were no traffic signals and few, if any, experienced drivers to learn from. Today his hobby is repairing watches.

In 1950 when he was sixteen, nine years short of the completion of his intense education as a spiritual leader, the Chinese invaded his country and he had to assume political authority. He had to negotiate with such ruthless men as Mao Tse-tung and Deng Xiaoping, then the leaders of China. In 1959, the Chinese occupation led the Tibetans to revolt, and, fearing for his life, His Holiness the Dalai Lama, then only nineteen years old, led many of his people into exile. Today he and the exiled Tibetans have established Dharamsala, India, as the capital of Tibet in exile. Yet he has never expressed hatred or anger toward the Chinese; he has always sought reconciliation and peace.

Recently, in Bloomington, Indiana, he was asked if he thought it was a good idea for people to boycott Chinese-made goods in order to pressure the Chinese into freeing Tibet. His answer surprised many of his supporters. He answered that the Chinese should not be isolated but befriended and brought into the community of nations. After all, as he has often said, the Chinese are our fellow human beings, striving for happiness in the only way they know how and are themselves victims of circumstance. In Buddhist theory we are all one and to hurt others is to hurt ourselves. His remarks were not unlike the Christian sentiment, "We are members one of another."

For his efforts to establish peace and harmony throughout Asia, His Holiness was awarded the Nobel Peace Prize in 1989. He is just as intent upon creating peace among the religions of the world, which he compares to items on a menu. If everyone ate the same food all of the time, our different tastes and needs would not be satisfied. Religions are our spiritual nourishment, and different people have different tastes and needs there, too. The Dalai Lama was an active participant in the 1992 parliament of world religious leaders that took place in Chicago. He does not suggest that Americans and Europeans should become Buddhists. Rather, he believes that it is more appropriate for Americans and Europeans to stick to their own Judeo-Christian traditions, although he recognizes the need of all people to make their own choices in spiritual matters.

As evidence of how interrelated we are all becoming in the emerging global culture, Tibet and the Dalai Lama have become increasingly well known to Americans in recent years. Movies such as *Little Buddha, Seven Years in Tibet,* and *Kundun* have featured Tibetan Buddhism or the Dalai Lama himself. Adam Yauch of the music group the Beastie Boys recently organized a Free Tibet concert held in Golden Gate Park in San Francisco that featured groups such as the Red Hot Chili Peppers, Sonic Youth, and Smashing Pumpkins. Actors such as Steven Segal and Richard Gere count themselves friends of His Holiness, as does Asian scholar Robert Thurman and his (perhaps better known) daughter, actress Uma Thurman. It is not His Holiness the Dalai Lama that seeks the recognition or company of these well-known figures; rather it is they who seek the presence of this remarkable spiritual leader.

Sources: Dalai Lama, *Oceans of Wisdom: Guidelines for Living* (San Francisco: Harper & Row, 1989); Henry Dreher, "Recite Your Mantra and Call Me in the Morning," *New York Magazine* (May 11, 1998), 24–31; Dinty W. Moore, *The Accidental Buddhist: Mindfulness, Enlightenment and Sitting Still* (Chapel Hill: Algonquin, 1997).

THE ROLE OF RELIGION IN A GLOBAL SOCIETY

With globalization comes the redrawing of many boundaries. As a result, we have begun to take personal and group identities less for granted than we did previously. Of special concern today is the increasing importance given to conceptualizing and understanding the global system itself and the role of each group (and each species) in it. Our economies and governments, along with modern medicine, education, and science, can offer specific practical solutions to limited aspects of our larger problems, such as programs that limit population growth or programs that increase the energy efficiency of production. But the larger and deeper issues that are increasingly facing us all do not allow for solution at this level. These larger issues (which include living with the uncertainty that is the result of nuclear proliferation, keeping our individual sense of place amid the rapid changes in values that globalization can bring, and defining what obligations human beings have to each other and to future generations) are not the sorts of issues that we can resolve by practical rational solutions, yet they represent deep concerns.

A recent book edited by political scientist Susanne Hoeber Rudolph and professor of Islamic studies James Piscatori, *Transnational Religion and Fading States* (1997), suggests that in this new era of globalization religion may surpass the nation-state as both a social force and source of identity for the first time in two centuries. The **nation-state** is based on the idea that the people who occupy a given territory share a common culture and common identity and should be governed by a unified political system. Existing nation-states developed from efforts of elite groups to unite diverse populations under a central authority. Today nation-states are under pressure from processes that act in two directions—internal divisions and external global forces. Many of the subgroups that have been parts of nations are asserting their differences once more. Meanwhile, groups that offer identities that extend beyond national limits (*trans*national identities) are becoming more important to some people. It is true that certain religions have inspired higher loyalties and identities across territorial boundaries for millennia. This is especially so of Christianity, Islam, and Buddhism. But today something new, namely globalization, is altering identities and causing social boundaries to become more permeable. Religions are helping to shape that process.

Contemporary globalization is being shaped both by the values and beliefs of modernism and by social reactions against modernism. Modernism, which began some 500 years ago in Western European societies, involved a concerted attack on *tradition*, that is, all those social and cultural patterns based on emulating the past. Attacks by the supporters of modernism against inherited status, power, and privilege led to important institutional changes. (Analyzing the social consequences of changes due to modernism [called modernization] has been a central concern of sociology since its origins.)

One of these changes was the emergence of the nation-state system. The members of a society became increasingly defined as a "nation," a group of people who because of birth in a given territory were assumed to share a common culture and identity. (The word *nation* comes from the Latin word meaning birth.) New political forms were needed to express the will of this "nation," or, as it was also said, "the people." Their collective well-being would be better served by a "rational" system of decision making that involved voting than by ancient systems that were based on the inherited power of privileged classes and ruling families.

Similarly, economies that involved social relationships defined by contract (and money) and were driven by the "rational" pursuit of profit replaced economic systems based on traditional relationships and values that restricted economic expansion. The forces of modernism also attacked the Roman Catholic Church because of its association with traditional political and economic patterns. They also attacked the Church for its corruption and its failure to meet the perceived spiritual (and social) needs of many people, especially those of the emerging urban classes who were intent on creating the new economic and political orders. Science became a major instrument in all of these changes, as it provided a method for finding answers to practical and theoretical questions. Because of its relative success in this regard, science and the philosophy of materialism that accompanied it became sources of authority that replaced religion in most matters of practical concern—medicine, agriculture, warfare, business, and the conquest of other nations.

The dominant institutions of modern society, the economy, the nation-state, and the instrumental rationality of science and technology (a standard of rational thought aimed at the efficient control of nature) have, however, generated problems that these institutions cannot solve. Economic and political systems have created both an ecological crisis and vast disparities of wealth, power, and opportunity among the world's people. These systems can produce high rates of economic growth, but they have not solved the problems of poverty and human exploitation. In fact, they often contribute to them. The incorporation of hundreds of millions of people into large centralized nation-states has not solved these problems either. Nation-states are often too large and too impersonal to handle the problems of the individuals and ethnic groups that comprise them. Conversely, nation-states, for all their supposed power, are too limited and narrow to be able to address problems of global ecological crisis, political tyranny, or international terrorism. The rationality that propels these modern institutions is mostly of the instrumental variety, typical of our scientific and technological age. Such a perspective involves finding efficient ways (means) to achieve selected goals (ends). This works well when the goals are material and the benefits of meeting them is clear to everyone. But instrumental rationality is not a vehicle for discovering what ends or goals we *ought* to pursue, and this makes it very hard for leaders of modern societies to justify social policies that require people to make sacrifices, other than in wartime when most people in the society can be persuaded of the necessity of making personal sacrifices for the larger good.

In contrast, in the world's religions, there is a recognition of the existence of a higher set of priorities beyond the immediate gains of the material world. As we will see in this chapter, that higher set of priorities has to do with the sacred, and therefore sacrifices (literally "making something sacred") are the "business" of religions. Furthermore, religions satisfy other profound human needs such as the need for a positive sense of worth and a meaningful role in life. Many individuals have resolved issues of self-identity by becoming embedded in groups. The nation itself has been such a group and great effort has been expended by national governments to instill national loyalty. The nation fails, however, to provide people with the larger identity that might help them address global concerns, and it fails to provide the sorts of reassuring meanings that people seek in the face of personal tragedy and death. Once again it is religion that more often serves these functions, although religious groups may also narrow a person's sense of self-identification.

Religion also addresses the kinds of ultimate issues that arise in the globalization process as diverse cultures come into intimate contact with each other and commonly face the mounting threat of poverty, war, and ecological catastrophe. In addition, religion also addresses many needs, both social and psychological, of persons who embrace it, all of which explains why it has continued to play an important role in contemporary societies. Sociologist Milton Yinger defines **religion** as "a system of beliefs and practices by means of which a group of people struggles with [the] ultimate problems of human life" (Yinger, 1970:7). According to this definition, many of the sorts of issues stimulated by globalization have a religious dimension. Many traditional religious groups have begun to address the global crises we discuss in this book. These ultimate issues, we should add, are also sometimes addressed by today's social movements. Although they are not viewed as religions, many of these social movements, such as the environmental movement, clearly have religious or spiritual themes. In this chapter we treat these movements as the functional equivalent of religion.

Religion as a Social Movement

Social movements, you may recall, develop outside of established social institutions. In time such movements must either become institutionalized patterns within established society or fade from existence. Most of the world's major religions—Buddhism, Christianity, Judaism, Islam, and Taoism—for example, began as social movements under the influence of charismatic leaders. Each of them has continued to spawn social movements throughout its long history. Thus, there is a strong affinity between social movements and religion.

A characteristic that somewhat distinguishes religious from other social movements is the idea that religion deals not only with ultimate issues but also involves an orientation to or an actual experience of the *sacred,* or spiritual dimension, of reality. We cannot say what the sacred is in itself, but we must acknowledge that throughout human history it has been the center of powerful and frequently life-changing experiences. At times these experiences have threatened the existing social order (as was the case when Jesus' view that one could know God threatened Rome's power); at other times such experiences have affirmed it (as is the case today in Saudi Arabia, where the prevailing religion, Islam, upholds the existing social order).

Approaches to Religion

There are two approaches that we may take with regard to religion, or the sacred (which can also be called the holy, the spiritual, or the supernatural), although each of these terms is a slightly different variation on the same theme. The first approach is called the **phenomenological approach.** According to comparative religion professor Mircea Eliade, proponents of the phenomenological approach do not deny sociological, psychological, or physical elements in religion but insist that we must take religion and religious experience at face value. That is, we must recognize them as means of expressing and embodying the sacred (cited in Cunningham et al., 1995). Whether or not we have had religious experiences, we must at least allow for the fact that many people have claimed to have them and have attempted to express them to others. The Bible, for example, is replete with accounts of visions and other religious experiences, and in today's bookstores and libraries it is possible to find any number of books on the topic, including such classic texts as *The Varieties of Religious Experience* (1902) by American philosopher, theologian, and psychologist William James. Later in this chapter we briefly discuss this type of experience. (While we may reasonably wonder whether some [or all] experiences of the sacred are *authentic,* that is, genuine, this valid question and its answers lie beyond the scope of this book.)

Many religious or spiritual traditions have practices or *injunctions* that, when adhered to diligently, will provide experiences of or insights into the sacred or spiritual world (Wilber, 1998). These injunctions include techniques of meditation and prayer. The validity of the resulting experiences and insights can be evaluated by groups of more experienced fellow practitioners. Among Native Americans, the visions a young man experiences during his vision quest are reviewed by the elders of the tribe, and in a similar way a Zen monk's experiences of enlightenment are tested by his teacher. Mainstream American religious groups do not typically perform this function, although, for example, the authorities of churches that require conversion experiences before administering baptism may be concerned that individuals prove that their conversion is genuine.

Another approach to religion and the sacred is called the **functional** (or pragmatic) **approach.** It involves looking at the effects that the sacred (and religion in general) has on persons, groups, and societies. People may receive great psychological benefit from their experiences of the sacred or their participation in religious groups. Experiences of the sacred often have life-changing effects on individuals. These effects may or may not seem beneficial, however. Religion can sometimes be toxic; the changes that deep personal experiences can bring about can result in social and psychological maladjustment—in this decade, the mass suicide of the Heaven's Gate cult is one such example. Perhaps of more relevance to the topics of this chapter is the fact that the sacred can deeply affect patterns of group life and can even transform whole societies. When the sacred appears as a more or less sudden and unexpected social force, it threatens to disrupt the set routines of a society. We will use German sociologist Max Weber's term *charisma* to describe this phenomenon. So for us, charisma is a socially disruptive and unexpected manifestation of the sacred in the life of a group or society. Charisma brings with it new values and new *cosmologies*—new patterns of social life that may in time become routine or set patterns, as happened when Christianity in Europe replaced much of the "pagan" culture and social order over time.

Religion, the Sacred, and Consciousness. One of the consequences of modernization is the weakening of tradition, especially religious tradition. Modernism, you may recall, involved a concerted attack on *tradition,* that is, all those social and cultural patterns based on emulating the past. It attacked inherited status, power, and privilege and led to important institutional changes, such as the emergence of market economies, democratic politics, and the nation-state.

Sociologist Peter Berger points out that the weakening of tradition puts great weight on personal experience. As Berger observes, "Man is an empirical animal to the extent that his own direct experience is always the most convincing evidence of the reality of anything" (Berger, 1979:32). This self-reliance has two consequences: (1) We tend not to believe anything out of the ordinary unless we have experienced it ourselves, and (2) we tend to believe what we have experienced and discount or deny anything else.

Since its beginnings, sociology has been concerned with the consciousness, that is, with how people both experience and think about themselves and their world. Emile Durkheim, one of the founders of sociological inquiry, held that our experience of the sacred was a function of social organization. Karl Marx, another founder of sociological thought, believed that human consciousness was itself transformed over the course of history by the interaction of social forces. According to Marx, for example, capitalist society would produce a new and anticapitalist mentality in the working class that would then impel them to overthrow capitalism and replace it with a more humane socialist order.

More recently, Peter Berger has pointed out that we simply cannot take for granted the way we experience and think about the world because history generates and dissolves one structure of consciousness after another. For example, Renaissance thought replaced medieval thought only to be replaced by early modern thought, which has in turn been replaced by advanced modern mentalities. Indeed, in some ways, each distinct cultural group bears its unique structure of consciousness (Berger, 1979). Because of this, no pattern of consciousness, worldview, or sense of reality is absolute. But society is not the only force that structures or transforms consciousness. Personal tragedy, a near-death experience, the use of mind-altering substances, certain experiences with nature, and religious or spiritual experiences can have profound effects on consciousness. However, for experience to become reality, it must receive the support and validation of a group.

How is this so? There is considerable agreement among scholars of religion that no individual experience is "pure," but rather all experiences, even the most dramatic and profound, involve elements of interpretation. That is especially true afterwards, when the experience is remembered and discussed. This means that cultural traditions and group processes affect even the person's most private world (Küng et al., 1993:173). Therefore, whatever the person's original experience might be, it takes on meaning or becomes "reality" through a social process.

Berger (1979) states that we experience not just one reality, but a number of different realities. For example, reality is different to a person who has just fallen in love than to a person who is asleep and dreaming. We typically accept one of these many realities as the basic and "really real" one. For most people, everyday waking consciousness is viewed as reality because it is the one that receives the most social support. It is after all the "real world" of business and politics in which practical things get done. Yet, Berger claims, this reality is in fact fragile and subject to "rupture." For example, a personal tragedy or a brush with death can call this reality into question. There is sometimes even the danger that we might get too hung up on an alternative reality, and we have to "snap out of it," "come down to earth," or "get real" again before we can resume acceptable roles in daily life.

One of the most important of these reality ruptures, according to Berger, is the experience of the supernatural or sacred. Berger says the supernatural feels like another world, as massive and real as the ordinary one. In fact, many claim that it is the ordinary world that seems flat by comparison. This experience of the supernatural may occur in a religious context but in today's world it is increasingly found in other settings. A growing body of research shows that certain near-death experiences exhibit a coherent pattern that resembles Berger's description of the supernatural (Fenwick, 1995; Ring, 1982; Sabom, 1982). These experiences occur spontaneously to people who were neither religious nor spiritually inclined before the actual episode.

In addition to the experience of the supernatural as described by Berger, there is also the type of experience labeled as *mystical* (Smart, 1995). The mystical experience has been called "non-dual" because it is associated with the sense of oneness or unity with nature, reality, or God. This experience also is a very common one and occurs spontaneously at times. Here the injunctions discussed by Wilber (1998) come into play. Serious seekers may engage in these practices if they want to find out for themselves.

Today many people argue that we may be on the brink of a major transformation in human consciousness. In the following sections we examine some of these claims as they arise in the context of interfaith dialogue and the radical ecology movement, both of which have addressed issues of the role of human beings in nature and the cosmological order. Some of those engaged in interreligious dialogue suggest that such dialogue promotes transformations of consciousness and human identity (Cousins, 1992). Many of those involved in the radical wing of the ecology movement, for example, argue that if we are to effect the kind of changes necessary to preserve life on this planet, profound and dramatic changes will first need to occur in the ways that we experience ourselves and the natural world.

Peter Berger: Religion in World Building and World Maintenance. In *The Sacred Canopy* (1967), Peter Berger introduces another aspect of the importance of religion in human society. Like many sociologists, Berger believes that existence is really quite chaotic. There is no real way to predict the action of the forces of nature, much less the behaviors of people. But people cannot live with such chaotic conditions. They therefore construct a social world that in their minds gives them control over nature, predictability in relation to each other, and stability in their personalities. Berger holds that every society is engaged in world building and world maintenance. Religion helps members of society by providing a "sacred canopy"—a sense of safety in this world, rooted in beliefs and experiences of the sacred.

Religion plays a vital role in world building by rooting the human world in the *cosmological order* (that is, in the structures that gave rise to the universe itself). The cosmos represented in religion both transcends humans and contains them. For most of human history, this cosmos has been sacred. It stands as a powerful "other" that confronts humans and sustains them. Standing in right relationship with the sacred has firmly rooted humans in such a fashion that it ensures that their worlds will not be swallowed up in chaos. "Religion implies that human order is projected into the totality of being. Put differently, religion is the audacious attempt to conceive of the entire universe as being humanly significant" (Berger, 1967:28).

Socially constructed worlds are notably precarious. That is, they are innately unstable. The maintenance of the legitimacy of the social world presents a major problem in the production of stability. Each new generation that comes along asks the basic question: "Why is it that we believe what we believe and do what we do?" When the members of a generation do not receive credible answers to this question, their culture is threatened. Religion effectively legitimates social structures by integrating them into a worldview that not only includes the material world, but also the greater spiritual reality that transcends it. Put another way, religion anchors precarious human social constructions in ultimate reality. Ultimate reality is by definition beyond the fluctuations of human activity and life. It is what enables people to go to bed at night with the external and internal realities of their social world safe and secure. After all, as they perceive it, their ways are God's ways, their salvation is God's salvation, their enemies God's enemies, and their structures are the eternal structures of the universe.

The Impact of Globalization on Religion

In the first two chapters, we discussed some of the changes wrought by globalization. We argued that globalization has called for the redefining of personal and group identity and the redrawing of group boundaries. Rapid transportation and instantaneous communication have brought together peoples and cultures from all over the world. Even as it has produced radical changes in the backdrop of civil society, globalization has also radically altered the context for religion. Sociologist Peter Beyer (1994) has observed that contemporary religions emerged in a much different context from the one in which they now operate. They emerged in tribal or agricultural societies, in which people lived in smaller groups with a strong sense of community. There was comparatively little specialization. Even hierarchical structures were not highly developed. Groups had a more coherent identity and were able to establish rather clear boundaries between themselves and other groups. Most people in these communitarian societies shared a common lifestyle and morality. Under such conditions, Beyer would agree that religion functions much as Berger has spelled out. That is, religion could be used effectively to build and maintain the social worlds of ethnic groups. The skills of persuasion and manipulation that religious authorities developed to defend their faiths (and their societies) and to expand their dominion emerged in preurban, preindustrial environments.

First modernism and now globalization have radically redefined the context in which religions operate. As people moved into modern urban industrial societies, they had to confront and deal with people unlike themselves as **pluralism** (the bringing together of people of different views, religions, nationalities, and/or races) became the rule. Cities grew to the point that their inhabitants could not know one another personally as most people had in preurban societies. The sense of *personalism* (being known personally by others) and community declined. The stratification system in modern societies became infinitely more complex. People's identities, consequently, became much more tangled, as there were now many more groups with which to identify. For example, modern men and women may identify themselves as members of a particular family, religion, ethnic group, and nationality, but also as members of a particular political party, social class, city, state, occupation, professional group, and as employees of a certain company, volunteers for a specific charity, and so on.

To make matters more complicated, people's identities frequently overlap. For instance, many, if not most, people in modern societies have several different bloodlines in their heritage. That is, they are multiethnic and/or multiracial. They may be married to mates of different class, religious, or ethnic backgrounds and work at jobs with others from numerous religious, ethnic, class, and educational backgrounds. Modern life may call on people to cooperate with persons from racial, ethnic, religious, or other groups that they dislike (and perhaps distrust) in order to accomplish common political, economic, environmental, or social goals.

This pluralistic tendency of modern societies has been heightened by globalization. A striking symbol of the global village was seen at the opening of the 1998 Winter Olympic Games in Nagano, Japan. A Japanese-born conductor led an American orchestra and choirs from the five inhabited continents in a simultaneous, real-time stirring rendition of Beethoven's "Ode to Joy," through the marvel of modern technology. Such integration means that peoples who at one time might not have even known of one another are constantly confronted with each other's existence. Additionally, the growing environmental, political, economic, and cultural integration of the planet means any given people has to cope with the fact that their fate is tied up with those "strange people over there."

The Reaction of Religions to the Global Context

According to Beyer (1994), prior to modernism, religions were more capable of maintaining dominion over their rather limited ethnic groups. That is, the group's identity frequently was linked not only with their ethnicity but also with their religion. To be an Italian was to be a Catholic Christian; to be an Egyptian was to be a Muslim; to be an Indian was to be a Hindu. Religion also functioned to help maintain group boundaries. Italians could separate themselves from Egyptians not only by cultural, political, and geographical differences, but also by the fact that they were Christians whereas Egyptians were Muslims. Under such conditions it is not difficult to see how religion functions in building and maintaining social worlds. It allows people to claim the power of the absolute for their particular social world.

In the pluralism of an increasingly global society, people's social worlds are constantly bumping against other people's social worlds. As we become more aware of other people's norms, values, practices, and religions, it becomes more and more difficult for us to defend the absolute correctness of our own social world. Our social worlds become **relativized;** that is, everyone's social world is increasingly seen as but one of many social worlds. Our sense of relativity makes it more difficult for us to believe in the superiority of our social world. This situation is especially trying for religions because each of them claims to be rooted in and to give insight into the Ultimate. When confronting competing claims to ultimacy, the average citizens of the global village may be excused for throwing up their hands and exclaiming, "Just whose absolute ultimacy am I to believe?!!!"

Debating the Social and Cosmological Order

This question drives to the heart of the problem of religions in the global context. How are religions to understand, defend, and/or extend their own claims to ultimacy? What is at stake in the debates within and among various religious traditions is the nature of both the social and the cosmological orders. Religious traditions bring to the table their understanding of human beings, human relations, and morality as well as how these concepts are related to the nature of the cosmological order. Many people see these debates as overwhelmingly significant. To have no cosmological anchor for their social worlds undermines their social and personal identities and leaves them adrift in the chaos of competing worldviews.

The Privatization of Religion. Beyer notes several reactions to the situation of religion in global society. One response has been the privatization of religion. The **privatization of religion** is the tendency to make religion a private and individual experience. This phenomenon underlies the statement, "Well, you have your religion, and I have mine." This statement usually is heard in pluralistic situations, where it is often employed as a mechanism to reduce potentially destructive religious conflict. However, underlying the statement is a deeper conviction—we cannot know or objectively prove anything about the nature of the transcendent realm that is the purview of religion. This conviction may be accompanied by an assertion that religion has no place in public life. For example, some would advise political candidates to keep their religious views private. The candidate should present issues as if they were divorced from religious beliefs. Otherwise, the candidate's religious views may become an issue in themselves and harm the chances of election to office. It has been argued that in America today there is an almost antireligious bias in our media and legal institutions (Carter, 1993).

Universalism and Particularism. Although the privatization of religion is often discussed by sociologists, universalism and particularism are also significant in the global dynamics of religion, according to Beyer. **Universalism** refers to the common principles or constructs that apply to all people everywhere. When applied to religion, this means trying to find common religious or moral principles that can form the basis for group interaction and be used to address the problems that threaten humankind.

At the other end of the spectrum, **particularism** stresses the uniqueness of a given group's ways, practices, and ideas. When applied to religion, particularism involves stressing the uniqueness (if not the superiority) of one's own religious tradition in comparison to other people's religions. In national and global discussions, particularism takes three forms: insular, militant, and embedded. **Insular particularism** seeks to insulate a group from outside interference. In essence, proponents say, "Our ways, practices, or ideas are our business and no one else's. Others should leave us alone." The aborigines of Australia are one example of insular particularism. Often, this type of particularism is defended on the basis of universal principles such as solidarity rights.

Militant particularism holds that a group's uniqueness is superior and should become universal. This followers of this brand of particularism seek through conversion, political means, or force to impose their group's unique characteristics on others. In the religious arena, militant particularism is represented by those branches of Christianity, Judaism, Islam, Hinduism, or other religions that seek to become the religious basis for defining the cosmos and for forming the basis of the global society. Leaders of the so-called Christian Right in the United States are another example. They continually reinterpret news events as evidence of the second coming of Jesus Christ, which they claim is about to happen any day and in which they and their followers will play a very special role.

Embedded particularism seeks to maintain the distinctiveness of groups practicing it but sees these groups as integral to the larger globalization process. Embedded particularists recognize the unifying tendencies of the globalization process but insist on maintaining diversity in the face of that unity. Groups practicing embedded particularism may even hold that they have a special role to play in global society. For example, many indigenous peoples contend that there are elements in their cultures that have much to offer to global society. They may point to their tribal wisdom, their sense of community, the ability of members of their society to work harmoniously with nature, or their knowledge of traditional technology as valuable elements that are necessary in global society. Although embedded particularists offer elements of their culture to the global community, they do not seek to impose these components on the global community as do militant particularists.

Before ending this discussion, we need to make two additional points. First, Beyer notes that religion is a part of that total interaction that occurs within societies, among societies, and between societies and the globalization process. As a result, religious dynamics also influence other elements of human societies. For instance, interaction between universalists and particularists forms the foundation for global debates in the political realm, on the environmental scene, and even about the proper relation between men and women worldwide. We refer to conflicts between branches of universalism and particularism in a number of places throughout this book. Beyer also observes that one of the functions that religion has frequently taken for itself is that of setting moral standards. This gives those moral standards the appearance of being anchored in God or the ultimate reality. Therefore, it should come as little surprise that many of the cultural wars worldwide should take the form of clashes over morality, in which at least one side, if not both sides, claims to be defending a morality that is absolute.

Universalistic Responses to Globalization

In the following sections we examine two of the major examples of ongoing efforts to pursue universalistic understandings of humanity's place in the cosmos. The first of these, interfaith dialogue, is rooted in established religions and faith communities and reflects interactions among the world's cultures that began at least a century ago, if not earlier. The second, the emergence of new views of nature in the form of radical ecology, is a cultural phenomenon that is new and difficult to classify. These two developments are interdependent in many ways. It remains to be seen how they will unfold in the twenty-first century.

Universalism and Dialogue

In a dialogue two or more participants typically seek to be understood and to understand the other. All seek to be understood as they understand themselves and to understand the others as those parties understand themselves. How can we know that we have understood the other? One of two processes is involved when we encounter new information, ideas, or perspectives. *Assimilation* is one of these processes. When we assimilate a new idea, we attempt to fit it into the pattern of ideas and the way of thinking we already possess. This process may involve distorting the idea somewhat. Such a distortion may be deliberate but usually is inadvertent—we ourselves probably do not appreciate that we have distorted the information, idea, or perspective. For example, many people have embraced the idea of recycling, but not the idea of avoiding wasted resources that goes along with it. For many, the fact that aluminum soda cans and TV dinner trays are recyclable suggests that using such items is ecologically sound. In making such an assumption, however, these individuals are interpreting the idea of not wasting resources in a way that enables them to continue to practice a form of eating and food preparation that continues to use nonrenewable global resources.

The other process we use as we encounter what is new to us is *accommodation.* That is, we find that we cannot grasp the new item without restricting or reconstructing our ideas or patterns of thought. We must change in order to grasp the new information, idea, or perspective. This self-change is more difficult than is assimilation and sometimes is painful. Yet in a true dialogue, we must accept the need to accommodate to the other's perspective and when this need arises, we must accept the cost. But we must also appreciate that the other, too, may have to change and that he or she may find that change uncomfortable or difficult. For example, today there is more and more dialogue among Christian scholars and Asian scholars, especially those steeped in Buddhism and Hinduism. These discussions have long since passed the level of talking about superficial similarities and differences among their religious traditions and have arrived at the point where virtually all participants find themselves and their views to have been profoundly changed by the process. This is not to say that participants have "converted" or ceased to believe in their original faith, but rather that the dialogue has deepened their understanding of their own religion and religious experience and expanded their views in new and more universal ways. Still, the process remains deeply disturbing at times to participants because true universalism rooted in dialogue challenges cherished beliefs, even those of people deeply committed to their own traditions.

From what we have said, we may be able to derive a simple explanation or definition of universalism. This definition makes universalism observable or testable. Suppose there are two people, A and B, who have different points of view. If A can understand B *as B seeks to be understood,* and B can understand A *as A seeks to be understood,* then we can say that person A and person B understand one another. Perspectives A and B are equally universal. A can understand both A and B; B can understand both A and B. Given two other perspectives, C and D, if D can understand C *as C seeks to be understood,* but C *cannot* understand D *as D seeks to be understood,* we can say that C and D are *asymmetrical* with respect to mutual understanding. In addition, we can say that D is more universal than C. Universalism, therefore, is a matter of perspective, that is, of which perspective is more comprehensive. Often, when two people or cultures disagree (or cannot comprehend one another), there is a possible third point of view that is different from both. But we must warn you that this possible third point of view requires a reinterpretation of *both perspectives,* and this can be a painful experience for people who are strongly committed (and who isn't?) to their own perspective.

Thus universalism can be seen to involve the more inclusive position, the one that accommodates other

Here the Dalai Lama is shown addressing the Parliament of the World's Religions, which met in 1993. At this meeting it was noted that religion has been the long-missing dimension in the global discussions that have ranged over such topics as the environment, women, peace, and population.

positions. Therefore, when we use the term *universalism* in this book we do not mean to suggest that there is or will be one final worldview embraced by all persons. Rather, we are assuming that the search for universals is the ongoing effort to be inclusive and to accommodate all voices in dialogue, including those who have been suppressed or ignored—the poor, women, tribal peoples, minorities. It is important, in this context, for all of us to be understood as we wish to be understood, to be listened to. It is also important that we listen to and hear others. All these require concerted effort. Even the rules of dialogue itself are evolving and will continue to evolve to accommodate these requirements. New similarities and new differences will emerge and all participants in the dialogue will come to redefine both themselves and the other. As the Dalai Lama points out, we need to be able to see religion as a feast that can satisfy a variety of tastes. Efforts to establish a single world religion are motivated by power seeking. In today's global dialogue, the encounter among the diverse traditions of the world in the arenas of religious beliefs and spiritual practices is becoming more intense and the process of dialogue is becoming better understood. However, we are still in the earlier stages of this activity.

Parliament of the World's Religions: Global Interfaith Dialogue

Robert Muller, former assistant secretary-general of the United Nations, stated that religion has been the missing dimension in the global discussions that have ranged over the topics of the environment, women, peace, population, and the like. He was speaking on behalf of the Parliament of the World's Religions that convened in Chicago, Illinois, in the summer of 1993 (Beversluis, 1995). Those aspects of life that touch men and women most deeply, that which they perceive as the highest, deepest, most meaningful dimension of their beings, had not been fully addressed until the parliament.

In that meeting, the parliament participants recognized the need for collaboration among the world's religious and spiritual leaders on issues of peace, the preservation of the planet, and the relief of suffering. Some members of the assembly (the group of religious and spiritual leaders of the parliament) agreed to take plans and projects aimed at dealing with the issues of human rights, peace, and ecology to their communities and to the leaders of their nations. The assembly also adopted a declaration about universal human rights called "Towards a Global Ethic" that was drafted and refined at the parliament. This declaration achieved a degree of agreement and forcefulness of expression in the area of common values and ethics that has inspired efforts to arrive at similar statements in other areas of global concern, such as the environment and the promotion of peace and nonviolence. The parliament also agreed to meet again to promote interfaith dialogue and to address possible solutions to common planetary problems.

The idea for the 1993 parliament began as a centennial celebration of the World's Parliament of Religions held in Chicago 100 years earlier, but it became much more. It is instructive to look at the earlier event because it shows the changes that have occurred in religion, not just in the United States, but in the world. For one thing, today's discussion among cultures and religions has become far more inclusive. The 1893 meeting, held in conjunction with the celebration of American progress called the Columbia Exposition (World's Fair), was itself an unprecedented event. The 1893 parliament was organized and financed by the commercial and governmental interests that organized the exposition. The steering committee that organized and oversaw the parliament's proceedings was composed of one Roman Catholic bishop, one Reform Jewish rabbi, and fourteen members of the leading American Protestant denominations. Richard Hughes Seager (1996), a historian who has written about the 1893 parliament, observes that for its time the parliament was an extremely liberal event that demonstrated immense openness and tolerance consistent with the great self-confidence of its organizers. Leading Protestant denominations of mostly English and Scottish origins were the custodians of contemporary culture. In the minds of many people, the triumphant emergence of the United States was intimately connected with its religion, science, and technology. Despite these intentions and assumptions, the 1893 parliament introduced Americans to the religious and philosophical traditions of Asia (Buddhism and Vedanta Hinduism in particular) and sparked an interest in these faiths that continued to grow.

The parliament held one century later differed in most respects from its predecessor. It was not supported by any major economic or governmental interests. The major Protestant denominations were notable largely by their absence. Another contrast was that minority group churches and religions abounded at the 1993 meetings. Representatives from the black Nation of Islam, African American Protestant churches, and Caribbean groups such as the Rastafarians were present. A wide range of Asian faiths, varieties of Buddhism and Hinduism, and many of the other Asian groups (like the Sikhs, Jains, and Zoroastrians) were also represented. Their numbers were swelled by numerous spiritual groups outside the conventional religious categories—Neo-Pagans, New Age groups, and Theosophists. Especially important when we consider the historical context was the presence of tribal religions represented by groups such as Native American and indigenous African groups. In the 1890s, representatives of such faiths were ignored because of the attitude that primitive peoples and their ways were superseded by modern technological society. It is a mark of how far we have come that today this attitude is rare. Globalism and the shared perception that we live in a global village have had a huge impact on how the religions of the world view themselves and each other.

The meeting in 1993 also testified to the nature of what has been called postmodern culture. The faith in progress and the belief that the dominant industrialized societies represent a superior form of civilization are rapidly receding into the past. The optimism that prevailed in 1893 about technology and the benefits of modern civilization has also largely died. The immense diversity of the groups represented testified to the nature of postmodernity. All of this also suggested hope to the participants. One of the main fears of organizers had been that a gathering of this many (8,700 participants) and this diverse a group (more than 200 distinct faith communities were represented, some of which had long-standing hostilities to one another), would lead to unmitigated disaster. Yet, as Jim Kenney (1996:1), one of the organizers, noted afterward:

> They gathered and they celebrated. They came together in extraordinary variety: Buddhists and Christians, Hindus and Jews, Muslims and Zoroastrians, Jains and Sikhs, Indigenous peoples, Pagans and New Agers. They came together to celebrate a remarkable idea, that somehow there is harmony in our incredible diversity.

Ecology and Spirituality

As we saw earlier, though not itself a religion, global ecology shares with religion a concern with the sacred or ultimate. Environmentalism involves concern about protecting the natural world for the sake of human survival and for the sake of nature itself. According to anthropologist Kay Milton (1996), one of the signs of the times is the emergence of *environmentalism* as a worldwide cultural phenomenon.

The broad category of environmentalism includes well-established groups like the National Audubon Society and the Sierra Club. Such groups receive a good deal of corporate funding and appeal to a middle-class constituency. They work to preserve the wilderness and wildlife in the United States and in other countries. They primarily seek legislation to gain their ends, and attempt to persuade legislators and the general public to support bills that protect the environment. The term *environmentalism* applies well to these groups because it suggests that there is something called "the environment" separate from human society and human life. It suggests that we need to do something about this environment if it is to continue to meet our needs and to support life.

Radical Ecology. In recent decades, a far more radical view of environmentalism has emerged, one that does not accept a boundary between nature (environment) and human beings. This movement has been called **radical ecology** (see Chapter 6 for more on this movement) because it rejects the basic assumptions on which modern culture is founded and argues that deep-seated institutions and values of modern society must be changed in the interests of all living things, including human beings. It is this view of the environment that is most closely connected to religion. This view embraces an alternative *organic worldview* (cosmos as living thing) rather than the still-dominant *mechanical worldview* (cosmos as machine). According to social historian Carolyn Merchant (1992), radical ecology embraces, among other ideas, the following general assumptions:

- *Everything is related to everything else.* Reality is a seamless web, a single whole, as both physics and the science of ecology suggest. Nothing exists separate from the whole and everything that does exist is a manifestation of the whole.
- *The whole is greater than the sum of its parts.* Components of systems work together to produce greater effects than could come about by adding up their separate contributions. Systems like organisms, ecosystems, and societies can exhibit properties not found in the separate parts. This is not true of machines but it is true of living systems.
- *Human beings and nonhuman nature are one.* According to the modern worldview, we human beings alone possess rational intelligence that gives us the power to observe nature objectively and the right to subject it to our control. This view was realized at the price of environmental health, and it also led to our feeling alienated and out of place in the cosmos. Twentieth-century science, in contrast, has shown that the human observer and the observed world are inseparably linked.

Radical ecology is an amazingly rich and diverse set of ideas, practices, and social groups, many of which have been around for centuries. The assumptions we have described tend to be shared by all schools of radical ecological thought, of which there are three main branches, according to Merchant. These branches are spiritual ecology, deep ecology, and social ecology.

Spiritual Ecology. At first glance, spiritual ecology would seem to have the most direct connection with the issue of religion. **Spiritual ecology** is based on the view that a transformation of consciousness is necessary if the present ecological crisis is to be averted. To avert it would require a total change in the way people experience and feel about the world of nature and their ongoing relationships with the natural world. More is required than merely a new "map" of reality. A change in direct experience or inner appreciation of the world is needed.

Spiritual ecologists recognize that most people in the world still value religious ideas and practices and therefore believe that a deep change in their relationship to the natural world is most likely to come through involvement in their own religion. Spiritual ecologists emphasize those religious concepts, practices, and attitudes that are conducive to nonexploitative relationships to the views of nature found in the world's established religions. For example, Western religious traditions, which tend to assert a personal creator, contain seeds of the idea that the earth has been given to humankind so that they can be its stewards or caretakers. Among Buddhists, in contrast, the practice of *mindfulness,* of always being aware of what you are doing and of its consequences, is applicable to our consumption of goods and other aspects of our relationship to nature. Tribal religions may regard some aspects of nature, such as sunrise or certain animals, as sacred and act with care and reverence toward them. Today, some who are involved in spiritual ecology are attempting to explore their own tribal roots by trying to rediscover the pre-Christian Pagan practices of their European ancestors. They argue, for example, that the view of God as a male found in Judaism, Islam, and Christianity has reinforced the attitude of domination and exploitation associated with the male-dominated patriarchal culture. To counteract this model, they are seeking feminine models of divinity that have been created within all the traditions in the hope that this will help reverse millennia of exploitation and empower women within society (Anderson and Hopkins, 1992; Eisler, 1987).

Deep Ecology. **Deep ecology** (see Chapter 6 for more discussion of this movement) is also a profoundly spiritual movement that sees nature and humanity as inseparable, thus challenging the most basic modern notions about the cosmos and about the human person (or self). Philosophers Arne Naess and George Session, and sociologist Bill Devall, among others, have developed this view (Merchant, 1992). Deep ecologists revere native or tribal cultures for their attitudes toward nature and have occasionally joined forces with tribal cultures to combat those whom they see as harming or destroying the natural world.

Historically, we human beings have regarded ourselves as the sole owners, as it were, of minds and personalities. This attitude has led us to treat nature as different and external to our innermost being—something that we can control but that is not a part of us. Deep ecology requires us to rethink this whole arrangement. Because nature and humanity are inseparable, we can and must relate to nature as like us in some key respects. In some important ways nature has awareness and can communicate with us; for example, when forests are too dry, they burn. From this we might learn ways of acting more carefully when we are in forests, such as not smoking.

Drawing on Asian philosophies and religions, deep ecologists insist that we must redefine the human self. They argue that the notion of the human self as a rational mind locked up inside the skull is an arbitrary and extremely limited idea. The separation between the rational human knower and the object of knowledge is simply a prejudice, not a fact. Deep ecologists insist that we must develop (or rediscover) a sense that we are part of a Greater Self as it exists in Hinduism or some other Asian worldviews. Deep ecology is an *ecocentric,* as opposed to *homocentric,* philosophy. What that means is that deep ecologists attempt to see everything from within the ecosystem; they put the needs of that system first and assess the needs of humanity in terms of the larger system.

A sense of deep ecology may be similar to the experience of unity and peace that many people feel watching the sun set over the ocean, or it may be the thrill of feeling yourself to be a very small part of a very big cosmos whole while looking at the night sky, or it may be the almost religious awe some people feel on seeing the Grand Canyon in the western United States. A sense of deep ecology occurs especially when such experiences crowd out the more petty concerns of life and really shake people to their core. At such times some people may experience a "Presence," which seems in some way also a self but a more inclusive one than a single human being, and they may feel as if they were merging their small, individual self with the larger whole. Others may experience a feeling of mutual recognition between themselves and an animal of another species such as a beloved pet. According to believers in deep ecology, these sorts of experiences are neither rare nor silly but are testimonies to the ever-present and fundamental connections between human beings and nature.

Social Ecology. **Social ecology** (see also Chapter 6) is a movement that draws attention to the issues of human suffering and social injustice at the root of the ecological crisis of our times. Social ecologists look to the work of radical social theorists of Marxism and anarchism. In European society a countercultural tradition has long existed that opposes the established modern culture that emphasizes crass materialism and the capitalist market economy. The conjunction of ecological and spiritual concerns is part of this countercultural movement, as is a critique of injustice and inequality.

The radical social theories of German social scientists and philosophers Karl Marx (1818–1883) and Friedrich Engels (1820–1895) owed much to this general movement. In his *Economic and Philosophic Manuscripts* (1844), Marx argued that nature is humanity's large body. He accused capitalism of polluting and destroying the natural environment in its effort to turn the natural world into an object for its own profit. In *Dialectics of Nature,* which was first published in 1927, Engels elaborated on the philosophical and scientific aspects of a more organic view of nature and humankind. Human beings, he suggested, have the unique advantage over other creatures of being able to learn nature's laws and apply them, but they cannot conquer and control nature. To attempt this, as capitalists attempt to do, will only wreck the fertility of the earth on which all life and all human wealth depend. Nature is an organic whole of which we are an integral part. The dualism of mechanistic thinking must be overcome. In its place, we must seek "to know ourselves to be one with nature," and to realize that there is no "contradiction between mind and matter, man and nature, soul and body" (cited in Merchant, 1992:139).

Unfortunately, the socialist movements influenced by Marx and Engels did not practice these attitudes toward nature. In fact, socialism in reality proved to be one more expression of the modern effort to control nature and to create a society of material abundance without much regard for other values or qualities. Thus socialist societies applied bureaucratic forms of organization that were strictly hierarchical and very rigid. They also encouraged little actual grassroots participation, although their own ideologies insisted on democracy and the participation of the workers in decision making. Moreover, they systematically repressed the spiritual in favor of a bland and oppressive materialism. In brief, their record is no better than that of capitalism at its worst.

Hierarchies, according to anarchist social ecologist Murray Bookchin, are not to be found in ecosystems, which are networklike structures in which all species participate to the mutual advantage of each. Bookchin refers to the "food web" rather than the food chain to point out that even the dominant species at the top are ultimate food for the lowliest bacteria and fungi at the bottom (cited in Merchant, 1992). The socialist societies were based on bureaucratic hierarchies of control that exempted those at the top from the costs of running these complex systems, while making the local ecosystem pay the costs in the form of the pollution and over exploitation necessary to maintain vastly inefficient economies. In their total ecological impact, these systems were as bad or, most would say, worse than that of capitalist societies.

Social ecologists want to rebuild society from its roots. This cannot be done simply by having new scientific ideas (a paradigm shift) or by practicing rituals. A change in social structure is what is necessary. Such change requires that repressed and exploited workers and tribal people, women, and other minorities become organized and motivated to make changes. Social ecologists are skeptical of deep ecologists and spiritual ecologists in part because they do not seem to realize the importance of mobilizing significant portions of society to make changes. Social ecologists also fear that the members of the other movements dangerously disregard human needs and human suffering while they lavish concern on other species.

Particularistic Responses to Globalization

In the previous section we discussed some of the religious groups and movements that advocate moving in universalistic directions. By and large these movements try to affirm the globalization process based on the assumption that universalistic principles provide direction for increasingly larger human collectivities. In this section we look at the other end of the continuum—particularism. Particularistic groups also contribute to the globalization debate, bringing their narrower assumptions about globalization, morality, and the cosmos to the table. Many of these groups reject the entire concept of globalization or selective parts of it and thus serve as a counterbalance to those who advocate the broader picture of universalism.

Like their expansive counterparts, particularists often are lead by charismatic leaders, are able to muster considerable social and physical resources, and may create social movements that promote their worldviews. It is beyond the scope of this book to review all of these particularistic movements. Rather, we look at some of the more significant of these groups that assume a religious, or at least a functional religious, form. We begin by examining in some depth the worldwide phenomenon of fundamentalism.

Fundamentalism: A Worldwide Reaction to Globalization

The term *fundamentalist* originated in the first quarter of the twentieth century in the United States. It came out of the controversies between liberal and conservative Protestants over how to react to modernism. The liberals (also called modernist

Protestants) made concessions to modernism in accepting scientific worldviews that included evolution, modern morality, and/or contemporary interpretations of scripture. To conservative Protestants such concessions seemed wrong, if not heretical. The conservatives believed that modernism denied cherished Christian doctrines such as the creation of the world by God or the virgin birth of Christ, undermined moral principles, and questioned the authority of the Bible. To many traditionalists, modernism was nothing short of an attack on Christianity itself. The most extreme of the conservatives vowed to defend the fundamentals of the Christian faith and accepted the designation "fundamentalists" as a description of themselves.

Fundamentalism Defined. The term *fundamentalism* currently is applied to a host of religious movements as diverse as Twelve Imam Shi'ites; Sinhalese in India; Pentecostals in Latin America; and Jewish settlers on the West Bank of the Jordan River adjoining Israel. These groups certainly do not share the same doctrines or goals. In fact, most might consider the others as their enemies. So, what is it that these diverse movements have in common? Whether Christian, Islamic, or Hindu, **fundamentalism** is a socioreligious reaction to the perceived threat posed by contemporary society. Fundamentalists believe that changes in society threaten their cherished way of life, values, and religious convictions. Changes in the religious realm wrought by globalization are threatening to fundamentalists. For example, the dialogue so important to universalists is seen as part of the threat by fundamentalists. Compromise equals surrender. Fundamentalists also are responding to changes in society that they find distasteful. For instance, many American fundamentalists believe that the more tolerant attitude toward homosexuality in contemporary society is a denial of Biblical morality, a threat to the family, and a sign of moral decay. Not only is their religion threatened, but their way of live is eroding. Whereas certain issues such as homosexuality may serve as "lightning rods" for religious ire, the actual causes or specifics of this erosion are generally broader and more vague, based on the sense (not rationally defined or coherently perceived) that society is slipping into religious and moral decay. Such religious absolutism that focuses on a limited number of issues (abortion, homosexuality, women in the clergy) serves as a way to express fundamentalists' beliefs that their social world is faltering.

One of the interesting features of fundamentalism is that it is not an all-out rejection of contemporary society, either in its modernist or its globalist form. Fundamentalists pick and choose. For instance, they may reject the materialistic assumptions of modern science but still rely on the benefits of science such as medical facilities or technology. But fundamentalism is more than simply a rejection of aspects of modernism. Fundamentalist religions generally serve to provide a model to change society into an environment more conducive to the fundamentalists' desired state.

This model usually involves reconstructing an imagined "past time" when society and morality were grounded on basic, traditional, religious values. The sacred story of the past time serves as a mechanism through which fundamentalists identify themselves and gives purpose to their activities. Religion and morality are the battleground for social restoration. It is the appeal to tradition that gives legitimacy to the fundamentalist program and agenda (Marty and Appleton, 1994).

Though much of fundamentalists' efforts claim to be aimed toward restoring the desired past time, they are not driven by an obsession with the past. Rather, fundamentalists believe that they are engaged in a struggle for the future. The future of the world, or at least their section of it, depends on restoring the religious devotion, social harmony, and moral purity projected onto the past time. Fundamentalists believe that they are God's instruments in a sacred mission to return morality and the true faith to the earth. It is this vision of the future, along with the deeply sacred convictions and unshakable assurance associated with the vision, that gives fundamentalism its powerful appeal.

Other Characteristics of Fundamentalism. This sense of mission feeds into other characteristics of fundamentalism. One such characteristic is that for many fundamentalists, compromise is unthinkable, as it amounts to surrendering to the enemy. The language of warfare dominates fundamentalists' rhetoric. Their opponents frequently are portrayed as the enemies of "God" (or, perhaps, of "truth" or "morality" or "the nation," or all of these). For instance, fundamentalists in and out of the Iranian government often refer to the United States as the "Great Satan" and blame this country for all the evils

For many fundamentalists, compromise is unthinkable as it amounts to surrendering to the enemy. Fundamentalists in and out of the Iranian government often refer to the United States as the "Great Satan" and blame this country for all the evils and moral decay of world society.

and the moral decay of world society. The appearance of the ability to draw clear and hard lines that define issues and group boundaries is especially appealing to persons experiencing the uncertainty of change. Fundamentalist movements tend to be authoritarian, if not dictatorial. Only specially selected, trained, or inspired members of the movement can interpret its morality, tradition, or vision. Ordinary members are not to be trusted. Questioning the leader (or leaders) is tantamount to questioning God. Since those outside the movement are enemies of truth, unjust treatment, force, or violence toward them may be justified.

Most fundamentalist movements are examples of what we defined as militant particularism. Most fundamentalists wish to expand their particularistic vision to their whole society, if not to global society. The expansive orientation of fundamentalism is especially troubling to advocates of human rights, dialogue, and democracy. In their zeal for their "divine vision," most fundamentalists show little respect for human rights. Freedom of speech and of the press should be denied. Pluralism is to be avoided. Women and children frequently are placed in subservient positions to men. Education is to teach only those truths that fundamentalists hold, not tolerance or critical thinking. Fundamentalists view themselves as upholders of absolute truths and seek to oppose all the forces of this world and of spiritual evil in an effort to maintain those truths. To their way of thinking, critical reasoning and tolerance of opposing views only play into the hands of evil and corrupt forces. This is why they often oppose the right to protest policies of fundamentalist-dominated governments.

Though fundamentalists tend to be conservative, their militant expansionist views and belief in their absolute authority separate most branches of fundamentalism from conservative movements. Conservatives generally have strong ideas regarding religion, morality, and society that they hope to build into government policies and laws. However, they tend to respect differences, rely on democratic processes, and exhibit concern for human rights. They also have less of a tendency to demonize their opponents, are open to dialogue, and reach compromises with opponents in the political process.

Fundamentalism and Nation-States. Many modern nation-states, including democracies, find strong fundamentalist movements very threatening. In part, this is because the religiously driven authoritarianism of fundamentalism undermines democratic principles. That is, militant fundamentalism does not accept pluralism, free speech, tolerance, and other similar practices that underlie modern democracy. Some fundamentalists seek to replace secular democracies with societies based on religious law. It was this assumption of a threat to democracy that was used to justify a military junta that seized power in Algeria in 1992. Fundamentalists appeared poised to take over the government by winning a majority in an upcoming election. Ironically, the military seized control over the government and invalidated the upcoming election in the name of saving democracy. Very few human rights groups, international agencies, or democratic governments protested the Algerian military's destruction of democracy. In fact, most tacitly supported the action. Perhaps this is an indication of how deeply human rights proponents and democracies fear fundamentalism.

However, the concerns of nation-states about fundamentalism are based on more than anxiety about democracy. Fundamentalism's assertion of a religious basis for government and law undermines the foundations of modern nation-states. Fundamentalist religions contend that their principles are rooted in the sacred realm, which transcends and supersedes the material world and the laws of humans. Religious insight or revelation gives believers comprehension of this sacred realm and its expectations. Modern nation-states rest on Enlightenment assumptions that support the power of rationality, tend toward secularity (i.e., they do not turn to religious authority for their legitimization), and hold the will of the governed as the ultimate ground for political authority. The naturalistic (or real world) bent of these assumptions is contradicted by the claim of fundamentalists that the transcendental realm, not the natural realm, is the source for government, law, and morality.

But the actual dynamics of the interaction between fundamentalist groups and governments are not quite as clear-cut as the above contrast indicates. In fact, room for considerable accommodation may exist. Fundamentalist religious groups often produce social movements that become active politically. Some of these movements are able to obtain a measure of political success, but they seldom gain complete power in their country. When fundamentalist movements attain some, but not total, political power, they often are forced to enter into coalitions with other groups, which allows them to partially accomplish their goals. Such coalitions mean that they must bargain and must compromise to some degree. In order to have a share in the power, Jewish fundamentalists in Israel's Parliament have entered into coalitions with political and religious conservatives. In the process, Jewish fundamentalists have had to tone down some of their more extreme demands, such as the expulsion of all Palestinians from "Jewish" lands or the imposition of strict observance of Jewish religious law in Israel. However, the coalition of fundamentalists and conservatives in the Israeli government has forced the government to take a hard line on such controversial issues as establishing Jewish settlements in land owned by Palestinians (the fundamentalists favor this) and returning land occupied by Israel to Palestinians (the fundamentalists oppose this policy). These moves have undermined efforts to establish peace between Israel and the Palestinians and Israel and its Arab neighbors throughout the Middle East.

On the other hand, some fundamentalist groups disdain the political process and attempt to impose their religious notions on others by force. For example, when Russian military forces that supported the government of Afghanistan withdrew from that country in the early 1990s, a bloody civil war erupted among the secular socialist government and various factions opposed to the government. One of these factions, known as Taliban, gained control of two-thirds of the country. Taliban is an Islamic fundamentalist faction that has as its goal the creation of a republic that imposes its strict interpretation of Islamic law on all of Afghanistan. When Taliban forces capture areas of the country, they frequently imprison, execute, or otherwise punish various "sinners." In the areas they control, women are forced out of jobs and must restrict their activities to the home. All people are forced to worship according to fundamentalist precepts. Most literature, art, music, and the like is suppressed. Freedom of speech, religion, and assembly and other human rights are eradicated (Tribune News Services, 1997; Faruqi, 1996; Lev, 1996).

We suggested that when fundamentalist groups share power in governments they have to tone down many of their more radical demands and cooperate with other political factions. However, secular governments often react negatively to fundamentalists and resort to violence to suppress their activities. In such circumstances, fundamentalists usually respond to the government's use of force with more violence. Such interactions have led to bloody guerrilla wars in a number of places around the world.

Foreigners in the country where the guerrilla war is occurring may also be targeted. The ongoing warfare and escalating violence between the respective governments and Islamic fundamentalist factions in Algeria, Egypt, and Israel are good examples of such conflicts (Hundley, 1998; Moseley, 1997; Abdo, 1994; Hundley, 1993).

Conflicts involving Religious and Functionally Religious Groups

A number of religious or functionally religious groups worldwide are involved in ethnic, class-based, and/or religious conflicts. *Functionally religious* refers to ethnic and class-based conflicts that are justified as religious struggles. Some of these conflicts can be called fundamentalist, but others cannot. It is beyond the scope of this book to look at each of these in depth. Rather, we mention just a few. The "troubles" in Northern Ireland is one of the longest standing of such conflicts. Though centuries of conflict have characterized relations between the English and Irish and between Irish Protestants and Catholics, the most recent phase began with the 1920 partition of Ireland into Ireland proper in the south and the six counties, called Northern Ireland, in the north. The people in the south are Catholic and staunchly Irish. In contrast, the people in the north are mainly Protestants with strong ties to England. In Northern Ireland, the Protestant majority refused to share power with the Catholic minority and favored maintaining the separation between their nation and Ireland. Most Catholics, however, were angered by their treatment at the hands of the Protestants and were desirous of reuniting with Ireland. Ongoing violence between the two groups ensued.

Each side formed politically oriented parties and underground terrorist groups and gained the support of various NGOs. For instance, the main Catholic political group is Sinn Fein and its militant arm is known as the Irish Republican Army (IRA). The Protestants have had political parties such as the Democratic Unionist Party and various paramilitary units dedicated to violent suppression of opponents. Protestant violence toward persons perceived to be threats has been met with Catholic retaliation. More than 3,000 persons died in Northern Ireland during the last three decades alone (Madigan, 1996). Violence toward Great Britain increased dramatically when its army assumed responsibility to provide internal security for Northern Ireland during the 1960s. Not only did British soldiers serving in Ireland become targets of IRA attacks, but civilians, hotels, airports, and other establishments in England were hit as well. Even though most Catholics and Protestants welcomed an agreement signed in 1998 that promised to bring peace to the region, militants on both sides threatened to subvert the peace process.

A host of other religiously oriented groups worldwide continues to use violence to support their causes. These range from the Aum Shinri Kyo cult in Japan, to Tibetan Buddhist separatists in China, to Sinhalese Buddhist and Tamil Hindu extremists in Sri Lanka, and to Joseph Kony Lord's Resistance Army in Uganda. Other antigovernment movements are not overtly religious but serve as what we described as functional religions. Such movements as the Basque separatist movement in northern Spain and the Maoist Shining Path guerrillas in Peru fit into this category.

Global Rise in Hate Groups

One of the more troubling developments in recent decades is connected to the functionally religious movements we have been discussing. There has been a marked growth of hate groups in many parts of the world. **Hate groups** are organizations that thrive on rhetoric, literature, or actions that foster acrimony and intimidation of other religious, ethnic, or national groups. The objects of hatred may be specific groups, such as Christians or Algerians, or may be directed toward less defined categories, such as so-called foreigners. In some cases, these groups have formed into political movements, but in others they are content to distribute propaganda and secure converts to their cause without exhibiting a specific political agenda. Most are relatively small in their own country, but they assert a disproportionate amount of influence because they build on the uncertainties and prejudices found in the larger population. Their influence is further magnified because they are willing to use violence or the threat of violence against the targets of their hatred as well as their opponents. The increase in hate groups is associated with the economic and social uncertainty fostered by globalization (see "The Human Face of Hate Groups: Nico Mietzelfeld").

You may be wondering why we are discussing hate groups, and especially such groups as Nazis, in a chapter about religion. Without exception all of the

THE HUMAN FACE OF HATE GROUPS

Nico Mietzelfeld

Nico Mietzelfeld of eastern Germany is a strong 24-year-old man with a shaved head who admits he has participated in attacks on foreigners. He lost his job as a metal worker six years ago and has not been able to find another. He survives on welfare. He has joined the National Democratic Party, the strongest extreme right party in eastern Germany.

Nico, along with 30 or so other rightists, attacked two Lebanese-run food stands. Workers at the stands were attacked with baseball bats, metal bars, and gas pistols, and several people were injured. Mietzelfeld explains the attack this way:

> We only wanted to talk to them at first. There was an exchange of words, and there was alcohol involved. Perhaps we started provoking them. It was because of frustration. So many of us are unemployed, and foreigners take away jobs. We were arrested, but they were let off. . . . Hitler was a totally stupid person. . . . As for Jews being gassed, it was probably not right that just one group was chosen for persecution. . . . [It may not be right] . . . to run around and beat people up in the street. The police are watching us very closely. Foreigners can work here, but Germans should get preference.

Source: Ray Moseley. 1998. "Germany's New Storm Troopers." *Chicago Tribune*, April 5:1.11.

great religions and all of their founders taught the unity of humanity (not racism or separatism of any sort) and without exception these great religions teach love and compassion toward others. In today's world, the leaders of the great religions condemn the ideas and the practices of hate groups as wrong. Indeed, such hatred and intolerance are among the issues addressed in interfaith dialogue such as that represented by the Parliament of the World's Religions. Yet, even the followers of the recognized religious traditions have at times practiced intolerance and hatred toward others, even to the point of engaging in violence that they justified in the name of their faith and its founders. As for members of hate groups, they embrace beliefs that, for them, serve some of the functions of religion. These beliefs offer them a sense of meaning and purpose, of belonging and relatedness that they must otherwise lack. In the twentieth century we have seen any number of secular (nonreligious) belief systems serving as functional equivalents of religion. Some of them, such as Nazism, Stalinism, or Maoism, are responsible for the mass slaughter of millions of people, as we show in later chapters.

Many of these functionally religious groups have actually incorporated rituals (Nazi mass rallies), veneration of past leaders (the reverence toward the embalmed corpse of Lenin in the former Soviet Union), even "holy scriptures" (Hitler's volume *Mein Kampf* or Chairman Mao's *Little Red Book*). This is not altogether surprising when we consider the historical contexts out of which movements like National Socialism (Nazis) and communism emerged. A number of reputable and not-so-reputable books have been written about the role of religious, spiritual, and occult pursuits during the emergence of the Nazis in Germany. Some of the more reputable work is described in *New Religions as Global Cultures* (1997) by Irving Hexam (professor of religious studies) and Karla Poewe (professor of anthropology). Likewise, the communist movement emerged in pre-Soviet Russia amidst a confusing welter of spiritual, philosophical, and religious activity that accompanied social changes of the nineteenth century, according to philosopher Nicholai Berdyaev's book, *The Russian Idea* (1992). Both the Nazi and the Soviet communist worldviews purported to govern the total lives of the societies they dominated. They functioned, in short, much as state religions do. Both emerged out of religious and spiritual traditions, although they became essentially nonreligious, or secular, ideologies. It would seem from these two examples that the power of shared beliefs and rituals is evident and that some of the functions served by authentic, traditional religions can be born by functional religions.

Rightist groups in today's Germany have come to serve as functionally religious groups. Like most of the rest of Western Europe, Germany experienced a prosperous economy during the 1980s. However, the economy has cooled in light of global competition, and unemployment has been relatively high during the 1990s. The German situation is complicated by difficulties produced by the reunification of East and West Germany following the end of the Cold War. East Germans were controlled by a totalitarian socialist regime after World War II. Workers were paid and their jobs were guaranteed even when factories lost money because of inefficiency and overstaffing.

In 1990, the two Germanys were reunited. The prosperous capitalistic West Germany has had to absorb most of the cost of this reunification. In the east, the many inefficiencies of the defunct socialist system produced even greater social and economic costs. Antiquated, polluting, and ineffectual businesses could not compete successfully when they were suddenly thrust into the global trading system. Plant closings and layoffs soon followed. Unemployment in eastern Germany still remains at 25 percent, compared to about 12 percent nationally (Moseley, 1998). Economic unrest and social dissatisfaction continue to be widespread.

Because the communist government of the former East Germany attributed all economic and social evils to capitalistic imperialism, people in that region still tend to hold others responsible for their misfortunes rather than see them as the product of a complicated and evolving political and economic situation. The communist leaders did not teach the people about the role rightist fascists played in the horrors of the persecution of minorities during World War II. Nor did students learn about the role of National Socialists (Nazis) in the Holocaust, as did their peers in West Germany. Moreover, as in most First World countries, a stream of immigrants from Third World nations has come to Germany seeking political freedom and economic opportunity. These people have become the new scapegoats for the frustrations of the workers of the former East Germany.

This volatile mix has led to an increase in the illegal and legal political activities of right-wing extremists in Germany. Many outsiders label these extremists Skinheads (because they shave their heads) and neo-Nazis, though they prefer to be called Nationalists. Figure 3–1 shows the escalation of hate crimes in Germany since the collapse of the Berlin Wall in 1989. This has been accompanied by

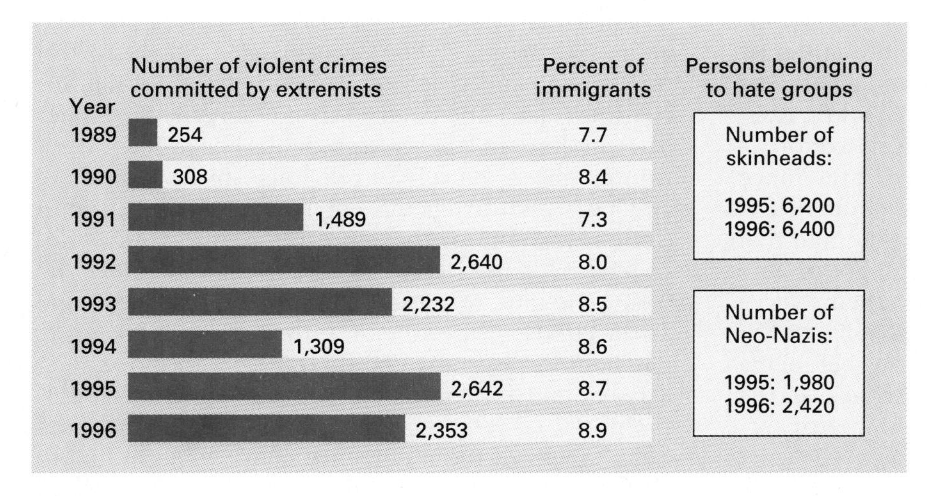

FIGURE 3–1 German Hate Crimes Increase

Source: Ray Moseley. 1998. "Germany's New Storm Troopers," *Chicago Tribune*, April 15: 1.11.

a significant increase in the power of extreme rightist political parties. The actual number of committed extremists is quite small (about 6,400 Skinheads and 2,400 neo-Nazis in 1996). But their influence is magnified because many less radical persons share some of their views. A recent poll in eastern Germany found that 65 percent of respondents believed there were too many foreigners in Germany, 48 percent believed foreigners took jobs away from Germans, and 14 percent agreed that a strong dictatorship could solve the area's problems better than the current democratically elected government (Moseley, 1998). There also is evidence of significant sympathy with rightist and neo-Nazi sentiment among the police and the German army. In Germany, like much of the rest of Europe, immigrant communities feel threatened and may respond with violence toward the larger society (Tribune News Services, 1995).

Religion-Related Issues in the United States

Earlier in this chapter we discussed the interplay between religion and human culture. Like other countries, the United States has been subject to the same forces of modernization and globalization that have affected the rest of the world. There should be little surprise that the same social, economic, political, and religious forces that vie to shape the global scene also operate in the United States. As with other places, these struggles take a unique form shaped by the history and culture of this country. Nothing exemplifies the American approach to religion better than the First Amendment to the U.S. Constitution.

The First Amendment Sets the Stage

Many of the women and men who founded this country migrated here in search of religious freedom. However, once on the shores of this country, they often suffered religious persecution from religious groups that had preceded them. Or, if they became members of the dominant group themselves, they used the power of the state to persecute religious minorities in their midst. For instance, the Pilgrims whom Americans celebrate at Thanksgiving were actually Puritan separatists who came to New England to establish a godly society in the American wilderness. Although they found religious freedom for themselves, they often used the apparatus of the state to persecute Quakers, Baptists, Catholics, and assorted "freethinkers" who migrated into their jurisdiction. These experiences, along with a long history of abuses in Europe where the power of the state and religion were combined, produced a strong desire among many colonists to limit the ability of religious groups to use the state for its purposes and the ability of the state to use religion for its purposes.

When in the late eighteenth century the original 13 colonies won their independence from England, many believed that the proposed Constitution of the United States did not go far enough to guarantee specific rights that difficult historical travails had proven were necessary for true freedom. This situation was rectified by adding 10 amendments to the Constitution in 1791. These 10 amendments specified a number of rights for citizens and came to be known collectively as the Bill of Rights. Among other rights, the First Amendment guaranteed freedom of religion. More specifically, it sought to guarantee that Congress would make no law that "establishes religion or inhibits the free practice thereof." That is, the First Amendment separates church and state.

The exact meaning of this separation has been and continues to be at the root of many controversies in the United States. As with other elements of the Constitution, the meaning of the First Amendment has been interpreted by the courts. The courts generally have declared unconstitutional any practice by which religious exercises or beliefs have been imposed by an agency of government, such as a state legislature or a public school system, on some relatively powerless category of people, such as employees or students. Public funds generally cannot be used to support strictly religious programs. Such a use might be seen as the establishment of a particular religion by the state.

But freedom of religion does not mean freedom from religion. That is, the First Amendment does not imply that the United States is to be a "religionless" society. Nor is religion strictly a private affair in this country. Religion can be an integral part of public life in the United States. Politicians in their official capacities frequently attend public religious affairs such as prayer breakfasts. Congress has official chaplains paid for by public funds, as do all branches of the military and government institutions such as public hospitals. Moreover, religious groups of all beliefs are free to attempt to influence public morality and public policy. Thus, the First Amendment compels our society to strive for that delicate balance between establishing religion and inhibiting the free exercise thereof.

Universalism and Particularism in Religion

In the United States the seeds of the contemporary conflict between universalists and particularists emerged in the nineteenth century as an ongoing religious struggle between modernists (liberals) and traditionalists (fundamentalists). The modernists were very accepting of the modern age. They believed in the findings of science, including English scientist Charles Darwin's (1809–1882) idea that the earth and its great variety of life were both the result of a long evolutionary process. Modernists also applied the tools of modern historical research to study of the Bible. This led them to question some cherished Christian beliefs, such as the belief that Moses wrote the first five books of the Bible, the virgin Birth of Jesus, and the historical accuracy of the New Testament about the life of Jesus and the early church. The revelations of God, many came to believe, were not directly transmitted to biblical authors, but developed as the authors struggled with the activity of God in their lives and within historical situations.

Modernists were more sympathetic to dialogue among various Christian denominations and to the ideas of those from other non-Christian faiths. For instance, liberals were responsible for the World Parliament of Religions that met in Chicago in 1893. Modernists also became heavily involved with the social gospel movements. The social gospel was a modernist interpretation of Christianity's message that said that Jesus did not teach a religion that involved only spiritual salvation; his message had social implications as well. Adherents of the social gospel believed that Christians were to be in the forefront in matters of social justice and were to be involved in solving various social problems such as poverty.

Traditionalists became alarmed at these tendencies in Christian theology and practice. They came to see modernism as a direct attack on the Christian faith. By the early twentieth century, conservatives believed they had to defend the fundamentals of Christianity; hence, they came to be called fundamentalists. Fundamentalists rejected Darwinian evolution and affirmed the literal truth of the account of six days of creation in the biblical book of Genesis and of other stories in the Bible such as that of Adam and Eve (the first human beings) in the Garden of Eden. They viewed the Bible as accurate not only in its doctrinal and moral teachings, but also in its historical and scientific facts. The scriptures were unerring because God verbally inspired them (i.e., God told the biblical authors what to write). Fundamentalists were less inclined to dialogue with nonfundamentalist Christians and persons from non-Christian backgrounds and were more inclined to proclaim the "truth," leaving it for others to accept or reject it. Twentieth-century fundamentalists and conservatives moved away from asserting the social implications of Christian teaching and toward the strong affirmation of personal salvation, individual piety, and private morality.

Battles between modernists and fundamentalists raged in denominational structures, churches, theological schools, and state legislatures across the country for the first quarter of the twentieth century. The early phase of the modernist-fundamentalist controversy came to an end in 1925 in a trial in Dalton, Tennessee. There, the State of Tennessee accused a young biology teacher, John Scopes, of violating a recent law that forbade the teaching of evolution in the classroom. Both modernists and fundamentalists saw the trial as pivotal in their struggle. Both sides brought in "big guns" to represent their positions, and journalists from all over the world covered it. The fundamentalists successfully convicted Scopes of violating the Tennessee law and fined him $150. This conviction was later overturned on a technicality, though both sides had hoped to take the case to the U.S. Supreme Court. (The Supreme Court has yet to rule on the constitutionality of laws that restrict the teaching of evolution.)

Although the fundamentalists won in the courtroom, they lost in the court of public opinion. The modernists were successful during the trial in portraying fundamentalists as uneducated, backward buffoons, with a pathological fear of the modern world. The direct attacks by the fundamentalists in the larger society died down. Most of the northern branches of mainline denominations such as the Presbyterians, Lutherans, and Methodists settled on policies that made room for liberals and traditionalists by agreeing to disagree on controversial topics. Fundamentalism was assumed to be put to rest, if not buried.

Resurgence of Fundamentalism and the Rise of the Christian Right

However, fundamentalism did not simply go away, as many scholars and theologians had predicted it would. In fact, the 1960s saw an increase of militant activity by fundamentalists. Initially, they set their sights on cleansing denominational schools of contamination from liberals and on seizing control of the leadership positions of their respective denominations. This phase of the modernist-fundamentalist controversy occurred in religious denominations whose membership was concentrated mainly in the southern part of the United States and that had been largely untouched by the religious strife of the first half of this century. For example, by the late 1960s, fundamentalists were able to gain control of the Missouri Synod branch of Lutheranism. By the early 1970s they undertook a purge of professors who did not hold fundamentalist views at Lutheran Concordia Seminary in St. Louis and at other denominational schools. Fundamentalist Lutherans have increasingly restructured denominational schools, literature, and agencies in such a way that their theological and moral agenda is supported. Similarly, the Southern Baptist Convention, the nation's largest Protestant denomination, is under fundamentalist control, though Southern Baptists of a more moderate bent are mounting a strong counterattack. While we have emphasized that the rebirth of fundamentalism arose out of southern roots, no denomination has been unaffected by it.

Fundamentalists versus Evangelicals. Before we proceed, a word of caution is needed about the labels we attach to various categories of people. Any label is slippery in that it can have multiple meanings. Fundamentalists now prefer to be called "Evangelical Christians," "conservative Christians," or "traditionalist" (though like fundamentalists everywhere they actually rewrite the religious traditions to which they belong to suit their purposes). Moreover, a substantial portion of the American population calls itself either conservative Christian or Evangelical Christian. Most of these same people may support some of the agenda of radical fundamentalists but strongly oppose some of their more radical positions. For instance, many Evangelical Christians may oppose homosexuals openly displaying their lifestyle and the legal and religious recognition of gay marriages. However, these Christians may also resist more radical positions of fundamentalists, such as denying human rights or employment to known homosexuals.

The Christian Right—A New Force in Politics. The rise of the Christian Right on the political scene parallels the success of fundamentalists in the religious arena. The 1970s saw the emergence of Evangelical Christians in the political realm. Their impact was significant enough that *Time* and *Newsweek* called 1976 the "year of the Evangelicals" (Kepel, 1994:117). At this point, the label "Evangelical" referred more to Christians who sought the moral regeneration of America than to those with a strictly fundamentalist bent. This situation changed by 1980 when a number of fundamentalist groups—the best known of which was Rev. Jerry Falwell's Moral Majority—claimed a strong share of the credit for electing Ronald Reagan as president. These groups interpreted Reagan's election as a triumph for their political agenda and as God's way of restoring Americans to their conservative political, religious, and moral roots.

The now-defunct Moral Majority continued to be a force in American politics in the early part of the 1980s, but its influence has waned as it increasingly became aligned with more extreme political positions that alienated it from the majority of Americans, including many who consider themselves political, social, and religious conservatives. In 1989, the causes of the Christian Right were furthered by the founding of the Christian Coalition. Working together, televangelist Pat Robertson and the head of the coalition, Ralph Reed, put together a highly successful organization. At one point, the Christian Coalition could boast of thousands of local chapters, tens of thousands of precinct and neighborhood coordinators, and a total membership of 1.5 million (Bawer, 1997).

The Christian Coalition was extremely vocal about directly confronting issues, supporting candidates to their liking, and openly opposing politicians who drew their ire. Their tactics and their ability to deliver votes gained them increasing influence on the national scene, especially in the Republican Party. The success of the open confrontation approach was apparent in the 1992 Republican National Convention held in Houston, Texas. There, it became clear that "Bible-believing Christians" had defeated more moderate Republicans at the precinct level with a carefully designed campaign to rescue the party from the "liberals" represented by Reagan-Bush conservatives

(Lind, 1996). It was these "liberals" who had driven the Republican Party to the extreme right, argued Christian Coalition proponents.

At that convention, Pat Robertson shared the presidential box with President Bush. Pat Buchanan, an extremely conservative journalist and politician, delivered the keynote speech filled with calls for cultural and religious wars against the liberal forces that was highly alarming to many Americans—Democrats and Republicans alike. Although after the convention politicians continued to court the fundamentalist vote, sentiment among many conservatives had changed. By the 1996 Republican National Convention, most mainline Republicans were seeking ways to separate their party from the extreme positions held by the Christian Right. This change of fortune led to an alteration of tactics by Evangelical Christians. Rather than concentrating on confrontation at the national level, they focused their formidable organizational machinery on gaining control of local-level political units such as local school boards, city and county councils, and state legislatures. They have had considerable success with this tactic.

As the year 2000 presidential election approaches, another branch of the Christian Right appears set to make an attempt to strongly influence the Republican Party's platform and campaign. This branch is led by James Dobson, founder and head of the Focus on the Family Institute. Dobson maintains a radio, television, and publishing empire and has begun to supplant broadcasters such as Pat Robinson and Jerry Falwell as leader of the conservative Christians. Dobson's political allies include Gary Bauer, the head of the political action committee known as the Family Research Council, and John Ashcroft, the Republican Senator from Missouri. Bauer and Ashcroft will probably be candidates for the Republican Party's nomination for president in the year 2000 (Tackett, 1998).

The Christian Right's Agenda. Like fundamentalists elsewhere, supporters of the Christian Right are convinced that they are engaged in a life-and-death struggle for the soul of America. They tend to demonize their opponents as "liberals," "modernists," "secular humanists," or, more recently, "one-worldists." Supporters of the Christian Right tend to believe that mainline denominations came under the influence of Satanic powers when they strayed from the traditional Christian view of the scriptures as the verbally inspired, inerrant Word of God. This fall from the truth was compounded when mainline denominations became too deeply involved in social justice issues such as the American civil rights movement, opposition to the War in Vietnam, the advancement of the cause of the poor, and the extension of human rights to such relatively powerless groups as women, the disabled, and homosexuals. The increased tolerance advocated for homosexuals, single parents, and working mothers is an indication of the moral decline of America.

The solution for this moral decline is a return to "Bible-believing America" through the recovery of our traditional roots and the governing of society according to the "laws of God." Part of this "returning to America's roots" involves restoring family values. For Evangelical Christians, family values mean keeping homosexuals in the closet (if not denying them political and social rights), restoring the "biblical model" of male-dominated homes, removing women from the workforce and placing them in their homes where they can care for their children, and reversing the 1974 *Roe* v. *Wade* Supreme Court decision that legalized safe abortions.

Church and State in the Classroom

The political arena is not the only arena in which liberals and fundamentalists have squared off. The public school classroom has been a place of conflict as well. A significant part of these conflicts centers on three issues: prayer in the public school, creationism, and control of the curriculum. Before looking at these separately, we need to define the context from which they emerged. The public schools present some problems when dealing with religion, as students are young, impressionable, and forced by law to attend. Thus, if religious services are in any way required at a public school, this amounts to forced participation in a particular religion that violates the First Amendment prohibition against "establishing religion." From the inception of public education, the values underlying it have been largely Protestant. The domination of the public school by Protestants led Roman Catholics to set up their own school system.

For the most part, the courts ignored the implications of conducting prayer in public schools. This policy changed in 1962 when the Supreme Court decided that mandatory school prayer violated the

First Amendment. By implication, other practices such as reading or posting scriptures on public school property or teachers teaching their own religion in class were also taboo. Liberals generally supported the decision, noting that it prevented the imposition of one form of religion on persons who might not share that set of beliefs. They, among others, noted that the decision did not prevent private prayer or scripture reading, nor did it prevent the formation of religious clubs as extracurricular activities.

Evangelical Christians saw the situation differently. They saw the efforts to remove mandatory religious practice from the public schools as an assault on the Christian faith and American's religious heritage. It also was a sign of the moral decay brought on by creeping liberalism. Removing prayer and other forms of religious observance from the classroom was also, in itself, a cause of that decline. The solution for problems ranging from declining test scores to drugs and violence in public schools was to bring prayer and the teaching of America's traditional religion back into the classroom. Conservative Christians have subsequently sought to restore prayer to the public schools through a number of means, including pushing national laws and a constitutional amendment to allow prayer. These efforts have not been very successful. Efforts at the local level have been more successful. Usually these efforts have taken the form of having moments of silence or meditation at the beginning of the school day or permitting students to voluntarily read scripture or lead prayer at the beginning of the school day. These efforts continue to be viewed with great suspicion by the courts.

Conservative Christians have sought to restore prayer to the public schools in a number of ways; efforts at the local level have been most successful. These efforts include having moments of silence or meditation, or permitting students to voluntarily read scripture or lead prayer at the beginning of the school day.

Another set of issues centers on the old question of teaching evolution in the classroom. While the fundamentalists were unsuccessful at preventing the teaching of evolution, their attack on evolution took a new form in the 1970s with the emergence of creation science. Believers in **creation science** (or creationism) contend that the biblical accounts of creation are as scientifically valid as explanations based on evolution. Supporters of creationism also contend that evolution is just a theory and that many scientists today find the theory controversial. They argue that in the interest of fairness and an open curriculum, creation science should be taught in science classes alongside evolution. Creationists have been successful in getting several southern states to require the teaching of creation science in public schools. Their opponents, including most scientists like paleontologist Stephen Jay Gould (1983), contend that the controversies within the scientific community concerning evolution usually center on questions regarding exactly *how* evolution occurred, not *whether* evolution occurred. More important, these critics claim that creation science is not science at all but is a thinly veiled attempt to introduce religion into the classroom packaged as science (Johnson, 1991).

Another set of problems associated with the public schools centers on the content of the curriculum and who controls that content. We address the issue of the control of the curriculum at greater length in

Chapter 10. Here we look only at questions raised by conservative Christians. Like other Americans, Evangelicals are concerned with what is taught in public schools. The more extreme among them believe that the curriculum has been taken over by secular humanists, liberals, feminists, homosexuals, and other disfavored groups, thereby contributing to the moral decline of this country. The tolerance of people who are different, which is taught in many public schools, is equivalent to advocating immoral behavior.

These concerns are especially strong when it comes to dealing with programs associated with sexuality. From the point of view of the religious right, sex education programs that recognize that many teens are sexually active and attempt to help sexually active teens be more responsible through such measures as using condoms encourage teens to be sexually active and to violate the only acceptable standard for teen sex—abstinence. Again, programs aimed at teaching toleration for people with alternative lifestyles such as homosexuals often draw attacks. A good example is the recent assault on New York City's proposed Rainbow Curriculum. This curriculum was intended for use in grade schools. It taught about alternative lifestyles such as those of ethnic or religious minorities and included homosexuals in the list of alternatives. The curriculum drew so much fire from opponents that school officials had to withdraw it. Conservative Christian parents, like parents of other persuasions, believe that their children should be taught a curriculum that reflects the beliefs and values taught at home. In this case, it was the conservative Christian parents and their supporters who won.

The Militia Movement

As we discussed earlier, there are a number of movements that are not specifically religions but are the functional equivalents of religions. The 1995 bombing of the federal building in Oklahoma City alerted many Americans to the growing web of interrelated organizations that form the militia movement in the United States. The militia movement is composed of extremist groups that practice their right to bear arms. These groups are generally driven by fear and anger that stem from conspiracy theories that claim that local, state, and federal governments and international agencies such as the United Nations are acting to deprive American citizens of their constitutional rights. Members of these groups are becoming progressively more fearful and, in many cases, more violent. These groups go by many names, such as Posse Comitatus, Freedmen, Sovereign Citizens, Christian Identity, state militias (i.e., Illinois Militia, Michigan Militia, and so on), independence movements (i.e., Kansas or Texas independence movements), Vipers, and Patriots, to name a few. Members often flow back and forth between these groups (Jackson, 1995). These groups represent an extreme version of a phenomenon common to American politics, referred to by political scientist Richard Hofstadter as the "paranoid style" (Hofstadter, 1965). What makes it paranoid, according to Hofstadter, is the more or less elaborate conspiracy theory that always is used to explain everything undesirable in the present and the past as the work of a group that is acting secretly behind the scenes of history. The group behind the scenes is, of course, very powerful and intent on keeping its secrets. Members of these extreme groups believe that they know about the secret and that it is very dangerous (and special) to possess this knowledge. They form their own secret organizations, arm themselves for confrontation with the conspirators, and sometimes engage in terroristic attacks, hoping to expose or topple the conspiracy. We can call them paranoid extremist groups for these reasons. They differ from simple hate groups because they subscribe to a paranoid conspiracy theory.

Members of these groups participate in a subculture that in many ways turns the beliefs and assumptions of most Americans upside down. For example, most Americans saw the bombing of the Oklahoma City federal building as a terrorist act that killed many innocent people. The trial and conviction of Timothy McVeigh (a sometime member of militant extremist groups) confirm this belief. Members of the militia movement, in contrast, trace the bombing to the actions of the federal government, which worked through the Federal Bureau of Investigation (FBI), Bureau of Alco-hol, Tobacco and Firearms (BATF), or some secret government agency. The militia movement holds these agencies are responsible for the bombing, the purpose of which was to discredit right-wing extremists.

These militant extremist groups may have somewhat different emphases, but they share a mistrust of the government, a fear of crime, and a sense of outrage over the loss of control of their lives—feelings that are expressed by many other ordinary

American citizens. Extremists, however, believe that the federal government is subverting the Constitution by illegally taxing; passing laws; issuing currency; and seizing property of (through foreclosure on unpaid bank loans), trying, convicting, and imprisoning ordinary citizens and patriots. The actions of the federal government (with those of state and local agencies) are directed by bankers who may belong to an international conspiracy of Jewish (or other) elites who successfully direct national (and/or world) policy in ways that deprive ordinary people of their rights, liberty, and property.

Under such conditions, the government is nothing but an occupying power that patriots have a right to resist, by violence if necessary. Beyond this, mainstream American society has been duped by the government into accepting an authority that is clearly denied by the Constitution. Because of the complicity of most Americans, ordinary citizens, like government officials, may be and have been targeted for harassment, intimidation, and violence.

These theories are fueled by a number of radio stations, publishing houses, magazines, preachers, political commentators, and Internet sites. We may have a hint of the content of these propaganda organs by looking at the web site of the David Koresh Foundation. Koresh was the leader of the Branch Davidians, whose compound near Waco, Texas, federal agents, under the order of Attorney General Janet Reno, attacked in April 1993 in an attempt to arrest Koresh on a variety of federal charges. Koresh, who perished with 79 of his followers, has since become a hero to various militia groups in the United States. According to the web site,

> ". . . a Jew who has connections with the ADL [Anti-Defamation League of B'nai B'rith]. . . . the ADL working with the BATF . . . stormed into Waco in May of 1993. The BATF flew a helicopter over the Davidians' Compound around 6 o'clock and sprayed high-caliber bullets into the Davidians' Compound, killing men, women, and children who were asleep." (Quoted in Coates and Dorning, 1995:1.14)

The fact that Janet Reno is not Jewish and that most of the other "facts" in this description are erroneous, or at best only partly true, seems not to register with the Americans who see in the militia movement a way to seize control of the runaway government and morals of the United States.

Hate Groups

While dissatisfaction with government intervention in their lives and a desire to preserve and protect fundamentalist religious values motivates many of the militia groups, hate groups focus their venom on religious, racial, or ethnic groups such as Jews, Catholics, African Americans, whites, Mexicans, or simply non-Americans (i.e., recent immigrants), much as we saw in the example of German skinheads earlier in this chapter. In addition to propaganda, these groups may encourage hate crimes. **Hate crimes** are illegal acts directed against persons or property such as physical attacks, defacing or destroying property, or acts of intimidation motivated by hatred of specific categories of people. The Southern Poverty Law Center (SPLC), a well-known group that tracks and opposes hate groups, divides hate groups into six categories—Klan, Neo-Nazi,

The Ku Klux Klan is a hate group whose activities have included physical attacks, defacing or destroying property, and acts of intimidation.

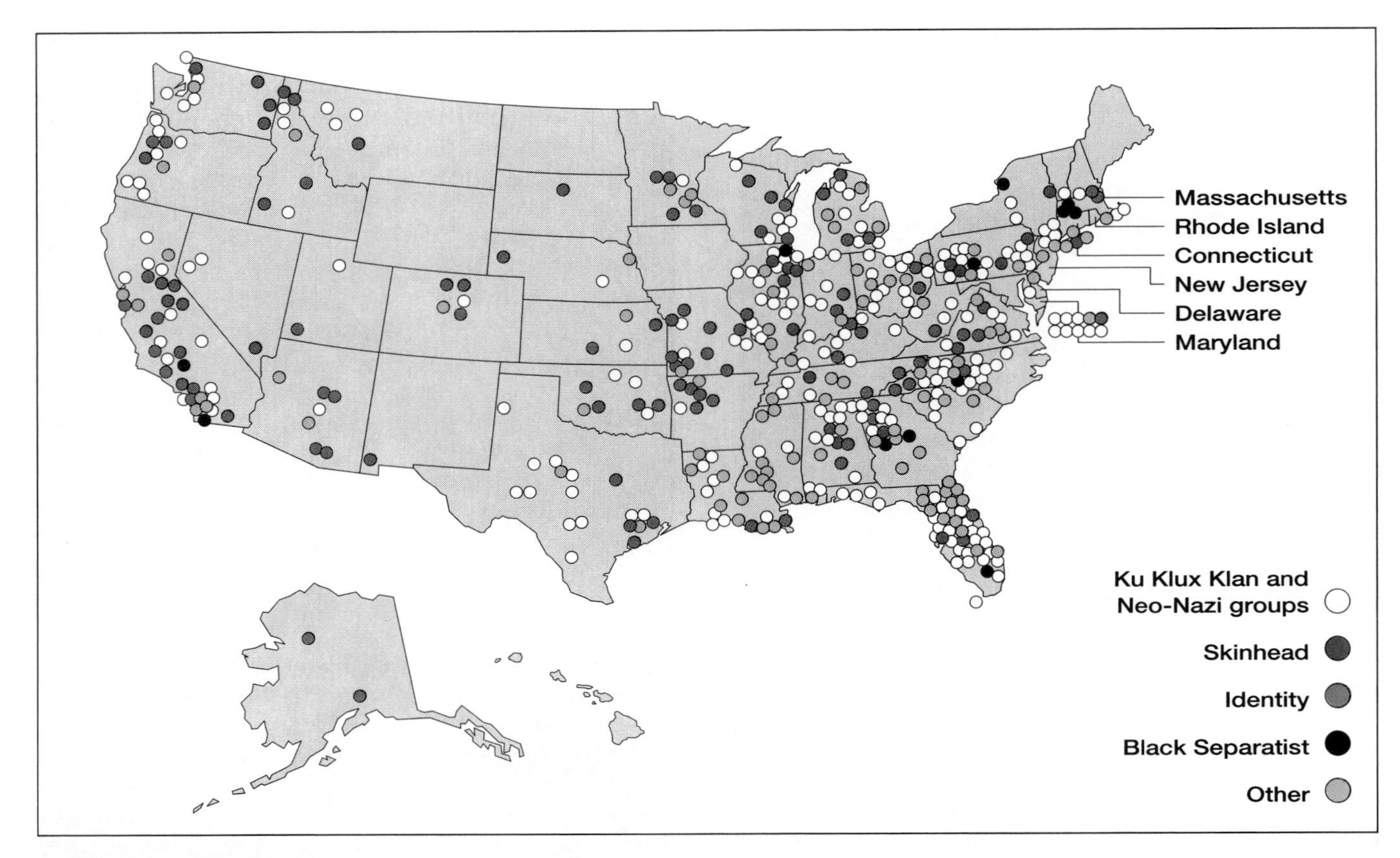

MAP 3–1 Hate Groups in the United States
Source: Reprinted by permission of Southern Poverty Law Center, Montgomery, AL.

Skinhead, Christian Identity, Black Separatist, and Other. Map 3–1 shows the distribution of these groups in the United States.

The SPLC believes the Oklahoma City bombing was the opening shot in a renewal of domestic terrorist attacks, which includes plans to bomb buildings and bridges, assassinate public and civil rights officials, invade military bases, commit robberies, collect illegal weapons, and engage in widespread illegal tax and other financial frauds. Driven by paranoia and religious zeal, extremist and race-based terrorist activities are on the rise. Shortly before the Oklahoma City bombing, the FBI was investigating 100 terrorist cases; now it is investigating more than 900 such cases. The total of identified hate groups was 474 in 1997, up 20 percent from the previous year (Southern Poverty Law Center, 1998a).

ASSESSING THE SITUATION

Our main purpose in this chapter has been to suggest the many roles that religion plays in the globalization process. There is reason to believe that the contribution of religion will be increasingly significant despite the fact that at the beginning of the twentieth century most social scientists had concluded that religion would wither away and be replaced by secular social and cultural forces (Berger, 1992). This thesis is referred to as the secularization hypothesis. Yet on the eve of the twenty-first century, the balance between religious and secular factors appears to have tipped once more so that religion is coming to the fore, while certain secular forces (such as the nation-state) are receding in importance. This is the conclusion of a growing number of social scientists, including prominent scholars convened by the Social Science Research Council to address issues of religion and global security (Rudolph and Piscatori, 1997). This view is gaining ever wider support by scholars of religion who see the growing tendency to fuse ethnic identities with religious support as a challenge to the sovereignty of national governments (Marty and Appleby, 1997).

Long before the formation of today's territorial nation-states such as Great Britain, the United States, and Japan, religion constituted a powerful international or intersocietal social force. Certain religions, especially Buddhism, Christianity, and Islam, spread over large territories, transmitting to the populations there a sense of meaning and identity that transcended local bonds of tribe, ethnicity, and political loyalty. These religions awakened in many of the persons who embraced them a feeling that they were participating in an ultimate reality, a sense of involvement in a greater context that lay beyond other more limited contexts and loyalties. Each of these religions in its own way recognized the equality of the human being in the presence of this ultimate truth and regarded all human beings as deserving of equal respect and compassion. In our century, these ideas became the basis for conceptions of universal human rights. But involvement in these religions also divided humanity along religious lines at various times, and religious loyalties fused with tribal, ethnic, regional, and racial identities have often reinforced a sense of social separation.

Modernism almost always challenges religious identities, along with other traditional statuses. This is because modernism focuses on the individual human beings as the center of interests and rights and on individual reason as the source of values and beliefs, rather than on tradition or the quest for ultimate truth. To a considerable extent, modernism empowers the individual person in secular (nonreligious) social contexts, in particular the market economy and politics, in which each pursues his or her own self-interest. This modernist approach, sometimes referred to as secular humanism, has aroused various religious responses.

One class of religiously based reactions to modernism has been clearly antimodern, rejecting the pluralism and tolerance of diversity, the belief in individual rights, and the reliance on the reasoning powers of the individual that characterize so much of modernism. This class of responses has tended to embrace tradition, although tradition has often been redefined to fit the needs of the antimodern reaction. This rejection of secular society and its culture includes rejection of other traditions and hence of other ethnic, racial, and religious groups in many cases. We have described many of these reactions as particularistic, as they favor limited identities and loyalties over more inclusive ones. In view of the need for some degree of order and cooperation in contemporary pluralistic societies, it is not an inherently bad thing to value a local or limited group identity and its traditions, provided that in doing so we extend to other groups the right to do the same. Early social scientists, from Karl Marx to Max Weber to Emile Durkheim, assumed that traditional and local subcultures would all eventually become subsumed by or be converted to the dominant modernist (and secular-rational) culture of the nation. The antimodern particularistic responses are largely opposed to equality of rights, societal pluralism, and genuine dialogue with other groups, however, and these reactions are flourishing at present in many social arenas both within nations and in the developing global context.

The persons to whom these reactions appeal tend to feel threatened by the loss of a sense of certainty about the meaning of life that so often accompanies the moral ambiguity and uncertainty of modernism and contemporary society. This is acutely felt when traditional beliefs that guaranteed immortality are lost with the acceptance of modern skepticism. In general, such people experience an extremely strong need for assurance, simple clear-cut answers, identity, and a sense of social order symbolized by powerful authority figures (Marty and Appleby, 1997). Membership in these groups may involve powerful conversion experiences or initiations in which the individual's sense of self becomes fused with membership in the group and the beliefs and myths of the group (Bourguignon, 1973). This fusion not only provides a sense of belonging and meaning, but also is frequently accompanied by the belief in some form of continuing life beyond death. Its flip side, however, is a tendency to project evil onto others (outsiders) and to be suspicious of anything or anyone different or unfamiliar (and thus threatening to these group beliefs) (Wilber, 1981; Wilson, 1973). Finding themselves in a pluralistic cultural context of competing ideas and knowledge that challenge their beliefs can generate a sense of deep moral and social uncertainty that in turn creates or intensifies psychological insecurity (Berger, 1992). This can account for some of the fanaticism or extremism found among a few members of these groups. Leaders of these groups may exploit this mentality for their own economic or political ends. Several recent studies show how leaders exploit the religious sentiments of their followers for their own personal purposes to the detriment of the spiritual aspirations and material well-being of the followers (e.g., Hexam and Poewe, 1997).

The mentality we just described is widespread and, to an extent, represents a normal part of social and psychological development, since all human beings have similar developmental needs and pass through similar developmental stages (Kegan, 1994; Fowler, 1981; Kohlberg, 1981). We all have the need to belong to groups, to find meaning in our personal lives, and to come to grips with the human condition that includes issues of good and evil, life and death (Fowler, 1981; Maslow, 1971; Frankl, 1963). Many readers may have heard of Abraham Maslow's hierarchy of needs, described in introductory psychology textbooks. Maslow's hierarchy shows that a person develops new sets of needs over the course of his or her development if and when earlier needs are adequately met. These needs begin with basic biological necessities and progress through various social-psychological needs such as security, a sense of belonging, the need for esteem, and so forth. The typical textbook states that these needs culminate in the need for self-actualization, the need for the individual person to develop and express his or her unique talents and interests in a way that benefits society. But what the textbooks generally do not state is that Maslow went on to document the importance of another whole class of needs, those involving the need for self-*transcendence* that he called Being-needs. The early developmental needs are deficit-needs that stem from what the individual lacks (food, love, social acceptance). Being-needs have nothing to do with lack or deficiency but call for the healthy person to seek that which is beyond his or her own self-centered wants—to seek beauty, knowledge, meaning, or social justice for its own sake. Being-needs are frequently met, or at least are stimulated, by powerful experiences (often, but not always, interpreted as religious) that Maslow calls *peak experiences* (Maslow, 1971, 1970, 1968). Religion has been used to meet virtually all human needs. Some would wish to limit "authentic religion" to meeting that class of needs that Maslow defines as Being-needs. But, empirically speaking, much religious involvement occurs because religion is a way to meet needs for identity, belonging, emotional and physical healing, and even to acquire such practical things as jobs and marital partners. These are legitimate human needs and wants, although they may not be purely spiritual.

The multiethnic and multireligious contexts in which we increasingly live present us with a unique set of challenges. In contemporary times, national educational systems, representative democracies, high rates of geographical mobility, mass media, the spread of modernist culture, the availability of military weapons to many subnational groups, declining resources, and other factors exacerbate tensions by bringing diverse groups into contact. Modernism, at least, has served and still serves a universalizing function when it treats all traditional and religious identities and beliefs as relative and private matters, as differences to be discreetly put aside in the public arena (politics, education, work, the mass media).

Yet these matters are not that easily put aside, and the mutual acceptance and tolerance required by such a point of view leave a perceived cultural and moral (or meaning) gap in the lives of many people, who may ask: "Besides tolerating other people's differences, what should I or what can I believe and how should I act?" In fact, throughout much of the world, including the newly independent nations of the former Soviet Union, underdeveloped or Third World countries (Marty and Appleby, 1997), reunified Germany (Hexam and Poewe, 1997), and other nations (Rudolph and Piscatori, 1997), religious identification is becoming (or continues to be) a powerful force for helping people and groups find a place for themselves in the contemporary world. This adds to the pluralistic mix and therefore increases the need for common ground and mutual tolerance while it intensifies some people's commitment to their particularistic identifications.

Religion has often served the function of helping groups and individuals make the transition from rural life to life in the complex and confusing urban centers, a transition caused by modernization (Bourguignon, 1973). In such circumstances, religion can and does provide moral guidelines, group support, new meanings and forms of decision making, ways of relieving stress, physical and emotional healing, and the sharing of services by members such as childcare and job placement. Religion offers powerful experiences of sacred community and also new forms of rationality more appropriate to the modernized urban setting. What may appear to the outsider as irrational, bizarre, or socially disruptive behaviors, such as trances and communications with the dead and other spirits, have been shown to be ways of helping people adjust to difficult new situations (Bourguignon, 1973; see also Marty and Appleby, 1997, for some of the important stabilizing functions of religion). Today's situation is, if anything, more stressful and disorienting than ever before. The framework or social scaffold provided by national governments, sometimes supported by foreign colonial powers or held in place by pressures of the Cold War and the role increasingly played by the global market and modern communications and transportation provide a context in which new identities are being forged that divide the members of nations as new connections are formed across national boundaries. Most people simply seek a place within this uncertain new and ever changing social environment, whatever we may think about the ways they seek this. Knowing who and what you are, where you belong, who are your friends and who are your enemies, whom you can count on and whom you cannot, what you can rightfully expect out of life and what you can be expected to give are the central issues involved in forming a social identity. Those groups that provide the clearest guidelines and the strongest contrasts between *us* and *them, insiders* and *outsiders,* those that make strong demands (including a willingness to die or kill to defend "the faith") are the ones that meet the need for a sense of identity most effectively (Marty and Appleby, 1997).

In the contemporary situation, these groups, although they define themselves over and against outsiders and assume rather exclusive (particularistic) attitudes and identities, also find that they must often justify their right to be exclusive (even as regards their right to claim a collective identity and to engage in "traditional" practices) in terms of *universal*—and globally shared—rights, especially the third generation of human rights, which has to do with rights of collectivities or groups. Some groups may deny outright that they do this or may claim collective rights in order to promote the violation of other internationally recognized human rights. In the long run, it will prove difficult for groups to claim one set of rights for themselves without being bound by (held accountable to) other rights.

Another religious or spiritual response to this contemporary situation is quite different from both modern and antimodern responses. This response can be called *transmodern,* in that it incorporates, but goes beyond, modernism. It can also be called *integral* because it attempts to integrate that which is valid in traditional teachings and practices and that which is valid in modern teaching and practice. These include the scientific method and an acknowledgment of universal human worth and dignity rooted in the great religious traditions that held human beings to be equal before God or the Ultimate Reality, however it was conceived (Ray, 1996). There is evidence that value changes are emerging in the more developed countries. A number of sociological studies suggest that the values of the most modernized populations of the world are shifting to less materialistic values and to concern with issues of human rights, spirituality, and ecology (e.g., Barbour, 1991). The emergence of what have been called *new social movements* that focus on quality of life issues (including social justice, human rights for others, and the environment) that have an increasingly global outlook is further evidence that cultural changes of a universalistic nature are occurring.

What is of most interest to us in this book is the extent to which a new cultural and social arena is being created by religious and other nongovernmental organizations (NGOs) such as human rights groups, environmentalists, and others. Thus a global civil society is coming into being (Rudolph and Piscatori, 1997; Wapner, 1996). Throughout the nineteenth and the twentieth centuries, national territorially based governments were perceived to be the most important and most enduring actors in the world arena. As global conferences on women, the environment, population, and religion itself become more frequent, NGOs of many varieties have emerged alongside national governments and their agencies as significant global actors. Traditional territorial boundaries define the arena of effective social action less and less. NGOs may act on their own, educate, and inform the "global public," or they may seek to constrain or direct the policies and actions undertaken by governments. These are developments the world has never seen before.

There are many ways in which this growing global context is manifested. For example, in the contemporary world, Hindus, Muslims, Buddhists, Christians, and tribal peoples, among others, are increasingly dispersed across the face of the earth. In the past, such extensive migration to some extent isolated groups of people and attenuated their social ties to their communities of origin. Today satellite communications and rapid jet transportation make it possible for traditional community and family ties to remain comparatively strong in the event of such migrations. This increases the cultural and religious diversity of all the world's societies. Increasingly, the sense of what is inside and what is outside a nation's boundaries is becoming blurred. The gradual erosion of the meaning of nation-state boundaries raises new security issues. As civil society becomes global, the prospect of civil war among religious, ethnic, and cultural groups increases. Indeed, today many nations and former nations are torn by civil strife and this has a tendency to spread. An example is the Ayatollah Khomeini's (the Islamic fundamentalist leader of Iran) worldwide call in 1989 to loyal fundamentalist Muslims to kill novelist Salman Rushdie (a modernist Muslim living in England) for alleged blasphemies against Islam in his writings.

Another very pertinent example of this globalization of civil society is an underlying change in the meaning of security that has been coming about with the decline of nations and the end of the Cold War (Rudolph and Piscatori, 1997). Increasingly, security has to do with environmental degradation, resource depletion, migration, population depletion and surplus, and the spread of infectious disease. As we will see in later chapters, these emerging threats to the survival (hence to the security) of groups and to the survival of the human species are complexly interconnected in ways that make it impossible to finally resolve them on the local level without global cooperation. This aspect of the global civil order would seem to require greater cooperation and continued dialogue among culturally and religiously diverse groups. It is to this greater inclusiveness and mutual understanding that we have applied the name universalism. Whether or not this cooperation will occur or, conversely, more groups will withdraw in efforts to protect particularistic identities and interests is beyond anyone's ability to predict at present.

Summary

1. The **nation-state** is based on the idea that people who occupy a given territory share a common culture and common identity and should be governed by a unified political system. Existing nation-states developed from efforts of elite groups to unite diverse populations under a central authority.
2. **Religion** can be defined as a system of beliefs and practices by means of which a group of people struggles with the ultimate problems of human life. Although not viewed as religions, many social movements, such as the environmental movement, clearly have religious or spiritual themes. Religion plays a vital role in world construction by rooting the human world in the *cosmological order* (the structures that gave rise to the universe itself).
3. **Social movements** are relatively large-scale, loosely organized forms of social action that develop outside established social institutions in an effort to deal with issues widely perceived to be problems. Most of the world's major religions—Buddhism, Christianity, Judaism, Islam, and Taoism, for example—began as social movements under the influence of charismatic leaders.
4. There are two approaches to religion: The **phenomenological approach** does not deny sociological, psychological, or physical elements in religion, but it insists that we take religion and religious experience at face value. We must recognize religious experiences as means of expressing and embodying the sacred. The **functional approach** (or pragmatic approach) involves looking at the effects that religion and the sacred have on persons, groups, and societies. The sacred can deeply affect the patterns of group life and can even transform whole societies.
5. As people moved into modern urban industrial societies, **pluralism**—the bringing together of people of different views, religions, nationalities, and/or races—became the rule. *Personalism* (the sense of being known personally by others) and community declined.
6. The **privatization of religion** is the tendency to make religion a private and individual experience. It may incorporate an assertion that religion has no place in public life.
7. **Universalism** refers to the common principles or constructs that apply to all people everywhere. Applied to religion, this means finding common

religious or moral principles that can form the basis for group interaction and can be used to address the problems that threaten humankind.

8. **Particularism** stresses the uniqueness of a given group's ways, practices, and ideas. When applied to religion, particularism involves stressing the uniqueness, and sometimes the superiority, of one's own religious tradition in comparison to other people's religions. The three types of particularism are **insular particularism**—the insulation of a group from outside interference; **militant particularism**—the belief that a group's uniqueness is superior and should become universal; and **embedded particularism**—the insistence on the distinctiveness of one's group while seeing that group as integral to the larger globalization process.
9. *Assimilation* of a new idea involves fitting it into the existing pattern of ideas and way of thinking. *Accommodation*, conversely, involves restricting or reconstructing patterns of thought in order to grasp the new information, idea, or perspective.
10. **Radical ecology** is a view of environmentalism that does not accept a boundary between nature (environment) and human beings. The branches of radical ecological thought are spiritual ecology, deep ecology, and social ecology. **Spiritual ecology** is based on the idea that a transformation of consciousness is necessary if the present ecological crisis is to be averted. **Deep ecology** sees nature and humanity as inseparable. **Social ecology** seeks to draw attention to the issues of human suffering and social injustice at the root of the ecological crisis of our times.
11. *Modernism* generally challenges religious identities because it focuses on individual human beings as the center of interests and rights and as the source of values and beliefs, rather than tradition or the quest for ultimate truth. Modernism empowers the individual person in secular (nonreligious) contexts. In the twentieth century, we saw secular belief systems such as Nazism, Stalinism, or Maoism serve as functional equivalents of religion.

Thinking Critically

1. Explain why those who promote dialogue among the world's religions might believe that it can contribute to the formation of a new global understanding of values and ethics. In a related vein, why have many in the ecological movement embraced spiritual questions and concerns?
2. Religion both divides and unites. Explain ways in which it does both. How can people of different religions come to be united without one religion trying to convert the others or without the sacrifice of the religious commitments of any one group?
3. What are some of the functions provided by functionally religious groups that correspond to the functions that religions provide? Are there functions or needs that functionally religious groups are unable to meet but that conventional religion can? How then would you distinguish the latter from the former?

Suggested Readings

Allport, Gordon W. 1954. *The Nature of Prejudice*. Reading, MA: Addison-Wesley.

Beyer, Peter. 1994. *Religion and Globalization*. Thousand Oaks, CA: Sage.

Kepel, Gilles. 1994. *The Revenge of God: The Resurgence of Islam, Christianity, and Judaism in the Modern World*. Translated by Alan Braley. University Park: University of Pennsylvania Press.

Lind, Michael. 1996. *Up from Conservatism: Why the Right Is Wrong for America*. New York: Free Press.

Marty, Martin E. and R. Scott Appleby, ed. 1991. *Fundamentalism Observed*. Chicago: University of Chicago Press.

———, ed. 1994. *Accounting for Fundamentalism*. Chicago: University of Chicago Press.

Merchant, Carolyn. 1992. *Radical Ecology: The Search for a Livable World*. New York: Routledge.

Rudolph, Susanne H. and James Piscatori, ed. 1997. *Transnational Religion and Fading States*. Boulder: Westview Press.

Teasdale, Wayne and George F. Carsons, ed. 1996. *The Community of Religions*. New York: Continuum Publications.

Web Sites

Interfaith Conference of Metropolitan Washington

http://www.interfaith-metrodc.org

This site describes interfaith dialogue among Christians, Muslims, Sikhs, Latter-Day Saints, and Hindus. The group's membership seems to be growing. It sponsors discussions, interfaith concerts, and other events in the interest of improving communication among faith groups. In addition to promoting understanding and a sense of community among members of diverse faiths and cultures, the group addresses issues of social and economic justice. It is located in Washington, DC. Persons of all faiths are invited to participate in the dialogue.

Common Spirit

http://www.commonspirit.org

This site also involves interfaith dialogue but focuses on activities and projects that involve sharing, exploring, and developing rituals, forms of meditation, and other religious practices. Theologian and priest Matthew Fox, famous for his Creation Spirituality, participates in this site.

Southern Poverty Law Center

http://www.splcenter.org

This site is mounted by the Southern Poverty Law Center (SPLC), which attempts to overcome hate and prejudice through education and litigation. Among other things, this site provides links to pages that offer updated information on the Ku Klux Klan, militia groups, and other hate groups in the United States.

International Association for Religious Freedom

http://www.interfaith-center.org/oxford/iarf

The organizations and information on this site affirm the right to religious freedom. The organizations embrace people from the many religious traditions of the world, including religious groups from Asia, Africa, the Middle East, Europe, and North America. This site contains information about the founding organizations (IARF and World Congress of Faiths), as well as links to religious resource sites, major indexes, and other sites of interest.

The American Center for Law and Justice (ACLJ)

http://www.aclj.org

The American Center for Law and Justice is a not-for-profit public interest law firm and educational organization dedicated to defending and advancing religious liberty and the sanctity of human life. At this site one can find out more about the organization, its legal services, and litigation in which it is involved.

Facets of Religion

http://sunfly.ub.uni-freiburg.de:80/religion/

Facets of Religion is a listing of the major faiths worldwide. It contains general and interreligious information, related topics, and scholary studies.

Galaxy: Religions

http://galaxy.einet.net/galaxy/Humanities/Religion.html

Galaxy's Religion page provides links to readings and discussion of religion in the contexts of the culture and philosophy. This site also includes collections, directories, discussion groups, and links to other organizations on the Internet.

Galaxy: Religion (Community)

http://galaxy.einet.net/galaxy/Community/Religion.html

Resources on religious communities worldwide, from Judaism to Voodoo, are provided here. This site also offers a variety of articles, collections, directories, discussion groups, and links to other religious organizations on the Internet.

CHAPTER ▪ FOUR

Technology and Society

Negotiating the Natural Order

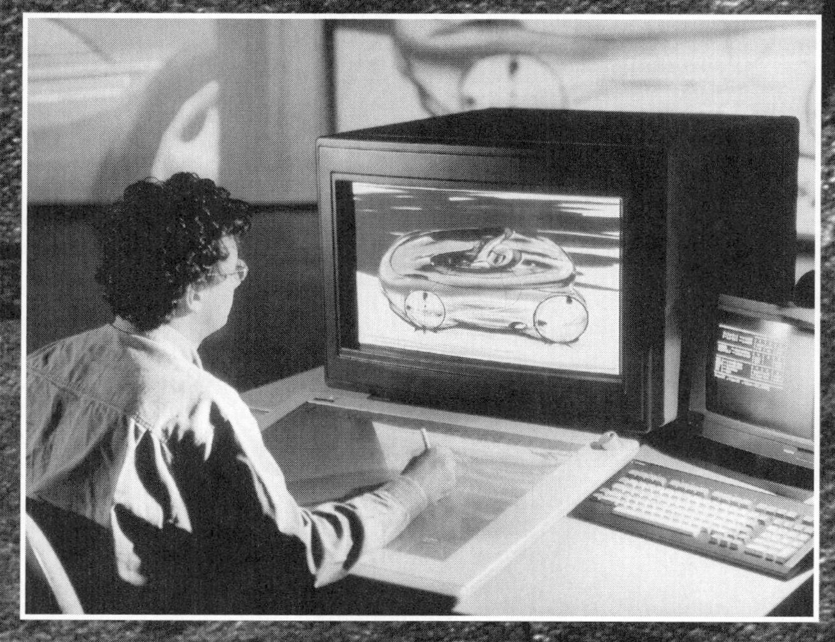

"Bishanial Kanojia's position in life was decided generations ago. He was born to be a *dhobi-wallah,* 'a washer person.' He was born to wash India's clothes. Up at dawn, Kanojia heads to an outdoor site called a *dhobi-ghat,* where he stands in a vat of sudsy water to stomp and squish clean the day's laundry with his feet.

"It is the work Kanojia's parents did, and their parents before them. The tradition is old enough and strong enough that most people working at the *dhobi-ghat* have the last name Kanojia. The work is their caste and their identity. They are the human washing machines of India.

"The *dhobi-wallahs* may not have that option much longer. A rapidly modernizing society could make irrelevant the only work they have known. This is the dilemma facing the *dhobi-wallahs* and countless other traditional occupations as mechanization and new ideas spread through the country. Call it India's version of downsizing—the casting aside of millions of manual laborers as the ancient nation races ahead.

"The concern for the *dhobi-wallahs* is simple and profound. As a middle class blossoms in India, their work is slowly being replaced by the washing machine. In the long run, technology and education should improve opportunities for the washers, as well as the carpenters, peasant farmers and even rickshaw drivers whose work is being usurped by modern times.

"But for now, India's government worries that new developments and new prosperity will result in the loss of millions of jobs for the people least able to react."

Source: From Michael Lev, "Traditional Jobs Washed Away in Modern India." *Chicago Tribune,* June 6, 1996: 1.1, 1.5.

Understanding the relationship of science and technology to the rest of human life takes us to the very roots of our intellectual and moral traditions. We need to explore these roots as best we can because science and technology are involved in every aspect of life, from issues of personal growth and fulfillment to those of social justice and participation to matters of sustainable development and ecologically sound social practices. One of the most significant effects of science and technology on society and human life is the introduction of novelty. New discoveries and newly developed techniques are the legitimate goals of science and technology, without which they would not exist. Without the novelty they create, a society will not survive or develop solutions to the problems of its way of life. Yet science and technological practices can become just as restrictive and repressive of novelty as other elements of culture such as religion or the moral values of a society.

We are so accustomed to mentioning science and technology in the same breath that it might surprise you to learn that it was perhaps only about 150 years ago that these two "streams" of human invention came together to form a powerful partnership. In traditional societies "science" was pursued by a leisured class with time to speculate about nature but not in the systematic way we think of science today. On the other hand, tools and techniques (technology) were used (but not always invented) by nonelite classes who applied their brains to easing the burdens of labor that fell upon them, rather than to understanding the natural world.

In this chapter we look at the social nature of technology and examine how it is embedded in social practices and patterns and in the cultural sphere of ideas and values. We then trace the emergence of modern science in the context of competing concepts of nature and see how one view in particular, that of the mechanistic philosophy, has dominated because of its compatibility with political and economic forces. We suggest that these forces, combined with the authority of science, have influenced our Western sense of identity, modes of engaging the world, and conception of the larger cosmic context in which we act. We next focus on how technology and science combined to create a powerful engine of invention through the formation of corporations and government research efforts. We describe how this Western-based process affected the rest of the world and how today's concern for the non-Western world is expressed in ideas such as that of appropriate technology. We then discuss some examples of technology that help generate a number of our global issues and describe alternatives that are emerging today. (Wherever appropriate, discussions of specific technology are reserved for other chapters in this book.) We discuss some of the implications for contemporary culture of ideas in the natural sciences, social sciences, and technology. Finally, we examine the role these ideas play in the debate between modern and postmodern culture.

Technology and Technology Practices

Technology can be defined as the systematic application of ideas to produce some desired outcome by manipulating the material world. This definition points to the fact that technology is rooted in the immaterial (ideas, wants, values) but finds expression in the material world, including our bodies. The goal of any technology is a desired state of affairs or condition, such as the production of material goods or good health.

A **technology practice** is the complex set of social and cultural patterns in which a society's technologies are embedded. It includes the organized individual and group activity that applies scientific and other knowledge to solving practical tasks (Drengson, 1995). A basic component of a technology practice is a given society's fundamental model of "reality," or the larger context in which human action occurs. This reality is often expressed in the stories and myths members of a given society cherish. Of special importance in a society's technology practice are the organized groups that promote specific technologies and the ideas and values underlying these groups. For example, during the 1970s agribusiness (massive business firms that operate for their own profit through the production and distribution of agricultural products and the implements and chemicals used to produce them; today these businesses often operate globally) supported efforts of leading U.S. research universities to develop products such as tough, juiceless (and largely tasteless) tomatoes that could be picked by machines without bruising. The underlying value in this instance was not the production of high-quality food, either in terms of nutrition or taste, but increased profits and reduced labor costs.

Natural systems survive and thrive only by means of self-correcting processes that enable them to resist the forces of disorder in the physical universe. Technology practices intervene in natural systems that are self-organizing structures. For example, the use of chemical insecticides has disturbed the natural balance between predators and the insects that eat many of our crops. This has resulted in increased crop losses resulting from insect pest populations that grow much larger without the restraints of natural predators. Human technology takes advantage of natural processes and redirects them toward human ends. The laws of nature dictate that imposing human order (novelty) comes at a price, which inevitably involves greater disorder (referred to as *entropy*) somewhere in the environment. This, too, is an aspect of technology practice. In contemporary times we are learning much more about the limits or boundaries of ecological systems in which we participate and are coming to understand the need to respect those limits.

All of this has led philosopher Frederick Rapp to describe our present age as the age of technology, which he sees as involving "constant technological alteration of the natural world; substantial alteration of daily human life through technology; and the continuous global expansion of Western technological processes" (quoted in Drengson, 1995:86–87). More than any previous people, we define ourselves in terms of technological processes. This age of technology, then, is dominated by the corporation-based, science-driven development of technology.

Protechnology and Antitechnology Responses

It is not at all surprising that today's highly technological world has led to diverse responses, some optimistic, others pessimistic. We review some optimistic and pessimistic views of the effect of modern technology on our lives.

Technological Optimism

Optimists accept some of the changes brought about by modern technology as unquestionably beneficial. For example, they point to increased standards of living that have resulted in greater longevity, better health, and more consumer goods and services. Furthermore, modern industrial technology and the type of society it supports have increased immensely the range of personal choice and freedom as well as the amount of leisure time. Technological optimists also cite the expansion of communication and knowledge that has occurred as a result of modern technology. According to the optimists, **premodern communities,** whether historical or contemporary, are based on ascribed statuses, close kinship ties, and, in many, if not most, cases, unquestioned patriarchy. Because of these conditions, such communities allow little personal freedom and few opportunities for self-expression except those allowed by the group and its customs.

Criticism of the Optimistic View. Recently, Ian Barbour, a scientist and well-known philosopher of science, has criticized the optimistic view of technology as too one-sided and incomplete. Technological optimists, he argues, ignore the institutional structures of economic power and self-interest controlling the directions of present technological development (Barbour, 1993). According to Barbour, technological optimists also (1) tend to overlook the environmental and human risks of technology; (2) ignore modern society's alienation from nature, which lies at the root of our approach to technology and hence of many of our current problems; (3) fail to recognize how technology has facilitated the concentration of economic and political power in the contemporary world; (4) underestimate the role that large-scale technology plays in the world today (for example, current technologies replace human labor with machines, receive disproportionate government support, and are subject to frequent and, potentially, devastating breakdown); and (5) accept the dependency of society upon experts as a good thing, but ignore such far-reaching effects as the disempowerment and alienation of the average citizen that such dependency can bring about. Technology-induced disempowerment, among other things, weakens democratic control while increasing people's sense of helplessness. Barbour also claims that the supporters of technology accept a linear view that sees scientific knowledge as the source of new technology that makes a positive contribution to society. This view does not take into account the ways that social dynamics, including social injustices, help to shape technology and even our scientific models of reality.

Technological Pessimism

Pessimists argue that technology generates a host of problems that are unsolvable by technological means. Pessimists believe that because technology has altered the ways we think about and experience the world, the ways we relate to one another and to the earth, and the ways we approach the solution of problems, it is not easy to understand the negative ways that technology has already influenced us.

Some of these negative effects, based loosely on Barbour's discussion, include the following:

1. Technological society creates mass society; as such it requires and enforces uniform thinking and behaving. Although uniform thinking was engendered by mass production society, critics of technology believe it is even more characteristic of today's

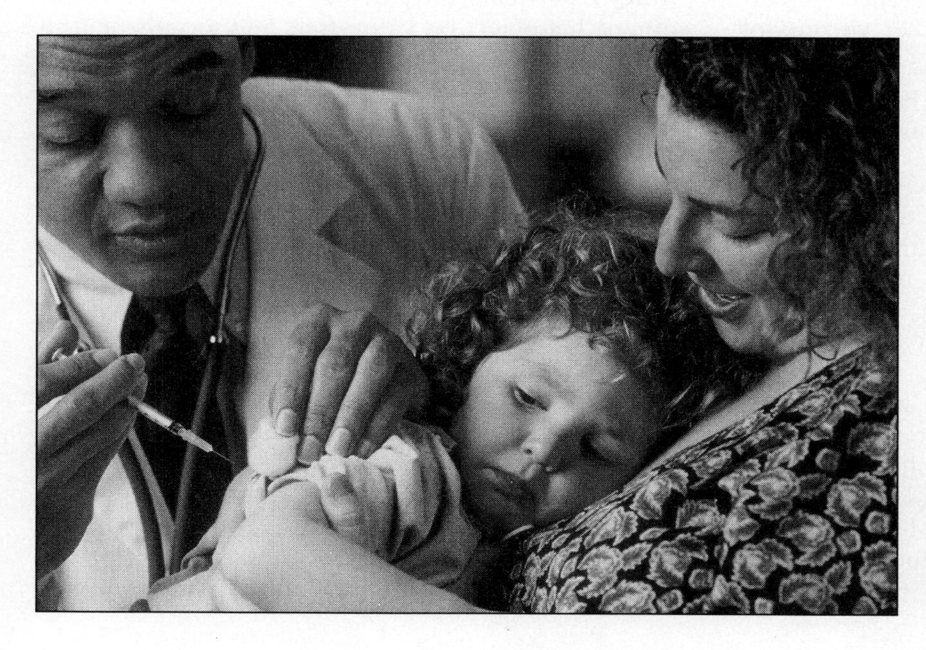

The optimistic view of technology fails to take into account the self-interest that controls the directions of technological development. An example is the pharmaceutical companies' preference for antibiotics over vaccinations for reasons of profit.

information age technology, because it involves ever more sophisticated methods of manipulating tastes, desires, and patterns of thinking. The prospect of genetically engineered human beings, with its implications for creating higher degrees of conformity, is even more hair-raising.

2. Quantitative criteria, such as efficiency, replace qualitative values such as natural beauty, friendship, meaningful work, and the sense of participation in society.

3. Real needs, like the need for economic well-being and protection against rights abuses, are ignored in the interest of creating desires for questionable new products.

4. Life becomes increasingly impersonal or depersonalized. This process has been ongoing, due largely to the restricted roles people play in modern work organizations, but it accelerates when machines are portrayed as superior to people and ways of manipulating human beings are perfected.

5. Complex, large-scale technologies are increasingly uncontrollable. Not only do catastrophic accidents like nuclear plant meltdowns (as in Chernobyl, the former Soviet Union, in 1986) and mass poisonings from industrial gas (as in Bhopal, India, in 1984) become "normal" and expected (Perrow, 1984), but the course of technological development itself seems to be outside the power of society to control.

6. Workers experience a general sense of alienation or powerlessness, not only with respect to their jobs but also with respect to the other citizens of modern society.

Criticisms of Pessimistic Views. Barbour offers three replies to the technology pessimists.

1. Great variations exist among technologies and among what we call technology practices. Some of these technologies clearly have the undesirable effects that the pessimists perceive, but others do not. Some technologies empower rather than exploit people, giving them satisfactions, such as meaningful work and self-expression.

2. The pessimists ignore the many avenues available to redirect technological development. There are always alternative forms of technology (or of scientific theories). These other technologies express alternative values and interests and have different effects upon human life and social structure than do our current technologies.

3. Technology can be made to be the servant of human values. Obviously, it is always the servant of the values of *some* human beings. But these values usually tend to be those of elite groups and are narrowly defined. This situation did not always exist, as in tribal societies when technical know-how was generally shared among all members of the group (with the possible exception of technologies that were gender-specific in a given society). Today there is growing interest in movements that advocate the development of *appropriate technology,* movements that work specifically on designing technologies to meet the needs of local communities.

Pessimists tend to accept some version of the **technological imperative,** the belief that technology will follow a set course because of an internal imperative and, therefore, human beings can do little to alter this course. But historians and sociologists who have studied the actual course of scientific and technological development find no evidence for this "imperative." Rather, the struggle for political power and control over material resources and over whose ideas will prevail in society are the forces behind what appears to be the "natural course" of scientific and technological change, not some hidden power inherent in technology itself.

The technological imperative has become an *ideology,* that is, a set of beliefs that justifies some real, or potential, social arrangement. Those who benefit from a particular technology attempt to convince others that objective, value-free, and socially neutral forces have created that technology. People who can be persuaded to accept this idea are more likely to believe that any harm or injustice that may come about because of technology is simply the unfortunate but inevitable result of "progress."

Related to the concept of the technological imperative is that of **technological determinism,** the idea that technology, driven by its own internal imperative, is an independent cause of social, cultural, and psychological patterns. Technologies do in fact often dictate, or shape, the patterns of behavior required to use them and may additionally require that groups of people be organized in specific ways to operate them. It is true too that some technologies enhance the power of some persons or groups. For example, an airplane needs a well-organized crew to execute with precision the orders of the pilot. Technology in this sense does have an effect

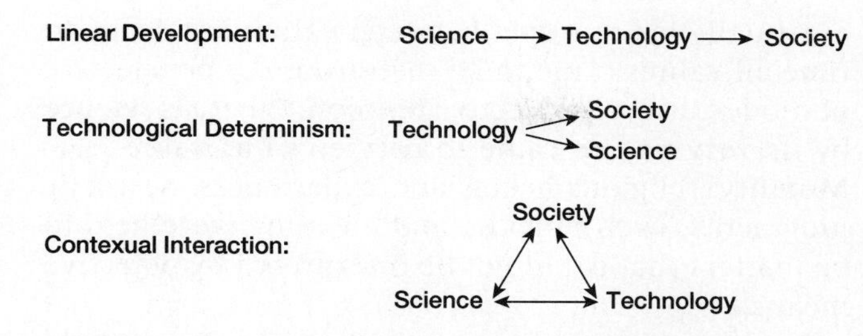

FIGURE 4–1 The Social Construction of Technology
Source: Ian Barbour. *Ethics in an Age of Technology: The Gifford Lectures,* vol. 2. Copyright © 1992 by Ian F. Barbour. New York: HarperCollins, p. 20. Reprinted by permission of HarperCollins Publishers, Inc.

on social patterns. Alternative ways can always be found for achieving the ends for which a technology is developed. But social and political forces intervene to influence which technologies are developed and widely used. For example, crop rotation is a cheap and effective means of maintaining soil fertility and controlling pests, but in the 1980s U.S. farmers who rotated crops were not given the subsidies that farmers who used chemicals to accomplish the same ends received.

Barbour offers an alternative to both the pessimistic and optimistic models that he calls contextual interaction. In the **contextual interaction model,** the three forces of society, technology, and science are related in such ways that each can be the cause or the effect of the other. This dynamic creates what Barbour refers to as the *social construction of technology.* In this model technology is ultimately the servant of political power, but political power does not have to be concentrated in the hands of a few select groups and organizations, as it is now. Democratic political pressures can, and, in fact, do, redirect technological developments and applications, at least upon occasion (see Figure 4–1).

Modernism

In our previous chapters we have dealt with culture as a process more than as a set of fixed elements such as beliefs, values, rules of conduct, or symbols. We have emphasized the dynamic quality of human consciousness (i.e., experience of, and thought about, the world). We have shown that in the course of interaction structures of consciousness emerge that constrain experience and thought. These structures of consciousness are the assumptions and theories, the models of reality, and the shared ways of experiencing the world constructed by human beings. These patterns evolve and change over time, as sociologist Peter Berger (1979) points out, but sometimes they persist beyond their usefulness and become too restrictive and lead to undesirable outcomes.

Beginning in the 1500s, and lasting for at least three centuries, a structure of consciousness was forged in Western Europe called modernism that influenced modern science and technology profoundly. We pointed out in Chapter 1 that modernism accompanied the spread of European culture and continues to be a factor in contemporary globalization. A value system oriented to the rational manipulation of nature and society in the interest of progress, modernism is actively opposed to traditional restraints on individual or collective choice. Modernism—here we are interested in it from the perspective of science and technology—emerged during the course of four great periods of historical change: the Renaissance, the Reformation, the scientific revolution, and the Enlightenment (Spretnak, 1997).

The Renaissance (early fourteenth to the late sixteenth centuries) involved the rediscovery of ancient ways of thinking. The legacy of the Renaissance to the developing ideology of modernism was the attitude called **humanism,** an optimistic faith in human creativity and intelligence. Although Renaissance thinkers sought power through means that today we would regard as magical and occult, their faith in human achievement contributed to the modern outlook.

In northern Europe the Protestant Reformation (beginning in the early sixteenth century and continuing for several centuries) was a second major contributor to the development of modernism as a philosophy. The Reformation started as protest against the corruption of the Roman Catholic Church. Although they recognized humankind as sinful, and did not in that sense share the optimism of Renaissance thinkers, Reformation thinkers believed that the remedy for sin lay in individual faith and in the grace of God toward the individual rather than in the institution of the Church and its rituals. Dominant Reformation thinkers emphasized religious individualism. Such an approach gave rise gradually to an emphasis on rational self-discipline and a rejection of much of the supernaturalism (the belief in nature, spirits, and magic) that had characterized so much of traditional European thinking, both inside and outside the Church.

The scientific revolution, which began in Europe in 1543, helped to complete the transition from an outlook that regarded nature as living and filled with spirits to an outlook based on the material world. The introduction of science as a rational mode of inquiry came to be associated over time with the *mechanistic worldview*. In this view the world is a complex but essentially lifeless and mindless machine. *Instrumental rationality*, a philosophy that propounds control over nature, accompanied the growth of the scientific worldview as human alienation from nature grew.

The last of the Western philosophies to emerge that contributed to modernism was the Enlightenment. This school of thought, which dominated much of eighteenth-century thought, was a social and political expression of the emerging modernist consciousness. Enlightenment thought insisted on the freedom of the individual from institutionalized restraints, which were regarded as irrational. Virtually all traditional obligations of kinship, religion, or inherited rank, then, were to be thrown off, because few of these controls could be justified by rational thought. Society needed to be set on a rational course. Although Catholics and Protestants alike might teach that sinful humankind was in need of divine assistance, Enlightenment thinkers tended to find the source of corruption in society and its institutions (including, very prominently, religion). Only the political, economic, and educational restructuring of society could allow human nature to achieve perfection, proponents of the Enlightenment argued. Beginning in the late eighteenth century, political revolutions in America and France, the rise of socialism, and the evolution of numerous reform movements expressed the ideas of social engineering that Enlightenment thinkers believed would result in human progress.

Modernism, then, created a positive attitude toward human nature and individual freedom. Modernism brought rationality to approaches to solving problems, and its proponents believed that the natural world and human nature could be controlled and improved. Modernist thinkers generally embraced Enlightenment notions of progress and saw in natural evolution confirmation of the law of progress. But modernism's reliance upon instrumental rationality and the methods of empirical science eventually led to a split between values and facts. In time all values came to be seen from the perspective of modernism as subjective opinion, whereas science by its very nature came to be viewed as value free. Morality, religious beliefs and experiences, aesthetic judgments, even purpose and meaning were held to be matters that could not be interpreted by objective means.

But the twentieth century brought two world wars, Nazism in Germany, Fascism in Italy, and the corruption of the socialist revolution in Russia. For many, especially in Europe, these events spelled the loss of faith in progress and the beginning of the end of modernist hope. The United States has clung to the fading belief in progress longer than Europe, perhaps because we came through the crises of the first half of the twentieth century largely unscathed, even rising to global prominence as a consequence.

Mechanistic Science and Alienation from Nature

Science refers to the systematic attempt to understand and explain any realm of human experience, including nature, society, and human mental processes, by methods that can be replicated and thus lead to socially shared knowledge. The birth of the modern phase of natural science was preceded by a transformation of human perception and consciousness. The way humans came to experience themselves in relation to the world changed. This can be seen in early fifteenth-century Florence, when painter and architect Fillipo Brunelleschi became the first human being to paint a picture in "true" perspective, an event that shows us that what we have come to accept as the "normal" way things look had, in fact, to be learned. Our neural pathways have to be conditioned in order to provide us with the visual experience of depth and three-dimensionality that we accept as natural (Talbott, 1995). The new visual imaging of the world, according to Talbott, ushered in by the Renaissance brought a growing sense of the separateness of the "ego"—that is, the experiencing and thinking self—from the world "out there." Talbott describes the medieval human being's sense of self as the feeling of being like an embryo embedded in a cosmic womb, in which space is a sort of amniotic fluid filled with countless threads connecting all parts of the person to minerals, plants, animals, stars, and planets (Talbott, 1995). But the abrupt appearance of perspective painting during the Renaissance, complete with mathematical laws for creating the illusion of spatial distance, enabled human beings to acquire a new sense of the self as spectator. The world became empty three-dimensional space in this construct, best represented by mathematics.

Renaissance Views of Science and Nature. Three philosophies of nature, organicism, vitalism, and naturalism, competed with one another in the Renaissance period of the fifteenth and sixteenth centuries, according to historian of science Carolyn Merchant (1980). The three philosophies incorporated much of the earlier belief that humankind participated in a living and meaningful nature, a world that was, in the language of German sociologist Max Weber, "enchanted." Mechanism, which by the seventeenth century had become the dominant philosophy of nature (especially in Britain and France, then eventually throughout the Western world), contrasted with these views. The mechanistic worldview, you may recall, saw all of nature as a machine—lifeless, mindless, and pointless. Whereas each of the earlier views held that nature was alive and possessed soul, mechanism refuted these beliefs. The first mechanists were not materialists who simply denied the existence of souls. Rather, they believed that human beings alone of all creatures in the physical world possessed souls.

Social Forces Supporting the Mechanistic Philosophy. As various social groups attempted to dominate the material and political resources of seventeenth-century society and to enforce their belief systems upon others, competing views of science were hotly debated. Political, social, and religious forces came together to promote the mechanistic worldview. These forces included

1. the theologians who defended biblical miracles against the claim that such events could have been instances of natural magic
2. the growing urban middle classes who embraced Protestantism, science, and technological innovation
3. the defeat and suppression of certain radical Protestant sects, who as "levelers" sought to eliminate the distinctions of social class and all the privileges that accompanied it. (These sects embraced radical religious beliefs concerning the end of the world and the development of social justice, which was to occur with the overthrow of corrupt and sinful orders. Levelers also espoused many of the nonmechanistic versions of science because they were more congenial to their mystical religious worldview.)
4. the alternative versions of science or philosophies of nature that included feminine elements and values.

Antimechanistic thinkers emphasized female or androgynous models of nature. Their laws of nature were organic rather than mechanistic and focused on life processes rather than machine processes (Griffin, 1993). Merchant suggests that supporters of the mechanistic worldview were quite explicit about their espousal of a "masculine" science—the language they used to describe their values as well as their attempts to control and dominate nature were typical of masculine sensibilities. Merchant also notes that mechanistic thinkers suppressed the "feminine" view that nature is alive.

The mechanistic worldview, Merchant argues, removed the ethical restraints against exploiting nature because proponents of mechanism believed that nature was neither alive nor senstient. The mechanistic philosophy retained the tradition of magic, which involves the effort to control the natural forces that govern the world, but denied that those forces were living or conscious. Furthermore, mechanistic thought removed what Merchant calls the feminine "World Soul" from our picture of the cosmos, leaving only a neuter machine and a male-oriented rationality. Mechanists believed the soul to be feminine in contrast to the Divine Spirit (God), which they thought to be masculine.

The mechanistic philosophy also sanctioned the expansion of commercial capitalism (Merchant, 1980). Especially in its mathematical form, the mechanistic philosophy proved to be a formidable intellectual defense of a way of life that involved expansion and the conquest of the natural world and other cultures. Although in the seventeenth and eighteenth centuries, scientific knowledge had yet to "deliver the goods," its proponents insisted that its ideology supported technological invention.

New technology developed largely independently of scientific knowledge, but it was encouraged by the same social forces that supported mechanistic science. Certainly, many inventions, such as the barometer (1643), contributed to scientific models of natural processes and also performed as precision instruments used to test those models. Technical invention became less haphazard as the methods of experimental science were systematically applied to it. But the traditional social separation between head (theory, science, mathematics) and hand (tools, inventions, techniques) persisted. There was a definite affinity between global expansion, new technologies, mechanistic science, the control over nature, and the economic materialism characteristic of the cusp of European cultural growth.

Choices and alternatives are always available to human societies and their members. For example, an international diversity of opinion existed among mechanists about scientific models of the natural world. (Then, as now, scientists construct mental, pictorial, mathematical, and even solid three-dimensional models of various aspects of nature—from the purely mathematical models of probability to wooden ball models of molecules.) This diversity was rooted in the cultural and political differences among the various regions of Europe. In Germany the mechanistic worldview was challenged by leading thinkers such as poet and scientist Johann Wolfgang von Goethe (1749–1832). The German antimechanistic approach maintained a sense of living nature, animated by a life force, or world soul. Its model was a living organic system whose overall actions and processes could not be explained by its separate parts but had to be understood through the functional unity of the whole and through its development over time. This distinctly different point of view turned out to be scientifically fruitful. German science was to make major contributions to embryology, cell theory, the concept of evolution, and the electrical nature of chemical reactions, among other areas; it may also have contributed to nonmechanistic developments in twentieth-century physics like quantum mechanics.

Mechanistic Philosophy and the Social Sciences. Although the social sciences are generally regarded as of secondary importance to the natural sciences (Kuhn, 1964), the application of mechanistic consciousness to the study of society was essential to the emergence of the world we now inhabit. Economic historian Karl Polanyi has argued that the social science of political economics justified the value of science to the capitalist middle class of Europe during the eighteenth and nineteenth centuries. These social "sciences" encouraged and justified ongoing social transformations by applying the mechanistic model to the study of society and of history (Polanyi, 1944).

In the political arena, for example, the idea of "revolution" was introduced from the field of astronomy, in which "revolution" referred to the cyclical motion of the planets. The revolutions that rocked Europe, such as the French Revolution (1789–1799), were viewed by contemporaries as the inevitable result of the laws of motion of human society itself. Members of the growing middle class used these doctrines to justify their own efforts to change society. Mechanistic thinking took deep root in European thought. For example, radical German political philosopher and socialist Karl Marx (1818–1883) portrayed himself as the Newton of political economics, after the English physicist Isaac Newton (1642–1727), who discovered the laws of motion. Marx claimed to have discovered the "laws of motion" governing human society.

Democracy itself even began to be viewed as the expression of the concept of the separate ego, in the form of the citizen-self—an atom of society—directed by rational opinion. Democracy, from this perspective, was a means to register the sum of individual opinions so that the motion of society as a whole could be directed toward the greatest good for the greatest number.

Mechanistic ideas shaped economic thinking too. According to this perspective, great impersonal laws, working with the precision of the planetary system, operated the economy. Scottish economist Adam Smith (1723–1790) said that the motion of the economy was regulated by something like an "invisible hand." Essentially, Smith argued that economic laws were out of human hands and therefore represented universal patterns. The ultimate triumph of the economy as a central institution of modern European civilization and its global extensions represented theory in practice. The attitudes of human beings toward themselves, their bodies, their labor, their crafts, their local communities, their religious traditions, and their local ecology all had to be transformed totally and finally in order for the capitalist economy to operate successfully (Polanyi, 1944).

Perhaps the most famous "scientific" theory in defense of Western civilization's global conquest arose in the late nineteenth century and was called *social Darwinism.* Some interpreters of Darwin's theory of natural selection saw competition among species as a law of nature that led to the idea of the survival of the fittest. Social Darwinism justified the ruthless competition of capitalist colonialism and imperialism on the grounds of the supposed law of nature

How the New Physics Transforms Culture

In 1976 a young physicist named Fritjof Capra published *The Tao of Physics,* a book that underscored many remarkable parallels between the worldview of the new physics and that of Eastern philosophies and religions such as Hinduism, Taoism, Buddhism, and Zen. Both the new physics and the ancient mystical teachings, Capra argued, recognize that there is a unity underlying all reality. Both physics and Eastern thought argue that the rational human mind is limited and that reality often has to be represented in paradoxes. An example of a paradox in physics is the idea that the quantum, the smallest packet of physical activity, can manifest itself either as wave motions spread across a region of space or as a particle, a tightly localized "object." These two manifestations represent such radically different types of being that it is impossible to imagine how any single thing could share both forms of being. Another convergence of science and mysticism is the dynamic, flowing nature of physical reality discovered by modern physics. (According to modern physics, "objects," on close inspection, are in constant motion and change. In fact, "objects" are really complex events resulting from the motion or flow of energy, and any object, or any event, can be expressed as the movement of waves.) These findings seem to agree with many of the Eastern philosophies, which teach that everything is impermanent (Buddhism) or that reality is an endless flux of interacting forces (Taoism). Both physicists and Eastern mystics speak of the existence of a timeless, spaceless field in which, or out of which, space, time, and all the processes of nature unfold.

The revolution in physics, Capra suggests, is part of a global transformation, or "turning point," in human consciousness that is giving rise to a new planetary culture (Capra, 1976). His view is not unique, but it reflects a widespread belief that contemporary humanity is experiencing or participating in an evolutionary leap of unprecedented proportions. The convergence of physics and mystical-spiritual views is a major signal of this new global awareness. The founders of the twentieth-century physics of quantum mechanics and relativity theory were in fact often "mystics"; that is, they perceived an underlying unity behind all phenomena, which they identified with consciousness, or mind. For example, English astronomer Arthur Eddington (1882–1944) described the physical world as abstract and without "actuality" except for its link to consciousness (Eddington, 1928).

Among those who have explored the connections between modern physics and the spiritual approach to reality in the latter half of this century were thinkers of the caliber of David Bohm (1917–1992), one of the most important physicists of the second half of the twentieth century. Another such scientist is the Indian-born quantum physicist Amit Goswami, currently at the University of Oregon, who argues that the only way to make coherent sense of the paradoxes of quantum mechanics is to recognize that consciousness is necessary to "bring" the physical world into existence in the form that we know it.

Today, experiments continue to affirm the crucial role played by human awareness in the physical universe. Whatever their outcome, even a cautious assessment of the implications of quantum physics forces us to accept that what is observed is not independent of the mind of the observer—that both the observer and the observed are part of a larger unity (Barbour, 1990). For these reasons, the basic assumptions on which the modernist mechanistic worldview were based—that the physical universe consists of distinct parts with definite properties and that it exists separate from the observer—must be radically revised or simply abandoned.

Sources: Ian Barbour. *Religion in an Age of Science: The Gifford Lectures,* vol. 1, 1989–1990 (New York: HarperCollins, 1990); Fritjof Capra. *The Tao of Physics* (Boulder, CO: Shambala, 1976); Sir Arthur Eddington. *The Nature of the Physical World* (New York: Macmillan, 1929).

(Sahlins, 1976). Thus, supporters of social Darwinism argued that the Western exploiters, especially the dominant economic classes and the political states of England, Germany, and the United States, were biologically superior. White Europeans and Americans were supposedly the "favored races," who were mentioned in the subtitle of Darwin's famous book *The Origin of Species by Means of Natural Selection or the Preservation of Favored Races in the Struggle for Life* (1859). In summary, inventions and technology enabled and even inspired conquest and exploitation as the "scientific" justification and moral implications of them were worked out by leading social thinkers and propagandists (see the box, "FYI: How the New Physics Transforms Culture," for a more recent interpretation of the relationship between science and culture).

Science and Technology Coming Together

Until the mid-nineteenth century, inventors flourished without possessing a great deal of scientific and mathematical knowledge. Then the demand for mass-produced muskets and accurately bored cannons encouraged greater precision in the development of machine tools. More efficient steam engines began to be designed because of the development of the science of thermodynamics (the study of the flow of heat) that resulted from studying technology rather than pure science. In other words, the need for technology was now driving scientific inquiry rather than vice versa. The first industries to make extensive use of scientific knowledge were the chemical and electrical industries. Perhaps there was simply no way to intuitively grasp the newly discovered and mysterious forces of electromagnetism and chemical affinity without studying the new sciences. Figure 4–2 provides historical perspective on the emergence of some important scientific and technological innovations as well as the philosophical ideas that contributed to such innovations.

The immense role that technology played in the global expansion of Europe dates from the sixteenth century. The mechanical clock, improved ship designs, more accurate astronomical tables, and the cannon contributed to improved navigation, improved transportation, and the growth of military power of the European "explorers" and imperialists. We may say that technology made possible or facilitated actions conceived of and motivated by other social forces, and this would be partially true. A stronger statement might be that new technologies made new courses of action feasible and hence conceivable. New technologies, in other words, altered the range of choices available while structuring the motivation and interests of persons and groups in society.

The technological development of ironclad steamships and rapid-fire weapons allowed a pattern of colonization and exploitation by Europeans. In this engraving, an English ship destroys Chinese junks in the Opium Wars in 1841.

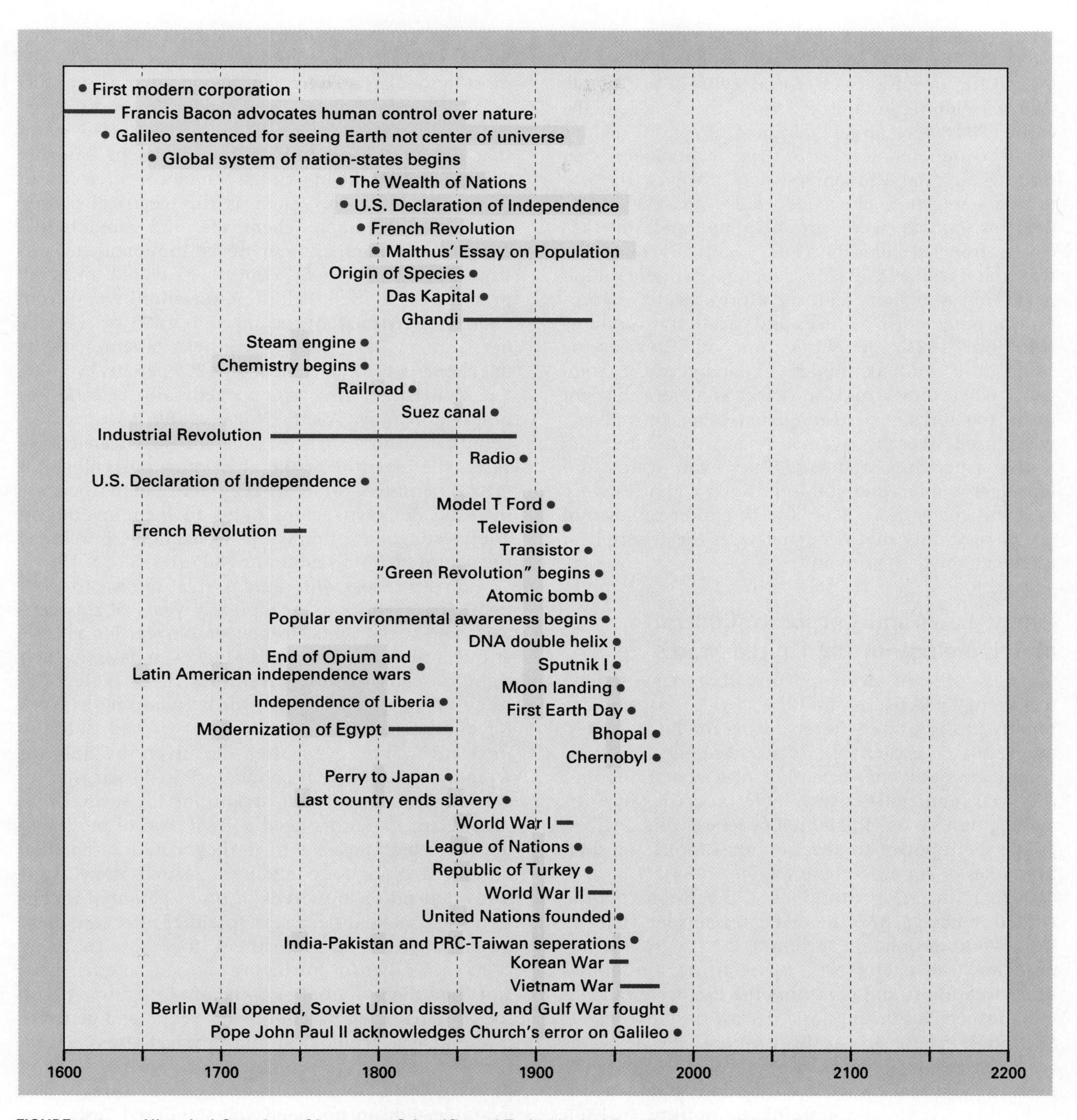

FIGURE 4–2 **Historical Overview of Important Scientific and Technological Developments, 1600 to Present**

Source: Adapted from *Global 2000 Revisited: Report to Parliament of World's Religions* by Gerard O. Barney. Copyright © 1993 by The Millennium Institute. Reprinted by permission of The Millennium Institute.

For example, the pattern of colonization and exploitation by Europeans was strongly influenced by specific inventions (McGinn, 1991). Most of the colonial empires established from the 1500s to the early 1800s were largely confined to coastal regions of the conquered territories. The technologies that made their establishment possible involved the improved navigation of wooden ships and the use of firearms (which were primitive by modern standards). Ironclad steamships and, eventually, rapid-fire weapons facilitated deeper geographical penetration into faraway regions and, therefore, greater disruption of indigenous cultures and local environments (McGinn, 1991). Machine guns and devastating "dum-dum" bullets, which expanded more than usual when they struck an object and were thought to be too terrible to use against other Europeans, were used liberally against Asians, Africans, and Native Americans, and sometimes even against defenseless women and children. Such activities were probably made more likely by the earlier removal of moral restraints that occurred with the triumph of the mechanistic worldview.

Patent Laws and Corporate Control of Technology in the United States

Some significant developments that have shaped technology practice around the world occurred very rapidly in the United States during the latter half of the 1800s. These changes concerned the nature of patent laws and the formation of corporations that acquired monopolies over whole industries by controlling thousands of patented processes and devices, giving them power to develop innovations and then to market or suppress them (Noble, 1984).

During the Constitutional Convention of the United States (1787), the delegates decided that the U.S. patent law should "promote the progress of science and the useful arts, by securing for limited times to authors and inventors the exclusive right to their respective writings and discoveries" (Article 1, Section 8). These practical inventions, the delegates reasoned, were beneficial to society; therefore, the persons who made such contributions ought to receive the rewards of a grateful community. In 1860 President Abraham Lincoln (president 1861–1865) praised the patent law because it "added the fuel of interest [material reward] to the fire of genius" (Noble, 1984).

The scramble for control of patents was part of the push to industrialize rapidly after the Civil War. Almost immediately following the war, many inventors (e.g., Thomas Edison) and many investors (e.g., Westinghouse) began an effort in the United States that led to the control of whole sets of valuable patents, not by the inventors, but by corporations. In numerous industries, such as the electrical power, telephone, telegraph, chemicals, and radio industries, certain companies achieved monopolistic control. Eventually, such control extended over all products. The Bell Patent Association went from control of two patents acquired in 1875 by Alexander Graham Bell, the Scottish-born inventor of the telephone (1876), to control of 9,255 patents by 1935. The Bell Patent Association eventually became another monopoly, AT&T (Noble, 1984). Meanwhile, genius inventors such as Croatian-American Nikola Tesla, the inventor of the alternating-current motor (1883), entered rather shabby retirements because they did not own patent rights to their inventions. The Westinghouse Company, for example, purchased the patent of Tesla's motor in 1885 (Davidson, 1989).

Many inventors who came to this country to work for U.S. corporations in the early years of this century sold their rights to their employers for as little as one dollar. In some cases, they even gave up their rights to patent future inventions. Even if they decided to try to get around this by planning to work for another company, their employer had rights to their inventions even after the inventors quit (or were fired). Intelligent people forfeited their right to get rich from their own inventions for several reasons. First, inventors need a great deal of money to develop their ideas, which they could often gain only by working for companies. Second, new inventions depend on hundreds of other patented inventions that make it necessary to either purchase these other patents or reinvent them. Inventors routinely sued each other for infringing on their patents. Such suits had the potential to bankrupt inventors, tie up the production of inventions for years, and generate intolerable psychological and physical stress. Third, inventors also were the objects of personal slander, physical intimidation, and even death threats. For example, Edison hounded and slandered Tesla over patent rights. In response to such problems, corporate research and development laboratories emerged in the beginning of this century as the main social force behind technological innovation.

Government and Military Encouragement of Technology Driven by Science

The government has been another force behind technological innovation. The government has traditionally invested money to support scientific and technological research in many and varied ways. Some of the less obvious ways have been financial support of education in the sciences, science and technology museums, World Fairs, and technological and scientific exhibitions. Examples of more direct government support in the United States are military contracts and the space program, as well as major subsidies to corporations for the development of new technologies. All of these are crucial aspects of contemporary technology practices, not just in the United States, but around the world.

The introduction of information-processing devices in manufacturing provide an example of government involvement in technological development. Supporters argue that by adopting "smart" machines and computerized control of production, businesses can reduce costs, increase production, and compensate for the shortage of highly skilled employees. But after reviewing actual studies of the effects of using computer-assisted design and manufacturing (CAD/CAM), David Noble, a Marxist historian of automation in industry, concludes that the evidence for the competitive advantage of using computers is ambiguous (Noble, 1977). He compares the contemporary introduction of information technology in industry with the industrial revolution in the nineteenth-century United States, when mass-production machines were first introduced in factories. The two periods are remarkably similar—in both periods the U.S. military had the money and the resources to invest in the rather expensive hobby of technologically redesigning industry. In addition, industrial changes were *not* in either example driven by the self-regulating market, but by forces operating apart from market forces—the army in the nineteenth century and the air force at the end of this century. Governments around the world continue to be a major source of investment in the research and development (R&D) of new technologies. Table 4–1 shows how R&D money is spent by typical contemporary governments.

TABLE 4–1 Research and Development Spending of Seven Major Governments

CATEGORY	TOTAL (BILLION 1995 DOLLARS)	SHARE (PERCENT)
Military	62.6	36
Advancement of Knowledge[a]	39.2	23
Health	18.2	11
Civilian Space	15.5	9
Energy	10.7	6
Industrial Development	8.0	5
Agriculture, Forestry, and Fishing	5.6	3
Infrastructure[b]	3.8	2
Earth and Atmosphere	2.7	1
Social Development and Services	2.5	1
Environmental Protection	2.3	1
Total[c]	171.6	100

[a] Includes advancement of research and general university funds.
[b] Includes transport, telecommunications, urban and rural planning.
[c] Includes other categories not listed separately.

Source: Based on National Science Board, *Science and Engineering Indicators 1996* (Washington, DC: U.S. Government Printing Office, 1996), Appendix Table 4–32.

Selling the Idea of Technology

The first great extravaganza whose goal was to provide propaganda for technological innovation was the Crystal Palace Exhibition in London, England, in 1851. The exhibition's goal was to show the industry of all nations, thereby celebrating progress and promoting trade. Such celebrations of technology tend to portray the role of technology in human life in an overly optimistic way. They seldom suggest the existence of problems that technology cannot solve or problems that technology actually creates (Segal, 1994).

The only certainty about predictions of future technology is that they will be proven false. Optimists who proclaim a bright technological future do not seem to understand how unpredictable the development of new technologies really is. The prophets of technology, for example, never anticipated radical new technologies like X-ray lasers (1984) or personal computers (introduced to consumers in 1974). Experts falsely predicted that by 1980 all cars, boats, and planes would be nuclear powered. Nevertheless, powerful propaganda efforts to portray technological change in a positive and hopeful light continue, supported by private corporate interests, such as the Disney Company, as well as governmental administrations, departments, or agencies such as the Department of Defense or the National Aeronautics and Space Administration (NASA) (Segal, 1994; McGinn, 1991; Noble, 1984). Such propaganda efforts are intended to counteract resistance to new technology and concern about the effects of existing technology, for human beings and human cultures have always been ambivalent about technology (Marx, 1964).

In summary, modern Western technology practices developed within a complicated social and cultural milieu. Technology is not an autonomous force following its own inner logic. Scientific theories are only models of nature, not the real world. Human beings, motivated by political, economic, philosophical, and religious concerns have shaped the direction of both science and technology. Science and technical inventions interpenetrate, changing the natural and the social environments. Much money and effort have been devoted to the attempt to give the public a positive view of science and technology, but an undercurrent of distrust remains, expressed in many mass media presentations depicting technologies as out of control.

Technology in the Third World

Remarkable global changes have occurred in the twentieth century. After World War II many former colonies of Europe freed themselves from direct domination. (There remain various forms of less direct domination of course, and very severe problems associated with the continuing underdevelopment of these Third World societies.) Most remarkable has been a shift in the moral consciousness from acceptance of the exploitation of other societies to a new concern on the part of the Western developed world toward the less developed peoples. Closely related to this change is the inclusion of Third World leaders and thinkers in the ongoing global dialogue. We do not want to exaggerate the concern and care of individuals living in industrialized nations for people living in nonindustrialized and industrializing societies. But the fact that the new concern has led to some policy changes by the First World in relation to the Third World suggests that sometimes, at least, the concern is genuine. Ironically, when efforts are undertaken to benefit Third World recipients, the depth and complexity of the task becomes clearer. Frustration, despair, and intensified conflict often result.

Technology Transfer

After World War II experts and the informed public hoped that much of the gap between the developed and the less developed world could be closed by means of **technology transfer,** or the direct sharing of the developed world's technology with the less developed nations of the world. This hope depended on a view of technology that was too narrowly focused and did not take into account technology practices. Any tool or productive process is embedded in a complex social system, which includes other technologies, educational systems, attitudes, skills, and support services. We cannot, therefore, introduce a complex modern technology into a nonmodern context and expect it to flourish without trained personnel to operate and manage it, troubleshooters to repair it, spare parts to keep it running, infrastructures like roads to transport it, telephone and power lines to communicate to and from it, universities to train technical people, and a host of other necessary supports. More advanced technology not only requires more of these supporting structures, but also tends to employ fewer workers and to require more capital. But Third World countries have a surplus of workers and a shortage of capital. Given this equation, benefits in the form of profits often go to the country that is supplying the technology. A more subtle and difficult issue is the incompatibility between the technology and the culture of the recipients. Recently, the proposed introduction in Papua New Guinea, of a biogas-generating plant that derived energy from human waste was rejected by most natives because of fears based on magical beliefs about the use of human excrement.

Since the publication of the E. F. Schumacher's book *Small Is Beautiful* (1973), the term **appropriate technology** has come to mean technology designed to fit the needs of the recipient culture. At first people interpreted the factors involved in this exchange too narrowly and saw the process simply as a kind of technology transfer, but today we have a clearer understanding of the factors that make technology "appropriate." These factors are:

- The technology must fit the given country's infrastructure, its social and technological support system—that is, its existing technology practices.
- The technology must be affordable and be able to be properly maintained.
- The technology generally must be of intermediate scale.

Such intermediate technology exists when the supporting social systems or group structures necessary to maintain and use the technology are neither too great nor too small for the society receiving the technology. In addition, appropriate technologies should

- meet real human needs
- empower users
- provide meaningful work and opportunities for personal growth and development
- involve consultation with users
- be environmentally sound and sustainable.

A further refinement of the idea of developing technologies appropriate to Third World contexts is that **indigenous technologies,** or technologies developed by local peoples themselves (e.g., traditional ways of harvesting and maintaining local forests, fields, lakes, and rivers, which have proven effective for generations), should form the core of appropriateness. That is, as far as is possible, technological developments must be based upon already existing local technology practices.

Energy and Information Technology Practices

There are many technology practices that we could consider here. Some will be discussed in Chapter 10 in connection with health and nutrition. We consider energy and information here. At the beginning of the twentieth century, it was discovered that matter and energy are interchangeable aspects of the physical world. Consequently, energy began to replace matter as the basic component in our models of reality. More recently, information has been found to be a ubiquitous aspect of the world as well. It seems appropriate, therefore, to single out particular technology practices associated with these two components—energy and information—of the universe.

Energy

The industrial revolution, which continues today for many countries, is closely associated with a shift to fossil fuels (at first coal, then later petroleum) as the main source of power and, ultimately, of the manufactured wealth of the industrial system. A great deal of the wealth and power of contemporary industrial societies results from having tapped this supply of stored energy and matter.

But there are severe drawbacks to the use of fossil fuels. First, these fuels are nonrenewable. This means that we are living off of our energy "capital" rather than our "income" and are depleting our reserves, thereby ensuring that future generations will be denied these resources. Second, the burning of fossil fuels is a main source of pollution, particularly in the form of carbon wastes. Carbon dioxide is a major contributor to the **greenhouse effect** (the phenomenon whereby the earth's atmosphere traps solar radiation, caused by the presence in the atmosphere of gases such as carbon dioxide that allow incoming sunlight to pass through but absorb heat radiated back from the earth's surface) and the changing worldwide weather patterns. Third, petroleum consumption has contributed to major power inequities in the world today. Petroleum is a highly concentrated source of energy that every nation finds very necessary, given the industrial world's extensive reliance on technologies that require petroleum. But it is located in only a few major underground reservoirs in the world, which has far-reaching consequences. For example, the nations controlling these resources—located mainly in the Middle East—have had a great deal of power over where the fuel goes and at what prices. The Organization of Petroleum Exporting Countries (OPEC) has, therefore, played a key role in world politics during the last few decades. Oil companies and other industries closely allied with them, such as the automobile industry, also have influenced domestic and international energy policies. Energy wasteful countries such as the United States are among those who most actively support the energy industry and the oil-producing nations in opposing alternative energy sources and legislation to limit carbon emissions. In addition, U.S. military interests remain focused on the oil-rich Middle East. Depletion of these resources will tend only to heighten their value and increase political tensions. Despite these factors, global fossil fuel consumption continues to rise, as Figure 4–3 shows.

There are, in fact, many alternatives to the reliance on fossil fuel. But in the United States, recent Republican presidents Ronald Reagan (1981–1989) and George Bush (1989–1993) showed little inclination to support these alternatives. (Democratic President Bill Clinton (1993–   ), on the other hand, has been more supportive of alternative energies.) Other

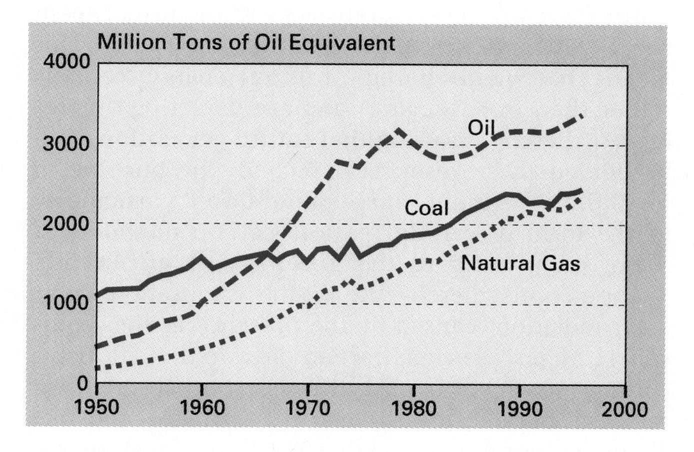

FIGURE 4–3 Global Fossil Fuel Use, 1950 to 2000

Source: *Vital Signs 1997* by Lester Brown et al. Copyright © 1997 by Worldwatch Institute. Worldwatch estimates based on DOE, BP, UN, PlanEcon. Reprinted by permission of Worldwatch Institute, Washington, DC.

sources of resistance to alternatives to petroleum involve public attitudes such as the high value many Americans ascribe to owning a car. Another obstacle has been that the costs of alternative energies are generally higher at present than costs of "traditional" energies.

But with continued research and development, alternative sources are rapidly becoming competitive in terms of price. One such alternative is nuclear power. Many national governments, scientific associations, and members of the existing energy industries have promoted nuclear energy. In the United States, nuclear power industries have advertised it as "clean" compared to coal, because nuclear power emits no carbon wastes. But on the downside, fission reactors produce deadly radioactive waste material that not only sickens and kills but also causes genetic damage and sterility in people and animals. Such wastes remain hazardous, in some cases, for tens of thousands of years. Public fears of these waste products, as well as of devastating nuclear accidents, such as the 1986 disaster at Chernobyl (in the former Soviet Union), have led to a virtual moratorium on new nuclear installations, except in a few countries, including France (Kane, 1996). An alternative form of nuclear energy, involving an entirely different nuclear process, is fusion. Although clean and potentially abundant, by most reports it has not yet proven to be practical.

One of the inherent problems of any form of nuclear power is that dealing with it is highly technical; consequently, nuclear power can be (and is, at present) monopolized in the same way that petroleum and coal have been. In fact the concentration of its control in the hands of corporations, governments, and a few countries may account for the strong support that nuclear power has enjoyed over the decades. This situation indicates another serious disadvantage of nuclear power as an alternative technology, especially in the Third World, where the technical expertise and capital needed to invest in its operation are less available than in the more developed nations.

More feasible and less controversial forms of alternative energy are solar and wind power. These two sources of power have been "taking off" in the last decade. A researcher for Worldwatch Institute, Hal Kane (1996), has referred to the "solar revolution" that has been taking place. As indicated in Figure 4–4, this revolution is facilitated by the falling price of solar power cells. The growth of both wind

The use of solar power has increased rapidly in the last decade, due to the falling price of solar power cells. Here, Niger villagers watch a solar-powered television.

and solar energy use is exponential when looked at from 1980 to the present. This growth has occurred despite resistance from powerful entities like the U.S. government and the automobile and energy industries. Wind and solar energy are virtually pollution free and sustainable; most areas of the world have abundant wind and solar energy waiting to be tapped. Indeed, use of wind energy is rising in many countries, as you can see from Figure 4–5.

Because solar and wind power are decentralized intermediate-scale systems of energy production, they work most efficiently when local communities, or even families, in some cases, have their own generating devices. Wind and solar energy also make sense for isolated Asian and African villagers. Developing countries that have not yet committed to the construction of the large energy grid systems (complex systems of energy that require wires and

FIGURE 4–4 Decline in Cost of Solar Energy

Source: *Vital Signs 1997* by Lester Brown et al. Copyright © 1997 by Worldwatch Institute. Reprinted by permission of Worldwatch Institute, Washington, DC.

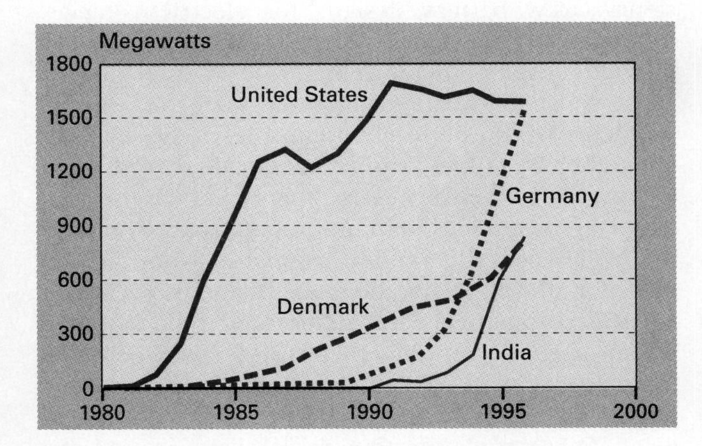

FIGURE 4–5 Wind-Generating Capacity: United States, Germany, Denmark, and India, 1980–1996

Source: *Vital Signs 1997* by Lester Brown et al. Copyright © 1997 by Worldwatch Institute. Reprinted by permission of Worldwatch Institute, Washington, DC.

booster stations) found in the developed world can move directly to these sources of energy. It also seems possible that a shift could be made within the developed nations to alternative energies without the loss of or great reduction in their rich living standards (Kane, 1996).

The generation of energy is only part of the solution to the energy problem. Efficient use is equally vital. By far the majority of the energy we use in producing and consuming goods is wasted. New technological developments such as advanced superconductors (which enable electricity to flow with no loss of energy) could improve the energy efficiency of offices by 75 to 80 percent (Peterson, 1994). By using such newer technologies, for example, a business could be run for four days on the energy it now requires in one day. Superconductors are based on the holistic or "cooperative" behavior of electrons that literally "bypass" the usual resistance that leads to energy lost as heat. Superconduction was first discovered at near absolute zero temperatures. Attaining such low temperatures is difficult and expensive, which makes the use of superconductors impractical for most ordinary uses like dishwashers or televisions. But superconductors that can operate at room temperatures are fast approaching reality; when this actually occurs, it could mean an immense leap in energy efficiency.

New engine designs and new engine materials are also currently being explored. Several alternatives to gasoline engines are being developed, while electrical automobiles are reaching higher levels of proficiency. New battery designs for electric vehicles, hydrogen fuel cells, and natural gas may be used to provide power in future vehicles.

The most radical possible solution to our energy problems would be to eliminate fuel as we know it altogether by tapping into what is called zero-point energy, the immensely dense energy known through quantum mechanics to fill up "empty space" (what is left over when you remove all matter from a given place, or, alternatively, the space that exists between particles of matter). According to physicist David Bohm, a cubic centimeter of empty space contains more energy than does all the matter in the universe (Petersen, 1994). Former U.S. astronaut and scientist Brian O'Leary claims that researchers around the world have demonstrated the ability to tap this vast, nearly infinite energy reserve (O'Leary, 1996).

The impact of zero-point energy on society and the future of humankind may outweigh just about any other change in the field of energy research. The zero-point energy generator would eliminate the need for fuels altogether, and it could easily free the masses of people from dependency upon corporations and governments to meet their energy needs. Such a generator would of course also eliminate our reliance on environmentally hazardous sources of energy such as fossil and nuclear fuels. The power monopolies of the developed world, the petroleum-rich countries, and those industries that have "mastered" nuclear technologies could dissolve overnight.

In Japan, a currently energy-poor country, there is support for the work of Shiuji Inomata, a highly respected senior research scientist at the Ministry of International Trade and Industry, or MITI (O'Leary, 1996). The Toshiba Corporation has contributed $2 million to help Inomata develop his prototype zero-point energy generator. Such explorations are not limited to one country. In India, Paramahansa Tewari, who is both a government official and a respected scientist, is currently operating a large-scale generator of zero-point energy that he calls a "space power generator" (O'Leary, 1996).

Information Technology

The technology that is currently transforming social life and the way we think about ourselves and the world most directly is the computer. Fierce debates will probably continue for some time about the impact of computers on employment, and about the nature and quality of the jobs that people will have in a world dominated by computers. Whether the computer will create more jobs than it eliminates is at present an open question. Still, a crystal ball is not required to realize that the answer depends largely on whose values and interests shape present and future choices. The democratic participation of employees and of citizens in these decisions is critical if we are to counteract the effect that the concentration of power in the hands of huge multinational corporations and First World nations may have on the elimination of jobs.

The quality and content of work and work relationships are also related to the use of computers. Some argue that the long-range trend of capitalism has been to replace the worker's thoughts, choices, and practical wisdom with management-controlled technological processes. Computers can and do aid management in accomplishing such an end. But a study of 24 U.S. plants using computer-controlled manufacturing showed that the majority had upgraded workers' skill levels, increased workers' flexibility and commitment to the job, and improved relationships between management and unions. The introduction of computers apparently redistributes skills more often than it replaces them. This research suggests that computers have the capacity to enrich jobs and to give workers more influence as well as more flexibility about when and where they work (Barbour, 1993).

How will information technology change the distribution of power in businesses and corporations? Control of information and knowledge has always been one source of management power; there will probably be considerable resistance to sharing information and knowledge with those lower in the workplace hierarchy. The first computers were large devices that centralized information and groups of experts. Today's information technology, in contrast, involves networks of small personal computers that can be most effectively used in flexible and decentralized ways. Too much top-down control will tend to interfere with the creativity, efficiency, and effectiveness of the new technology. If such a situation develops, it may hamper a corporation's ability to adapt to the rapid changes in today's economy (Peters, 1987). Efforts to use computers more creatively may also lead to new approaches to management and decision making that will reduce hierarchical structures (Senge, 1990). However, such changes will have to be introduced within the context of strong managerial power, which will be difficult.

Direct voting by citizens made possible by cable hookups and computers has been proposed as one contribution that information technology can make to the political process. But someone will still have to define issues and choices, and these can be subtly manipulated. Citizens may be uninformed, deceived, and easily swayed by emotional factors during the process. Many poor people will not have access to the channels of information necessary to register their opinions. Voting may be monitored by "Big Brother," and so forth.

Professor of history and critic of contemporary culture Theodore Roszak (1994) notes that for the average citizen desirous of more democratic participation and discussion, Citizen Band radio offers an even better means of achieving this goal than do computer hookups. Yet that has not been the use to which CB radio has been put. To some extent, the computer has been used to connect citizen interest groups, not only across the country but also around the globe. Such a use is particularly vital for environmental groups and/or groups concerned with empowering Third World people who are otherwise isolated. Connecting these groups to each other and to the peoples of the Third World may turn out to be a far more effective and democratic use of computer technology than direct voting. Such connections can be two- or three-way exchanges of information and services. But of course the peoples of the Third World would have to gain greater access to computers. Still, having said this, we need to point out that there is also a potential political "downside" to computers—they may allow governments or other groups to engage in surveillance and to compile information about citizens and citizen groups for the purposes of manipulating them, undermining their power, or otherwise harming or deterring them.

Information and information technology have been monopolized by the developed world for some time, but that too is changing. In 1984 Brazil banned the import of computers. Less than 10 years later, 270 Brazilian companies had entered the computer business (Barbour, 1993). This situation is obviously not typical of Third World countries, but it does suggest what is possible in some cases. A report made in 1987 to the UN by a commission to study environment and development (called the Brundtland Report) maintained that microelectronics could facilitate sustainable development, and the International Labor Office (ILO) proposes the integration of computers with traditional methods of agriculture and production (Barbour, 1993). International agreements now make it possible for every nation to have orbital positions available if and when they have their own communication satellites on the principle that space is the common heritage of humankind.

Still, what is transmitted via much of the cable and satellite media is not the "common heritage of humankind," but largely Western commercial mass media fare. Beamed into Third World and tribal cultures, these programs sometimes have devastating effects. For example, television viewing among these peoples disrupts traditional patterns of transmitting culture from elder to younger generations and undermines the elders' authority (Macionis, 1996). Furthermore, the content of these messages replaces traditional values with the consumerism, moral relativism, and individual self-indulgence that abound in the Western media. Traditional people may have, if anything, less resistance to the persuasiveness of

CONTEMPORARY DISCUSSION

Information Technology

No reasonable person today denies the immense value that information technology has in contemporary life. Computers are indispensable in monitoring and modeling changes in the atmosphere caused by pollution, for example. The space program would be impossible without computers, as would be many forms of new medical technology. Information technology also has many business applications, including allowing increasingly sophisticated record keeping. Nevertheless, a lively dialogue is shaping up among those optimists who see information technology as a largely positive force and those less optimistic about it.

The Upside of the Information Age

We are essentially the first generation to live in the *information age*—a transformation of society and culture as great or greater than those wrought by the shift from nomadic hunting societies to agricultural societies and the onset of the industrial revolution. Today the most important new resource is "information" or "knowledge," which is different from other resources such as money or land because it is the one resource that can be increased by our sharing it. Power and influence will pass to those who possess this "social" resource. Already we see the impact of information technology on businesses, which are shifting from hierarchical structures to "flatter" structures based on the sharing of information among flexible work teams.

Access to global networks of information will probably enhance democracy. People who have access to information tend not to be easily manipulated, and the ability to communicate issues globally will help to focus public and professional opinion about the plight of groups previously exploited simply because they were isolated. In addition, increased access to technical, scientific, and medical information; to social and political skills; and to national and international markets will empower people around the globe. The net result of these ongoing changes is most likely to be enhanced participation and the formation, for the first time, of a truly worldwide community.

Moreover, information technology and the perspectives it generates are altering our assumptions about the very nature of reality. Many sciences are finding that the concept of "information" is necessary to explain the organization of natural systems (a system is a set of interacting components that produces an overall effect, i.e., that act as a "whole") and this recognition is leading to the "dematerialization" of our worldviews, according to some observers. Thus we think less and less about the material components of systems and look more and more to the information content and processes of those systems. Matter and energy flow into and out of living organisms at a rapid rate, yet they maintain their stability and basic structure because of information processes, for example. Perhaps the following example will make this clear. After seven years *all* of the matter and energy in a human body has been replaced (while many organs and tissues replace themselves in a matter of months or even days). Yet if you meet a friend you haven't seen for seven years, you can still recognize her because her body has a genetic information "blueprint." This blueprint is a set of instructions (information) that directs the matter and energy flowing into and out of her body, so that from day to day and year to year, her body and face continue to display a familiar pattern. Even our economic production seems dematerialized because of the new reliance on information, and its wider and faster spread has resulted in our using fewer materials to meet our needs. Increasingly, we rely on information to serve this purpose. Finally, our reexamination of the nature of reality and of the mind and of the relationship between them has led to the recent introduction into our language of terms like "cyberspace" and "virtual reality." New concepts like these themselves open up new conceptual possibilities and stimulate creativity. We are more able to think in terms of dynamic systems (e.g., living organisms or human groups, whose present activity is based in part on their own past activity; thus, they change over time in response to their own activity), which is precisely what the "real" world is all about.

The Downside of the Information Age

People cannot eat, wear, or drive information. Information technology will not enable us to transcend our need for basic resources, no matter how valuable information or knowledge becomes. Moreover, some applications of information technology (e.g., genetically engineered grains) are not delivering all that they promised in areas of basic needs. In addition, power has not shifted from transnational corporations and the developed societies to smaller companies and less developed societies; nor does it show signs of doing so in the near future. Besides, the sorts of knowledge that are truly useful in the world require extensive university education and access to scientific research, communication skills, and languages, which are not generally available to most of the world's people. Indeed, the reduction in the need for raw materials in this "information age" will have devastating effects on poor countries that depend almost entirely on the export of one or two natural resources.

Moreover, within the developed world, the chief impact of information technology may be the elimination and deskilling of jobs. Mental functions and decision making that used to require human beings are now routinely taken over by machines, reducing even the little mental skill once necessary. Just as the demand for factory labor has been greatly reduced by the introduction of "smart" machines, clerical and service (e.g., health care aides, fast-food attendants) jobs continue to decrease, with no new types of work in sight to absorb those seeking jobs. To whose advantage is it to deskill or eliminate jobs? In such a situation, owners and managers will benefit by gaining their share of higher profits engendered by the smaller labor force needed to produce and sell products. The future will bring relatively few jobs, and even those few new jobs created will require high levels of education and mental skills. The majority of people will thus become an "information proletariat," a group lacking the information skills and knowledge base necessary for success in contemporary society. In addition, because most people in developing nations will lack access to information technology and to information networks altogether, the new technology will only reinforce the growing gap between many of these nations and the developed world.

The much-hyped Internet will be used chiefly for the trivial pursuit of pleasure. It is already being exploited by commercial interests, not to mention pornographers and others of questionable motives. The suggestion of some that being "online" will encourage grassroots democracy is not likely to be realized. Although, obviously, some people will make good use of the Internet to expand grassroots democracy, others will use it to indulge in escapist behavior.

Indeed, the concepts of the new information sciences and technology tend to debase rather than to elevate the human spirit by confusing knowledge and meaning with information and information processing, and with the more creative process called thinking. Further, the new information sciences and technology confuse the rather depersonalized and often dishonest interactions via the computer with true human communication. In face-to-face settings, and even over the telephone, we reveal a great deal of our identity and social status—age, sex, and race—and to an extent display our intentions. These important social markers are absent when we use electronic communications in which persons can easily misrepresent who and what they are by disguising their identity. The Internet makes it much easier to manipulate or exploit others (e.g., adults have used the Internet to seduce children). Indeed, what is real may come to be confused with the computer-enhanced fantasy of "virtual reality." The effects on human identity (at least for some people) may be unfortunate, leading to greater isolation and mental difficulties.

◇ **For Critical Thought** 1. What assumptions do the opponents in this debate hold? 2. What are the human rights issues raised by this debate? 3. What are some of the upsides of the information age? The downsides? 4. How may it be possible to resolve the controversy expressed in this debate?

these media than do the members of the developed countries.

Other issues about the effects of computers focus on the availability of and access to information, as well as its content and quality. When access to databases and information networks requires a fee, information is available only to those who can afford it. When access is too available, or simply free as a public service, the quality of the information and communications may tend to become degraded, as some critics of the Internet, the leading public access computer network, suggest (Stoll, 1995). The promise of an "information superhighway" will probably never be fully realized for many reasons. The main reasons are seemingly unresolvable issues of property rights over information and ideas and lack of control over the quality of what is available. Moreover, most books and journals will never be placed on computers, and most readers of books and journals will probably never want them to be, mainly because people like and find it convenient to hold a book or magazine in their hands. A particularly frequent problem may turn out to be the online traffic jams that result as the participation of people in the network increases (Stoll, 1995). The box, "Contemporary Discussion: Information Technology," debates the upside and downside of the new information technology.

Science, Technology, and Worldviews

Many of our present ideas about medicine, nature, human nature, and most other large issues facing human beings and the life of this planet have been deeply influenced by the lingering effects of the mechanistic worldview. Despite the emerging worldview engendered by the information revolution, the mechanistic perspective continues to influence how we try to deal with the problems that face us. For example, we still generally believe that if a little bit of a pesticide or an antibiotic is good, a lot more is even better. This type of linear thinking, which assumes that each additional input will give the same output, is an aspect of mechanistic thinking. But linear thinking does not work when you are dealing with nonlinear systems, and most of the natural and social reality we have discovered in this century is nonlinear. Ironically, the science of physics itself dealt the fatal blow to simple mechanistic thought in the early days of this century when the new physics, consisting of relativity theory and quantum mechanics, was developed. One of the founders of quantum mechanics, German physicist Werner Heisenberg (1901–1976), said that quantum mechanics radically challenged the old worldview in the following ways (Moore, 1994):

1. Quantum mechanics refutes the materialism that has characterized science since the days of Newton. Today we can no longer think of the world as comprised of solid bits of matter. Rather, the reality that underlies observable physical properties is a field of probability, not a collection of things. What this means is that the "objects" studied by quantum physicists are not objects at all in our everyday sense of the word. They are events that exhibit a certain likelihood of occurrence depending on how researchers choose to probe the world. The quantum word can be described, then, as a field composed of nothing more than overlapping probabilities, or potentialities, of manifestation.
2. Quantum mechanics shows that there are no separate things at all. There exists one unified whole; everything that seems to exist is a manifestation of that one unity. Causality and determinism are no longer adequate explanations of reality. Complete predictability and complete control are not even remotely possible.
3. The human observer plays an essential role in the universe as we know it. The mind must once more be taken seriously in our understanding of the natural world.

Perhaps developed nations overvalue physics as a source of new ideas and perspectives, especially today. The biological sciences, psychology, and sociology, as well as philosophical inquiry, have, after all, made equally important contributions to emerging perspectives. But the prestige of physics in the popular mind and among academics has given physicists great authority in the eyes of many people. This focus allows us to sometimes forget that one of the most pervasive influences that has changed the way people view and talk about their world has been the impact of technology. For example, in the nineteenth century steam engines and electromagnetic devices gave rise to ideas of energy, entropy (the inevitable decrease in energy available to do work), and force fields (a force field is a region of space throughout which the force produced by a single agent, such as an electric current, is operative) that eventually culminated in the proof by German-American physicist Albert Einstein (1879–1955) that mass and energy could be converted into each other. Einstein's discovery led to the realizations that "everything is energy" and that nonmaterial fields govern the behavior of material objects. But the meaning of matter has since radically changed; matter itself has become "dematerialized."

Chaos Theory

In the last few decades new developments in the physical sciences and related mathematical concepts have emerged that may have as much revolutionary import as have quantum mechanics. Sometimes called "chaos theory," new scientific models of complexity, or of the dynamic behavior of nonlinear systems, have demonstrated the existence of previously unsuspected forms of order (Hayles, 1990; Briggs and Peat, 1989; Gleick, 1987). Although called chaos theory, these developments deal with order as much as they do with chaos. Most, if not all, "real world" systems are nonlinear in that their actions feed back on the system itself. This effect could be the wear and tear on an automobile, the growth of a population of bacteria or humans, or even a conversation between you and your best friend. What happens at each point in the process has an ongoing effect on the process as it unfolds that is more than merely cumulative. Scientists have shown repeatedly that systems seemingly in stable order one moment can suddenly and without warning enter into unpredictable and seemingly random (chaotic) behavior. This change occurs, for example, when airplane wings suddenly shear off, a tornado appears on the edge of a rainstorm, a freight ship suddenly lists and capsizes, or a person's heart goes into random motion called fibrillation and he or she dies. What seems incredible to observers is that an increment of change at one moment can have no apparent effect on the stability of a system, but the same increment of change at another moment (due to feedback effects) can push the system over an invisible rim of stability into chaotic behavior. Even more remarkably, it has been found that the boundaries of stability and instability correspond to a new form of mathematical model called a fractal.

Scientists have also discovered that out of a period of chaotic behavior may emerge a new order within the system that had not been there previously. Chaos, in other words, emerges from order and order from chaos (Briggs and Peat, 1989). The new emerging order enables the system to deal with a higher level of stress than did the previous order. This reorganization is holistic, involving the system as a whole. Such discoveries demonstrate the "self-organizing" capacity of some nonlinear systems (Waldrop, 1992; Prigogine and Stengers, 1984). These developments may give new insights into the evolution of systems, including ecosystems and organisms, society and culture, perhaps consciousness itself. Some insights already emerging from chaos theory and nonlinear systems include the following:

Scientists have shown that systems in stable order one moment can suddenly and without warning enter into unpredictable and seemingly random (chaotic) behavior. This type of change occurs, for example, when a tornado appears on the edge of a rainstorm.

1. Systems behave as wholes.
2. Chaos and stability are different phases of a single system.

3. A mathematical order underlies patterns of chaos.
4. Despite the mathematical pattern governing periods of chaos, during chaotic periods the actual behavior of the system from moment to moment is unpredictable and uncontrollable.
5. There are points of instability at which very small changes can have large and unpredictable effects.
6. New order can emerge out of chaos.
7. Many nonlinear systems are self-organizing.

How does chaos theory affect society both nationally and globally? If we properly understand the notions of chaos, dependency on top-down control in order to gain technological control of nature and to engineer society must fail. Systems have their own internal and dynamic process of growth, self-maintenance, and change.

The Information Model

Scientist Stephen L. Talbott (1995) lists the following four points as key aspects of the emerging *information model* of the world:

1. "Information" is quickly replacing "matter" (and energy and force) as the central topic of scientific interest.
2. The increasingly blurred distinction between subject and object, knower and known, is fundamental to the information model. This blurring is especially true in the field of virtual reality. Participants in virtual reality use their minds to generate the world they interact with. Thus, the mind creates the experienced (virtual) world to which it then responds as if that world were reality.
3. Software evolves independently of hardware. In the material and Darwinian universe, the evolution of intelligence, consciousness, and culture depended on the prior evolution of brains—the equivalent of hardware. Today, however, more and more people are beginning to recognize, via the information-processing industry, that there can be nonmaterial evolution that does not depend on material evolution.
4. Intelligent patterns may be transferred from one computer to another without the transfer of any actual matter. Informational software is independent of hardware. Thus, mind is as real as matter.

These four ideas emerging from information technology are closely related to the three effects of quantum mechanics described by Heisenberg listed earlier in the chapter. In addition, information technology is having or probably will have other effects on our sense of reality. For example, wealth and power will depend increasingly on the possession of knowledge and symbols (intellectual property), not on the control of production of material goods as in the past. Intellectual property in the form of information has the potential to become so valuable that conflict over its control seems probable.

Impact of Social Sciences on Models of Reality. Although often overlooked in discussions of science, culture, and society, throughout the modern and postmodern eras the social and psychological sciences have played a key role in influencing how we perceive and participate in society. It was the social sciences that originally lent support to the idea of progress and offered the hope of creating rational social institutions. The early political economists, including both advocates of the free market and socialists, believed in the rationality of society and the eventuality of progress. They also believed in what was considered the dominant institution of modern society—the economy. Economics, a social science, is the "science" most often consulted by governments in their search for workable policies. This fact may seem odd, partially because economists rely upon abstract mathematical models that are seldom empirically tested (Etzioni, 1988). When tested with actual government policies, these economic models frequently fail. In addition, like other scientists, economists often disagree strenuously over interpretations and courses of action. Still, economists are consulted in virtually all policy decisions of governments around the world. Indeed, to be "rational" and "realistic" is to rely on what economists tell us.

The social sciences have influenced popular culture as well. Contemporary American popular culture has been pervaded by psychological ideas, so much so that people now speak of "psychobabble," the frequent and loose use of pseudopsychological terms in everyday life. In other parts of the world, such as Latin America or eastern Europe, we often find concepts drawn from Marxist social theory embedded in the social fabric. To call a person "bourgeois" is a common insult in such contexts.

One of the most important and significant developments in the social sciences in recent decades was the articulation of the idea of the social construction of reality, a concept we introduced in Chapter 1. The expression was first coined by sociologists Peter Berger and Thomas Luckmann in a book with that title published in 1966. At about the same time historian and philosopher of science Thomas Kuhn published *The Structure of Scientific Revolutions* (1962), in which he suggested that even the physical sciences were strongly affected by social forces.

Kuhn showed that when the scientific community operates with a shared model, called a paradigm, it produces cumulative research that apparently constitutes scientific progress. Under these conditions we have "normal science," in which each researcher builds upon what previous scientists have accomplished, extending the work by small increments. Kuhn describes this kind of science as "puzzle solving." But every so often science encounters anomalies that cannot be solved by standard puzzle-solving procedures. Older, established scientists struggle to resolve these anomalies without seriously changing the scientific paradigms on which they have staked their careers and reputations. Younger scientists with less at stake in defending the old paradigm and much to gain by creating new models make bold leaps, thereby beginning a paradigm shift to which there is tremendous resistance. The new ideas are rejected as nonsense, heresy that is unsupported by evidence. But eventually the older generation of scientists retire and die. By implying that even the "progress" of the natural sciences is a function of social and political factors, Kuhn reinforced the idea that all reality is socially constructed. All worldviews and beliefs about cultural progress are politically motivated and serve the interests of the groups holding them.

These ideas—that reality is a social construct serving political ends, that all views about reality are relative, and that no consensus is possible—generally characterize what has come to be called postmodern culture. Postmodernists examine written and spoken "texts" to show how nothing has meaning in itself apart from its context and how all contexts are socially and politically self-serving. This form of postmodernism, called *deconstruction*, involves the application of modern assumptions, the reduction of human action and communication—of meaning—to psychological and social constructs. No meaning can remain valid in the face of this method, except, paradoxically, the assumptions on which the method itself rests.

Today a small but significant group of thinkers are trying to reconcile the diverse cultural developments we have described. On the one hand they want to extend and explore the implications of some of the developments in the natural sciences, as well as developments in the study of consciousness, body/mind interactions in health, and other new approaches. On the other hand, they acknowledge that "reality" is not a given—different cultures and different periods of history, as Berger (1979) said, exhibit different structures of consciousness. This diverse group of thinkers and practitioners may be representative of the first phase of an emerging *integral culture* (Ray, 1996). Some attempts are in fact being made to describe what the integration of modern science and social science—those cutting-edge developments in fields of science and technology—with more traditional points of view and practices might look like. Physicist David Ray Griffin (1989) speaks of "postmodern organicism," whereas social scientist Charlene Spretnak (1997) calls it "ecological postmodernism." Neither of these formulations intends to reduce culture to biological dimensions, although the names chosen may suggest this. To reduce culture to biology is a tactic of some modern schools of thought but would not be appropriate for the sort of integration we are describing.

Spretnak maintains that although modern thought attempted to reduce the world to simple mechanical components, postmodernism has asserted that the "world," at least insofar as it is accessible to us, is nothing more than the stories we construct about it. In contrast to both sets of ideas, ecological postmodernism argues that there is a self-generating and self-organizing cosmological process, of which human thought and action are essential aspects. The modern world sought to control nature and the human body out of a deep mistrust and fear of their reality. The postmodernists saw this as impossible, because the only "realities" are our diverse cultural views about "nature" and the "body." We never experience either nature or the body directly, according to postmodernist thought; we experience only our interpretation of them.

But ecological postmodernism holds that nature and the body are neither machines (apart from us) nor merely our ideas about them. Rather, nature and the body are intelligent, self-organizing systems that include human culture and human consciousness in interaction with biophysical components. We can, moreover, "trust" these systems. In modernism, the primary truth was universal, revealed by the scientific method. Postmodernism denied the universal and upheld the particular (we each have our own truth). According to Spretnak, ecological postmodernism holds that truth is to be found in the particular in context.

In Chapter 3 we called this embedded particularism. Any expression of truth is particular and occurs in a limited context, but knowing these limitations does not render this "truth" untrue. We can actually acquire a deeper and more comprehensive grasp of truth by understanding it from multiple contexts. In fact, the more profound the truth, the more valuable it is to see it from multiple perspectives, even when they may be incompatible and contradictory. This is an idea that makes many people very uneasy because it seems to make things extremely complex. Yet there has always been difficulty applying laboratory findings to the real world, because the laboratory context and the "real world" context are quite different.

People are most uncomfortable in regard to religious truths. But here Spretnak's ideas seem especially useful. The profoundest thinkers in every religious tradition have acknowledged that the ultimate source of truth is itself a mystery. In modernist thinking the ideal world and society were an orderly whole organized from the top down in which every part found its appropriate functional niche. Postmodernism sees nothing but fragmentation, separateness, and difference. Ecological postmodernism also sees no hierarchy, no possibility of top-down control, but what it does see is an organic process in which unity continually emerges out of diversity.

One conclusion that can be drawn from our discussion is that we cannot take for granted the views held in the past. Science and technology continue to confront us with new challenges. The academic world in general struggles to make sense of what is going on and to then teach it to others. In fields like medicine, new alternatives have emerged that call into question older assumptions about health and illness and the role of the patient and his or her physician in personal well-being. There are no easy answers. We cannot simply rely upon the experts, especially when the experts do not agree or when the choices they offer are unacceptable or too new even to assess.

Assessing the Situation: Science, Technology, and the Future

Originally, science held out the hope that we could know the physical world with certainty. Such a construct made science appear superior to both religion and philosophy. Science also held the promise that humankind could master and control natural forces. On the basis of these claims, scientists assumed authority to define human nature and our place in the world. No contemporary philosopher of science would now claim that scientific knowledge is certain. Today the mastery and control of nature also seem an idle hope. The philosophy of mechanistic materialism at the root of both of these ideals lies in shambles because twentieth-century science and our understanding of its place in culture lend little or no support to it. This fact is often not recognized, even by many scientists, who still embrace some version of materialism and the mechanistic worldview. Despite this, modern science (and technology) is helping to redefine both our identity as a species and our relationship to nature. We have discussed how developments in the sciences such as quantum mechanics, chaos theory, information technology, and the applications of social science concepts to culture are reshaping some of our basic assumptions.

Modern culture involves a split between the realm of values (the subjective) and the realm of facts (the objective). More accurately, this split involves the idea that whereas our measurements and observations of the physical world can be socially validated, and therefore shared, our judgments about values cannot. Postmodern thinking acknowledges that we cannot really speak of "objective" facts because we cannot share the point of view of an object. But we can speak of *intersubjective* truths, or those truths that can be validated, and so shared, by others. As we discussed in Chapter 3, religious experience—or any experience—becomes reality when it is socially shared. The instrumental rationality of science and technology claims that we can agree upon the most efficient (rational) means to achieve our goals but cannot agree upon what goals are worth pursuing. But we have seen in Chapters 2 and 3 that in relation to human rights and religion, this claim is not altogether true. There is more convergence among societies about basic values than extreme relativists would ever guess. The ability of religiously and culturally distinct groups to come together, to recognize common ground, and to build the basis for collaboration to solve many of the world's problems is increasingly demonstrated, as we discussed in Chapters 1 and 2. This fact suggests the possibility of the convergence of value judgments among persons even when they are members of diverse cultures. Given that scientists often disagree over interpretations of their data and theories, there may be only minimal distinctions between judgments in the realm of value and that of fact.

In discussions about the problems that science and technology seem to create for society, the concept of cultural lag (Ogburn, 1964) is often cited. **Cultural lag** refers to the fact that some aspects of culture (science and technology in particular) change rapidly, whereas other parts of culture (especially values and customs) lag behind, causing considerable social stress. Consider, for example, how our advanced life-support technology has created much uncertainty about when it is proper to "pull the plug" and allow a person to die naturally. The cultural lag thesis seems to suggest that values and social norms (mores) are a sort of brake on forward progress. Social scientists, too, have generally tended to accept the inevitability of scientific "progress" and the need for society to adjust its (somewhat stodgy) thinking accordingly. But a good deal of the cultural lag in our society has been due to a social structure in which those who are developing technology are guided by instrumental rationality in the interests of profit, power, and scientific recognition. This phenomenon has been coupled with the fact that moral or ethical judgments have been rendered somewhat less effective in modern societies because they have been relegated to secondary institutions like religion (in many societies), or to less important decision-making bodies ("ethics committees") within more powerful organizations. Some of the cultural lag in our society has been caused by the tendency for many of the assumptions of the mechanistic worldview to remain, even though the most advanced science of our day has shown them to be obsolete. We discuss some examples of these obsolete but troublesome assumptions next.

Many undesirable effects of science and technology can be traced to four mechanistic assumptions about nature. The first assumption, *linearity,* is the idea that if a little of something is good, more will be that much better. For example, the overuse of pesticides and antibiotics (see Chapter 10) has led to results that are the exact opposite of those intended because linear thinking conflicted with the nonlinear aspects of natural systems. A second assumption, *separability,* holds that the cosmos is composed of distinct and separate parts that can be dealt with without affecting the whole. For example, we use an antibiotic to kill an isolated bacterium and somehow do not expect it to affect other bacteria in our body or in the environment. A third assumption, *reversibility,* is the notion that we can undo anything that we can do. For example, we believe that we can pollute the environment because eventually we will be able to clean it up. But we cannot in fact reverse the extinction of species or the depletion of fossil fuels. The fourth assumption, *uniformity,* is the belief that sameness is good. This belief underlies mass production and mass education, both of which aim to produce an endless stream of identical products. The concept of uniformity has been used to justify humankind's destruction of other species, as well as racial and cultural imperialism, both of which are attempts to eliminate all who are not just like us. The value placed on uniformity is also frequently supported by propaganda that argues that everything is simply a matter of "survival of the fittest." But nature prefers variety, and survival demands not uniformity but diversity. Many scientific innovations of the twentieth century described earlier (quantum mechanics, chaos theory) recognize assumptions that are direct opposites of these four mechanistic assumptions about nature: nonlinearity, nonseparability (or interconnectedness), irreversibility, and diversity.

The science and technology of today raise more and more difficult questions. Most people are at a loss to know what to make of them. For example, one difficult issue is who owns the intellectual property rights over genetic information. Companies and university research laboratories in the United States and other advanced industrial societies have begun scouring the world for genetic information and other biological resources (as they appear in animals and plants) believed to have potential applications in medicine and industry. But because so many of the animal and plant species on this planet are found in tropical rain forests, tensions have arisen between the industrialized nations with the know-how to exploit the information and the nations where the rain forests are. The advanced industrial nations claim that they should have rights to the information that they gather, whereas the host nations claim that since it is their rain forest and their species, they too should have some rights.

But the situation gets even stickier. Because this information is contained in organisms, including human beings, it raises the issue of "property." Already genetic codes of human beings have been collected and stored in computer data banks. Who owns *your* genetic information? You may think you do, and at present probably nobody else does. However, your genetic code can be extracted from one single cell of your body (including blood cells) and you lose millions of cells a day without noticing it. At present the law doesn't give you exclusive rights to your own genetic information, to the cells of your body, or to the enzymes and other products of your cells. Now and in the future increasing use will be made of biological organisms and the information contained in them. It will be done for profit. Shouldn't a person at least get some compensation for contributing his or her genetic information to a profit-making venture? You did not create your genetic information, but neither did those who might make use of it. If it were land or minerals that you owned, you would still have rights to them even though you didn't create them.

As you can see, the discoveries and developments of contemporary science have presented us with potential problems, which, partly because of their newness, are particularly difficult for our society to resolve at present. As this book goes to press, the question of whether we should (and whether we will) clone human beings is being debated. Cloning consists of making an exact biological copy of an organism by using that organism's DNA (genetic information) to form a new organism. A clone would be an exact copy of you (genetically speaking), based on inserting your genetic data directly into a host cell that would then grow into a human being. The value-free instrumental approach of science has led some in the scientific community to contend that if we can make clones, we might as well do it. Others have argued that the scientific community and other interested and responsible parties need to assess the situation and come to an agreed-upon set of ethics governing this and other similar potential situations. The fear is that the impact of any cloning on society will be devastating. Already we battle over abortion, surrogate motherhood (a woman carrying another woman's egg to full term), and prolonging life by artificial means. Opponents of cloning argue that as a society we are not ready for the complications that cloning will bring.

Throughout modern times our technical ability, what we *can* do, has far outrun our cultural agreement about what we *should* do. In fact, today no way exists to prevent someone, somewhere, from cloning human beings should it prove possible to do so. Yet the unanswered questions are staggering. Consider the following: Assuming that you are not yourself a clone, who would own your clone and what would the clone be used for? Suppose that you have a rare blood type or that your body produces a valuable enzyme. Your clone could be used to make money from those rare substances. Or a clone's organs could be harvested, and you might be the principal recipient of those transplants. Of course, the clone would have been produced in a laboratory by the government, a university, or a large corporation, making it possible that you would not have a say about where those organs go, which brings us back to the question of who owns the clone.

So far we have spoken of the clone as an "it." Yet a clone would be a human being. Who then are its parents? As it is a copy of you, it has received your parents' genes. Biologically, it is your parents' child and so stands to inherit their money and property. As the rich may want to clone themselves for the purpose of organ donation to prolong their lives, the problem of the inheritance of their fortunes may become especially problematic. Suppose, though, that the clone has come about entirely from your cells, by your choice. So in a sense you are its parent. If a fertilized egg is raised in the womb of a surrogate mother, in what sense is she also its parent? We haven't yet figured that one out. If you are a woman, your clone may have matured in your womb. In this case you can sort of give birth to yourself. Would that definitely make you the parent of the clone, entitled to its inheritance? But what about the lab technicians or the university or the corporation whose technology has made it all possible? Do they have any claims to parenthood?

From the point of view of the clone, "it" will presumably have thoughts and feelings of its own. What would be the psychological effect on those raised with the knowledge that they are clones and carbon copies? Would your clone be willing to give you its organs, if that is what you wanted it for? Presumably it would have human rights and its rights would be equal to yours.

For some people, an especially acute issue is whether or not a clone would have a soul. This issue of human identity is of great concern to religious people. The possibility of a human being cloned in a laboratory presents difficulties for those who believe in a unique individual human soul. The choice is that either a clone, as a living conscious human being, has no soul or that God is "forced" to create a soul for a human being who was not produced in the way God presumably intended. Either of these ways of thought may be intolerable for many. If a conscious human being can exist without a soul, how do I know that I have a soul? Or, if cloning is against the will of God, how can he be forced to go along with this and make a soul to fit the clone? If cloning is not against the will of God, why isn't it, since it is such a problem for human beings? (This issue may present less of a dilemma for those such as the Buddhists who do not believe in an individual soul.) All these issues and others demonstrate cultural lag.

We have seen that contemporary science-driven technology and technology-driven science are fairly recent inventions, making unprecedented powers available to human beings. At present this power is held by a few—among others, multinational corporations and the military. Throughout this book we will examine the consequences of this concentration of power. In medicine, agriculture, manufacturing, and warfare, new technologies are introduced and hailed as the cutting edge of progress. Often technological innovations bring positive effects, but they also can disempower local groups, undermine traditional communities, wreak havoc on natural systems, and shift power to fewer and fewer hands. This is true in developing countries, but as we saw with the possibility of cloning, some technological developments threaten to disrupt even those societies that have so far absorbed much technological change.

One encouraging fact is that alternative technologies exist and that some are being developed in scientific laboratories around the world. There is often little financial support and much resistance to these alternatives. Alternative technologies threaten both existing power arrangements and deeply held assumptions. Some of the alternative technologies have been in use for hundreds, if not thousands, of years and have been thoroughly "field tested" in traditional and tribal settings. These are traditional techniques embedded within the technology practices of non-Western and nonmodern societies. Preindustrial forms of food production are far more energy efficient and make use of natural processes that maintain ecological communities of diverse species. These forms of food production require community cooperation and involve complicated property rights as well as traditional knowledge and skills. They are the property and heritage of these communities, whose rights are threatened on at least two levels. As communities, they stand to be destroyed as their technology practices are uprooted and replaced by those of others. Such a situation involves violations of the third generation of human rights, that is, the rights of collectivities. In other cases, their property rights may be violated by those who take over local technologies, such as medicinal substances, for the private profit of outsiders.

A major issue today is clearly which technology, or better, *whose* technology will prevail in a given situation. The large-scale, high-tech, science-rich, and capital-intensive technologies sponsored by corporations and modernizing forces around the world are designed to eliminate workers and ignore local conditions of culture and ecology in the interests of enforcing a centrally controlled uniformity. Traditional and tribal technologies are rich with information about the local setting, embody local values and ways of life, and are generally more respectful of nature and more sustainable over the long haul. They tend, therefore, to empower local people and respect their "right" to maintain a distinct way of life.

SUMMARY

1. **Technology** is the systematic application of ideas in order to produce a desired outcome by manipulating the material world.
2. Technological optimists accept the changes brought about by modern technology as beneficial. Technological pessimists argue that technology has generated a host of problems that are unsolvable by technological means.
3. Pessimists tend to accept some version of the **technological imperative,** the belief that technology will follow a set course because of an inner necessity and, therefore, that human

beings can do little to alter this course. **Technological determinism** is the idea that technology is an independent cause of social, cultural, and psychological patterns.

4. **Science** refers to the systematic attempt to explain any realm of human experience, including nature, society, and human mental processes, by methods that can be replicated and that lead to shared knowledge.
5. During the latter half of the 1800s in the United States, corporations rather than inventors gained ownership and control of patents and valuable ideas. Corporate research and development laboratories emerged at the beginning of this century as the most important social force behind technological innovation.
6. Government support, in the form of military contracts, the space program, and major subsidies to corporations for research and development, is often the source of technological innovation at the end of the twentieth century.
7. **Technology transfer** is the direct sharing of the developed world's technology with the less developed world. **Appropriate technology** is technology designed to fit the needs of the recipient culture.
8. Issues relevant to the information industry include the number and quality of available jobs, the sharing of information in the workplace, the content of information transmitted around the world, and access to information. The information model of the world introduces four key points: Information is replacing matter as the central topic of scientific interest; distinctions between subject and object, knower and known, are increasingly blurred; software develops independently of hardware; and intelligent patterns may be transferred from one computer to another without any transfer of matter.
9. Negative effects of science and technology can often be traced to four mechanistic assumptions about nature: *linearity,* the idea that if a little of something is good, a lot is better; *separability,* which holds that the cosmos is composed of distinct and separate parts that can be dealt with without affecting the whole; *reversibility,* the notion that we can undo anything that we can do; and *uniformity,* the belief that sameness is good. Many scientific innovations of the twentieth century recognize the opposite assumptions of nonlinearity, nonseparability (interconnectedness), irreversibility, and diversity.

Thinking Critically

1. How is it possible for the scientific community to create novel ideas despite the powerful influence of dominant groups in society that finance and sponsor scientific discovery? In other words, how can new scientific discoveries or new technologies be developed and spread when the rich and powerful may be opposed to them?
2. How can we achieve democratic influence over the process of technological development in the United States? How can we do it globally? How can the recognition of alternative models in science and technology help to empower people? How can the average citizens of a nation, or of the world, have a voice in deciding the appropriateness of technologies such as human cloning? Should issues like this be left to experts?
3. How may some of the new scientific and technological discoveries mentioned in this chapter help to bring about social transformation?

Suggested Readings

Barbour, Ian. 1990. *Religion in an Age of Science: The Gifford Lectures.* Vol. 1: 1989–1990. New York: HarperCollins.

———. 1991. *Ethics in an Age of Technology: The Gifford Lectures.* Vol. 2: 1990–1991. New York: HarperCollins.

Briggs, John and F. David Peat. 1989. *Turbulent Mirror.* New York: Harper & Row.

Capra, Fritjof. 1976. *The Tao of Physics.* Boston: Shambala.

Drengson, Alan. 1995. *The Practice of Technology: Exploring Technology, Ecophilosophy, and Spiritual Disciplines for Vital Links.* Albany: State University of New York.

Ferkiss, Victor. 1993. *Nature, Technology, and Society: Cultural Roots of the Current Environmental Crisis.* New York: New York University Press.

McGinn, Robert E. 1991. *Science, Technology, and Society.* Englewood Cliffs, NJ: Prentice Hall.

Merchant, Carolyn. 1980. *The Death of Nature: Women, Ecology, and the Scientific Revolution.* San Francisco: Harper & Row.

Roszak, Theodore. 1994. *The Cult of Information: The Neo-Luddite Treatise on High-Tech, Artificial Intelligence, and the True Art of Thinking.* Los Angeles: University of California Press.

Segal, Howard P. 1994. *Future Imperfect: The Mixed Blessings of Technology in America.* Amherst: University of Massachusetts Press.

Stoll, Clifford. 1995. *Silicon Snake Oil: Second Thoughts on the Information Highway.* New York: Doubleday.

Talbott, Stephen L. 1995. *The Future Does Not Compute: Transcending the Machines in Our Midst.* Sebastopol, CA: O'Reilly and Associates, Inc.

Web Sites

Links and Resources for Energy and the Environment: Environmental Studies Program, University of Oregon

URL: http://zebu.uoregon.edu/energy.html

This very rich source from the University of Oregon gives access to numerous other sites. Includes many topics such as environmental impacts of energy technology, political aspects of energy questions, Environmental Protection Agency guidelines, and extensive descriptions and practical advice on various forms of alternative energy, including solar, wind, geothermal, fusion, and biomass technologies.

Energy and Environment Sites

URL: http://www.worldbank.org/html/fpd/em/network/links.stm

This site is provided by the World Bank and also gives access to many other sites. Deals with various aspects of technology and the environment. Summarizes numerous papers on a wide variety of issues. Information relevant to students, researchers, governments, and private industries is provided here.

Mind Uploading Home Page

URL: http://sunsite.unc.edu/jstrout/uploading/MUHomePage.html

This fun site is an extended argument for uploading your mind and personality from your brain to a computer! The site argues that mind is nothing more than what the brain does, and the brain is a slow computer. Philosophical issues are addressed, such as whether you are still a person after your mind has been uploaded. (The authors of this book do not endorse the theories put forward here.)

PART ▪ TWO

Globalization and Changing Institutions

The globalization process is fueled by a growing realization that the realm of human activities (the sociosphere) is crashing through the limits set by the ecological systems that support all life on Earth (the biosphere). That is, the powerful technology of the modern industrial world is rapidly destroying our environment. This destruction is enhanced by the rapid expansion of the world's population. Not only do more people consume more, but people worldwide are adopting the aspirations of Western materialistic society. This means they are increasingly defining the "good life" in terms of the acquisition of more and more material possessions. The increased adoption of these aspirations has dramatically increased global consumption and waste.

In turn, population growth and the escalation of material expectations is putting pressure on economic systems and political systems, forcing them to change. Economic and political systems as we know them emerged with modernism and were influenced by Enlightenment thinking. Enlightenment ideas evolved into a rejection of religion and other forms of nonempirical thought and practice, the idea that humans and their activities were separate and apart from nature, a faith in the ability of reason and science to solve all problems, and a belief that human efforts and technology could control society and even nature itself.

Ultimately, however, neither society nor nature has proved to be amenable to so-called rational control. In fact, the effort to turn human groups into machines governed by hierarchies of power (bureaucratization) has repeatedly proved to generate irrationality and inefficiency, not rationality and control. The lack of a common value system and a sense of larger purpose plagues modern life and has in the past spawned efforts to transcend the limits of what many saw as amoral instrumental rationality. Socialism was one answer to the issues that emerged from Enlightenment humanism. The collapse of the Soviet Union and Eastern European socialism, which may be viewed as testimony to the failure of centralized hierarchical control systems, has dealt a severe blow to socialism and no one knows whether it will ever recover. Today's lack of a shared value system has led to many responses—from global interfaith dialogue to the emergence of fundamentalism and new ethnic-religious movements all over the world.

Toward an Ecologically Sensitive Sociology

Western culture, and sociology in particular, has failed to recognize the value of the natural world, especially with respect to the limits and constraints that nature imposes on human activity. Natural limits and constraints do not cease to affect social patterns just because members of a society are not conscious of them. These limits may actually be all the more effective to the extent that they are not recognized. In sociology the term latent *is used to refer to factors in social life that are unrecognized or unacknowledged. Such factors may play a very significant role in human activities even though members of society do not consciously take them into account. Factors having to do with natural systems, such as the effects of infectious bacteria in the great plagues of Europe, played a major role even though they were unrecognized. If anything, ignorance lends more power to natural restraints. During the bubonic plague of fourteenth-century Europe, people killed cats because they thought them to be agents of the devil that spread the plague, when in fact cats would have helped to control the flea-ridden rat population that was really responsible for the epidemic.*

The Dominant Western Worldview

Today some social scientists are still reluctant to acknowledge that latent natural factors such as soil depletion, deforestation, climate change, and infectious disease have played major roles in the rise and fall of societies and are likely to do so in the future. Catton and Dunlap (1980) ascribe this reluctance to the dominant Western worldview, *which consists of the following assumptions:*

1. *Human beings are different from all other creatures, over whom they have dominion.*
2. *Through our capacity for free choice and learning, we are masters of our destiny.*
3. *The world provides unlimited opportunities for us.*
4. *The history of humanity, which is one of progress, proves that for any problem, we human beings will find a solution.*

This worldview is thus a version of modernism. Sociology, like the other intellectual pursuits of Western humanity, has grown out of these assumptions. They have led to the belief that we human beings are exempt from the constraints and limitations that bind other living organisms. Catton and Dunlap propose that sociologists adopt the new ecological paradigm. *This emerging sociological view holds that despite what is truly unique about human beings, we are still bound by the laws of nature, within which we must live if we are to survive and prosper.*

Ecology, Society, and Life Support

We agree with the new ecological perspective that human activity in the sociosphere is deeply embedded in the biosphere. This relationship can be expressed by thinking of our lives as interconnected with three essential life-support systems.

The Planetary Life-Support System. *The first and most fundamental of these is the* planetary life-support system, *or biosphere. This system is the global ecological system that makes all life on the planet possible. If this system were to be seriously disrupted or damaged, our society and, perhaps all life, might be threatened. The biosphere operates on principles not invented by human beings that are beyond our power to alter or to escape. These principles include the following:*

1. Biological diversity. *Our continued existence on this planet depends on the immense variety of species, ecosystems, and genetic variations that comprise life on this planet. Nature favors variety, not sameness.*
2. Solar energy. *The earth is a vast living engine that transforms solar energy into life through the variety of organisms just described.*

3. Cycles of renewal. *Our atmosphere, soil, and water are renewed and replenished by natural cycles. The planetary system is extremely dynamic and maintains itself in a highly improbable state of unstable order unlike that found on "dead" planets (on which no life exists), such as Mars or Venus (Lovelock, 1988). Such a system is self-regulated by means of feedback processes that keep it in balance. In the following chapters, we will see how the violation of these principles is leading to situations of life-threatening peril.*

The Societal Life-Support System(s). *The second, and most problematic, life-support system is the human-designed societal life-support system(s). By* societal life-support system, *we mean those humanly created systems by which we support our existence. Because they are built by human beings, these systems reflect human values and beliefs. The capacity to use symbols enables us to invent and to accumulate knowledge. This ability, which distinguishes human beings from all other species, also makes it necessary for us to create our life-support systems. Human culture is the overarching societal life-support system in that it contains other societal life-support systems, such as the economy and the government. Both the economy and the government seek to (or perhaps should seek to) support and also to protect the lives of citizens.*

There is a gap between human creative imagination and the natural world sufficient to allow for a wide range of human cultural variation. This gap also allows human societies to be out of harmony with natural systems. Symbols are what allow human culture to escape the immediate bounds of space and time. We do this, for example, when we plan for the future, accumulate knowledge, and create global systems of trade and communication that enable us to escape the limitations of the immediate biophysical environment. But this freedom from the limits of nature is not infinite. It enables us merely to postpone *the recognition that the finite globe on which we live ultimately imposes limits on us.*

In the broadest sense, the societal life-support system may be called the "economy" if we remember that the original meaning of that word is "household" (i.e., economic activity is the support of the human household) and if we remember to include sexual reproduction, waste disposal, eating, and dying as household activities of the human family. Speaking in terms of physical facts, all economic activity is the transformation of energy into human activities and material products that are guided by the ideas and values of a society. Economic activity, like all activity, involves the inescapable degradation of part of the energy used. Degraded energy is called entropy, *and it can be equated with both waste and disorder. If entropy becomes too extensive within an ecological system or a social system, that system's continued existence is threatened.*

The Personal (or Primary Group) Life-Support System. *The third type of life-support system is the* personal *or* primary group life-support system. *This system consists of all the practices in which a human being engages that enhance or hinder his or her own physical and psychological well-being and that of his or her primary dependents, such as children or aged parents. It includes nutrition and exercise, contraception and other sexual practices, exposure to dangerous and unhealthy environments, knowledge of remedies and use of medicines, and even such things as yoga and self-defense. Clearly, any individual's primary life-support system greatly depends on that of his or her society, but a degree of choice is also involved. Today, for example, people in both modern and traditional societies are choosing from among a variety of alternative medicines to supplement or to replace modern scientific medicine.*

Modern Capitalism

Modern capitalism incorporates both competition and hierarchy. Capitalism is an economic system that is based on competition for profit among privately owned firms. This

form of society is particularly dynamic and has unleashed the productive powers of human beings to a degree that even its most serious critics have admired. Although it is less unequal than the peasant-based agricultural societies that preceded it, capitalism creates inequality in terms of the control of wealth, influence in politics, and domination of the economy by large corporations.

Capitalism is driven by the profits of the few and requires continuous growth at a fairly high rate. This dynamic produces far more products than persons need, and psychologically powerful forms of advertising have been developed to promote correspondingly high levels of consumption. Indeed, a value system has evolved that can be called consumerism *because it promotes the idea that high levels of consumption are natural and good and the idea that consumption promotes happiness and well-being, neither of which seem to be corroborated by fact. But in both the most developed nations and on the globe as a whole, contemporary capitalism is behaving according to the predictions of its severest critics by generating increased inequity and environmental damage. As we document in Chapters 6 and 8, the biosphere is in danger. Income inequality is soaring. Global employment is shifting to the lowest-paid workers. This may be a boon to them, but it lowers wages across the face of the earth and makes well-paid jobs harder to find in the wealthier societies.*

A viable alternative to hierarchical and competitive societies has yet to be found for the industrial or postindustrial stage of societal development. The only modes of viable and sustainable societies that we have are ones that are both small in size and use relatively simple technologies. Our hope today is to find a way of life that enables us to both feed and care for the people on this planet and provide them with a life of dignity and worth. We must to be able to do this at the same time that we protect natural resources for future generations.

Conclusions

The chapters in this section explore our relationship with our natural ecology. We examine the impact that human beings have had on our world and the continuing effects of the earth on human beings. Human activities are governed by socially expected patterns of action, called norms. Norm-governed activities include biological processes such as sexual reproduction and the consumption of food and other necessities. We try to understand how these have changed over time and how new patterns of social expectations are made necessary by globalization and the present planetary ecological crisis.

On the eve of the twenty-first century, we can no longer accept the assumptions that dominated Western culture on the eve of the twentieth century. Democracy and the market economy cannot be expected to bring about universal improvement of the conditions of humanity; nature and natural limits are not likely to be overcome and subjected to human whim; the spheres of moral values and religious belief are not likely to continue to be of purely private concern; and we cannot count on a gradual increase in reason and rationality in all areas of culture and social life. New assumptions, values, and beliefs must be developed that enable the biosphere and our sociosphere to exist in harmony. We examine what some of these may be in the chapters of this part and again in the Epilogue.

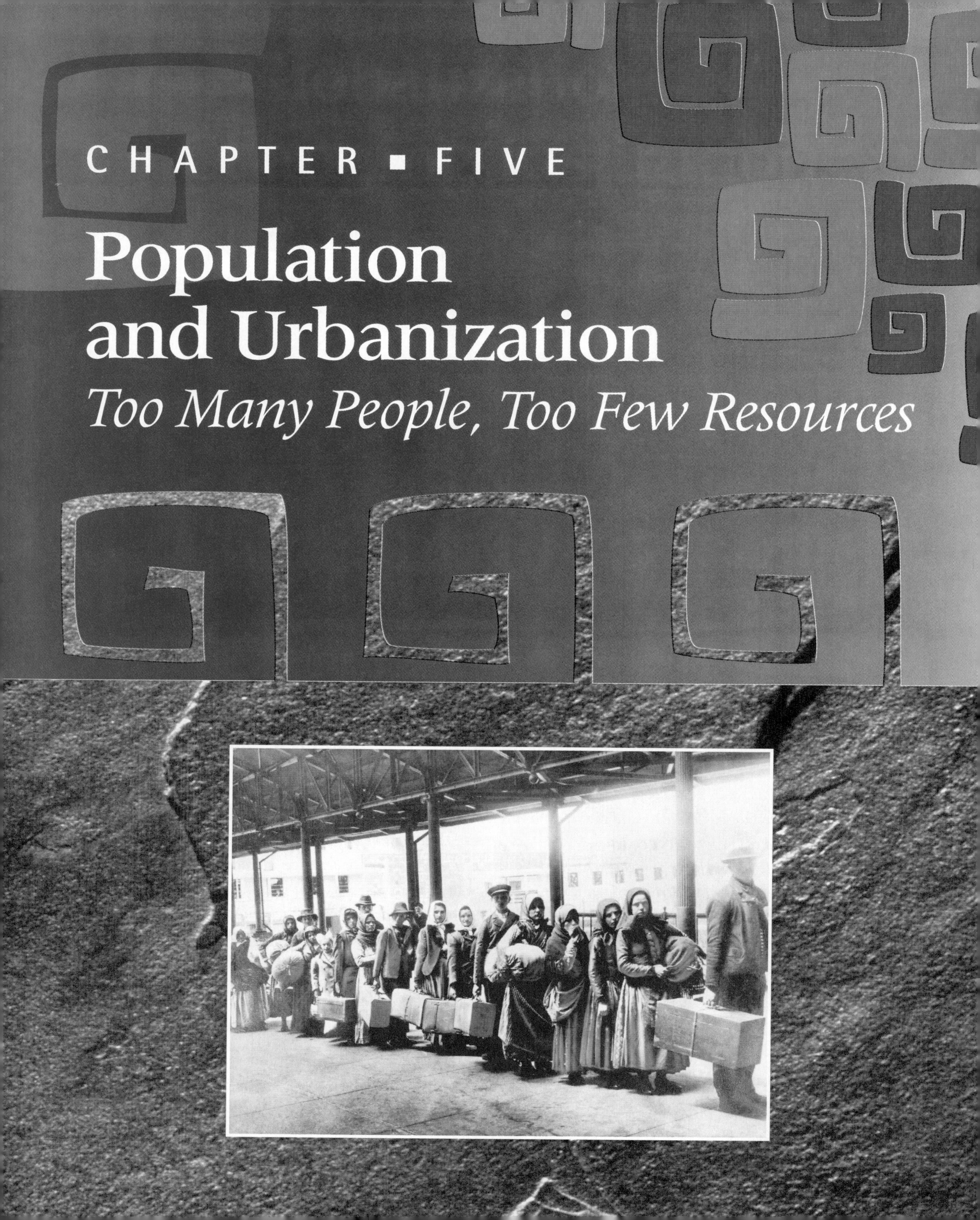

CHAPTER ■ FIVE

Population and Urbanization

Too Many People, Too Few Resources

There once was a time when children and big families equaled wealth in an Africa of vast resources. The simple economics: More children meant more hands to till the soil, tend the cattle, produce food and care for the aged. Those days are fast disappearing. Seventy percent of Africans still live off the land, even as its productivity is being drained. Stagnant local economies struggle to keep pace with the highest population growth rates in the world. People are growing poorer, and this rich continent's once lush farms are steadily losing their fertility.

Africa, a continent that occupies nearly 20 percent of the Earth's surface but accounts for only 10 percent of its population, can no longer feed itself. Some Africans are starting to realize that large families are a burden, not a blessing. Consider Stephen Makope, from Zimbabwe. He wishes he had fathered eight children, the ideal number for a traditional African family, he explains, enough to secure comfort in one's old age and assure respect for the family name. It is too late for hindsight. Makope has 57 children, and at age 73, a time when many men his age are starting to take things easy, he is struggling to support the 15 youngest who are still dependent on him, along with the six of their 11 mothers who still are alive. "It's too many. I feel troubled now, and I have regrets. . . . "

Zimbabwe's population is now more than 11 million, a 550 percent increase in Makope's lifetime, with all competing for a place in an economy that has failed to grow at the same rate as the population.

The story of Makope's expanding family during these years mirrors the history of Zimbabwe's population explosion and the problems it has caused. Now, as those born into a more crowded world challenge the age-old assumptions about family size held by their parents, there is a shift in attitudes.

Improvements in health care during Makope's lifetime mean more children are surviving to adulthood and adults are living longer. In 1950, a quarter of all children born did not live beyond their fifth birthday and life expectancy was 42. Today, 92 percent of Zimbabwean children reach age 5, and life expectancy has risen to 60. Makope would have had 65 children, had eight of them not died—during the early years—but he might have had just 43 had infant mortality remained as high as it was in his youth.

From Liz Sly, "Father of 57: 'It's Too Many,' " *Chicago Tribune*, 30 January 1996.

Population explosion is a term used to describe the huge increase in the number of people in the world. It is easy to think that the population explosion is a problem in developing nations like Zimbabwe. But this is not true. Problems such as homelessness, drug addiction, pollution, poor health conditions, and high crime rates are not just related to living in a "bad neighborhood." They are to some extent the result of population pressures and problems caused by so many people moving to urban areas.

Population pressures and the problems of urbanization are not merely social problems, but in a very real sense they are linchpins to most of the global social problems we discuss in this book. They contribute to, influence, or set in motion many other social problems in the world. For instance, population pressures often create environmental problems. When the need for food is so great, more and more land is turned over to agriculture, which can result in a loss of timber, overcultivation, and, ultimately, desertification.

Population pressures sometimes create political problems within a country or among sovereign nations. Population is also directly related to the global economic system and the flight of jobs from the developed world to places where labor is much cheaper. Racial and ethnic concerns and women's issues also influence changes in the population. For example, there is a clear link between the level of education girls receive and the birthrate: More education means fewer children. This topic is covered in more depth in Chapter 9.

As population rises, many people move to urban areas in search of jobs and opportunities. The rise of vast cities has led to unprecedented social changes with which we are still trying to grapple—changes such as rural people moving to cities with few of the job or life skills they need in an urban environment. It is almost impossible to overemphasize the importance of population pressures in the world today.

Adaptive Regimes

All human and animal groups experience population pressures. Human communities are unique, however, presenting special problems when it comes to population. Some animals defend territories and possess harems (in which a dominant male controls many females), whereas other animal societies exhibit dominance hierarchies (in which some, usually male, acquire more power, status, and food than others). These structures are similar to some of those found in various human groups. These patterns aid the animal group in maintaining a sustainable population density. In addition, these patterns are unique to a particular species and are genetically controlled.

What is unique about the human species is that our communities are not genetically regulated but, instead, are based on shared customs, norms, and cultural ideas. These are transmitted and maintained through the use of language. Sexual conduct, childbirth, and family size are regulated, not by genes, but by *social norms* (rules by which society guides the behavior of its members). These social norms are taught through the use of symbolic language and are supported by group pressure. Equally important, human consumption of resources (the most basic of which is food) is also regulated by norms.

The fact that norms, not genes, govern basic social patterns of human beings is explained by two factors—variety among human groups and, over time, new adaptations that develop in response to changing circumstances. No other species can adapt to changing circumstances to the degree that humans can. Changes in biophysical conditions, to which human societies must adapt, can be the result of natural processes beyond human control, or these changes can be the result of human activity itself. The second scenario is increasingly the case.

Human societies have developed various normative patterns that we will call "adaptive regimes." These involve how a society utilizes environmental resources (ultimately, energy) in an effort to maintain its way of life. An **adaptive regime** is comprised of a society's normatively regulated practices relative to population size and to the consumption of environmental energy. The adaptive regime is basically an aspect of a society's technology practice (Maybury-Lewis, 1992). Of particular importance in defining a society's adaptive regime are social patterns regulating birth, family size, and consumption of material goods and natural resources. We briefly describe the three basic adaptive regime patterns.

Tribal Equilibrium Regimes

The earliest regime to evolve seems to have been the **tribal equilibrium regime.** A tribal society is a relatively small social system capable of meeting the needs of all of its members without the aid of political authority invested in a state. Once thought to be "primitive," tribal societies are being reassessed as alternative forms of society rather than as an outmoded or "backward" stage of society (Bodley, 1990). Rather than being "simple," these societies are complex in ways that have not yet been fully appreciated.

Societies that adopt the tribal equilibrium regime are so structured as to maintain a level of population well below the carrying capacity of their environments. This may be accomplished by various means. The Yanomamo, in Brazil, practice continuous warfare that is linked to a preference for males and,

Once thought to be "primitive," tribal societies are being reassessed as alternative forms of society. Rather than being simple, these societies are complex in ways that are still to be fully appreciated.

hence, the practice of female infanticide. The resulting shortage of adult women encourages the capture of women in war. This self-balancing feedback loop maintains a relatively limited population and a sufficient level of protein consumption.

The Toda, in India, also practice female infanticide but suppress any tendency to warfare. As with the Yanomamo the shortage of women maintains a limited population. The sharing of wives among brothers, a practice called *polyandry* (literally many husbands), along with a complex social structure based on a division of society into dual sections that must depend upon each other, maintains a peaceful and compact unit (Queen and Habenstein, 1974). Both of these societies seem to follow practices that they do not consciously comprehend. These practices appear to have evolved over time without deliberate planning; the practices survive because they work. Other societies, such as the Desana (who live in a tropical rain forest on the Brazilian-Colombian border), are quite aware of why they choose to have only two children and why they use herbal contraceptives to prevent unwanted births (Bodley, 1990).

Population size is not all that these tribes limit. They also have norms that restrict the overconsumption of natural resources. These include rules about not hunting during breeding seasons, not stripping a tree of all its fruit, and not killing all the members of a herd, as well as different food taboos for different sectors of the tribe. Both reproduction and consumption are limited by these social norms.

Pronatalist Expansionist Regimes

A second type of regime may be called a **pronatalist expansionist regime,** a society that favors more births. Usually based on more complex agricultural or herding techniques than those found in tribal-equilibrium regimes, pronatalist expansionist regimes favor large kinship and family groups. Using these techniques and the domestication of food resources, people in these societies attempt to increase production and, hence, increase the capacity of their resource base to provide for them. Achieving this goal requires large numbers of people, which means that there must be many births per woman. Often it means that men will marry multiple wives (called *polygyny*) to increase their own and their kinsmen's wealth and social standing. Stephen Makope's prolific fertility illustrates the pronatalist expansionist regime.

There is often rivalry within and among societies of this type. Pronatalist societies tend toward a hierarchical stratification, although in the earlier stages of expansionist regimes there may be powerful norms leading to the sharing of wealth. The redistribution of wealth is an aspect of tribal organization, which means that some tribal groups actually fall within this category rather than in the tribal-equilibrium category. Population expansion tends to lead such societies into a seesaw pattern of population growth over many generations. When the carrying capacity, or ability of the environment to sustain the population, is exceeded, the population declines.

The population tends to be regulated by Malthusian factors, or the notion that with overpopulation comes widespread malnutrition and other problems. (See our discussion of the theories of Thomas Malthus later in this chapter.) These societies intensify or expand territory and productive output. The right to consume is *not,* however, equally shared.

A high degree of stratification or social inequality tends to accompany the pronatalist expansionist regime—at least as it is applied in large-scale societies. The dominant groups consume vast quantities of all that is produced. The lower ranking members of these societies live much closer to *subsistence* (exploiting food and other resources directly from the environment). These societies often "rank" the relative status of all occupations. In addition, they frequently have some type of *sumptuary laws* that define what individual members can wear and what goods they can consume; these decisions are based on social rank. High rates of consumption are the privilege of high rank. An example: Aztec nobles could wear the feathers of colorful tropical birds, but if commoners usurped this right, they could be put to death.

Industrial Consumptionist Regimes

The third, and most recent regime to emerge is the **industrial consumptionist regime.** This type of regime emerged with the development of the industrial mode of production. The populations of industrial societies pass through a series of stages referred to as the demographic transition (which will be discussed in more detail later in this chapter). In brief, the demographic transition process unfolds in the following way: In the first stage, population growth is dramatic. Over time, growth slows as the mass of people take up residence in the cities and begin to limit births. Eventually, a stable state is reached consisting of a large population made up of numerous small families. In this phase the standard of living is unprecedented. The chief characteristic of this regime is its emphasis on continuous growth of industrial output and, hence, of consumption. Industrial consumptionist regimes are far more egalitarian and "democratic" than those described earlier because they favor high rates of consumption for all.

Socialist versions of industrial societies emphasize production and the more or less equal distribution of basic necessities. In recent years this model has been eclipsed by the openly consumption-oriented model followed by capitalist societies. However, both models are based on the premise of expansion of output and both exhibit similar population patterns. In truth, one of the failures of the socialist system is an insufficient supply of consumer goods to citizens. Industrial consumptionist regimes will not be able to sustain themselves, certainly not at present rates of production and consumption. Nor does it appear to be possible to raise the majority of Earth's human inhabitants to the exorbitant levels of consumption enjoyed by the most developed industrial societies.

Population Issues in Historical Perspective

Over the past quarter century, the aspect of the population problem attracting the most attention has been the population explosion and the threat it poses for the world. According to most experts, such a rapid population growth is pushing the demand for food (and other resources) beyond the earth's capacity to produce them. Even though agricultural productivity continues to increase, in recent years the world's food reserves have been seriously depleted. According to a report by the Worldwatch Institute (Postel, 1994), cropland is scarcely expanding, a good portion of existing agricultural land is losing fertility, and the world's seas are being drastically overfished.

In the last decade of the twentieth century, in many parts of the world (particularly in sub-Saharan Africa), famine is an ever present danger. In addition, most experts see a link between overpopulation and environmental issues such as degradation of the water and air supply, global warming, and deforestation. For example, rural people who burn wood for fuel use an average of 7.5 trees per person per year—and few people replant trees. Population pressures also promote extensive poverty and the likelihood of war.

Current Trends and Statistics

According to **demographers** (scientists who study population), about 250,000 people are added to the world's population every day (United Nations, 1995). That's approximately three people every second. At present our population is about 5.9 billion people (Population Reference Bureau, 1997). Answering the basic needs—food, fuel, shelter—of each of these people has an enormous environmental impact, both in the countryside and, increasingly, in urban areas.

Currently, overall world population is growing at an astonishing pace. This growth is more pronounced and has a greater impact in particular countries and regions of the world. Asia is by far the most populous continent. It contains roughly 3.5 billion people, or about 60 percent of the world's total (Population Reference Bureau, 1997). Although the rate of increase is lower in Asia than in Africa or Latin America, Asia's net gain in population surpasses that of any other continent because of the sheer size of the existing population base. Two-thirds of the world population growth in 1996 and 1997 took place in Asia alone (Bryjak, 1997).

In discussing overpopulation and its attendant problems, another important fact needs to be added to the equation. Although the developed world is not "overpopulated" (it has less than one-fourth of the world's people), its population consumes three-fourths of the earth's raw materials and energy and produces three-fourths of the earth's solid waste. If we look at the facts, it is indisputable: In one lifetime a newborn American has many more times the environmental impact than a child born in Asia or Africa. The American will use (or waste) far more food, water, and energy than a member of the developing world.

Of every ten people in the world today, four live in either China or India. If we add to this total the people in the United States and the former Soviet Union, we have accounted for half the world's population. The other half of the world's people are distributed unevenly among the remaining countries. Although the population explosion is a global phenomenon, it is important to note that the population is growing faster in the poorer, developing nations (see Table 5–1).

TABLE 5-1 Population Growth-Rates and Doubling Times (in selected countries)

ANNUAL RATES OF NATURAL INCREASE		DOUBLING TIME IN YEARS
1.5%	World	45
0.2	Europe	332
0.7	North America	105
0.7	United States	105
2.3	Middle America	30
2.2	Mexico	34
1.8	South America	38
−0.6	Russia	?
1.0	East Asia	66
1.1	China	62
0.3	Japan	277
1.9	Southeast Asia	37
2.3	Vietnam	30
2.1	South Asia	34
1.9	India	36
2.2	Latin America	32
2.5	North Africa	28
2.3	Egypt	31
3.0	Sub-Saharan Africa	23
2.7	Zimbabwe	26

Source: Adapted from de Blij and Muller, 1997: A-1–A5.

As shown in Table 5–1, the time it takes to double the population (the doubling time) for Europe, North America, and Japan is more than a century—in the case of Japan, it is 277 years. For the People's Republic of China, the doubling time is 62 years. But for Africa the doubling time is less than half that, 23 to 26 years.

Decline in the Death Rate. The industrialized world has greatly lowered its death rate. This is not a recent development. In the industrialized countries, the death rate declined as the Industrial Revolution progressed and industrial consumptive regimes emerged. During the eighteenth and nineteenth centuries, advances in agriculture, transportation, and commerce made better diets possible. As manufacturing operations became more sophisticated, clothing, housing, and other amenities became more affordable and widely available. A rise in real income facilitated the growth of public sanitation, medical science, and public education. For the industrialized nations, then, medical advances had little to do with the decline in the death rate.

To compute population, demographers use the following formula:

$$\text{Population} = \text{Births} - \text{Deaths} \pm \text{Migration}$$

If the deaths dramatically decrease but births and migration do not change much, there is an increase in population. In developing regions today, modern medical technology and the use of pesticides to control mosquitoes that carry malaria are prompting an extremely rapid decline in the death rate. Developing nations have experienced a much faster drop in death rates than Europe or the United States ever did when they were developing.

The idea that the population pressures experienced by developing nations are the result of a high birthrate turns out to be false. The accurate explanation is the drastic *decline* in the death rate. Citizens of developing societies are not having more children but, as the case of Makope and his family illustrates, the problem is that more of the children they do have are surviving in unprecedented numbers.

Death rates have plunged in the world's poorest regions because UNICEF (United Nations Children's Fund), the World Health Organization, and other international organizations have brought medical advances. Thanks to recent medical discoveries, widespread communicable diseases such as malaria, yellow fever, yaws, syphilis, cholera, plague, typhoid, smallpox, tuberculosis, and dysentery can now be controlled on a mass basis at a low cost, using antibiotics, vaccines, and better diagnostic instruments like the portable X-ray machine.

Preventive public health measures, instituted and organized by governments and private organizations with only a handful of specialists, can save millions of lives at costs ranging from a few cents to a few dollars per person, per year. These preventive measures do not require citizens to change their habits, nor do people need to understand the disease, or take any personal initiative. But this swift decrease in mortality, coupled with high fertility, yields a huge swelling of the population. Our opening vignette of Makope and his family shows how one

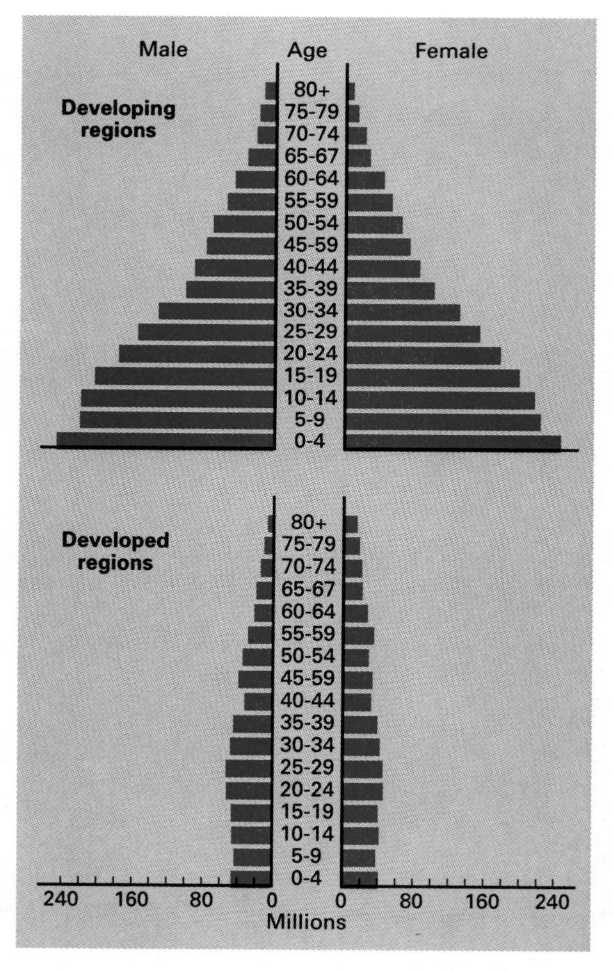

FIGURE 5–1 Population Pyramids: Population Structure of Developing and Developed Regions of the World

Source: Rentzetti, Claire M. and Daniel J. Curan. 1998. *Living Sociology.* Boston: Allyn and Bacon, p. 502. Used with permission.

man's personal situation—multiplied by thousands—becomes a population problem for the nation, and perhaps, for the world.

Because most of the people whose lives are saved are young, the drop in mortality means that preindustrial nations have very young populations. In fact, many of these countries have the youngest populations the world has ever known. In developing countries, nearly everyone is under the age of 40. For example, 36 percent of all Mexicans are below the age of 15. In the United States, by contrast, the figure is 22 percent (Population Reference Bureau, 1997). Figure 5–1 graphically depicts the age disparity between the developed and developing regions of the world.

Note that the developing world (often called the "Third World") faces the prospect of continued population growth, as a substantial proportion of its population has yet to reach childbearing years. The left-hand side of the figure shows the number of males in the population; the number of females is on the right-hand side. The numbers in the middle are the ages of the population, starting at newborns to age 4 and rising in increments. In this particular chart, the oldest group are those who are 80 or older. The chart allows you to see a quick profile of the population. The wider the base of the pyramid, the more children in that particular population. Such young populations have meant that these developing countries are (1) facing the problem of rapidly rising numbers of people while (2) struggling with a burdensome *child-dependency ratio* (the large number of children who must be supported by adults).

As if to compensate for the heavy child-dependency drag, agrarian societies tend to put children to work at a very early age. However, child labor is neither efficient in the short run nor conducive to economic development in the long run. A nation needs a skilled workforce, so children must be educated. Failing to educate children deprives them of the opportunity to acquire ideas and attitudes that are conducive to development and desirable social change. In Chapter 9, we discuss this issue in more depth.

Education might help thwart the role of young people in making and breaking dictators or in participating in the social upheaval that has often been present in developing countries. People need information in order to make intelligent decisions and not be swayed by propaganda from a powerful speaker. An educated citizenry serves both economic development and political ends.

Population before the Modern Period

According to demographers, for 97 percent of human history overpopulation was not a problem. Throughout the world only tribal-equilibrium regimes were

Agrarian societies tend to start children working at a very early age; here a young Napalese boy carries harvested tea on his back. Child labor is not efficient in the short run, however, nor is it conducive to long-term economic development.

found. In most places underpopulation was the problem. Populations expanded slowly, increasing temporarily in some places, but declining in others. For thousands of years, the net increase was infinitesimally slow.

During this long period, the number of people living in any given area was directly determined by the **fertility rate** (the number of children the average woman has). Geography and climatic conditions set limits on how many people an area could support. Our earliest human ancestors—hunters and gatherers—were dependent on the environment for sustenance, consuming roots, leaves, fruits, berries, nuts, seeds, fish, shellfish, and small animals—whatever foods were available.

Having children is largely influenced by the social contexts in which people live. So the transition from food gathering to food production was a crucial technological change in human development. Although from our best evidence this shift did not prompt an immediate increase in the population, over time, however, it did.

Three Escalations in Human Population. Three periods in human history saw populations surge rapidly. The first population spurt occurred in the *Neolithic Revolution,* about 8000 B.C.E., and was sparked by technological advances in agriculture. In various parts of the world, people began to settle down, grow food, domesticate animals, and store grains and other food for future consumption. These developments speeded up the rate of population growth; people had a more dependable food supply. This escalation was based on the transition from primarily tribal-equilibrium regimes to pronatalist expansionist regimes.

For nearly ten thousand years, population grew rather slowly, increasing in some areas and declining in others in response to climate and other factors. But around 1750 C.E. the *industrial revolution* began, sparking the second escalation in population. In England and then in other parts of Europe and the world, the shift to industrial consumptionist regimes took place.

You might wonder how the industrial revolution could affect population growth. Consider the impact of modern transportation. Foodstuffs are usually heavy, bulky, or both, and before a network of serviceable roads was developed, even local famines were often catastrophic. A sizable proportion of the people in a given area might die from malnutrition, if not outright starvation. Elderly people and small children were particularly vulnerable.

The first major improvements in transportation touched off by the industrial revolution were comprised of a network of canals, built around 1750 throughout Great Britain and eastern Europe. In fact, the eastern United States also underwent a period during which a lot of money was spent constructing canals. Barges operating on these canals could move foodstuffs relatively quickly and cheaply. But after a few decades an even more economical and efficient transportation system was devised: steam-driven railroads. Even today, barges and railroads are the most economical ways to move bulky and heavy goods. When shortages of food in one area could be met quickly and efficiently by shipping food from another area, populations grew, not because more people were being born but *because the death rate fell.*

In addition, the industrial revolution brought improvements in public sanitation, safe water supplies, and the like. Eventually, even agriculture was mechanized, increasing food production. All these developments helped people to live longer, healthier lives and made the population grow.

The third escalation in human population occurred in the late 1950s, after World War II. This *modern period's* population spurt was caused by advances in medicine and technology. During the industrial revolution medicine was far from a science. On occasion the cure was more dangerous than the illness—as when practitioners used leeches to "bleed" patients. But by 1945, all kinds of medical innovations were bursting onto the scene. Vaccinations were developed for various diseases, including smallpox, diphtheria, and cholera. In addition, researchers developed pesticides to rid areas of mosquitoes that spread illnesses such as malaria. All these advances saved lives and prompted a worldwide surge in population (see Figure 5–2).

Note that in all three of these population spikes, the reason for the increase was not that people were having more babies. Rather, people were living longer because of a more stable food supply and, by the mid-twentieth century, because of medical advances. For most of human history, the death rate was exceedingly high; most humans died as infants. If one reached the age of 5, one was likely to live to 45 or 50. The most vulnerable age was infancy.

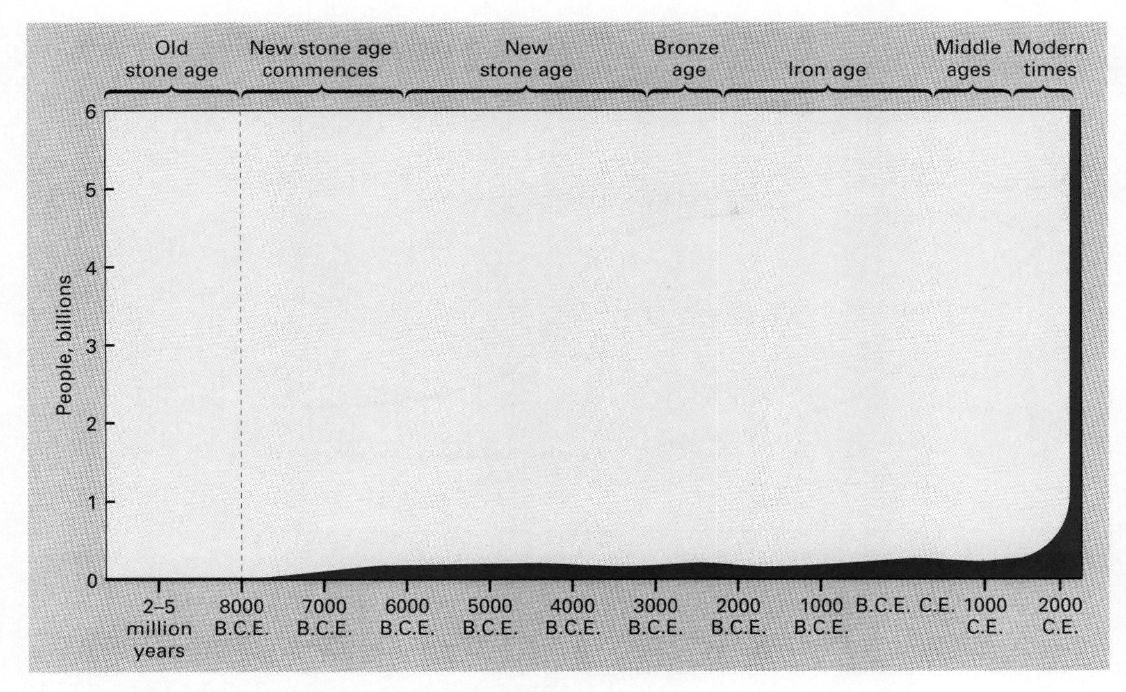

FIGURE 5–2 **Timeline of World's Population Growth**
Source: Population Reference Bureau, 1994.

Demographic Transition Theory. Demographers argue that the human population's current rate of increase is just a temporary deviation from the annual growth rate that prevailed during most of humanity's history. This notion is based on the concept of a **demographic transition,** which has taken place in the industrialized region of the world during the past few centuries. Demographers maintain that as countries industrialize and become more modern and as more of their people live in cities, individual families voluntarily limit the number of children they have. When enough people do this, the population falls.

Historically, industrialization, modernization, and urbanization have produced a gradual decline in birthrates that is usually accompanied by improvements in agriculture, transportation, and preventive and curative medicine. These technological advances raise the standard of living and produce an even more rapid and dramatic drop in **mortality rates** (the incidence of death in a society's population).

As industrialization, modernization, and urbanization have spread over the globe, we have seen a large net gain of births over deaths, sparking a rapid explosion in the world population and a surge in new social problems. In preindustrial nations, hundreds of thousands of peasant farmers have been forced off the land by the mechanization of agriculture; these peasants flood into cities, particularly the capital cities. This movement has resulted in **overurbanization,** a situation in which so many people are concentrated in cities that they overwhelm the city's capacity to provide basic services and necessities like housing, safe water, and sufficient jobs. We will discuss overurbanization in more detail later in the chapter.

Demographers have developed a theory to explain changing rates of recent population growth and to predict future trends. **Demographic transition theory** postulates that as nations industrialize, they tend to pass through four stages (see Figure 5–3). In *Phase I,* the preindustrial stage, birthrates are high because little is known about birth control, but death rates are equally high due to food shortages, disease and accidents, and poor or absent medical care. A combination of high birthrates and high death rates means the *annual increase* (the growth

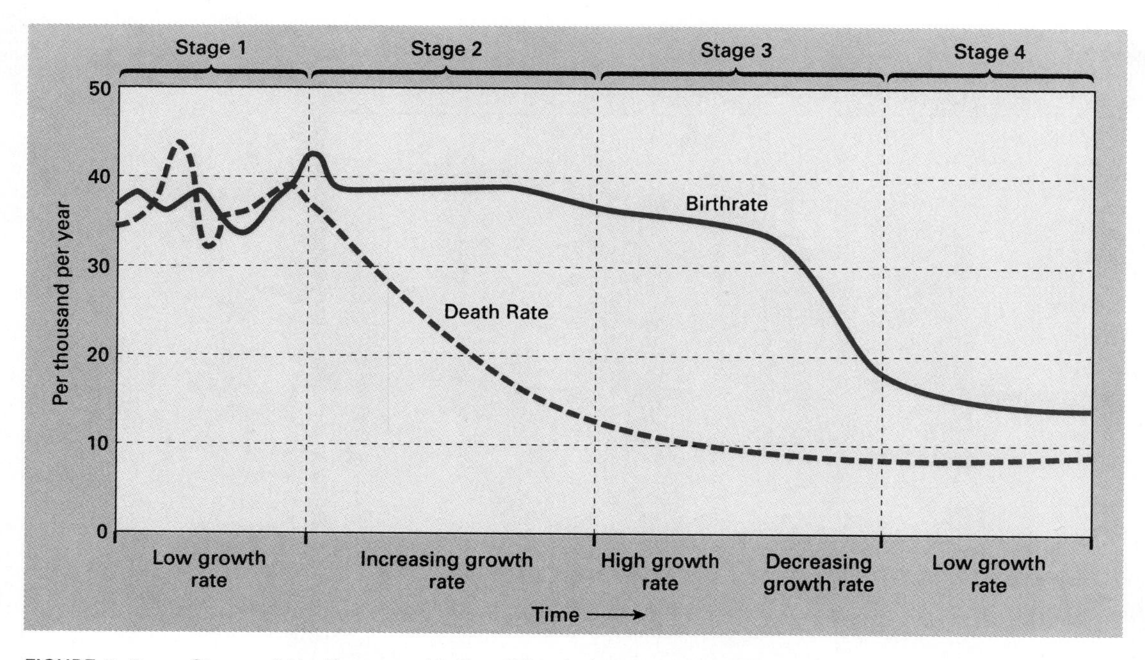

FIGURE 5–3 Stages of the Demographic Transition in Industrializing Nations

Source: Macionis, John J. 1998. *Society: The Basics*, 4th Edition. Upper Saddle River, NJ: Prentice Hall, p. 372.

rate) is small. For most of human history, we were in Phase I.

During *Phase II* the birthrate slowly begins to decline. Thousands of individual couples decide to have fewer children so that they can better provide for the ones they have. In a parallel development, death rates decline more quickly because of improved transportation to ship food to population centers, better sanitation, and, eventually, modern health services. With slowly falling birthrates, but rapidly declining death rates, the annual increase is large. Europe and North America went through this stage a century or so ago, as the industrial revolution unfolded. Today much of the underdeveloped world is in Phase II. Families in these countries are beginning to have fewer children, but the population is growing at an alarming rate because the death rate has plunged at a much faster rate than the birthrate.

In *Phase III,* the drive to technological maturity, smaller families become the norm. Families realize that they do not need so many children to provide for them in their old age. As contraception improves, couples can choose between having another child or spending money on something else. Often consumption wins out over procreation, and the overall birthrate declines. India is an example of a country in Phase III: The government endorses inexpensive birth control and vasectomies so that individual families can curb their family size.

In *Phase IV,* a period of full industrialization or postindustrialization, both the birthrate and the death rate stabilize at a low level, yielding low population growth. North America, most of Europe, and Japan are in Phase IV.

Few people seriously quarrel with demographic transition theory. Low population growth accompanies development, and it must prevail if the population is to remain within the earth's carrying capacity. But the big question is: How long will it take poor nations to reach Phase IV? If it takes only a matter of decades, the globe can probably handle the additional people. But what if it takes as long as a century or two? Then the world will face major problems. Demographic transition theory cannot predict how long this transition is going to take.

Time to Double the Population. In examining contemporary population concerns, we must consider not only the high rate of population growth but also the absolute base of people, which has become larger than ever before (see Table 5–2). The United Nations has been issuing population projections for decades.

TABLE 5-2 World's Population Growth and Time It Took to Double

YEAR	WORLD POPULATION	TIME TO DOUBLE POPULATION
8000 B.C.E.	1/4 billion (est.)	?
1650 C.E.	1/2 billion	9,650 years
1850	1 billion	200 years
1930	2 billion	80 years
1975	4 billion	45 years
2015 (est.)	8 billion (est.)	40 years

In 1975, for the first time, the UN revised its projections *downward.* Demographers believed world population growth rates peaked in the 1960s (Ray, 1995). Today's population is estimated to be about 5.9 billion, and the forecast for the year 2000 has been revised downward from 8 billion to 6.3 billion (Ray, 1995).

The Population Reference Bureau (a U.S. government agency) estimates that in developing countries, population is doubling very swiftly: every 26 years in Africa and every 37 years in Asia, excluding China (Population Reference Bureau, 1997). That means to maintain even their present state (which is grossly inadequate) developing nations must double their natural resources, food production, schools, hospitals, highways, railroads, teachers, and doctors. All essentials must double in the same period for the people to maintain their present lifestyles.

But the citizens of these countries aren't satisfied with their current circumstances. Thanks to advances in communication and travel, many of them are aware of the lifestyles of people in the developed parts of the world, and they want "a piece of the pie." They are demanding more and better food, improved communications, better education, scientific advances, and higher standards of living, even though the resources and capacities to produce these hallmarks of the good life are already severely strained.

Currently there is serious disagreement about population projections. Some believe that unless birthrates fall precipitously, the death rate will climb because competition for scarce resources will ferment war and bring on famine and disease. The other view points out that in recent decades, fertility in developing countries decreased by 30 percent: "If the decrease continues, it will surely be the most astonishing demographic shift in history" (Mann, 1993).

The good news is that for a variety of reasons, the growth rate of the world population appears to be slowing. Much of this decrease is occurring in the industrialized parts of the world. For instance, Belgium, Croatia, the Czech Republic, Finland, Greece, Iceland, Romania, the Ukraine, and Russia now have a negative rate of natural increase (de Blij and Muller, 1997). But in addition, the rate of increase is slowing, sometimes minutely, in the developing parts of the world as well. Considering the size of the population in those countries, a drop of even one-half percent means a significant decrease in the population, particularly over time. Unborn people cannot have babies.

The Malthusian Debate

In the nineteenth century, English economist and clergyman Thomas Malthus (1766–1834) wrote a troubling and highly influential book entitled *Essay on the Principle of Population.* English naturalist Charles Darwin (1809–1882) maintained that Malthus's essay provided him with one of the keys that opened the door to the principle of natural selection that formed the basis for his theory of evolution (Robertson, 1987). Malthus lived and wrote during the second escalation of population, in a time when the population was too high, little new land came under the plow, rural-to-urban migration increased, and society was very unstable. Alarmed at the continued increase of population, Malthus decided to investigate the matter. He maintained that in order to get to the heart of poverty and human misery, it is necessary to consider the population itself, and especially the rate at which it increases.

Mathus theorized that if allowed to increase without checks of any sort, the world population would double every 25 years. He pointed out that population increases *geometrically* in accordance with the series 1, 2, 4, 8, 16, 32, 64, 128, 256, and so on. On the other hand, the food supply—even in the most favorable circumstances—could not possibly increase in more than an *arithmetic* progression, in accordance with the series 1, 2, 3, 4, 5, 6, 7, 8, 9, and so on. At these rates, Malthus concluded, in two centuries, the population to food ratio would be 256:9. In three centuries it would stand at 4,096:13, and so on; in 2,000 years the difference would be incalculable.

The mathematical formula, not so much as the facts, made Malthus's theory so persuasive. Others had pointed out the relationship between the productive powers of the earth and the reproductive potential of the human race, but the mathematical ratio seemed far more precise and convincing than any verbal statement.

However, Malthus realized that population does not increase without checks. These checks were of two kinds, which he called "positive" and "preventive." In Malthus's view positive checks were those that shorten the natural life span by increasing the death rate; these included epidemics and other diseases, wars, plagues, famines, unwholesome occupations, hard labor, and climatic exposure. Up to that time in the world's history, only positive checks curbed population increases.

According to Malthus, preventive checks (which function to decrease the birthrate) include celibacy, late marriages, and sexual abstinence—or as Malthus put it, "moral restraint." Because Malthus recognized that the sexual urge was very strong, the outlook for the future did not appear very bright to him.

Malthus was the first to focus attention on what came to be known as the *Malthusian trap* (the theory that with overpopulation comes widespread malnutrition and possible armed conflict between nations). Malthus may not have grasped all the nuances of demography, but his essay captured people's attention. However, things did not work out the way he anticipated. The world has not fallen into the Malthusian trap, at least not yet. Neither the increase in population nor the increase in the food supply conforms exactly to Malthusian predictions. Three developments permitted Great Britain (and ultimately the world) to escape the dire fate Malthus predicted:

1. *Large-scale emigration became common.* Within a century, 20 million people left Britain and northern Europe for less populated lands in the New World. The United States, Canada, and Australia were often the destination.

2. *Significant improvements occurred in farm output.* These advances were brought about piecemeal and included developments such as the enclosure of common lands, drainage of wetlands, publicity about improved farming methods, and better access to markets.

3. *The industrial revolution provided rising standards of living and brought about a number of social changes.* These changes included a decrease in the average number of children that families had, more years of schooling, improvements in the status of women, enhanced consumption, and growing urbanization. Later, demographers identified these social changes as hallmarks of the second phase of the demographic transition.

Other countries followed Britain's lead, including Belgium and Germany. They imitated British practices and followed the upward spiral of increased productivity, wealth, and rising standards of living. Eventually, this transition occurred in all industrial nations.

Other factors, which Malthus could not anticipate, have also influenced population growth and food production trends. Improved birth control methods (especially the "pill"), chemical fertilizers, the mechanization of agriculture, irrigation, and so-called miracle seeds (hybrid seeds of basic grains like corn, wheat, and rice that dramatically increase production compared to that of ordinary, nature-pollinated seeds). But even with these technological advances, increasingly we realize that at some point, we may outstrip the earth's capacity to sustain a soaring population. The population growth rate of developing countries reached its peak in the period 1965 to 1970, but the children born in these years are just beginning to have their own families. Sometimes this is called the baby boom echo.

Impact of Increased Population

Since the 1950s, the confluence of three trends has put excessive pressure on the world: (1) rapid population growth coupled with a high absolute base; (2) the rapid consumption of nonrenewable resources and concomitant environmental pollution; and (3) the widening gap in the distribution of income between the "haves" and the "have-nots" (Brown, 1994; Worldwatch Institute, 1994).

At the end of the twentieth century, most of the major crises affecting the world are directly related to the problems of the growth and distribution of population. These crises include

- severe food shortages
- deterioration of the biosphere and the environment
- war and social unrest

- imbalances in the worldwide distribution of wealth (de Blij and Muller, 1997)

At issue is human survival. Many experts believe world population is growing faster than our ability to produce food. Others disagree with this view and maintain that the problem is more one of distribution than supply.

Severe Food Shortages. According to the United Nations, one out of five people worldwide is malnourished (UN Population Fund, 1990). It is true that in developing countries, almost 60 percent of the population still live on the land, but most of the best and most accessible farm land is already in use. What is left is either less fertile or harder to clear and work. During the 1980s, the area available per person actually declined at the rate of 1.9 percent a year (Sadik, 1991).

Food production per person is falling, not rising, and in many developing countries, malnutrition threatens life (Bryjak, 1997). As a whole, in the last quarter century, developing countries have suffered a serious decline in food self-sufficiency. Their deficits have been met by surpluses in the industrialized nations, primarily North America, but these surpluses are disappearing, too (Linden, 1996). Absolute poverty has risen worldwide. Now at least 1 billion people cannot meet the most basic needs of food and shelter (Sadik, 1991). The falling death rates are primarily a phenomenon of Western industrialized nations, but in the developing world, where people are malnourished, relatively minor ailments can sometimes cause death.

Deteriorating Biosphere and Environment. The combination of rapid population growth and poverty in developing nations has begun to make permanent changes in the environment. Already millions of acres of soil have been degraded by wind and water erosion, much irrigated land is too salty for food production, rain forests are threatened by peasants who use slash-and-burn techniques to convert forests to short-lived farms, forests in the upper hemisphere are damaged by acid rain, the ozone layer is thinning, and global warming has become a concern. The environmental impact of so many people on the planet has been enormous. Increasing numbers of people are damaging the ecological system and absorbing resources at an ever quickening pace. The next chapter will discuss environmental issues in more detail.

According to the Worldwatch Institute, nearly one out of every three people in poor nations lacks access to a safe supply of water (Worldwatch Institute, 1994). Many experts contend that marine fishing is facing a global crisis; these fish supply the world with more animal protein than any other source, including pork, beef, or poultry (Weber, 1994). Quality of life demands of a growing population, such as the demand for automobiles, are also polluting our air and water. All these problems bring up the question: What are the limits of the earth? We will address this later in the chapter.

Potential for Social Unrest and War. Rapid population growth also creates social unrest and economic and political upheavals. Western industrialized nations are inundated with emigrants (both legal and illegal) who "vote with their feet" and move to lands of more freedom and opportunity. Sometimes the pull is economic, sometimes it is political, and sometimes it is based on the search for fundamental human rights.

Population surges in Third World nations, coupled with the growing gap in standards of living, increase the possibility of warfare, including chemical or nuclear war, not because such surges spawn aggressive ideologies, but because of desperation brought about by the exhaustion of a nation's capacity to feed its people and supply them with the materials they need for survival (Klare, 1992).

Imbalances in Distribution of Wealth. The gap between the "have" nations, such as the United States and most Western countries, and the "have-not" nations continues to widen. Overpopulation in developing countries exacerbates imbalances in the worldwide distribution of wealth, too. During the 1980s, the number of poor people in the world increased dramatically, but even more significant, the proportion of the population that is poor also rose. In both Latin America and sub-Saharan Africa, poverty deepened during the decade, meaning that the poor fell further and further below the poverty line (Worldwatch Institute, 1994). This also happened in individual countries, including the United States.

Contributing to this problem is the fact that developing nations are faced with abnormally young populations, which means that they are struggling not only with the problem of rapidly rising numbers of people, but also with the problem of a burdensome child-dependency ratio. A high child-dependency ratio generally results in low per capita income, educational levels, and living standards. Whatever economic advances a developing country makes may be literally eaten by its increasing population, with the result that poverty continues unabated. If 40 to 50 percent of the inhabitants are children, much of the labor of the workforce is done to feed these relatively unproductive members. There is a lag of 15 to 20 years between the peak of population growth and the peak growth in the labor force.

As an example, sub-Saharan Africa has the dubious distinction of being the fastest-growing region in the world. In 1992 this region had just over 500 million people. The population there is very young; most people have not yet reached their childbearing years (Bryjak and Soroka, 1994). On any indicator of well-being, this area ranks poorly: Per capita income is stagnant or declining, illiteracy is high, people are starving, and the life expectancy is one of the lowest in the world. For instance, the average life expectancy in sub-Saharan Africa is 51, compared to a life expectancy of 66 for the world. In Sierre Leone, the life expectancy is 34 years! In the United States, life expectancy is 76 years, more than double that of Sierre Leone (Population Reference Bureau, 1997).

Solutions to "the Population Problem"

Only three demographic factors can produce population changes: alterations in the birthrate (fertility), variations in the death rate (mortality), and migration into or out of a particular territory (the formula we mentioned earlier). Since migration is not a factor for the world as a whole, only fertility and mortality need be considered in explaining past and present world population trends. However, there are political, economic, and cultural obstacles to these options.

At the present rate of population growth, 90 million people are added each year (Brown, 1994), a rate that is unsustainable and that will force us to reduce living standards, if it continues unchecked. But keep in mind that in much of the world, these standards are already below the level necessary to sustain life.

Lower the Birthrates. Analysts note that the industrialized world has reduced birthrates primarily through the use of contraception and abortion. When these are made medically safe and legal, large numbers of women take advantage of the opportunity to limit family size.

In some areas of the world, this goal has been helped along by postponement of marriage and childbearing. In the Middle Ages, a man could not marry until he could prove that he could support a family—no easy task. Even today in Ireland and in the People's Republic of China, the average age of marriage for women is over 25 years, which removes several potential childbearing years.

Many planners have taken gloomy demographic forecasts to heart, and some governments have imposed dramatic measures to curb their population growth. The harshest measures have been implemented by the People's Republic of China. In 1997, 1.2 billion people (Population Reference Bureau, 1997), or about one out of five people on the planet, lived in the People's Republic of China. Although China spans a large area, much of it is not suitable for agriculture. Regarding its huge population as a barrier to economic and social development, the government instituted a two-child limit for families that was later revised to a one-child policy.

This family policy has worked better in urban areas than in the countryside. Close supervision to detect second pregnancies and bonuses for reporting unauthorized pregnancies are more successful in cities. In particular, peasants resist government efforts to restrict population because they believe that it is necessary to bear a son. Traditionally, sons are thought to bring more happiness—boys can do the heavy work in the fields, and sons offer security for their parents' old age. Thus, culture stands in the way of a seamless implementation of a reduction in birthrate.

Census data indicate that hundreds of thousands of individual Chinese families are aborting or killing infant girls in an effort to have the desired son as their only child. The government is aware of this and has now made it illegal to use ultrasound to determine the sex of the fetus. China anticipates keeping the one-child-per-family policy in force for an entire century, slashing the population in half. But this will mean that every child will be an only child, with no aunts or uncles or cousins. No country has ever attempted such a drastic change. It remains to be seen how successful the Chinese will be. In Chapter 9, we discuss another aspect of this policy—the sex imbalance created by parents aborting or abandoning their girls.

Another example of government policies affecting birthrates comes from Europe. In 1957, the Romanian government legalized abortion and made contraceptives available. The birthrate fell dramatically. Within a decade, about 80 percent of pregnancies ended in abortion. In 1967, in an effort to increase the population (and the number of future workers), President Nicolae Ceausescue restricted contraception and abortion to women who were over 45 or who had already had four living children. Romanian orphanages became overwhelmed by children when families who could not feed their babies put them up for adoption.

In the past, most organized religions opposed contraception and abortion. Many have changed their positions, but not all. The Catholic Church and many Moslem groups still oppose contraception. In a sense, this is a holdover from preindustrial times when the problem was not one of too many babies, but of too few babies surviving. The position of the Catholic Church and some Islamic groups is that the purpose of sex is not pleasure, but procreation. According to this view, life is sacred.

As we have seen, the contemporary plunge in the death rate, which has more than doubled the average life expectancy, has eliminated *the need for prolific reproduction.* Prior to the medical advances of the last 40 years, individual families wanted to ensure that they had enough children to outlive the parents. Adult children were, in a sense, the "social security" that would care for parents in their old age. Even in parts of the world where that is still true, parents no longer need six or seven children to ensure that one will survive them. Nor are children an economic asset these days. In preindustrial days, children were important producers. For the most part, that is no longer true. But the old values endorsing large families have not disappeared. This is an example of *cultural lag.* Changes in the material culture (like advances in health care) are accepted more quickly and easily than changes in the nonmaterial culture (beliefs and norms, for example, that it is important to have many children). At one time, all Jewish and Christian groups opposed contraceptive devices, but most Protestant groups and Reformed and Conservative Jews have changed their views to conform to changing conditions. As the century draws to a close, relatively few religious groups are still unequivocally opposed to contraception and abortion—but such groups do exist.

Increase the Death Rate. Demographers agree that the key ways of reducing fertility are through economic development, family planning programs, and social change. If we do not bring about these changes, and thus voluntarily limit the number of people who are born, the only other way to reduce population is to increase the death rate. In the past, death frequently served as either an intentional or unintentional population control measure. Some societies killed elderly or incapacitated people; more often children were killed, either deliberately or unintentionally, by contracting fatal diseases. Death through warfare has killed huge numbers of people. Genocide attempts, such as the Nazis' annihilation of 6 million Jews during World War II, is another example.

Today we hold the sanctity of human life and the desirability of keeping people alive as one of our fundamental and highest values. A policy of deliberately destroying life is considered taboo—by most (see the box "FYI: An Alternative View on Overpopulation").

Yet even setting aside concerns of compassion and humanity, death does not work well as a solution to overpopulation simply because there is no inherent limit to the death rate. Entire populations can be wiped out. As an example, in the fourteenth century, it is estimated that the plague killed off three-fourths of the population of Europe, the Middle East, and Asia. Another example would be the experiences of the indigenous peoples of North America and Hawaii after the arrival of Europeans. Because the native population had no immunity to common European diseases (such as measles, smallpox, and venereal diseases), huge numbers of them died. Anthropologists and historians believe that between 50 and 90 percent of Native Americans died because of contact with Europeans. Because the death rate is potentially without limit, people are driven to try to find other less drastic solutions to the population problem.

Migration. Migration is another possible solution to the population problem, but, like raising the death rate, it is not ultimately effective. The population problem in developing nations is directly linked to the lack of industrialization and jobs. Thanks to the widespread diffusion of American and European movies and television programs, poor people all over the world have come to realize there is an alternative to their misery. The more ambitious and industrious often decide to migrate to places where jobs and opportunities are greater. Interestingly enough, every migration stream also produces a counterstream of returning migrants who are unable to adjust or are persuaded to return home, but the counterstream is usually much smaller than the outmigration (de Blij and Muller, 1997).

According to sociologist Martin Marger, from about 1850 to 1950, the traditional pattern of global

An Alternative View on Overpopulation

There are some people who propose drastic schemes to confront what they perceive as an overpopulation problem. Here are the views of one man, Pentti Linkola.

What the world needs now, Pentti Linkola believes, is famine and a good war. In his solitude, Mr. Linkola, a Finnish thinker and amateur biologist, ponders the world's problems—overpopulation, dwindling natural resources, industrial trashing of the biosphere. And he has come up with a modest proposal to save the earth: annihilating most of the human race.

End Third World aid and asylum for refugees, he advises, so millions die. Try mandatory abortions for women who already have two children. And then find some way to get rid of the extra billions of people. Another world war, he says, would be a "happy occasion for the planet," given a population 2.5 times greater than the population that the earth can support.

Living alone in primitive style here, without running water or a car, the fisherman likes to compare humanity to a sinking ship with 100 passengers and a lifeboat that can hold only 10. "Those who hate life try to pull more people on board and drown everybody. Those who love and respect life use axes to chop off the extra hands hanging on the gunwale."

He warns of human extinction within decades unless we violently thin ranks. "Everything should be done to save the human race." This is the only way to stop man, "Homo destructivus," from depredating the planet.

He particularly singles Americans out for annihilation. No more than "a few million" would live in his utopia. "The U.S. symbolizes the worst ideologies in the world: growth and freedom."

Source: Dana Milbank, "In His Solitude, A Finnish Thinker Posits Cataclysms, *The Wall Street Journal,* 20 May 1994.

migration occurred mostly within Europe and between Europe and North and South America. That pattern began to change after 1950. From then on, international migration encompassed virtually every part of the globe, with three streams predominating: (1) from Latin America and the Caribbean to the United States and Canada; (2) from south and east Asian countries primarily to the United States, Canada, and Australia and secondarily to western Europe, and (3) from North Africa, the Middle East, and southern Europe primarily to northwestern Europe and secondarily to the United States and Canada (Marger, 1997). Estimates of the number of international migrants are likely to be inaccurate. Illegal, or undocumented, migrants make it difficult to arrive at an accurate number, but we know that the figure is substantial. Many from Third World countries emigrate to Western industrial nations in search of work. In Europe, these individuals are often called "guestworkers." They usually come from southern European countries (Italy, Greece, Turkey), from France's former colonies (Algeria and Morocco), and from Finland. In other parts of the world, they may come from Asia or South and Central America.

When members of a population migrate to areas where there are jobs, the immediate dilemma of unemployment is overcome, at least in the short term, as a solution for individual nations. However, if we are thinking about the world population as a whole, migration is no help. At best, it is only a local remedy, not a solution for the world as a whole. In some cases migration can bring substantial (if temporary) relief, as it did in Ireland after the potato famine in the 1840s; in Norway, Sweden, and Switzerland in the later part of the nineteenth century; and for the Jews of Czarist Russia in the late nineteenth century. But to address the problem of overpopulation in some parts of the world (most notably in the developing world), the volume of migration would have to be 80 times the level it was during the height of international migration (the late nineteenth and early twentieth centuries). From 1870 to 1914, almost 25 million Europeans emigrated to the United

States (de Blij and Muller, 1997). Thus, in today's world, 2 billion people would have to migrate (80 × 25 million).

Emigration on such a large scale is almost inconceivable today. For one thing, emigration on that scale presumes that host countries such as the United States, Europe, or Australia would agree to the surging in-migration, which is hardly realistic. In these countries, and others, there is a resurgent **nativism** (a movement that strongly espouses a halt to large-scale immigration). This will be discussed in more detail in Chapter 11. Besides providing an unsatisfactory solution to the problem of overpopulation, international migration will most likely continue to present problems for the industrialized nations (such as the United States and Germany) both ethnically and practically (Simmons, 1992).

The globalization of the economy has set the stage for more and more people to seek a better life in the West. The communication revolution has enabled people everywhere to see what life in the industrialized West has to offer. It is estimated that at present 60 million people are on the move around the globe (Simmons, 1992). This figure includes at least 19 million who are considered refugees, fleeing from violence and persecution (Newland, 1994). Some refugees are displaced by war, others by other types of civil strife, and many others by political repression. The circumstances prompting emigration include environmental catastrophes, the threat of starvation, economic hardship, and a desire to improve personal circumstances. Barriers to migration, such as strict immigration laws and raised quotas, are doomed to failure. If people truly want to migrate, they find a way to do so, illegally if necessary. All over the world, a thriving business exists that smuggles aliens, provides false identification papers for them, finds jobs for them, and the like. As long as there are new avenues and opportunities for migrants, they find their way around the obstacles.

As more people seek to move to the industrialized nations of the North, developed nations react with alarm. Xenophobia and racism are rising. An example of this response to immigration is California's Proposition 187, a 1994 measure approved by voters that denies illegal immigrants access to welfare benefits, health care, and public schooling (Marger, 1997). (See Chapter 11 for a more detailed look at this topic.)

A lack of economic growth is not the only cause of migration. Even poor countries that have experienced growth may have high levels of unemployment and significant out-migration. For instance, Puerto Rico in the 1950s, Mexico in the 1960s and 1970s, and Korea in the 1970s and 1980s all had spectacular economic growth, but at the same time they lost workers and families through international migration. This apparent paradox may be attributed

Circumstances prompting simple immigration include environmental catastrophes and threat of starvation, both of which can be seen in this African landscape.

to the dual trends of high population growth and the mechanization of business and agriculture, which make it impossible for developing nations to absorb all their workers (Simmons, 1992).

Today, globalization is sharpening both the awareness of differences and the real distance between the rich and the poor. Most developing nations are products of the colonial system, through which Western nations controlled their political, economic, and social destinies. Economically, the developing nations of the world are still locked into a system in which they must operate in a marketplace controlled by the rich industrial nations. Even when industrialized nations export factories and jobs to developing nations, the number of jobs and benefits created are still inadequate to meet the needs of the resident populations. These structural changes in the world economy have caused hardship to workers in places like the United States, without markedly increasing the welfare of workers in developing nations. Their pay is still very low.

The gap between "have's" and "have-nots" continues to widen. On the one side are the nations of the developing world. Not only are these nations less industrialized and less wealthy but they also must face the many problems of rapidly growing populations and urban regions with few resources to spend on solving them. On the other side are the industrialized nations of the world who want to keep whatever gains they have secured over the years. The migration of people from one region to another within a country or from one nation to another is often perceived as threatening. Frequently migration creates unrest. We examine these issues in more detail in Chapter 8.

As the twentieth century draws to a close, economic problems and the resulting political crises in developing countries create both pressure and potential for immigration. In addition, globalization of products and industrial development create an international division of labor. Jobs in fields ranging from science and technology to design, finance, and management are concentrated in the industrialized North, whereas labor-intensive and manual jobs are primarily found in the agricultural South. This means that economic growth in the West creates an expanding demand for low-cost support and service jobs. Emigrants from the developing countries are more than willing to fill that need. These jobs pay little by Western standards, but by Third World standards, they are good jobs, much better than the menial opportunities available in the Old Country.

Population Issues in the United States

So far we have reviewed population-related problems from a global perspective. We will now turn our attention to various issues resulting from changes in the population structure of the United States. Those of us who live in the United States and other industrialized parts of the world are often lulled into a false sense that difficult problems occur somewhere else. Unless they specifically apply to them (or to people they know), many Americans minimize problems in other regions of the world. On television news we see situations in nations that are dramatically worse than problems in the developed world and we tend to distance ourselves from them.

Although our nation is blessed in many respects, the advantages we have do not exempt us from the population problems and pressures affecting other societies. Only two countries in the world have a larger population than ours: China, with more than 1.2 billion people, and India, nearing 1 billion. (The U.S. population is well over a quarter-billion now; Population Reference Bureau, 1997.) (If we look at population densities, rather than total numbers, there is some shifting in rank; India goes to the top of the list as the most densely populated, with about 350 people per square mile. China is next, with about 200; and the United States ranks third, with more than 55 people per square mile.)

Earlier we mentioned the "population explosion." This is not a problem in our country. Our birthrate is low, and it takes more than a century to double by natural increase. But paradoxically, even a slowly declining population can present political or economic problems. One of these is that as our population ages (some call this the "graying" of America), we are confronted by new issues that could pit older people against younger ones over issues such as Social Security. A dwindling workforce will be faced with paying for these expensive programs. In later chapters, we will discuss these issues in more depth.

The U.S. population continues to grow older. In 1991, the median age of Americans was 32.8 years. Reasonable estimates project that the median age will increase to 35.7 by the year 2000 and to 39.3 by 2050 (U.S. Bureau of the Census, 1993:4). (See

Figure 5–4.) This dramatic increase is fueled by the aging of the baby boomers, the first of whom will reach age 65 in 2011 and the last of whom will turn 65 in 2029. These and similar statistics indicate that the problems of the aged will be magnified in the near future. We address some of those areas of concern later in the chapter.

Interestingly, the U.S. population growth from roughly 4 million people in 1790 to 63 million in 1890 follows Malthus's predictions for all populations almost exactly. During this one-hundred-year period, the population doubled every twenty-five years, and the curves of the actual population growth and Malthus's projections almost overlap. The actual growth of our population was even slightly higher than the Malthusian rate because of the effects of immigration, which continued until 1920. But from 1890 to the present, another one hundred years, our population did not increase nearly as fast as Malthus had predicted. Why was this?

The declining rate of increase stems in part from a drop in the birthrate during this period. In 1955, the rate of growth further decelerated, so that we approached zero population growth in the mid-1970s. But since then our birthrate has increased somewhat, and almost half a million immigrants settle in our country each year, further boosting our population. Within the United States, population changes are related to the same forces that affect population worldwide—alterations in birth and death rates, and in- and out-migration.

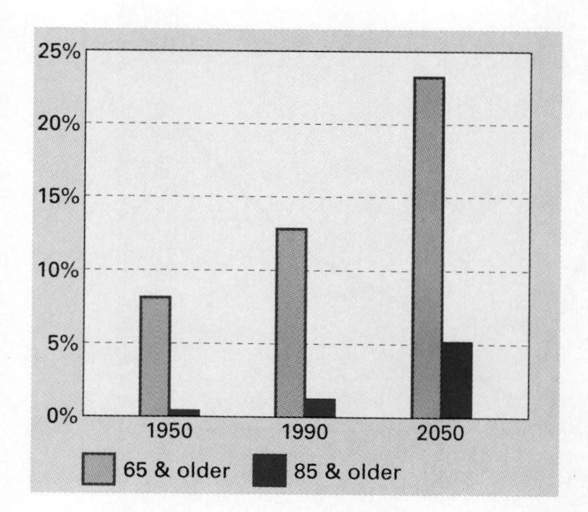

FIGURE 5–4 Percentage of the U.S. Population over 65 and 85

Source: U.S. Census, 1993 and U.S. Senate Special Committee, 1991.

Although people do leave the country, the balance of migration is into the United States. *Push factors* influencing the movement *out* of other countries include political oppression, economic need, and social instability. *Pull factors* influencing the move *into* the United States (as well as into other industrialized nations) include the perception of political and personal freedom, economic opportunity, and social stability available in this country. Even though the United States has its detractors, and the reality experienced by immigrants seldom lives up to their expectations, the United States is still viewed by many as the land of freedom and opportunity.

In this country, as elsewhere, a variety of social and historical forces have conspired to produce lower birthrates, along with lower death rates. The United States, for example, industrialized in the nineteenth century, and so at a relatively early period many consumer goods were available to its citizens. Hundreds of thousands of individual families elected to have fewer children and more consumer goods. Such individual family decisions can greatly affect a nation's total population.

Social Factors Affecting Fertility Rates

A number of social factors influence the birthrates in this country and in other nations as well, leading couples of different social classes, religions, and racial and ethnic groups to have different fertility rates.

Certainly *religion* is one of those social factors that influence fertility. For instance, the Roman Catholic Church has a staunch stand against any kind of birth control. Until recently, Catholic couples had larger families than other Americans, but for the past two decades, that has changed. Apparently, for many Catholic families, the norms and values of the larger society in regard to birth control and family size have become more influential than the views of the Church.

Race and *ethnicity* are another important pair of variables but this, too, is beginning to change. Today there are only minor differences in fertility rates among different races and ethnicities within the country. White women aged 34 to 44 have an average of just under two children per woman (1.9), African American women in this age group average 2.2 children, and Hispanic women in the same age group average 2.6 children (U.S. Bureau of the Census, 1991). Japanese

Americans have lower fertility rates than whites, but Vietnamese Americans have higher fertility rates than whites.

Socioeconomic status is also related to fertility. The old adage, "The rich get richer and the poor get children" seems to be valid. Higher fertility in many respects correlates with lower socioeconomic status. In contemporary American society and the industrialized West, no matter how you measure socioeconomic status—by education level, occupational status, or income—women from a higher socioeconomic status have fewer children. Of these three indicators of social status, the educational attainment of women is the strongest predictor of fertility patterns.

Immigration to the United States

In absolute numbers, the United States remains the principal destination of immigrants. In the 1990 U.S. Census, the number of foreign-born was 19.8 million, which was 7.9 percent of the population. In 1910, the foreign-born comprised 14.7 percent of the population (Pedraza and Rumbaut, 1996).

Figure 5–5 illustrates the general trends in immigration since the 1820 Census, the first year that the United States recorded the place of birth of its residents. However, the earliest arrivals, Native Americans, predated European immigrants to North America by about 35,000 years (Wax, 1971). European migration began in the sixteenth century, and the importation of slaves from Africa began in the early seventeenth century (Marger, 1997). The eighteenth century saw considerable migration from several European countries. But the great period of immigration occurred in the nineteenth century, when successive waves of immigrants arrived from Ireland, Germany, Scandinavia, Italy, Poland, Russia, China, and Japan, among other places. The motives for immigration varied from place to place. Sometimes emigrants left because of push factors, like years of mandatory service in the military (as in Germany) or religious persecution (as in Russia). Sometimes emigrants were drawn by pull factors, like the lure of jobs (as for Chinese emigrants). But whatever the reason, they came in vast numbers.

The great period of immigration to the United States reached a peak in the first decade of this century. Immigration then "tailed off" as a series of laws reflecting isolationist and nativist sentiments closed the borders of the United States to foreigners. Nativists Madison Grant and Lothrop Stoddard published books in the early twentieth century that convinced millions that the American population would suffer if southern and eastern Europeans were allowed to become citizens and intermarry

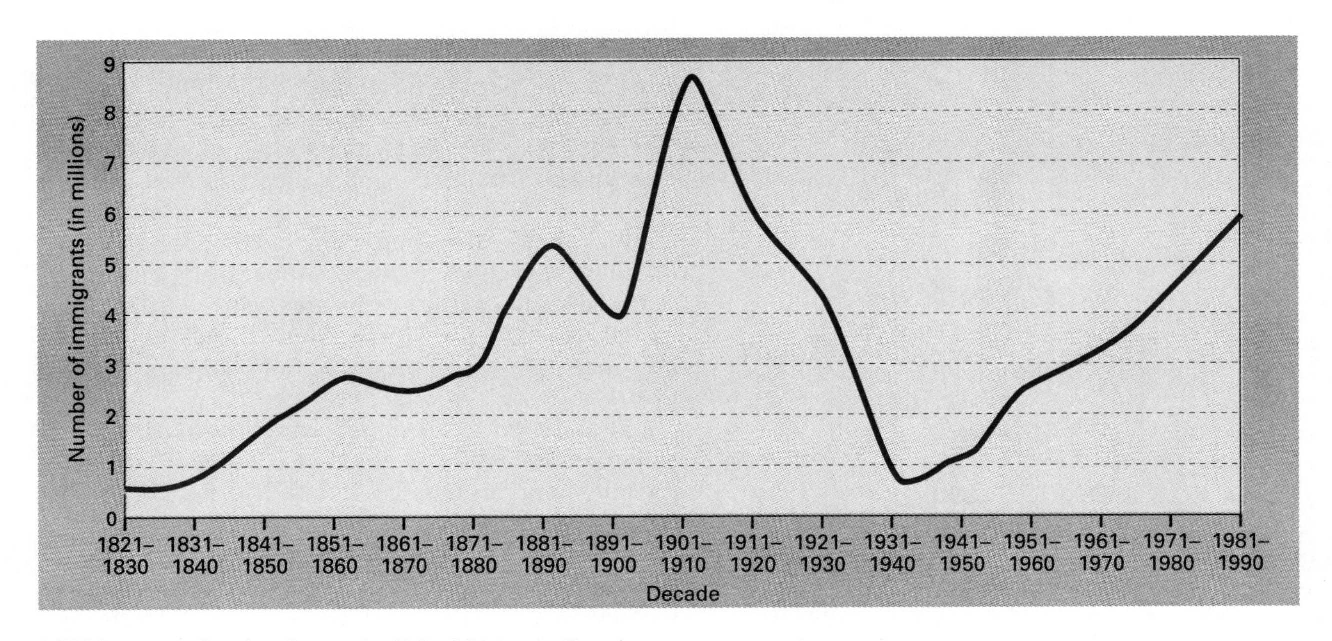

FIGURE 5–5 Immigration to the United States, by Decade

Source: U.S. Immigration and Naturalization Service.

with Americans. After World War II, legal immigration resumed, increasing less than 100,000 to 600,000 per year in the 1980s (U.S. Immigration and Naturalization Service, 1991). A 1990 change in immigration laws now permits 750,000 legal immigrants to come to this country annually.

Although this level of immigration is not as high as it was during the peak of the great migrations of the nineteenth century, it is very high when compared with the immigration rate during the earlier part of this century. Extensive migration into the United States has touched off a renewed immigration debate, which centers not only on the rate of migration but also on the ethnic composition of the newcomers themselves.

Some people have been alarmed that since 1970 there has been a large influx of people from non-European countries such as India, the Philippines, and China. Combined with low rates of natural population increase and higher fertility rates among minority groups, the "face" of America has been radically altered. Without this influx of immigrants, the population of the United States would have actually declined. In the next century, any increase in the population of the United States will depend on immigrants and their descendants. Our low natural population increase, together with current levels of immigration, is significantly altering the racial and ethnic composition of this country. We will discuss the effect of the new immigrants on the United States in Chapter 11.

Migration within the United States

Immigration is only one of the factors affecting the population of a nation. Another is internal migration, the movement of people within the boundaries of a nation. People move from region to region within countries, as well as back and forth between rural and urban areas. The majority of both interregional and rural-urban migrations are prompted by economic concerns. Internal migration reflects as well as magnifies the changing economic fortunes of particular areas. For instance, since the mid-twentieth century, there has been a huge exodus from what is sometimes called the rust belt (the industrial northeastern and midwestern states) into the sunbelt (the southern and southwestern states, where unions are less prevalent). Figure 5–6 shows regional population changes from 1960 to 1990.

Significant population shifts inside this country have had a profound impact. Push forces affecting these migrations include declines in the economies of the Northeast and Midwest (the so-called rust belt), disillusionment with the problems of the central cities, harsh northern climates, and a variety of personal dilemmas. Pull factors encouraging persons to move into southern and western states as well as

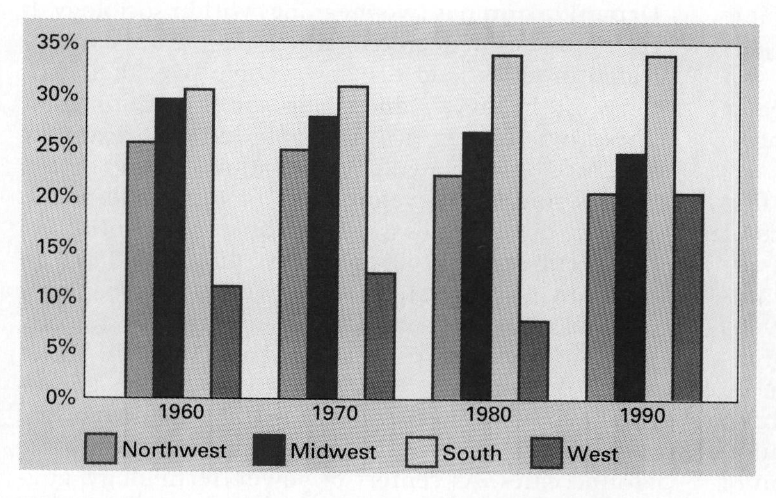

FIGURE 5–6 Regional Population Changes in the United States
Source: U.S. Bureau of the Census, 1991.

the suburbs of larger cities include the lure of better jobs, a more favorable climate, and lower taxes.

Americans have always been mobile. From early settlements along the East Coast, European immigrants spread out across the continental United States, generally moving from north and east to south and west. By the end of the nineteenth century, settlers had reached the Pacific Ocean. Reaching the far side of the American frontier brought to an end one phase of migration.

Implications of Internal Migration in the United States. What do all these population shifts mean over the long term, as population and jobs move out of cities and out of the Northwest? Wealth and income might also be expected to follow population. Although this is not an unreasonable theory, it also has its limits. To some extent there was a "hollowing out" of the central section of the country over the last decade that included slow population growth and an exodus of jobs and economic opportunity. The Northeast also experienced a net outmigration of manufacturing jobs and sluggish population growth. In addition, both regions suffered more than other sections of the country from a recession that began in the mid-1980s, and they recovered more slowly than the rest of the country. Yet the Northeast remains the wealthiest section of the country. This anomaly arose because the loss of blue-collar manufacturing jobs was not matched by a corresponding decline in better-paying white-collar professional, managerial, and investment positions. A higher proportion of wealthy people live in the Northeast than in other parts of the country, and it is the Northeast where better-paying blue-collar jobs continue to disappear. As a result, the income gap between the wealthy and the less fortunate is greater in the Northeast than in most places in this country.

During the first 60 years of this century, our nation underwent another major realignment, as first whites and then blacks began to move from the rural South to northeastern and north central cities. Although most blacks still live in the South, many migrated out of the region before 1960. The 1960s ushered in yet another change in the direction of internal migration. Americans once again began to move from the Northeast and Midwest into southern and western states. Although the overall population in each region continued to grow, the proportion of the total population living in the Northeast and Midwest declined precipitously, and the percentage of Americans residing in the South and West increased dramatically. Population surges in these sunbelt regions had two key sources: internal migration and immigrants from abroad, who settled predominantly in these areas.

Long-range predictions involving population are difficult to make. For instance, as population and jobs shift, wealth and income might also be expected to move with the population. Thus wealth should move from the Northeast and Midwest to the Southwest and the West Coast. It should also move from central cities to the suburbs. Suburbs come in a variety of "flavors." Affluent commuter communities are one type, but there are also working-class suburbs and industrial park suburbs. Historically, they were named suburbs because "sub" indicated they were not economically self-supporting. The suburbs were originally simply appendages of the central city. That distinction is no longer valid.

The population of the United States (and Canada) has been on the move almost from the very beginning. Americans are the world's most mobile people. In the 1990s, migration continues to reshape the United States. The most persistent and significant movement has been a shift from the rust belt toward the sunbelt. The 1980 U.S. Census revealed that for the first time, the geographic center of the United States was west of the Mississippi River (de Blij and Muller, 1997).

Urban Issues in Global Perspective

Urbanization has two meanings within sociology. It refers to (1) the degree to which people are concentrated in cities, and (2) how people live, their patterns of behavior, and their social relationships. These two aspects (*where* people live and *how* they live) are interrelated. Urbanization is one of the most significant developments of the modern era. The rise of vast cities is essentially a nineteenth- and twentieth-century phenomenon, directly related to the growing population of the world. As urban values and behaviors spread to the countryside, the distinctions between rural and urban diminish. Cities affect the ways in which nearly everyone lives—even people who never visit them. At the turn of the millennium, all over the globe, human lives revolve around cities. As centers of power, technology, government, finance, industry, and culture, cities have a tremendous influence on everyone.

Preconditions of City Life

Urbanization itself dates back almost ten thousand years, but in comparison to today, early cities were small. For humans to be able to concentrate in towns or cities, certain things were necessary. Gideon Sjoberg (1960) calls these the "four preconditions of city life."

The first precondition is a *favorable physical environment,* which for most of human history meant fertile soil and a location near water (to provide transportation for food and other supplies, irrigation for crops, and consumption by the residents and any animals they might own).

The second precondition for city life is a relatively advanced technology so that agriculture can create a *social surplus.* It was not until ten thousand years ago that a substantial portion of any society's population lived in cities. Most people lived in the countryside because of the difficulty of feeding large numbers of people. The agricultural surplus was due to several factors. People settled down in one place, cultivated grain, domesticated animals, and eventually developed rudimentary agricultural technology. This technology enabled families to produce more than they needed for their own survival—in other words, they produced a surplus.

A third precondition necessary to the development of cities is a well-developed social organization with some *division of labor.* As some people are freed from the obligation to grow their own food, they become the priests, soldiers, tax collectors, weavers, midwives, and merchants who live in settlements. One of the things that distinguishes an urban area is that residents make their living in some way other than farming. It has only been in the last two hundred years—after scientific and technological advances and improvements in industry, agriculture, commerce, transportation, and sanitation—that substantial numbers of nonfarming people could be fed, housed, and *employed.* That allowed for the growth of huge cities. In earlier times the populations of "cities" or "towns" were only a few hundred people, for the most part. Early cities, which developed about 6,000 years ago, demanded some social organization, but compared to the cities of today, their economic organization seems quite primitive. An example of one such ancient city is Babylon, the capital of Southern Mesopotamia (present Iraq).

The fourth precondition for city life to develop is the *formation of distinct social classes.* This process involves creating social surpluses beyond food. Such a surplus allows for the expansion of goods and services, which leads to greater differentiation and, ultimately, to a hierarchy of occupations and social inequality.

In the industrial West, the processes of modernization and industrialization played a significant part in urbanization. *Modernization*—a process of economic, social, and cultural change that facilitates the transition from preindustrial to industrial society—took generations to occur. It was accompanied by industrialization (the shift to mechanized production) and urbanization (the movement of people to cities), which took several generations. The growth of Western cities was a response to gradual economic advances led by individual capitalists and entrepreneurs. Governments had relatively little to do with it.

The growth of cities was the result of several factors, including increases in population, rural-to-urban migration, and technological advances in agriculture that left many rural people unemployed or underemployed. As technology made farming more efficient and reduced the need for rural labor, new industries developed in the cities. These industries supplied the growing market for new goods and services. The first cities could not have grown much in size except for the near constant migration of people from rural areas.

With the growth of industrial cities came far-reaching and unprecedented cultural and social changes. These early industrial cities (mostly in Europe) produced a great deal of wealth but, by any standard, they were characterized by serious overcrowding, unsanitary conditions, diseases, and epidemics. But the large-scale urbanization in Europe and North America had one advantage that urbanization in the developing world does not have: The process spanned more than a century. It involved massive economic and social change, spurred by industrialization. Also, early cities in Europe and the United States were not as large as Third World cities at the end of the twentieth century. Mexico City, Manila, and Calcutta are far larger than New York or London ever were (Palen, 1987).

In 1965, North America (including the United States and Canada) contained the most highly urbanized region, followed by Europe and Latin America. About a fifth of Africa's population and less than a fourth of Asia's people lived in urban areas. What a difference a few decades make. North America and

Europe are still highly urbanized, but the developing areas of the world are now also rapidly urbanizing.

Urbanization in the Developing Nations of the World

In the developing nations of the world, the process of urbanization is highly visible and much more dramatic and rapid than the process was for the Western industrial nations. In the Third World, urban explosion can be attributed both to rising populations and to in-migration from rural areas. By the twenty-first century, there will be at least 21 cities with more than ten million inhabitants, and 17 of them will be in developing nations (Massignon, 1993). The reversal or slowing down of urbanization is not likely to occur for years, for three reasons: (1) the expected rapid population growth of city dwellers who are young and of childbearing age, (2) the fact that more and more workers are being pushed off the land as farms are mechanized, and (3) the hope many people harbor of finding work in cities (Massignon, 1993).

Such a situation presents problems for Third World cities. Even prior to industrialization, Western nations were the wealthiest countries in the world. In contrast, much of the developing world is poor by almost any standard of measure. As developing nations attempt to industrialize and more and more of their citizens move to their cities, they are forced to compete with the highly advanced economies of the West. To feed, house, and find work for all these people is almost impossible. These nations lack virtually everything—capital, infrastructure, an educated workforce, and an industrial base. When the West was industrializing, private entrepreneurs and businesses took care of much of this, but in the developing world today, to provide all these things is simply beyond the abilities of private businesses or corporations. Moreover, much of the business in these countries is run by transnational corporations, which have little incentive to provide these commodities. It is "better business" to go where all (or most) of these things can be provided at no cost to the corporation.

Western industrial societies have had the luxury of time to make the transition from preindustrial societies. Even so, those people who couldn't find jobs, or housing, or adequate food were seriously harmed by the transition. But in today's developing societies there is the phenomenon of very rapid transformation from a rural society largely based on agriculture to an urban society based on industry. The result of this accelerated change is frequently a great deal of social disorganization. Because individuals (or perhaps a family unit) move to the city alone, the loss of family and community connections frequently means that people lose the social support and comfort of being part of a larger group. Often, people in such circumstances feel powerless and alienated.

Unlike in the West, the growth in the cities of the developing world is not the result of growth in the private sector. Cities in the Third World grow because peasants see them as their only hope. As agriculture becomes mechanized and fewer hands are needed, agricultural workers find themselves unemployed in the countryside. They move, not because private companies in the city need workers, but because there are no jobs in the countryside. The "engine of growth" is totally different for developing world cities; it is not opportunity in the city that

In the cities of the developing world, housing presents a particularly intractable problem. New urban residents often live in squatter settlements such as this favela (slum) in Rio de Janeiro, Brazil.

draws peasants, it is the total lack of opportunity in the countryside that pushes them to the city lights.

Most Third World governments do not have enough money and resources to promote and manage urban growth on a massive scale. Infrastructure (transportation, housing, water and sewage systems, schools, hospitals) are all expensive. Although some developing world cities add some of these amenities before housing projects are completed, so many people move into communities that these amenities quickly become inadequate. Huge population growth (some of these countries double their populations in 25 to 30 years) further complicates the problem.

The enormous population increases in developing countries, particularly in rural areas, have meant that many people are literally pushed off the land in search of jobs. Unfortunately, rural migrants are among the poorest and least skilled members of their society. These surplus workers crowd into cities at a much higher rate than the city can absorb them, that is, provide them with jobs and housing. This trend is sometimes called *overurbanization* (the disparity between the opportunities and services that are available and the demand for those opportunities and services). Overurbanization is usually the result of a migration from rural to urban areas that takes place far faster than the expansion of possible jobs in the city. But for peasants pushed off the countryside, although life in the city may be difficult, at least it offers hope for something better for them and their children.

The term overurbanization implies that the proportion of people residing in cities is too large in relation to the nation's or community's economic development. Developing societies, though unique in some respects, have many common problems, including relatively high unemployment, inadequate housing, poor transportation, insufficient medical services, inadequate school systems, and high rates of pollution. The result is harmful to the health and well-being of the people of such societies.

In the cities of the developing world, housing presents a particularly intractable problem. New urban residents often live in *squatter settlements* (makeshift arrangements that often have no access to water, sewers, or other amenities). Sometimes they have access to electricity; sometimes they do not. In squatter settlements the house/shelter is built and owned by the residents, but they do not own the land itself. Legally, they are trespassing and could be required to move at any time. These squatter slums are often on the outskirts of the cities of the developing world, but sometimes they are located in neglected pockets of land within the city that have been bypassed because they are too hilly or too wet or are undesirable for some other reason.

Cities are often unhealthy places, but the extent of their problems is magnified many times over in the developing world. Take Mexico City for example. Most experts agree that Mexico City is either the largest city in the world today, or will be within the next decade or so. Because of a number of factors, including the fact that the city is built in a geological basin that traps pollutants and prevents winds from dispersing the contaminants, it is a city plagued by smog.

In a country like Mexico where many people drive old, fuel-inefficient cars powered with leaded gas, the city's air pollution is extremely unhealthy. When it is particularly bad, the Mexican government orders that cars with license plates ending in even numbers may drive on Tuesdays, Thursdays, and Saturdays, while those ending with odd numbers may drive the other days of the week. (Wealthy people get around the restriction by purchasing two cars and making sure one license plate ends in an even number, the other in an odd number.) In 1992, the problem became so bad that the government banned all automobile traffic in the city for two days a week. The health ministry frequently advises against outdoor exercise.

Another factor that contributes to Mexico City's unhealthy environment is that fully 30 percent of the city's residents lack access to toilets. Human waste is carried both in the city's dust and in the air as harmful gasses. Nevertheless, the city continues to grow, both from natural increase and from in-migration from the rural areas. Since the majority of people who leave the land are young people, poverty often rises in the rural areas. Because of the mechanization of agriculture, fewer people are needed to till the land, but cities, even Mexico City, cannot provide enough jobs for the displaced workers.

Mexico City is not unique. All across the globe, large numbers of people are moving from the countryside to the cities. This migration is changing the world's demographic landscape. All governments (including ours) find it difficult to provide the expensive infrastructure required by cities. Someone has to pay for the streets, waterlines, sewage systems, schools, health care systems, roads, and electric lines. To provide an adequate infrastructure is especially difficult for cities in the developing world.

Urbanization within the United States

The population of the United States has migrated from rural to urban regions from the earliest days of nationhood. The industrial revolution occurred almost a century later in the United States than it did in Europe, but it took hold so successfully that within 50 years the new nation surpassed Europe as the world's mightiest industrial power. The far-reaching social and economic changes that Europe's industrializing nations experienced were accelerated in the United States. Of particular significance was the arrival of nearly 25 million European immigrants who, no matter what their occupations in the Old Country, headed for American cities and urban jobs (de Blij and Muller, 1997).

TABLE 5–3 Urban Population of the United States, 1790–1990

YEAR	POPULATION (IN MILLIONS)	PERCENT URBAN
1790	3.9	5.1%
1800	5.3	6.1
1820	9.6	7.3
1840	17.1	10.5
1860	31.4	19.7
1880	50.2	28.1
1900	76.0	39.7
1920	105.7	51.3
1940	131.7	56.5
1960	179.3	69.9
1980	226.5	73.7
1990	253.0	75.2

Source: U.S. Bureau of the Census, 1996.

Early Urban Growth

In 1790, only 5 percent of the American population lived in urban settings; by 1990, more than 75 percent of Americans resided in towns, cities, or their suburbs. These figures are somewhat misleading because the Bureau of the Census uses an outmoded definition of "urban" to refer to any community with 2,500 or more residents. (See Table 5–3.)

The nineteenth century was a period of increasing urbanization in the United States. Early urbanization was based on the traditional role of cities, providing goods and services for the hinterlands in exchange for raw materials. Preindustrial cities fostered handicraft production and commercial activities, while the emerging movement toward industrialization tended to favor further growth of urban centers. The nineteenth century was a period in which power, population, manufacturing, and finance concentrated in urban areas such as New York, Boston, and Philadelphia (Palen, 1987).

Nineteenth-century urban centers provided concentrations of both investment capital and labor; transportation and communication networks were already in place. In addition, these cities could absorb the vast numbers of immigrants who clustered around the new factories built within city limits or in nearby communities. There was money to be made, and it provided the capital for cities to invest in better infrastructure as well as housing. Each round of industrial expansion accelerated the trend toward urbanization (de Blij and Muller, 1997).

The rapid rise of U.S. cities was an unintended, but crucial, by-product of industrialization. Together, industrialization and urbanization profoundly altered the economy. As a result of technological changes, the standard of living improved for most people. In time, a large, mainly white, urban class was created that was as concerned with consumption as with production. In earlier times that consumption might have included electric refrigerators rather than iceboxes. Today consumption can include microwave ovens and VCRs.

Without industrialization the United States would not have had the rapid economic development that it did. The period of greatest growth of American cities was from 1870 to 1920, but the growth of cities predated even the Civil War. During earlier times, small production units were more common. By the end of the nineteenth century, large-scale enterprises were emerging. But no matter the size of the business, the growth of cities in America and of its industrial-based economy were based on shifting employment opportunities.

Urbanization in the Twentieth Century

The flow of people moving to cities accelerated dramatically in the twentieth century. At the start of the century, even though large industrial centers had emerged, the country was predominantly rural and agricultural. However, the fast pace of industrialization gave people incentive to leave farms to work in urban factories, businesses, and offices. By 1990, only about 5 million people—less than 2 percent of all Americans—lived on producing farms (U.S. Bureau of the Census, 1993).

The phenomenon of U.S. residents migrating to follow jobs is not new. In addition to moving from one region of the country to another, in the 1950s people began to move out of central cities into rapidly growing suburbs. Most shifts occur within central cities or within the suburbs themselves. When people move between the central city and its suburbs, the flow of population is heavily in the direction of the suburbs. Even when people move from rural regions to urban areas today, they go directly into the suburbs rather than living for a few years in cities. The net result of all these migrations to suburbs has been a withering of central cities and a blossoming of suburbs.

To make matters worse for the central cities, the people moving out of them have tended to be wealthier than those they leave behind. Corporate America has also abandoned the cities, especially those in the Northeast, transplanting facilities and jobs to suburbs, more favorable southern areas, or out of the country altogether. This outflow of people, wealth, and jobs has set in motion a vicious cycle: As central cities experience a declining tax base, a decreasing job base, and a deterioration of housing stock and infrastructure, they also face increased demands for services, such as police and fire protection, calls for money to provide education for disadvantaged children and the children of immigrants, public health services, and public assistance. In a strange twist, most U.S. metropolitan regions are characterized by poor, decaying inner cities surrounded by relatively affluent suburbs, whereas in the developing world, new, gleaming, prosperous central cities are usually surrounded by miles of slums inhabited by the poor and the unemployed.

Today America's central cities are often places of pathology and decay. The crime rate is high, the drop-out rate from school is high, the amount of drug abuse escalates, thousands (perhaps hundreds of thousands) are homeless, the housing inadequate, and the list goes on. One of the major issues central cities face is urban funding. Who will pay for upgrading the infrastructure? How should limited urban funds be spent? Should we try to revitalize the economies of the old central cities? Or should we permit cities to contract to a size at which they are economically viable? These choices are of more than academic interest. The decisions made influence the lives of hundreds of thousands of urban residents and millions of taxpayers.

It seems likely that most rural sections of the country will continue to experience a net out-migration, as better educated citizens and young adults leave in search of improved job prospects. A further decline in population and wealth is likely in most of the central cities as well. More and more poor people will find themselves trapped in decaying central cities.

While it is no longer true that a move to the city is a stepping-stone to a better life, everything is not rosy in the suburbs either. Many suburbs are growing so fast that they are overwhelmed by the need for services, infrastructure, schools, and the like. Traffic jams clog roads designed for much smaller populations. Pollution problems, crime, and street gangs are among the undesirable by-products of an increased population. Not all suburbs are prosperous; some older suburbs are growing poor themselves, as affluent residents move to newer areas. Moreover, many poor people are migrating directly to suburbs, bypassing central cities altogether. As a result, some suburbs have affluent neighborhoods alongside poverty-stricken ones.

Assessing the Situation

This chapter brings together two major problems that are dramatically altering the world scene—population and urbanization. Developing countries tend to have high growth rates. Poor rural people flock to cities in large numbers, which causes Third World nations to have most of the world's largest cities. Traditionally, industrialization has preceded urbanization, but that sequence is being reversed in developing nations today. Jobs and other amenities simply are not available in sufficient quantity or quality.

Population

Increasing population pressures are an important factor that drives the trend toward globalization at both the objective and subjective levels. Objectively, many people travel, migrate, or come into contact with people from other cultures. On the subjective level, significant changes are occurring in the ways people think about themselves. For instance, television and the mass media have made it more difficult for citizens of the developed world to ignore the conditions of poor people in the developing world. At the same time, the power of the mass media also has made the rapidly growing populations of Third World countries more aware of the discrepancy between their own standard of living and that of those living in wealthy nations. Increasingly, people everywhere want "a piece of the pie," consumer goods that will make their lives easier. One result is the spread of consumerism and expectations for material well-being, even if on a modest scale. Such expectations may fuel further environmental decline. As an illustration, in the late 1970s, one of the authors spent two summers in the rural mountains of Mexico. Far from any community of any size was a beautiful group of scenic waterfalls in a horseshoe shape. Below the falls was a huge, brightly colored eddy. Close inspection revealed that it was made of various colored plastic detergent and bleach bottles. Women upstream continue to wash clothes along the banks, as their mothers and grandmothers have done before them. But now they use modern products, and when the bottle is empty, they throw it in the stream.

Fear of Overpopulation. Urbanization and population increase come together with devastating consequences. There are some people who believe that the world need not fear overpopulation. They maintain that food shortages occur not because of the danger of running out of foodstuffs, but, rather, because the distribution of food has become a political issue. If that is true, one option is to stop concentrating on producing more food, per se, but instead to stress redistribution of resources, especially food and potable water. Such a redistribution would probably require government supervision to artificially lower the price of some staples so that poor people could afford them.

Another option is to try to achieve "optimum population," a term that is used in contradictory ways, but which generally refers to the number of people who can be supported at a given standard of living, rather than the most people who could possibly be supported at a minimum standard of living.

Nearly all experts agree that population cannot continue to grow unchecked. There is a finite limit to human population on our planet, but debate centers on what that figure is. In addition, a question of fairness surrounds the status quo. If people in the industrialized North would compromise on a reasonable standard of living, there would be more food and energy available for those in the poor agricultural nations clustered in the South. Economist Herman Daly (1991) uses the analogy of a ship to make this situation clear. Ships have a mark on them called the plimsoll line. If the water level rises above this line, the vessel is too heavy and in danger of sinking. He points out that the ship we call earth is in danger; we are currently sailing with water almost above the plimsoll line, surpassing the carrying capacity of the planet.

UN Human Rights and Population Policies. The United Nations would like to stabilize the world's population at 7.27 billion by the year 2015. The UN proposes three basic guidelines to help reach that goal (UN Population Fund, 1990). These programs are closely related to human rights issues. Specifically, this program of action includes the following:

1. *Universal access to family planning services, information, and advice on all aspects of fertility, with national goals set by each country.* Family planning programs have three basic elements: provision of information about reproduction and contraceptive techniques, provision of contraceptives at no or low cost, and a propaganda campaign that promotes the ideal of small families and the acceptability of contraception.

2. *Primary health care for women and infants that emphasizes the need to space pregnancies and seek postnatal care.* Changes in the role of women will be a factor. In some parts of the world, women are isolated and do not have the opportunity to participate in activities outside the home. Their status (or worth) depends upon their ability to bear and rear children, particularly sons. Societal changes that improve the status of women lead to decreased fertility rates (Barr, 1992). Better health care for girls and women is just the starting point.

3. *Basic education for all girls by the year 2015 and equal enrollment for both sexes in secondary schools.* Studies have shown that when women are given greater educational and employment opportunities, fertility declines (Barr, 1992). As we discuss in Chapter 9, as long as children have any economic value to parents (however small), they are less likely to receive an education, and without it, are more likely to continue the tradition of large families.

Theoretical Concerns about Population. Earlier, we discussed how human societies often develop patterns that have unforeseen and undesired effects. In some cases once these patterns are set in motion, they tend to continue even though their effects are harmful. In some cases the harmful effects even reinforce the pattern itself, making it very difficult to halt the damaging consequences before it is too late.

One example of such a self-reinforcing feedback loop is found in the way human population growth follows the pattern known as the "tragedy of the commons." In 1977, biologist Garrett Hardin described human population growth as a process similar to the destruction of the British commons that took place on the eve of the industrial revolution. English villages had by tradition maintained common land accessible to all villagers to use for grazing, hunting, the gathering of firewood, and the like. When markets for wool, mutton, and beef developed, villagers discovered that it was in their private interest to exploit the common land by grazing a few extra head of sheep or cattle. The resultant overgrazing caused a decline in the actual size of the animals, but still this was not viewed as a signal to stop overgrazing. Rather, individual villagers saw it as an incentive to increase their own family's herd in an effort to keep themselves afloat. Their decision to do this led to even faster depletion of forage, which gave each individual family even more incentive to enlarge its herds in an increasingly desperate effort to maintain the family's standard of living.

The essence of tragedy in literature lies in the fact that the protagonist is compelled to act in ways that lead to his or her own destruction. And so it was for the English villagers, compelled to destroy their livelihood in the very effort to improve their lot. This example is a prime case in which the individual good and the collective good are in opposition. The logic of the system seems to favor more sheep or cattle for the individual farmer, yet this response dooms the system as a whole.

Hardin was not particularly interested in long-dead Englishmen and their sheep. Rather, he was pointing to a common and recurrent pattern in many places in the world today. In particular, he was concerned with population in the poorer regions of the world. Here the "commons," or free resource, is human reproductive capacity. Poor families throughout the world invest in having more children, which are a poor family's prime means of improving its lot. Yet when hundreds of thousands of poor families have an extra child or two, the overall effect is to reduce the income each child provides for the family. This falling family income is not, as in the case of the English villagers, interpreted as a signal to cease and desist (that is, to have fewer children). Although it is not necessarily true that the poor rural villagers in developing countries cannot see this larger picture, for any poor family to refuse to have another child seems almost a guarantee that it will not prosper and will fall behind its more "fortunate" neighbors whose families are larger. And though poor rural villagers in the developing world may also recognize that such expansionary logic is true only in the short run, we all live in the short run—especially the poor who must be concerned about feeding themselves and paying their debts today, in the process perhaps saving enough so that one of their children might receive a smattering of education and be able to benefit the family tomorrow.

Fortunately, a society is made up of many interconnected processes and not merely one negative feedback loop. As we have seen in this chapter, there are ways that the cycle of population and poverty has been broken. Educating women helps; the development of an urban economy helps; the redistribution of some of society's wealth, so that the poor who generate so much of it may receive minimal economic security, helps. These are among the factors that encourage people to gradually cease investing in their reproductive capacity to have another child.

Urbanization

The worldwide trend of people moving to large urban regions is the other central topic of this chapter. The world's demographic, environmental, and social problems are most acute in cities, particularly in urban areas in the developing world, where hundreds of thousands of peasants migrate from the countryside or small villages to urban centers. Yes, there are problems in the city, but there are also the possibilities of cash employment, education, medical care, chances for advancement, and the excitement and entertainment of a modern lifestyle. For the young and ambitious, the pull factors are difficult to resist.

Rural Land Reform. One possible solution to urbanization problems in the developing world is some sort of land reform to help prevent large numbers of peasants being pushed off the land. For instance, perhaps by extending irrigation or clearing forested areas, new land could be put under the plow. This is expensive, but in some places it could be accomplished. This is a possible catch-22 in that such practices could cause environmental problems such as a lack of firewood or global warming.

Another possibility is the confiscation of large estates and redistribution of the land to the peasants. This could reduce pressure on cities to provide jobs and other amenities and could boost agricultural production as well. Land reform has been tried in several Central and Latin American countries, with mixed results.

However, land reform is expensive. Peasants would need credit to purchase seeds, fertilizer, and equipment. Another disadvantage of land reform is it would involve bitter political confrontations with those who own the large estates.

Overurbanization. The population increases in the developing world, coupled with the lure of big city amenities, leads to the phenomenon of overurbanization. The sheer numbers overwhelm the capacity of developing countries to provide urban infrastructure and even basic services, such as housing, jobs, and transportation.

Overurbanization contributes to social disorganization. We have seen this in the United States, where businesses move from the central cities to the suburbs or even rural areas. The poorest of the urban dwellers remain, while the more affluent follow the jobs and the prospects of a safer, more attractive environment. The flight of both the middle class and jobs results in what has been the traditional subject matter of social problems courses—crime, drug and alcohol abuse, and family breakdown.

In the cities of the developing world, these problems are even worse, and developing cities have far fewer resources with which to combat them. Many of these communities (and countries) do not have the industrial base or other resources to tackle these problems, so they keep getting worse. In both industrial nations and the Third World today, urban problems seem to defy solution. What can be done?

Early sociologists were not in agreement about the merits or drawbacks of urbanization. Some (such as Ferdinand Tönnies and Louis Wirth) stressed that personal ties and the traditional values of rural life diminish in the rush of anonymous, impersonal city life. Others (such as Emile Durkheim and Robert Park) emphasized the positive features of urban life, including more autonomy and a wide range of life choices.

Sociologist J. John Palen (1987) suggests three approaches to urban social planning and social problems. The *conventional approach* assumes that urban problems can be solved by existing mechanisms, by allocating money and other resources more wisely. *Reformist approaches* assume that cities need major modification and changes. Proponents see the system as the source of the problem and will accept quasi legal methods, such as those used by the civil rights movement or the environmental movement. The *radical approach* is pessimistic and assumes that urban problems cannot be solved. Proponents believe that the existing system is so flawed that little can be done to save it.

Summary

1. The **population explosion,** the huge increase in the number of people in the world, contributes to or sets in motion many global social problems, including environmental, political, economic, racial, women's, and ethnic issues.
2. An **adaptive regime** is a society's normatively regulated practices relative to population size and to the consumption of environmental energy. Examples include the *tribal equilibrium,* the *pronatalist expansionist,* and the *industrial consumptionist regimes.*
3. In modern times,the death rate has declined because of improvements in diet, housing, sanitation, and medical science. **Demographers** (scientists who study population) compute the population as follows: Population = Births − Deaths ± Migration.
4. In human history, population has escalated rapidly during three periods: the Neolithic Revolution (about 8000 B.C.E.), which was marked by agricultural development; the Industrial Revolution (around 1750 C.E.); and post–World

War II (late 1950s), when major medical advances saved many lives.

5. **Demographic transition theory** posits that as nations industrialize, they pass through four phases: Phase I, the preindustrial stage, marked by high birth and death rates; Phase II, the industrial phase, characterized by a slowly declining birthrate and a quickly declining death rate; Phase III, during which smaller families become the norm as technology matures; and Phase IV, during which both birth and death rates stabilize at a low level as industrialization is fully developed.
6. Among the results of the increased world population are food shortages, a deteriorating biosphere and environment, and imbalances in the distribution of wealth.
7. Solutions to the population problem include lowering birthrates, increasing the death rate, and migration.
8. The United States has the third largest population in the world. Social factors related to fertility rates include religion, race and ethnicity, and socioeconomic factors. The overall trend in internal migration in the United States has been a dramatic decline in the proportion of the total population living in the Northeast and Midwest and a sharp increase in the proportion living in the South and West.
9. Preconditions of city life include a favorable physical environment, a well-developed social environment with some division of labor, and the formation of distinct social classes.
10. **Overurbanization** is usually the result of migration from rural to urban areas far faster than the expansion of possible jobs and infrastructure in the city.
11. In the United States, each phase of industrial expansion accelerated the trend toward urbanization, with the flow of people to the cities increasing dramatically in the twentieth century. Starting in the 1950s, people as well as corporations began to move out of central cities into rapidly growing suburbs.
12. The UN proposes three action goals toward stabilizing the world population: universal access to family planning, primary health care for women and infants, and basic education for all girls by the year 2015.

Thinking Critically

1. Most demographers place world population today at about 5.9 billion (Reuters Service, 1994). Population experts disagree about what the optimum population of the world should be, but they do note that two issues are paramount when we address the question of optimum population: (a) the maximum carrying capacity of the globe—that is, the number of people who can be fed and cared for and (b) the optimum population in relation to a given standard of living. We could keep millions more alive, but the standard of living of some, or all, might be below the level most of us consider satisfactory. With this in mind, do we have a worldwide population problem, or is the problem located in individual countries, some of which, like China and India, have too many people? What do you think? Why?
2. Finnish thinker Pentti Linkola maintains that the earth is already 2.5 times more densely populated than the optimum population (see "FYI: An Alternative View on Overpopulation"). Most authorities would probably cite a larger optimum population figure than Linkola, and they certainly would not support his drastic solutions. But what is the magic number? And what is a realistic standard of living? No one argues that the kind of life we have enjoyed in the United States and the industrialized West can be sustained by even the 5.9 billion alive today. That leaves a key problem: Would those of us who are citizens of the industrialized countries willingly accept a lesser standard of living so that others in the developing world could live a better life? If so, in what areas would we compromise? Less calories consumed? The same

number of calories but fewer of them obtained from meat? Colder houses? Smaller dwellings? Less extensive wardrobes? Abandoning private vehicles in favor of public transportation? In what areas would we willingly cut back? Or will we decide that the industrialized West, including the United States, does not have a population problem? These are all significant questions, and they are not easy to answer. But in a very real sense, the future of humanity on this planet turns on how we respond to these critical concerns today.

3. Consider the social effects of population measures such as the one-child policy in China. How would such measures affect social institutions like the family, education, and the economy? If the need arose, do you think that the citizens of the United States could ever support such a drastic policy?
4. As the twenty-first century approaches, more and more people throughout the world are becoming urban dwellers. Considering the serious problems of cities throughout the world today (crime, lack of jobs, drug addiction, insufficient affordable housing, the crumbling infrastructure), what are some possible remedies? What might experts from a conventional, reformist, and radical perspective suggest?

Suggested Readings

Daniels, Roger. 1990. *Coming to America: A History of Immigration and Ethnicity in American Life.* New York: HarperCollins.

Farley, John E. 1995. *Majority-Minority Relations,* 3rd edition. Englewood Cliffs, NJ: Prentice Hall.

Feagin, Joe R. and Clairece Booher Feagin. 1996. *Racial and Ethnic Relations,* 5th edition. Upper Saddle River, NJ: Prentice Hall.

Hewlett, Sylvia Ann. 1993. *When the Bough Breaks.* New York: Basic Books.

Schaefer, Richard T. 1993. *Racial and Ethnic Groups,* 5th edition. New York: HarperCollins.

Worldwatch Institute. 1994. *State of the World, 1994: A Worldwatch Institute Report on Progress Toward a Sustainable Society.* New York: W. W. Norton.

Web Sites

The following web sites are especially useful for understanding population and urbanization issues and keeping up to date on recent developments.

The U.S. Census Bureau, Population Division, has a "pop clock" that provides up-to-the-minute estimates of U.S. population and world populations. It also provides extensive data on human population as far back as 1000 B.C.E.:
http://www.census.gov/ftp/pub/population/www/

Princeton University publishes the Population Index, *which is especially useful for demographic information about the decade 1986–1996:*
http://popindex.princeton.edu/

Princeton also has a research center on population (Population Research Bureau) that tells about the latest developments in population research:
http://opr.princeton.edu/research

The Homepage for the Cairo International Conference on Population and Development includes fact sheets, statistics, press releases, and full-text documents from the conference:
http://www.mbnet.mb.ca/linkages/cairo.html

CHAPTER ■ SIX

Environmental Destruction

Depleting the Global Commons

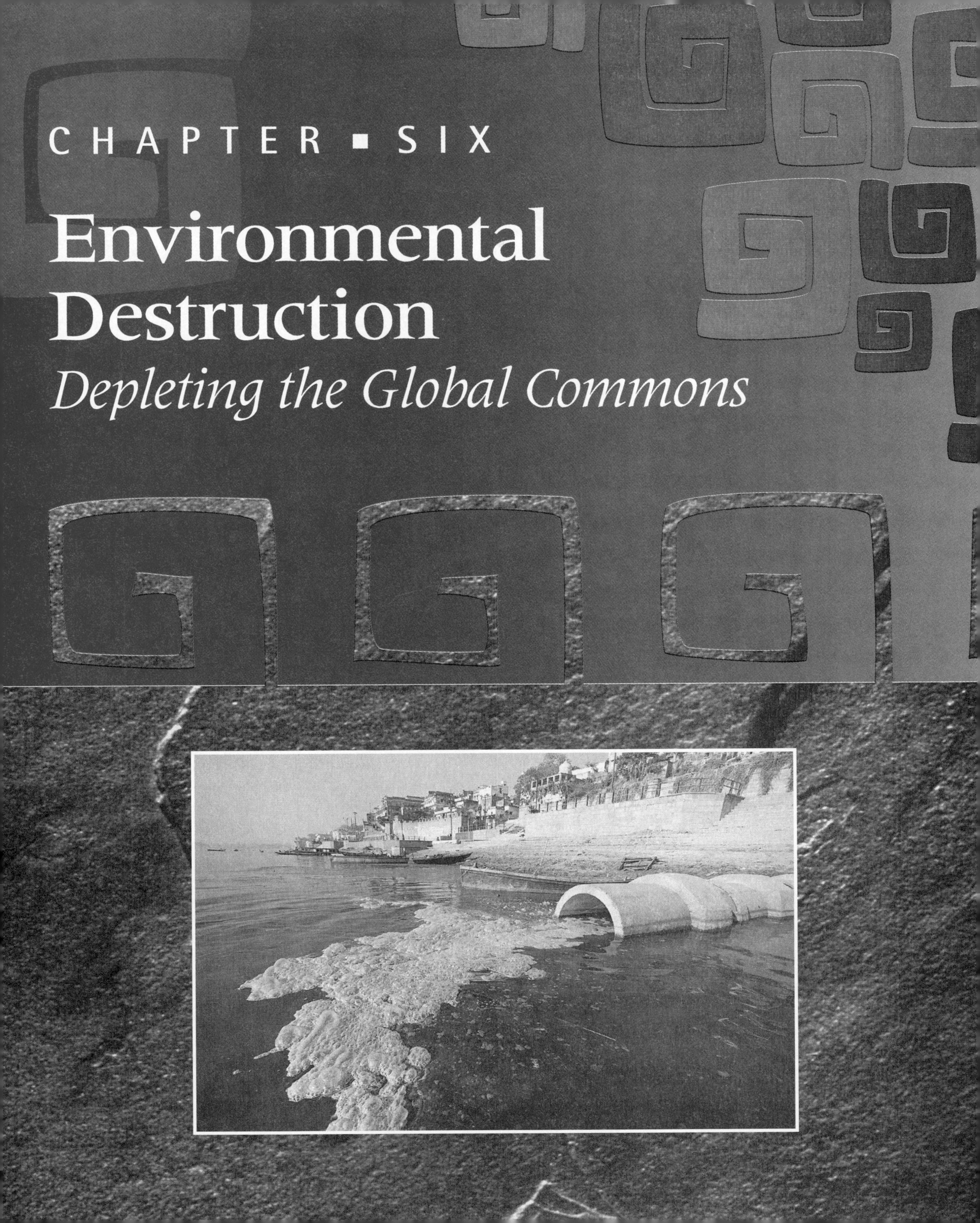

Gede is a resident of a slum in Jakarta, Indonesia. Each day during the rainy season, black, polluted water flows down from the surrounding hills in the morning and floods his home. At times he is forced to stand chest-deep in the brackish liquid, his meager furniture is soaked, and his children must take to the rafters of the house until the water recedes in the afternoon. Like other poor residents of the city, Gede must cope with pollution from auto exhausts, noise from traffic and machines, and toxic wastes from Jakarta's rapidly expanding industries.

Yet, in many ways, Gede and the other poor like him are their own worst enemies. He and his neighbors use the banks of a nearby river for a privy because they cannot afford the 50 cents a day it costs to use the public toilet in their neighborhood. They dump their garbage and household trash in the muddy streets in front of their houses. Their wastes are washed along with other pollutants into the same foul waterways used to provide household drinking water. Occasionally, these grimy channels provide fish, which proves a welcome tidbit in an otherwise bland diet.

These conditions are not entirely the fault of the impoverished. The slum dwellers flock to the city from the surrounding countryside in hope of finding jobs and a better life. Often jobs are unavailable, and such employment as is found provides only scant income. Moreover, the government has been unable to create streets, sewers, safe water, schools, and health facilities for the 60 percent of Jakarta's population living in poverty, in part because the city is expanding so rapidly. Officials are in a genuine bind. Money to address these problems is very difficult to obtain, but the alternative of doing nothing is even more costly. It is estimated that Jakarta's air and water pollution alone costs the city 6,000 lives and $6 billion in economic losses annually. Already, a liter bottle of mineral water costs almost twice as much as a liter of gasoline.

Under pressure from Western countries, the Indonesian government has begun to take measures to improve Jakarta's environment. By 1994, the government had developed a plan to improve the quality of drinking water and hoped that within a year all gasoline-powered engines would use unleaded gas. Attempts are being made to enforce automobile emission standards. And industrial pollution is no longer accepted as the price of economic development. Still, the task is formidable. Jakarta's environment will likely be significantly tainted well into the next century.

Adapted with modifications from Sheila Tefft. 1994. "In Search of Solutions for a Polluted Jakarta." *The Christian Science Monitor.* September 19: 9–11.

Gede's story illustrates the common plight of Third World cities. In fact, the poverty, pollution, and destruction of the environment in Jakarta is found to some extent in all modern cities. Indeed, it is the smog of a warm day, the stench of a polluted waterway, and the toxic waste spill that many associate with the world's habitat problems. But as injurious as these may be, they are not the most harmful problems facing people at the beginning of the twenty-first century. In this chapter, we review the more significant global environmental problems and assess some of the options for dealing with them. In addition, we discuss several of America's more pressing environmental dangers, although most of these cannot really be separated from similar problems found elsewhere on the planet.

Environmental Degradation and Ecology

It is necessary to present some background information before we discuss specific habitat problems. We first allude to the long history of nature's degradation and try to answer the question of why we are only now concerned with environmental issues. Then we present some ideas from the science of ecology useful for assessing problems and possible solutions to them.

Perspectives on Environmental Degradation

Pollution, habitat destruction, and the degradation of the natural environment are not new phenomena. In the natural world, all organisms produce wastes as a byproduct of living that, if untreated, would have a detrimental effect on their habitat. Fortunately, a variety of natural processes have evolved to purify waste products to some degree and frequently to turn them into something useful. For example, waterways are cleansed of limited amounts of harmful debris through such processes as sand filtration and oxygenation. **Symbiotic relationships,** in which dissimilar organisms live together in mutually beneficial associations, are also quite common in the natural world. In such processes, the waste product of one organism becomes the "fuel" that provides life for another. For instance, in Africa, dung beetles harvest elephant dung, which then becomes the prime source of food for the beetles and their young. The harvested dung is rolled into balls and stored in the ground, where it fertilizes the soil.

But even with such built-in natural controls, many living organisms have a tendency to be destructive to their native habitat. For example, deer can devastate plants in the areas where they live, especially if the deer are not controlled by predators. When it is uncontrolled, the deer population can increase to the point that its normal food supply is exhausted. The deer begin eating small trees, bark, leaves, and plants to the extent that the area becomes denuded of vegetation. In such a scenario, a large portion of the deer population will die of starvation and disease as nature seeks to restore the proper balance between plants and animals.

Human beings are also no strangers to destruction of the environment. The following are some of the numerous historical examples of humanity's negative impact on the environment. Biologist Edward O. Wilson attributes the extinction of numerous species of large land animals in Africa, Australia, North America, Madagascar, and New Zealand to the arrival of human beings in these regions (Wilson, 1992). The overgrazing of domesticated animals around the Mediterranean and in the Middle East left once lush mountain slopes bare and formerly thriving ancient ports silted up (Wagner, 1974). Lead, sulfur, and other toxic metals belched into the air by silver smelters in Sweden 2,600 years ago still pose a health threat to humans ("Centuries-Old Lead," 1994). European settlers destroyed forests in the eastern United States (Wagner, 1974). In London during 1952, the infamous "black fog" caused by coal smoke from household and industrial sources combined with fog to reduce visibility to one yard in some parts of the city. The metropolis was paralyzed for two weeks, and 4,000 people died (Coleman and Cressey, 1990). This litany of human despoilage could be extended ad infinitum.

Since humans (and other animals) have always polluted their habitat, why has so much concern about protecting our environment arisen only in recent decades? Several factors, some of which we have already mentioned, explain this phenomenon. First, there are many more people in the world now than at any other period in history (see Chapter 5 for more on the population explosion). For most of history, groups of people could ravage their local surroundings with relatively little impact on other parts of the planet. Because a relatively small population meant limited amounts of degradation, the natural processes of the earth could correct much of the damage. But in this century the sheer volume of humans, their demands for natural resources, and the magnitude of their waste conspire to produce monumental environmental stress.

Second, industrial society itself has a negative impact on the environment in several ways. The manufacturing processes upon which industrial societies depend demand high quantities of raw materials at the same time that they generate wastes that are destructive and often potent. Industrialization exchanged the muscle power of humans and animals for machine power. But to run, machines need fuel. The type of propellants most often used are **fossil fuels** (coal, oil, gasoline, and natural gas, found in deposits created by decaying plant and animal remains buried underground for millions of years). Fossil fuels, however, have a somewhat limited supply; frequently cause environmental damage during their extraction, refining, and transport; and produce pollutants when they are burned. In addition, the science and technology underlying most modern production has created products hitherto unknown in nature. The most familiar of these products are the thousands of unique chemical compounds formulated each year. Although most are benign to the environment, many are not. Because such chemical compounds are different from elements derived through eons of evolution, the earth's natural cleansing processes are unprepared to dispense with them. If unattended to, these compounds can often cause great harm to the environment.

Third, modern capitalism itself plays a powerful role in the current environmental crisis. Modern capitalism, you may recall, is based on the idea that continued economic expansion is necessary and possible. (Modern socialism shares the same notion.) Economies must grow or they are in peril; markets must continually expand or the system is in danger of collapse. Capitalism offers the promise of a constantly improving standard of living when such expansion is pursued. Such "improvement" tends to be popularly defined as a steady elevation in material prosperity. This expectation was first incorporated in the popular mindset of the First World, where to some degree material prosperity has been realized. But the expectation of increasing material prosperity has also been transmitted to developing nations and the rapidly expanding populations of undeveloped countries, leading them to pattern their consumption after the West. But the Western nations, which have a relatively small portion of the world's population, do tremendous damage to the biosphere. To extend such high rates of consumption and waste to the rest of the world's population would be ecological disaster.

The demand for economic well-being has combined with an attitude in the West that sees humans as separate from and dominant over nature. Some argue that this attitude stems from the biblical injunction in Genesis in which God tells humans to be fruitful, multiply, and subdue the Earth and gives them "dominion over the fish of the sea and over the birds of the air and over every living thing that moves upon the earth" (Genesis 1:28). The dominant position in the West has been to see this command as an injunction to control, manipulate, and exploit the natural world (Passmore, 1974). In this view, we need not look at the consequences of our actions on nature, for the cosmos is there to serve our needs. The legitimacy of society's control over nature received its strongest support with the triumph of the mechanistic philosophy of nature in the eighteenth and nineteenth centuries (see Chapter 4). Among other things, this attitude shows our ignorance of scientific ideas such as the notion of entropy, the inevitable degradation of energy, and the disorder that results when energy is used to produce anything.

Pollution, environmental exploitation, and materialism are often viewed as solely the purview of Western industrialized society. The opposite is in fact the case. Most of the Second World nations are total ecological disasters. Typically, these countries contain dead lakes (lakes so polluted that they are unable to support living systems), denuded forests, and rivers so laced with chemicals that it is not unusual for them to catch on fire. Large areas are so decimated that they present an eerie landscape resembling regions ravaged by war and fire. These scenes are typical in Russia. Environmental quality is so bad throughout Russia that an adviser to President Boris Yeltsin recently forecast a decline in the Russian population as a result of the ecological damage (Gallagher, 1994). The level of environmental destruction in the former socialist states is largely the result of the way those societies were governed. That is, the consequences of entropy are magnified when they come into contact with an unyielding hierarchy. In such a situation, higher levels of power and influence are able to force the chaos generated by entropy to lower levels of both the sociosphere and the biosphere. We may conclude then that top-down management such as that found in the former socialist states also rapes the earth.

Indeed, the surviving major socialist country, China, is acknowledged as one of the world's worst polluters. Pollution there is so severe that snowflakes are black in China's heaviest industrial areas. The Chinese government's indifferent and sometimes hostile attitude toward the environment was evident in its recent announcement that China was going to build 100 new factories to produce chlorofluorocarbons, the major cause of ozone depletion, as discussed later in the chapter (Schmetzer, 1994). During the Cold War, such excesses by the socialist nations were justified by the push to bury the capitalist economies. Now, with the demise of most socialist regimes, the excesses are rationalized as a necessary cost of extending the benefits of capitalism to an expanding populace. The same pressures inform the attitude of many Third World nations that contend that they cannot afford to be concerned with environmental protection because they must pursue economic development at all costs.

Although, as we have seen, capitalism is not to blame for all habitat destruction, for several centuries trends originating in the West that have a negative environmental impact have spread throughout the globe. Progressively larger portions of the planet have been integrated into a worldwide system of assumptions, practices, and values that affect our habitat and human life disastrously (see the box "FYI: U.S. Government Frequently Released Radiation"). The world's exploding population, combined with the practices of consumption-oriented, capitalistic, industrial society, has already reached, and perhaps exceeded, the biological **carrying capacity** (the largest number of any species that the planet can sustain for an extended period of time) of the earth (Postel, 1994).

Relevant Concepts from Ecology

The contemporary concern for population and environmental issues began in the 1960s with the publication of biologist Rachel Carson's book *Silent Spring*

U.S. Government Frequently Released Radiation

Human experimentation has long been considered unethical except under extremely controlled conditions, in which the subjects of the experiment give their consent after they have been fully informed about its potential dangers. But evidence is mounting that the U.S. government (especially the military) performed widespread secret tests to determine the effects of radiation on unsuspecting people during much of the Cold War. The Advisory Committee on Human Radiation Experiments appointed by President Bill Clinton recently reported having documented hundreds of cases of intentional release of radiation on unsuspecting Americans. Additionally, at least 400 instances of human medical experiments involving radiation have been well documented, and fragmentary evidence supposedly exists of 1,000 more. In many of these cases, the subjects were not informed about the nature of the experiment.

Adapted from "Panel: U.S. Radiation Released Frequently." 1994. *Chicago Tribune.* October 22: 1.23.

(1962), which traced the impact of insecticides on animal life. Other similar books such as Paul Ehrlich's *The Population Bomb* (1968) became bestsellers. Although many of the more dire predictions of such books have proved incorrect, they expanded public awareness of environmental problems beyond simple localized pollution toward the complex interrelationship of sociosphere and biosphere discussed throughout this text.

Much of the material about environmental issues is rooted in the biological science of ecology. **Ecology** is "the study of households, including the plants, animals, microbes, and people that live together as interdependent beings" (Odum, 1993: 23). Ecologists see the biosphere as composed of an intricate web of interacting ecological systems, or ecosystems. An **ecosystem** is an identifiable network formed by a community of living organisms interacting with their environment. The environment of an ecosystem may be large or small but is relatively separable from the surrounding ecological systems. A given mountain range, a particular valley, or a certain pond may be discussed as a distinctive ecosystem. Within each of these networks, living plants and animals have adapted, possibly over a very long period of time, to the specific conditions in their environment. Each ecological system exists in mutual dependency with other systems. A change in one system may have many unanticipated ripple effects, or consequences for interrelated ecosystems. Ecological systems also arrange themselves in a **nested hierarchy,** or a series of graded levels in which a number of lower-level ecological systems reside within the next higher level of the biosphere. These natural nested hierarchies allow for the flow of information among the various levels; in contrast, humanly constructed hierarchies frequently inhibit the proper flow of information both within natural hierarchies and within social hierarchies.

At the bottom of the nested hierarchy are numerous ecological systems, which tend to be minute and simple, teeming with life. These combine to form a larger, more complex system that unites with other networks to create still larger and more intricate ecological systems. The low-level systems are unstable and are dependent on a narrow range of environmental conditions to maintain themselves. Conversely, in addition to being more complex, higher-level systems are more stable and approach a steady state: "In other words, large ecosystems as a whole, such as oceans or large forests, are more stable than their individual components" (Odum, 1993: 27). Thus, the total biosphere, which contains all the inhabitable soil, air, and water, is more stable than any of the separate ecological systems upon which it is based. A number of ecological systems can be changed or eliminated in the biosphere without totally destroying it because numerous natural systems operate within the large web of life to maintain the proper balance. Considerable ecological damage can be absorbed or made relatively innocuous.

A word of caution is in order: The biosphere and its ecosystems exist only in a *relatively* stable condition. The proper balance necessary to maintain life is a dynamic equilibrium capable of rapid, unpredictable alterations when certain limits or thresholds are exceeded (Homer-Dixon, 1993). For example, within limits pollutants can be added to the atmosphere with little or no perceptible change. But once a critical (generally unknown) threshold is crossed, the whole ecological system "jumps" to a new state of equilibrium, one capable of accommodating the existing level of pollution, but one that may not support many of those species that depended on the old level of balance.

In Chapter 4, we discussed a new development in science called chaos theory that is relevant to the system patterns described here. According to chaos theory, complex systems behave as wholes, exhibiting overall patterns of stability and change while maintaining fluctuations at the lower levels. Some versions of chaos theory hold that leaps to higher order organization may occur when thresholds of energy and entropy are exceeded. For example, once air pollution crosses a critical threshold, the atmosphere's composition may suddenly become so altered that most animals, including humans, can no longer breathe it.

According to this version of chaos theory, we humans have evolved in such a way that we can live only within a relatively narrow range of environmental conditions. If our activities cause a sudden and significant change in these perimeters, we human beings may cease to exist. The eradication of the dinosaurs 66 million years ago after a very long reign as the dominant species is one example of many species extinctions in the history of the evolution of life on Earth. Humans could well be next.

The photograph of the earth rising over the moon taken from Apollo 8 during the first manned mission around the moon in 1968 is one of the most famous images of the twentieth century. More than any other image it illustrates that even if many of us conceive of the earth as infinitely large and resilient, it is only a small globe suspended in the vastness of space. Our planet is, in essence, Spaceship Earth, carrying a fragile cargo of life through the void of the universe. If we use up Earth's limited resources and foul its life-support systems beyond all repair, then that fragile cargo is destined for oblivion. Many scientists believe that we are at a crucial juncture. The limits of our global resources are being reached,

This photograph of the earth rising over the moon, taken from Apollo 8, illustrates the fact that even if many of us think of the earth as infinitely large and resilient, it is only a small globe suspended in the vastness of space.

but we may still have time to make life-sustaining choices.

Global Environmental Problems

We hope that enough background ideas have been presented that you can begin to assess the issues relevant to our planet's habitat-related enigmas. We now turn our attention to several of the world's pressing environmental problems. These problems concern common global resources (global commons) that are currently being depleted or seriously degraded through inappropriate or excessive use. Although in one sense all natural resources are free gifts of nature available to humanity as a whole, some in particular have a planetary role. These resources are often in the form of *circulating planetary media,* such as the air and the oceans. Circulating planetary media literally flow across the face of the earth carrying life-giving matter and energy or, conversely, pollutants. These media are necessary to the maintenance of the entire planetary life-support system.

Other parts of the global commons do not circulate around the earth. For example, plant life (forests, photoplankton) and the genetic information it contains directly affect both atmosphere and water cycles as they convert vital solar energy into organic substances necessary for all life, including our own. Air, water, the world's forests, and increasingly, the genetic information contained within the earth's millions of life forms have been treated until recently as common resources, free for the taking. Such an attitude has encouraged competitive pressures to build human-made structures and create products, thereby hastening the rate of exploitation. This type of pattern we call a tragedy of the commons.

We define each of the following dilemmas as a tragedy of the global commons because it meets one or more of the following criteria: (1) An entire planetary media such as the atmosphere, or the **hydrosphere** (the earth's surface and groundwater), is in danger; (2) adverse conditions are widespread enough that they threaten universal ecological networks; or (3) injurious circumstances undermine large portions of the sociosphere and the biosphere to the extent that they undermine the planetary life-support system.

Global Warming

Life as we know it is able to exist only in a comparatively narrow temperature range. Few, if any, living organisms can survive at temperatures above 212°F (100°C) or below 0°F (−17.78°C). The closer the average temperature gets to either of the two extremes, the less variety of life is found. Taken as a whole, living organisms have proven remarkably adaptable to variations in environmental conditions. Each species develops adaptations that enable it to operate effectively within a particular niche in its ecosystem (Odum, 1993). An **ecological niche** is the function or job of a particular organism within the community of organisms comprising its habitat. Because everything has its own ecological niche, even small changes in habitat conditions, such as a flux in the average temperature, a slight change in the warm and cool weather in a specific ecosystem within the timespan of a single week, or alterations in the amount or timing of rainfall due to temperature change, can result in species extinctions and disruptions of ecological systems.

Although we have little control over climate variations caused by nature, we are likely to have more success dealing with environmental change produced by activity in the sociosphere. Most experts agree that **global warming,** or the rising of the world's average temperature, is one largely human-made situation in which action is needed. In 1896, the distinguished Swedish chemist Svante Arrhenius predicted that the burning of fossil fuels by the industrial nations would significantly raise the earth's average temperature (Kemp, 1990). This increase, he argued, would occur because when gases emitted by burning fossil fuels become lodged in the upper atmosphere, they produce a "greenhouse effect."

Figure 6–1 illustrates the greenhouse effect. When energy from the sun strikes the earth's surface, a certain amount is absorbed. But a significant proportion is reflected back into space. The greenhouse gases linger in the upper atmosphere, where they bounce heat that would have otherwise escaped back to land and water. The result is a warming of the global climate. A trace gas, carbon dioxide, is the chief culprit in the greenhouse effect. Other trace gases such as the chlorofluorocarbons (CFCs), methane, and nitrous oxide account for the rest of the greenhouse effect.

The presence of these trace gases increased dramatically with industrialization. Although a causal

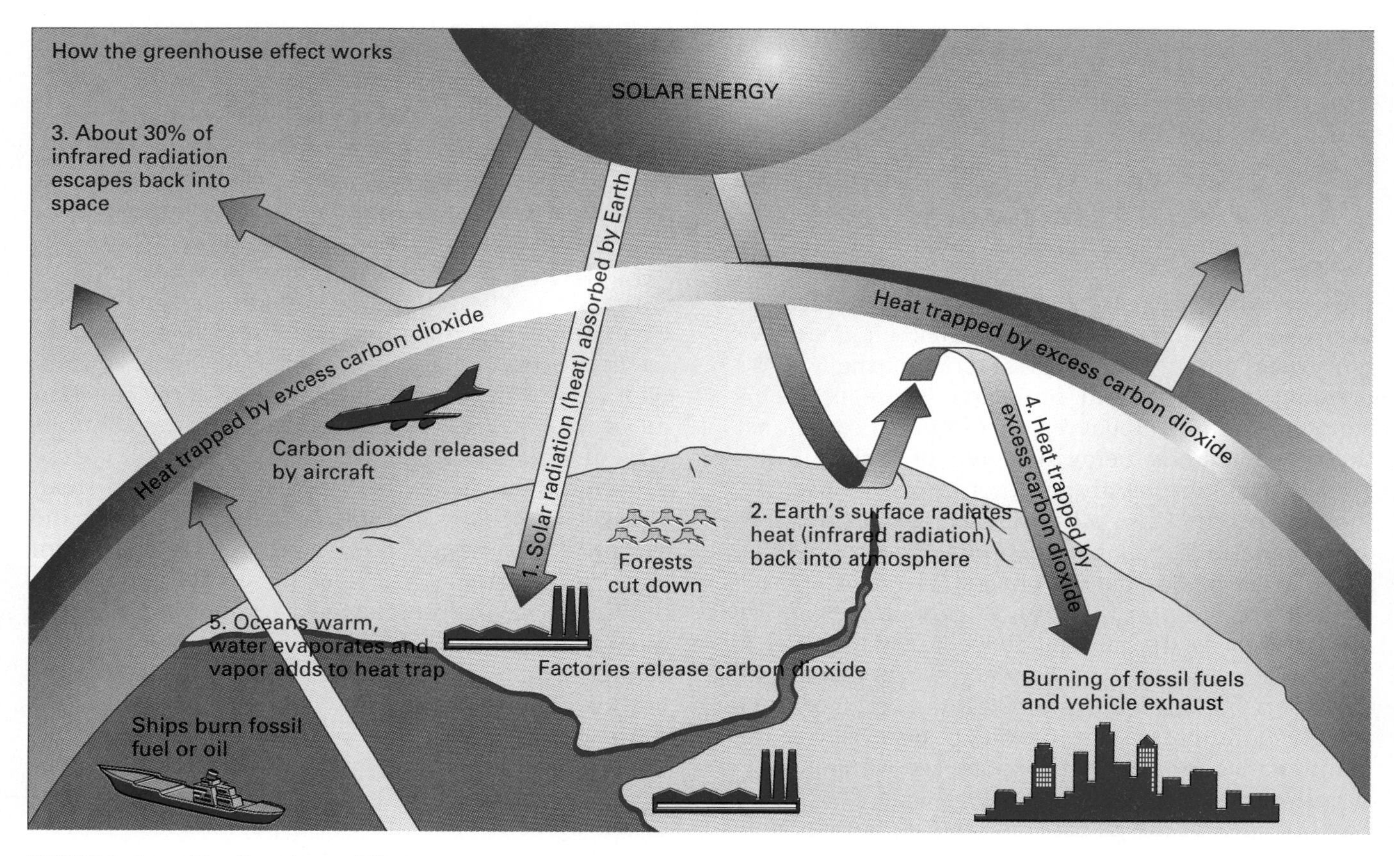

FIGURE 6–1 The Greenhouse Effect

Source: From *Green Facts: The Greenhouse Effect and Other Key Issues* by M. Allaley. Copyright © 1989 by Hamlyn. Reproduced by permission of Hamlyn, a division of Octopus Publishing Group Ltd.

relationship cannot be proven conclusively, the mean global temperature has risen about 3.6°F (2°C) over this century, an increase consistent with the pattern predicted by Arrhenius (Kemp, 1990). The mean global temperature is currently rising at about 0.5°F per decade. The Intergovernmental Panel on Climate Change (IPCC) (sponsored by the UN) and the World Meteorological Organization recently supported the estimate that the global average will climb by 2.34°F (1.3°C) by 2020 and 5.4°F (3°C) by 2070, the most rapid climate change in history (Intergovernmental Panel on Climate Change, 1992).

The impact of this change is unclear, partly because the models used to predict habitat variation are not sophisticated enough to handle such complex phenomena as global climate modification (Cowen, 1994; Pielke, 1994). Moreover, the influence of global warming is not uniform. Map 6–1 shows projected effects of global warming on temperatures and rainfall in specific regions of the world. But even though scientists' models may not allow them to predict effects with absolute certainty, some generalizations from average temperature variations can be made.

One possibility is that the entire global climate may be forced into a new equilibrium. If this occurs, dramatic changes in the extent and type of vegetation are predicted in many places, especially in the earth's temperate regions. Much of Earth's food is grown in temperate zones in areas such as southeast Asia, Russia, Europe, the United States, and Canada. These regions will likely become hotter and dryer. The expected temperature increases in North America could also cause a 15 to 20 percent decrease in soil moisture (Homer-Dixon, 1993). Soil moisture is a key variable for growing grain and other crops. In many productive areas of the United States and Canada, grain output is likely to decrease. The United States alone can expect to see a one-third drop in its crop yield and a decrease of 70 percent in the amount of food it has to send to other countries.

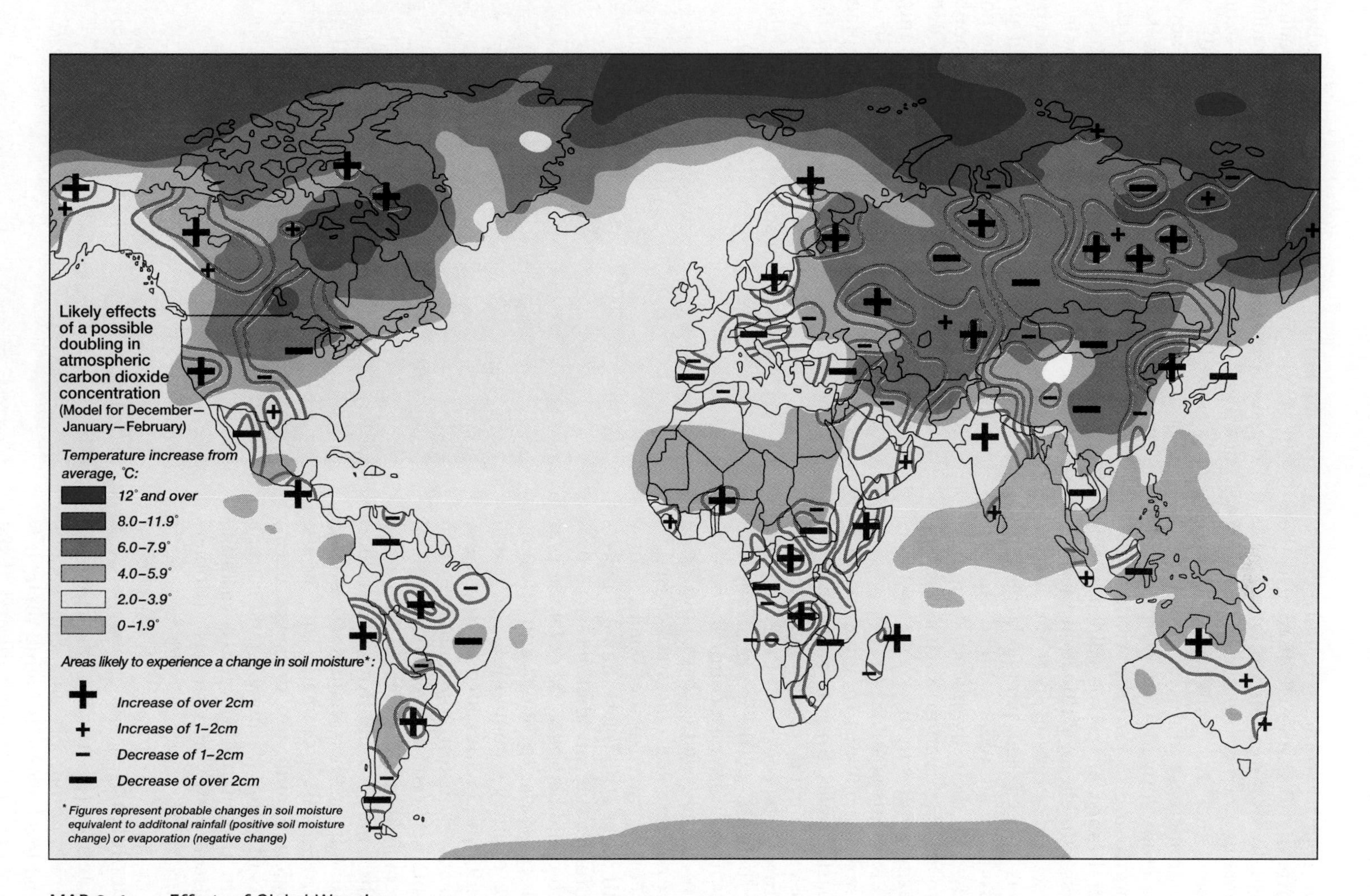

MAP 6–1 Effects of Global Warming

Some parts of the country could be totally devastated, as were parts of Texas and Oklahoma in the 1930s when unusually dry weather combined with poor soil management practices to create the dust storms that created the dust bowl. In contrast, Canada might see an increase in the total amount of land available for crop cultivation as warmer temperatures move northward toward the Arctic Circle. However, in general much of the soil gained in this fashion will be less suitable for cultivation than the soil already in use. Therefore, even if the world's total food supply is not reduced, persons depending on agriculture produced by today's bread and rice baskets will likely see their livelihood disappear; mass migrations to avoid starvation (such as the trek by Great Plains farm families to the West Coast during the dust bowl) are thus possible.

Another trend already obvious in some places is the flooding of coastal zones. Such flooding may become more severe as the polar ice caps melt because of rising temperatures. The prospect of their melting is especially dire because of the concentration of population in coastal areas in most countries bordering the sea. Many islands, deltas, bays, and other coastal regions are vulnerable to disasters caused by rising sea levels. For instance, in the Asian country of Bangladesh, half of the land is less than 4.5 meters above sea level. Studies indicate that about 18 percent of Bangladesh could be under water by the year 2050: by 2100 this could rise to 34 percent, affecting 35 percent of the country's population (Lean and Hinrichsen, 1994: 93). U.S. cities such as New York, Boston, New Orleans, Houston, and San Francisco could find parts of their land areas flooded. All of southern Florida could be underwater. In fact, a rise in sea level of only 1 meter could drive 200 million people worldwide out of their homes (Lean and Hinrichsen, 1994). Even if a dramatic shift in the world's climatological equilibrium does not occur, the minimal effects of global warming "could cause a sudden increase in the chance of crop-devastating droughts, floods, heat waves and storms" (Homer-Dixon, 1993: 21).

Ozone Layer Depletion

Ozone layer depletion (destruction of the earth's protective ozone) is another pressing atmospheric problem. At ground level, ozone is highly toxic; it is one of the main components of acid rain and of the smog that makes life hazardous in many major cities. However, ozone is dispersed between 6 and 30 miles (10–50 km) in the upper atmosphere, where it filters out very high volumes of ultraviolet radiation from the sun (see Figure 6–2). Ultraviolet radiation is so deadly that the filtration function of ozone makes life as we know it possible (Kemp, 1990).

Human activities in the sociosphere now threaten this vital ozone shield. Several trace gases come into play here. These gases drift upward from natural processes and as industrial by-products. Oxides of nitrogen and methane play a noticeable part, but chlorofluorocarbons are the chief offenders in ozone destruction. CFCs are extremely useful products at ground level. Because they are inert (do not interact with other chemicals), highly stable, nontoxic, and nonsoluble in water, they have been widely used in industrial societies, where they are employed as coolants in refrigerators, freezers, and air conditioners and are released during the manufacturing of products such as styrofoam (Lean and Hinrichsen, 1994; Kemp, 1990). It takes about 10 years for CFCs to reach the upper atmosphere from the ground.

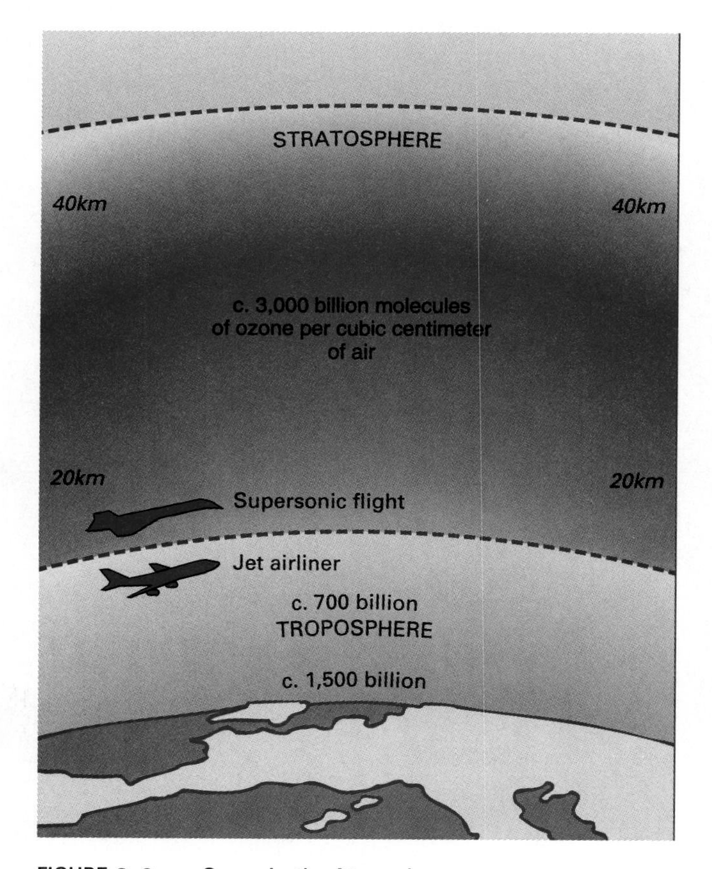

FIGURE 6–2 Ozone in the Atmosphere

Once there they react with the intense ultraviolet radiation by breaking down into chlorine and bromine. These elements serve as catalysts in the destruction of ozone.

The "hole" in the Antarctic ozone layer is the most dramatic effect of this process yet observed. Since the late 1950s, scientists at the British research base in Halley Bay, Antarctica, had been measuring seasonal fluctuations in the continent's atmosphere, including a thinning of the ozone layer during the springtime there (October through December). Beginning in the early 1980s, the British researchers noticed a quite unexpected near-total disappearance of ozone.

This ozone hole grew (see Map 6–2) until by 1991, it was 13 times larger than it had been 10 years earlier (Lean and Hinrichsen, 1994). Although the hole appears only during the southern spring, the length of time it remains open has been extending. Additional investigations have revealed large quantities of chlorine (which probably foretell a decline in ozone) in arctic regions during late winter, and an actual abatement in ozone at all latitudes (UNCED, 1991). The decline in ozone has already been measured in large areas covering the United States, Europe, northern China, and Japan.

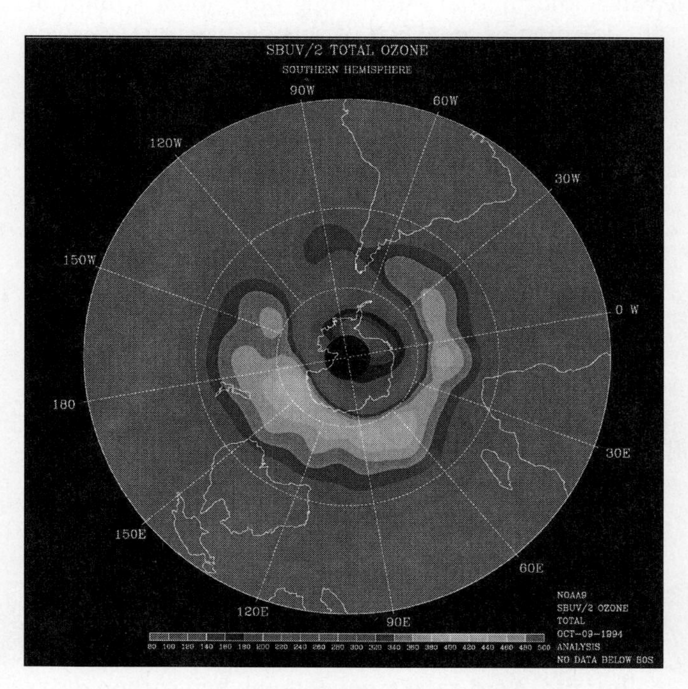

The destruction of the earth's protective ozone layer is another pressing atmospheric problem—in the upper atmosphere ozone filters out ultraviolet radiation from the sun. This map of Antarctica shows a hole in the ozone layer (it shows up as white in this photo), first discovered in the 1980s.

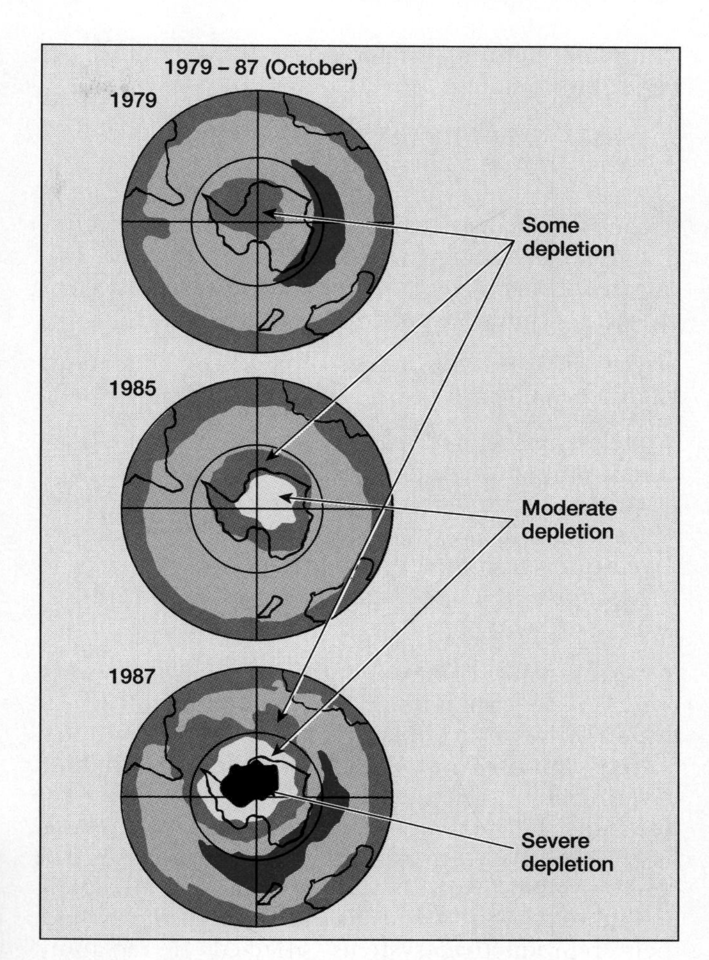

MAP 6–2 Growth of Antarctic Ozone Hole

Additional evidence indicates that the denuding of ozone has occurred at a much more rapid rate in the last 10 years than it had during earlier decades. Despite international efforts to reduce production of CFCs and other ozone-destroying elements (discussed later), the worst is yet to come; ozone depletion will continue at an increasing pace into the next century because controls are only being phased in and because of the long lifespan of the destructive gases themselves ("The Worst Is Yet to Come," 1994).

Even a minuscule increase in the amount of ultraviolet radiation reaching the surface of the earth can have dire consequences. Human health will suffer.

Ultraviolet light is a major cause of skin cancer. As one scientist states,

> Recent research suggests that a 1 percent decrease in stratospheric ozone produces about a 2 percent increase in the incidence of cancer-causing ultraviolet radiation on the surface of the earth, which in turn produces about a 3 percent increase in nonmelanoma skin cancer rates. (Homer-Dixon, 1993: 22)

In the United States alone, skin cancer kills about 12,000 people each year:

> Melanoma, a dark mole that becomes malignant and is usually lethal, has doubled in frequency worldwide over the last two decades. However, in Australia, where the ozone depletes each summer, the melanoma incidence has doubled in the last ten years. (Caldicott, 1992: 20–21)

Increased ultraviolet radiation may also suppress the immune system, making people vulnerable to a multitude of afflictions. Approximately 12 million persons worldwide are blind and another 18 million have impaired vision because of cataracts caused by ultraviolet light (Lean and Hinrichsen, 1994). These figures will probably escalate as the ozone layer becomes thinner. Humans and other animals alike will not only suffer numerous illnesses, but also may find their reproductive systems affected if radiation reaches high enough levels. In addition, scientists predict that crops, forests, and other vegetation will suffer negative effects. Ultraviolet light increases may destroy the plankton (tiny organisms floating near the surface of the sea) that form one of the most important bases of the oceanic food chain and absorb much of the world's excess carbon dioxide. Plankton destruction would disrupt the balance of aquatic life and speed up global warming.

Other Problems with Our Habitat

We have given extended treatment to the issues of global warming and ozone depletion because they have an immediate effect on our total environment. We discuss more briefly in this section several problems concerning the pollution of air, water, and land; habitat destruction; and biodiversity, each seemingly more localized in its impact than the problems previously discussed. But because these more local problems are frequently related to one another and are intertwined with population increase, among other things, they also have an overall effect on the global biosphere and sociosphere.

Atmospheric Pollution. Agricultural and industrial chemicals play a significant role in modern life. According to the United Nation's Environmental Programme, more than 7 million chemicals have been discovered or concocted by humans. Several thousand new substances are created each year for use in agriculture or in the manufacture of consumer products from food to clothing to medicine to plastics. Annual world "production of organic chemicals [alone] has soared from 1 million tons in 1930 to 7 million tons in 1950, 63 million in 1970, and a half billion in 1990" (Gore, 1992: 147–48). At the present rate, production will double in six to seven years. The government permits companies to market the vast majority of these chemicals with little or *no* research on their impact on the biosphere or their effect on human health.

We have already noted how by-products of industrial civilization interact detrimentally with the atmosphere. Climatic warming and ozone destruction are not the only negative consequences of these contaminants. In fact, impurities released into the air, water, and land are degrading our global habitat at an alarming pace. Much of this destruction involves the type of fuels used in contemporary civilization (see Chapter 4 for a discussion of some alternatives to fossil fuels). Pollution and environmental damage have increased as humans have moved from technology powered by human muscles to technology driven by animals to technology dependent on fossil fuels. Two effects of this change are immediately observable: urban air pollution and acid rain.

Urban air pollution is not confined solely to urban areas but is spread throughout the globe. Even the most remote regions of the world, such as the Arctic, periodically suffer from smog resulting from heavy doses of airborne contaminants. The effects of these contaminants vary from respiratory difficulties to increased lead levels in newborns to proliferating risks of lung cancer to a host of other maladies. Airborne toxins also contribute to the death of plants and animals and to the deterioration of buildings, monuments, and other human creations.

Acid rain is another problem produced by airborne pollutants. **Acid rain** is generated when carbon dioxide, oxides of nitrogen, or sulfur dioxide interact with water vapor in the air to form mild levels of acids that then precipitate out as snow, ice, or raindrops (Kemp, 1990). When acid rain falls, it contributes to the increasing acidity of our soil and water and makes them unsuitable for sustaining life. Acid rain, ironically, was created by efforts to improve local air quality in the 1970s. Many local and federal governments in the industrialized world required taller smokestacks for factories and electrical generating facilities. The new stacks carried the pollutants higher into the atmosphere, thereby spreading them away from their points of origin, which enhanced the local air quality. But the pollution was often carried hundreds of miles away, where it fell as acid rain. According to physician and environmental activist Helen Caldicott,

> acid rain has devastated forests around the globe. In New England, the maple syrup crop has been halved in recent years because the magnificent maple trees are dying. Fifty percent of Germany's Black Forest has been killed, and similar figures pertain elsewhere—to the East Coast forests of North America to other European forests, and to the forests in China and South America. Eighty percent of the lakes in Norway are dead . . . . Sixty-seven percent of the trees in Britain are sick . . . [and] acid rain and snow—originating in European, Soviet, and Chinese factories—is polluting the lakes, rivers, and trees of Alaska. No country is immune. (Caldicott, 1992: 53)

Besides the effect of acid rain on living things, it is highly detrimental to buildings, artwork, and other exterior artifacts. Many of the world's architectural and outdoor artistic masterpieces (such as public monuments) are deteriorating rapidly because of acid rain's onslaught.

Ground Pollution and Waste Disposal. The soil of our planet is also being despoiled. Some of this degradation is caused by airborne or waterborne impurities and accidental spills. In addition, farming methods employed worldwide such as open ditch irrigation (i.e., letting irrigation water run into fields through open ditches) and slash-and-burn agriculture (in which farmers cut down and set fire to grass and trees so that the ashes fertilize the land they wish to cultivate) eventually render much soil unusable. Clear-cutting of forests, in which loggers remove all trees in the area being harvested, causes valuable topsoil to wash away and rivers to become plugged with sediment. Much rich soil is also covered each year by concrete or polluted by runoff because of urban development. Mining too, especially strip, or surface, mining destroys large tracts of land. Still another source of ground pollution are mining operations or factories that deliberately discharge destructive chemicals onto the ground.

Waste disposal of all kinds is a huge problem of contemporary life. Even disposing of the ordinary products of modern society has become a formidable task. The widespread use of chemicals in consumer products has made human garbage more harmful to the biosphere. The volume of waste and its noxiousness present numerous difficulties to every country in the world. In industrialized nations, the most common method of waste disposal is to bury it in landfills. But landfills are currently filling up at an alarming rate. Moreover, poisonous elements frequently leak into the surrounding soil and contaminate the groundwater. As more people have become aware of such dangers and assumed the activist position "not in my backyard" it is becoming increasingly difficult for waste disposers to find suitable places for new landfills.

These problems are compounded when dealing with the huge volume of hazardous wastes generated worldwide each year. Poisonous substances are frequently released by manufacturers into the air or waterways, stockpiled or buried on land, or dumped by roads or in isolated places. Figure 6–3 illustrates the methods used to dispose of hazardous wastes in four countries.

Placing toxic wastes in legal and illegal landfills is the technique most often employed in industrialized nations. This practice has resulted in numerous known and unknown toxic waste sites in most nations of the world, which in themselves pose significant hazards. For example, the Netherlands has more than 4,000 sites, about 1,000 of which pose substantial risks to human health and the environment, while roughly two-thirds of Poland's annual production of 30 million metric tons of toxic wastes is discarded in unregulated locations (Lean and Hinrichsen, 1994). Cleaning up degraded locales will cost hundreds of billions of dollars.

Adding to the difficulties involved in waste disposal is that it has become a common practice to transport hazardous wastes across international boundaries, a practice that makes tracking and regulating them particularly difficult. In addition, because of increased regulation at home, many First World nations now send part of their deadly wastes to Third World countries for disposal; there the method used is typically haphazard. This practice

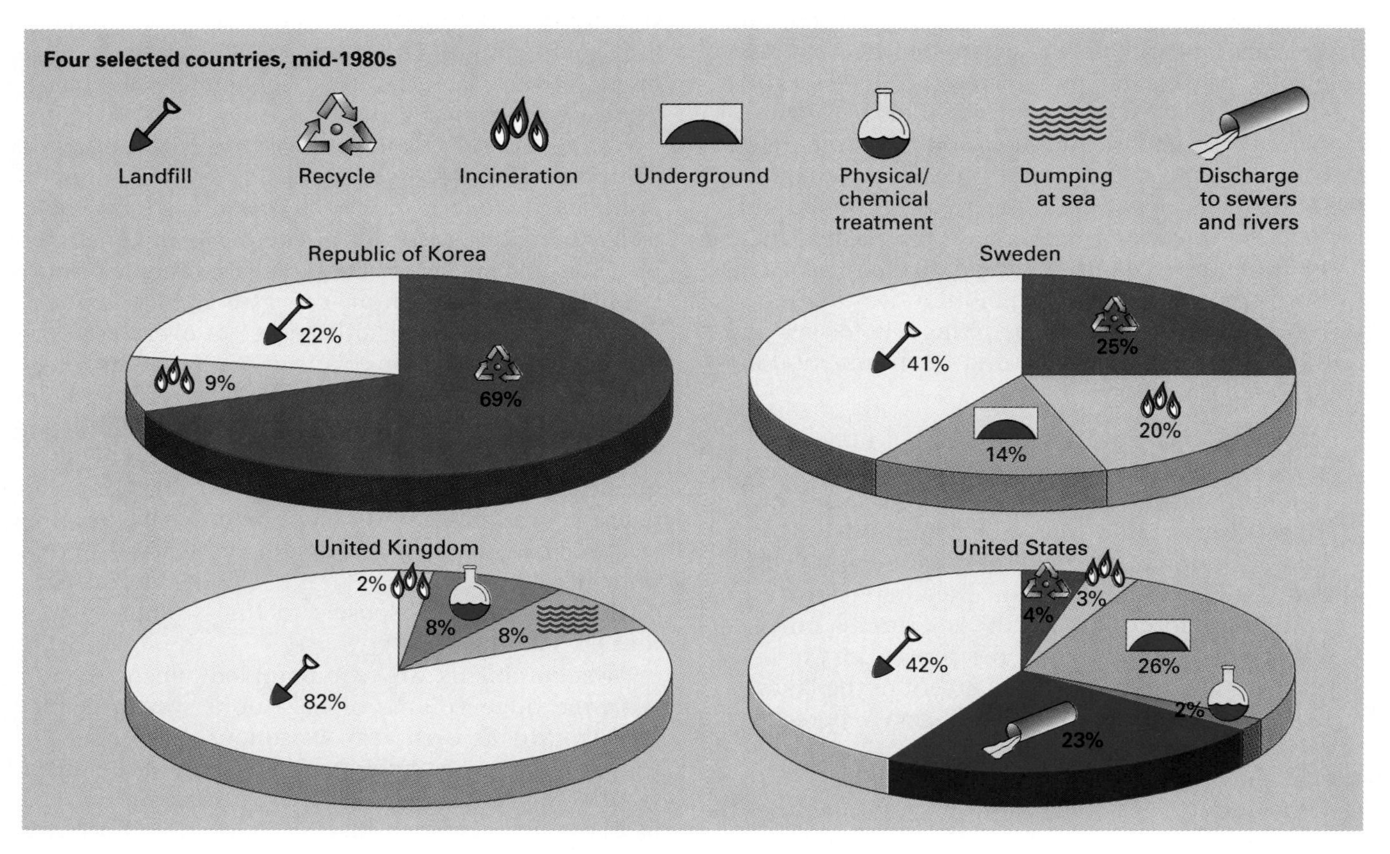

FIGURE 6–3 Hazardous Waste Management

may gain some income for nonindustrialized regions (though the money usually goes only to wealthy individuals), but it costs the areas receiving the waste dearly in terms of environmental decline and the destruction of their citizens' health (though usually only the poor suffer directly).

Habitat Destruction and Biodiversity. Researchers have noted the disappearance of several species of frogs in isolated mountain regions of the American Northwest and deep in the jungles of Costa Rica. Marine biologists have found coral reefs bleaching (turning white because they have died) in places far removed from regions of modern commerce. These findings are significant because amphibians and the tiny creatures that make up living colonies of coral are directly immersed in their environment and thus highly susceptible to changes in it. The fact that frogs and the inhabitants of living coral colonies are dying means that airborne and waterborne pollutants have reached even the farthest flung places in sufficient strength to do damage. This fact does not bode well for the rest of life on Earth; all of life may be in deep trouble.

Species of living organisms are disappearing at alarming rates. Edward Wilson contends that although we know about 1,413,000 species of plants and animals, the total number of species existing is between 10 and 100 million (Wilson, 1992). He concludes: "In the small minority of groups of plants and animals that are well known, extinction is proceeding at a rapid rate, far above prehuman levels. In many cases the level [of extinction] is calamitous" (Wilson, 1992: 255). We may only guess at the rate of extinction among the millions of unknown species of living things. Conservative estimates hold that we are losing 27,000 species each year, or 74 each day, or 3 per hour (Wilson, 1992). At this rate, by the year 2050, half of the species now extant will have disappeared.

Many people will probably fail to understand how the death of a species of frogs, the disappearance of a variety of monkeys, or the demise of genus of plants has any significance for them. Yet "biodiversity is our most valuable but least appreciated resource" (Wilson, 1992: 281). Biodiversity is nature's survival mechanism. By **biodiversity,** we mean the great variety of living systems, from differing ecosystems to varieties of species within given ecosystems to genetic variations within species. Such wide variation assures that at least some species will survive to reestablish an ecosystem, even if a calamitous change destroys many plant or animal groups.

A given species' death usually means that the entire habitat is threatened; thus, the extinction of a species warns of larger changes looming. One species' demise often wreaks havoc with other species. For example, many plants depend on bees for their pollination. The future of numerous types of vegetation would be imperiled should their service bees disappear. Like bees, numerous kinds of flora (the plants in a particular place) and fauna (the animals in a particular place) have a special ecological niche, one that is filled by no other species. If they became extinct, the entire ecological system would be threatened. Moreover, the extinction of key species or simply a large number of varieties may signify the crossing of an unknown threshold by which the entire ecosystem is forced to some new equilibrium that significantly alters or threatens the lifestyle of all species in the region, including humans. Finally, numerous types of plants and animals have direct (sometimes unimagined) value to people. For instance, 40 percent of all pharmaceuticals are derived from living organisms (Wilson, 1992). Table 6–1 shows a few of the numerous plants that have been indispensable to modern medicine to prolong and improve the quality of life for innumerable people. Interestingly, many of these medicinal plants have been known to practitioners of folk medicine for centuries but only now are being discovered by scientists (Cox and Balick, 1994).

Not only is declining biodiversity an epidemic on land, it also is menacing the oceans (Holloway, 1994).

TABLE 6–1 Some Plants Used as Medicines

PLANT	DRUG	USE
Amazonian liana	Curare	Muscle relaxant
Annual mugwort	Artemisinin	Antimalarial
Autumn crocus	Colchicine	Antitumor agent
Belladonna	Atropine	Anticholinergic
Coca	Cocaine	Local anesthetic
Common thyme	Thymol	Antifungal
Ergot fungus	Ergotamine	Analgesic
Foxglove	Digitoxin, digitalis	Cardiotonic
Indian snakeroot	Reserpine	Antihypertensive
Meadowsweet	Salicylic acid[a]	Analgesic
Mexican yam	Diosgenin	Birth-control pill
Nux vomica	Strychnine	CNS stimulant
Opium poppy	Codeine, morphine	Analgesic (& antitussive)
Pacific yew	Taxol	Antitumor agent
Recured thornapple	Scopolamine	Sedative
Rosy periwinkle	Vincristine, vinblastine	Antileukemia
Velvet bean	L-Dopa	Antiparkinsonian
White willow	Salicin[a]	Analgesic
Yellow cinchona	Quinine	Antimalarial, antipyretic

[a] Compound formed from salicylic acid and acetic acid is called acetylsalicylic acid: better known as aspirin.

Source: Lean and Hinrichsen. *Atlas*, p. 130.

TABLE 6–2 Reasons for Loss of Biodiversity

Reason	Percentage
Destruction of physical habitat	73% of species
Displacement by introduced species	68% of species
Alteration of habitat by chemical pollutants	38% of species
Hybridization with other species and subspecies	38% of species
Overharvesting	15% of species[a]

[a] Percentages total more than 100% because many species face multiple sources of threat.

Source: Edward O. Wilson. 1992. *The Diversity of Life.* Cambridge, MA: Harvard University Press, 254.

This decrease has many causes, most of which are directly or indirectly attributable to human activities. Table 6–2 illustrates the major sources for species loss as identified by the International Union for Conservation of Nature and Natural Resources (IUCN). The most common threat is loss of habitat due to chemical pollution and direct incursion by expanding human populations.

Environmental Problems in the United States

As in the rest of the world, overpopulation (in some areas), the problems of industrialization, and increasing energy needs, among other factors, contribute to the deterioration of the environment in the United States. In recent decades, environmental issues have captured the interest of many Americans and as a nation we have begun to work on these concerns, although much remains to be done (see the box "Contemporary Discussion: The Dioxin Question").

In some respects, Americans have been in the forefront of identifying serious problems and trying to deal with them. The United States can afford to develop and apply new technologies to protect our soil, water, and air. It is in the country's best interest to be environmentally concerned. The growing scarcity of many natural resources increases their value. This economic incentive has sparked interest in greater conservation of energy, minerals, wood, and water. But even though Americans have more environmental awareness and concern than possibly ever before, we still have serious environmental problems. Much of what has been done amounts to little more than applying Band-Aids. The following is a

CONTEMPORARY DISCUSSION

The Dioxin Question

Environmental issues are frequently controversial. Often debates center on how much pollution can safely be allowed. Nowhere is this more obvious than in the rekindling of the long-running dioxin debate. The highly toxic dioxin group of chemical compounds is found in the defoliant Agent Orange used by U.S. forces during the Vietnam War. Dioxins are released into the atmosphere as unintended by-products of the manufacture of certain chemicals and herbicides, the burning of wastes (particularly those from medical facilities), the chlorine bleaching of pulp to make paper, and other industrial processes. Dioxin discharges eventually settle in streams and on grasslands, where they are absorbed by the flesh of fish and other animals and so find their way onto the American dinner table through fish, meat, and dairy products. Dioxins cause cancer, birth defects, and other maladies in humans.

A controversy concerning dioxins has raged because of the small proportions of the chemical discharged. A pivotal question is: How much dioxin can be allowed in the environment before it is harmful to human health? The latest phase of this debate was ignited by a 1994 EPA brief discussion of some of the most pressing environmental concerns in this society.

Water Pollution

In many parts of the world, water has been polluted and unsafe to drink for centuries. This situation, however, has not typically occurred in the United States. But in the last 50 years, the quality of our drinking water and the water in streams and lakes has become a major concern. Federal clean water legislation has led to significant improvements in the quality of our surface water (water in rivers, streams, and lakes), but groundwater (water contained within the earth) is a different story. Groundwater has become increasingly contaminated by various chemicals such as agricultural pesticides, household cleaners, and industrial wastes. The federal Environmental Protection Agency (EPA) estimates that three-quarters of the known toxic waste disposal sites leak their contents into aquifers. Once polluted, groundwater is almost impossible to clean up. But more than half of all Americans rely on groundwater for domestic use. Major sources of water pollution in the United States include industries, farming, cities, and thermal pollution.

Air Pollution

Another major environmental problem for Americans is chronic air pollution. After a century of dumping noxious gases and particulates (minute separate particles) into the atmosphere, the United States, like most industrialized nations, now tries to enforce clean air standards. But clean air is a relative matter (see "Contemporary Discussion: The Dioxin Question") and even with laws to enforce such standards, vast amounts of pollutants still discharge into the air.

When it is not overtaxed the atmosphere cleans itself through natural processes, but human activity is overburdening the atmosphere. In many areas of the United States, air quality is dangerously substandard. Internal combustion engines, industrial processes, power generators, refineries, smelters, home heaters, waste incineration, and aerosol use have caused this decreased air quality. We now realize that continued long-term exposure to airborne pollutants has cumulative effects, including the increased incidence of such illnesses as asthma, bronchitis, emphysema, and lung cancer. Air pollution also contributes to less serious health problems such as allergies and eye, nose, and throat irritations.

report released after extensive study. The conclusion of the report was that present dioxin releases represented a significant hazard, and should, therefore, be severely limited, as they had been in other countries.

Environmental groups contended that the report was too cautious, and that the recommended restrictions should be even more strict. These groups essentially agreed with the notion that any dioxin is too much. In response, the National Cattlemen's Association and the Chlorine Chemistry Council, which represents the chemical industry, argued that the report overstated the risks. These opponents of the environmental groups argued that dioxins were useful in numerous manufacturing processes and that discontinuing their use would cause financial hardship. The small quantity found in America's food supply, they also suggested, might prove to be safe once all the facts are known. Additional study should be required before taking drastic steps to curtail the use of products whose by-products are dioxins.

◇ **For Critical Thought:** (1) What are the assumptions of each side in this discussion? (2) How do these issues relate to major theoretical themes in this book? (3) What are the implications of strictly limiting the use of chemicals believed to be dangerous or restricting only those pollutants that can be conclusively demonstrated to be harmful? (4) What practical problems are created by each position?

Adapted from Brad Knickerbocker. 1994a. "Exhaustive Report on Dioxin Satisfies Few in Scientific Debate." *The Christian Science Monitor.* September 21:2; Casey Bukro. 1994b. "The Debate on Dioxin: Is It the No. 1 Environmental Hazard?" *Chicago Tribune.* September 22: 3.1.

Carbon monoxide is an example of a pollutant that compromises the quality of American air. The National Public Health Service estimates that 68 million tons of carbon monoxide are added to our atmosphere each year. Exposure to carbon monoxide is obviously greatest in urban areas. High concentrations can cause drowsiness, slowed reflexes, and possible death. Auto emission controls have reduced this quantity by more than 30 percent from earlier levels.

In 1970, the U.S. Congress passed the Clean Air Act. The goal of this legislation was to ensure air pollutants did not exceed safe levels. Proponents of the act argued that the government needed to protect health, halt pollution, stem damage to crops and forests, and prevent damage to buildings located near industrial sites. Within 15 years after the law went into effect, the amount of suspended particulate matter, sulfur oxides, nitrogen oxides, carbon monoxide, and lead in the air dropped dramatically. Nevertheless, many Americans believe much more needs to be done.

Despite its worthy goals and its success, the Clean Air Act has its enemies. Some industrial producers, particularly those most directly affected by the legislation, have lobbied intensively to weaken the act's main provisions. In response, environmentalists have worked equally hard to resist changes. A stalemate developed and neither side won a decisive victory. This situation was altered by the congressional elections of 1994, which we discuss later in this chapter.

Acid Rain

Acid rain is a major air pollutant. It is found primarily in heavily industrialized areas of Western Europe and the Northeast and northern Midwest of the United States. Smokestack industries such as the coal-burning industries in the East and the Ohio River Valley produce acid rain (or acid snow). The acids contained in this precipitation damage forests, agricultural production, fish, and other life in lakes, streams, and rivers, even eroding concrete and metal structures hundreds of miles from the source of the pollution.

Acid rain has international political implications; it is, for example, a major source of ongoing contention between the United States and Canada. Acid rain originating in the United States and falling on Canada has been highly detrimental to Canadian forests, waterways, and agriculture. Canadian authorities estimate that acid rain has already destroyed the fish and normal plant life of 200 Ontario lakes and threatens 48,000 of the nation's more than 180,000 lakes (Henslin, 1996). The Canadian government wants the United States to strictly enforce emission regulations already in place, particularly those for major polluters like power utilities and companies that burn coal during their manufacturing process.

Solid Waste Disposal

How to safely dispose of solid waste is another major environmental concern in the United States, as it is in much of the rest of the world. One of the ironies of industrial societies is not that we consume too much, but that we waste too much. The problem is that many of the things we consume are not really used up. We are a throwaway society; rather than fixing most items that no longer work, we discard them and buy new models. Each year, consequently, we dispose of huge volumes of solid waste. The most commonly used methods of waste disposal involve putting refuse in sanitary landfills or incinerating it. But many landfills are in violation of safe disposal laws, and improperly designed incinerators are major contributors to air pollution. Moreover, we are reaching the point at which most landfill sites are full. Fears of groundwater contamination make it difficult to find new, safe areas to use.

How to dispose of wastes of all kinds is an enormous problem of contemporary life. Even disposing of the ordinary products of modern society has become a formidable task. For example, every U.S. citizen generates approximately 3.5 pounds of garbage each day. This adds up to 200,000 tons of garbage created daily throughout the country. Each year, Americans throw away 1.6 billion pens, 2 billion razors and blades, 220 million tires, and 16 billion disposable diapers (Langone, 1989).

Adding to the problem is that many coastal communities use the ocean as a dumping ground. The sheer volume of wastes has overwhelmed the capacity of the seas to handle them. Another problem involves the types of wastes produced by modern society, namely, the plastics and other synthetics that do not decompose readily in the environment. They essentially persist forever, which means that they have been found all over the ocean, even far from land or shipping lanes. When synthetics like plastic are burned, they produce hydrocarbons and nitrogen oxides, which dangerously pollute the air.

How to safely dispose of solid waste is a major environmental concern in the United States and the rest of the world. We are a throwaway society; rather than fixing most items that no longer work, we discard them and buy new models.

Chemical Hazards and Nuclear Wastes

Americans face several other environmental hazards, including chemical hazards and nuclear wastes. Because we are a capitalist nation, there are always financial pressures to push new products on the market, which has resulted in ill-advised uses of various pesticides and herbicides. Such products are inadequately tested for their long-term cumulative effects on people and the environment. DDT (dichloridiphenyl-trichlorethane), a synthetic insecticide, provides a classic example of this problem. The residue of DDT can last for decades in the soil or water. In addition, the residue accumulates in the food chain. This means that all the residue taken in by plants and animals at lower levels in the food chain is transferred to those higher up that consume them. The increasing concentration of DDT residue has greater impact on animals the higher up the chain they are. For instance, the bald eagle, the symbol of the United States, was seriously imperiled by it. The eagle fed on fish that had fed on insects that had fed on plants covered with DDT. As all the residue imbibed by plants, insects, and fish below them on the food chain concentrated in the eagles, the shells on their eggs became so thin they broke before the baby eagles were ready to hatch. As a result, bald eagles were failing to reproduce, leading to their placement on the endangered species list.

Fortunately, once the use of DDT was banned in this country, a considerable increase in the bald eagle population (and other species affected) was noted. Unfortunately, DDT is still manufactured by First World nations for sale in the Third World. Persistent chemicals like DDT are spread to even the most remote areas by global air and water currents.

Because of rampant consumption and waste, the average citizen of the First World produces several times more pollutants, including chemically hazardous wastes, than people in the developing world. We in the United States are particularly at fault. Helen Caldicott drives this point home:

> The U.S. population, a mere 4 or 5 percent of the world total, creates half of the world's toxic waste. . . . Of the 375 to 500 million metric tons of hazardous waste manufactured on the planet each year, the United States produces 260 million . . . or more than one ton per person. (Caldicott, 1992:66)

So much toxic waste has been produced in the United States that "8 of 10 Americans live near a toxic waste site. There are 15,000 uncontrolled hazardous waste landfills and 80,000 contaminated lagoons in the States" (Caldicott, 1992:69). The federal government has established a superfund to clean up contaminated sites, but the sum set aside seems insufficient to deal with the problem; in addition, the money reserved has often gone unused because of bureaucratic red tape, among other obstacles.

The existence of toxic waste sites, many of which still may not be known, is often a threat to persons living nearby. The infamous events at Love Canal, New York, provide one example. From the 1930s to 1952, the Hooker Chemical and Plastics Corporation had used an old canal bed in the area as a chemical dump for more than 44 million pounds of hazardous chemicals. In 1953, the company sold the filled land to the city of Niagara Falls for a token sum of $1 without warning anyone about the chemicals. The deed stated that Hooker was not liable for any deaths or injuries that might occur on the site. A new elementary school and a housing tract were subsequently built on the filled land.

The existence of the hazardous waste dump was only discovered many years later as officials began to investigate the causes of unusually high clusters of abnormalities and illnesses among neighborhood children and adults. Investigators were able to trace the source of these medical problems to toxic liquids that had begun leaking in the early 1970s through the clay cap sealing the dump. In the end, Hooker disclaimed any responsibility, and the state paid $10 million to buy some of the homes, another $10 million to stem the leakage, and relocated about 1,000 families.

Among hazardous wastes, nuclear wastes present some of the most difficult challenges of waste disposal. One source is nuclear power plants, which produce millions of gallons of liquid radioactive waste and large quantities of radioactive solid wastes (such as spent fuel rods used in the generation of electricity). America's aging nuclear weapons arsenal is another source of dangerous nuclear materials.

The Spotted Owl Controversy

Many people believe that stricter environmental protection costs jobs. This kind of thinking was a major factor in the debate over the northern spotted owl that raged in the American Northwest during the late 1980s and early 1990s. Much of the economy in the Northwest is based on logging in old growth forests in the country's national forests. The federal government has traditionally subsidized the timber industry, allowing it to sell its products below costs. The U.S. Forestry Service has even built roads into remote national forests for timber company use.

Environmentalist groups, who are opposed to what they view as the destruction of old growth forests, have tried to slow logging in national forests by citing the Endangered Species Act (1973) that protects the vital habitat of any endangered species. The national forests, environmentalists have argued, should be protected because they are the habitat of the endangered northern spotted owl. Embattled loggers and many area residents responded by predicting extensive job loss and economic ruin for the region should larger sections of the forests be declared off-limits to the timber industry as a way of protecting the owls' habitat.

The environmentalists eventually won the battle over the northern spotted owl. Larger sections of the forests came under federal protection, and about 15,000 timber-related jobs were lost. Still, the region's economy is flourishing, as additional jobs were created in environmental protection programs and tourism. In addition, new companies have chosen to locate in the region because they can pay their employees substantially less than in other sections of the country. University of Oregon economics professor Ed Whitelaw maintains that such lower salaries are possible because of the attractiveness of living in the locality. In effect, employees receive a second paycheck comprised of forested mountains, clean streams, scenic vistas, and a low probability of being the victim of crime. Some small local towns hit hard by the layoffs have also received unexpected windfalls in the form of government programs established to ease the transition from heavy dependence on logging.

Adapted from Brad Knickerbocker. 1994. "Owls Nest, Jobs Grow in West as High Tech Supplements Forestry." *The Christian Science Monitor.* November 11, 1994.

Smaller quantities of radioactive wastes are also produced by the medical industry via techniques and equipment used to diagnose and treat diseases and by industrial, governmental, and university-based research projects. Nuclear wastes are not only highly toxic, but have a half-life (the time they are still radioactive and dangerous) of thousands of years. Where and how to store or safely dispose of these products is still largely unresolved and has become a matter of national debate.

The Attack on Environmental Policy

In the congressional elections of 1994, the Republicans gained control of both the House of Representatives and the Senate. Republicans saw their victory as a mandate to implement their campaign platform, which they called the "Contract with America." The "contract" called for a significant reduction in the size of the federal government and a decrease in the number of government rules and regulations. This agenda was combined with an attack on social programs and federal agencies that had fallen into disfavor with conservative elements in society. By the spring of 1995, the Republican Congress had turned its attention to environmental regulations, launching attacks on the three centerpieces of national environmental policy—the Clean Air Act, the Clean Water Act, and the Endangered Species Act. These attacks were combined with efforts to weaken significantly the U.S. Environmental Protection Agency, whose chief function is to enforce laws and regulations in order to control environmental decline.

For sociologists analyzing these assaults on environmental regulation, it might be useful to ask, "Whose interests are thereby served?" Although the Congress claims to be obeying the will of the people (after all its members were elected by the people, who must therefore supposedly support the ideas expressed in the "contract"), this seems questionable. Environmental laws protect citizens against hazardous threats to themselves, their property, and the nation's natural resources. Moreover, recent polls have shown that the vast majority of Americans are environmentally aware and expect environmental protection to be a high priority of government. Environmental regulations seek to protect the people, and Americans expect their elected officials to provide such safeguards. Other interests are being served by assaults on the environment. Some industrialists, businesspeople, and owners of ranches, mines, and timber enterprises have long contended that environmental protection is too expensive, stops them from plying their trades, and/or costs employees jobs (see "FYI: The Spotted Owl Controversy"). In fact, the Republican majority permitted some lobbyists from these groups to dictate legislation designed to undermine more than two decades of U.S. environmental policy.

Development and Resource Problems in the United States

Like most of the world, Americans face problems brought on by modernization and the development it promotes or causes. The demands stemming from efforts to feed an increasing global population, combined with modern scientific farming techniques, are depleting water supplies, threatening the safety of our drinking water (through agricultural and industrial pollution), and eroding fertile soil. Our natural resources are further threatened by the settlement into ecologically sensitive areas by people seeking pristine environs. Such relocation not only causes environmental decay, it pits competing interest groups against one another, which has led to a series of cultural wars, mainly in the American West.

In this section, we look at some of the difficult issues affecting the environment caused by population and development. Two of the most pressing issues involve the twin crises of water scarcity and water pollution. We also review land degradation and the destruction of wetlands and forests.

Water Scarcity

In some parts of our nation, such as the Southwest, the amount of water available is insufficient for people's needs. Irrigation and other human uses have caused the withdrawal of immense amounts of water from aquifers (large geological formations containing the world's underground water supply). Here, and in many other parts of the country, wells drilled into these aquifers extract water much faster than it can be replaced. As a result, water tables (the depth below which the ground is saturated with water) are receding, and wells must be dug deeper for people to obtain suitable amounts of moisture. In our country, the amount of water in the aquifers is seriously depleted. For example, the water table of the great Ogallala aquifer underlying eight Great Plains states is falling by about a meter a year (Lean and Hinrichsen, 1994). A quarter of the entire U.S. irrigated crop land is kept watered by depleting ground water supplies, and some has even had to be abandoned (Lean and Hinrichsen, 1994: 57). Water in the aquifers is necessary to support the land above them. In some places, the land is literally sinking as the water table drops. If the predicted global warming produced by the greenhouse effect occurs, the American West, already plagued by water shortages, will receive dramatically less rainfall.

In western states a tremendous competition over water use among various special interest groups already exists (see the box "FYI: Culture Wars in the American West"). There are intense competitions between agricultural requirements (for irrigation and livestock needs) and recreational demands (for boating, fishing, or lush golf courses), between farmers (who use it to grow crops) and urban dwellers (who use water for flushing toilets, taking showers, and consumption), and between environmentalists (concerned with wildlife habitat and spawning grounds) and developers (who want to build additional communities or water-intensive industries).

Another difficulty is that persons living farther downstream from the source of the contamination receive progressively less water than people living more close by. Not only does this negatively affect relations among segments of our population, but international conflicts also have erupted because of limited supply and high demand for fresh water. For example, the Colorado River used to run from the

Culture Wars in the American West

The "water wars" represent only a small portion of the conflict gripping the West as a result of development. This conflict is summarized by reporter Michael Elliott and his colleagues in the following excerpted article:

> With their gentrified new houses and chic art galleries, affluent newcomers are turning the traditional Mountain States into the nation's most fashionable—and most socially divided—region. Can the cowboys coexist with the Feds, the militias—and cappuccino bars?. . .
>
> Cows against cars [is but] one of the many skirmishes unfolding across the mountain west. Clashes that pit survivalists against the government are dramatic, political and . . . well known. Other economic and cultural conflicts are less sensational but equally important in this, the nation's fastest-growing region. Ranchers lose grazing land to California software writers buying up real estate; small towns with shared values are swamped by chic new settlers. The West is at war with itself. . . .
>
> For established Westerners, everything is fundamentally changing—and fast, as thousands of newcomers consume the available property. The West's traditional industries—mining, ranching, and logging—are clear losers in the new order. That old economy, based on "extracting" wealth from rocks, grass, and trees, is dying, pushed aside by high-skilled workers in high-tech companies. . . . So cowpats and coal mining are out; cappuccino and cilantro are in. . . .
>
> The Old West won't go quietly. Its stalwarts will fight, and fairly or not, one of their main targets is the federal government, blamed for regulating the old extractive industries to death. Throughout the West, federal rangers have been threatened; in some towns militiamen openly swagger, guns in holsters. The Bureau of Land Management warns its Idaho employees never to leave their compounds without radio communications and to "avoid areas with a known potential for conflict."

Source: Elliott, Michael, Stryker McGuire, Andrew Murr, and Daniel Glick. 1995. "The West at War." *Newsweek*. July 17: 24–28.

western United States to the Gulf of California in Mexico. Now, because Americans withdraw so much water from the river for agriculture and urban demands, its waters no longer reach the Gulf (Gore, 1993). This alteration has produced tremendous stress on Mexicans, who have depended on the river for their water and livelihood. Sharp conflicts between the governments of the United States and Mexico have ensued.

Water Pollution

A recent report by the Natural Resources Defense Council and Environmental Working Group indicates that as many as 53 million Americans may be drinking contaminated tap water because scores of communities have failed to meet federal standards for safe water. It is estimated that almost 1,000 Americans die annually from polluted water and another 403,000 become sick in varying degrees from it (McNulty, 1995). Water is contaminated from four primary sources—industries, farming, cities, and thermal pollution.

Industrial Water Pollution. In the not-so-distant past, industries dumped all types of waste into rivers, lakes, and oceans. This practice continues to some degree to this day in the form of illegal dumping of waste products. Accidents such as oil and chemical spills from ruptured pipelines and wrecked ships also pollute water.

Water contaminants include acid, ammonia, asbestos, lead, mercury, radioactive isotopes, and discarded items from manufacturing processes. Most water treatment facilities cannot remove all of these contaminants, many of which can cause severe health problems. For example, chronic exposure to lead (which also can be released in the atmosphere) can lead to anemia, convulsions, and kidney and brain damage. Other contaminants like mercury and pcvs (polyvinyl chlorides) in drinking water are similarly dangerous. Often, in an effort to make river water safe to drink, municipalities purify the water supply by adding even more chemicals, such as chlorine.

Agricultural Pollution of Water. In order to increase production and profits, most of American agriculture has turned to greater application of chemical pesticides and fertilizers, such as nitrates and phosphates. But rain and irrigation cause the runoff of these materials into rivers and lakes.

Large-scale hog, cattle, and chicken farms produce enormous amounts of animal wastes that also contaminate rivers, streams, and groundwater. The end result is that the drinking water of individuals and communities downstream may become tainted. In the spring of 1994, Milwaukee, Wisconsin, experienced an outbreak of flu-like illnesses. Thousands experienced diarrhea, vomiting, and high fever. The source of these ailments ultimately was traced to bacteria in runoff manure from farm animals, which found its way to Lake Michigan, the source of the city's water supply. Ken Midkiff, program director of the Ozark Chapter of the Sierra Club, summarized the threat from large-scale livestock operations: "With industrial strength pork production comes industrial strength pollution" (Ganey, 1995: 1.1). The Milwaukee outbreak points to an already common but increasing phenomenon.

Another pollution problem occurs when fertilizers and the decomposition of animal wastes produce algae blooms (or masses) in fresh water, which quickly grow and die. These algae consume much of the oxygen in the water, causing fish and other animals that draw their oxygen directly from the water to die. After the algae die, their decay settles on the bottom and kills the life forms there. In the 1960s, when Lake Erie was considered a dying lake, its bottom was covered by a 20- to 125-foot layer of this muck. Environmentalists, working with and for government agencies, grappled with the problem. In some cases their efforts have stopped pollutants from being discharged into the lake and nearby waterways; in other cases their efforts have reduced such discharges. Lake Erie, consequently, has been saved from total destruction. Such successful cooperative efforts can serve as models for dealing with other environmental issues.

Cities' Contribution to Water Pollution. Communities also contribute to water pollution. Many cities and towns deposit their wastes in rivers; the wastes then end up downstream in the drinking water of other communities. In 1990, 25 percent of the U.S. population was not served by sewage treatment facilities (U.S. Bureau of the Census, 1993:728). Another 21 percent are serviced by treatment plants that release significant amounts of raw sewage. The bacteria in untreated sewage is a serious health hazard for both consumers and swimmers. It is also unsuitable for many industrial uses. In addition, city garbage dumps leach toxins into underground aquifers and nearby waterways, endangering humans and animals alike. According to Caldicott, "So dangerous was municipal waste in 1990, that more than half of the hazardous waste dumps flagged (for cleanup) under the Superfund were municipal garbage dumps and landfills" (Caldicott, 1992: 69). As our population continues to grow, the problem of waste disposal and safe drinking water becomes more serious. No longer can we afford to ignore it.

Land Degradation

Our biophysical environment is vulnerable and does not have unlimited capacity for renewal. But as the twentieth century draws to a close, nations all over the world, including the United States, are placing new and drastic demands on the environment. Every ecosystem is made up of interrelated and interacting organisms and processes; therefore, change in any part of the local ecosystems triggers alterations in every other. For example, consider the dust bowl in the Great Plains region during the 1930s. It was caused largely by then-current agricultural practices. Marginal land that should never have been put under the plow was used for agricultural production. In good years, such land did produce a crop, but when a number of dry years came, the land turned to dust and literally blew away. Not only was soil lost to wind erosion, thousands of families lost everything they owned in the resulting catastrophe. Unfortunately, the loss of the nation's valuable topsoil did not stop at the end of the dust-bowl era.

Soil erosion is still occurring. The type of agriculture favored by most American farmers—deep fall plowing—means that much of the topsoil is lost to wind and water erosion during the winter and spring. A large portion of the threatened land lies in the midst of the Midwest corn belt. The federal government's General Accounting Office estimates that 84 percent of American farmland has lost more than five tons of soil per acre. This loss is significant because five tons per acre is the amount that the ecosystem can replace in a reasonable length of time. Moreover, the rate of loss has accelerated. During the dust bowl, soil was lost at an annual rate of 3 billion tons. Now, more than 6 billion tons is lost each year (Cunningham and Saigo, 1992). This acceleration is partly the result of farmers abandoning soil conservation practices established to stabilize the land during the dust bowl. Combined with the depletion of aquifers in the western United States, soil loss poses a serious threat to our agricultural future.

In 1985, Congress passed a farm bill that linked federal farm subsidies with progress in grassland conservation and wetlands protection. But a 1991 survey raises doubts about how effective this legislation has been (World Almanac, 1993). One hopeful sign is that farmers appear to be shifting to no-till farming, in which fields are not plowed after the fall crop harvest. The remaining stubble from the previous crop holds the topsoil that blew away under the old practice of turning over the soil. No-till farming also saves on time and energy costs and has no detrimental effect on future crop yields.

Wetland and Forest Destruction

Development threatens many of our nation's most important wetlands and forests. **Wetlands** are grounds on which standing water can be found for 15 consecutive days in any year, or which was saturated to the surface for at least 21 days a year. Many wetlands have been drained, to the detriment of wild life. In periods of too much rain, flooding of farmland, homes, and communities often occurs because wetlands have been developed and thus are no longer available to absorb excess rain water. Another problem caused by erosion or destruction of wetlands is that numerous forms of wildlife depend on them as their year-round home, whereas other migratory species such as ducks and geese use wetlands as migration stopovers and as breeding grounds. Destruction of these wetlands, then, imperils not only those populations that live there, but also numerous migratory species.

Destruction of forests, including our own rain forests, is another problem. The continuing debate on the health of U.S. forests, both public and private, centers on three issues—the quality of the forests, the maximum sustainable harvest on these lands, and the protection of endangered species that live in them. In addition, both Canada and the United States have a variety of rain forests (referred to as old growth forests), characterized by some of the oldest trees and most diverse ecosystems on Earth. These coastal temperate rain forests stretch from Alaska across British Columbia and the state of Washington into Oregon. Large parts of these forests have been logged or eliminated and the land has been put to other uses, such as housing. Much of the remainder is in peril. (Worldwide at least 55 percent

The destruction of the rain forests in Canada and the United States is another environmental problem. Large parts of these forests have been logged or eliminated, with the land being put to other uses such as housing.

of the coastal temperate rain forests already have been destroyed [Brown, Kane, and Roodman, 1994]).

Lumbering is big business in the United States. The industry operates on vast expanses of land owned by the federal government, especially in the western United States. Trees are not merely a source of lumber and jobs. They also provide a habitat for a wide variety of wildlife and plant species. Trees produce oxygen and clean the air of contaminants. Despite the necessity of forests for human survival, deforestation continues throughout the world and in the United States.

Assessing the Situation

Issues centering on environmental concerns tend to be very controversial. Often, there is debate within the scientific community about the exact cause of environmental problems as well as how best to address ecological concerns. Further, various interest groups such as business, labor unions, ranchers, loggers, and environmental activists push their agenda with local, state, and national governments. These interest groups seldom realize that their interests may complement one another, not conflict. Often, the controversies are put in terms of simple contrasts and zero-sum games, such as environmental protection versus jobs, food for hungry people versus preserving the rain forests, and so on.

As we have seen in this chapter, the choices are seldom so simple and environmental issues are seldom zero-sum games, especially when we look at long-range goals. For example, environmental regulations may not cost jobs as frequently as is argued. Even if jobs are lost in some areas, new and more lucrative positions often emerge in areas such as providing environmentally sound technology. Still we must assess short-term gains or losses against the background of the effects of ecological collapse if problems caused to the biosphere by human activity are not soon solved. In this section, we look at some issues we must address if we are to prevent environmental disaster.

Environment and Human Rights

The environmental problems we have discussed raise a number of human rights issues. The emerging area of intergenerational rights has strong environmental implications (see Chapter 2). Destruction of the environment by the present generation leaves little hope for future generations. The third generation of human rights (collective rights) also has a number of implications for environmental issues. Often, it is native peoples whose land is exploited and whose habitat is destroyed by incursions from dominant groups and by the modernization process. The world's poor also bear a disproportionate share of the shock of environmental decline. For example, more often than not, they suffer the most from environment-related diseases because they must rely on polluted water or live near hazardous waste dumps. One question humankind must answer is: Do not the poor as a collectivity have the same rights to a clean and safe environment as those who possess more material resources?

Human rights issues come to the forefront even when we confine our attention to those rights spelled out in the UN Universal Declaration of Human Rights (see Chapters 1 and 2). The rights to safe and secure living conditions, to health care, and to livelihoods that provide a dignified standard of living are all impacted negatively by environmental destruction. Political rights frequently are imperiled by environmental destruction, as powerful members of society require access to declining resources or demand exemption from regulations that protect the majority of citizens. Perhaps most significantly, humanity's right to exist is threatened by destruction of the biosphere. In summary, protection of human rights depends on environmental and habitat protection.

Toward a Sustainable Future

One of the basic contentions of this book is that there are no perfect solutions to the problems we are studying. This is certainly true when we look at environmental issues. Nevertheless, we have made some progress. There is a much greater awareness of the effects of irresponsible action on the biosphere than there was three decades ago when environmental concerns first started to receive wide attention. In industrialized nations at least, many people are now questioning whether pollution, ecological destruction, and deteriorating human health are the necessary costs for economic advancement. Consumers in industrialized nations are more concerned with buying green (purchasing ecologically friendly items) than in the past. Habitat concerns also have made their way into elections in most First World nations. Numerous NGOs push the "green agenda" in one form or another at local, national, and international levels.

Internationally, programs and agencies such as the United Nations Environmental Programme have emerged to deal with different aspects of environmental degradation. Their efforts have been supported by conferences and international treaties such as the Convention on International Trade in Endangered Species of Wild Fauna and Flora (CITES). The goal of CITES is to protect endangered species from exploitation, with special attention to banning the ivory trade that threatens the existence of the African elephant. The 1992 Earth Summit in Rio de Janeiro, whose goals were to stop global warming and protect biodiversity, is another example of such environmental conferences.

National governments in developed countries and in many developing nations also have begun to address environmental issues, passing laws and creating agencies to deal with ecological problems. For example, the 1970s in the United States saw the passage of clean air and water acts in addition to legislation designed to protect endangered species. The attack on environmental problems was bolstered by the creation of the Environmental Protection Agency and the creation of a superfund that provided money for cleaning up hazardous waste sites. Such pro-environment acts have filtered down to the state and local levels, where laws have been passed and agencies established to improve the quality of the local habitat.

Despite the passage of such laws, it is necessary to note that many remain unenforced because of lack of commitment, incompetence, or corruption. Moreover, many such regulations or agreements are watered down because of powerful political opposition or public hostility. Both undeveloped and developing nations still have dubious loyalty to environmental protection and even when there is a desire to improve their ecological record, they are prevented from doing so by lack of resources or by population pressures. In addition, First World nations are just beginning to acknowledge their obligations to help fund environmental campaigns in less developed countries. At best, all of the efforts made to date to confront ecological problems represent but the first faltering steps toward much more fundamental changes that many experts see as necessary if environmental catastrophe is to be avoided. Whether these alterations can be made rapidly enough remains to be seen.

Possibly one of the most important things that needs to be done is for people and governments to shift from an emphasis on short-term gains to a view of our actions from a long-term perspective. It is the stress on the immediate that has allowed depletion of natural resources, despoilment of the land, and pollution of the habitat without regard for the future impact of our behavior. A new attitude is needed, in which humans see themselves as part of, not separate from, the natural world and contemporary action is viewed from the perspective of how it affects future generations.

Some have suggested that this new ethic must be introduced to First World Nations from outside of the Western tradition because that tradition has been grounded in exploitation. But an ethic originating in non-Western beliefs might be difficult to introduce and is perhaps unnecessary. Philosopher John Passmore (1974) argues that there exists a "minority ethic" within the Judeo-Christian heritage that can serve as a basis for a viable ecological philosophy. This is the principle of **stewardship,** by which humans are viewed not as masters over the universe, but as creatures along with all of God's other creatures. The planet does not belong to humans to exploit as we please, but is God's property that we hold in trust while we are living. As stewards of Earth, Passmore suggests, it is our responsibility to not only return God's property in as good a condition as we received it, but to return it in a better state than when we acquired it. Considerations such as those enunciated by Passmore, have in fact resulted in a call for **sustainable development** or "development that meets the needs of the present without compromising the ability of future generations to meet their own needs" (UNCED, 1991:14).

Theoretical Concerns

Much of the environmental destruction occurring in the world today is directly or indirectly the result of practices governed by the assumptions of modernism, especially in its mechanistic version. Modernism has found expression both in the capitalism of Western Europe and the United States and in the socialism of the eastern bloc (the former Soviet Union and its allies in Eastern Europe). As a philosophy, modernism encourages us to see ourselves as distinct from nature, and the instrumental rationality it entails encourages us to exploit nature for our own ends. The larger context in which we see ourselves (the cosmos or natural world) is viewed as indifferent, if not hostile, to human values in much of modernist thought.

In pursuit of self-interest, we modern human beings organize ourselves into competing ethnic groups, corporations, and nations with which we generally feel a strong identification. Competition within and among these groups reinforces our sense that we live in a world that is threatening, thus intensifying our sense of isolation and struggle, our sense of "us against them." These attitudes often lead to a sense of scarcity and urgency. The sociosphere is perceived to be separate from a biosphere that threatens human survival but on which society must depend for its survival. The struggle to gain a share of the resources necessary for survival and growth is held to be intense and inevitable. In the modernist view, nature is unforgiving toward failures.

This mentality results in our use of common resources such as the atmosphere, ocean waters, and rivers to dispose of wastes; even the rain forests at times have been treated as essentially free for the taking. No market price or fee has been regularly set for their use. But these are our global commons. Since it has cost very little up front to exploit them, we have come to overuse and damage these resources. Costs are paid later, sometimes many generations later. Often, the payment is indirect or by those who were not responsible for the damage—for example, taxpayers directly and indirectly bear the costs associated with increased illness. Even when these damaging patterns are recognized, our assumptions lead us to underestimate the extent of the harm. Linear thinking leads us to believe that we can continue to obtain the same output for the same input and ignores natural thresholds that can trigger negative reactions, even breakdowns, in inherently nonlinear natural systems. Our assumption of reversibility causes us to think that we can always clean up any mess we create, but again natural systems have thresholds that make some level of damage irreversible. Thinking otherwise is part of the problem.

Will changing the way we see ourselves and our world alter these patterns of exploitation? Such changes seem to be happening for a number of people. Part of the globalization process involves a change in our sense of identity and our modes of engaging with the world. Frustration with the ways that governments, corporations, and mainstream environmental organizations have responded to the environmental crisis has led to the emergence of radical ecological movements, among which are the deep ecology movement (Merchant, 1992) and the social ecology movement, both of which are discussed in Chapter 3. Here we revisit them to look at their potential impact on environmental problems.

Deep Ecology is a social movement based on the assumption that we must expand our self-identity to include a sense of oneness with all living things and with the earth itself (Fox, 1990). To achieve this, we must transcend the subject/object distinction inherent in the modernist concept of rationality. The resulting sense of unity will replace our feelings of alienation from nature, thereby presumably restoring harmony between humankind and the ecosystem. These ideas represent a total rejection of rationality and of Enlightenment (modernist) ideals. But will the intuition of oneness with nature actually result in workable policies and practices that enable human society to be sustainable and allow ecosystems to thrive? The deep ecology movement seems to ignore social, political, and moral issues, as they involve the use of rational discussion.

The ideals underlying deep ecology thought are consistent with any political agenda, including a repressive one that denies basic human rights. We have seen that human rights violations, including the denial of civil, social, and economic rights, are frequently linked to ecologically destructive practices. Any philosophy of nature, such as the one articulated by members of the deep ecology movement, that purports to address ecological concerns must also articulate a coherent social and political policy that links human rights to ecological concerns and thus is committed to reestablishing the connection between the sociosphere and the biosphere. A solution that ignores these linkages is unworkable.

Social ecology is also a radical ecology movement, but unlike the deep ecology movement, it is rooted in socialist and anarchist social theories that trace ecological problems to the maldistribution of wealth and power in both capitalist society and Soviet and Chinese state-dominated socialism. For social ecologists, the link between social injustice and environmental degradation occupies the center of attention (Merchant, 1995). Social ecologists believe that a new sense of what it means to be human and to live on Earth is needed if the planet is to survive, but such a perspective must be well articulated and complex. It must go well beyond the instrumental rationality that now governs the relationship between human beings and nature and between human beings and other human beings (White, 1995). We must root our identities, modes of engagement, values, and patterns of social organization in a more comprehensive rationality that not only includes our intuitions of nature but also opens dialogue about social values, human rights, roles of men and women, political and economic structures, and worldviews. But change cannot come on the level of abstract beliefs alone. Social ecologists say that we can effect change only through active social agents who have a stake in making changes and who are willing to make the effort and the sacrifices necessary. Thus social ecologists predict that oppressed people like the poor will be agents of change. Yet today changes are taking place not only among the oppressed and exploited groups but also within the educated and professional upper middle classes with regard to ecological consciousness. This changing consciousness and growing ecological awareness are what set the stage for dealing with our ecological crisis.

We may be seeing the emergence of a new adaptive regime. We looked at three patterns in Chapter 5: tribal equilibrium regime, pronatalist expansionist regime (agrarian), and industrial consumptionist regime. The transition from one of these regimes to the next seems to have been driven by population growth, increasing population density, and depletion of vital resources. Much the same is happening today. Our industrial-age, high-consumption approach is beginning to show signs of breakdown.

As each regime gave way to the next, societies made great leaps in greater organizational complexity and in the total amount of environmental energy they captured and consumed. The societies able to make these leaps absorbed or destroyed smaller rivals, despite the fact that the smaller societies were often far more efficient and sustainable (Sahlins and Service, 1960). Indeed, the general evolution of social systems has not favored sustainable systems—not in the short run, at any rate. This fact seems to run contrary to the argument that what we need now is a sustainable way of life. The contradiction is only apparent. In the past, successful societies were capable of expanding and conquering new territories and/or new resources. In today's world, human activities are now global in scope, humans exploit the resources of the entire planet, and the effects of environmental damage are worldwide, affecting everyone and every region of the planet. The earth is now full; that is, we are coming close to its human carrying capacity. All previous societal types depended upon more or less specific ecosystems, but contemporary humanity, with its emerging global society, depends not on a particular ecosystem or set of ecosystems but upon the biosphere as a whole

(Dasmann, 1976). The strategy for survival has now shifted. To maintain ourselves, we will have to build a more complexly organized social and cultural system, not by using more resources, as was the case in each of the past transitions, but by using fewer resources. Still, new energy resources may be developed, as they were in the earlier transitions between adaptive regimes.

SUMMARY

1. **Symbiotic relationships,** in which dissimilar organisms live together in mutually beneficial associations, are quite common in the natural world. In such processes, the waste product of one organism becomes the "fuel" that provides life for another.
2. **Fossil fuels** like coal oil, gasoline, and natural gas, found in deposits created by decaying plant and animal remains buried underground for millions of years, have a somewhat limited supply; frequently cause environmental damage during their extraction, refining, and transport; and produce pollutants when they are burned.
3. The number of humans, their demands for natural resources, and the magnitude of their waste conspire to produce monumental environmental stress. The world's exploding population, consisting of a consumption-oriented, capitalistic, industrial society, has reached, and perhaps has exceeded, the biological **carrying capacity** (the largest number of any species that the planet can sustain for an extended period of time) of the earth.
4. An **ecosystem** is an identifiable network formed by a community of living organisms interacting with their environment. Ecological systems arrange themselves in a **nested hierarchy,** or a series of graded levels that include a number of lower-level ecological systems. The number of ecosystems can be changed or eliminated in a biosphere without totally destroying it because numerous natural systems operate within it and help to maintain a proper balance.
5. Tragedies of the global commons meet one or more of the following criteria: (1) An entire planetary medium such as the atmosphere or the hydrosphere—the earth's surface and ground-water—is in danger; (2) adverse conditions are widespread enough that they threaten universal ecological networks; or (3) injurious circumstances undermine large portions of the sociosphere and the biosphere to the extent that they undermine the planetary life-support system itself.
6. **Global warming,** the rising of the world's average temperature, results when greenhouse gases lingering in the upper atmosphere trap energy that would normally have escaped back to land or water. Possible effects of global warming are flooding of coastal zones, a shift in the world's climate, droughts, heat waves, and storms.
7. Water pollution results from groundwater contamination resulting from solid waste disposal in landfills, illegal industrial dumping of chemicals and waste products, and accidents such as oil and chemical spills. The most difficult to dispose of are hazardous wastes and nuclear wastes, which are highly toxic and radioactive for thousands of years.
8. Acid rain and substandard air quality are the results of chronic air pollution. Acid rain is found primarily in industrialized areas and is detrimental to forests, waterways, and agriculture. Long-term exposure to air pollution may cause asthma, bronchitis, emphysema, and lung cancer.
9. Soil erosion (the loss of topsoil to wind and water erosion), the erosion or destruction of wetlands (ground on which standing water can be found for 15 consecutive days in a year), and the destruction of forests all contribute to land degradation.
10. **Biodiversity** is nature's survival mechanism. The great variety of living systems, from differing ecosystems to varieties of species within given ecosystems to genetic variations within species, ensures that at least some species will survive to reestablish an ecosystem even if a calamitous change destroys many plant or animal groups.

Thinking Critically

1. To what extent is industrial expansion necessary to sustain rapidly developing populations? Are there alternatives to industrialization? How can industrialization be accomplished without environmental damage?
2. The assumption frequently is made that environmental protection is too costly, and that businesses that pursue environmentally sound principles of operation cannot succeed. Is this assumption correct? In what sense is pollution costly to business? In what sense is the cost of pollution shifted to the lower rungs of society and onto the environment? How can the costs of pollution be shifted to those who produce the pollution?
3. Much environmental damage results from humans psychologically identifying themselves as separate from the material universe. This attitude has combined with an instrumental mode of engagement to lead industrial society to exploit the environment. Is industrialization possible without this instrumentality? Are there alternative modes of engagement that could enable production to increase to meet the demands of an expanding population, but would allow us to work in harmony with nature? What lessons about this can we learn from preindustrial traditional societies? How might we behave differently if we identified ourselves as part of nature?

Suggested Readings

Anderson, Bruce N. ed. 1990. *Ecologue: The Environmental Catalogue and Consumer's Guide for a Safe Earth.* New York: Prentice Hall.

Barnet, Richard J. and John Cavanagh. 1994. *Imperial Corporations and the New World Order.* New York: Simon & Schuster.

Caldicott, Helen. 1992. *Love This Planet: A Plan to Heal the Earth.* New York: Norton.

Gore, Al. 1993. *Earth in the Balance: Ecology and the Human Spirit.* New York: Plume.

Hawken, Paul. 1994. *The Ecology of Commerce: A Declaration of Sustainability.* New York: Harper.

Lewis, Martin W. 1992. *Green Delusions: An Environmentalist Critique of Radical Environmentalism.* Durham, NC: Duke University Press.

Odum, Eugene P. 1993. *Ecology and Our Endangered Life-Support Systems,* 2nd ed. Sunderland, MA: Sinauer.

Passmore, John. 1974. *Man's Responsibility for Nature: Ecological Problems and Western Traditions.* New York: Scribner's.

Smil, Vaclav. 1994. *Global Ecology: Environmental Change and Social Flexibility.* New York: Routledge.

Wilson, Edward O. 1992. *The Diversity of Life.* Cambridge, MA: Harvard University Press.

Web Sites

Econet

http://www.econet.apc.org/econet/en.issues.html

Econet is a nonprofit computer network hosted by the Institute for Global Communications (IGC). There are a variety of environmental resources here, covering issues relevant to health, frugal living, wildlife, and sustainable development. The site contains links to IGC's other progressive networks.

Envirolink

http://www.envirolink.org/

This site is a large resource that provides the most understandable and current environmental resources available. It contains a great variety of searchable databases, news reports, and a chat room. The site also provides a directory of environmental resources.

Environmental Protection Agency

http://www.epa.gov

The homepage for the U.S. Environmental Protection Agency. This site provides access to databases at the EPA and to other government agencies that do research and collect data on environmental issues.

Greenpeace International

http://www.greenpeace.org/

The homepage for Greenpeace, this site includes information on the organization and its international campaigns and has many subpages and access to gophers. Here browsers also can access an index that directs them to other international organizations, political sites, and environmental organizations other than Greenpeace.

University of Oregon Energy Site

http://zebu.uoregon.edu/energy.html

This site is a valuable tool in that it contains links to numerous energy-related sites. It also has links to a number of sites containing environmental data.

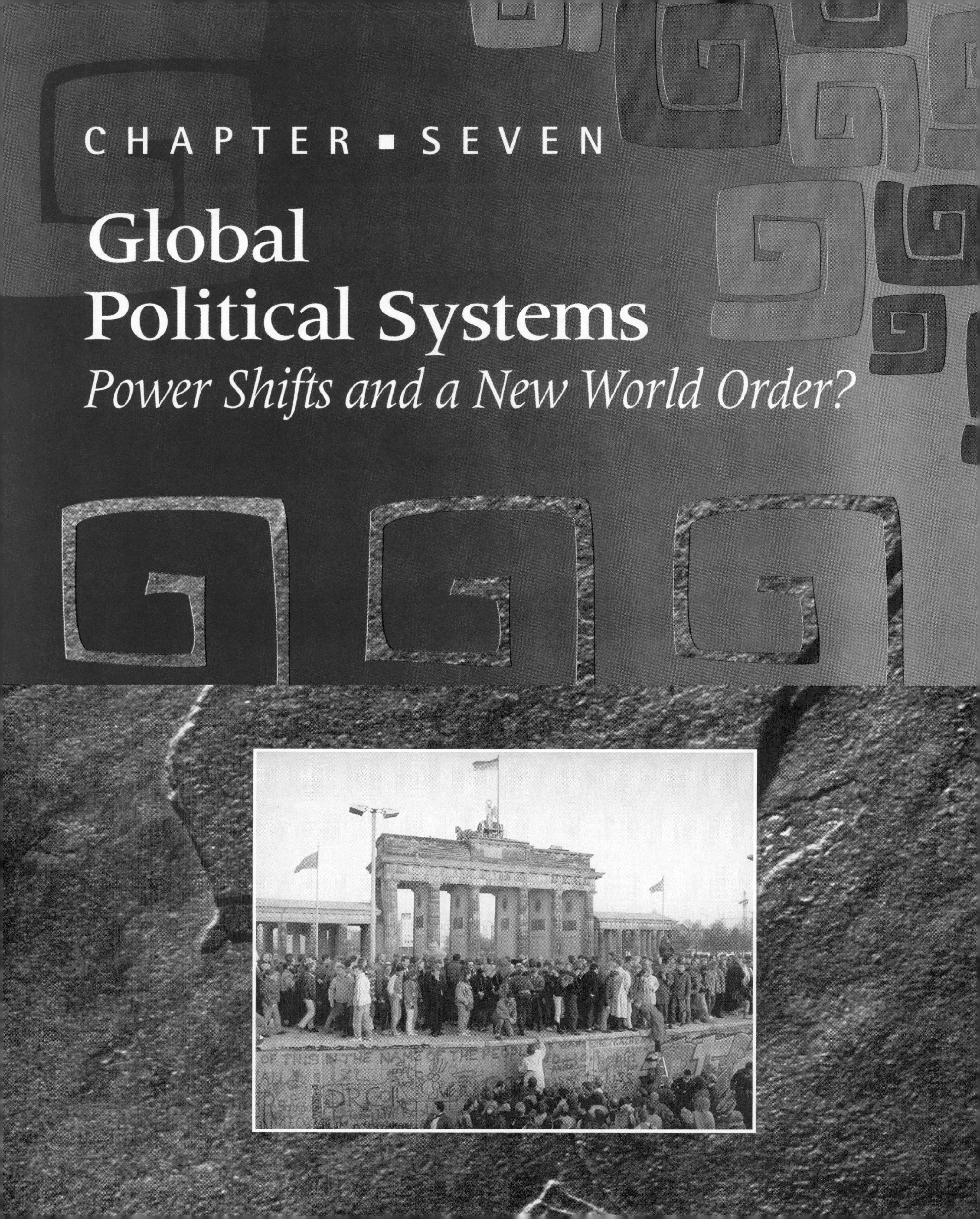

C H A P T E R ▪ S E V E N

Global Political Systems

Power Shifts and a New World Order?

NATO and Russia. In 1949 U.S. President Harry Truman signed a treaty that made the United States part of the North Atlantic Treaty Organization (NATO). NATO was designed as a military enterprise to protect Western Europe against the Soviet menace. For more than 40 years, the organization focused on its primary objective of containing Soviet expansion. The collapse of the Soviet Union in the early 1990s has left NATO without a clear purpose and the Western European, Canadian, and American governments that are members of NATO without coherent policies concerning its future.

Questions about NATO abound. Should the role of NATO be expanded to include dealing with regional or even global political problems? How would NATO then relate to the United States, the last surviving superpower? Would the organization be dominated by the United States? Would the interests of the United States and those of NATO always be the same? As NATO is primarily a military organization, could the United States depend on the organization to help it assert military power in other parts of the world? Under what conditions, if any, could the United States expect NATO to support American ideas and policies in Europe as well as in other parts of the world?

Many of the countries of Eastern Europe that were occupied by the Soviet Union have applied for membership in NATO as a deterrent to a feared resurgence of Russian attempts to control them. But Russia is at present weak politically, economically, and militarily and is likely to remain so for the forseeable future. What justification then is there for including Eastern European countries in NATO? And how might Russia view their inclusion? Will Russia see the expansion of NATO to its very borders as benign or as a threat? Will Russia decide that the Western powers seek to take advantage of its current weakness? If Russians view the expansion of NATO as a threat, is it likely that such expansion will contribute to the growth of democracy in Russia? Or will it encourage authoritarian, nationalist forces that promise to gain respect for Russia internationally by restoring its military prowess and so becoming a threat to its neighbors and the rest of Europe? Will the expansion of NATO ensure peace or will it produce a greater likelihood of war with Russia?

The questions we have raised about NATO reflect the changing world scene as we approach the twenty-first century. Nearly all governments and their citizens and political organizations face confusion about their direction. During the twentieth century the world's citizens have witnessed a culmination of social processes that began in the sixteenth century and have led to the beginnings of a worldwide political order. Much of the confusion we now witness may well be the birth pangs of this new order.

In this chapter we examine the emergence of that new global political order, beginning with its roots in colonialism and World Wars I and II. Although it is still early to draw a definitive portrait of what that order will be, by looking at the historical threads that make up its fabric—the postwar ascendancy of the United States, the creation of the United Nations, the effect of the Cold War, and the impact of communism's fall on the global balance of power—we can perhaps begin to discern its pattern. We examine, too, a number of problems that have emerged in the post–Cold War era, issues produced by the insecurity of the post–Cold War years. Finally, we review two important and interconnected political issues in the contemporary United States.

The Emergence of Nation-States and the Two World Wars

As strange as it may seem to readers today, the emergence of the nation-state as the primary unit of political organization is fairly recent. The **nation-state** is a modern form of political system in which a single governmental body claims to act on behalf of a group of people who share a common identity and territory. The nation-state as a social and political unity has two aspects: the **nation,** which refers to a group of people (often of diverse origins) inhabiting a common territory and (in theory) sharing a common identity, and the **state,** which refers to the governmental apparatus by which decisions are made and enforced on behalf of this group of people. The nation-state is sovereign; that is, it governs a contiguous territory over which it claims supreme authority. It is essentially bureaucratic and rational; that is, it governs by means of impersonal rules and roles.

For most of history, nation-states as such did not exist; the majority of the 192 contemporary nation-states were established in the last century and a half.

Previously, there were tribal territories or larger entities, such as kingdoms and empires. In some cases, tribal groups, such as the Mongolians or the Aztecs, served as the source of power for an empire; in others, the empire's power was based on that of its city-states, such as Athens, Sparta, Carthage, or Rome. In premodern Europe princes and kings governed by personal decree rather than by impersonal (and, presumably, more equitable and universal) rules. Their territories were often disconnected patchworks scattered across the face of Europe, in contrast to the coherent territories that make up today's nation-states.

By the late fifteenth century, several important political units resembling modern nation-states started to emerge in places such as France, England, Spain, and Portugal. By the time the Protestant Reformation reached its peak in the sixteenth century, **nationalism,** or love for, and devotion to, one's country, was becoming a powerful political force. The emergence of nation-states in the sixteenth century was accompanied by efforts to establish worldwide empires. Venetian traveler Marco Polo (ca. 1254–ca. 1324) journeyed to China and Mongolia, where he visited the court of the great Mongol ruler Ghengis Khan (ca. 1162–1227), thus opening routes of trade and cultural communication that had been closed since the decline of Rome. It was only after 1492, when Columbus discovered the so-called "New World" in an effort to open sea routes to India, that European conquest and colonization of the Americas began. Europeans were often amazed at the wealth, size, and sophistication of the civilizations they encountered in Asia, the Americas, and Africa. Over time the European powers managed to conquer or exploit them all.

Colonialism and the Emergence of a "World Order"

Columbus's discovery touched off a race among seafaring nations to establish colonies in many parts of North and South America that was initially dominated by Spain and Portugal. These initial incursions were followed by efforts from Holland, Britain, and France. **Colonies** are geographical regions ruled by an external sovereign power and whose political and economic activities are controlled to enhance the economic and political strength of the sovereign power rather than those of the indigenous peoples. European nation-states eventually extended their dominance to four-fifths of the world. By the twentieth century, the colonial holdings of Great Britain had surpassed those of all other European nations. There was a saying that "the sun never sets on the British Empire" because as the sun was setting in England, it was rising in the British colonies of India and Hong Kong. The United States also acquired colonies of its own in such diverse places as Cuba, Puerto Rico, Nicaragua, the Philippine Islands, Hawaii, and American Samoa. Africa was not carved up among the colonial powers until the early twentieth century.

By the end of the nineteenth century, Germany had organized itself into a modern nation-state with imperial ambitions. Turkey also controlled a significant empire in Asia Minor and parts of eastern Europe. Efforts to dominate the world political scene by these empires were opposed by Great Britain, France, and Russia. The formation of alliances based upon the principle that an attack on one nation would be an attack on other nations in the alliance, combined with increasing tensions and an escalating arms race, resulted in the "accidental" start of World War I.

Two World Wars and the Creation of a New Order

Although all the world's nations were not involved in either or both world wars, many, including the United States, participated. During World War I, large sections of Europe were devastated. More than 37 million combatants died, as did 10 million civilians. The immense death and destruction associated with World War I weighed heavily upon people's minds throughout the twentieth century. World War I ended with the signing of the Treaty of Versailles (1919), which exacted a heavy toll on the defeated Germans. The treaty also created the League of Nations. The purpose of the league was to mediate disputes and safeguard the peace, but it failed in its efforts partly because of its own internal weaknesses—it did not have the ability to enforce its edicts—and partly because of the retreat of the United States into isolationism (see Chapters 1 and 2 for more about the league and American nonparticipation).

The period immediately after World War I was tumultuous. Economic insecurity became widespread.

Depressions occurred in many countries worldwide. Citizens of the countries experiencing economic chaos turned to political leaders who promised easy solutions to their economic problems. Political extremists on both the right and the left vied for power. Fascists gained control of the governments in Germany and Italy, while a strong militaristic totalitarian state appeared in Japan. Germany was still smarting from World War I and the humiliating terms of the Treaty of Versailles. This, combined with a weak government and economic instability, made the country ripe for takeover by frustrated nationalists, which led to the rise of a strong authoritarian government under the leadership of Adolph Hitler (1889–1945).

Once Hitler dominated his own nation, he turned to empire building. He formed an alliance with Italy and Japan; these nations became known jointly as the Axis Powers. In 1939 Hitler attacked Poland, thereby beginning World War II. Because of treaty obligations, the Soviet Union, France, and Britain soon entered the war, eventually forming the Allied Powers with the United States and a host of smaller nations. The United States itself entered the war in December of 1941 after the Japanese attacked the U.S. fleet at Pearl Harbor, Hawaii.

World War II raged for six years; millions died on both sides. Eventually, the Allies triumphed over the Axis Powers. The war was finally brought to a close in August, 1945, with the surrender of Japan following the United States decision to drop two atomic bombs on the Japanese cities of Hiroshima and Nagasaki earlier that month.

Hopes for Stability and the Cold War

Even before the end of World War II, the three major Allies—the United States, the Soviet Union, and Great Britain—conducted a series of meetings intended to establish a more stable world at the conclusion of hostilities. They took two steps to ensure greater global stability. First, in 1944, they (and the forty-one other Allied nations) met in Bretton Woods, New Hampshire, where they laid the basis for a more stable world trading system designed to avoid the economic chaos of the post–World War I period that had contributed to the start of World War II. The economic restructuring established at the Bretton Woods Conference is discussed in more detail in Chapter 8.

The United Nations and the Hope for Stability

The other step the Allies took was to found the United Nations in 1946. The purpose of the UN was to produce political stability by providing a forum in which to discuss and solve issues before they led to open warfare. Since 1946 the mission of the UN has expanded to include a variety of humanitarian assistance and human rights charges. The UN is divided into two main bodies (see Chapter 2). In the General Assembly, each member nation, large or small, has one vote. Here, issues can be debated and courses of action proposed. The second division of the United Nations is the Security Council, composed of five permanent members, the United States, Russia, Britain, France, and China. The 10 other seats on the council are reserved for other member nations, which rotate on and off the council. The General Assembly debates issues, makes recommendations, and proposes resolutions, but it can perform no action. Only the Security Council has the power to undertake a range of actions—from economic embargoes to direct military intervention—that include sending peacekeeping troops into errant countries to enforce UN rulings. Each member of the Security Council has one vote, and each of the major powers may veto any action proposed by the Security Council.

The Cold War Develops

Hope was initially high for the UN, but this early optimism soon met with a dose of reality. Early on it became obvious that the cooperation between the Western powers and the Soviet Union that had been sustained by World War II could not be maintained in the era of peace. By the late 1940s, a Cold War had emerged between the United States and its allies and the Soviet Union and its allies. Politically, and to some extent economically, the world quickly developed into a bipolar system. One pole was the United States; the other pole was the Soviet Union (see Map 7–1).

For four decades, these two political and economic rivals carried on a tense global chess match. Each of the superpowers, for example, frequently distributed foreign aid, not for humanitarian reasons but to further its foreign policy goals in a particular geographic

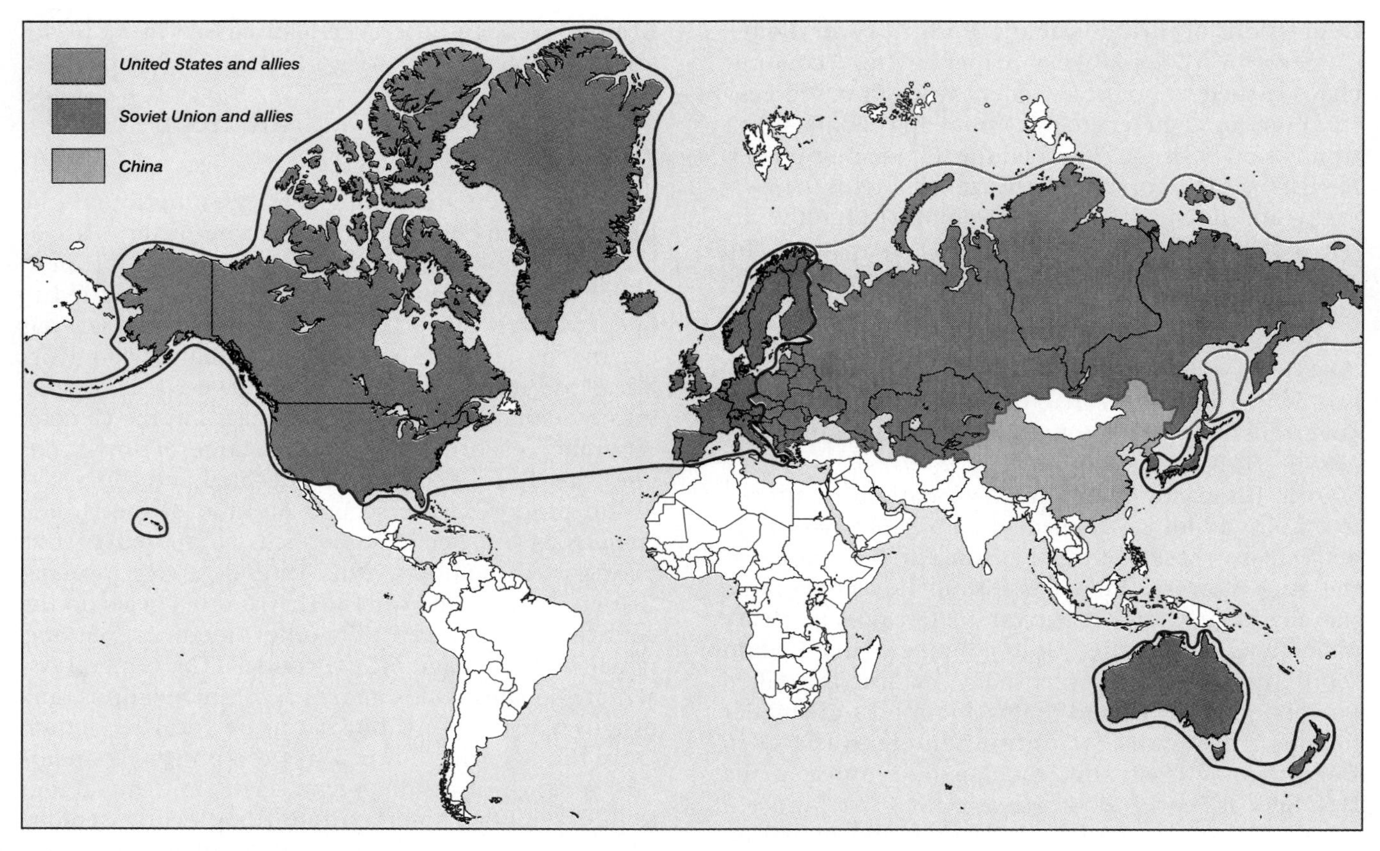

MAP 7–1 Bipolar World of the Cold War
This map illustrates the two main poles of world politics during the Cold War era. One pole is focused in the United States and its Western European NATO allies. The other is centered in the Soviet Union and its Eastern European Warsaw Pact allies. China played an unusual role in the Cold War. The world's largest socialist country did not ally itself with the Soviet Union. In fact, China often confronted the Soviet Union and its expansionist efforts. Most of the other nations of the world allied themselves with either the United States or the USSR; some changed alliances as their political situation changed. Some countries consistently pursued an independent course, sometimes using the superpower rivalry to their advantage.

area. Another tactic employed by the United States and the former Soviet Union consisted of using surrogate nations to make direct military incursions on their behalf. Throughout the period, the military forces of the superpowers also played a dangerous game throughout much of the world.

This gamesmanship was further exacerbated by the fact that the United States and the former Soviet Union tended to have **mirror image concepts** of one another. That is, they each viewed the other as an exact opposite. When the United States looked at the Soviet Union, it saw an untrustworthy "evil empire" bent on expansion. It saw itself, in contrast, as mainly peaceful and trustworthy. Conversely, when the Soviet Union looked at the United States, it saw an opportunistic capitalist empire bent on expansion and acting in an untrustworthy manner in international affairs. In contrast, it saw itself as largely peaceful and trustworthy.

The mirror images the two superpowers had of themselves and of each other illustrate the important role that identity plays on the stage of global politics. Based on the identities the United States created for itself and for its adversary, our government developed a policy of containment to prevent further expansion of Soviet-style communism. One of the unfortunate results of "identifying" the Soviet Union as it did was that the United States tended to view any type of insurrection or political instability around the globe as Soviet inspired. As a result, the American government frequently supported the suppression of democratic movements in the name of preventing Soviet expansion and defending democracy. For example, during the 1980s, the United States supported the right-wing government of El Salvador, a government that U.S. government officials knew was brutalizing its own population. One of the Salvadoran government's most infamous acts was the murder of six Jesuit priests, their housekeeper, and her daughter in 1989. Although this incident gained international media attention, the United States still considered the Salvadoran government a staunch ally in the fight against communism and refused to pressure it to bring those responsible for the murders to justice (Krauss, 1994).

The Arms Race

A huge international arms race was another result of the Cold War period. The Soviet Union and the United States spent tremendous amounts of money on military armament and the development of new weapons, and the entire world was flooded with weapons. The two superpowers frequently armed their surrogate nations to the teeth. Surrogates included many Third World nations that obtained levels of armament far beyond what they needed for their own self-defense.

In both the United States and the former Soviet Union, the use of so much money for military purposes diverted funds from domestic spending and more socially profitable investments such as the improvement of health standards, agricultural research, or humanitarian assistance. The most obvious and threatening example of this effort to attain superior military status was the competition to stockpile nuclear weapons. Shortly after World War II, the Soviet Union detonated its own atomic bomb and the race to develop ever more numerous and more destructive weapons—and more accurate means to deliver them—began. The absurdity of the nuclear arms race was highlighted by the fact that between the 1950s and the 1990s, each side relied on a doctrine known as MAD (mutual assured destruction) to guarantee that the other did not attack first.

This ongoing game was played around the globe between the air, land, and sea forces of the opposing sides. Consequently, there was always the possibility that some miscalculation or accident would lead to war between the superpowers and perhaps ultimately to a nuclear holocaust. In 1962 the dangers of such game playing were made evident when a confrontation occurred after the United States discovered that the Soviet Union was constructing missile bases in Cuba, just 90 miles off the coast of Florida. These missiles were capable of being launched into the United States. The threat to U.S. security of having Soviet weapons so close to home led President John F. Kennedy to demand that the Soviets dismantle the missiles or face the prospect of a military response. Kennedy's ultimatum pushed the two superpowers and the rest of the world to the brink of nuclear war. (The crisis ended peacefully; the Soviets withdrew the missiles and the United States pledged not to invade Cuba.) Because the Cuban Missile Crisis pointed out the folly of nuclear confrontation to both sides, it resulted in a number of steps that led to a reduction of nuclear tensions between the superpowers. Most important were a series of treaties that limited or reduced the number and types of nuclear weapons of each superpower (e.g., a 1963 treaty binding the United States, Great Britain, and the former Soviet Union not to test nuclear weapons in space, the atmosphere, or underwater and the 1968 Nuclear Nonproliferation Treaty), controlled the testing of new nuclear weapons, and prevented the proliferation of nuclear weapons to nations without them. (These treaties worked to a large degree, but sometimes nations defied them, as did India and Pakistan in 1998, when each tested nuclear weaponry.)

Foreign Aid, Decolonization, Gridlock, and Warfare

The period since World War II has been the greatest period of nation creation in history. Since 1945, 103 nation-states have emerged from former colonies. There were a number of reasons for this development. Possibly the main cause was that most of the European colonial powers either voluntarily divested themselves of colonies or had their colonies torn from their control through insurrection. For these former colonies, political independence often brought not only the promise of democracy but also hope for a marked improvement in economic conditions. At the same time, the Cold War produced a flow of foreign aid into the developing countries, and although much of this aid was military, a great deal entered these nations under the guise of technical assistance and funds for economic development. Unfortunately, much of this aid was diverted by dictatorial strongmen who came to power in many newly independent nations. These leaders subverted the democratic process and used the aid to gain money and greater power for themselves and their political cronies (see the box "The Human Face of Political Change: Killing the Messenger"). The result was more political unrest, which the superpowers generally exploited for their own ends.

With necessary programs and actions held hostage to Cold War politics, a kind of **gridlock,** the inability to deal with key issues as the result of power politics, developed in the UN and other international organizations. By the middle of the 1970s, the United States

THE HUMAN FACE OF POLITICAL CHANGE

Killing the Messenger

Even when a nation has established a more or less viable democracy, there is often no support for the democracy in its civil society because the society lacks those values, principles, and social structures necessary to sustain democratic practices. This is illustrated by the dealings with the free press of some apparently democratic nations. A free and independent press is vital in order for a democracy to function. Whether the medium is radio, television, or print, the press ideally informs citizens, criticizes the misuse of power, and points out social problems that need solving. Yet, in some societies, powerful political leaders, corrupt officials, and criminal elements who regard the free press as their enemy seek to repress it.

For example, in Peru, Alfonso Castiglione Mendoaz opened a radio station in a small town where he also became active in local politics. Although his station criticized government policy, his views were so moderate that he actually became the target of leftist guerrilla threats. Despite his status as a journalist and the guerrilla threats against him, he was arrested and tried before masked military judges for collaborating with the guerrillas. Even though no substantial evidence was offered against him, he received a 20-year prison term. After three years in one of Peru's harshest prisons, he was freed by a special government commission established to investigate the cases of many who may have been wrongly convicted through the years. The Peruvian government touted Mendoaz's release to show that justice had been restored to the judicial system. Peruvian journalists saw another message for the Peruvian people, namely that freedom can disappear as fast as the "crack of a whip."

Peruvian journalist Mirko Lauer provides another example of the way his government has treated journalists. Lauer is accustomed to almost constant intimidation because of his writings. He is closely followed by police and is the constant target of threatening phone calls. He believes that most of his antagonists are government agents. Asserting democratic rights in his country, he suggests, is made more difficult because the Peruvian public does not support the press in its battles for democracy.

China, Turkey, Yugoslavia, Algeria, Chechnya, and a host of other countries could be substituted for Peru. In Turkey, 150 journalists were subjected to violence by police in 1996; one journalist, Metin Gokteppe, was even killed. Algerian journalists have witnessed the murder of more than 60 of their colleagues in recent years. Worldwide, 38 newspersons were killed and 246 were imprisoned because of their work in 1996. For the same year, Freedom House, a well-known human rights international nongovernmental organization (INGO), counted 1,820 violations against journalists, an increase from the 1,445 it counted in 1995.

Source: Based on Stephen Franklin, "Shooting the Messenger," *Chicago Tribune,* February 23, 1997, sec. 1, pp. 1 and 8.

and other Western nations were frequently on the defensive in the United Nations General Assembly because of their support for repressive regimes and economic policies that appeared to exploit less developed nations. Many of the newly independent nations subscribed to *economic dependency theory* (discussed in Chapter 8), which holds that the lack of economic and social development throughout much of the world is the result of exploitation by the rich capitalist nations of Europe and the United States. The dependency of the poor nations on trade with the rich nations, according to this theory, made exploitation possible. This realization caused many poor nations to nationalize numerous industries, take control of domestic businesses to protect themselves from foreign competition, and otherwise insulate themselves from what they saw as the capitalistic global trading regime.

Another result of the Cold War was almost continual warfare in various parts of the globe, generally in newly independent nations. This warfare usually was supported by either the United States or the Soviet Union. Both countries also became bogged down in several large-scale confrontations that involved commitment of considerable troops and resources. The United States was the main military ally of South Korea when it fought communist North Korea in the Korean War (1950–1953) and of South Vietnam when it fought communist North Vietnam in the Vietnam War (1954–1975). The communist North Vietnamese were supplied by the Soviet Union. Similarly, in the late 1970s, the Soviet Union became progressively more entangled in a major Vietnam-style confrontation in Afghanistan, where it fought rebels against the communist puppet government. The United States was indirectly involved in the war; many Afghan rebels were trained and armed by the U.S. Central Intelligence Agency (CIA). By 1989 the Soviet Union was forced to withdraw all its forces from Afghanistan, but only after at least 15,000 Soviet soldiers and more than 1 million Afghans lost their lives.

The two superpowers also sponsored smaller-scale insurrections in a number of other countries. For example, the United States encouraged insurrections against Soviet-leaning regimes in Ethiopia, Somalia, and Nicaragua, and the Soviet Union sponsored insurrections against Western-leaning regimes in Ethiopia, Somalia, and the Philippines. Thus, at different times the United States and the Soviet Union each sponsored insurrections against the governments of Ethiopia and Somalia. When governments came to power that favored the Soviet Union, the United States supplied rebel forces against those governments. When governments came to power that favored the United States, the Soviet Union funded rebellions against those regimes. Such "side switching" among less developed nations was not unusual during the Cold War.

The United States and the Soviet Union also covertly sponsored various forms of terrorism against their enemies. For example, like the United States, the Soviet Union supported governments that used repressive and terrorist activities against their own populations. Similarly, the Soviets covertly supported nation-states such as Syria and Libya that trained, armed, and financed terrorist groups that represented a variety of causes that were generally anti-Western in their thrust. Both the United States and the Soviet Union also sponsored or supported various forms of terrorism against their enemies. For example, the United States supported repressive governments in Vietnam during the 1960s and 1970s and in El Salvador in the 1970s and 1980s because of the anticommunist stance of the leaders of these nations.

The Cold War's End and a New World Order

The collapse of the Soviet Union in December of 1991 signaled the end of the Cold War period and the beginning of a new phase in international relations. Some experts speak of the end of the Cold War as the beginning of a new world order. This new world order in some ways offers greater possibilities for world security and peace. Now, without the threatening distractions of the Cold War, there exists the possibility of focusing on pressing ecological, economic, and human rights issues. If this can be done, the world can move toward a brighter, more secure, and more prosperous future. On the other hand, the changing global situation also exhibits what appears to be an increase in ethnic and religious violence, a rise in terrorism, the dwindling of natural resources, and the threat of ecological collapse. Although many experts agree that we are at the beginning of a new era, few are bold enough to predict with absolute certainty the direction in which the global community is moving. This section briefly looks at some of the issues raised by this changing situation, reviews the role of the United

States in the new world order, and assesses other contemporary global political issues.

The Changing Global Situation

On the positive side, the collapse of the Soviet Union has apparently signaled the beginning of an era of greater international cooperation on political, economic, and social issues (see the box "Contemporary Discussion: Global Culture or Diverse Civilizations?"). For example, in 1992, Russian President Boris Yeltsin indicated that his nation's nuclear missiles no longer targeted U.S. cities and that his people no longer saw the United States as an adversary. In addition, Russia began seeking international funds and investments from the West to convert its socialistic centrally planned economy to a capitalistic **market-driven economy.** In a market-driven economy multiple producers of goods and services compete with one another (at least in theory) to make a profit. This system of buying and selling (the market) affects prices, profits, and wages without the need (again, at least in theory) for government control. In contrast, in **centrally planned economies** the government decides what goods and services are to be produced in the country and regulates how much of them are produced, which means that prices, wages, and profits are largely determined by government bureaucracies.

Partially driven by the desire for economic assistance, Russia has begun to cooperate with the West in a number of international political situations. For example, in 1991, Russia supported UN sanctions and the U.S.-led military intervention in the Persian Gulf War against Iraq's Saddam Hussein. Russia also assisted the United States to broker a peace in the bloody war among Croats, Muslims, and Serbs in Bosnia. Possibly even more remarkable, that peace involved the deployment of heavily armed NATO troops close to the Russian borders to enforce the peace agreement.

Significantly, the international community has begun to intervene in the affairs of nations in defense of human rights and for humanitarian reasons, not simply because of national, political, or economic reasons (see Chapter 2 for more detail about the international community's involvement in human rights issues). Additionally, there has been a marked decline in global political tensions as competition between the superpowers declined. For instance, the world's political leaders generally agree that we now have less likelihood of global nuclear warfare than we did during the Cold War. Decreasing tensions also raise the possibility of a significant **peace dividend:** Money spent for arms worldwide now can be diverted to more productive uses, such as improving health care,

CONTEMPORARY DISCUSSION

Global Culture or Diverse Civilizations?

Many scholars, including the authors of this text, are attempting to make sense of the political and economic scene emerging from the end of the Cold War. One of the issues they are considering concerns the shape of the global system(s) in the twenty-first century. Will some sort of unified global culture with global values, norms, laws, and political and economic structures dominate? Or will a group of diverse civilizations dominate regions of the world?

Global culture proponents point to the key role of the United States at the end of the twentieth century. They note the spread of market capitalism, accompanied by materialism, human rights, and democratic principles. They argue that the expansion of Western ideology and its economic and political structures overwhelms traditional cultures and challenges individuals worldwide to see themselves in a larger global context. Ultimately, this process could result in a type of global culture based upon Western foundations. Thinking along these lines has led American scholar Francis Fukuyama (1992) to proclaim the demise of the Cold War the "end of history," in that it represents the final triumph of American liberal democracy.

eliminating hunger, and slowing environmental degradation.

The Role of the United States in the Post–Cold War Era

The end of the Cold War also had a number of implications for the United States. The most important is that the United States is the sole surviving superpower. For the foreseeable future, "The United States . . . sits alone at the apex of the international hierarchy" (Kegley and Wittkopf, 1995:100). But American supremacy poses a number of questions regarding the role of the United States in the post–Cold War era. For example, how is the United States to use its political and military power now that it no longer has to focus on winning the Cold War? Most of the world looks to the United States for political, economic, military, and perhaps moral leadership. Yet Americans have tended to be skittish about exercising such power without a clear military threat to U.S. supremacy; when no apparent threat existed, we have tended to opt for basically isolationist policies.

Policing the World? The question of what America's global responsibilities are is usually posed in terms of the question, "Should the United States police the world?" According to some politicians, political thinkers, and strategists, the United States should exercise extensive widespread global leadership. Proponents of this position argue that as the victor in the Cold War, the United States now must assert global political, economic, and moral leadership. This means that the United States must become an active participant in the global community, including direct involvement in numerous political and military situations. Others argue that the United States should become involved only when one of our worldwide interests is directly threatened. The motivation to protect U.S. political and economic interests would be stronger than a concern for global well-being. If its interests were not threatened, in other words, there would be no need for the United States to become directly involved. Still others favor extreme isolationism. They believe that the United States should become directly involved in international political or military conflicts only when the conflicts pose a threat to our nation itself; otherwise, there is no need to spend U.S. money or shed U.S. blood.

Obviously, the United States should not become involved in every dispute that arises worldwide. Some situations have a better chance of resolution when the major powers do not get involved. For

Others, however, see the situation as more complex. For example, political scientist Samuel P. Huntington argues in *The Clash of Civilizations and the Remaking of World Order* (1996) that those who expect the rest of the world to adopt American-style democracy and capitalism will be greatly disappointed. Huntington points to what he identifies as the eight great world civilizations: (1) the Western, led by the United States and Western Europe; (2) the Sinic, dominated by China; (3) the Hindu, centered in India; (4) the Orthodox, led by Russia; (5) the Japanese, anchored in Japan; (6) the Islamic; (7) the African; and (8) the Latin American civilizations—these last three have no obvious leaders. Each of these eight civilizations is so distinct that deep convergence of values or institutions among them is impossible, Huntington believes. The Cold War forced much of the world to choose between the communist East and the capitalist West, but now each of the eight civilizations will be free to develop along its own lines. The result will be more diversity, not convergence (see Map 7–2).

◆ **For Critical Thought:** (1) What are the assumptions of proponents of each side in this discussion? (2) What are the political, economic, and cultural implications of each side in this discussion? (3) What practical problems are created by each position? (4) Are there possibilities other than the ones presented?

Sources: Francis Fukuyama, *The End of History and the Last Man Standing* (New York: Free Press, 1992); Samuel P. Huntington, *The Clash of Civilizations and the Remaking of World Order* (New York: Simon & Schuster, 1996).

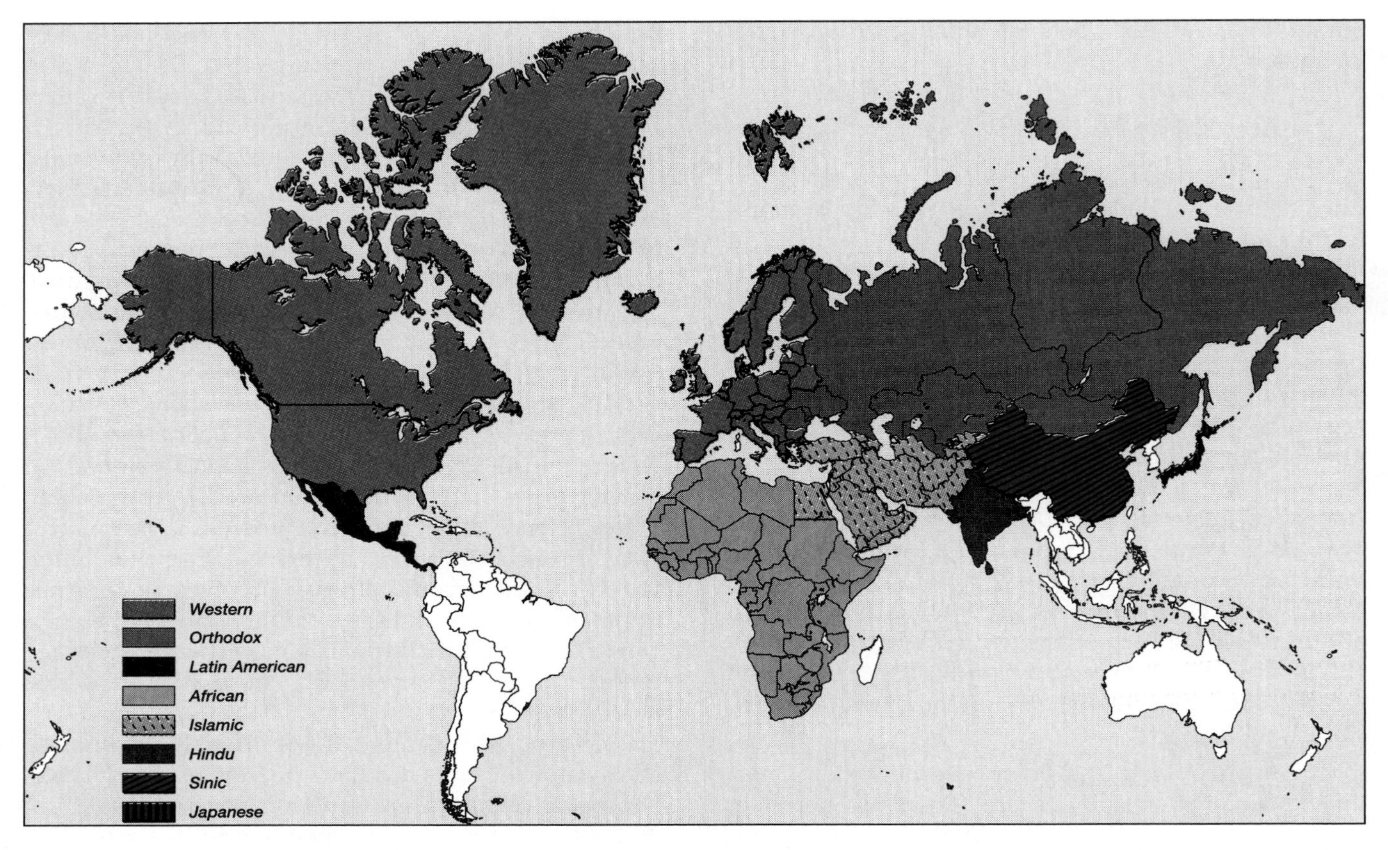

MAP 7–2 Huntington's Competing Civilization Centers
Political scientist Samuel P. Huntington sees the world of the twenty-first century as divided into eight competing civilization centers.

Source: Based on ideas presented in Samuel P. Huntington, *The Clash of Civilizations and the Remaking of the World Order* (New York: Simon & Schuster, 1996).

example, in many instances alliances of local nations can handle dangerous political or military situations more effectively. However, extreme isolationism or very limited involvement in world affairs does not appear to be a practical or viable option. In many international situations, the problems simply will not be solved without our help. For example, the warfare in Bosnia did not stop until the United States started to play an active political role that included its decision to commit ground troops and military support to enforce a peace within the region. Similarly, the peace accords secured in the Middle East involved direct U.S. brokering of deals and guarantees of security. Without this intervention, the steps toward stabilizing the Middle East would probably not have been taken.

Nevertheless, it is likely that in the future the United States will encounter fewer opportunities and fewer situations that call for "go-it-alone" solutions. That is, in the current global political scheme, most operations will be undertaken by some type of political or military coalition. For example, the United States operated in conjunction with the UN when it sent troops into Somalia in 1992. Something similar occurred when political chaos threatened Haiti in 1994. Previously, the United States had been prone to take unilateral action when something was amiss in the Caribbean. However, in 1994, President Clinton was careful to put together a UN coalition under U.S. leadership before he took direct action in Haiti. Even the Persian Gulf War fought under President Bush was waged as part of a coalition under the auspices of the UN. While the United States provided leadership and the bulk of the military power to support the operation, a number of Arab and other allies also supplied troops, money, and military hardware.

Even with such broad parameters, questions still remain. What should U.S. foreign policy look like? What are the conditions under which the United States should involve itself politically or militarily with situations occurring throughout the world? What interest could compel us to risk U.S. lives? Answers to these and many other questions have yet to be resolved as U.S. foreign policy, as well as the foreign policy of many other nations, evolves under the new political reality.

The Role of the Military. The changing military situation also deserves a great deal of attention. Since the 1950s, the main role of the U.S. military has been to contain and potentially defeat communism. The particular target of most military operations was the Soviet Union and its allies. Most sophisticated weapons systems developed as well as the military planning associated with them centered on defeating a numerically superior Soviet army. As a result the U.S. military establishment came to rely heavily on high-tech weaponry to compensate for its numerical disadvantage. President Ronald Reagan justified the huge military buildup during the 1980s by emphasizing the threat posed by the "evil empire" of the Soviet Union.

The Need for Low-Tech Weapons. This focus causes problems as the United States prepares its military for the post–Cold War era. For example, the United States during the Cold War put so much emphasis on high-tech all-out warfare that it was unprepared for the regional, relatively low-tech operations useful in most local disputes. For instance, during the summer of 1988, Iran and Iraq were at war. As a part of its tactics, Iran threatened to cut off shipping in the Persian Gulf. As tensions escalated, U.S. forces began flying limited sorties against Iranian naval vessels and oil rigs in the Persian Gulf area to keep shipping lanes open, thereby ensuring a continued flow of the petroleum so necessary to the West through the gulf.

The United States Navy was well prepared for defeating Soviet adversaries on the high seas, but it had difficulty adjusting to the more limited assignment of dealing with this relatively low-tech regional conflict. Large U.S. vessels were at a decided disadvantage in the confines of the Persian Gulf. Moreover, the low-tech weapons of the Iranians, such as World War I–vintage sea mines, often proved the bane of sophisticated U.S. ships.

Regional Conflicts and Emerging Superpowers. The role of the U.S. military in dealing with regional and smaller conflicts is likely to become increasingly important in the near future. The end of the Cold War has seen the unleashing of regional conflicts resulting from nationalistic or ethnic tensions previously held in check by the superpowers. It may well be that the U.S. military will have to become involved with a number of minor or major local or regional conflicts simultaneously—something to which the military is having to learn how to adapt. Yet even though regional or more limited conflicts seem to pose the greatest immediate challenge, the world is not entirely free from the threat of major confrontation.

China is beginning to reassert itself militarily and economically at a time when its impending change of leadership may produce a degree of political instability. In fact, the idea of a resurgent, somewhat politically unstable China concerns many of its Asian neighbors. A large number of these countries look to the United States for both defense and a measure of security in the face of the threats from their larger neighbor. The potential for danger in the situation was highlighted in 1996 when China conducted highly threatening military exercises in the Taiwan Strait. Taiwan is the island to which Chinese nationalist forces fled when the Chinese communists took over the mainland in 1949. Although the island subsequently developed into a flourishing capitalistic nation-state with a democratic government, mainland China has continued to regard it as a breakaway province run by an outlaw government. The recent show of force was regarded by most observers as an effort by the Chinese communist government to dampen democratic and independence-oriented elements in Taiwan. The implied threat of military action prompted the United States to dispatch powerful naval forces to the strait to assure the Taiwanese that they are not unprotected against the far larger nations.

Russia itself continues to have the potential to become a significant military threat. Although at present its government seems intent on carrying out democratic and economic reforms as well as maintaining a peaceful coexistence with the United States

When China conducted military exercises in the Strait of Taiwan in 1996, the United States sent naval forces to the strait to assure the Taiwanese that they would be protected against any show of force by the Chinese.

and its allies, the situation could change quickly. The efforts to move Russia from a centrally planned economy to a market-driven economy have caused numerous people to become impoverished and to lose their jobs. This situation has spurred much political unrest. Another potentially destabilizing factor is the great degree of dissatisfaction among the members of the Russian military who have seen their status decline considerably under the new Russian regime. The general discontent has already spurred two movements whose avowed purpose is to overturn democratic and economic reform. One of these is led by Communists who vow to return to the former system in which people had greater economic security. The other movement is led by nationalists who promise to return Russia to its former imperial glory. In 1996 these forces posed a real threat to President Boris Yeltsin's reelection. The specter of a return to aggressive anti-Western foreign policies by a resurgent Russia is formidable, especially when we consider the size of the nation's military forces and the thousands of nuclear weapons still remaining from the Cold War. One of the great challenges for Western capitalistic democracies will continue to be how to encourage democratic and economic reform in Russia without giving further support to Communists and nationalistic groups.

Instability in the "New World Order"

We have already discussed a number of political issues apparent in the changing global scene. In this section we consider three threats to global political security: continued warfare and the proliferation of weapons of mass destruction; the resurgence of national, ethnic, and religious violence; and the pressure resulting from an increasing population and dwindling resources. Each of these factors, alone and in combination, calls into question the ability of single nation-states or even alliances of nation-states to cope with various global crises.

World Order or Disorder?

Early in 1991 the United States headed a coalition of nations empowered under a UN mandate to dislodge invading Iraqi forces from the Middle Eastern country of Kuwait. The success of this coalition in the Gulf War led then President George Bush to declare a "new world order." Despite the president's enthusiasm and the contention of this book that we are seeing the early stages of an emerging structure, many still question the existence of this new world order. Let us review some of the issues in this debate.

People supporting the new world order viewpoint note that the end of the Cold War has left the United States the leading political and military power. The end of Cold War hostilities has also opened the possibility for a level of cooperation among nations to solve humankind's pressing problems that was unimaginable in the bipolar world of the Cold War. Since even powerful nations seldom can act alone to handle political or economic crises, international organizations such as the UN and the International Monetary Fund (IMF) are increasingly more involved in initiating action intended to address global issues. Universal standards frequently come into play in considering economic, political, environmental, or human rights issues. For example, the UN Declaration of Universal Human Rights is widely used to judge human rights issues (see Chapter 2), and *Agenda 21* (the action plan developed at the 1994 global Conference on the Environment held in Rio De Janeiro, Brazil) is used as a standard to evaluate development and environmental concerns (Sitarz, 1994). Further, widespread use of the Internet and satellite-based communication technologies make the development of a global culture more possible, while at the same time economic integration of most nations into the world trading system moves forward.

Despite these factors, the world may in some ways actually be more unsafe and unstable than it has been for the last 50 years. During the Cold War the superpowers engaged in dangerous game playing that held the constant possibility of miscalculation leading to widespread warfare. But as time passed the United States and the Soviet Union began to behave in a more rational fashion. Each side could be assured of a measure of predictability on the part of the other. It became obvious to both sides that widescale warfare between the superpowers was in no one's interest. Although each superpower sponsored insurgencies against governments thought to favor the other superpower, their combined power was able to keep some degree of control in surrogate states.

With the end of the Cold War, much of this predictability and control has disappeared. Major powers have less ability to manage situations such as those in which religious, ethnic, or nationalistic groups seek to carve out a portion of global prominence for themselves. Although the United States in its role as the sole surviving superpower may attempt to assert leadership, many nations, including former allies, frequently choose not to follow its lead, contending that no clearly defined system of power relationships has yet emerged. Acting on such principles, Germany is asserting dominance in Europe, Russia in central Eurasia, Japan in Asia, and the United States in North America (Klare, 1993). We may also add China, Iran, Iraq, India, Pakistan, and Libya to this list as countries seeking regional, if not global, influence. The increasing availability of weapons of mass destruction, the many ethnic and religious conflicts already apparent, continuing terrorism, and declining resources lead many to conclude that the end of the Cold War did not give us a new world order, but a new world in disorder.

Nationalism and Ethnic Violence

The Cold War's end has increased the possibility of regional or subregional conflicts. These conflicts may occur on two levels. The first level is discord between nation-states. For example, the absence of control by the superpowers has unleashed regional competitions for power in east Asia, south Asia, and the Middle East, each of which carries the possibility of armed confrontation. The rivalries between China and Taiwan, North and South Korea, India and Pakistan, India and China, Iran and Iraq, Iran and Saudi Arabia, and Israel and Syria are potentially among the most ominous (Klare, 1993).

The second level is violence within nations, which has also greatly increased since the end of the Cold War. This violence originates from two sources. The first source is **ethnonationalist movements,** movements by ethnic groups within multiethnic nation-states whose goal is to establish separate nations or, at least, a measure of political autonomy for themselves. Examples of participants in these movements include French-speaking Canadians in Quebec; separatist groups in Georgia, India, China, Indonesia, and the former Yugoslavia; the Kurds in Turkey and Iraq; the Palestinians in the Middle East; the Tamils of Sri Lanka; the Shan and Karen in Burma; and the Basques of France and Spain (Klare, 1993).

Revolutionary movements in numerous countries are a second source of violence within nations. **Revolutionary movements** propose sweeping changes in society, often demanding that existing institutions be demolished and replaced with new institutions deemed more desirable by the revolutionaries. Revolutionary movements may be secular in nature, frequently aiming to establish more egalitarian societies, like the Shining Path in Peru, the Khmer Rouge in Cambodia, and the New People's Army in the Philippines. Or revolutionary movements may be comprised of religious revolutionaries who seek to replace corrupt secular states with those governed by religious law, such as members of the fundamentalist Bharatiya Janata party in India, the Islamic Salvation Front in Algeria, and the Islamic Jihad of Egypt. Fundamentalist groups are especially troubling as members of revolutionary movements because they combine political zeal with "righteous" religious fervor, which allows them to attack or destroy "enemies of God" with little conscience. Fundamentalism as a reaction to globalization was discussed in Chapter 3.

Population Increase and Resource Decline

In Chapter 5 we saw how the population of the world is increasing most rapidly precisely in those regions that can least afford it—the poorest of developing nations. Throughout this book, we detail how our resources—including sources of energy, farmable land, water, and fisheries—are declining. Separately and together, population and environmental pressures have a destabilizing effect on global politics.

Thomas Malthus, as noted in Chapter 5, contended that factors that increase the death rate would multiply as population outstripped available resources. In such a scenario, not only are disease and famine more likely, but warfare over available resources becomes more probable. In fact, a growing population confronting declining resources does represent a major threat to global security (Homer-Dixon, 1994 and 1993). This threat can come from several directions. Internal conflicts among religious, ethnic, or class groups become more likely as these groups compete with one another for available assets. Rising prices in the face of declining resources can throw national and global economies into chaos. Nation-states may go to war with their neighbors, either to acquire resources or to divert the attention of their own citizens from internal crises. Ruling regimes may "harden" against internal dissenters to preserve their power as pressures for change build, thereby increasing the possibility of repressive terrorism and human rights violations.

Initially these conflict-ridden scenarios will probably be enacted in the poorest nations, but developed countries are not immune. In the 1970s the economies of developed nations were seriously crippled when the Organization of Petroleum Exporting Countries (OPEC) increased the price of oil. Some have argued that the 1991 Gulf War was waged more to protect the oil supply of industrial nations than to liberate Kuwait from Iraqi bondage. (See the box, "FYI: Oil and Global Security.")

The Future of Nation-States

Although nation-states will remain powerful players in global politics for the foreseeable future, they appear to be losing ground in their efforts to continue as the primary focus of power (Klare, 1993). They are being challenged on the *suprastate* and *substate* levels. On the suprastate level, market capitalism has become the driving economic force by transcending national boundaries. Multinational corporations that owe loyalty to no one country increasingly threaten the ability of nations to control their own economies and, at times, even to conduct an independent foreign policy. Rather than national interests guiding foreign policy, global and regional trading apparatuses such as the World Trade Organization (WTO) and the North Atlantic Free Trade Association (NAFTA) will determine the conditions of commerce.

This process is already being hastened by television, radio, computers, and other instruments of mass communication that foster a kind of global culture. On one level the globalization of culture involves internationally recognized sports stars, popular music, and well-known commercial items such as Coke or Nike running shoes. But even commercials and popular television series carry other messages, messages that have to do with values about dress codes, standards of living, and patterns of conduct. These sometimes new values inevitably conflict with both traditional standards of non-Western societies and the values of conservative groups within Western societies. At times these seeds planted by media grow into challenges to the traditional culture, raising questions of women's rights, marriage for love, and the quest for independence from parental authority, among other issues. These challenges can lead a culture to develop more open and universal standards but are just as likely to generate strong antimodern reactions.

Often these more open and universal shared values and norms are enforced by INGOs or international agencies to the detriment of national sovereignty. For

FYI

Oil and Global Security

The relationship of oil to modern society in the context of issues associated with globalization illustrates the interconnectedness of environmental, social, economic, and political problems.

The shift to an oil-based economy is the hallmark of modernism and industrialization in the twentieth century. In modern societies, oil, gasoline, natural gas, and oil-related products not only provide fuels, they also are the major components in a wide array of vital products, such as the chemicals used in plastics, pesticides and fertilizers, food preservatives, and clothing. As a result, nearly all sectors of industrial societies are affected by the availability and price of oil and oil supplies. Major sectors of our own economy, such as the auto, airplane, furniture, and electronics manufacturing; farming; transportation; and electrical generation industries depend on oil. For example, petroleum is used not only to transport goods but also to manufacture plastics for computers.

The heavy use of oil-related products has a major impact on the biosphere. For example, global warming, ozone depletion, acid rain, smog, pesticide poisoning, and the destruction of life in our waterways are all directly tied to pollution from oil-based products. Moreover, the availability or scarcity of oil affects almost all elements of the sociosphere: the price of commodities to consumers, elections of political figures, job security, the economic health of nations, and issues of peace and warfare, among others.

In the early 1970s, the members of OPEC decided to increase their revenues by limiting the amount of oil sold in the international market, thus inflating its price. Oil and gasoline for fuel were severely restricted. Lines formed at filling stations, and fights broke out as consumers scrambled for limited supplies of gasoline. As the price of oil doubled, economic recessions in most nations rapidly followed. The price of everything—from fuel oil to food to clothing to housing—soared. Inflation became rampant. The cost of borrowing money skyrocketed. Most nations of the world saw the quality of life of their citizens decline precipitously. People lost their jobs as well as their possessions. It took more than a decade for the world to recover from the shock induced by such a significant limiting of available oil.

Today experts estimate that the world has no more than a few decades of oil reserves left. As reserves decline, the balance of power will shift to nations that still have oil available. One consequence is that some developing countries will have newfound economic and political power. Another consequence will probably be that environmentally sensitive areas such as the arctic tundra zone will be opened to oil exploration and production, causing ecological distress. Oil prices will also rise to new highs, throwing the world's economy into turmoil once again. Political and social unrest will also probably occur. Nations may go to war to protect or secure oil.

---

example, INGOs such as Amnesty International work actively on behalf of human rights and democratic procedures in ways that alter the political climate within a nation. The Guatemalan village women of Nuevo Mexico serve as an example. In the early 1980s, a number of these women spent a dozen years in Mexico while fleeing civil war in their own country. During this time, national women's groups, political activists, and INGOs exposed them to ideas of how women could and should assert influence on their families, villages, and nations. Upon returning to Guatemala, many of these women assumed activist roles, staging sit-ins at government offices, blocking highways, and preaching organization and solidarity as members of an INGO called Mothers of the Earth. The result has been that these women have begun to exert considerable influence on both their own communities and national life (McMahon, 1996).

On the substate level, nation-states are becoming much more fragmented as groups defined by race, religion, ethnicity, class, sex, or economic interests (among others) enter into competition with one another. Often, this rivalry undermines efforts to find

Japan's Ginza, in Tokyo, is often called Japan's Fifth Avenue, with deluxe department stores, elegant boutiques, and luxurious restaurants. A kind of global culture is expressed in such stores, with messages about dress codes, standards of living, and patterns of conduct.

common interests that could unite competing collectivities into nations. This fragmenting of society is enhanced by grassroots movements that tend to form when these loosely defined interest groups claim certain rights for themselves. In the United States, for example, some members of fundamentalist religious movements, claiming the right to have their views heard, have pressured public school boards to include creationist science literature (based on a literal reading of the book of Genesis) with the more standard texts teaching evolution. This example reveals the ongoing fragmentation of American society, which is sometimes referred to as the culture wars. (The so-called "collective" or "solidarity" rights of groups were referred to as the "third generation of human rights" in Chapter 2, where we discussed problems that these rights raise in more detail.) When such grassroots movements as fundamentalist Christianity or radical environmentalists claim special privileges or protections for themselves, they undermine national control. Perhaps another factor contributing to the erosion of nation-states is that some problems are too "small" to be dealt with on the national level. For example, issues like neighborhood pollution may be best addressed by local authorities or agencies. Conversely, many of the problems we have been discussing in this text, among them global warming, increasing inequality, warfare, and the spread of infectious disease, need to be addressed on a global scale. The long-term weakening of the influence of nation-states, then, is occurring both from the top down and the bottom up.

Power, Voter Apathy, and the Political Process in the United States

We have addressed a number of political issues in this chapter that have direct or indirect impact on the United States. In this section we look at several issues in the United States that have particular relevance for U.S. democracy. First, we discuss who has power in U.S. society. Next, we examine the issue of voter apathy and its effect on the political process.

Power: Who Rules America?

The United States is often viewed as one of the world's great democracies. Our form of government and respect for political and civil rights provide symbols of hope for people still living under totalitarian repression. Ideally, our political system produces a "government of the people, by the people, and for the people," as President Abraham Lincoln observed. But ordinary citizens and social scientists frequently question whether our government is really run for and directed by "the people." We might assume that elected officials, for instance, have the authority to make laws and decide policy. Therefore, they rule America, but is this actually true?

Sociologists are aware that the situation is far more complex. One reason is that the real sources of power frequently are hidden. Elected officials from those on the local town council to U.S. senators and representatives may appear to have the power to rule, but real power seldom is exercised in the open. Elected officials may actually be figureheads, people without real clout. Real power may be in the hands of individuals remaining in the background who manipulate officials. For example, business and other special interest groups that contribute significantly to congressional campaigns may influence congresspersons to favor their interests even at the expense of the needs of ordinary Americans. Because of this complexity, in the sociological literature answers to the question "Who rules America?" fall into two broad categories: those reflecting elitist models of power and those reflecting pluralistic models of power.

Elitist Models of Power. Understanding who rules America is dependent on determining who has power within this country. *Power* is the ability to make decisions that shape the direction or quality of social life. Numerous social researchers subscribe to **elitist models of power,** the view that power is really in the hands of a relatively few people (Domhoff, 1990, 1983; Dye, 1990). For example, Robert Michels (1991) argues that voters in democracies often become apathetic and are content to leave governance in the hands of an **oligarchy,** a relatively small circle of elites.

In *The Power Elite,* sociologist C. Wright Mills (1956) contended that America is actually run by a small **power elite,** a group composed of top-ranking business, government, and military officials. Not only do these individuals hold power in their own realm, they also frequently interact with and support each other's actions in other realms. Additionally, a kind of "revolving door" exists, enabling elites in one field to rotate among jobs in other fields. A well-known example of this is Alexander Haig, who retired as a general from the military, held high positions in business, served as secretary of state under President Richard Nixon, and then ran for president of the United States on the Republican ticket. If Mills is correct, this power elite decides the course of the American economy, the laws of the American government, and the direction of American foreign policy. In addition, this power elite determines whether the economy will have a recession or a boom, whose grievances are addressed and whose are not, and if the country will experience peace or war.

Pluralistic Models of Power. A number of sociologists believe that elitist models fail to account for the complexity of power in American society (Dahl, 1982; Polsby, 1959). They argue that American society is too large and too diverse for any individual or oligarchy to assert power over all segments of our population. Rather, they see pluralistic models of power as better characterizing America. **Pluralistic models of power** operate on the assumptions that power may exist at a number of different levels in the social structure and that there are competing centers of power within the social system. Teachers may have a degree of power over the classroom, but little authority elsewhere, even in the schools where they work. A mayor may have power in a city, a governor may have power in a state, or a business owner may have power in that field of business, but they may have no power outside of their limited sphere of influence. Moreover, a person at a higher level within the social structure may have little influence on lower levels. The president of the United States, for example, may set general domestic policy for our nation but may have little influence in determining the actions of a local mayor, a neighborhood businesswoman, or a city council.

Frequently, sources of power compete in the larger society or in a particular sphere of influence. For example, the owner of a business may wish to set the salary of her employees, determine their working conditions (such as safety rules, hours worked, or vacation time), and hire or fire workers. In any of these areas, she may find that her ability to act is limited by the competing power of several groups. These groups may include labor unions; local, state, and federal agencies; and various nongovernmental organizations (NGOs), which may be involved in regulating salary and working conditions and setting procedures for hiring or firing employees.

The framers of the Constitution were fearful of concentrating too much power in the hands of a few. As a result, they divided power among the legislative (the Congress), executive (the president), and judicial (the Supreme Court) branches of government. Democrats, Republicans, and a host of smaller parties that also vie for national political power have emerged over the years. The division of power and political party systems that developed at the national level are reflected at most echelons of government, from the national level to the local level.

Power is further fragmented in industrial urban societies like the United States because of pluralism. Our society is comprised of many different class, religious, ethnic, and interest groups. We may often have difficulty identifying with one another and finding common ground for problem solving. Pluralism always has the potential to become divisive, especially

Our society is made up of many different class, religious, ethnic, and interest groups, and we may often have difficulty identifying with one another and finding common ground for problem solving. This pluralism has the potential of becoming divisive.

when sociologists, news media, and politicians so emphasize our differences that we begin to believe we share nothing.

This perception may be enhanced because of the proclivity of political, business, and religious leaders and groups to exploit these differences to further their agendas. In the 1980s and 1990s, for example, in order to secure votes from pro-life advocates, some Republican politicians represented their party as more pro-life than it really was while representing the Democratic party as more pro-choice than it really was. (Other Republican politicians, however, sought pro-choice voters by pointing out that their party contained those who favored a woman's right to choose whether to have an abortion.) Many Republican women, including Barbara Bush, wife of former President George Bush are, in fact, pro-choice, a view that is largely a function of their relatively high social class status. Meanwhile, during the same period some Democratic politicians, seeking the votes of pro-choice advocates, represented their party as more solidly pro-choice than it really was while representing the Republican party as more pro-life than it really was. In fact, many working-class Democratic women sided with pro-life advocates. (Other Democratic politicians, however, seeking to woo pro-life voters, did point out that the party, as represented by its members, was not solidly pro-choice.)

Opposition and segmentation within society are also advanced when the relationship among groups is cast as a zero-sum game. Additionally, in the United States, the forces of compromise and bitter factionalism have coexisted from the start, with one or the other in the ascent. However, in recent decades American politics has become increasingly divisive. Conservative Republicans especially have been on the attack, treating liberal opponents with particular contempt. It may basically be political rhetoric, but treating "liberal" as the dirty "L-word" expressed the sort of all-or-nothing attitude characteristic of zero-sum thinking that undermines real discussion and fosters fragmentation.

This loss of common ground means that there are relatively few issues that may be used to appeal to Americans as a whole. Their absence has meant that narrowly defined issues that appeal to one segment of society or another have assumed heightened significance. For example, a politician may or may not receive votes mainly because of his or her stance on abortion, women's rights, affirmative action, or gun control. In other words politicians may not be judged on their record as a whole or their vision for the country, but by their stand on a single issue. What that single issue is will vary with individual constituents, depending on what each views as important, an agenda that is itself most often set by interest groups concerned with little else than their particular issue. One reason narrow, divisive issues have begun to figure so prominently in American politics is that voters tend not to participate unless their direct interests are at stake.

One implication of this trend is that power tends to center on specific issues. People who mobilize followers may influence political processes on that key issue but have no generalized influence on the direction of the country as a whole. Another seemingly paradoxical implication is that a relatively small group of organized voters can have an effect out of all proportion to their numbers. For example, a small group of well-organized protesters may prevent the construction of a nuclear power plant in a given area, even though the construction is favored by powerful business and government interests. This example shows how organization is one of the keys to power in modern societies. An example of this is discussed in the box "FYI: America's Cuban Policy—A Decaying Relic of the Cold War." The box shows how a comparatively small group of Cuban exiles who hate Fidel Castro influence America's Cuban policy.

Perhaps there is no single answer to the question "Who rules America?" Little doubt exists that those with wealth, power, and access to resources such as the media exert disproportionate influence in this society. There is a power elite, but even its power is circumscribed because it is unlikely that all of the interests of the various elites correspond. In fact, at times the interests of government, business, and military elites conflict. Moreover, because our society is both large and complex, it is doubtful that any elite group can control all areas of it. Still, as we have seen, issue-oriented groups not necessarily composed of elites can be influential. Perhaps the one safe conclusion that can be drawn is that the masses of unorganized voters have potential power but may not be motivated to or be capable of using it effectively.

Voter Apathy or Anger?

We observed that many if not most Americans are not active in politics. Only 61 percent of the eligible voters voted in the 1992 presidential election. Voting rates are even lower in years in which there is no presidential election. They are still lower in state or local elections when there are no national elections. Participation in elections at all levels has decreased for the last several decades. For example, in 1982 less than half of eligible voters (49 percent) cast ballots in off-year congressional elections. In 1992 only 45 percent of the electorate elected congresspersons (U.S. Bureau of the Census, 1995a, Tables 433 and 459).

Some say that satisfaction with the system explains voter apathy. Most voters, according to this view, are fairly content with their lot in life; otherwise, they would be voting for change. But considerable evidence indicates that the reason people do not vote is because of dissatisfaction with the American political system. At best, they believe their vote will not count; at worst, they are very angry toward politics and politicians (Kaplan, 1995; Kline, 1995).

Gridlock, Narrow Issues, and Voter Frustration

Most Americans support the division of power established by the Constitution, but many are frustrated with the gridlock resulting from the political games that Democrats and Republicans play. These games have become more and more obvious over the last decade. For example, political games between the Democratic president and the Republican-controlled Congress over approval of the annual federal budget led to a partial shutdown of the federal government in the spring of 1995, an event that angered many ordinary Americans.

Narrow issue-oriented politics is a key factor in voter frustration for several reasons. First, issues that assume national prominence usually do not greatly concern most voters, whereas problems that do affect the majority of the electorate are often neglected by politicians. For instance, making abortion illegal is an issue that has played a highly visible role in American politics since the 1980s. Although most Americans have opinions on abortion (and to many, especially women, the issue is important), the vast majority are not passionate enough about abortion to make it a pivotal consideration of politicians. The abolition of abortion is kept alive as a political problem by a small minority of conservative citizens, many of whom are supported and encouraged by the religious right (see Chapter 3). While the abortion issue has been highlighted, Congress has, however,

FYI

America's Cuban Policy—A Decaying Relic of the Cold War

In 1960 Cuban revolutionary Fidel Castro overthrew a corrupt dictatorial regime in his country. After the revolution many wealthy, land-owning, and professional Cubans fled to the United States, where they concentrated in the Miami, Florida, area. Initially, Castro was not a committed Communist, but his nation's isolation (due largely to U.S. policies) eventually forced him into the Soviet camp. Before the revolution the United States had been Cuba's major trading partner. Afterwards, the United States, opposing what it saw as Cuba's descent into communism, imposed economic sanctions in the form of quotas on sugar cane imports. These sanctions later evolved into a full-scale economic embargo of Cuba. U.S. companies and citizens were forbidden to trade with Cuba. The United States also pressured other countries to participate in the embargo. As domestic economic conditions worsened because of the embargo, Cuba received much-needed aid from the Soviet Union, and Castro became a committed socialist revolutionary.

The goals of U.S. political and economic policy toward Cuba were to overthrow Castro and prevent him from spreading socialist revolutions to Central and South America as well as to other parts of the world. The policy was successful in preventing the spread of Castroism but has proved futile in replacing Castro himself. Castro has now outlasted seven U.S. presidents who have pursued the same policy.

Few objective observers question that Castro's regime has been a violator of human rights. Basic political and civil rights are consistently denied in Cuba. But the Cuban government has been diligent in providing social and economic rights for its people. For example, education and quality health care were supplied free of charge to all Cubans. Now, with the collapse of the Soviet Union, Cuba can no longer afford to give its citizens such an array of benefits. The fall of Soviet communism left Cuba without the massive amounts of foreign aid that had propped up the country's inefficient and underdeveloped economy.

The continuing U.S. embargo has caused severe hardship for the Cuban people. Adequate health care delivery, adequate supplies of food, and an adequate education system have each become compromised in Cuba since the U.S. embargo—one could say that the viability of the society is at risk. The infrastructure is decaying. Unemployment is high. The people are in desperate need of external trade. But rather than relaxing trading restrictions and moving toward more productive relations, the United States is turning up pressure on Cuba by attempting to tighten the trade embargo. The recently passed Helms-Burton Act (1996) allows Americans to sue in U.S. courts companies that engage in trade with Cuba. This act has placed the United States at odds with most of the rest of the world, including close allies like Canada and the European Union. These allies have even threatened to bring a case before the World Trade Organization against the United States for unfair trade practices.

The suffering that the U.S. trade embargo causes the Cuban people is still defended by politicians in terms of trying to punish Castro for human rights violations and hasten his political demise. Ironically, some of the same political forces in this country that advocate such a strict policy to punish Castro are willing to trade with China and other nations that violate human rights. If we trade with other human rights violators, and Castro is not being brought down by the embargo while the Cuban people continue to suffer because of it, whose interests are served by this relic of the Cold War?

been unable to productively address issues such as the protection of Social Security and Medicare benefits and health care reform—issues extremely important to many Americans.

Special Interest Groups and Voter Frustration

Most Americans also are aware of the clout of special interest groups. **Special interest groups** are collectivities organized to promote a political agenda that advances their concerns. Well-known special interest groups include the American Association of Retired Persons (AARP), the National Rifle Association (NRA), and the Sierra Club, but there are thousands more. These groups have come to have an inordinate amount of power in our society. For example, the NRA has successfully prevented the passage of national gun control legislation for three decades, although the vast majority of Americans consistently favor some type of regulation of the possession of firearms. Here, as in so many other instances, a small, well-organized group has successfully promoted a political agenda in opposition to the wishes of the majority of Americans. This agenda may have a serious negative impact on the health and safety of Americans, as guns remain one of the leading causes of death in our country.

The NRA has successfully prevented the passage of national gun control legislation for three decades, although the vast majority of Americans consistently favor some type of regulation.

Special interest groups are so successful because they lobby in Washington, D.C., state capitols, and/or local seats of government. **Lobbying** is a process of influencing legislation that is usually conducted by professional lobbyists and involves contact with lawmakers and their staff, the cultivation of grassroots support, and the allocation of contributions to campaign funds. Special interest groups frequently use **political action committees** (PACs), which funnel large amounts of money to election campaigns. Table 7–1 illustrates that key people in both parties receive large contributions from PACs. Many Americans are asking, "What do PACs expect in return for their money?"

PACs usually cover all bases by contributing to politicians representing divergent positions, but they tend to contribute the most money to candidates that support their agendas. Although PACs cannot directly require that a politician receiving money promote legislation that favors their interests, there is little doubt that the contributions have influence. For example, during the 1996 presidential race, Republican candidate Bob Dole caused a stir when he suggested that tobacco was not addictive. This assertion conflicted with scientific opinion as well as with the experience of millions of Americans who had tried to stop smoking. One possible influence on his remarks was the $350,000 Dole had received in donations from the tobacco lobby to finance his campaign (Page, 1996). In the same election, President Bill Clinton received numerous contributions from foreign interest groups, causing many Americans to worry about foreign influence on his administration. Although both Republicans and Democrats have pledged to initiate and support campaign financing reform, little serious effort in that direction has been made.

Special interest groups also influence the government by supplying expert witnesses to testify before

TABLE 7-1 Largest PAC Contributions to Congresspersons—1994

SENATE		HOUSE	
Kay Bailey Hutchinson, R-TX	$1.98 mil.	Richard Gephardt, D-MO	$895,616
Jim Sasser, D-TN	$1.08 mil.	Dan Rostenkowski, D-IL	$699,906
Kent Conrad, D-ND	$1.07 mil.	Vic Fazio, D-CA	$686,885
Dianne Feinstein, D-CA	$1.05 mil.	John Dingell, D-MI	$633,910
Frank Lautenberg, D-NJ	$926,624	Alan Wheat, D-MO	$602,413
Orrin Hatch, R-Utah	$914,877	Tom Foley, D-WA	$591,497
Pat Moynihan, D-NY	$895,128	Jon Kyl, R-AZ	$568,098
Richard Bryan, D-NV	$894,118	Bob Carr, D-MI	$536,192
Joseph Lieberman, D-CT	$874,733	Peter Bacra, D-WI	$535,937
Conrad Burns, R-MT	$853,551	Martin Frost, D-TX	$526,641

Source: "Largest PAC Contributions to Congresspersons—1994" by Susan Hadden and David Bowermaster in *U.S. News and World Report.* October 10, 1994.

committees considering regulations or laws. Additionally, many of these groups are able to initiate call-in and write-in campaigns supporting or opposing legislation that affects their interests. Whereas politicians may recognize these as pressure tactics, they cannot escape the perception that special interest groups also have the ability to deliver voters during elections. On the one hand, special interest groups and their lobbying operations may be seen as democracy in action in that they represent citizens organizing to promote their viewpoints. On the other hand, special interest activities also may be seen as undermining democracy, for they generally represent minority concerns that take precedence over those concerns of the majority. These factors have led to the popular quip, "American government is government of the special interests, by the special interests, and for the special interests."

Globalization and Voter Frustration

Globalization also contributes to a sense of alienation from the American political process, for it gives substance to the belief that government does not respond to the needs of American citizens. For example, issues associated with the economy are vital to many Americans, who typically feel insecure about employment and the economy. Yet companies have used the excuse of having to downsize for effective global competition in order to lay off both white- and blue-collar employees. In addition, some manufacturing operations have moved off shore, that is, moved to countries where wages are low and regulations lax. Furthermore, several hundred thousand legal immigrants and countless illegal immigrants enter the United States annually. Rightly or wrongly, they are often viewed as competitors for scarce jobs. Their presence sometimes makes some voters believe that the government is not treating the needs of its own citizens as a priority.

Taken together, the issues we have been discussing raise a great deal of ire among voters. Globalization may also leave voters feeling that they are being manipulated by forces beyond their control and comprehension. Again, the fact that our government cannot direct these forces makes it seem out of touch and uncaring. All of these factors conspire to leave many people uncertain, anxious, and suspicious of government. Such conditions provide fertile ground for the growth of the hate groups and extremists discussed in Chapter 3.

Assessing the Situation

In this chapter we have reviewed a number of issues emerging from changes in the global political systems. It is beyond the scope of this book to deal with solutions to these issues in detail. Rather, we look at some general options that have the potential to set the framework in which to address specific challenges.

The United States, Developing Nations, and the Global Order

It will be some time before a tightly organized global political system emerges, if indeed one ever comes into being. Nevertheless, even now there is little doubt that the nations of the world are so interrelated that their fates are linked. Even though nation-states may eventually disappear as the primary unit of global political organization, they will remain a real presence for the foreseeable future. The solution to global problems will entail international effort and cooperation.

The United States came out of the Cold War as the premier political, military, and economic nation on the globe. Because of this unique historical position, it has grave leadership responsibilities. The United States, experts assert, must now strike a careful balance between isolationism and excessive involvement in world affairs. Additionally, as the United States exercises its leadership, it must be careful to avoid "go-it-alone" situations. We have noted the significance of coalitions and international cooperation in resolving world problems. Not only does the United States need to work with other nations, but it also may need to work with worldwide governmental agencies, regional associations, and/or INGOs. While at times the United States has exercised its leadership in a wise fashion, at other times it has made what many consider to be grave errors. For example, in 1996 two bills were passed in this country that legislated punishment for nations trading with Cuba, Libya, and Iran. Unfortunately, the passage of these laws put America at odds with allies such as Canada and the European Union, because the allies had trading ties to the prohibited nations. America's allies have threatened to retaliate if the provisions of the bills are carried out. These and other unilateral actions have left many friendly nations alienated from what they view as American arrogance that borders on chauvinism.

Many developing nations stand at the opposite end of the global power continuum from the United States. Their problem is not how to exercise power, but how to obtain enough power to assert themselves on the global scene. During the Cold War, Third World nations gained some prominence by manipulating relations between the Soviet Union and the United States. Cold War politics also allowed developing nations to form alliances such as OPEC and the Nonaligned Movement (a group of Third World nations that used their numerical strength in the UN), which gave them some success in obtaining a degree of economic and political power.

The end of the Cold War has left the Third World without an effective bargaining chip. As a result, developing nations have little hope that their issues will receive adequate attention. But the United States and other developed countries may find it necessary to address Third World problems out of self-interest, if for no other reason. If their concerns are ignored, developing nations may resort to extreme measures such as the creation of or use of weapons of mass destruction or the support of terrorist activities. For example, in 1998 India tested nuclear weapons and its arch rival Pakistan soon followed with its own tests, despite international pleas against such testing. Political or economic instability in these nations will almost always spread, eventually involving developed nations. Environmental degradation as a result of growing populations in developing nations frequently threatens the biosphere. For instance, a growing population of subsistence farmers in Brazil uses slash-and-burn farming techniques in the ecologically sensitive Amazon areas in their efforts to scratch out a living. In the process, they destroy ever increasing sections of the world's irreplaceable rain forests (see Chapter 5).

Democracy and Human Rights

We have seen that abuses of political and civil rights abound in today's world. Around 80 percent of our planet's population live in societies that routinely suffer a significant degree of repression. Even those societies that may be labeled "free" frequently have noteworthy abuses. Moreover, the swing toward right-wing politics in the liberal, industrial democracies is already combining with a backlash against immigrants to these countries, raising concerns about increasing abuse even in free countries.

Nevertheless, there is some reason for optimism. Human rights (especially political and civil rights) are in the forefront of global concern to a degree never before witnessed in history. The UN, regional alliances, and individual nation-states have exhibited a willingness to become involved in the internal affairs of other nation-states whenever rights violations are obvious. At least partially successful interventions have been carried out recently in removing a repressive military regime in Haiti and conducting free elections in Cambodia. The global community's greatest success at intervention has been its role in the end of apartheid in South Africa and the establishment of a multiracial government under Nelson Mandela. The establishment of a peace process between Israel and the Palestinians that involves restoration of some territory occupied by Israel to Palestinian control holds promise, though there is likely to be more bloodshed before a lasting peace can be established (see Chapter 2 for a more detailed exploration of global human rights).

Perhaps even more important, a wave of democracy is engulfing the globe. The last 20 years has seen a doubling of the number of democratic states ("Democracies Double," 1994). The decade from 1981 to 1991 has witnessed the greatest wave of democratic growth in history (McColm, 1992). The impetus for most of this change has been the demand for democracy from citizens of nation-states; only after such demands has pressure been brought to bear by outside forces. Modern technology has also spread democratic ideas to an extent never before known. The ready availability of radios, televisions, satellite disks, computers, fax machines, and cellular phones has meant that the traditional elite have controlled information with increasing difficulty, including the information that promotes democratic revolutions. With the transition to democracy, we may reasonably expect to see an increasing respect for political and civil rights, because democracies generally have better human rights records than do undemocratic governments.

Still, caution is in order for several reasons. Some of the transitions to democracy are in name only. Powerful individuals, parties, or ethnic groups dominate the political scene in some countries to the extent that true universal democratic participation is impossible. In addition, even where genuine democracies have been established, the new governments may be fragile. New democratic governments often exist in regions like Russia and Central and South America, where there is no democratic tradition upon which to draw. Therefore, these new democracies often lack commitment to such principles as the sharing of power, instituting change through the ballot instead of with violence, tolerating the opposition or unpopular ideas and behaviors, or granting freedom of the press, religion, and speech. As we have seen, powerful religious or ethnic divisions within a new democracy may create unbearable tensions.

Many democratic revolutions are linked with promises of economic reform that may threaten the effectiveness of the new regime (Petras and Morley, 1991). It is comparatively easy to change government leadership; it is much more difficult to overhaul the economy, especially when it requires some kind of leveling of the distribution of wealth. Powerful elites may resist losing their assets. In addition, short-term economic pain for large segments of the population may have to be endured before long-term improvements can be realized. Citizens may lose patience with "democracy" when it does not produce the expected economic gains. This is one of the major hurdles faced by most of the new democracies in Central and South America, as well as in Russia and South Africa.

In addition, corruption and crime threaten many of the new democracies. Corruption and crime create inefficiency; even in democracies the delivery of benefits to citizens is compromised when these forces are unchecked and scarce resources are diverted to criminals. Moreover, corruption and crime encourage the continuation of repressive and unjust forms of power. For instance, drug cartels have a powerful influence in several Latin American nations, where they successfully divert money from the legitimate economy, corrupt the political and judicial systems, and use terrorist tactics against opponents. Many new democracies may have difficulties confronting the consequences of their repressive pasts. For example, most of the Central and South American democracies are now having to deal with the legacy of the "disappearances" discussed in Chapter 2. Powerful elites often use their influence to undermine these governments, but a government's failure to prosecute perpetrators causes it to risk losing the confidence of the populace in the judicial and democratic processes.

We would expect the wave of democratization to produce an improvement in the observance of political and civil rights. But we must remember that democracy is fragile. Most democracies have failed. Human rights and the democratic institutions intended to perpetuate them must be protected.

Theoretical Concerns

In Chapter 1, we argued that the redefinition of self-identity is a significant change that has resulted from the globalization process. Just as globalization fosters rapid changes in political and territorial boundaries, so does it also precipitate changes in cultural and social boundaries. These changes encourage painful identity shifts. For instance, the end of the Cold War has seen a number of nation-states break up altogether or nearly break up into premodern ethnic enclaves. The former Yugoslavia is a nation-state that divided into ethnically defined regions. The French-speaking province of Quebec has threatened to withdraw from Canada because many voters there believe that their French heritage is submerged in largely English-speaking Canada. In such cases, citizens of the nation-state must decide whether their primary identity is with the nation-state or with their ethnic heritage. Another difficulty new democracies face is that political and economic expansion expose previously isolated groups to the rest of the world. This exposure has tended to intensify intergroup conflict while strengthening in-group identity.

Additional insight into why nationalism and ethnic identities produce increasing conflict may be gained by considering the role such identities play in modern people's lives. A national identity requires people to subordinate ethnic, religious, and class identities to their identity as citizens. In the United States, for example, citizens are called upon to regard themselves first and foremost as "Americans" regardless of their ethnic or religious backgrounds.

The shift to national identity is never total. Many people continue to put their religious or ethnic identities first. The histories of many religious and ethnic identities reach back thousands of years, whereas virtually all nation-states were formed within the last two hundred years; many have emerged only since 1945. The borders of nation-states were often arbitrarily drawn, cutting across traditional ethnic or tribal lands. As a result, some ethnic groups were split by national boundaries or clustered together with traditional enemies and rivals. Some interethnic hostilities have been held in check by the state; in some cases, ethnic groups in conflict have been dominated by a foreign power. When the hegemony of the state is broken, as it has been in parts of the former Soviet Union and Eastern Europe, suppressed hostilities may reassert themselves.

Multiethnic nations almost always relegate some ethnic groups to minority status. The dominant ethnic group or groups are more likely than minority groups to benefit from national identities. Therefore, it is in the self-interest of minority groups to promote ethnic and/or religious identity over that of national identity.

Conflict between groups has become even more likely because of the complexity of identity within modern nation-states. Traditional societies have a relatively simple set of statuses that serve as sources of identity. These consist mostly of ethnic, religious, familial, and gender statuses. Industrialization has added job, class, educational, age, and special interests statuses that are competing sources of personal identity. So an individual may be called upon to view himself or herself in terms of occupation, gender, education, religion, race, age, and any number of other possible ways of defining the self. Since personal identity is tied to this complex system of statuses, there is more in modern societies to fragment people and less and less to remind them of their common identities. We saw earlier in this chapter the key role that special interests play in American politics and, indeed, in global politics. Given the significance of social identity to a personal sense of well-being, it is easy to see why passionate, even violent, struggles are occurring worldwide as subnational, national, and supranational units compete to define who they are, to whom they are loyal, and what their place is in the cosmos.

During the Cold War, nations and political groups of all sorts were expected to define themselves in terms set by the USSR and the United States according to their rather abstract sociopolitical models of communism and capitalism. The collapse of this polarized global structure is causing a confusing and too-often violent redefinition of boundaries and identities. The conflict among Muslims, Serbs, and Croats in the former Yugoslavia and the warfare between Hutus and Tutsis in Rwanda are two examples of this dynamic. We will take a closer look at the Yugoslavian situation to further illustrate this point.

Map 7–3 illustrates the complexity of ethnic divisions in the former Yugoslavia. Here we see ethnic and religious divisions originating centuries before the formation of the modern nation-state. Croats and Slovenes are Roman Catholic and tend to align with Western Europe. The Serbs, Montenegrins, and Macedonians are Orthodox Christians and historically have aligned with Russia. The Bosnians are Muslim. During the Cold War years, Yugoslavia's first Communist leader, Marshal Tito (1892–1980), was able to suppress ethnic violence. However, after Tito's death, ethnic tensions increased. In 1990, with the demise of the Soviet Union, Slovenia and Croatia declared independence from Yugoslavia. In short

MAP 7–3 **Ethnic Divisions in Yugoslavia**
This map illustrates one of the main problems of nation-states. They are pluralistic; that is, they often are composed of numerous ethnic groups. Globalization is forcing many of these groups to examine their identities. When these groups decide that their primary identity lies with their ethnic heritage and not with the nation-state, the unity of the nation-state is threatened.

Source: Albert M. Craig, William A. Graham, Donald Kagan, Steven Ozment, and Frank M. Turner. 1997. *The Heritage of World Civilizations,* 4th ed. Upper Saddle River, NJ: Prentice Hall, p. 1029.

order, the European Union extended recognition to the new nations. Serbia was determined to keep the two newly independent states in a greater Yugoslavia dominated by Serbs. Civil war soon ensued. The war raged on with instances of ethnic cleansing and genocide occurring from all sides of the conflict. This bloody conflict was brought to an end when NATO intervened militarily in 1995. Later that year, the United States successfully negotiated a peace treaty. That peace is, however, maintained by a heavy commitment of NATO troops including some twenty thousand from the United States. Actual peace in the absence of international peacekeepers seems far away indeed.

Other aspects of globalization are dissolving the boundaries between domestic and foreign policy. Nations and their leaders once maintained fairly clear distinctions between domestic and international areas of concern. Today this distinction is being eroded by the increasing interconnectedness characteristic of globalization. Some analysts speak now of *intermestic issues* (Jowitt, 1993), in which international and domestic matters have become inseparable.

Today the issue of identity is not limited to national versus subnational identifications. New and old identities transcend the geographical and political limits of nation-states. Roman Catholicism is, for instance, an older basis of supranational identity. New identities may increase as a global civil society emerges and with it a sense of global citizenship rooted in issues such as democracy and human rights, feminism, ecology, and the AIDS crisis. For example, people worldwide are now called upon to ignore their immediate economic and political interests and make ecological decisions with the future of the planet in mind. This process requires people to move beyond their family, ethnic, and national identities and view themselves as citizens of the world. Similarly, feminists challenge women around the world to adopt wider norms in determining their proper role in families and society. Women are challenged in international meetings sponsored by the UN and other agencies to move beyond patriarchal definitions of them as second-class citizens to exercise their full rights as human beings as defined in the UN Declaration of Universal Human Rights (see Chapter 9).

SUMMARY

1. The **nation-state** is a modern form of political system in which one governmental body acts on behalf of a group of people who share a common identity and territory. **Nation** refers to a group of people that inhabits a territory, while **state** refers to the governmental apparatus that makes and enforces decisions for this group.
2. **Colonies** are regions ruled by an external sovereign power whose politics and economic activities are controlled to enhance its own economic and political strength rather than benefit the indigenous people.
3. In response to the massive death and destruction of World War I, the United States retreated into **isolationism,** a policy whereby a country cuts itself off from foreign involvement. But the United States eventually entered World War II, forming an alliance with the Soviet Union, France, and Britain that was known as the Allied Powers.
4. The United Nations was created to produce political stability by providing a forum for solving issues before they lead to war.
5. A huge international arms race that diverted funds away from domestic investments was among the results of the Cold War, which ended in 1991 with the collapse of the Soviet Union.
6. Some politicians, political thinkers, and strategists believe that the United States should exercise extensive widespread global leadership, or act to police the world; others believe that the United States should become involved in political and military conflicts only when one of our worldwide interests is directly threatened; still others believe in extreme isolationism.
7. Global culture proponents argue that the expansion of Western ideology overwhelms traditional cultures and could result in a unified global culture. Others argue that there are eight civilizations—Western, led by the United States; Sinic, led by China; Hindu, centered in India; Orthodox, led by Russia; Japanese; Islamic; African; and Latin American—each so distinct that convergence into a global culture is impossible.
8. Three threats to global political security are continued warfare and the proliferation of weapons of mass destruction; resurgence of national, ethnic, and religious violence; and the pressure resulting from an increasing population and diminishing resources.
9. **Elitist models of power** hold that power is in the hands of a relatively few people, such as an oligarchy, a small ruling faction, or a **power elite** (a group of top-ranking business, government, and military officials). **Pluralist models of power** assert that power may exist at a number of different levels in the social structure and that there are competing sources of power in the social systems.

Thinking Critically

1. We noted that the foreign policy of the United States is in a state of flux because of the dramatic changes in the world since the end of the Cold War. What should be the five most important guiding principles of U.S. foreign policy? Show how one or more of these direct American actions in a given international conflict.
2. Ethnic conflict that often results in genocide or other war crimes has become common. Under what conditions are international interventions in ethnic conflicts likely to be successful? What rights should subnational or supranational groups have? How can these rights be used to solve ethnic conflict without resorting to violence?
3. Campaign financing has become a major problem in the political life of the United States. Is significant reform of financing likely to occur? Why or why not?

Suggested Readings

Amnesty International. 1986. *Voices of Freedom: An Amnesty International Anthology.* London: Amnesty International.

Bing, Leon. 1991. *Do or Die.* New York: HarperCollins.

Bonner, Elena. 1986. *Alone Together.* New York: Knopf.

Deese, David A., ed. 1994. *The New Politics of American Foreign Policy.* New York: St. Martin's.

Domhoff, G. William. 1990. *The Power Elite and the State: How Policy Is Made in America.* New York: Aldine deGruyter.

Fukuyama, Francis. 1992. *The End of History and the Last Man.* New York: Free Press.

Huntington, Samuel P. 1996. *The Clash of Civilizations and the Remaking of World Order.* New York: Simon & Schuster.

Klare, Michael T. and Daniel C. Thomas, eds. 1993. *World Security: Challenges for a New Century,* 2nd ed. New York: St. Martin's.

Mandelbaum, Michael. 1981. *The Nuclear Revolution: The Politics of Nuclear Strategy.* New York: Basic.

Web Sites

U.S. Congress
URL: http://congress.org
This site provides complete and up-to-date information on the U.S. Congress, including information on members, committee assignments, and how you can communicate with members of Congress.

Geneva International Forum
URL: http://geneva.intl.ch/geneva-intl/gi/egimain/edir.htm
This site provides links to various international organizations, including intergovernmental associations, INGOs, and private companies.

The Jefferson Project
URL: http://www.voxpop.org:80/jefferson
This site is a searchable index containing links to publications, issues, online forums, political parties, and other resources on both U.S. and international political topics. The feature "Issues and Activists" provides links to NGOs and INGOs operative in national and global issues.

National Endowment for Democracy

URL: http://www.ned.org

This is the homepage of the National Endowment for Democracy, an organization dedicated to the promotion of democracy worldwide. It contains links to excellent information, scholarly journals, and discussion groups.

Russian Web

URL: http://www.sitek.ru/~admcomer/xsu.htm

This site provides access to information about Russia and the Commonwealth of Independent States, as well as links to numerous state, university, institute, business, and NGO sites.

United Nations

URL: http://www.un.org

This site contains a wealth of information about the United Nations and its activities. Numerous links are provided to databases containing information collected about many global issues, including up-to-date information about political crises.

CHAPTER ■ EIGHT

Global Economic Systems

From Exploitation to Interdependency?

"Until he had to pick up a load of free groceries last week in a modern version of a soup line, Larry Bragg figured he had outfoxed the system. The 55-year-old Vietnam veteran last September voluntarily agreed to a layoff from his job at the Thomson Consumer Electronics, Inc. television plant here because he thought it was going to close and he could beat the stampede into the job market. 'There's nothing,' Bragg grumbled. . . . I've been from one end of Bloomington to the other and got only one bite.' . . .

"Thomson, the Indianapolis-based subsidiary of the French-government-owned Thomson SA, announced it was closing the Bloomington [Indiana] plant, once the world's busiest television manufacturer, next year. Thomson will transfer its production of RCA, GE and ProScan TV sets to Juarez, Mexico. . . . For Bragg and the 1,300 employees at Thomson, the primary question is this: In a time of industrial migration and technological change, where do veteran industrial workers left behind turn for jobs? . . .

"Workers in Bloomington receive an average of $19 an hour in wages and benefits, but the comparable pay rate in Mexico is only $2.10. . . . That factor should enable Thomson to save $350 million over the next 10 years. [However, the impact on former employees is another matter. In addition to a general lack of available well-paying jobs, persons laid off] 'don't have the skills or the education to find jobs elsewhere in the labor market.' . . .

"[Many workers believe that they are too old to find work.] Jim Miller . . . is an example. At age 47 and with two kids in college, he will be pounding the pavement next year with a résumé that includes a high school diploma, 9 credit hours of college and 28 years of experience in television assembly and warehouse work for Thomson. 'Without a degree and at my age, companies are going to hire a 25-year-old with a degree and train them for the job.' "

Source: From David Young, "Starting Over, All at Once." *Chicago Tribune*, February 27, 1997:5.1 and 7.

Larry Bragg's story illustrates one of the many effects of globalization. Whether we live in advanced industrial, industrial, or industrializing societies, globalization affects us, undermining traditional social and economic arrangements, replacing human workers with technology, and calling our economic security into question. Even the nature of work itself is changing.

In this chapter we examine the impact of globalization on the world's economic system. We first present a brief history of the emergence of the key institutions in the global trading system and discuss the global inequity perpetuated by the world economic system. We go on to consider the idea of "development," a buzzword for global efforts to alleviate all sorts of conditions, including such diverse problems as poverty, the exploitation of women and children, and environmental concerns. Finally, we survey economic issues in the United States.

Development of the World Trading Order

One goal of the United Nations was to improve political stability by offering a forum for people to discuss political issues and seek justice for their causes. It was hoped that this political forum would help prevent wars. However, underlying the political chaos between the world wars was economic chaos. The Great Depression in the United States during the 1930s was our national expression of worldwide economic decline.

The Bretton Woods Conference

Economic discord led to the political unrest that fueled the fascists' rise to power in Germany and Italy that set the stage for World War II. By the time World War II was drawing to a close, the Allies recognized that political security was unalterably tied to economic stability. Before the end of World War II, President Franklin Roosevelt met with British Prime Minister Winston Churchill and the premier of the Soviet Union, Joseph Stalin, in a series of conferences to map out the postwar world order. The three leaders not only planned instruments such as the UN to stabilize the political scene, they also envisioned a number of mechanisms to balance the economic situation. The most important economic tools emerged from the 1944 Bretton Woods Conference (see Chapter 7).

Three important mechanisms for handling economic issues emerged from the conference: the International Bank for Reconstruction and Development (or the World Bank, as it came to be known), the International Monetary Fund (IMF), and the General

Agreement on Tariffs and Trade (GATT). The initial function of the *International Bank for Reconstruction and Development (IBRD)* was to rebuild war-ravaged sections of the world, concentrating especially on Europe and Japan. Once this initial task was accomplished, the IBRD was to turn its attention to developing nonindustrialized countries. The *International Monetary Fund (IMF)* was designed to promote balanced expansion of international trade as well as to encourage stability in the world's financial markets. The *General Agreement on Tariffs and Trade* was a negotiated treaty that was intended to stabilize the world economy by producing fair regulations for international trade. Because charges were frequently made that GATT favored wealthy nations through the establishment of unfair trading rules that kept poorer countries dependent, it was renegotiated several times between 1945 and 1995. In 1995, GATT was replaced by the *World Trade Organization (WTO)*, an international organization designed to regulate global trade and ensure fair trading practices.

Free Trade

Since World War II, free trade has been prescribed as both the antidote to global economic woes and the most effective way to prevent widescale economic upheavals. **Free trade,** or trade based on the unrestricted international exchange of goods without protective customs tariffs, originates in the idea that all nations will increase their prosperity by mutually opening their markets to trade. One of the fundamental concepts of free trade is that goods and services should be produced where they can be made most efficiently at the lowest cost. Unfortunately, as the cases of Larry Bragg and Jim Miller illustrate, the movement of production can cost jobs. Whole industries may decline or disappear. For example, the northeastern section of the United States once had a

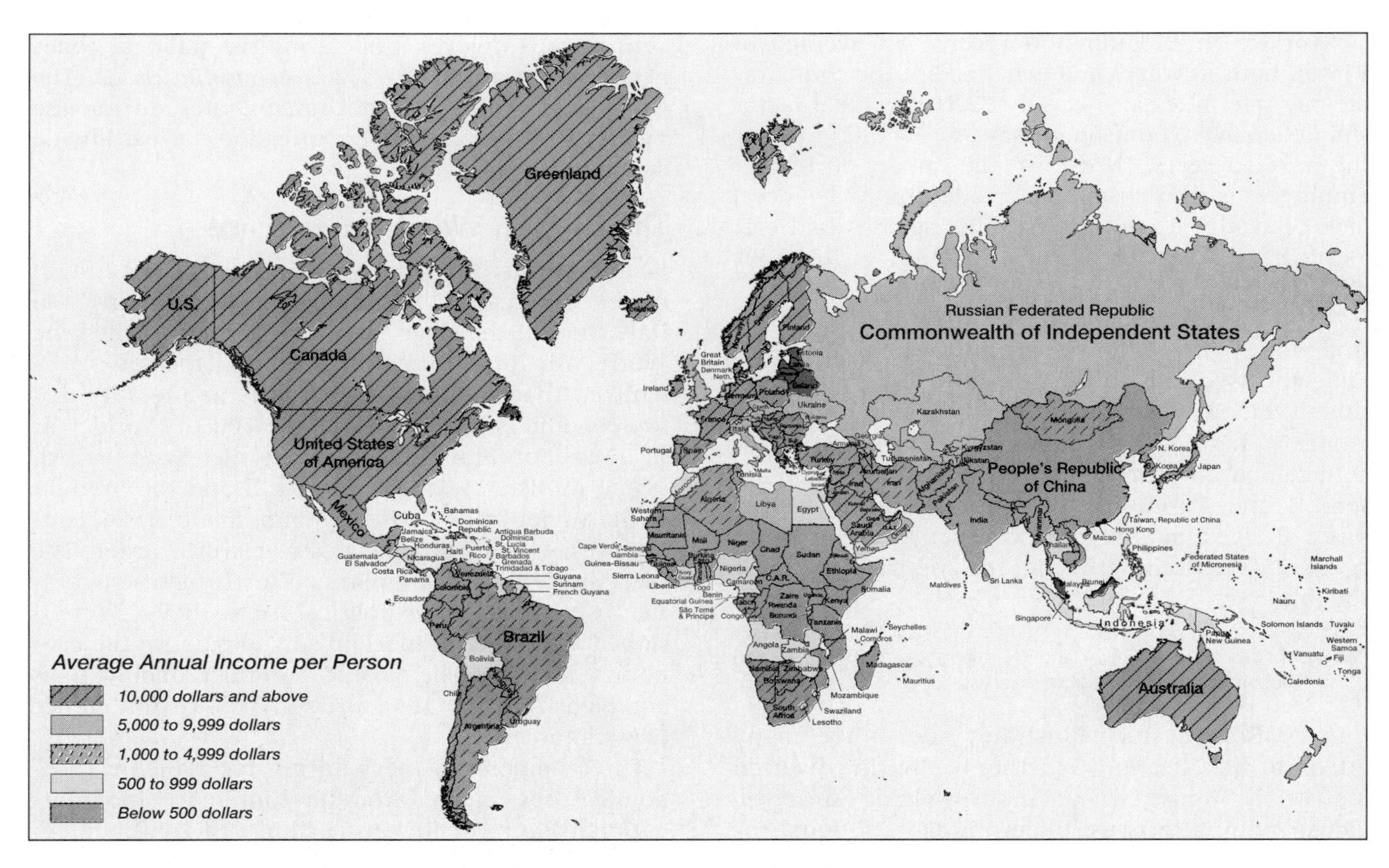

MAP 8–1 Per Capita Income in Global Perspective

Source: © 1994 by Prentice-Hall, Inc. A Paramount Communications Company. Upper Saddle River, New Jersey 07458.

very strong shoe manufacturing base. Now, however, few shoes are made anywhere in the nation. Despite such drawbacks, the United States continues to be one of the strongest advocates of free trade in the world. The tendency toward global free trade has been given a boost in recent years by the creation of regional free trade zones, such as the European Union (EU) and the North American Free Trade Zone (NAFTA). Whether these regional trade blocs will further global free trade or inhibit it in the long run is uncertain.

Global Inequity

The existence of inequity in wealth, income, and quality of life among nations is widely recognized. Global inequity has numerous serious implications. Map 8–1 shows global per capita income. **Per capita income** (income for each person), an indicator of the wealth of a nation, is derived by dividing the total *gross national product* (GNP) by the nation's population. GNP is the total market value of all the goods and services produced in facilities owned by a nation's citizens regardless of where they are produced during a specified period such as a year. GNP does not include production by foreign-owned facilities within the nation. In other words, per capita income shows how much income each man, woman, and child in a nation would receive if each received an equal share.

The people of the industrialized nations make up roughly 15 percent of the population of the world, but they receive almost two-thirds of its income(see Figure 8–1). The Second World contains around 10 percent of the earth's population and shares about 15 percent of the world's income. The Third World has almost 80 percent of the world's population but shares only about 20 percent of the world's income.

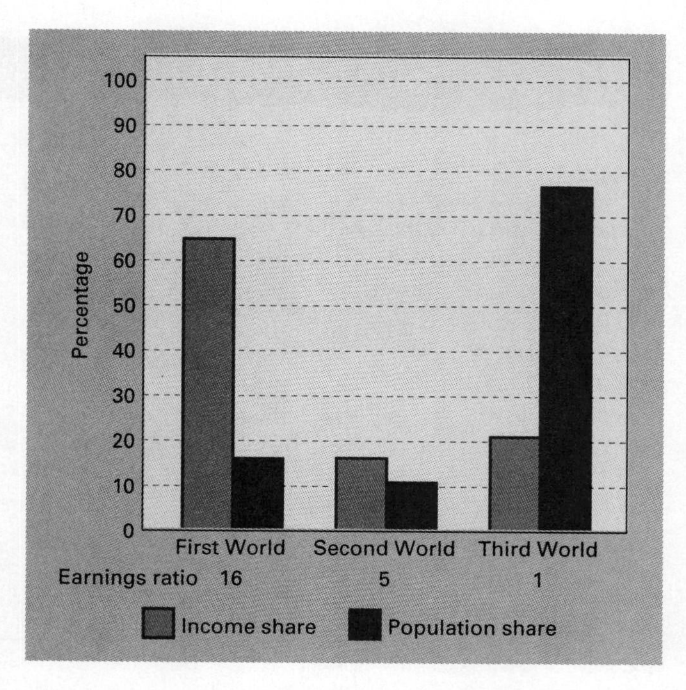

FIGURE 8–1 Division of World Income by Nation Type

Source: © 1994 by Prentice-Hall, Inc. A Paramount Communications Company. Upper Saddle River, New Jersey 07458.

Measuring Quality of Life

Global inequity significantly affects the overall quality of life in developing nations. Selected data from a quality of life index created by the UN to measure factors that affect how people live are presented in Table 8–1. The human development index (HDI) is based on average life expectancy, average years of schooling, and adult literacy. The index clearly demonstrates a positive relationship between per capita income and quality of life in a country. Thus, the citizens of those nations with the highest *gross domestic product* (GDP, this index is similar to the GNP but excludes production by facilities owned by a nation's citizens if the facilities are in another country and includes production by foreign-owned facilities within the nation) and the highest per capita income generally have a higher standard of living.

Although the United States has by far the largest economy (GDP), its quality of life score of .942 ranks fourth in the world. Moreover, when we review the quality of life index in Table 8–1, we find that the inhabitants of some countries with smaller economies and a lower per capita income than the United States, such as Poland and the Czech Republic, actually have a good standard of living.

The complicated relationship among GDP, quality of life, and per capita income is illustrated by some of the former socialist countries. The former Soviet Union and its allies were able to house, feed, provide medical care, and, in the case of adults, give jobs to virtually all their citizens. The economic and social suffering that was a consequence of the system was much more evenly distributed than in most capitalist countries. But the focus of these economies on providing social needs led to their being unable to

TABLE 8–1 Quality of Life in Selected Countries

COUNTRY	GDP	REAL GDP PER CAPITA INCOME	HDI INDEX SCORE
Advanced Industrial (Capitalist)			
Canada	$694 billion*	$21,459[b]	.960**
United States[a]	7.3 trillion	26,397	.942
Industrial (Socialist)			
Poland	227 billion	5,000	.883
Czech Republic	106 billion	9,201	.882
Russia	796 billion	4,828	.792
Developing (Industrial/Nonindustrial)			
China	3.5 trillion	2,604	.626
India	1.4 trillion	1,348	.446
Zaire[b]	16.5 billion	429	.381
Sierra Leone	660 million***	660	.176

[a] The United States ranks fourth in the world.

[b] Now the Congo.

Source: *Central Intelligence Agency (CIA), *CIA Handbook of International Economic Statistics.* (1995 Figures.) Electronic transmission: http://www.odci.gov/cia/publications/heis96/index.htm

**UN Human Development Programme, "Human Development Index." 1997 Figures (Real GDP Per Capita and Index Scores are 1994 Figures). Electronic transmission: http://www.undp.org/undp/hdro/hdi.htm

***World Bank, *World Development Report 1995: Workers in an Integrating World.* 1993 Figures (New York: Oxford University Press, 1995).

compete in the global marketplace. This largely explains why Second World nations have rushed to embrace market capitalism since the collapse of communism. But the switch to a market economy is having a terrible impact on the former Soviet Union and other East European countries. For example, the political ramifications are ominous, as we discussed at length in Chapter 7.

Similar patterns are emerging in the developing nations. The People's Republic of China has a very large GDP. China recently moved up to become the third largest economy in the world, surpassed only by the United States and Japan. Because of China's enormous population, the Chinese people have a per capita income of only $2,604. Nonetheless, China still has a moderately high quality of life index. As Table 8–1 also indicates, sub-Saharan Africa contains many of the poorest countries—those with the lowest standards of living in the world—yet even here a relatively high GDP and/or per capita income do not automatically translate into a higher quality of life (see the box "FYI: GDP as a Measure of Economic Health"). For example, the people of Sierra Leone enjoy a higher per capita income than the people of Zaire, but Sierra Leone's HDI score is less than half that of Zaire.

It is a fact that citizens of nations with more productive economies usually have high standards of living. And it is also accurate to say that increasing productivity and limiting population growth is one way to improve the quality of life in a given country. But there is no simple one-to-one correspondence between economic measures, such as the GDP and per capita income, and the quality of life. A country may choose to spend its funds from increased production on military hardware or on

FYI

GDP as a Measure of Economic Health

We have noted that the GDP is not a good indicator of the quality of life in a society or its economic health. First, the GDP and its surrogates, such as the GNP, are based on the assumption that consumption drives prosperity. By this logic, increased consumption is necessary to improve the quality of life. In addition, according to this logic, people are viewed more as consumers than as producers.

Another limitation of the GDP is that it measures only certain kinds of economic activity. It concentrates on transactions that involve direct monetary exchange, thereby leaving out two very large segments of the economy that contribute significantly to economic well-being: (1) nonmonetary contributions, such as those made by family members who care for other family members (e.g., parents raising children) or by community volunteers (e.g., volunteers at the local hospital) and (2) the condition of the natural habitat, upon which all human systems, including the economy, depend. Because neither of these factors involves the direct exchange of funds, they are not taken into account in calculating the GDP.

A third problem with using the GDP (and other measures of the economy) is that they fail to distinguish between beneficial and harmful and sustainable and unsustainable activities, and between costs and gains. The GDP measures only the *quantity* of economic activity, not its *quality,* nor the overall positive or negative direction of that activity. Because *all* monetary transactions contribute equally to increasing the GDP, down actually becomes up. That is, money spent on activities indicating a decline in the quality of life in a society is counted as an increase in the GDP and, by inference, an improvement in the society's quality of life. Thus money spent on controlling crime, combating disease, or dealing with a natural disaster contributes to the growing GDP as much as an increase in exports does. The increase in exports could indicate an improvement in quality of life, but crime, disease, and a natural disaster negatively affect a society. Applying this faulty formula for assessing economic health (i.e., all money spent equals improvement) can lead to absurd thinking about how to improve the nation's economy. For example, it might lead us to deduce that widespread riots in our cities, necessitating an extensive military and police intervention, would be one of the best ways to improve the economic health of the United States! For not only would such rioting increase money spent for these services, it would also require more spending on cleanup and rebuilding. To really help the economy, Cobb, Halstead, and Rowe (1995) argue, these humanmade disasters should be combined with heavy and destructive snowstorms, major forest fires, and a hurricane that destroyed large sections of Florida. The "national health" would be further enhanced by rising rates of child abuse because such an increase would necessitate extensive payments for prosecution against the abusers. Finally, a war defending our borders against say, the Canadians, would do wonders for our economy's well-being and thus show what a healthy society we have.

Source: Adapted from Clifford Cobb, Ted Halstead, and Jonathan Rowe. "If the GDP Is Up, Why Is America Down?" *The Atlantic Monthly* (October 1995):59–78.

projects that aggrandize its leaders (such as public monuments dedicated to them), but such spending may have a limited or even a negative impact on the standards of living of most of its citizens. Another nation may invest in programs to provide improved education, adequate health care for all, or improved housing, all of which directly benefit the lives of its citizens. The distribution of wealth within the society is also important in determining a country's standard of living. Growth in the GDP is often accompanied by an increasing division between the rich and poor.

Historically, there was not a great disparity in well-being in many places in the world. But economic stratification within and among nations is now growing. For instance, in 1950, the richest one-fifth of the Mexican people had an income ten times higher than the poorest one-fifth. But by the 1990s, the richest Mexicans had an income twenty times higher than the poorest one-fifth (Kerbo, 1991).

Third World Poverty

One of the net results of global income disparity is extensive poverty in much of the Third World. The extent of Third World poverty is overwhelming. Although poverty is expected to decline throughout the developing world, the year 2000 will see at least 750 million poor people in the developing nations alone (World Bank, 1990). However, these figures do not give an accurate picture of the depth of poverty in the nonindustrial world. In the United States and the rest of the industrialized world, most of the poor live in **relative poverty,** that is, they are poor when compared to the rest of the domestic population. In contrast, many of the poor in the nonindustrialized world live in **absolute poverty,** that is, they are so poor that they live in life-threatening situations. For example, in Bangladesh 51 percent of the population do not have safe water; 55 percent have no access to health care; and the average life expectancy is only 51 years (Institute on Hunger and Development, 1992). Table 8–2 demonstrates that the populations of many developing nations are descending into more extensive poverty.

TABLE 8–2 Developing Countries: People in Absolute Poverty

COUNTRY	ABSOLUTE POVERTY 1992 (MILLIONS)	ABSOLUTE POVERTY 2000 (MILLIONS)
Africa		
Algeria	5.8	6.9
Egypt	20.1	23.5
Kenya	11.1	13.2
Nigeria	40.7	49.1
Sudan	17.0	19.9
Asia and Europe		
Afghanistan	8.6	13.6
Bangladesh	58.4	70.0
China	108.9	109.2
India	340.3	392.7
Americas		
Brazil	61.8	67.6
Guatemala	6.7	8.3
Mexico	13.2	14.4
Peru	12.5	14.4

Source: Richard A. Smiley. 1995. "Developing Countries: People in Absolute Poverty." Electronic transmission: http://www.partners-bsbdc.org/sumpover.htm

Transnational Corporations

Transnational corporations (also called multinational corporations) play a mixed role in the global economic system. **Transnational corporations** are businesses that are headquartered in one country but operate in one or more other countries. Most of the world's big corporations have subsidiaries and plants in many different countries. For example, Ford and Mazda and GM and Toyota have formed joint ventures to manufacture and sell cars all over the world. The same globalization is found in oil production, banking, and the production of computers and computer software, among numerous other fields. These transnational companies have become so powerful that they not only operate outside of national boundaries, they also operate outside the control of nation-states. One way to grasp the power of transnational companies is to look at the revenue they generate. These giant corporations have steadily increased their share of the world's wealth. In 1995, the world's largest companies actually accounted for 28 percent of the total $252 trillion gross world economy. According to one expert, "More than half of the 100 biggest economies in the world are corporations, not nations" (Longworth, 1996:1.1). Table 8–3 compares the revenues and GDPs of several selected Third and First World nations with those of some of the world's largest companies.

Fully one-half of all global trade passes through a handful of transnational corporations, giving these businesses tremendous power to determine what happens in developed and developing nations alike (Braun, 1997). Moreover, transnational corporations often build their manufacturing plants in Third World nations, where critics have often charged them with exploiting natural resources and a cheap labor supply. Defenders of transnational investment practices defend them against such criticism by pointing out that foreign companies frequently pay higher wages and provide better working conditions than do native businesses.

TABLE 8–3 Revenues of Selected Transnational Corporations Compared with GDPs of Selected Nations

CORPORATION	REVENUE (1995)*	COUNTRY	CLASSIFICATION	GDP (1993)**
Mitsubishi	$184.5 bil.	Guinea-Bissau	3rd World	$241 mil.
Mitsui & Co.	181.7 bil.	The Gambia	3rd World	303 mil.
Itochu	169.7 bil.	Mongolia	3rd World	539 mil.
General Motors	168.8 bil.	Lesotho	3rd World	609 mil.
Sumitomo	167.7 bil.	Sierra Leone	3rd World	660 mil.
Marubeni	161.2 bil.	Finland	1st World	74 bil.
Ford	137.1 bil.	Israel	1st World	70 bil.
Toyota	111.1 bil.	New Zealand	1st World	44 bil.
Royal Dutch/Shell	109.9 bil.	Ireland	1st World	43 bil.

Source: *R. C. Longworth, "Corporate Giants Dwarf Many Nations." *Chicago Tribune.* October 11, 1996: 1.1 and 28; **World Bank, *World Development Report 1995: Workers in an Integrating World.* (New York: Oxford University Press, 1995).

Nevertheless, multinational corporations typically are in a position that enables them to dictate prices, set wages, and keep operating costs down with impunity in the host country. They bring comparatively little money into the country as they drain local funds offered to them as loans and other concessions to attract them to the host country. Another result of transnational involvement is that such companies can so dominate a poor country's economy that they produce a small, elite, relatively well-paid workforce and drive most other workers into unemployment (Braun, 1997). Being plugged into the global trading system benefits the upper and middle classes of developing nations, but the portion of income going to the lowest 20 percent actually decreases (Braun, 1997).

Furthermore, the majority of the wealth created by investment from transnational corporations flows to the home countries of the companies. There are indications that for each dollar invested in Latin America, $2.70 leaves the region, via loan repayments to First World banks, interest charged on these loans, and profits of foreign corporations (Dos Santos, 1970).

In addition to cheaper labor costs, multinational corporations enter Third World nations because of lax environmental and safety regulations. Many transnational companies and native businesses in developing countries feel no moral obligation to protect the environment or the safety of workers. For example, along the border between Mexico and the United States, pollution has become endemic. The Rio Grande, running between Texas and Mexico, has become one of the most polluted rivers in the northern hemisphere. Most of this pollution originates on the Mexican side. Mexican, U.S., and transnational companies have built factories on the Mexican side of the border because the area is close to U.S. markets, and they can exploit cheap labor while not having to observe the same safety regulations and environmental restrictions imposed on manufacturing inside the United States. NAFTA was designed to address some of these issues by requiring Mexico to commit to bring its environment and safety laws up to the standards of the United States and Canada. Whether this agreement will have a significant effect has yet to be seen.

The absence of global safety and environmental standards means that if a country becomes "too tough" on transnationals, the transnationals go elsewhere. Moreover, although factories owned directly by transnationals may be exploitative, they usually are not the greatest exploiters. The most significant exploitation frequently results from the practice of "farming out" manufacturing to plants run by locals. Many of these plants operate as sweatshops. A **sweatshop** is a factory in which workers are forced to work long hours in unsafe conditions for very low wages. No one knows exactly how many workers toil in sweatshops globally, but the practice is extremely widespread. Prices to consumers in industrialized nations are thus kept artificially low through the exploitation of labor in less developed nations.

Development and Solving Global Problems

"Development" is a term that summarizes many of the philosophies and trends that have shaped the twentieth century (Rich, 1994). The term is often equated with modernization and the installation of capitalistic, market-oriented economies that operate on the principle of free trade. Although development has created riches for some, it has impoverished many. Moreover, development typically perpetuates an environmentally disastrous consumption-focused culture.

Definitions of Development

Development can mean many things (Jackson, 1995). Development has been interpreted by many, particularly by Americans, as the idea that nations can improve the standard of living of their citizens only by rapidly increasing their GNP/GDP. The general prosperity of the economy will "trickle down" to those most in need. Others see development largely in terms of spreading democracy and/or strengthening political institutions in Third World countries. According to this view, the prosperous industrial nations are democracies with relatively efficient, honest governments that deliver admirable services to their citizens. Conversely, many nondeveloped nations are hampered not only by a lack of resources, but also by both governmental inefficiency and corruption that prevent them from addressing many of their most pressing problems.

A number of difficulties may be seen with each of these optimistic views of development. For example, although there is little doubt that the general prosperity of the developed nations was wrought by industrialization and global competition, simply exporting industrialization to the Third World does not ensure that the quality of life of citizens will be improved. In fact, there have been numerous instances in which the overall quality of life of a country declined as it industrialized and entered the global marketplace. In the early 1980s, Mexican industrial exports increased 130 percent. At the same time, however, the portion of Mexico's GDP going to wages declined from 37.2 percent to 24.9 percent. Meanwhile, inflation rose to 25 percent. Mexico had to import half of its grain. Personal consumption of beans, rice, and corn had to be cut in half (Braun, 1997).

Similarly, increasing a nation's GNP/GDP does not, as indicated, guarantee an improvement in the quality of life for most of its citizens. Just as the gap between rich and poor nations has grown wider (even in countries for which growth is phenomenal), so, too, has the gap between the rich and the poor within those countries (Kidder, 1988). For example, over the last decade Chile's economy has expanded so rapidly that it is now frequently called the "Tiger of the Andes." Yet during this period, the gap between the rich and the poor has reached the point that it is accurate to speak of two Chiles—one rich, privileged, and growing wealthier; the other poor, deprived, and becoming more endangered (Epstein, 1994).

Finally, democratization and efficient governmental structures do not automatically translate to an improved quality of life for citizens. Even in industrialized nations like the United States, people often

Increasing a nation's gross national and gross domestic product does not guarantee an improvement in the quality of life for most of its citizens. Just as the gap between the rich and poor nations has grown wider, so, too, has the gap between the rich and poor within those countries.

complain that the government is unresponsive to their needs. Democratic institutions in such countries frequently come to be dominated by the rich and powerful to the detriment of the poor and powerless. Meanwhile, continued economic stress itself often undermines democracy, leading to popular discontent that encourages chaos.

Another definition of development better reflects the quality of life in countries and thus provides a more viable standard for measuring successful development. In this definition, **development** is an improvement in the fundamental quality of life of the citizens of a country. This definition leads to the measurement of development in terms of improvement in the most basic aspects of life—infant mortality rates, life expectancy, disease rates, literacy rates, sanitation, and so on (Jackson, 1995). Such an approach represents a movement away from the equating of development with GNP or industrialization. Viewed according to this perspective, development may be used to assess the element it is supposed to improve—the quality of life of a country's citizens.

Theories of Development

Several theories of worldwide economics have had an impact on efforts to foster development. Although numerous theories have been employed to explain and correct global inequity, the more important fall into two major categories: modernization theory and dependency theory. In this section we look at the basic tenets of these two theories. We then explore some of the current issues and thinking likely to influence the future direction of development.

Modernization Theory. The idea driving development efforts for most of the period since World War II is modernization theory (Kegley and Wittkopf, 1995). According to **modernization theory,** underdeveloped societies are hindered both by their failure to employ advanced technology in production and by traditional modes of thought that stress family and relationships rather than the individual and economic efficiency. The antidote, modernization theorists argue, is to promote modern ways of thinking and acting.

From this perspective, the solution to the Third World's problems is for the developed world to help modernize it, that is, to assist in turning traditional societies into industrialized, consumption-oriented nations. First World nations, along with the World Bank, UN agencies, and other international venues, provide resources to aid industrialization. The funds invested encourage the creation of capital that can then be used for more modernization, expressed by the generation of new industry or the protection and growth of existing industry.

Although modernization theory emphasizes the economy, other aspects of culture are also targeted in the drive for modernization. Contemporary technologies are substituted for traditional ones, even when the new technologies are not appropriate for promoting the desired ends. For example, during the 1980s, the Indian government, with the assistance of the World Bank, undertook the building of five large dams in northern India. The dams were intended to provide hydroelectric power to Indian cities and thus improve the life of India's people. But whether these dams have in fact benefited the larger population remains questionable. What is clear is that the dams have flooded rich valleys and have driven several hundred thousand people out of their homes. People had lived comfortably in these valleys employing traditional farming methods that both provided them with sufficient food and protected the environment. Today these people and their descendants live in poverty on nonproductive highlands above their flooded former homes.

The impact of traditionalism in less developed societies was also decreased by such practices as introducing modern medicine, fostering the values of individualism, stressing achievement and efficiency, attacking customary family arrangements (such as hiring relatives to fill jobs for which they are not qualified), educating the young about scientific principles, and encouraging urbanization. Seen from this perspective, modernization has proven a mixed blessing. In some cases, ordinary people have had their income and quality of life improved by modernization. But, in many other cases, modernization has led to increased poverty, social disruption, and environmental degradation. For instance, as people all over the globe have moved from rural areas into cities, traditional family patterns have been disrupted, and divorce has increased.

Dependency Theory. Another major theoretical approach has also played a significant role in efforts to develop nonindustrial countries and to shape the interaction among the First, Second, and Third Worlds. During the 1950s, there was hope throughout the world that once underdeveloped nations received independence from their European colonizers, the economic conditions of their citizens would considerably improve.

However, by the 1960s, it was becoming obvious that there were winners and losers in the post–World War II global economic system. Some Third World countries had made strides toward the advancement of material conditions in their societies, but most had not, despite considerable aid from First and Second World nations. Overall, the gap between the First and Third World nations had widened as many newly independent nations slipped into political chaos and economic decline. One theory that developed seemed to explain the plight of the Third World.

This theory, called **dependency theory,** argues that the condition of underdeveloped countries is not the result of internal weaknesses, but is the product of a global economic system that favors wealthy nations and exploits poorer nations. According to dependency theory, capitalistic First World nations deliberately keep Third World nations economically and technologically underdeveloped and dependent. This situation allows the transfer of wealth from the poor peripheral societies to the world's rich societies. Transnational corporations are the chief instruments of this transfer. Investment by First World corporations allows these organizations to exploit the natural resources, environment, and cheap labor supply of the underdeveloped nations to the benefit of themselves and First World countries.

Dependency theory, because of its close association with Marxist ideology, was especially attractive to many developing nations during the Cold War. In addition to blaming the industrial countries for their problems, many Third World leaders also saw international economic institutions such as the International Monetary Fund (IMF) and the General Agreement on Tariffs and Trade (GATT) as mechanisms for maintaining neocolonialism by perpetuating the economic control of the former colonial powers (Kegley and Wittkopf, 1995). By the 1970s, much of the Third World began to aggressively pursue a *new international economic order (NIEO)* to replace the *liberal international economic order (LIEO).* Third World countries argued that the LIEO, which had been created at the Bretton Woods Conference, protected the privileges of First World countries. The NIEO, its supporters argued, would facilitate a redistribution of global wealth from wealthy nations to poor nations through grants, aid, investment, improved trading rules that favored developing nations, and the transfer of technology. Many Third World countries maintained that it was the moral responsibility of First World nations to redress the wrongs they had done by giving up their wealth and advantages. With the support of socialist countries, the developing nations tried to push the NIEO through the UN but were largely unsuccessful in changing the international trading regime.

Transnational corporations are the chief instruments of the transfer of wealth from the poor peripheral societies to the world's rich societies. Here an employee works on an IBM factory assembly line in Mexico.

Many Third World nations followed internal policies that isolated them from the LIEO and/or discouraged foreign investment. For example, the governments of countries such as Egypt, India, Zambia, and Mexico *nationalized* industries, or took over the control or ownership of some private companies. Commonly nationalized industries include banking, mining, manufacturing, transportation, and communications. Growth in such countries was frequently, though not exclusively, pursued through import substitution. *Import substitution* is the process by which a Third World nation seeks to develop itself by encouraging domestic industries to manufacture goods previously purchased from First World nations. The governments of Third World nations that nationalized industries and employed import substitution usually put substantial funds into social programs for education, housing, or health care. The overall goal of such policies was to create self-sufficiency by discouraging foreign business activity and limiting the impact of the inherently unfair global market economy believed to favor First World countries.

Like modernization theory, dependency theory offers only incomplete explanations of the workings of the global economy. Whereas programs based on dependency theory have had some successes in addressing the plight of the world's poor, they have proven to be flawed models for development because they have failed to produce a viable economy that could sustain the growth needed to improve the lives of the people in the long run. On the other hand, as we have said, some nations have made great strides since the 1950s toward increasing (on a long-term basis) their GNPs and improving the living conditions of their people. For example, Japan and South Korea, two of the poorest countries in the world in the 1950s, are now countries with strong economies and good standards of living for most of their citizens. They accomplished this growth by participating in the international trading regime, not by isolating themselves from it. Dependency theory has great difficulty in explaining such successes given its emphasis on the inherent inequity and exploitativeness of the LIEO. Moreover, according to dependency theory assumptions, societies that isolated themselves from the LIEO and pursued policies like import substitution should have progressed, whereas societies more closely allied with the global marketplace should have languished. However, nations that became involved in the global marketplace and pursued policies such as export-led growth to improve their standards of living have fared well. Countries that pursued dependency theory–based programs that led them to isolate themselves from the LIEO have generally been devastated socially and economically (see the box "FYI: Africa—The 'Basket Case' of the World?").

The World Bank and Third World Debt

Third World debt is a major hindrance to development. Although many factors contribute to this problem, we focus on the role of the World Bank in the Third World debt crisis and on the implications of the bank's actions to relieve the crisis. During the 1970s, Third World nations were encouraged by the World Bank and the International Monetary Fund to undertake development projects funded by international public and private monies, often at the inflated double-digit interest rates common at the time. Lending nations and private sources were prompted to make money readily available to developing nations on the faulty assumption that projects advocated by the bank had been thoroughly investigated and were therefore economically, socially, and environmentally sound. Another fundamental concept that fostered easy lending was the belief, based on customary practice, that a sovereign nation could never default on its loans.

But the lagging world economy of the late 1970s caused a severe slump in the exports of developing nations. Most borrowing nations began to find it difficult to make interest payments on ballooning debts, much less pay down the principle they owed. As these countries fell behind on debt payments, the World Bank advocated that they borrow still more money to service the debts. Although this practice accorded with the prevailing economic principles of the time, the net result was that most borrowing nations descended deeper and deeper into debt. In 1982, debt in developing nations totaled $700 billion (Raymond, 1993). By 1991, this debt, which now included that of the former Second World, totaled $1.3 trillion (World Bank, 1991). The escalating difficulty in paying debts further strained the economies of debtor nations. Quality of life suffered as unemployment increased and social services diminished because growing levels of resources were dedicated to servicing the national debt.

The debt crisis reached a critical point in 1982 when Mexico threatened to default on its $100 billion debt to foreign banks. Mexico's threat raised the

Africa—The "Basket Case" of the World?

Although the gap between the world's richest and poorest countries has continued to widen since the 1950s, all sections of the developing world have not fared equally poorly. Sub-Saharan Africa is the one region where there has been a consistent drop in quality of life. The region's prospects for improvement, most experts agree, are practically nil. All the intertwined problems reviewed in this book, such as poverty, environmental degradation, chronic illness, and political instability are rapidly coming to a head in Africa, especially in sub-Saharan Africa. In a recent series of articles for the *Chicago Tribune,* journalist Liz Sly discussed the many challenges facing this region:

> The [African] continent's 720 million people represent 13 percent of the world's population, but control only 1.3 percent of its wealth. . . . In 1993, per capita GNP for most African nations was less than $695, compared to $24,750 for Americans. In Sub-Saharan Africa, the 1993 per capita GNP was only $560. Since the end of colonialism, African economies have lagged behind other areas of the developing world. Africa, the region of the world most in need of development, grew the least. (Sly, 1995:1.7)

Africa's development, as Sly points out, is further hindered by illiteracy and the poverty it is supposed to help relieve. For example, many of the women and children of Africa have had to forgo an education to do whatever they can to survive economically. Consequently, few adult Africans, especially females, can read or write. The day-to-day struggle for existence of the vast majority of Africa's poor impedes development in other ways. According to Sly, finding food, water, shelter, and fuel dominates the lives of homeless peasants and unemployed urbanites and keeps them out of the workforce.

Inadequate health care and poor nutrition are the norms. More than 1.2 million people died of AIDS in 1994; this is more than 20 times higher than AIDS-related deaths in North America. Health problems are compounded by malnutrition and polluted water. For example, only about 45 percent of the population of sub-Saharan Africa have access to clean water.

As discussed in Chapter 5, all of these problems are multiplied by Africa's ticking population bomb. Africa has the highest rate of population growth in the world. North Africa's population will double in 29 years; sub-Saharan Africa's in 23 years. Escalating population fuels environmental devastation, not only of water supplies, but of forests as well. In some parts of Africa, it is now difficult to find firewood.

Longstanding tribal rivalries within the nation-states—legacies of colonialism—are also creating havoc in much of Africa. For centuries Europeans engaged in trading activities in Africa, including the slave trade, but they made little effort to politically dominate the continent until the end of the nineteenth century. Then, between 1879 and 1913, the European powers divided the continent among themselves. Because the borders of the resulting nation-states did not respect traditional tribal lands, the new states generally contained diverse cultures with little in common except a long history of conflict. After their independence, Cold War–related conflicts spread throughout the continent in places as geographically separate as Angola and Ethiopia. In addition, tribalism once again asserted itself, resulting in ethnic violence. According to Sly,

> War has become a way of life in much of Africa, but superpower-backed conflicts of the past have given way to blood anarchy. Traditional tribal rivalries have reignited as factions battle for control of Africa's young nations. Countries such as Somalia, Rwanda, Sierra Leone, Liberia, Burundi and Sudan hemorrhage from self-inflicted wounds while millions of people flee as refugees across borders or are displaced and homeless within their own countries. (1995d:1.13)

Source: Sly, Liz. 1995a. "Metamorphosis of a Continent." *Chicago Tribune.* July 9: 1.1, 6, and 7; 1995b. "The Curse of Tribalism." *Chicago Tribune.* July 26: 1.1 and 8; 1995c. "Signs of Economic Hope." *Chicago Tribune.* September 13:1.1 and 12; 1995d. "UN Fails Test Case in Somalia, Humanitarian Use of Military Falls Flat." *Chicago Tribune.* February 26: 1.1 and 12; 1995e. "War as a Way of Life." *Chicago Tribune.* July 12: 1.1 and 13; 1995f. "Warlords Ready to Feast in Somalia." *Chicago Tribune.* February 21: 1.1 and 11; 1996. "Father of 57: 'It's too Many'." *Chicago Tribune.* January 30: 1.1 and 8–9.

real possibility of global financial collapse. In response to the Mexican crisis, the World Bank and the IMF imposed a series of austerity programs on debtor nations intended to stabilize and restructure their economies. The goals of the restructuring programs included decreasing domestic spending, lowering imports, and increasing exports to generate more revenue (largely intended to service debts owed to First World lending institutions). In return for undertaking austerity programs, the World Bank assisted in negotiating more favorable conditions for loan repayment such as lowering interest rates and extending the time for repayment.

Bank officials spoke in sanitized terms such as "structural adjustments," "policy reforms," and "stabilization," but the effects of these programs were disastrous for Third World countries. The policies forced debtor nations to withdraw funds from programs such as health care and education and place them into servicing the debt (Rich, 1994). Even a decade after these "reforms," economic growth in Africa and Latin America is still not expected to equal population growth. Other data are equally alarming. Roughly 100 million children in the Third World do not attend school; in two out of three developing countries, the education budget has shrunk by more than 25 percent. Increased poverty has been accompanied by a rising tide of hunger and malnutrition (Raymond, 1993). By 1996, the UN's International Labor Organization estimated that 1 billion workers worldwide were unemployed or underemployed ("World's Jobless Hits 1 Billion," 1996).

Admitting that its policies have had negative impacts on the poor in developing nations, the World Bank now advocates programs to lessen their adverse consequences. In addition, the World Bank contends that it has shifted from debt rescheduling programs to debt reduction programs. For example, new programs encourage First World nations to forgive debt in Third World nations such as Brazil in exchange for the Brazilian government's promise to protect sections of the rain forest.

But the World Bank continues to insist that adjustment programs will succeed in turning around economies in developing nations. Moreover, the World Bank claims that it is shifting more of its funds away from large-scale projects that proportedly help large segments of a developing nation's population (such as building hydroelectric dams) toward smaller programs that will more directly benefit individuals (such as improving irrigation systems of local farmers). In addition, the World Bank now states that it is looking more carefully at the human, cultural, and environmental impact of its projects. However, many of its critics, both inside and outside the Third World, remain skeptical of such claims.

Development during the Cold War

For four decades after World War II, history was shaped by the Cold War. This global ideological and military competition also had notable economic ramifications. Most obviously, the money spent on armaments was unavailable for dealing with environmental and social problems at home. In the Soviet bloc, the civilian economy suffered significantly, as scarce resources were diverted to military uses.

Developing nations that were perceived to favor one side or the other received a great deal of foreign aid from the side they supposedly supported. Much of the aid from the superpowers came in the form of military assistance or other grants intended to keep a friendly leader in power. As a result, huge sums of money went to support the lavish lifestyles of dictators and/or were stashed by such leaders in foreign bank accounts as a hedge against the time when they might be overthrown. Much well-intended aid was siphoned off by corrupt officials and never reached those it was intended to help. In this way external assistance supported unproductive economies and state policies. Indeed, the generous subsidies from the two dueling superpowers saved numerous inefficient Third World economies from ruin. Loyalty to the supplier of aid, not accountability for funds or improved standards of living, was required.

The dismantling of the Berlin Wall in 1989 symbolized the collapse of the Second World and the triumph of market capitalism. Russia is now suffering the pains of converting to a capitalistic state that operates on more democratic principles than the Russian people have ever known. The other great communist nation, China, has yet to fully embrace capitalism; rather, it practices a hybrid of capitalism and socialism sometimes referred to as "Market-Leninism" (Kristof, 1993). At the same time, the Chinese government severely abuses human rights and resists movement toward true democracy.

The Current Situation

It is not yet clear how the end of the Cold War and the transition to market economies will affect development. It is obvious that the less developed nations must now cooperate with the more developed societies if they are to succeed in improving their standard of living. The confrontation between the First and Third Worlds, which characterized much of the 1970s and early 1980s, has largely given way to mutual cooperation. Developing countries can no longer pursue unproductive economic and political policies. Increasingly, they are being held accountable for the impact of their programs on the efficiency of their economies and the quality of life of their citizens.

It also is still uncertain how the end of the Cold War will influence direct foreign aid policies of the First World, such as extra help from the IMF or the World Bank. Possibly some of the money committed to Cold War military expenditures could be diverted to help less developed countries improve their quality of life. Yet much of the aid extended by First World nations during the Cold War was for political purposes; that is, it was intended to counter moves made by Second World nations. Since the strong Cold War incentive for contributing to the developing world no longer exists, industrial nations may decrease their contributions to the Third World. This trend already is apparent in the United States, where some legislators have called for decreasing foreign aid in order to use the savings to ameliorate pressing domestic problems or provide tax breaks. These new isolationists no longer believe that foreign aid contributes to the "vital interests" of the United States.

This trend has also surfaced in other First World countries. The total amount of money expended by the industrial world in various aid programs has continued to grow, but contributions have declined from 0.47 percent of the GNP of the developed nations in 1965 to 0.34 percent in 1991 (World Bank, 1994). In addition, part of Western aid now supports the development and capitalization of the former Second World. Judging from such recent policies, it seems likely that the First World's future posture toward underdeveloped nations will be one of benign neglect (Kegley and Wittkopf, 1995).

Increased participation in the global capitalistic economy and intensified free trade are now touted as the primary mechanisms for the development of the Third World. However, governments, businesses, and development people are moving away from the simplistic assumptions of the modernization model. Growth in the GNP is no longer seen as the automatic harbinger of improved standards of living. As a corollary, there has been a shift away from stimulating economic growth toward meeting basic human needs. One indication of this change is the creation of various indexes, such as the human development index of the United Nations Development Programme, that represent attempts to gauge directly the living conditions in nations.

Another post–Cold War change is the growing recognition that the relationship between industrialization and improved standards of living is not a one-way street. Improving citizens' health, education, and general welfare is positively correlated both with enhanced productivity and the attracting of industrial investment (World Bank, 1991). As the World Bank (1991:43) has noted, "Increasing the average amount of education of the labor force by one year raises GDP by nine per cent. This holds for the first three years of education; that is, three years of education as compared to none raises the GDP by twenty-seven per cent."

Similarly, people involved with development increasingly recognize that assistance is most effective when those in need are targeted directly. Often this involves creating programs aimed at women, children, indigenous people, and the landless, all of whom are disproportionately affected by poverty. The Grameen Bank of Bangladesh represents one such targeted effort to alleviate the situation of the most needy. Founded by Dr. Muhammad Yunus, the Grameen Bank makes small loans averaging about $100 to very poor people who cannot ordinarily qualify for commercial credit. The money must be used for something that directly improves the recipient's and his or her family's life. Usually the money is employed to start small businesses. For example, recipients of such loans may use the money to purchase items from fellow citizens, which they resell to tourists for a profit. The profits from these businesses are then used to repay the loan, hire other workers, provide for children's education, or improve the family's home. The efforts of such NGOs have been replicated by government endeavors like the U.S.-supported Inter-American Development Foundation and Appropriate Technology International. These organizations provide small grants and loans, typically less than $500,000, to local communities, small businesses, farmers, entrepreneurs, NGOs, and cooperatives in the Third World (French, 1994).

Additionally, there is growing realization among people and groups involved in development of the ineffectiveness of centralized agencies such as the World Bank and nation-states to deal with certain global issues (Rich, 1994). For example, the World

Bank may lend money to nation-states for economic development, but it cannot loan money to individuals directly for the type of small-scale improvement projects previously discussed. The needs of people vary from nation to nation and even region to region within countries. Centralized agencies cannot understand the complexities of each locality in which they operate. Consequently, development agencies are now actively seeking local input into planning for development.

Conversely, local resources may be inadequate to significantly improve negative conditions. Cooperation between localities, nation-states, and the international community is required. For example, in spring 1998, several southwestern states (especially Texas) had such heavy air pollution, caused mainly by fires in northern Mexico, that the American government committed large amounts of supplies, equipment, and personnel to assist the overwhelmed Mexican government to control the fires.

Another current trend is the growing recognition of the necessity to evaluate the impact of development on the quality of life of citizens and on the environment. Governments and experts are becoming aware that it costs less to limit environmental destruction before it happens than to attempt to deal with the results afterwards (World Bank, 1991). There also is strong international pressure to practice **ecological economics** that take into account the price of environmental destruction and resource depletion when figuring a company's costs of producing goods. The practice of ecological economics encourages the limitation of environmental damage, recycling, and switching to more abundant resources for manufacturing, thereby saving scarce resources.

The Changing Nature of Work

Globalization is a process that is radically remaking the entire context in which economic development must occur. One powerful element of this reshaping is described by economist Jeremy Rifkin in his book *The End of Work* (1996). By "the end of work" Rifkin means the end of employment and the rise of unemployment that is rapidly occurring not only in the postindustrial economies of Europe, the United States, and Japan but is also spreading to the less developed economies of the Third World. The reason for this loss of employment is new technology, which has boosted productivity and eliminated the need for human workers. The *Wall Street Journal* estimates that this restructuring will cost from 1 to 2.5 million U.S. jobs each year for the foreseeable future (Rifkin, 1996). Economist Mike Hammer (cited in Rifkin, 1996) says that reorganizing a company to accommodate the greater productivity and efficiency of information technology eliminates at least 40 percent of the employees of that company and may eliminate as many as 75 percent. Technology's negative impact on jobs is a major issue that has not been addressed adequately.

A Shift in the Social Contract. One solution to the problem of job loss created by the implementation of new technology would to be create new jobs. The economies of most First World countries in fact have been doing this. But the types of jobs being created in advanced industrial nations do not bode well for employees. The industrial revolution created many well-paying manufacturing jobs. In recent decades, industrial societies have created service jobs, and the number of people employed in manufacturing has steadily declined. *Service jobs* are those positions that provide some type of service to others in response to need or demand. Economist Beth Rubin (1996) notes that clearly there are "winners" and "losers" in the new service economy. The winners are those who can manage, utilize, and create new technology; their jobs are likely to have the most stability. To compete successfully in the new service economy, individuals need to possess specific knowledge in areas such as computers, coupled with an ability to combine that knowledge in novel ways and/or the ability to create new knowledge with commercial applications. Unfortunately, such jobs will be possible for a relatively small elite. Most service jobs will go to "losers"—unskilled workers with low levels of education. Jobs available to the poorly prepared will have low pay, few benefits, and very limited security.

Rubin believes that the dramatic increase of low-end service positions represents a violation of the basic social contract between owners and workers that has governed business relationships through much of this century. There was a basic understanding that if workers worked hard and were productive, owners would reward them with job security and an improved standard of living. Company profits translated to increased income and benefits for blue-collar and white-collar workers alike. Workers then had more available money to purchase goods produced by industry. As the number of low-paying, unstable jobs has escalated dramatically, increased profits no longer translate into improved standards of living. Rather, they often result, as our opening vignette illustrated, in the transfer of jobs to less developed economies overseas. This process undermines workers' loyalty and job satisfaction. In the long term, this situation may result in declining profits for business, as workers have less money with which to purchase goods. As workers buy less, companies are likely to lay off more employees. Great social upheaval is likely to follow on the heels of massive unemployment if nothing is done to alleviate the frustration and suffering it causes.

The Social Economy. Modern political and economic thinkers have tended to divide the social and economic world into two broad sectors. The **public sector** consists of all economic activity and exchanges involving the use of government money and other capital, which originates largely through the collection of taxes. For example, taxes collected by the federal government may be used to improve the interstate highway system or to support the military. The **private sector** consists of all economic activity based on personal (or corporate) sources of capital undertaken for personal or corporate profit. The economic activities of families and households are part of the private sector. The rise of a social economy, Rifkin suggests, represents a new, "third sector" of the economy.

By **social economy** Rifkin (1996) means those networks of NGOs that are actively carrying out those tasks (e.g., organizing and providing medical care to people in areas where famine exists) necessary for the viability of local, national, and global society. These organizations, such as women's groups, peace activists, and church groups, are not associated with either the public or private sectors.

In carrying out these essential tasks, they are laying the basis of a "new social contract" based neither on the public nor on the private sector (Rifkin, 1996). For example, in Eastern Europe and Russia, the spread of democracy has been facilitated by NGOs. In India, women's organizations have been especially instrumental not only in addressing "women's issues" and "family issues," but also in reforestation and the environmental movement. Elsewhere in Asia, movements and groups are actively engaged in providing goods and services when neither governments nor the market economy can do so. These movements and groups are also actively resisting the environmental, political, and economic exploitation of the people in the societies they serve. Throughout Latin America, much of the new social economy has sprung out of Christian-based communities that have been spawned by liberation theology. Africa, too, is witnessing the spread of the social sector of the economy; churches are playing a vital role in this change (Rifkin, 1996).

While it is undeniable that the social economy is contributing significantly to reducing suffering and addressing problems of societies worldwide, it is equally clear that the preponderance of the work in this sector is conducted by unpaid volunteers. The question remains, therefore, exactly how can these social economy "jobs" help provide financial support for people who cannot find adequate employment in the public and private sectors? Rifkin offers several possibilities. One is to allow employees to work part-time in the public or private economies but still pay them full-time wages if they also work in the social sector. A second possibility is to tax the excess profits that corporations reap when they lay off workers through downsizing. These taxes would then be used to pay workers in the social sector. Neither of these options, however, is likely to find a favorable reception with powerful business interests.

Economic Issues in the United States

The remaking of the world economic system through globalization has serious ramifications for the American economy. In this section, we briefly discuss the central role of the United States in the world trading system. Next, we consider the reasons for and implications of the expanding wealth gap in this country. Finally, we review issues associated with poverty, welfare, and "wealthfare."

The United States and Global Trade

After World War II, the United States had the only major economy in the world left intact. At war's end, Americans were able to convert their economy from war production to the manufacture of consumer goods. A war-weary world was ripe for buying items for home use. The desire for consumer goods was also fueled by a backlog of frustrated need from the depression, which had lasted until the war. Sales, therefore, were brisk, and the global demand for American products was very high.

By the 1960s, Japan and Western Europe had developed very strong economies that were beginning to compete with that of the United States. American industry was slow to recognize this turnabout. Owners of U.S. companies had so long operated in a situation in which there was little real competition that they believed that they could sell nearly anything they manufactured. Quality had slipped. Pricing was out of line. Little attention was given to improving outdated and inefficient plants.

To make matters worse, American industry had lost touch with consumer desires. For example, auto manufacturers continued to insist that consumers wanted only big gas-guzzling cars, but a significant market had risen for small economical cars. The German Volkswagen "Bug" was the first to fill this niche. The Japanese also began to make significant inroads into the American domestic market with smaller high-quality cars at a reasonable price. By the 1980s, however, improved quality combined with more responsiveness to consumer needs and more efficient manufacturing helped restore American competitiveness. Today the U.S. economy remains sound, but other nations' economies have improved to the point that we now experience brisk global competition. The United States no longer has a corner on the market; it does, however, have its own corner of the market.

The twentieth century has witnessed the steady increase in the political and economic importance of east Asian nations (Borthwick, 1992). For much of the 1990s, some of the most dynamic economies in the world were found in places such as Japan, Korea, Hong Kong, Taiwan, Singapore, and China. The emergence of these regions as major economic powers brought a shift in American trade patterns away from Europe and toward the Pacific Rim (those nations that border the Pacific Ocean). Although this shift has great promise, it has also left the United States vulnerable to economic changes in Asia.

The Wealth Gap—A Threat to the American Way of Life

Earlier in this chapter, we looked at some major changes in the nature of work associated with the movement into the global economy. We asserted that the move to an economy dominated by information and service jobs produced clear winners and clear losers. In this section we look more closely at some of those winners and losers in the American economy. Specifically, we examine the stagnation of family income, the growing gap between the richest and poorest Americans, and some of the causes and consequences of this disparity. Then we turn our attention to the nature of poverty in the United States, and look at issues centering on the welfare system in this country.

Stagnant Income. Overall, the vast majority of Americans are beginning to look like losers in the global workplace. The evolution of the median family income (the money earned during a given year) in the United States from 1950 to 1992 seems to indicate a significant increase in family earnings. In 1950, the median family income in this country stood at just over $3,000. By 1991, it had multiplied more than 10 times to reach about $35,000.

But this is not an entirely accurate picture. When we hold family income constant in 1991 dollars, we see significant gains until 1973. During the period 1950 to 1973, median family income increased some 65 percent. But since 1973, the median family income has not changed significantly. Some argue that the U.S. worker has actually lost ground because of increases in such key expenses as medical care, college tuition, and automobiles, while median income has remained stable and benefits have decreased. The lost ground has occurred despite the fact that families today are more likely than families in the 1950s to have multiple wage earners. Employed workers also are working longer hours and are more likely than they were in the 1970s to have two jobs. Americans are working more, harder, and longer in a futile attempt to maintain their standard of living.

Growing Disparity in Income. The growing disparity in income between the richest Americans and middle- and lower-income earners is another indication of fundamental problems in the economy. In 1994, the upper 20 percent of our population received almost 47 percent of the nation's income. The highest two-fifths of families received more than 70 percent. In contrast, the lowest two-fifths of the population earned only a little more than 14 percent of U.S. annual income, and the lowest one-fifth received only 4 percent of the total national income. Our richest Americans are better off and our poorest are worse off than in any other industrialized nation except the United Kingdom (Braun, 1997).

Although most countries in the world have seen a significant increase in the disparity of income between the richest and poorest, the United States has the biggest increase in the First World. We can see the sweeping nature of this change by looking at the *ninety-ten ratio,* the total income of those persons who receive more than 90 percent of the nation's income, divided by the total income of those who receive less than 10 percent of the nation's income. The ninety-ten ratio shows how well the top 10 percent of the population is doing in relation to the bottom 10 percent. In 1995, the United States had the highest ninety-ten ratio of the industrialized nations (5.94). In the industrialized world, the country with the next highest ratio of rich-to-poor, Canada, was well behind, at 4.02 (Braun, 1997). Moreover, comparing changes in the rich-to-poor ratio over time reveals some significant shifts. During the decade of the 1980s, Australia, Canada, and New Zealand showed some reduction in the ratio of wealthy to poor; other industrialized countries saw an increase. The largest increase by far was in the United States, which showed an annual increase of nearly 3 percent in the gap between the rich and the poor. The very rich got much richer in the 1980s and the very poor became much poorer, especially in the United States.

Growing Disparity in Wealth. As striking as the disparity in income is, the increasing gap in wealth is possibly even more ominous. *Wealth* is the total worth of all material objects that have a money value or an exchangeable value, such as stocks, bonds, and property minus outstanding debts. Wealth in the United States is even more concentrated in the hands of a few individuals and families than is annual income. Thus, in 1993, 20 percent of the population received nearly one-half of this country's income but owned 80 percent of the country's wealth. Another way to illustrate the concentration of resources in a nation is to divide wealth into thirds and see what portion of the population controls each third. In 1986, 90 percent of Americans controlled 33.4 percent of this country's wealth. The next 9 percent held 35.1 percent of the nation's wealth. The final 1 percent of the U.S. population owned the last 31.5 percent of the nation's wealth (Braun, 1997).

The concentration of resources in the hands of the few has been escalating rapidly. Looking at income alone, almost 60,000 families became millionaires during the 1980s—an increase from 4,424 families at the beginning of the decade to 63,642 families at the end. Similarly, in 1991, 2.1 million families had wealth of more than $1 million, a figure that is 62 percent higher than it was just 7 years earlier. A recent study compared 1983 with 1989 and found that 55 percent of the total expansion of real household wealth went to just the top 0.5 percent of the American population; another 29 percent went to the next 9.5 percent. Eighty-four percent of the nation's increase in wealth over this six-year period went to only 10 percent of our population (Wolff, 1995).

Middle Class Slide and Other Results. Obviously, the wealthy, especially the very rich, have been the winners in the "getting richer sweepstakes" over the last few decades. But who were the losers? Figure 8–2 demonstrates that all categories of Americans lost wealth except for the richest fifth. The largest losers were the near-poor to solid lower class (the second fifth). The poorest fifth also saw a considerable deterioration in their situations. For many Americans, this meant a slide into poverty, as income and wealth decreased and debt mounted.

Middle- to upper-middle-income workers also saw a significant erosion of their prosperity. The erosion of the economic position of middle-income families and their intensifying financial instability is called **middle-class slide.** The trend toward middle-class slide is especially significant because for most of this century the middle class had grown in numbers and in wealth.

A progressive erosion of the prospects of the middle class and the upper rungs of the lower class will likely result in economic and political disorder. Economist Ravi Batra (1988) has argued that since the birth of this country periodic highly skewed accumulation of wealth has been associated with times of political, economic, or social upheaval that have resulted in the redistribution of affluence into more equal portions. The present accumulation of wealth by the richest Americans is approaching the record that was set at the beginning of the Great Depression in 1929. Other effects of affluence gap include a decline in the numbers of persons from lower- and middle-income families who attend college; a reduction in low-skilled workers who seek to upgrade their skills through further education; the increasing disruption of the American family; and a rise in extremist groups as faith in the American dream erodes and people turn toward devious activities to improve opportunities or to vent their frustrations. (Usually, higher crime rates accompany affluence gaps, but at present, crime rates are dropping due to a variety of factors, including improved policing techniques.)

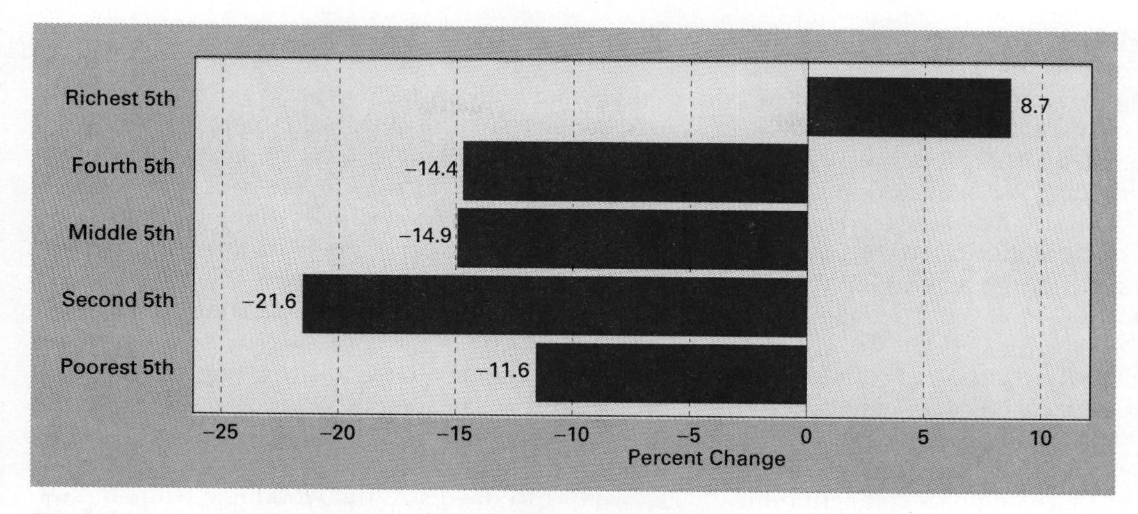

FIGURE 8–2 Percentage Change in Wealth by Income Class, 1984–1991

Source: Data from *The State of Working America, 1994–95* by Lawrence Mishel and Jared Bernstein. Copyright © 1995 by Lawrence Mishel and Jared Bernstein. Reprinted by permission of M. E. Sharpe, Inc., Armonk, NY 10504.

Causes of the Disparity. The changes in the American economy that have resulted in the growing affluence gap are produced by a multitude of interrelated internal and external factors, some of which we have discussed. Three factors are directly related to the global economy—a decline in manufacturing jobs, corporate downsizing, and the change in the type of jobs now being generated by the U.S. economy. Other factors have more to do with the response of the United States, especially the government, to the emerging global economy. The more important of these are government policies that favor the wealthy, a decreased social commitment to Aid to Families with Dependent Children (AFDC) and other social programs, and the weakening of labor unions.

Middle-class families in the United States saw a significant erosion of their prosperity in the 1980s. This is expressed in the growth of stores such as Costco, shown here, where thrifty shoppers buy groceries and other goods in bulk to get the most out of a shrinking household budget.

Effects of the Global Economy. Global economic competition and technological changes such as robotics and computerization have resulted in a decline in American manufacturing jobs. It was these jobs that expanded throughout much of the century, thereby providing the mechanism for improving the lives of most American workers. But now American industry has greater productivity and is showing record profits at the same time that the number of Americans employed in industry is sharply declining.

The demise of manufacturing and other fairly high-paying jobs has been further accelerated by corporate downsizing. American companies have typically employed the excuse that they need to become "lean and mean" in the face of global competition in order to rationalize their attempts to significantly reduce their workforces. But the real causes of most downsizing are more complex and have more to do with corporate greed than with the global economy. Beginning in the early 1980s, many companies initiated *leveraged buyouts* (the buying by one company of enough shares of another company's stock that it could force that company to sell itself to the company or group that bought the stock). Other companies sold themselves or merged with still other companies to create larger corporations. All these transactions cost large amounts of money to complete. Some companies "downsized" to cut costs enough to service loans they had undertaken to finance takeovers and mergers. Another factor that encourages downsizing is the emphasis on increasing shareholders' profits. In the process, positions occupied by older, more expensive, workers were typically the first to be cut, leaving these workers to the difficult task of finding comparable-paying jobs elsewhere. As our opening vignette illustrates, those workers forced into early retirement frequently have had to survive at a standard of living significantly below that at which they had expected to retire. Another factor, as indicated, is that most of the jobs created in recent decades are relatively low-paying positions in the service sector.

America's Response to the Global Economy

These changes in the U.S. economy only partially explain the growing disparity between winners and losers. After all, each of the other advanced industrial societies is experiencing similar market forces, but economic stratification in many other countries has decreased, in contrast to the situation in the United States. Several elements of the reaction of the U.S. social system to globalization are especially significant in explaining this discrepancy. The first is the reaction of wealthy people and transnational corporations to the possibilities of the global marketplace. Large U.S. corporations have been especially quick to turn their attention to the global workforce and the possibilities of emerging markets. They have largely disregarded the consequences of their actions for the U.S. labor force and their long-range impact on American consumers. American business has been more prone than business elsewhere in the First World to move operations outside the country as well as to downsize the workforce. Human concerns such as growing underemployment and declining standards of living have taken a back seat to the goals of increasing profits and raising stock prices.

Closely related to this is the U.S. government's response toward actions of the business community. During the 12-year period from 1980 to 1992, the White House was occupied by conservative Republican presidents Ronald Reagan and George Bush. Both pursued pro-wealth policies under the banner of *supply-side economics,* the economic theory that argues that the best way to stimulate the economy is to allow the wealthy to accumulate more wealth, which will then be reinvested in the economy. In theory this will create more jobs and ensure greater prosperity for all, including the developing nations. But this "trickle-down" notion of prosperity has proved ineffective in improving the lot in life of poor people in the United States and in Third World countries.

Embracing this theory, the conservative Reagan and Bush administrations undertook a widescale reshaping of government structures and regulations. Their goal was to free American business to engage in more open competition. Deregulation is one example of this probusiness activity. Many conservatives saw government regulation as a major hindrance for business. To change this, a broad array of federal regulations were relaxed—from environmental and safety rules to banking regulations and restrictions on mergers of corporations. When deregulation was not politically feasible, funding to regulatory agencies was cut, ensuring lower levels of enforcement of existing regulations. In theory, these actions should have allowed the marketplace to operate more freely, encouraged greater efficiency, stimulated competition, driven down prices to consumers, and created more jobs.

In some cases, there were short-range benefits from deregulation, but the long-range impact has been negative. For example, deregulation of the banking and savings and loan industry proved to be another boondoggle for the American public. A number of financial institutions, especially savings and loan institutions, took the opportunity afforded by lack of federal supervision to engage in highly risky speculative loans. Although the loans offered the possibility of huge profits over short periods of time, they frequently were not adequately secured by sound collateral. When these loans faltered, financial institutions failed. The federal government has insured citizens' deposits in banks and savings and loans since the Great Depression. Therefore, the government and, ultimately, the taxpayers were saddled with paying for losses incurred by depositors resulting from slipshod lending practices. The total cost to taxpayers of the bailout of the savings and loan industry has yet to be determined, but it may run as high as $500 billion (Braun, 1997).

American tax laws have changed over the last several decades in a number of ways that promote the interests of the rich. We are moving away from a **progressive tax system,** a system that compels wealthier taxpayers to pay increasingly higher percentages in taxes as their income rises. In other words, the more one makes, the higher portion of one's income is paid in taxes. Progressive tax systems are used by governments to redistribute the wealth of the nation by requiring the richest to turn over more of their money to the government as their incomes increase, thus making it difficult for them to accumulate vast sums. The government may then use these monies to support programs that benefit the less affluent. Obviously, a progressive tax system is not favored by the well-to-do. Even with the movement toward a more regressive system, in which the less affluent pay higher portions of their income than previously, most prosperous Americans complain that their taxes are too high. But in fact wealthy Americans pay substantially less than do the affluent in most industrialized nations.

Since 1980, the after-tax income of the richest one-fifth of the U.S. population has grown by almost 29 percent. The next two-fifths of the population had slight increases in after-tax income, but the poorest two-fifths of Americans lost ground. In the mid-1980s, a new tax bill was passed. It supposedly simplified the tax code and redistributed the tax burden more equitably. Although legislators recognized that this new tax code would also reduce the burden on the rich, it was justified in part because it closed *tax loopholes,* or special provisions in laws permitting citizens to either not pay taxes at all or to pay reduced taxes on certain types of income. Although some of the provisions of the new tax laws—such as the exclusion of mortgage interest payments and some state and local taxes from taxable income—benefit a wide range of American taxpayers, many of the new laws enrich only the most prosperous because they apply to those types of income that only the wealthiest possess. In addition, many loopholes that were closed in the 1980s have since slipped back into the law. In summary, these changes in federal law, combined with the shifting of a larger portion of funding for government operations and programs to state and local governments (which typically have more regressive tax systems than that of the federal government), have further eroded the economic situation of middle- and lower-income taxpayers.

As middle-income workers began to shoulder a larger share of the tax burden, services were substantially reduced. Under the guise of increasing governmental efficiency by eliminating costly, ineffective, and unneeded "entitlement" programs, President Reagan dismantled many of the social reforms instituted during the 1960s and 1970s. Although he promised to maintain a safety net to protect the truly needy, abundant evidence indicates that the assault on social programs has left not only the poor but the average American worker in much worse condition than before. Moreover, as social programs were being decimated, the Reagan administration began one of the largest military buildups in American history. Much of the increased allocation for the military was financed by deficit spending. The result was an ever growing national debt and even less to spend on social programs, which were cut even further.

During this period, labor unions and the gains they had helped workers achieve came increasingly under attack. Probusiness government policies encouraged assaults on unions. This stance, combined with the threats of employers to take jobs abroad, undermined union strength. Many unions were forced into "give-back" postures, in which salary increases and worker benefits were traded for promises to keep plants operating.

The combination of stagnant wages, pro-wealth government policies, cutbacks in social programs,

CONTEMPORARY DISCUSSION

Why Are Poor People Poor?

In recent years, debate has escalated about how to answer the basic question, "Why are poor people poor?" The way we answer may have serious implications for strategies to assist those living in poverty.

Conservatives Blame the Poor for Their Plight

Conservatives argue that opportunities are available for anyone to succeed if a person has the discipline and initiative to seize them. Success requires hard work and sacrifice. The poor lack both of these virtues. We can see this early in life, as the children of the poor do not do well in school. For example, they often do not do their homework or do it in a slipshod fashion; they also drop out of school at a higher rate than do the children of the more affluent. Then, later in life, the poor tend to have a spotty work record, dropping in or out of a series of jobs. Many do not work at all. When some money is accumulated, it is squandered on goods or activities that have nothing to do with improving their economic lot. In short, the poor are poor because they are lazy, waste their opportunities, and are unwilling to make the sacrifices necessary to succeed. A more sophisticated version of this logic is presented by those who offer some variation of the "culture of poverty" approach to destitution (Banfield, 1974; Lewis, 1961). This line of argument holds that many of the poor are trapped in an endless, self-perpetuating cycle of poverty. Nothing in the world of the poor gives them the idea that they can escape this cycle. For example, they do not have positive role models of people who have succeeded. It is very difficult, if not impossible, this argument asserts, to escape this vicious cycle.

and weakened unions explains why the standard of living of most Americans has been threatened, and why the gap between the rich and poor has widened and continues to expand. Although most of the European countries have been subject to the same market forces as the United States, the conditions of their average citizens have not worsened to the same degree, nor has the gap between the richest and poorest grown as dramatically. These nations have lessened the impact of globalization on their advanced industrial societies by pursuing pro-worker policies. In the process, they have maintained an adequate safety net for their citizens and helped to keep labor unions relatively strong.

Poverty

One of the great ironies of the twentieth century is that the United States, one of the wealthiest and most powerful nations in history, still has a relatively high rate of poverty. Moreover, many Americans seem to have very little sympathy for the poor and exhibit a great deal of suspicion of the needy (see the box "Contemporary Discussion: Why Are Poor People Poor?"). The nation's more affluent citizens simply do not trust the poor, but put a great deal of faith in those like themselves who are financially successful.

Attitudes toward the rich and the poor are part of a country's socially constructed reality. In the United States, the country's Calvinistic religious heritage was translated into the **Protestant work ethic,** the belief that if a person works hard, success will follow. This belief inclines many affluent Americans to assume that the poor are poor because they do not work hard and/or waste their resources. Additionally, the popular perception of the United States as a "land of opportunity" still prevails; those who are not successful are seen as not availing themselves of all the opportunities open to them. Such a view ignores the ways in which discrimination means that not all citizens have equal access to the same measure of opportunity. Finally, Americans place a high value on individualism. Perhaps more than in any other country, in the United States the individual is seen as responsible for his or her

Liberals Blame Society for the Plight of the Poor

Liberals argue that a society, not its individual members, decides how its assets are distributed. Societies do this by establishing systems that favor some groups and make it more difficult for other groups to succeed. For example, in the United States, individuals who are born into wealthy families, European Americans (whites), males, the better educated, and those who attend prestigious churches (such as the Episcopal and Presbyterian churches) fare better economically than minorities (especially African Americans), women, the less educated, and members of lower status denominations. Through no fault of their own, most of the poor are born into disfavored categories of people. Poor children often are malnourished; have less access to medical care, computers, books, or opportunities for enriching experiences (such as trips to museums or historical sites) than other children; and are, moreover, reared by parents who are poorly educated. When they start school, poor children are already far behind their more fortunate classmates. In such a context, school often becomes a frustrating experience in which they fall increasingly behind children from more privileged backgrounds. Additionally, many young poor students may have difficulty buying school supplies, getting money for school trips, or obtaining acceptable clothing. Poor children may also have more pressure in the teen years to drop out of school to help support their families. Poor people experience the same types of frustrations repeatedly when they enter the workforce and participate in family life. Whether the activity involved is purchasing housing, providing food, or paying for utilities, it is most common that society conspires to ensure the poor are always "a day late and a dollar short."

◇ **For Critical Thought:** (1) What are the assumptions of each side in this discussion? (2) How do these issues relate to some of the major theoretical themes in this book? (3) What are the political, economic, and cultural implications of each side in this discussion? (4) What practical problems are created by each position? (5) Are there possible ways of looking at the situation of the poor other than the ones presented?

actions as well as his or her successes or failures. Because our national ideology stresses individualism, some Americans find it difficult to distinguish between failures that occur because of personal inadequacies and those that occur because of systemic obstacles to success.

The Extent and Nature of Poverty in the United States. We indicated earlier in this chapter that poverty in most First World nations is relative poverty, whereas more absolute poverty is found in Third World nations. But in stating this fact we do not mean to imply absolute poverty is not found in First World nations, including the United States. For example, the United States ranks twenty-first in the world in *infant mortality,* the rate of death per thousand children during the first year of life (Braun, 1997). This statistic is significant because infant mortality rates reflect such factors as the quality of health care and the nutrition available for mother and child. The vast majority of infant deaths in the United States occur in poor families. Moreover, the Children's Defense Fund estimates that 10 million American children die annually from poverty-related causes (Braun, 1997).

In 1995, the official poverty threshold was $15,141 for a family of four (U.S. Bureau of the Census, 1996b). The poverty threshold is based on the amount of money a family needs to supply food and other necessities for itself. The threshold changes over time, as the standard of living shifts. According to this measure, more than 6 percent of Americans can be classified as severely poor; that is, they have to manage on 50 percent or less of the official poverty threshold. Additionally, one-fourth of Americans can be classified as near-poor, because they have annual incomes of only 50 percent above the poverty threshold.

In 1960 more than 22 percent of Americans were classified as poor. Another one-fifth of the population was described as deprived, in that they did not have enough to provide adequately for their needs. This rate fell dramatically until 1973, when the official rate reached a low point of 11.1 percent. This extraordinary reduction was influenced by a strong economy and President Lyndon Johnson's War on Poverty. The resulting programs and new ones created in the early 1970s by President Nixon raised as many as 15 million citizens out of poverty. New poverty programs such as free school breakfasts and lunches for poor children and food stamps helped reduce hunger in the 1960s and 1970s. Medicaid, a medical services program for the poor, made some inroads in providing health care for the needy.

But a severe economic recession in the early 1980s brought a dramatic upsurge in poverty. Although it declined from its peak in 1982, poverty returned with greater ferocity in the 1990s. In 1995, 36.4 million people, 13.8 percent of all Americans, were classified as living in poverty, as Table 8–4 shows (U.S. Bureau of the Census, 1996a). Moreover, as poverty has been rising, more elements of America's "safety net" are being dissolved. The drastic overhaul of the welfare system, which began in 1997, will probably drive more people deeper into poverty. We discuss this overhaul in more detail later in the chapter.

When Americans think of the poor, they often assume that most of the poor are African Americans or members of other minority groups. This image is perpetuated by the popular media, which often use minority group members in their stories about poverty. In fact, the vast majority (67 percent) of poor are whites; non-Hispanic whites compose the largest portion (44.7 percent) of American poor. At the same time, *poverty rates* (the poverty rate is the number in poverty per 100,000 of the population) are 4.5 times higher for black and Hispanic families than they are for non-Hispanic white families. Families headed by females are another large part of the American poor. The poverty rate among female-headed families is 32.4 percent, but these families compose more than 53 percent of all poor families in this country. Poverty rates are even higher for female-headed African American (45 percent) and

TABLE 8–4 American Poor in 1995

CATEGORY	NUMBER (IN MILLIONS)	% IN POVERTY	% OF TOTAL POOR
Total Poor (Number of Individuals)	*36.4*	*13.8*	
All whites	24.4	11.2	67.0[d]
Non-Hispanic whites[a]	16.3	8.5	44.7
Blacks	9.8	29.3	26.9
Hispanic[a]	8.6	30.3	23.6
Poor Living in Families	*27.5*	*12.3*	*75.5*
Children under 18	14.0	20.2	38.4
Children under 6	5.6	23.7	15.3
Total Poor Families	*7.5*	*10.8*	
Married couples	2.9	5.6	38.6[c]
Female-headed[b]	4.0	32.4	53.3[c]

[a] Hispanic means Spanish-speaking. Hispanics may be of any race.

[b] No husband present.

[c] % of poor families.

[d] Figures in this column add up to more than 100%.

Source: U.S. Bureau of the Census, 1996a. "Income and Poverty, 1995." Press briefing transcript. Electronic transmission: http://www.census.gov/ftp/pub.hhes/income95/prs96asc.html; ———. 1996b. "Table A. Persons and Families in Poverty by Selected Characteristics, 1996 and 1995." 1996. Electronic transmission: http://www.census.gov/ftp/pub/hhes/poverty/pov95/povest1.html

Hispanic (49.4 percent) families. This represents a departure from the past, when a majority of the adults in poor families were married couples. The tendency toward more female-headed households over the last four decades has been fueled especially by a higher divorce rate, which has left more females to singlehandedly provide for their families. Second, there has been a greater tendency among females who become pregnant outside of marriage to have their children and rear them without marrying. Third, males who divorce or father children outside of marriage often have little or no financial responsibility toward them. For example, many fathers refuse to pay court-ordered child support or are not legally required to pay much support. These factors combine to concentrate poverty among females in American society. The escalating numbers of females living in poverty is called the feminization of poverty. Of course, this trend has serious implications for children as well.

Historically, the largest age category among the poor has been the elderly. At the end of the 1950s, around 60 percent of those 65 and older were poor. This dropped to 10.5 percent by 1995. This dramatic decline was caused by improved benefits from private pensions and increases in government Social Security payments. During the same period, poverty among America's youngest citizens increased significantly. In 1995, more than one in five people under 18 lived in poverty. In the short run, poverty among children is manifested as malnutrition, hunger, mental retardation, higher death and disease rates, poor performance in school, and more physical and emotional abuse. In the long run Americans will pay for tolerating poverty and withdrawing support from children with higher crime rates, an increase in other antisocial behavior, increased spending for prisons and penal support personnel, more illness, a poorly prepared workforce, and the need for more extensive social services.

Welfare, Wealthfare, and Welfare Reform

In the broadest sense, welfare means well-being. When thus understood, **welfare programs** are any of a host of federal, state, and local programs that contribute to the well-being of the American people or specific segments of the population such as the elderly, the young, the poor, the wealthy, the disabled, farmers, businesspeople, and the like. Social Security and Medicare are two of the most expensive and most effective welfare programs in the United States. In the context of our definition of welfare as well-being, programs to immunize children or provide for their education can be considered welfare programs. Similarly, programs or institutions such as rehabilitation facilities or state mental hospitals designed to treat or care for the mentally or physically challenged represent another type of state involvement in welfare. American farmers benefit from a multitude of agencies, programs, and direct subsidies paid for out of federal tax receipts that contribute considerably to their financial well-being.

Many welfare programs involve giving preferential treatment to special-interest groups with lobbies in Washington, D.C., or in local seats of government. For example, in 1997, the attorneys general of a number of states reached a record settlement of several hundred billion dollars for their class action suits against the tobacco industry. Shortly afterward, Congress passed a bill putting into effect a major budget agreement hammered out with the White House that moved the country toward a balanced budget. In this massive bill, congressional supporters of the tobacco industry incorporated a segment that permitted the industry to deduct from its taxes $50 billion of the money paid to the states. Adding amendments that favor special interest groups to long, important bills is a common strategy of lawmakers.

These tax breaks do not always entail direct expenditures, relief from taxes, or the creation of widescale programs. Sometimes they take the form of policies that permit or even encourage higher incomes for privileged segments of the population, such as sugar growers. Through a combination of subsidies and import limitations that severely hamper foreign competition, American sugar prices are kept artificially high. The General Accounting Office estimates that inflated sugar prices cost Americans $1.4 billion annually, or $5.38 for every man, woman, and child in the country (Chapman, 1997). Such expensive endowments are comparatively small and seldom noticed by the American people. American sugar growers are thus allowed to reap windfall profits at the expense of the rest of the American people. Although support for special interest groups flies in the face of the doctrine of free trade supposedly favored by American businessowners and policymakers, these sectors make exceptions when their own interests are involved.

The term **wealthfare** is used to describe those programs, policies, and preferential treatment given by the government to more affluent members of society. Wealthfare is more extensive and costly to American society than is the sum expended on welfare programs aimed at the poor. For example, the federally funded Aid to Families with Dependent Children program (AFDC) costs about $25 billion annually. This is about half the $50 billion in tax deductions taken by homeowners for interest paid on mortgages and half the previously mentioned tax break for the tobacco industry. AFDC comprises roughly 8 percent of the $300 billion in Social Security benefits paid out yearly to elderly Americans, many of whom are quite wealthy. And the program is miniscule when compared to the hundreds of billions given each year to corporations in the form of various tax breaks (Macionis, 1997). While it is not necessarily true that every wealthfare break is undeserved or unnecessary, it is true that controversies about the welfare system usually focus on programs directed at the poor but seldom mention this wider context of American welfare.

When welfare programs are reformed, programs for the poor are the usual targets. We already have noted numerous attacks on the safety net beginning in the early 1980s. In recent years, welfare reform has come to focus on one program—AFDC. Conservatives have been particularly critical of this program as the number of poor families with children headed by females has increased. They often criticize women who stay home drawing welfare checks rather than working, even though the targets of their attack generally have full-time jobs as mothers. In addition, a good portion of women on welfare do work for wages at least part time. Ironically, these same conservatives often chide middle-class women for working instead of staying home to take care of their children.

Nevertheless, the concerted attack on AFDC resulted in the passage of a law effective in 1997 that was intended to put physically healthy adult AFDC recipients to work. The Personal Responsibility and Work Opportunity Act of 1996 replaced AFDC assistance to poor families with Temporary Assistance to Needy Families (TANF) grants to states. The law provided for two more years of assistance for families of nonworking adults. Then payments will be ended. Moreover, a healthy recipient (and his or her dependent family) will receive a lifetime maximum of five years of benefits. States that fail to reach the mandated reduction in welfare recipients will lose their federal aid grants. In addition, no federal funds are allocated to assist recipients to make the transition from welfare to work. As many as 4 million families will be affected by this law, making the Personal Responsibility Act one of the largest social experiments in recent American history. Moreover, this experiment has been undertaken without the slightest idea of whether or not it will work (see the box "The Human Face of Welfare Reform: The Door to College Is Closed Ma'am").

The destruction of the AFDC program is based on the value judgment that the poor should work. Three other assumptions also underlie the act. The first assumption is that welfare assistance is all that prevents the poor from working. The second assumption is that once the poor are kicked off the dole of welfare dependency, they can work. The third assumption is that the work they obtain will provide sufficient income to move them to self-sufficiency. These assumptions are taken as matters of faith by supporters of the Personal Responsibility Act, but as we have seen, they are simply part of a socially constructed reality that originates in the Protestant beliefs of many of the nation's first settlers.

Despite the zeal of conservatives, several practical problems with these assumptions threaten to transform the promise of self-sufficiency into the reality of greater human suffering. One set of difficulties centers on the lack of social capital possessed by the recipients themselves. These persons generally are not highly educated individuals with good job skills and impressive résumés. Most are poorly educated, have high school diplomas or less, have spotty work records, and possess few necessary job skills. They may not know how to look for a job, how to prepare an application or résumé, or how to conduct a successful interview. Current welfare recipients may not have those items that many of us would take for granted, such as money to purchase clothes for a job. Furthermore, the poor often do not have reliable transportation to get to jobs, suffer from a lack of daycare or other childcare provisions, and experience greater levels of poor health, mental illness, and drug addiction than do affluent people. Many of the nonworking poor have a host of problems that may prevent them from obtaining and keeping jobs.

Still other practical difficulties stem from the U.S. economy itself. For example, it is not clear that there will be enough suitable jobs available when former welfare recipients start searching for them. The U.S.

THE HUMAN FACE OF WELFARE REFORM

The Door to College Is Closed Ma'am

Sociologists often note that any given policy may have *latent functions* (unintended and unrecognized consequences). In fact, some of these unintended consequences may be *dysfunctional,* or actually prevent or hinder the policy from reaching its intended goal. We have noted some of these in the text. However, the dysfunctions of the Personal Responsibility Act deserve special attention. Since all recipients must find jobs within two years, AFDC mothers now attending colleges under welfare-to-work educational plans must soon quit school to take low-paying jobs and will lose their educational benefits.

Not only do such parts of the act make dubious political sense, they also extract a human toll. One Oregon college administrator noted that 10 years ago 50 percent of AFDC recipients were enrolled in two-year college programs in that state but that today only 5 percent are enrolled. Welfare recipient Sabrina Gillon needed two more semesters to complete an associates degree but was forced to comply with the work-and-off-welfare mandate. Now, rather than graduating, she registers students at the same college she attended. An associates degree would have helped her get a higher paying position and to remain off the welfare rolls.

Sandi Sabrowicz, a 36-year-old single mother of a four-year-old, went on welfare after she lost her job. Armed with only a high school education, she believed that being on welfare would allow her to obtain a degree from an institution of higher education. Then she would be able to get off welfare and provide for herself and her son. But her caseworker has been pushing her to take a full-time job even though she needs only a few credits to complete her degree in computer information systems. Her instructors have had to run interference in order to help her remain in the educational program.

Cases like this suggest it may be that the short-term benefits of the Personal Responsibility Act are disastrous in the long run for the most ambitious former welfare recipients.

Source: Based on Ginger Thompson, "Welfare Reform Slamming Shut Door to College." *Chicago Tribune.* Nov. 19, 1997: 1.1 and 19.

economy has been generating about 2 million new jobs a year since the mid-1980s. But many of these jobs are not the kind for which the former welfare recipients are qualified. They will compete in a labor market already flooded with job seekers. Although the national unemployment rate is currently in the 5 percent range, unemployment among women under 34 years old with a high school diploma stands at 11.3 percent; for those without a high school diploma, the unemployment rate is 19.1 percent. Researchers in a recent Northern Illinois University study of employment opportunities for low-skilled job seekers in the Midwest found 104,000 job hunters in Minnesota, but only 40,000 openings; in Indiana there were 133,000 seekers, but only 44,800 jobs; and Ohio had 324,800 job hunters for 80,500 positions. Other states in the Midwest posted similar figures (Goozner, 1997). At the time of this study, the economy in the Midwest was one of the most robust in the country.

Moreover, even if jobs are available, they may not be located in areas where welfare recipients live, such as inner-city neighborhoods or rural areas. One irony in the current situation is that there are many low-skilled job seekers in inner-city areas where there are few jobs, while in the affluent suburbs openings for low-skilled jobs cannot be filled because of a lack of workers.

Some have suggested that workfare may be the answer to the problem of too few low-skilled positions. **Workfare** is a program of public sector jobs created so that welfare recipients can work for their checks. These jobs may include providing janitorial services in public buildings, cleaning streets, or repairing infrastructure. The match initially may seem perfect:

Workfare is a program of public sector jobs created so that welfare recipients can work for their checks. Here men pave a street as a part of a workfare jobs program.

welfare recipients have the dignity of working for their check, while the public receives needed services for its money.

However, unions have been hesitant about such proposals for fear that they may cost union members their jobs. Where workfare has been tried, there appears to be a tendency to replace more highly paid private sector employees with lower-paid welfare recipients. One other potential problem with workfare must be mentioned. The economies of advanced industrial nations, as indicated, have been creating high-paying jobs for people with advanced education (for which most welfare recipients would not be qualified) and low-paying positions (many of which are temporary or part time). Low-end jobs often do not have benefits such as health insurance and retirement programs. Even if individuals were to be lucky enough to be hired in these positions on a full-time basis, the pay probably would not be enough to lift them out of poverty. Additionally, they are likely to have difficulty earning enough money to pay for health care plans or save for retirement.

In brief, the Personal Responsibility and Work Opportunity Reconciliation Act may have dubious consequences. And of course the children supported by welfare will also suffer from the cutoff of welfare funds.

Assessing the Situation

This chapter brings together a number of themes underlying many of the issues addressed elsewhere in the book. Population increases, social and economic systems, and environmental limits are coalescing to create a world economy with a bundle of problems that cannot be addressed adequately without coordinated international action. Efforts to solve these pressing issues often are summed up under the rubric of "development." Yet, as we have seen, development, at least as it often has been conceived, is as much a part of the problem as the solution.

In this section, we consider both the concept of sustainable development and the concept of development itself from the perspective of human rights. After reviewing some key issues associated with capitalism, the political system, and the free market, we assess current economic conditions in light of some of the theoretical constructs discussed earlier in this book.

Sustainable Development

Because the world's population continues to grow, utilization of natural resources and development will have to continue. Yet development cannot continue to equal exploitation and overconsumption; development must become sustainable. *Sustainable development* is "development that meets the needs of the present without compromising the ability of future generations to meet their own needs" (UNCED, 1991:14). The idea of sustainable development was popularized in 1987 by the World Commission on Environment and Development (1987) in its report *Our Common Future*.

Often referred to as the Brundtland Commission and the Brundtland Report (after the group's chairperson), this report was the basis for work begun through the United Nations to organize a global meeting to move the planet toward a sustainable future. These efforts culminated in 1992 with the United Nations Conference on Environment and Development (often called the Earth Summit) held in Rio de Janeiro, Brazil. Despite continuing disagreements, the conference was able to release the Rio Declaration on Environment and Development and *Agenda 21*.

Agenda 21 represents a recognition that development, environment, and the quality of life in societies are interrelated. The document seeks to address many of the core problems discussed throughout this book. *Agenda 21* states that sustainable development rests on positive answers to two fundamental questions: (1) Can we increase the standard of living of the world's population without depleting the planet's natural resources and environment? and (2) Can we step back from the brink of disaster and lift the standard of living of the world's poorest residents? (Sitarz,1994). *Agenda 21* presents an extensive plan to move the world toward the goal of sustainability in the twenty-first century. It seeks to ensure participation from the local level to the global institutional level to create a "global partnership based on common interests, mutual needs, and common, yet differentiated, responsibilities" (Sitarz, 1994:6).

In *Agenda 21* the environmental deterioration in nondeveloped nations is viewed as primarily the result of the actions of industrialized countries. Much of the responsibility for correcting these problems, therefore, lies with the industrialized nations, as they have the capacity, technology, and education necessary to assume the lead in solving them. Yet underdeveloped nations must find a way to develop livelihoods that do not destroy the environment and undermine their resource base. They cannot duplicate the patterns of production, consumption, and waste of the industrialized nations. Industrialized and nonindustrialized countries must cooperate to break these destructive patterns (Sitarz, 1994).

Development cannot rest on the traditional consumption-based economy that may produce short-term gains but is globally unsustainable. Achieving a sustainable standard of living requires a bold new approach that requires long-term vision (Sitarz, 1994).

Development and Human Rights

Development is a human rights concern because it is associated with those issues necessary to produce a dignified human existence. Considering development as a human rights issue implies viewing development in terms of improvement in the quality of life of a country's citizens. Any effort to enhance the quality of material life must be accompanied by efforts to increase personal security and must be attempted within the context of democratic participation and the implementation of all other political and civil rights.

As spelled out in the UN Universal Declaration of Human Rights and other such documents described in Chapter 2, authorities violate human rights whenever they impinge upon citizens' political or civil liberties, seize property without due process, or attack an indigenous people's cultural heritage in the name of development. When the privileges of businesses take precedence over the needs of citizens, or the World Bank measures success on the basis of the quantity of loans it gives out and not the quality of programs it supports, human rights have been violated. Similarly, when development is undertaken at the cost of irreplaceable resources and threats to the biosphere, human rights have been violated.

Agenda 21 does an admirable job of addressing basic political and civil rights. It attempts to protect and advance the rights of particularly vulnerable groups, especially women, children, and indigenous peoples. In addition, *Agenda 21* reflects current ideas about how these rights are to be implemented, such as democratic participation and economic empowerment of vulnerable groups.

One area *Agenda 21* leaves unclear, however, involves the third generation of rights—the rights of collectivities or peoples. Whereas the Universal Declaration recognizes unspecified cultural rights for nationalities, it is unclear whether ethnic or religious groups occupying *subnational* (a territory smaller than a nation) or *supranational* (a territory not confined to a nation) regions have rights at all.

The idea of sustainable development implies the fourth generation of rights, intergenerational rights, in that it requires that this generation's needs be balanced against those of future generations. Yet the exact nature of the rights of future generations still has not been spelled out. More important, it is unclear just how much this generation should sacrifice for future generations. It may well be that the industrialized countries should drastically reduce their waste and consumption for the sake of the future. These nations could substantially reduce their standards of living and still maintain a more than adequate lifestyle for their citizens (assuming that they solve the problem of maldistribution of wealth within their own borders). But what about persons living in desperately poor societies? Should they be required to sacrifice resources that could be used to alleviate suffering today for the sake of future generations? To reduce this issue to its barest terms, how many lives should be sacrificed by this generation—a thousand, a million, a hundred million, a billion—to conserve resources for future generations?

Our point is this: The rights of future generations have still to be defined, especially whether the rights of future generations should supersede those of present generations. But what is apparent is that the industrial nations can decrease their levels of consumption and waste without endangering citizens of the current generation. Whether they have the political will to make the necessary changes is, however, doubtful.

The U.S. Constitution and Economic Issues

The Preamble to the U.S. Constitution states that one of the reasons for forming the new government was to "provide for the general welfare." Although we may debate what constitutes the general welfare, there can be little doubt that the framers of the Constitution believed that government has a responsibility to look out for the needs and interests of the American people. In the broadest sense, welfare may be seen as the well-being of every American.

We suggest this point because it has been popular in recent years for politicians to argue that government has little responsibility to provide for the welfare of its people. Some Americans in fact want freedom from government interference and want to take care of themselves. They argue that the best government is the least government. Under the guise of cutting government waste, getting the government off citizens' backs, and shrinking "bloated" government, much of the dismantling of our society's social safety net has occurred. Those who have attacked government policies, from environmental laws to safety requirements to nursing home regulations, justify their positions by pointing to what they consider to be unnecessary expense and governmental intrusion. Additionally, they argue that changing these policies will provide more opportunities for more individuals.

Entitlements (or entitlement programs) have drawn especially heavy fire. **Entitlements** are various types of government bequests that people can expect as givens. Critics tend to view entitlements as special privileges that certain groups demand. For example, gays may demand health care benefits for their partners. Inmates and the poor may assume they can expect to file an endless array of "frivolous" legal cases against authorities or business. The poor may expect a constant dole from the government to support themselves and their children. Often these special privileges are presented by their critics in such a way that they seem to come at the expense of the majority of hardworking, family-oriented Americans.

Supporters of entitlements, in contrast, see them as basic rights that cannot properly be denied to human beings. Indeed, they argue, some entitlements that have been strongly attacked by conservatives are basic civil rights outlined in the U.S. Constitution and the UN Universal Declaration of Human Rights. For example, civil rights, such as the rights to seek redress from the government or to have competent legal counsel, are fundamental to U.S. and international legal codes. Moreover, economic well-being, education, a living wage, and health care are rights protected by the Universal Declaration. A fundamental principle of democracy is the idea that the minority must be protected from the tyranny of the majority. From this perspective, attacks on the safety net and on entitlements are assaults on fundamental human rights.

The Global Economy

The tendency of modern capitalism to pursue short-term gain to the long-term detriment of the environment, workers, and economic stability has largely been controlled in the First World through governmental regulation. Each of the industrial capitalistic nations of the First World has learned through experience to control the most dangerous forms of speculation and the most questionable financial practices. Elsewhere, however, much of the global economy is out of control. In Russia and in other Second World nations, the retreat from socialism and the move toward capitalism have resulted in the extreme wealth of a few and increasing crime rates. Many of the masses in these countries are out of work, out of home, and out of luck. More recently, the rapidly expanding boom economies of southeast Asia have experienced sharp downturns that have resulted in economic chaos and human suffering. Speculation (loans made to persons without proper collateral), overbuilding, and inflation in these countries led to varying states of economic collapse starting in 1997, during which many people lost their savings, their jobs, and their homes.

Much of the blame for this economic collapse is placed on the inability of the international financial community to control the global economy effectively. For example, in the nations of the First World, economic safeguards and regulations limit speculation and risky loans. These help minimize the risk of economic collapse. But such devices are almost nonexistent in the global marketplace. Moreover, technology presents new challenges to economic stability. New information technologies enable huge sums of money to move around the world totally outside the control of the regulations imposed within the borders of advanced industrial nations. For example, $400 trillion are traded each year in the global currency markets (25 times the amount needed to finance all world trade). What remains after this trade is financed is used for unregulated speculation (Longworth, 1997). Although capitalist theory shuns government intervention, this situation has led many economists and even businesspeople to call for government curbs on international trading and the creation of strong supranational structures to ensure fairer trading and financial stability.

In addition, the global trading structure represents a threat to democracy. One of the functions of a democracy is to ensure the distribution of wealth in a fashion that benefits the majority in a society. The global trading system, as it currently exists, places decisions concerning how wealth is distributed in the hands of a few, who work for their own self-interest to the detriment of the interest of the many. It is ironic, some experts contend, that with the demise of socialism, the great enemy of democracy may turn out to be unfettered capitalism. For example, political scientist David Marquand observes:

> Either democracy has to be tamed for the sake of the market or the market has to be tamed for the sake of democracy. . . . Society cannot indefinitely tolerate alienation, social fragmentation and insecurity on the present scale. Globally and nationally, we shall sooner or later have to choose between the free market and the free society. (Quoted in Longworth, 1997: 10.1)

Theoretical Considerations

Terms such as "the economy" and "economic behavior" are abstractions. Actual human conduct is embedded in social contexts and affected by cultural and psychological influences of which economic factors are, at best, only one aspect. Yet these terms have come to be viewed by many as important out of all proportion to other institutions and aspects of human life (i.e., family, religion, community). The significance attributed to economic matters did not develop in a social vacuum but reflects the rise of urban middle-class merchants and manufacturers, the territorial expansion of Europe (imperialism), the development of more productive technology, the shift to fossil fuels, the ascent of the nation-state, and the decline of traditional religious restraints on making money by means of business transactions. By the end of the twentieth century, even politics and political ideology have fallen prey to the belief that the market is an all-powerful force for good in human relations. In this view, if left alone the market will make the proper adjustments necessary for human well-being.

Such assumptions rest upon the ideas of Enlightenment thinkers such as Adam Smith (1723–1790). For Smith, the market was a self-regulating distinct system, directed by its own universal laws and governed by an inherent rationality. Smith referred to an "invisible hand" that ruled over all the apparent chaos and self-centeredness of economic transactions and ensured the good of the whole. The expression "invisible hand" was used in the eighteenth century to refer to the unseen guiding hand of God, or Providence. To this day many still argue as if they too believe that "market forces" are guided by a built-in unerring wisdom and that economic principles are eternal and universal verities rather than relative and limited patterns.

A more empirical sociology of economic behaviors recognizes that the production and exchange of goods and services and social (and physical) processes are governed by social norms and cultural factors. In other words, economic behaviors are part of the societal life-support system (those social activities necessary for humans to sustain their lives). According to this view, economic behaviors are made up of the transformation of energy (and the generation of entropy, or the accumulation of waste within a system). Ideally, these processes operate in ways that help to sustain a societal way of life that enhances most of society's members. For example, the economy should be directed by societal norms and laws that encourage a reasonably equitable distribution of wealth. To effectively operate as part of the societal life-support system, the world economic system must be linked to other aspects of the sociosphere (e.g., the family and the political system) as well as to the biosphere. These linkages take the form of feedback loops that serve to reinforce certain tendencies while altering or correcting others. For example, effective feedback loops are essential to the market economy, in which items that are manufactured are put out for sale. If an item sells, this represents positive feedback, in that it encourages the manufacturer to produce more of that item. But if an item does not sell, this represents negative feedback, in that it discourages the manufacture of more of these items.

When these interconnections are recognized and allowed to function freely, markets can play a vital role in providing feedback to producers, consumers, workers, governments, and other interested groups. Markets have the potential to contribute significantly to societal well-being. For example, consumer choices could determine what type of goods are produced, how many are made, and the price paid for these items. As the demand for goods increases, production increases, profits escalate, and pay to production workers could rise. The taxes consumers and workers pay would escalate and various interest groups and citizens would benefit. Market mechanisms based on consumer choices, as this example suggests, can provide feedback that enhances ecological sustainability.

Such an ideal functioning of the economy requires several conditions. The first, and possibly most important, is that social values must define the primary purpose of the economy as the support and the quality of social life and the general well-being of citizens. In the current situation, the main purpose of the market economy is to make money for investors. Too often, little thought is given to the effects of economic activity on workers, citizens, the fabric of society, or the biosphere.

Second, feedback loops must be allowed to operate freely. For example, the market can take appropriate corrective measures only when the full range of costs involved in the production, exchange, and consumption of goods is expressed in prices. At present, costs to workers' or consumers' health, damage to natural ecosystems, or the depletion of scarce resources are almost never taken into account in the calculation of true costs of the production of items. The result is that prices are kept artificially low. If the total cost of production were to be taken into account, it is conceivable that the price of goods would rise, consumers would stop buying costly items, and companies would search for less detrimental and less costly means of production. But when the full cost of production is not accounted for, corrective feedback does not reach decision makers, destructive behavior is reinforced, and corrective changes are resisted. This interruption of the feedback loop undermines the long-range economic well-being of both individual nations and the global population.

Third, bureaucracies must stop interfering with the ideal operation of feedback in economies. *Bureaucracy* is an application of rationality to social organization that stems from early modern or premodern times. Its practical application often results in hierarchical top-down systems of social restraints that involve several levels of decision making. Bureaucracy was the preferred means of regulating economic production and distribution in the former Soviet Union. Bureaucratic hierarchies tend to block the "upward" flow of corrective information so that it is conveyed in distorted form to top-level decision makers, if the information reaches them at all. In bureaucracies social positions become sources of power and privilege to be protected at all costs, which defeats organizational efforts to innovate and adapt. Bureaucratic environments, then, undermine efficiency, the main purpose of bureaucracies.

Market societies also employ bureaucratic methods of organization that develop or maintain systems of hierarchical stratification. Although we often perceive social class and other inequities as basically economic in nature, issues of power may be more central to the explanation of these inequities. Although to some extent different rewards for different kinds of work and different levels of skill determine inequalities, the accumulation by some individuals of power and the resulting disempowerment of others that results cause the most persistent and socially debilitating forms of stratification. Although it is arguably beneficial in complex societies for there to be a degree of unequal reward, such societies become far more unequal than necessary due to the exercise of power (Lenski and Lenski, 1987).

Often considerations of race, ethnicity, and gender are used to designate who will and who will not participate fully in societal rewards and decision making. This is always costly and inefficient from an economic perspective because the society as a whole loses the contribution of those who have been marginalized. Additionally, the society suffers additional costs in terms of ill health, waste, crime, and lost productivity. For example, when a minority group is marginalized, it often receives limited education, which results in low-paying jobs (or no jobs at all) that may lead in turn to other negative consequences such as malnutrition and ill health. Treating ill health is costly for society. Or people with inadequate jobs may be tempted into crime. Overstratification inevitably costs a society and harms the ecosystem because it disrupts feedback loops at very critical junctures, those points at which people are closest to the natural and biological foundations of society. Agricultural workers, indigenous people, and women with children provide examples of groups who live and work at these critical junctures. The degree to which their needs are met is indicative of the health of a society.

Another problem with efforts to solve economic problems stems from modernity's strong stress on rationalism as the chief component of human character. Rationality enters into economic decision making at a number of levels. For instance, German sociologist and economist Max Weber (1864–1920) distinguished among several different varieties of rationality. One form is rationality with respect to goals; a second form is rationality with respect to means (instrumental rationality). Although changes are occurring, decision makers in critical positions of power, such as officials at the World Bank, often assume that they are employing the best, or most rational, means to achieve the goals of economic growth. Their emphasis on rationality, when used in this way, tends to render them blind to the consideration of all possible means of achieving economic growth, such as alternative or indigenous technologies.

It is seldom accurate to assume that such agencies as the World Bank or even corporate leaders are simply cynical and uncaring, driven by nefarious motives such as greed. Nor is it accurate, as some critics contend, to regard them as simply ignorant. Indeed, sociologists at their best do not attribute the actions and choices of actors in complex social positions to such purely psychological motives as greed or the desire for power. They find it far more accurate and useful to assume that these persons are shaped by commitments to social norms and their involvements in ongoing relationships, that they are subjected to numerous pressures and limitations, and that they make unquestioned assumptions about the nature of the world, which they then act upon. Among these unquestioned assumptions are the prevailing economic models themselves.

At one level, the economic models that governments, corporations, some economists, and other powerful organizations use to make decisions and assess economic situations tend to assume that human beings act as if they are unattached and unaffected by social commitments, that they reason logically and attempt to maximize their own material advantages, and that they have full knowledge of relevant facts. In truth, no economist would assert that these assumptions are all literally true, but those economists who attempt to create more realistic models of human economic conduct have tended to modify and tinker with these assumptions, rather than to discard them.

In opposition to these views, sociologist Amitai Etzioni (1988) argues persuasively that even those persons from whom we would expect the most scientifically rational decisions concerning actions—physicians, scientists, and the like—make choices largely on the basis of normative and affective (emotional) grounds and follow steps in thinking that are not very logical. Thus, economic models, which are themselves taken as the norm or guideline for many important public decisions, fail not only with respect to ecological systems, but also because of the way human actors behave in economic (i.e., social) situations. For example, the marginalization of minority groups is not logical and defies the rationality of many economic models. The socially learned prejudice of some businesspeople may lead them to decide against selling to minorities who have the money to buy their goods. Thus, the irrationality of prejudice can cause such businesspeople to act against their economic self-interest.

To put this in terms we developed earlier, the core of the matter is often identity. The prevailing economic model assumes that human beings see themselves as isolated and unattached, acting only according to self-interest. Another model is both more realistic and more sociologically sound because it recognizes that people have strong social attachments and identify themselves with other persons and the groups to which they belong. In this other model, personal identity is connected with identifying with groups to which a person may belong. Thus, to be self-interested (concerned about the well-being of the self) has a different meaning for individuals who strongly identify with their children or ethnic group than it does for individuals who identify themselves only with the self. Such group-based identities significantly alter economic behavior. For example, childless adults typically allocate their financial resources differently than do adults with children.

Economic and social stress tend to motivate people to escape or change the situation. We can view *social stress* as the accumulated tensions, strains, and discontent resulting from the persistent failure of social structures to respond to corrective feedback. At times these failed efforts culminate in social movements, organized group efforts to resist or promote the social forces of change perceived as causing the stress. As we suggested in Chapter 3, contemporary social movements differ from nineteenth- and early twentieth-century social movements. Indeed, although power and economics are not absent from their agendas, contemporary social movements focus far less on the redistribution of economic rewards and political power than previous movements did. This change in focus, no doubt, reflects underlying changes in culture and social structure. These contemporary movements include *ecological resistance movements* (Taylor, 1995). Examples include the resistance of indigenous peoples to the destruction of the environments that are the source of their livelihoods or organizations, or self-appointed defenders of the natural world such as the NGO *Earth First!* Indeed, modern technology, combined with changes in values, worldviews, and identities, has led to a proliferation of national and international NGOs, of which there are upwards of 100,000 in the world today.

NGOs and related social movements build linkages among public and private sectors and within the social economy. In establishing these linkages, they construct social patterns that attempt to relieve perceived stress. Environmentalist groups are among those groups that try to forge such linkages in order to bring about change in the global arena. To create the linkages, they direct their efforts at selected levels of the developing global social system. For example, an NGO may bring together business interests, indigenous peoples' organizations, national and international government agencies, and human rights groups in international conferences to discuss the areas in which their common problems and interests intersect.

Such efforts help create networks of interaction and exchanges of information among the groups involved. These serve to construct social and normative entanglements and to reshape worldviews, identities, and value systems. For example, such international conferences may help redefine the worldviews of businesspeople, environmentalists, and indigenous people by creating a vision of how each group interfaces with the biosphere and how each group can contribute to sustainable development. All this activity has the effect of generating a social texture of assumptions, norms, and relationships that aid in the collective governance of human conduct outside the direct effects of states and ultimately help forge a global civil society. Such a global civil society may provide the impetus and the means to confront our pressing economic problems.

Summary

1. Three important mechanisms for handling economic issues emerged from the 1944 Bretton Woods Conference: the *International Bank for Reconstruction and Development* (or the World Bank), to rebuild war-ravaged sections of the world; the *International Monetary Fund (IMF),* to promote balanced expansion of international trade as well as encourage stability in the world's financial markets; and the *General Agreement on Tariffs and Trade (GATT),* a treaty that was intended to stabilize the world economy by producing fair regulations of international trade.

2. **Free trade** is trade based on the unrestricted international exchange of goods without protective customs tariffs; one of its fundamental concepts is that goods and services should be produced where they can be made most efficiently at the lowest cost.
3. **Per capita income** is an indicator of the wealth of a nation and is derived by dividing the *gross national product* (GNP), or the total value of the goods and services produced, by the number of residents of a nation during a specified period. The human development index (HDI), a UN measure of how well people live, shows a complex relationship between per capita income and quality of life in a country.
4. In the United States and the rest of the industrialized world, most of the poor live in **relative poverty**—they are poor when compared to the rest of the domestic population—while many of the poor in the nonindustrialized world live in **absolute poverty**—they are so poor that they live in life-threatening situations.
5. **Transnational corporations** are headquartered in one country but operate in one or more other countries. These businesses enter Third World nations because of low labor costs and lax environmental and safety regulations. The introduction of industrialization and global competition to some Third World countries has increased the disparity between the rich and the poor and, in some cases, has caused a decline in quality of life for the poor.
6. According to the **modernization theory** of development, underdeveloped societies are hindered both by their failure to employ advanced technology in production and by traditional modes of thought that stress family and relationships rather than the individual and economic efficiency. **Dependency theory** argues that the condition of underdeveloped countries is not the result of internal weakness but is the product of a global economic system that favors the wealthy nations and exploits poorer countries.
7. Enormous Third World debt and a threatened financial collapse of the world economy in the 1980s caused the World Bank to shift from debt-rescheduling policies to debt reduction policies in the 1990s.
8. The changing nature of work may cause a shift from dependency on the public and private sectors for employment to the social economy. The **social economy** is that sector of the economy based on volunteer activities. The **public sector** consists of all economic activity involving the use of government money. The **private sector** consists of all economic activity based on personal (or corporate) sources of capital undertaken for personal or family gain.
9. In the United States, the richest 1 percent of the population holds 31.5 percent of the *wealth*, or the total worth of all material objects that have a money value and all property minus outstanding debts. The combination of stagnant wages, pro-wealth government policies, cutbacks in social programs, and weakened labor unions explains why this gap between the rich and poor continues to expand.
10. In the United States, 44.7 percent of the poor are non-Hispanic whites; the number of females living in poverty is rapidly escalating; and the number of children living in poverty is also rising. Explanations of poverty are often rooted in the **Protestant work ethic,** the belief that if a person works hard, success will follow. In reality, the poor have a host of problems—including a lack of transportation, a lack of adequate childcare, and poor health—that may prevent them from getting or keeping jobs. **Workfare** is a program of public sector jobs created so that welfare recipients can work for their checks.

Thinking Critically

1. Describe the differences between modernization theory and dependency theory. How would proponents of these two approaches propose to close the wealth gap between the First and Third Worlds? Are there alternatives to these views? How might these two theories be combined to present a more comprehensive solution to Third World poverty?
2. Development usually has been imposed in a top-down fashion on Third World countries. If

you were to plan a development project, how would you ensure input from people who are often excluded from the decision-making process, such as local villagers, indigenous peoples, young people, women, the landless, or other disempowered groups? How might you balance the competing interests of various collectivities, national governments, local or national businesses, and international business?

3. Sustainable development requires that we balance the needs of this generation with those of future generations. What, if any, rights have future generations to scarce resources? Who must sacrifice today for the sake of future generations? Outline five principles for making these decisions. How would you make sacrifices politically viable?

4. What constitutes the "general welfare"? Are there areas of social life in which the federal government should not become involved? Why or why not?

Suggested Readings

Berger, Peter. 1986. *The Capitalist Revolution: Fifty Propositions about Prosperity, Equality, and Liberty.* New York: Basic Books.

Bloom, Allan. 1987. *The Closing of the American Mind: How Higher Education Has Failed and Impoverished the Souls of Today's Students.* New York: Simon & Schuster.

Braun, Denny. 1997. *The Rich Get Richer: The Rise of Income Inequality in the United States and the World,* 2nd ed. Chicago: Nelson-Hall.

Ehrenreich, Barbara. 1990. *Fear of Falling: The Inner Life of the Middle Class.* New York: HarperCollins.

Garbarino, James. 1992. *Toward a Sustainable Society: An Economic, Social and Environmental Agenda for Our Children's Future.* Chicago: Nobel.

Goodland, Robert J. A., Herman E. Daly, Salah El Serafy, and Bernd von Droste, eds. 1991. *Environmentally Sustainable Development: Building on Brundtland.* Paris: United Nations Education, Scientific, and Cultural Organization (UNESCO).

Hurst, Charles E. 1992. *Social Inequality: Forms, Causes, and Consequences.* Boston: Allyn & Bacon.

Kinlaw, Dennis C. 1993. *Competitive and Green: Sustainable Performance in the Environmental Age.* Amsterdam: Pfeiffer.

Kozol, Jonathan. 1991. *Savage Inequalities.* New York: Crown.

Meadows, Donella H., Dennis L. Meadows, and Jorgen Randers. 1992. *Beyond the Limits: Confronting Global Collapse—Envisioning a Sustainable Future.* Post Mills, VT: Chelsea Green.

National Commission on Excellence in Education. 1984. *A Nation at Risk: The Full Account.* Cambridge, MA: USA Research.

Rich, Bruce. 1994. *Mortgaging the Earth: The World Bank, Environmental Impoverishment, and the Crisis of Development.* Boston: Beacon.

Rodgers, Harrell E., Jr. 1987. *Poor Women, Poor Families: The Economic Plight of America's Female-Headed Households.* Armonk, NY: M. E. Sharpe.

Sitarz, Daniel, ed. 1994. *Agenda 21: The Earth Summit Strategy to Save Our Planet.* Boulder, CO: EarthPress.

U.S. Department of Education. 1987. *Schools That Work: Educating Disadvantaged Children.* Washington, DC: U.S. Government Printing Office.

Wilson, William Julius. 1987. *The Truly Disadvantaged: The Inner City, the Underclass, and Public Policy.* Chicago: University of Chicago Press.

World Commission on Environment and Development. 1987. *Our Common Future.* New York: Oxford University Press (The Brundtland Report).

Web Sites

Bureau of Labor Statistics

http://stats.bls.gov/blshome.html

This site provides links to data collected by the U.S. government's Bureau of Labor Statistics. It also provides links to other web sites containing relevant data.

Educational Index

http://www.educationindex.com/educator/

This site contains links to other sites covering the full spectrum of education-related topics and problems.

Global Economic and Social Development

http://www.un.org/esa/

This web site, a good jumping-off place for searches, provides links to information about development issues around the world, including aging, children, families, human development, natural resources, alleviation of poverty, women and gender, and youth.

United Nations Educational, Scientific and Cultural Organization (UNESCO)

http://www.education.unesco.org

This site is the homepage of UNESCO's Educational Information Service. It provides links to a variety of international education sources, from news of programs and activities to web sites of IGOs and NGOs involved with international education to statistics and databases.

The World Bank Group

http://www.worldbank.org

This site provides access to World Bank statistics, other data, reports, departments, and programs. The site is very useful for information on a wide variety of issues concerning global inequity, development programs, and sustainable development.

PART ▪ THREE

Globalization, Victimization, and Empowerment

In this section, we turn to major issues involving victimization and empowerment. By victimization *we mean those social processes that substantially reduce the social status, quality of life, life opportunities, and/or the sense of worth of selected categories of people. For example, most societies around the world are male dominated. As a result, women have lower status, work harder, have less food available to them, have less opportunity to find profitable employment or receive an education, and possess lower self-esteem than do their male counterparts. Conversely,* empowerment *means providing people with the tools and resources they need to live healthy, productive, and dignified lives.*

Often, people who experience sexual or racial discrimination are seen by sociologists, among others, as victims of unjust societies. However, in many ways people who cannot obtain quality health care or education also are victims of social systems that substantially reduce the quality of their lives. Similarly, individuals who live in fear of violence or crime or who find that substantial portions of their nation's wealth is drained by crime or diverted into needless arms races rather than being allocated to meet more basic human needs may also be considered victims—of malfunctioning social systems.

In this section, we look at issues of victimization and empowerment in several key areas of the global scene. At first, empowerment might seem to be a straightforward matter of giving powerless people the resources they need to live more effective lives. However, this is not always the case. In designing empowerment efforts, a number of factors have to be taken into consideration (e.g., the level of personal social and psychological development of targeted persons) so that efforts can be directed toward the most effective intervention.

Life-Support Systems and Empowerment

In the introduction to Part Two, we discussed three life-support systems that are essential for human survival—the planetary life-support system (biosphere), the societal life-support system (sociosphere), and the personal (primary group) life-support system. These three systems are interrelated and are not mutually exclusive. That is, empowerment at the planetary level most certainly affects the societal and personal levels and vice versa. This explains why some interventions for empowerment must be directed at all three levels. For example, efforts to empower women probably should be directed at all three levels. The primary life-support system often has different implications for males than for females. For one thing, females in various societies are often fed after males have had their fill. When food is scarce, therefore, females are more likely than males to experience malnourishment, although they are usually responsible for the feeding of other members of the family and the community.

On the other hand, societal empowerment may involve international conferences and campaigns that raise awareness of the global plight of women and address women's problems as human rights issues. These activities may pressure nation-states to enact laws to outlaw the worst practices against women, as well as to see that food is adequately distributed to all citizens, especially female citizens. Societal programs may have to be developed to change attitudes and behaviors toward women and female children in the most intimate groups to which they belong, such as their families, to encourage allowing them to receive their fair share of available food, an issue discussed in Chapter 9.

At the same time, some issues may be better addressed at the level of the planetary life-support system. For instance, dealing with environmental problems may involve empowering people everywhere to insist that their needs take priority over those of corporations and governments, especially when it comes to issues of the exploitation of scarce resources or the destruction of the environment.

Some issues can best be addressed by empowering people at the societal level. In the United States, for example, our approach to controlling illegal drugs (Chapter 12) should be a matter of national debate and possibly should involve a national policy shift. If people were empowered by participation in such a debate, they might be more inclined to lobby for government programs that might lead to the possibility of the emergence of a more effective approach to illegal drugs. Finally, some issues might best be handled by empowering people at the personal life-support system strata. For example, in the United States, giving families more choice in choosing the educational setting for their children could empower them to obtain quality education for their children (Chapter 12).

Personal Development and Empowerment

Effective empowerment also involves looking at the needs of individuals who themselves are at different levels of social and psychological development. We will look at the three levels of personal development to illustrate this point. These three levels represent increasingly more effective and adequate psychosocial adaptation. We can view them as a sequence of stages through which persons may pass. The person must reach level one before he or she can reach level two, and so forth. This is a normal direction of development for the individual, but many factors, including age and a challenging yet supportive social environment, must be in place in order for people to traverse all stages of development. Transitions from one level to the next are never automatic and may be psychologically difficult. Since these levels represent ranges or degrees of development, those in the advanced ranges of one level resemble those in the early stages of the next higher level and vice versa.

Level One

Psychologically speaking, people at this stage may be said to possess an impulse-self. They are their desires and fears, their pleasures and pains, simply because they are unable to stand back and gain perspective or control over these biological and psychological components of themselves. Socially speaking, this developmental stage can be called the preconventional stage because social rules and roles (conventions) have not become an effective part of the individual's makeup. People at this level may conform to rules, but they do so out of fear of punishment or hope for reward rather than out of any appreciation for the significance these rules have.

At this stage people tend to identify the self with physical things like possessions and territory and to view the social worth of people in concrete terms. They greatly admire (or fear) people with more wealth or power or people who are physically large. They may esteem God simply because he is more powerful than anyone else. People in this mode of adaptation are not fully able to grasp the social perspectives of others. Therefore, people in the preconventional stage do not realize how much they themselves may be projecting their own wants and fears on others, that is, seeing others not as they are but in light of how those others relate to their own wants or fears.

In addition, people at this stage develop relatively simplistic and unsophisticated worldviews. Constructing a view of social life that is insufficiently complex, neither taking into account the perspectives of others nor using generally accepted evidence, they are likely to fall prey to conspiracy theories that explain present frustration in terms of an evil group secretly working behind the scenes of history (Lipset and Raab, 1970). Such a view enables them to project their pain and frustration on an external target. Marginal persons who have experienced life as a series of setbacks and frustrations are likely to operate at this level.

Simplistic views of social issues lead to simplistic solutions. For example, the hope that a savior, divine or otherwise, will intervene to set things right has frequently been a part of peasant movements throughout history (Wilson, 1973; Hobsbawm, 1959). Sometimes the belief is that a single dramatic action (like a bombing) is all that it will take to bring about transformation of the social order. The "paranoid style" of American politics (Hofstadter, 1965), also referred to as the "politics of unreason" (Lipset and Raab, 1970), reflects this level of adaptation. People who enter adulthood at this level of adaptation may be called sociopaths (Kegan, 1990; Yablonsky, 1970). Also called antisocial personalities, extreme sociopaths are in repeated conflict with society, do not feel guilt, and are unable to learn from experience or punishment or to take into account the well-being of others.

Empowerment at Level One

What is most needed to empower persons at level one are such basics as a steady job, a decent home life, a modicum of social respect, and recognition in the form of social roles that are not coercive. For people at level one, empowerment requires a degree of social participation and the experience of security, predictability, and acceptance, along with simple, reliable rewards for conforming behavior. Such empowerment can help prevent social pathologies of crime, interpersonal violence, and paranoid rejection of others.

But for such empowerment to occur, brutal conditions of life, punitive working and family conditions, exploitation, alcoholism, and conditions of social disorganization all need to be eradicated from human societies. Obviously, this is easier said than done, but we need to recognize that these conditions tend to breed people who, as adolescents and adults, are not capable of leading socially productive lives *in the modern world. Economic growth, literacy, and redistribution of social benefits that go beyond physical care are required. Conditions of social destitution contribute to the deep psychological disempowerment of people in the form of the absence of moral and social development that characterizes this level. This absence leads to the forms of social pathology that are so disturbing to most people.*

If the empowerment process is to be successful for people at level one, care must be exercised. Traditional practices, especially the exploitation of women and children under conditions of patriarchy, need to be abolished, but efforts in this direction may harden attitudes in ways that simply perpetuate the problem. It is important for persons at this level to learn a degree of compromise. For example, they may need to learn that believing in the adage "half a loaf is better than none" is superior to blowing up the "bakery" (or the society's institutions).

Level Two

Level two people—those who have developed a self that can negotiate roles and rules—are defined by membership in groups. They possess a rule-role self. This is the level of group-centered, or ethnocentric, people and can be called the conventional stage. *The ability to grasp the perspectives of others, at least those within one's own group, is essential at this level. An understanding of how others view one and the desire to maintain their approval gives social norms a psychological potency absent at level one. The sense of having a unique personal identity, one that is individuated from the group, however, is comparatively weak at level two. A person's sense of self at this level may go something like this: "I am a nurse, Ricardo's wife, José and Maria's mom, and a Roman Catholic."*

By and large the process of socialization in most societies seeks to produce this sense of self and this level of commitment to the society's roles and norms. At this stage the person may take part in the organized defense of the group and/or its cultural and moral codes, which are treated as absolutes by both the group and the individual. The person is able and even willing to sacrifice his or her own well-being for others in the group or for the group as a whole. But this self-sacrifice is balanced by a degree of rationality and appropriateness of response absent in level one adaption.

The more advanced stages of level two are likely to appear in pluralistic contemporary societies among the more experienced members, especially those of urban communities. In pluralistic societies a degree of toleration and cooperation is required among groups that are diverse, in competition with one another, and potentially hostile. National identity, that is, identification with the nation-state as the individual's master identity, has been the major social mechanism that has made it possible for multiethnic societies to flourish in modern times. A critical characteristic that emerges at this level is the ability to see rules and roles as at least partially negotiable within a larger framework of consensus. People who are different need not be seen as a threat, and people can be judged as "good people" even if they believe differently and have different goals than oneself. People at level two can view social reform as a matter of changing rules *rather than as a matter of finding the evil culprits and destroying them (a stage one response). Power does not define who is right. In fact, people at level two can recognize that social power must be made to reflect the moral consensus of the group, and that moral consensus may require negotiation and interpretation.*

Empowerment at Level Two

The removal of all ascriptive barriers to full participation and advancement in a society is necessary for empowerment at this level. That is, all limitations placed on people because of gender, race, ethnicity, social class, or other arbitrary social statuses must be removed. People at level two need opportunities to make a valuable and valued contribution to society and to develop talents and abilities. For those in the early stages of level two identification with a group, the recognition of collective rights is essential. First, the ethnic, national, religious, or cultural group as such must gain recognition and be established as legitimate in the larger community.

As people become more individuated or psychologically differentiated from their groups, it becomes especially important for them to have the chance to participate in voluntary groups that represent their interests, beliefs, and value commitments, such as labor unions, political parties, community groups, church groups, and so forth. This sort of participation enables persons to have some access to the decision-making and opinion-forming institutions of the larger society. These institutions provide training in compromise, bargaining, and negotiation. The acquisition of such skills requires a degree of tolerance and mutual respect. People at this level are capable of negotiating not only who gets what but also the rules of the game. They also are capable of taking the perspectives of others into account both antagonistically, as in competitive situations, and sympathetically, as in cooperative ones. The real challenge to a society, however, is whether people limit their perspective, associating only with those they perceive as like themselves. This is, after all, the ethnocentric level of normally socialized persons. True dialogue, in which persons come to know the perspectives of others in such depth that they risk conversion to the other's viewpoint, is usually too threatening to persons at level two.

Level Three

Persons at this level have constructed a personal or autonomous self. That is, they believe themselves able to play roles in society but understand that their identities are not limited to these roles. At this level people come to question society's taken-for-granted beliefs and values. They are able to see the world from the perspectives of many persons, that is, to recognize that society is made up of many persons who all have legitimate but often conflicting claims. People at this level realize that they alone must choose their beliefs, make their own moral judgments, form commitments, and suffer the consequences of these decisions. There are many stages within this level, but in modern societies there is a strong cultural and social pressure to achieve at least the first stages of level three autonomy. Often, many persons who speak as if they have achieved this level of adaptation actually have not. People at this stage may be called postconventional, *as they have the ability to transcend the conventions of their membership groups.*

Empowerment at Level Three

The buzzword "empowerment" probably was coined for people of level three. Here the issue of empowerment has to do with enabling people to pursue social and cultural alternatives, experiment, and adopt new "paradigms" (perspectives or worldviews). Whereas level one empowerment meant having an accepted and largely uncoerced role in contemporary society, and level two empowerment involved political rights and equal opportunities, empowerment at this level seems to mean having the chance to be authentic. By this we mean the chance to act on commitments to higher principles and to pursue new untested ideas. In one sense, society cannot grant these opportunities and perspectives. These are postconventional and world-centered (rather than society-centered) perspectives. Harvard psychologist Robert Kegan has studied the many ways in which contemporary American society demands that people function at level three, but he also points out how difficult this demand is to fulfill, causing us to feel that we are "in over our heads" (Kegan, 1994).

Self-knowledge is important in this type of empowerment. The two greatest dangers people encounter when

they are approaching this level are a pseudouniversalism that is really an unrealistic, or overly idealized, group ideology of holism and tolerance, or a postmodern cynicism and narcissism. In the first scenario, people believe that they have adopted a new paradigm that would make the world rosy if everyone else would believe it. These people believe that they have achieved a high level of psychological and spiritual growth—usually fairly painlessly. They become involved in self-exploration that is really disguised self-indulgence. The other scenario involves the adoption of an extreme relativism that ultimately denies all values; thus, all courses of action become equally pointless. Either of these reactions is disempowering. Actual involvemen in groups committed to dialogue and to solving global or local problems is an antidote to either of these tendencies. Today's global arena offers many opportunities for involvement in issues and in dialogue.

Conclusions

In this introduction we have seen that empowerment is not effective when a "one-size-fits-all" approach is employed. Some issues require focusing on one level or the other of life-support systems. In addition, people at each level of social and psychological adaptation need different things to empower them. Social change, however, must occur more holistically; it involves simultaneous changes on all three levels if social systems are to meet the needs of their members. The changes necessary to empower a person at level one require support from changes at the other two levels and vice versa.

CHAPTER ■ NINE

Women, Children, Families

Empowering the Building Blocks of Society

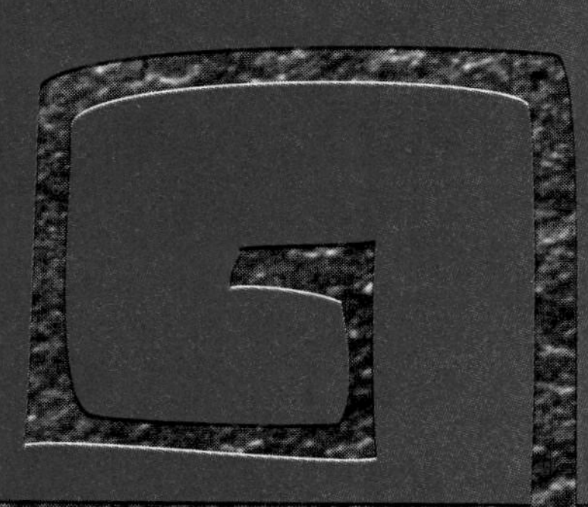

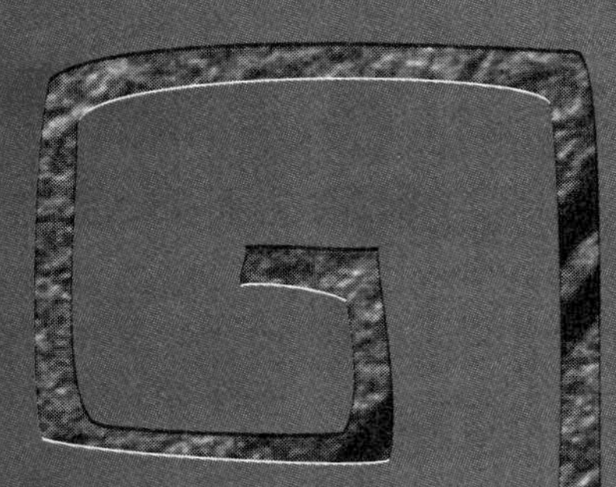

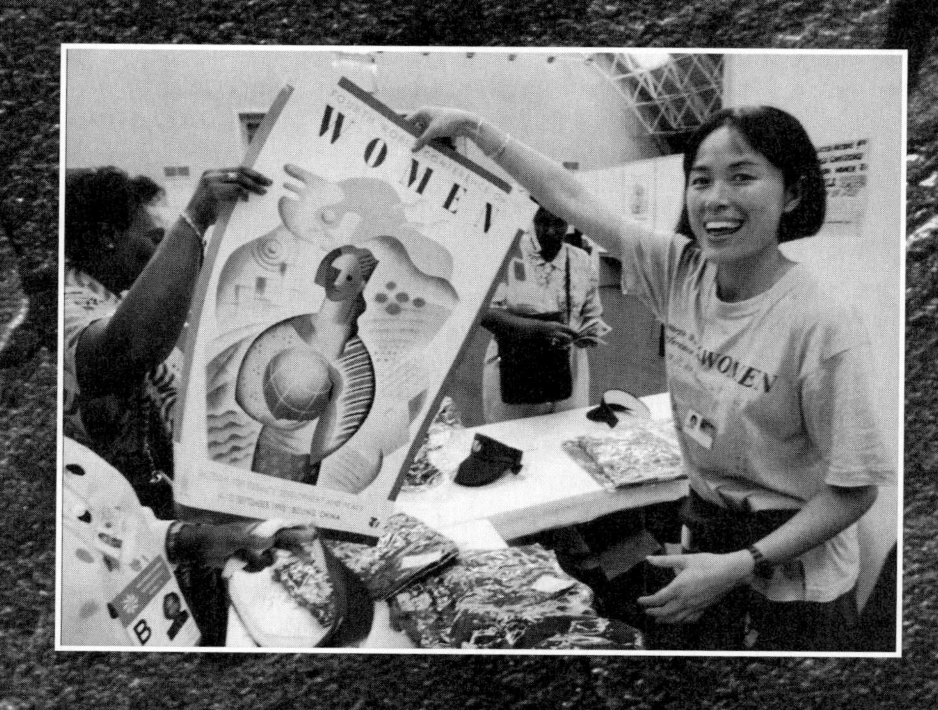

Case 1. In Pakistan in the late 1980s, a young blind girl was raped. Because of her blindness she was not able to identify the rapist. She and her family would have hidden the incident but during the rape she was impregnated. According to Islamic law, she was guilty of illegal sex. Her sentence—to be stoned to death (adapted from Rhoodie, 1989).

Case 2. In India during the early 1990s, a woman returned from the hospital with her newborn daughter. With her mother-in-law's assistance, she prepared a mixture of oil and mashed oleander seeds (which are poisonous). She then forced the mixture down the infant's throat. After burying her baby girl in a shallow, unmarked grave, she said, "I never felt any sorrow. There was a lot of bitterness in my heart toward the baby. The gods should have given me a son" (adapted from Anderson and Moore, 1993).

Case 3. According to U.S. Justice Department figures, about 1 woman in 22 (at least 2 to 4 million women) are victims of abusive violence every year in the United States (cited in Strong, DeVault, and Sayad, 1998). Of that number, about half are beaten at least three times a year. In 1992, 1,510 U.S. women were killed by husbands, former spouses, or boyfriends. That is an average of four female homicides each day (cited in Lamanna and Riedmann, 1997).

These are true stories. Are these isolated incidents? Probably not. A wealth of evidence indicates that being born female means that you are treated differently—and less fairly—than if you are born male. Many times the simple fact of being born female is hazardous to your health.

In this chapter we concentrate on families and the individuals who live in them. It is true that families include women (and children), but the typical sociological approach concentrates on the larger unit. Usually, that means that sociologists lose sight of the fact that the experiences of women and children may be different from those of males.

When people are poor, or female, or young, they are especially vulnerable to mistreatment. Unfortunately, there is a near universal tendency to exploit the weakest members of society, which in most countries includes women and children. We focus on women and children in this chapter because all too often their experiences are neglected or subsumed within those of males.

The Family and Marriage in History

Prior to industrialization, most families were units of both production and consumption. (In contrast, in Western nations today, families are primarily consumers.) Families worked together on the land or engaged in craft production. Any adult who was not married was expected to live and work in the family settings of others. Selection of marriage partners was usually not determined by love or affection. Rather, practical social and economic interests determined the choice. Often, the fathers of the couple in question had an especially large say, but sometimes even landlords' permissions had to be granted. (The landlord might want a particularly hardworking spouse for the individual who rented his land.)

In those preindustrial days, even small children were producers; they were put out to work at young ages. Frequently they labored for parents, but sometimes children were sent off as apprentices to learn a skill or to become domestic workers. Most children who were sent to work in other households seldom, if ever, saw their parents and siblings again.

In the contemporary United States, we often hear of high divorce rates. But even in preindustrial days, families were impermanent. Divorce was not the culprit; marriages ended because of premature death. In those days, women often died from complications of pregnancy and in childbirth. Adult men frequently died of accident, injury, or disease.

Family Types over Time

Family life in Europe and other Western countries has gone through three dominant phases since the sixteenth century. In the first phase, the usual family form was a type of nuclear family, but a family firmly enmeshed with other kin and the community. Over time, the notion that individuals could choose their own spouse became the norm. But even then, love or emotional attachment was the least of considerations. A woman wanted a good provider, someone who could support her and her children. A man wanted a healthy woman who could successfully bear and raise children and run the household (although married working-class women often contributed to the household finances by taking in boarders, doing laundry for pay, or performing paid work at home, e.g., making suspenders or hemming trousers). Other considerations, like attractiveness, a good personality, or a sense of humor, were minor.

Over time, this type of family evolved in Western societies into a second phase, or transitional family form, first found among the upper classes. Here the nuclear family became a separate entity, distinct from ties to other kin and the outside community. The importance of marital and parental love increased, but so did the authoritarian power of husbands and fathers.

Gradually, a third type of family form emerged. This third phase looks familiar to most of us. The family is tied by close emotional bonds, there is a norm of privacy within the family, and the major preoccupation is the successful raising of children. Unlike its predecessors, this family is oriented more toward consumption than toward production. Husbands and fathers work outside the home for a salary. Home and work are spatially separated (Giddens, 1991).

Recent Transformations in Family Life. A great deal of diversity in family forms still exists in the world today. In some of the less developed parts of the world, the old traditional family still exists, largely unchanged. But in most Third World countries, widespread changes are occurring. The origins of these changes in family life are complex, but several factors are identifiable. The spread of Western culture, especially through movies and television, has introduced the notion of romantic love. In addition, the power of national governments replaces the influence of villages and tribes. As an example of this influence, some governments today often deliberately attempt to alter family life by advocating smaller family size, whereas other governments encourage couples to have more children. The People's Republic of China is the classic example of a government advocating smaller families; the former Soviet Union (which suffered so many deaths in both World Wars and in the Stalin purges) encouraged women to have more children by providing a public award called "Heroine of the People" for women who had seven children. Another catalyst to change in families is rapid urbanization in the Third World. In Chapter 5 we saw that people perceive that employment and educational opportunities are in cities. Mass migrations to urban areas are the result of this perception. As it spatially separates families, this migration further weakens the influence of the extended family.

Sociologist Anthony Giddens identifies six changes occurring worldwide to families (Giddens, 1991):

1. The influence of family and kin is declining. Individualism (the belief that the happiness and welfare of individuals comes before the rights of the family or state) is spreading.
2. Throughout the world there is a strong trend toward the free choice of spouse.
3. The rights of women (in both the initiation of marriage and in decision making within the family) are increasingly recognized as legitimate.
4. A wider choice concerning who may be considered an appropriate spouse is becoming the norm. No longer is a potential spouse automatically excluded on grounds of group membership (race, religion, nationality, social class, or ethnicity).
5. In many nations more sexual freedom is accepted. In the not-so-distant past, traditional families were exceedingly restrictive about sexual behavior. There was a clear consensus about what was and was not acceptable sexual behavior. For instance, throughout much of the world, divorce was considered largely unacceptable as was premarital sex. But today there is no longer consensus about sexual norms in many societies, which leaves individuals increasingly freer to make up their own minds about how they are going to behave sexually.
6. There is a general trend toward extending children's rights. Most governments have passed laws protecting children from arbitrary decisions that might be against the best interests of children.

Patriarchy

Some of the difficulties of women and children stem from age-old traditions of patriarchy. **Patriarchy** is the practice of giving males more status, power, and authority than women, both at home and in the larger society. The suffix *-archy* means "the rule of." Patriarchy then literally means "the rule of fathers." A form of social hierarchy, patriarchy not only endows males with authority at home and in the political arena, it also decrees such a lowly status for women and children that they are virtually without rights.

There is a general trend toward extending children's rights, but many children, such as this young Bangladeshi boy, are forced to work long hours at menial labor, under dangerous and unhealthy conditions.

In the family context, patriarchy usually refers to the family form in which fathers had control over wives and children, even adult unmarried children. Patriarchy defined and directed all social relations between the sexes and between parents and children (Gordon, 1988).

Patriarchy, in one version or another, is near universal, so much so that many people assume it has always existed. But that is not true. In fact, considering the relatively short time humans have been on this earth, patriarchy is a recent invention (probably dating back about ten thousand years). **Male dominance,** the right of males to control women's behavior and treat women as inherently inferior, is both a socializing and a structural force. Male dominance has tended to intensify during historical periods when state power emerged. Social institutions (political, economic, religious, educational, military) in virtually every society throughout history have been developed by men, and even today tend to be dominated by males. Patriarchy exists at all levels of society all over the world. This male dominance almost inevitably results in the subordination of women.

Nowhere in the world today do societies exist in which men as a group possess less wealth, status, and influence than women. There is no known society in which women as a group are more powerful than men. That includes the United States, despite women's liberation, the feminist movement, and a rhetoric of equality. Throughout the world, women's primary roles are seen as those of homemaker and child rearer. Industrialization and the shift toward wage labor in the nineteenth century tied women more closely to these cultural roles. Prior to industrialization women's work was visible and perceived as needed. Once "work" was defined as wage labor performed by men outside the home, the notion that women were tied to hearth and home became the standard that virtually everyone accepted. Only middle- and upper-class families attained this norm; working-class families generally needed income from female members of the household.

Historically, then, gender inequalities and male dominance are deeply rooted. But if we go back in human history to the time when most people were hunters and gatherers, not all men had a monopoly on wealth, status, and power. There is a linkage between economic productivity and women's status. Anthropologists tell us that because the work women did in hunting and gathering societies—gathering roots, berries, and fruit—was crucial, people living then recognized it as essential for day-to-day survival. Because of their work women had more power and their status was high in many tribal groups (Giddens, 1991). The separation of work and home brought about by the industrial revolution made women's contributions less visible and less valued (Giddens, 1991).

History of the Status of Women and Children

Gender inequality, discrimination, and oppression are found worldwide, including in advanced Western societies like our own. Poor women especially are victims. In some parts of the world, women are deprived of basic human rights by culture, or religion, or laws. For instance, in poor countries like India, infants and young girls are fed less, denied education, sexually mutilated, forced into early marriages, and sometimes bought and sold for prostitution or slave labor. In some parts of the world, wives and mothers are treated little better than hired help or baby machines. There are societies in which a wife who outlives her husband may be banished from her home, denied any inheritance, and forced to live on the streets as a beggar (Anderson and Moore, 1993). In many Third World countries, well-entrenched social and cultural attitudes decree that women are inferior.

Throughout the world women continue to be disadvantaged relative to men. This is true across a wide range of **social indicators** (ways of judging where a group ranks). As we mentioned in the first chapter, what is, or is not, considered a **social problem** (a condition affecting a significant number of people in an adverse way) varies from place to place and from time to time. Only relatively recently has the unequal treatment of women and children been defined as a social problem.

On any social indicator you select, all over the world women and girls as a group receive or possess *less* than men—less education, less compensation for the work they do, less medical care (or care of an inferior quality), fewer vocational and occupational choices, less political clout, and less prestigious positions in organized religious groups. The key question is *why*? Why do women and girls as a group receive less? The traditional division of labor that assigns tasks by gender has meant that throughout most of recorded human history, women have been accorded fewer rewards.

Sociologists usually define rewards as money (or wealth), power, and prestige (or status). Until recently, most people, including women themselves, never questioned this unequal treatment. (In the United States, although women's rights activism dates from the 1840s, nineteenth-century feminists were a distinct minority.) It was considered "natural" and therefore inevitable. In a sense, there was an unwritten contract: Women would be dependent on men for sustenance, protection, and safety. In return they agreed to provide men with respect, housework, children, and sexual favors. It was an agreed-upon exchange. As the twentieth century draws to a close, however, more and more people (perhaps mostly women) question this exchange. As divorce and desertion rates increase, many women challenge these old assumptions of male dominance.

What we are really talking about here is **social inequality**—the fact that women as a group have unequal access to society's valued resources, goods, and services. Social inequality is a significant force in people's lives. It influences our chances of getting an education, holding a good job, being able to support a decent and adequate standard of living, and having a long and healthy life. Social inequality even affects how we think and behave in our everyday activities (see the box "FYI: Not a Pretty Picture").

Gender Stereotypes

Stereotypes about women and men persist partly because many people assume that gender role expectations and biological sex are the same thing. They are not. Sociologists call the physical differences between men and women **sex.** The evidence is inconclusive about what, if any, effect biological sexual differences have on human behavior and personality. What is clear is that every society places different behavioral expectations on children based on their sex. These different expectations based on sex are called **gender roles,** or expectations about which behaviors are appropriate for girls and boys or men and women.

When they are born, humans are usually considered either male or female, but their gender roles are socially learned. Very little human behavior is instinctual. Most of what we consider inborn and innate is learned, but learned so young and so well that most people do not acknowledge that their behavior is the product of *socialization* (the lifelong social experience by which individuals develop human potential and learn the patterns of their culture).

In recent years, a considerable amount of empirical research on gender roles has been conducted. But until the last few years, research studies were considered to be gender blind. That meant that women were invisible or viewed as unimportant or uninteresting. This gender-blind attitude clearly has

FYI

Not a Pretty Picture

Journalist Joan Beck, who based her research on a UN Human Development Report, writes that since 1970, women around the globe have progressed considerably in education and health but still lag far behind men in earnings and political power. According to Beck:

- The market value of women's work that is unpaid or underpaid, and so goes unaccounted for—and underappreciated—in the total world economy: $11 trillion.
- Two-thirds of the total amount of work women do is unpaid in both developing and developed countries.
- The percentage of all paid and unpaid work that is done by women: 53 percent in developing countries, 51 percent in industrial countries.
- The average number of working hours a day for married women in industrial countries who are employed and have children: 11 hours.
- The percentage of seats in legislatures held worldwide by women: 10 percent.
- The percentage of cabinet-level posts held worldwide by women: 6 percent.
- Among the 1.3 billion people in the world living in poverty, the percentage who are women: 70 percent.
- The number of children (mostly girls in Asia) forced into prostitution: 1 million.
- The number of girls who suffer genital mutilation: 100 million.
- The number of countries in which women hold at least 30 percent of decision-making economic and political jobs: 6 (Denmark, Finland, the Netherlands, Norway, the Seychelles, and Sweden).
- The proportion of girls and women who are raped over a lifetime: 1 in 6.
- The average wage of women, worldwide, compared to men: 75 percent.
- *The number of countries in the world where women are as well off as men: None.* [italics added.]

Source: Joan Beck, "Not a Pretty Picture." *The Chicago Tribune,* August 20, 1995, Section 4:3.

political or economic ramifications but in some areas it has life-or-death implications. For instance, until recently, when new medicines or procedures were tested, they were tested only on males. The logic was that one could generalize the findings to everyone, male or female. We now know in many cases that this is not so.

Until recently, the social division of labor using gender as the criteria for who did what also seemed natural and appropriate. When there is a great deal of work to be done and perhaps few machines or technology to help, assigning some tasks to males and others to females is an efficient way of dividing up the necessary work. But in much of the world what was originally a convenient division of labor is no longer necessary. For example, in many parts of the globe, their lesser physical strength than males does not exclude females from jobs previously requiring manual labor. Now machines (run by either males or females) often perform such work. Similarly, it is no longer true that only females can nourish infants. The development and widespread distribution of infant formulas mean that males can feed babies too.

Another example of gender stereotypes concerns the ways that patriarchy perpetuates male dominance through the use of language. Most languages, including English, often ignore women or subsume them with men. Examples include the generic terms "he" and "mankind" to refer to people in general.

Female "qualifiers" specify that women holding certain jobs represent an exception to the rule, for example, "woman attorney" or "female doctor." Communication and interpersonal behavior also reflect male dominance. For instance, research has found that contrary to public opinion, in the public arena men talk more than women and interrupt far more often. Males also control the topics covered in conversation (Tannen, 1990).

Current Status of Developing World Families

In 1995, the United Nations reported the following (United Nations, 1995):

- Women (half the world's population) do two-thirds of the world's work.
- Women earn one-tenth of the world's income.
- Women own one-hundredth of the world's property.

In addition, women around the globe experience unaddressed health problems far more often than do men. Women's inferior status saps their physical and emotional vitality and undermines their confidence, both of which are vital to achieving widely held goals for human progress, especially in the Third World (Heise, 1989).

Women and Work

In every country, women are crucial participants in their societies, but too often their contributions to the well-being of their families and their nation are unrecognized and unacknowledged. For example, the cheap labor of women in the poorest countries has helped create the Asian miracle, the tremendous burst of industrialization and productivity in places like South Korea.

In the Philippines and other Asian countries, large numbers of women leave their families to work in other countries as migrant (sometimes called "guest") workers. Much of the money they make is sent back home, relieving pressure on their governments to provide enough jobs and social services to their citizens. Because of this, home governments are reluctant to closely supervise the treatment of migrant workers. The government does not want to supervise working conditions, abuses of workers (including sexual abuses), or wages. These authorities generally prefer to let the situation of female migrant workers continue unregulated—because they do not want to deal with the problems they know exist (Human Rights Watch, 1995).

The majority of female migrant workers are domestic servants. Female migrants who work as domestics face serious problems. Because they are not citizens of the country in which they work, they lack legal protection. These women have no rights of citizenship, no families to stand up for them, and no permanent ties to the countries in which they work. This means that they are easy to exploit. In addition, in the host countries, women are frequently viewed as lesser beings, so they suffer exploitation and discrimination based on their gender too. The work they do as maids and domestic workers is not respected and, consequently, is underpaid (Human Rights Watch, 1995). The isolation they experience as domestics, frequently combined with a "slave-owner" mentality among their employers, sometimes leads to serious mistreatment, including withholding of wages, beatings, and rape.

The UN's International Labor Office says that most migrant women workers come from the Philippines, but increasingly they have come from Sri Lanka, Indonesia, India, Pakistan, and Thailand (Human Rights Watch, 1995). These migrant women work primarily in the Middle East (particularly Saudi Arabia) but also in Singapore and other parts of Asia. You might ask: Why do they put up with low wages and harsh treatment rather than leave? Remember that these women (and their families) perceive few options in their home countries.

The Feminization of Poverty. The work of women in low-paid jobs at home or abroad, in part-time work, and in the informal economy and the growing trend toward single-parent households have contributed to a worldwide trend. This trend has been labeled the **feminization of poverty**—an increase in the proportion of poor people who are female. The term emphasizes that now the poorest of the poor tend to be women and their children. From 1970 to 1990, the number of rural women living in poverty increased 50 percent, reaching a figure of 565 million women worldwide (New Internationalist, 1995). The reasons for this increase are complicated, but certainly one factor is that as men leave their families to seek work in distant cities, more women are left to head rural households whose members live in poverty.

Poor women are especially vulnerable to discrimination and oppression. In much of the world, poor women are not educated or, at best, are barely educated. Few jobs exist and there is much poverty. These women do what they believe they must to ensure their own survival and the survival of their families. The situation has perhaps even worsened in recent decades, as business and industry practices have changed in the industrial nations, thus creating a worldwide shift to more precarious employment. True, jobs have been provided but, in many cases, job security has diminished.

Manufacturing jobs in the industrialized nations have been increasingly shifted overseas, and foreign women have been hired to fill the jobs. But these Third World women earn only a fraction of what workers in the industrial nations earn when they do the same work. The wages paid to these women are low even by the standards of their own countries. Typically, women around the world receive wages 30 to 40 percent lower than those of men doing the same jobs (Human Rights Watch, 1995).

Working for wages, even unfair wages, is important for women; it changes the balance of power in families, especially when women provide a substantial portion of the household income. When women work for wages, they are in a better position to demand fewer children, and women with fewer children find it easier to work.

In many cases, jobs in the formally paid economy are scarce or nonexistent in the Third World. Many women in these nations work in the *informal economy* (irregular and sometimes illegal work). They may do such things as sell small items on the street, find and sell firewood, and make and sell home brewed alcohol. This kind of work pays very little and cannot be counted on. For those women who remain in their home village or in a large city in the home country, long hours of labor are required to make very little money.

Third World Women's Unpaid Work. Unpaid family work includes all the necessary tasks needed to keep a family and household running. It includes attending to the emotional needs of family members, meeting the practical needs of dependent family members (children, the disabled, the elderly), and maintaining the house.

In the Western world, the *family-based economy* (in which all members, including children, directly contribute economically to the family) dates from the seventeenth century to the mid-eighteenth century. Productive activity for household use was considered work; all members of the household, including children, contributed directly to household labor (Anderson, 1993).

For the majority of people in the underdeveloped parts of the world, productive activities and the activities in the household remain closely connected. The household is the basic unit of the economy because most production occurs in the home. The family works as a unit to provide for necessities. Usually, the father serves as the "boss," with the wife and children (and sometimes the adults' aged parents) contributing what they can. (In the United States, the nineteenth-century household depicted on the long-running television series *Little House on the Prairie* was an example of a family-based economy.)

Research confirms that all over the world, women typically work more hours than men do. This work includes both paid employment and the unpaid work they perform at home (see Table 9–1). Who does housework is an indicator of how a society constructs gender. For example, in American households, the vast majority of the time used for housework is spent by the wife, about 70 percent on average. Men perform a small selective amount of housework—typically cooking rather than cleaning or doing the laundry or ironing (Ollenburger and Moore, 1998). When only women do the tiring, repetitive tasks that must be performed for the family to live, the social dominance of men and the low social status of women are illustrated.

In Third World countries, housework is overwhelmingly the domain of girls and women. Even in some Western countries, such as in Europe and modern Japan, women do almost all of the housework. The United States is more egalitarian with regard to housework than most of the countries in the world.

Everywhere, it is usually women who do household labor, such as tending children, preparing food, and taking care of the house. But in the villages of the Third World, women, nevertheless, put in extraordinarily long days of other unpaid labor for their families. For instance, in Africa and other parts of the world, there is a shortage of firewood. Women may spend many hours a week searching for, and

TABLE 9–1 The Female Disadvantage

COUNTRY	ADULT LITERACY RATE OF WOMEN	LIFE EXPECTANCY OF WOMEN	MATERNAL MORTALITY PER 100,000 LIVE BIRTHS	WOMEN'S MANUFACTURING WAGES AS A PERCENTAGE OF MEN'S MANUFACTURING WAGES
China	71%	71 yrs.	95	NA
Costa Rica	95	79 yrs.	60	74%
Egypt	37	65 yrs.	170	68
El Salvador	69	69 yrs.	300	94
Hong Kong	87	82 yrs.	82	69
Kenya	67	57 yrs.	650	74
Paraguay	90	72 yrs.	160	66
South Korea	96	75 yrs.	130	50
Zambia	69	49 yrs.	940	73

Source: The World's Women 1995: Trends & Statistics, Human Development Report, 1996.

hauling home, wood for cooking. (The example of cooking with wood also illustrates a health hazard particular to women in these regions of the world. The smoke produces carcinogenic pollutants that are the equivalent of smoking 20 packs of cigarettes a day [Anderson and Moore, 1993].) In India, women and girls collect cow dung, pat it into flat rounds to dry, and burn it as fuel. Solar-powered cooking stoves have been invented, and some areas of the undeveloped world are beginning to use them. They save the woman of the house untold hours of hard labor, to say nothing of being better for her health.

Another problem is the issue of potable water (water that is safe to consume). In much of the world, safe water is scare. It is usually the job of women (or of children) to haul it to the home. Sometimes this involves a journey of many miles several times a week. Add to this job cooking, caring for children, working in the garden or in fields, cleaning the house and washing clothes, and you have a very long workday and workweek. These jobs represent unpaid and unrewarded work that for the most part is invisible and unacknowledged. For today's world, unpaid labor is not considered "real" work because no wage is earned. It is not counted by governments or acknowledged by most men as a vital component of family life and survival.

Health Issues

One of life's basic necessities is physical health. At first glance, you might think it is something solely determined by individuals—by their diet, their genetic background, and their health habits. But the reality is that physical health is greatly influenced by social and cultural factors, one of the most crucial of which is gender. Gender roles influence how long we are likely to live and what we will die from. Sociologist Margaret Andersen observes that the possibility that a person will encounter stress, become overweight, have hypertension, or fall chronically ill is significantly influenced by the person's sex (Andersen, 1993).

Although there are significant differences among various Third World countries, one common denominator is that the majority of people continue to live in dire poverty. Typically, most families in the less developed countries are poorly housed, poorly nourished, and chronically diseased. They have barely enough to eat, so malnutrition is a fact of life. Rarely do these families have enough potable water, so dysentery and other waterborne diseases are common. Health services are thinly spread and financially out of reach for millions of people, particularly women and children.

American writer Henry Thoreau (1817–1862) said that "The masses of men live lives of quiet desperation." His observation is particularly relevant to Third World women today. In some societies, there are cultural disparities based on gender. For example, norms specify routines for eating and which foods are permissible for women to eat. Many cultures also stipulate that males eat first; women may eat anything that remains, assuming any food is left. In places where this is the norm, food is seldom available in sufficient quantity that everyone gets enough. This means that women may be weaker, smaller, more lethargic, and more disease prone and have shorter lives than their husbands.

In many developing nations there are no public systems of social security to cushion the unemployment, sickness, or death of the family wage earner, so the threat of a destitute old age always looms over the future. Although this is true for most residents of Third World countries, it is particularly true for women in these countries. In industrial countries, the life expectancies of women tend to be longer than those of men. That is not true in Third World nations, where women die of the conditions we have mentioned, plus complications of childbirth.

The Status of Children

In developing countries, socioeconomic setting combines with poverty and ignorance to limit the choices open to the family. Earlier we mentioned that the weakest members of a society are the most exploited. Children are members of society, but they cannot survive alone. That means that the problems of their society affect their lives. They are particularly vulnerable to exploitation, both within the family and outside of it. In parts of the Third World, children (particularly girls) suffer from malnutrition and outright starvation. (It's true that some U.S. children suffer from malnutrition, but food is generally available in sufficient quality and quantity for children in this country.)

Experts argue that there is enough food to offer everyone in the world enough to eat, but the problem is poor distribution and lack of purchasing power. Infants and small children are particularly vulnerable to this shortage. In southern Asia, 30 percent of babies are born undernourished because their mothers have an inadequate diet. Malnutrition tends to become a way of life for most girls. Often, their physical growth is affected. One such effect is the formation of narrow pelvises, which may later cause problems during childbirth (Dorkenoo, 1994). Chapter 10 discusses these issues in more detail.

In the Third World, children from rural areas also have extensive duties and chores such as carrying water and wood, taking care of younger children, and herding animals. These duties fall on them at a very young age (sometimes as young as six or seven) (Reuters Service, 1996). Many children are forced to work long hours at menial labor to supplement a meager family income. This work is often dangerous or has long-term health hazards, but the money the children earn outweighs these issues for families. Many employers prefer children because children are easily intimidated and they are not organized into unions. The International Labor Organization reports that at least 73 million young children are engaged in child labor worldwide (Reuters Service, 1996). Two-thirds of these child workers live and work in Asia. Most of the rest are from Africa or Latin America.

Children are also vulnerable to physical violence. In Brazil, it is reported that more than 200,000 children spend their lives on the streets, and 1 in 4 are murdered every day. The killing of minor children in Brazil increased by 40 percent in 1994. Since then, there has been an international outcry about the practice, but not much evidence exists that it has substantially changed. In Thailand, Sri Lanka, and the Philippines alone, the combined number of child prostitutes is put at one-half million. We discuss child prostitution in more detail later in the section on violence against girls and women.

Preference for Boys and Female Infanticide. In many parts of the world, violence and discrimination against females is endemic, and it often begins at birth. Research has documented a strong parental preference for sons throughout the world (see Map 9–1), particularly in regard to firstborns (Lindsey, 1997). Baby boys are usually greeted with thanksgiving and joy. For instance, in China, the birth of a son is called "a great happiness." The birth of a daughter is less celebrated; it is called "a small happiness." In some places the birth of a girl is worse than a small happiness; it is a tragedy, something to mourn (Anderson and Moore, 1993).

In many developing countries, sons are considered essential. They support the aging parents, a fact of life crucial in societies with no social security system or pension benefits. In many places, such as China, it

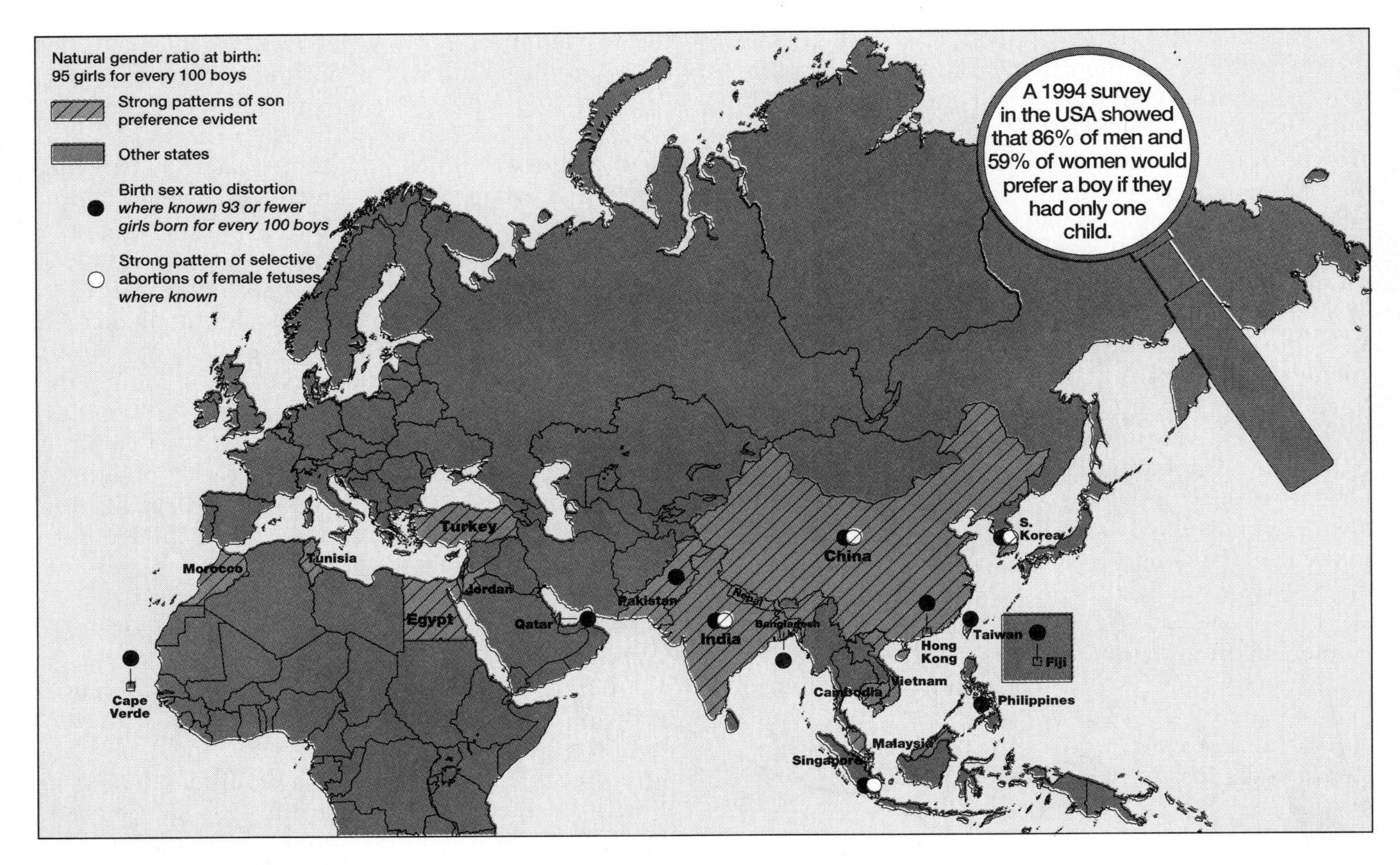

MAP 9–1 Son Preference: Early 1990s

Source: Joni Seager, *The State of Women in the World Atlas*, 2nd edition. Copyright © Myriad Editions Limited, p. 34.

is thought that only sons can conduct the proper funeral rituals that guarantee eternal happiness for a parent's soul. Daughters are viewed as liabilities, unable to perform either economic or ritual benefits (Bonvillain, 1998).

In China, India, and many other Third World countries, the preference for boys has resulted in outright neglect and even murder of girl babies. Recent census data in China and India show that in the last decade something is happening to the makeup of their populations. In both nations, the **sex ratio** (the number of males for every hundred females in a given population) has become skewed in favor of males. Demographers tell us that China's strict one child policy has resulted in a 3 to 2 male-female ratio in the population of people over the age of 15 (Goodwin, 1996). Literally *millions* of females are "missing"—aborted, killed at birth, or dead from malnutrition (because the limited food is fed to their brothers). Or they die because parents cannot, or will not, seek medical treatment for their daughters (Kristof, 1991).

In some countries such as India, discrimination and violence against females begins in the womb. Amniocentesis and ultrasound are used to determine the sex of the unborn child and if it is female, abortion follows. The destruction of daughters occurs in all socioeconomic classes in India, but mortality rates are highest among the affluent. Recently, the People's Republic of China made ultrasound illegal if the purpose is to determine the sex of the fetus.

The Chinese government is aware that the nation's sex ratio is becoming unbalanced. According to government reports, entrepreneurs have started a new business—kidnapping young women for the purpose of making them forced brides. In 1990 this trafficking

There is a strong parental preference for sons throughout the world, particularly in regard to firstborns. Thus in some countries the sex ratio has become skewed in favor of males.

in brides involved 50,000 Chinese women (Goodwin, 1996). These women are sold to families who want a bride for their son. He then rapes the female the family bought. Now "defiled" in a culture that rejects nonvirgins, she marries her rapist, as no one else values her as a bride.

India also practices **female infanticide,** or the aborting of female fetuses. In India, even the poorest village has ultrasound equipment to determine the sex of a fetus. If it is a girl, an abortion is usually performed. The Indian saying goes, "Better to spend $40 now than $400 on dowry later." Decades ago in India, a dowry was a sum of money (or goods) provided by the bride's father to help set up the young couple in marriage. Now the dowry has become an important part of premarital negotiations and refers to the wealth that the bride's parents must pay the groom as part of the marriage ceremony (Heise, 1989).

Education of Women and Children

Many young children around the world work for low wages to help support their families, but the policy of permitting them to work long hours for low wages is short-sighted. Children who work long hours cannot attend school, get an education, or improve their lives. Today's child workers typically will become tomorrow's uneducated and untrained adults, trapped eternally in poverty.

As nations industrialize, there is an increasing emphasis on teaching children how to read and write. In most countries, both girls and boys attend school, but until recently the education available differed significantly by gender. Even today, females are particularly discriminated against in education. In the world's poorest nations, especially in rural areas, the work a young girl can do is considered more important than her education. In poor countries, parents often choose to send only their sons to school or to send daughters for a significantly shorter period. Female children are frequently taken out of school to help care for younger siblings, to work around the home or in the fields, or to help their mothers trade goods. This practice is especially common in parts of Africa. There, women serve as small traders, typically selling goods that they made themselves (e.g., home-brewed beer) or as middle people, buying goods in small quantities and selling them for a little bit more. Women traders work either in the street (as street vendors), in the marketplace, or in front of their homes. Their daughters help out by selling these goods too (Stockard and Johnson, 1992).

When literacy rates of females and males are compared in much of the world, males have a much higher rate. Many research studies indicate that even when Third World females are allowed to pursue an education, most of them are channeled into traditional female majors, such as education and nursing. This results in **employment segregation,** and the female-dominated occupations receive significantly less pay and benefits. Until 25 years ago, this pattern was apparent in the United States as well.

Depriving women of an education does not simply affect individual women; it has consequences for population growth and the development of the entire society. Teaching girls to read and write has significant implications, not only politically and economically, but also for such basic decisions as family size preferences. Educated females have a "pay-off" for themselves, their families, and the country as a whole. Women who can read and write have fewer infant deaths, as high infant mortality is associated with high fertility.

Education empowers women and allows them to make crucial decisions. Research indicates that women who have completed at least primary school have fewer children than females who have no education (Barr, 1992). For women, knowing how to read and write often means marrying at a somewhat older age, working for wages, learning about family planning, and understanding the advantages of having fewer children (while providing more for those she has). There is a definite relationship between a woman's education and the number of children she has.

Violence against Women

According to many experts, there is also a relationship between discrimination against females and the violence frequently committed against them. In a very real sense, discrimination is a deadly disease. More women and girls die each day from various forms of gender-based discrimination than any other type of human rights abuse (Human Rights Watch, 1995).

Violence against women, experts agree, is global in nature, cross-cultural, and at epidemic proportions. Two questions arise: (1) Why is there so much of this kind of abuse? and (2) Why are women so often the victims? Throughout the world, the level of official and social acceptance of violence against women has seldom been an issue for public debate or government concern. For the most part, it has been considered an "individual matter" (private) or simply the consequence of being female (see the box "The Human Face of Violence against Women").

A recent development in the international efforts to protect women against violence has been to redefine such abuse and violence as a human rights issue. Lori Heise, a senior researcher at the Worldwatch Institute, maintains that violence against women is the

THE HUMAN FACE OF VIOLENCE AGAINST WOMEN

In 1991, a Saudi Arabian woman stepped off the plane at Montreal's Mirabel Airport and reported to immigration officials. She told them she was seeking refugee status in Canada. When they asked why, she replied, "Because I am a woman."

Nada (as she asked to be known in order to protect her family) had been repeatedly stoned in the streets of her country because she refused to wear a veil, was denied permission to study English, and was sexually harassed while she worked as a secretary, one of the few jobs open to her. The *mutawim,* the semiofficial religious police of Saudi Arabia, had tried to arrest her several times for not wearing the veil, but Nada—whose greatest illegal wish was to become a physical education teacher—had always managed to outrun them. Finally, she decided that as a woman and a feminist, she had no choice but to flee Saudi Arabia.

Her claim was rejected by the Canadian Refugee Board on the grounds that "she would do well to comply with the laws of general application which she criticizes" and that she should "show more consideration for the feelings of her father." Nada then went underground, where she waged her campaign through the media and was supported by human rights and women's organizations around Canada. As Nada persisted this support continued; meanwhile, other women in Canada and the United States began to make their related immigration cases public.

On January 28, 1993, partly in response to Nada's case, Bernard Valcourt, Canada's minister of immigration, announced that a new set of guidelines would be issued to immigration officers, instructing that rape, domestic violence, and gender persecution should be considered valid grounds for refugee status, and that Nada would be allowed to stay in Canada under these new guidelines.

Nurjehan Mawani, the head of the Canadian Refugee Board, released the new guidelines on March 8, 1993. Canada's initiative, she pointed out, is an international first.

Source: *Womanspirit: Moving Toward Peace and Justice, 1997 Peace Calendar.*

most pervasive but least recognized human rights issue in the world today. Included in this expanded definition of human rights abuses is violence against women and girls in the forms of female infanticide, domestic violence, murder, international sexual enslavement, rape, sexual mutilation, and extreme neglect (Heise, 1989).

According to the Women's Rights Project at Human Rights Watch, it is women's secondary status around the globe that sets them up as victims of violence, causing them to be powerless to challenge what is happening to them. If nobody sees anything wrong with the abuse, nobody sees any reason to end it (Goodwin, 1994).

Domestic Violence and Abuse of Women. For centuries **domestic violence** (physical violence within the family) has existed throughout the world. It remains an international problem. The problem of domestic violence crosses borders, classes, and cultures. Within the family, the unequal power balance legitimated by patriarchy permits wife beating to go virtually unpunished in most nations. According to Heise, in Bangkok, Thailand, it is reported that 50 percent of wives are beaten regularly by their husbands. In the barrios of Quito, Ecuador, 80 percent of women are said to have been physically abused, while in Nicaragua, 44 percent of men admit they have beaten their wives or girlfriends (Heise, 1989).

An extreme example of informally "sanctioned" domestic violence occurs in India. In the media, the practice is often called **dowry deaths** or sometimes the "burning brides." This is an all too common practice in India, especially in the north of the country, in which husbands and in-laws deliberately set a wife on fire if her parents cannot come up with the large, agreed-upon dowry. Because dowries keep escalating in amount, the Indian government outlawed them in the 1960s. But this action did not stop the practice of dowry deaths. Rather, the formal language changed; what used to be called a dowry is now called "gifts." Because the sum is so large (often equal to the annual income of the bride's father), many families have difficulty coming up with the entire amount. Following the marriage, if the gift payments are not forthcoming, both the husband and his family may begin to harass the bride. Harassment involves verbal abuse, but it may also include physical abuse. Sometimes the harassment drives the bride to suicide, thus freeing the husband to make another, perhaps more lucrative, union.

In India, thousands of young wives each year are also murdered by their husbands' families. Such deaths are usually made to look like cooking accidents, using kerosene or some other flammable liquid. The problem is widespread but notoriously underreported. In 1992, the number of reported female deaths in India attributed to in-laws was 4,785 (Ruth, 1998). Of course, accidental kitchen fire deaths do occasionally occur, but Heise reports that in urban Maharashtra and greater Bombay, 19 percent of all deaths among females between the ages of 14 to 44 are caused by accidental burns. In other Third World countries, such as Guatemala, Ecuador, and Chile, the same statistic is less than 1 percent (Heise, 1989).

International Sexual Enslavement. Forced prostitution is another form of violence against women. In the early decades of this century, in fact and fiction, there was a lot of publicity about *white slavery* (the kidnapping of white women from various parts of the world to be sold abroad for use as prostitutes). Sociologist Anthony Giddens (1996:32) defines slavery as "an extreme form of inequality, in which certain people are owned as property." As the twentieth century draws to a close, we are once again hearing of women being sold into slavery, but now Asian women and women of color are also involved in the **international slave trade,** or the kidnapping of women in one country to be sold abroad into prostitution.

Women who become victims of international prostitution are procured by several methods, including kidnapping, purchase, and false job offers (Yoon, 1996). In the 1990s, the trafficking of women from one country to another for forced prostitution involved tens of thousands of women and girls, some as young as 9 or 10 years old (Yoon, 1996).

Kidnapping threatens many females in Third World countries. Women and girls are abducted in one country and brought to another to engage in forced prostitution. Some of these kidnappings are reported, others are not. The women who are detained have a difficult time escaping or reporting the crime. In Asia, much of the prostitution business is run by gangs who kidnap women from Burma, Laos, Vietnam, and China. These gangs send the women to Thailand, where there is a thriving prostitution business aimed at tourists. It is estimated that more than 40,000 Burmese women and girls have been kidnapped and shipped to Thailand to work in this trade. But the problem of international sexual slavery is not exclusively Asian. It happens in Europe, Africa, the Middle East, and even North America (Yoon, 1996).

Kidnapped females often suffer terrible abuses, including being underfed and denied medical care. Because they are not allowed to negotiate the terms of sex, victims of forced prostitution are exposed to all kinds of health risks, especially sexually transmitted diseases. In addition, the global epidemic of AIDS means that sexual slavery is often fatal. Because kidnapped females are forced to have unprotected sex with a large number of men, they are particularly vulnerable to AIDS and other sexually transmitted diseases (Human Rights Watch, 1995).

As an alternative to infanticide, some females are sold into sexual bondage by their families. The sale of daughters happens most frequently in the Third World. For example, some Indian parents sell their daughters to Arab men. In return, the families receive needed cash and do not later have the burden of providing their daughters with a sizable dowry. In Thailand, some parents sell their baby daughters. When the girls reach the age of 9 or 10, they are resold into the prostitution circuit to serve foreign tourists. Some Third World parents say that selling their children (usually girls) into prostitution is better than letting them starve, an argument given little credibility by the global community.

Another method of procuring women for forced prostitution in a foreign country is by false promises of work. In Japan, many foreign prostitutes seem to have been brought into the country by this method. In 1989, the United Nations Human Rights Commission was told that of the approximately 300,000 foreign women working in Japan as prostitutes, 93 percent had been promised jobs as entertainers (Yoon, 1996).

You might wonder why foreign women are sought as prostitutes. There are several reasons. The demand for prostitutes may be greater than can be met by the number of local women willing to enter the trade. Another reason is that it is much more difficult for foreign women to escape from prostitution. They often do not know the language and are unfamiliar with their surroundings. In addition, many prostitution clients prefer foreign women. For instance, in Tokyo, blonde women are the most sought-after prostitutes.

One of the obstacles in dealing with the problem of traffic in women and girls for prostitution is the absence of enforcement mechanisms for international laws. Such laws exist but they are often not enforced because of corruption of law enforcement agencies, lack of government interest in the topic, and lack of sympathy by local police for the plight of foreign women (Human Rights Watch, 1995). Clearly, an international criminal court system would be useful as well as an international law enforcement agency to enforce international court decisions. Because creating structures like these is a formidable task in the face of obstacles such as corruption in the local law enforcement agencies, whose cooperation is essential, they are not likely to emerge soon.

Rape and Sexual Assault. **Rape** (forcing sexual relations on someone without consent) is another common form of violence women all over the world endure. Until recently, it was assumed that rape was a *victim-precipitated phenomenon*—an act the victim brought upon herself by being in the wrong place at the wrong time, wearing "provocative" clothing, or being "a tease." But increasingly, the activity traditionally called "rape" is being called "sexual assault." Although we may not agree on the exact definition of rape, experts do agree that it involves an act of power in which one person dominates another (Cyrus, 1993). As such, rape is increasingly being viewed as a hate crime rather than a sex crime.

Rape is sometimes a political act. (We use the word *political* to refer to any belief or behavior based on power-structured relationships or arrangements whereby one group of people is controlled by another group.) In these types of situations, which most typically occur in times of war, rebellion, or political oppression, women (and girls) are in double jeopardy. Not only are they discriminated against as females, but they are often more likely to become victims of human rights violations (Human Rights Watch, 1995).

Political rape is a way of demoralizing the enemy; the goal is to humiliate and humble. Perhaps some acts of rape in war represent simple lust or sadism, but as a weapon of war, rape works, sometimes even more effectively than killing (see the box "FYI: Rape and War"). Killing may create martyrs, thereby inspiring and strengthening the morale and solidarity of the victims. But rape of wives, mothers, sisters, and daughters not only defiles and shatters the individual women (especially in traditional societies), it also wounds morale and identity, destroying the pride and cohesion of a people. When a woman is

FYI

Rape and War

Rape and killing are chief among the vicious pleasures, a man's "recreations" on the dark side. Medieval kings reserved for themselves alone the right to do such things, at least in peacetime. In war, the privileges were distributed to the lowliest foot soldier; every man became a king.

Killing is what soldiers are trained to do. The disciplined destruction of the enemy is their military duty. In fact, soldiers may be court-martialed for not killing. Apparently, rape has always been an inevitable part of war; certainly it has been since Rome was founded upon the rape of the Sabines. In 1945, Soviet soldiers raped 2 million German women as a massive payback for everything the Nazis had done to Russia. In 1971, Pakistani troops raped more than 250,000 Bengali women and girls in Bangladesh.

Once there were elaborate rules about permissible rape in war. There was an early European convention: If a besieged town surrendered in timely fashion, its women would be spared rape. If the town resisted, wholesale rape was justified. That kind of rape had a political reason—to intimidate other towns to surrender without resistance.

Then and now, part of the enduring disaster of rape is this: The husband often blames the woman who was raped as much as he blames the man who raped her. All the dynamics of rape are ingeniously destructive. It tears the social fabric apart. It profoundly degrades the women and disgraces—absolutely—the men who were unable to protect them.

Source: Based on an article by Lance Morrow, "Behavior: Rape and War," *Time Magazine*, February 22, 1993, pp. 48–50.

raped in war, she, her family, and her community are all victims.

Political rape is not limited to war zones. Human Rights Watch reports that police also use rape when women are in police detention. In Peru, the victims are generally mestiza, women of mixed European and Native-American ancestry, from urban areas. Arrested as suspected subversives, they are incarcerated alone or in small groups and raped before their appearance before judicial authorities. Many of these rape cases have been documented (Human Rights Watch, 1995).

We have already mentioned the practice in the People's Republic of China of kidnapping and raping women so they would become potential brides for their rapists. Rape is increasing in much of the world, partly because women are relatively safe targets for aggression because of their secondary status.

Female Genital Mutilation. Female genital mutilation, or the removal of healthy tissue from the female genital region, is a widespread phenomenon, affecting an estimated 100 to 120 million females worldwide at the rate of about 2 million a year. The mutilation typically occurs between the ages of 5 and 11 (Ruth, 1998). The severity of the practice varies in different cultures. For example, one type of genital mutilation involves removing the clitoris and labia minora of young girls. Another type consists of removing all the external genitalia and then sewing up the vaginal opening. Whatever its form, the effects of mutilation are surgically irreversible. The procedure is usually performed by older village women, or sometimes by traditional birth attendants. Rarely are mutilations carried out by doctors or nurses in the hospital. Anesthetics are never used (except in the few procedures occurring in hospitals). The girl is usually held down by village women.

Female genital mutilation is a custom that has gone on for hundreds of years, justified by religion, or hygiene, or custom, or the rationale that it keeps women from being promiscuous. Map 9–2 shows the parts of the world where female genital mutilation is most common.

No religion requires female genital mutilation, but the practice is passed on from one generation to the next, enforced by custom and mistaken religious beliefs. The health risks and complications of female genital mutilation depend on the extent

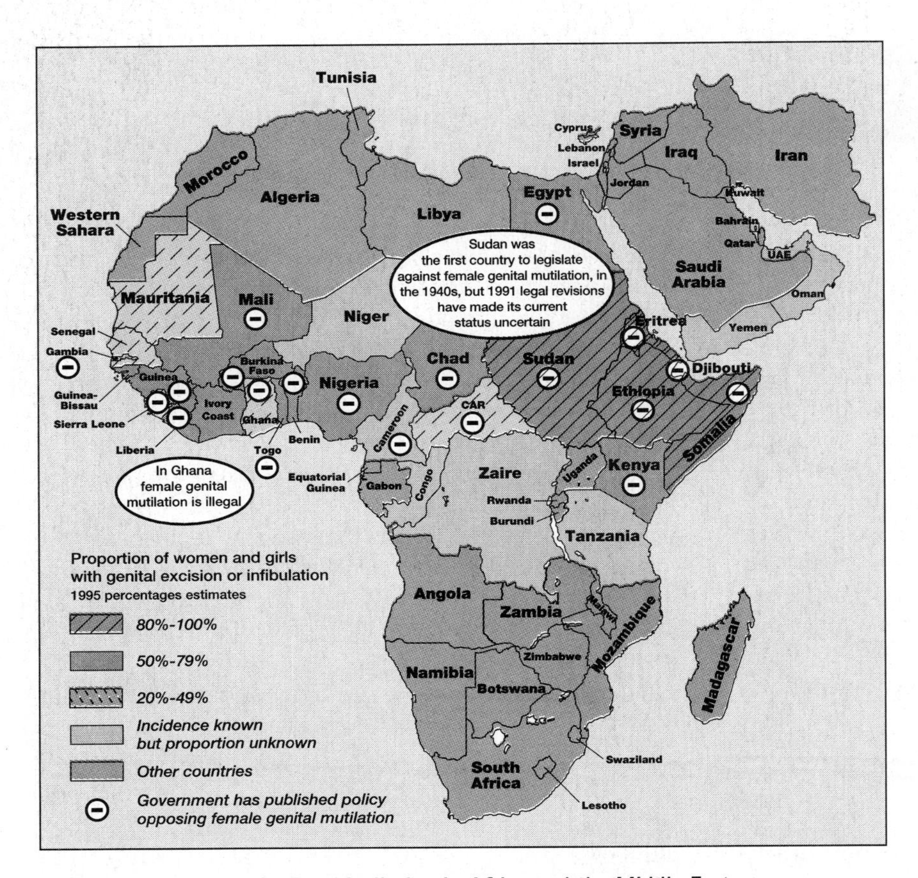

MAP 9–2 Female Genital Mutilation in Africa and the Middle East

Source: Seager, Joni. 1997. *The State of Women in the World Atlas* (new edition). London: Penguin Reference, p. 53.

of the procedure, hygienic conditions, the skill and eyesight of the person who performs it, and the struggles of the girl undergoing it (Dorkenoo, 1994). Immediate complications include violent pain, hemorrhage, tetanus, and blood poisoning from unsterile and often primitive cutting instruments (a knife, a razor blade, or even a piece of broken glass). Sometimes these complications, coupled with the shock from the pain, result in death (Heise, 1989). Although the age when the mutilations are done varies from one region to another, most experts agree that it is occurring at progressively younger ages.

It is impossible to determine the number of deaths resulting from the procedure. The majority who are fatally harmed live in rural areas, where accurate death records are not kept. The nature of the procedure means that the deaths are concealed from strangers and health authorities, but a Kenyan gynecologist estimates that 15 percent of all circumcised females die of bleeding or infections (Dorkenoo, 1994).

Until recently, female genital mutilation was something that most people in the West were unfamiliar with or, if they knew about it, tended to ignore or minimize. The euphemistic term "female circumcision" was the usual terminology, but the term "mutilation" is more accurate. (Physicians refer to any removal of healthy tissue as a mutilation.) As emigration from the more than 30 countries (mostly in Africa) that practice these rituals increases, we are hearing more about female genital mutilation. It is now found all over the world, but the major region where it occurs remains Africa. Increasingly throughout the world, sexual mutilation is being redefined as a human rights issue, and there are growing grassroots efforts to stop the practice.

Female genital mutilation is an extreme example of the subjugation of women. Another such example was the burning of Indian widows on the funeral pyres of their husbands, a practice called suttee, or sati. This practice was based on the position of widows in Indian society. Indian widows traditionally were shunned, forbidden to remarry, and turned out of their homes. This situation led to the practice of suttee, which was common for centuries, especially among high-status castes. The practice was officially outlawed in 1829, but even today occasional instances are reported (Bonvillain, 1998).

Foot-binding, a Chinese practice, is another example of female subjugation. In traditional Chinese society, tiny female feet were considered very beautiful. A foot length of three inches was the ideal. The practice of foot-binding meant that the feet of young girls (from the ages of 4 to 5) were bound with tight strips of cloth so that their toes curled under their feet. In the following years, their feet became increasingly deformed, causing them to be unable to walk normally. Only very poor Chinese girls were spared the ritual because they were needed to work in the fields and around the farm. This meant they had to be able to walk unassisted. Foot-binding was officially banned in China in 1902, but not until the Communists took over (in the late 1940s) was the practice totally eliminated (see the box "FYI: The Hidden Costs of Gender-Based Violence").

Women, Government, and Politics

Governments make rules (laws) that influence every aspect of public and private life. Yet the interests of female citizens are frequently ignored; women are grossly underrepresented in governments around the world.

The Hidden Costs of Gender-Based Violence

Gender-based violence, such as enforced prostitution, rape, genital mutilation, or domestic abuse does great damage to both the women who experience it and society as a whole. Only recently have activists, health officials, and development agencies begun to quantify the full costs of such violence. Currently, they are focusing on two aspects of the violence—the medical costs and the effects on economic productivity.

The most visible effects of violence are those associated with physical injuries that require medical care. Female genital mutilation, for example, often causes severe health problems. Typically performed in unsterile environments by untrained midwives or barbers working without anesthesia, the procedure causes intense pain and can result in infection or death. Long-term effects include chronic pain, urine retention, abscesses, lack of sexual sensitivity, and depression. For the approximately 15 percent of mutilated women who have been infibulated (which involves cutting away all external genitalia, leaving only a tiny passageway for excretion of urine and menstrual blood), the health-related consequences are even worse. Not only must these women be cut and stitched repeatedly (on their wedding night and again with each childbirth), but sexual dysfunction and pain during intercourse are common. Infibulated women are also much more likely to have difficulties giving birth. Their labor often results, for instance, in vesico-vaginal fistulas—holes in the vaginal and rectal areas that cause continuous leakage of urine and feces. An estimated 1.5 to 2 million African women have fistulas, with some 50,000 to 100,000 new cases occurring annually.

Infibulation also greatly increases the danger to the child during labor. A study of 33 infibulated women delivering at Somalia's Benadir Hospital found that 5 of their babies died while 21 of the infants suffered oxygen deprivation.

Only a few studies have attempted to assign an actual dollar value to gender-based violence, but their findings suggest that the problem constitutes a substantial health care burden. For instance, a study by a health insurance company estimated that violence against women cost the state of Pennsylvania's health care system approximately $326.6 million in 1992.

Source: Based on an article by Toni Nelson, "Violence against Women," *World Watch*, July-August 1996, pp. 33–38.

Women have long sought political rights, but it has been a lengthy struggle. Following the French Revolution (1789), women organized in groups to call for the application of the revolution's ideals of freedom and equality to women as well as men. These women's groups were particularly interested in equal rights in education, employment, and government, but the response of men was less than sympathetic (Giddens, 1991).

Women achieved the right to vote long after men did in virtually every nation in which citizens vote. For women, the right to vote has been seen as a symbol of political freedom and the means of achieving greater economic and social equality. Women leaders endured considerable hardship to win suffrage for their sex (see Table 9–2).

Despite widespread fears that women's involvement with politics would trivialize political life or undermine the stability of the family, such participation has not altered much political life. Women's voting patterns, like those of men, are shaped by a number of factors. In fact, on the whole, women voters tend to be more conservative than male voters.

The influence of women on politics involves more than just the right to vote. Feminists in many countries have played a significant role in the passing of equal opportunity laws and the placing of women's issues on the political agenda. They are concerned that women are underrepresented in decision-making structures and overrepresented as victims of gender-based discrimination, violence, and other types of human rights abuses. The issues concerning feminists around the world include equal rights at work (including equal pay for equal work), the availability of abortion, and changes in divorce laws.

Perhaps somewhat surprisingly, women in some developing nations have often wielded more power than in countries like the United States. In the last few decades, for example, women have been heads of state in a number of non-Western countries. Examples include Golda Meir in Israel, Indira Gandhi in India, Benazir Bhutto in Pakistan, and Corazon Aquino in the Philippines. Great Britain and France are the only large Western nations to have had female heads of state. (In England, Prime Minister

TABLE 9–2 The Year in Which Women Achieved the Right to Vote on an Equal Basis with Men, by Country

Year	Country
1893	New Zealand
1902	Australia
1906	Finland
1913	Norway
1915	Denmark, Iceland
1917	Soviet Union
1918	Canada
1919	Austria, Germany, the Netherlands, Poland, Sweden, Luxembourg, Czechoslovakia
1920	United States
1922	Ireland
1928	Britain
1929	Equador
1930	South Africa
1934	Brazil, Cuba
1936	Costa Rica
1937	Philippines
1941	Indonesia
1942	Dominican Republic, Uruguay
1945	France, Hungary, Italy, Japan, Vietnam
1946	Albania, Rumania, Panama
1947	Argentina, Venezuela
1948	Israel, Korea
1949	China, Chile
1950	El Salvador, Ghana, India
1951	Nepal
1952	Greece
1953	Mexico
1954	Colombia
1955	Nicaragua
1956	Egypt, Pakistan, Senegal
1957	Lebanon
1959	Morocco
1962	Algeria
1963	Iran, Kenya, Libya
1964	Sudan, Zambia
1965	Afghanistan, Guatemala
1977	Nigeria
1979	Peru, Zimbabwe

Source: Lisa Tuttle, *Encyclopedia of Feminism* (New York: Facts on File, 1986).

Margaret Thatcher was a true head of state; in France the role was more of a figurehead.)

For the most part, women are underrepresented as political representatives, particularly on the international, national, and state levels. At the local government level, women are generally more represented. What is surprising about the statistics on women's political involvement is not the low numbers per se, but rather how slowly the situation has changed. Women's political advancement is retarded because it takes a lot of time, effort, and money to succeed in politics. It seems that women, who have major domestic burdens and generally fewer financial resources than men, find it more difficult to produce those commodities in sufficient quantity to be as politically successful as men. Sometimes it is argued that, as a group, women do not want to enter the traditionally male domain of politics, but that seems a spurious argument: Most males do not want to enter politics either.

Today most countries provide for women to have the vote. Many nations have more political representation of women in government, both as elected and appointed officials, than we do in the United States. As more and more of the world's women vote and participate in government, we may expect more issues crucial to women (and families) to emerge as important issues for consideration.

Women, Children, and Family Issues in the United States

Social scientists are beginning to accumulate solid empirical evidence about human behavior, but even scientists tend to accept stereotypes about gender abilities. In the late nineteenth and early twentieth centuries, the scientific research of that day upheld traditional notions—ideas such as girls could not participate in vigorous sports; young women should not receive the same education as males; and women were designed, by nature, to be only wives and mothers.

In this country, and others, many laws based on those beliefs restricted the rights of women in order to enforce Western conventional gender roles. Judicial systems upheld these notions and legitimized discrimination against women. For example, in 1872, the case, *Bradwell* v. *the State of Illinois,* brought before the U.S. Supreme Court, focused on the issue of whether a married woman could practice law. In this case, the Court ruled that both nature and human beings themselves have designated separate spheres and destinies for women and men. The man should be the woman's "protector and defender," the judges decided, while affirming women's unfitness for some occupations—such as being an attorney (Rosenblum and Travis, 1996).

In Western nations, most of these restrictions have slowly and gradually been declared unconstitutional. For example, in the summer of 1996, the U.S. Supreme Court ruled that Virginia Military Institute cannot bar admission of women and still remain a public institution supported by state funds. Similar recent decisions in the United States have upheld the rights of women to hold jobs traditionally held by men.

Current Status of Families

Many of the social problems affecting families (especially women and children) are global in nature—they affect Americans as much as they do citizens of the Third World, although the intensity of the problem and how critical it is may vary. But in many respects, the West has been in the vanguard of many of the changes in the family.

As American women move steadily into higher education and full-time careers, new pressures for change occur both within and outside the family. The family structure has responded to the new economic position of women, albeit unevenly. Upper-middle-class Americans with dual incomes are adapting to the new, more equal balance of power between men and women. Similar changes are beginning to appear in other parts of the world, too. All over the globe, there has been a major shift in the lives of middle-class educated women. As they have become empowered by education, it has become acceptable, perhaps even desirable, for them to seek not simply jobs but careers, or positions in the professions and business open to them that are full-time and have similar career paths as those of men. The globalization of the economy has meant that many high-paying U.S. jobs have been exported to countries with lower wages. As a result, many American couples believe that it is essential that wives have careers with good incomes and adequate benefits. Two-income families provide a cushion against downward economic mobility; even if one wage earner loses his or her job, the other wage earner still has a good income and benefits for family members. In this section, we discuss some related issues affecting families today.

Women and Work. During the past quarter century, unprecedented numbers of women have entered the paid labor force, but many of these jobs are in traditional women's positions, in which the pay and benefits are inferior to those of men. Even that is progress of sorts. Historically, having a job and a family life was the norm for men, but for women, the sexual division of labor within the family made a paid job outside of the home incompatible with the homemaking role. For more than a century after the so-called feminine professions were established, women in the United States had an either/or option. They could become homemakers *or* have a career in nursing, teaching, or social work. These professions were seen as alternatives to marriage and homemaking. Until the late 1960s or early 1970s, white middle- and upper-class American women generally tended to accept these traditional sex roles defined by society. (African American women, immigrant women, and poor white women, usually for economic reasons, had to work after marriage; moreover, a significant proportion of married women have worked for wages since the 1890s in the United States.) Today most women are not faced with those limited choices.

By 1990, 58 percent of all American women were in the paid labor force (Ries and Stone, 1992). More than half of all married mothers with young children (under age six) were in the paid labor force. Although there are many objections to mothers of young children working outside the home, many Americans feel the need for two incomes.

As mentioned in the section on education, women are not equally distributed throughout the economy. Even today, a disproportionately large percentage of women are in the occupations defined as "feminine." Women work in all the occupational categories, but they are overrepresented in the lowest status jobs, work that receives the least earnings and benefits. Perhaps more important than the type of work women do are the wages they earn. The income of women still tends to be substantially lower than that of men, even when education, work experience, ability, and motivation are the same (Lindsey, 1997).

Many of us have heard about the **glass ceiling,** an invisible barrier that limits advancement of women and some minorities along their career paths. Subtle discrimination impedes women's progress and limits their opportunities. It is so subtle that the word "glass" connotes how hard it is to see. Glass ceilings may not be all of the problem. Julia Wood, a professor of communication studies, uses the metaphor *glass walls* to describe sex segregation on the job, by

Women are not equally distributed throughout the economy; they are overrepresented in the lowest status jobs. More important, the income of women still tends to be lower than that of men, even when education, work experience, ability, and motivation are the same.

which stereotypes about the type of work women should do puts them in traditional female jobs (Wood, 1997). And, of course, those traditional jobs (secretaries, typists, childcare workers) pay less money.

Many people believe that the wage gap between what women and men are paid has narrowed considerably over the years, but that is not true. This gap has changed relatively little. For the last three decades, women's income has hovered between 60 and 70 percent of what men earn. Only in the mid-1990s has the gap narrowed. A woman (doing the same work and with the same educational background as a man) now makes about 75 cents to every dollar he makes (Lindsey, 1997). For younger women (ages 16 to 24), the female to male earnings ratio is higher—young women earn 90 cents for every dollar earned by young men (Ries and Stone, 1992). (This statistic may reflect that younger women are receiving more education and thus can command more money.) Not only are wages lower for women, but female employees are less likely than male employees to have employer- or union-sponsored pension plans. That means that older women are more likely than older men to live in need in their retirement years.

For many women, full-time employment (and benefits) simply are not available (Negrey, 1993). Many women can only find part-time or temporary work. This reduced work has implications for work schedules, income, job security, personal autonomy, and quality of life concerns, to say nothing of retirement benefits.

Another reality for many females in the workplace is something that has come to be called **sexual harassment** (comments, gestures, or physical contact of a sexual nature that is deliberate, repeated, and unwelcome, creating a *hostile work environment*). Only recently has this behavior had a name. Because it was unnamed, it was difficult to recognize, think about, or stop. As Julia Wood points out, "'Making advances' and 'being pushy' fail to convey the abusiveness of sexual harassment. Only when the term was coined did we call attention to the wrongs of unwanted behavior that objectifies and humiliates individuals and ties sexuality to security and advancement" (Wood, 1997:158). Many companies and businesses now make efforts to sensitize employees to what constitutes sexual harassment, but it remains a major problem in the workplace.

Today many American women can combine career and family, but there are costs, emotional as well as financial, for doing this. We live in a place and time when caring for a house and children is still seen as primarily a woman's responsibility. If she can manage—or afford help in managing—both, fine, but ultimately if the family is slighted, it is still seen more as her fault than her husband's. One of the most urgent needs families face is childcare options. Until recently, young children were left with relatives (mostly grandmothers), or neighbors, friends, or other family members were pressed into service. But in today's world, many of these people are no longer available for childcare because they, too, are employed. Finding safe, adequate daycare is particularly important for single-parent households and those in which both parents work. One proposal to deal partly with this problem is to have a system of parental leaves that would enable fathers and mothers to take time off to care for a new baby without losing their jobs. Sweden has such a system; parents are given a six-months' leave at the birth of a child, and the leave time can be divided equally between the father and mother, if they so desire (Safilos-Rothschild, 1974).

Feminization of Poverty. The problem of the feminization of poverty (the trend toward women representing an increasing proportion of the poor) is not confined to the Third World. Higher rates of divorce and separation and single-parent families have placed women at a particular disadvantage. Almost half of all poor families are supported by women with no spouse present. When women with children divorce, their income falls dramatically. The average income in such households is 23 percent below the official poverty line (The New Internationalist, 1995). In the United States, although some women pursue higher education and careers, many do not have that opportunity. It is difficult for unskilled or semiskilled low-income women to simultaneously raise children by themselves and to find and hold a job that would lift the family above the poverty line.

Structural changes in the American economy are part of the reason for the feminization of poverty. The downsizing of American businesses, coupled with the flight of U.S. manufacturing jobs abroad, has cost thousands of Americans their jobs. And although it is true that new positions have been created, most new jobs pay too little to keep a family above the poverty figure. In addition, throughout the 1980s, the federal government systematically cut spending on antipoverty programs, thereby removing the "safety net" for hundreds of thousands of Americans. All of these changes have most harmed the weakest members of society, those least able to take care of themselves—women and children.

Women's Unpaid Work. The entry of women into the paid labor force has not seen a restructuring of household labor. Sociologist Arlie Hochschild (1989) calls this a *stalled revolution.* Our cultural traditions and social institutions give women primary responsibility for hearth and home and these old notions persist.

This issue of who takes care of children and does housework is not a trivial one. In the past, there was no debate: Childcare and homemaking were women's concerns. But as more wives and mothers enter the paid labor force, the question comes up in more and more families. No longer is it seen as fair that men do only minor home repairs and women continue to perform the rest of the unpaid work at home. Hochschild did a seven-year study on families in which both parents worked in the paid labor force. She found that in an era of fragile marriage and easy divorce, the strongest unions were those in which the husbands "pitched in" (Hochschild, 1989). It is true that husbands are spending more time on housework and childcare than in the past, but women are still overwhelmingly responsible for these duties.

In recent decades, increased immigration has provided a group of women who do childcare and cleaning for some dual career families (or affluent single-parent households). But most two-salary families cannot afford this solution. The women in these families, and indeed most American women, spend as much time on housework and childcare as did women in earlier times, when women were not employed outside the home.

Health Issues

Historically, we know that patterns of health change in response to the social arrangements and popular notions of the time. In the late nineteenth century, Western females were considered to have "fragile nerves" and to swoon (faint) easily. Smelling salts close at hand were a necessity. (The fact that fashion dictated a tiny waist bound by tight corsets that made it difficult to get enough oxygen was probably a contributing factor.)

Women's health (like that of men) varies according to sociological factors. As an example, there have been numerous research studies indicating that housewives have more reported illnesses than do females who work outside the home. There are a number of possibilities why this is so, including that the housewife role is devalued, which may have health repercussions. In the United States, social class and race are other sociological variables that greatly affect women's health, both physical and mental. As an example, African American women are four times more likely to die in childbirth than white women (Andersen, 1993). This statistic can be attributed to the higher birthrate and the greater frequency of high-risk pregnancies among African American women, particularly those who are poor.

Another health issue that greatly affects females is weight—both too much and too little. We live in a culture obsessed with thinness and physical attractiveness. Women especially are supposed to be thin as a key measure of their attractiveness. One consequence is the high rate of eating disorders among American women related to thinness, such as anorexia nervosa and bulimia. A large percentage of females fall into the other extreme and are obese. Sometimes American males are also grossly overweight, but few suffer from anorexia or bulimia.

Another gender difference concerning health relates to medical research. For decades, medical researchers spent most of their resources on studying medical problems of men. Because more men die of heart attacks than any other medical problem, most of this research was devoted to work on heart disease. But little time or money was spent on women's heart attacks, and much less funding was spent on breast cancer research, a leading cause of women's deaths (Applebaum and Chambliss, 1995). Feminists attribute this to the fact that until recently, most physicians were male and, consciously or unconsciously, were more concerned with male problems and diseases.

The Status of Children

Until recently, the rights of children has not been a topic that concerned many people. Because of social norms, what went on within the family was considered private. Only if death or serious injury occurred did the police or the public hear of abuse. Still, maltreatment of children did occur. Maltreatment of children can be one of three general types—physical abuse, sexual abuse, or neglect.

Increasingly, the outrageous atrocities committed against children by their parents, siblings, neighbors, and strangers in the United States are being publicized. Many states now have compulsory child abuse reporting laws so that more of these cases are reported to authorities. In addition, the definition of child abuse has gradually been expanded in some states to include things like malnutrition, the child's witnessing violence between parents or adult caretakers, and the taking of sexually suggestive photographs of youngsters.

The amount of violence against children is astonishing in a country that gives lip service to being a child-centered society. Even with new laws and increasing awareness, we do not hear of most cases of family violence because they never come to the attention of welfare authorities or the police. In the past, many people who suspected problems were reluctant to report them to authorities in case they were mistaken. Although the situation is better today, people are often still hesitant to intervene.

Until the twentieth century, children were often considered the property of parents and, as such, could be disciplined in any way the father or mother saw fit. Today standards of acceptable child discipline vary according to culture and social class. Precise figures are difficult to obtain. There is a problem in that people define "abuse" in markedly different ways; moreover, it is an underreported phenomenon. There is also the problem that the definitive research on child abuse was done in the 1980s, and little new research has been undertaken (perhaps because of the costs). But there is some evidence that the incidence of child abuse has declined in the last decade or two (Lamanna and Riedmann, 1997). Reported cases of parental physical abuse against children are about equally divided between mothers and fathers. This fact flies in the face of popular assumptions of a "maternal instinct."

Part of the problem is that sometimes physical punishment escalates into abuse. In the United States, parents have a constitutional right to rear their children in accordance with their own beliefs. There is no legal prohibition against parents spanking their children; most state laws permit parents to use "reasonable" corporal punishment. Most of the world also permits parents to use corporal punishment, but in some places this is changing. In 1979, Sweden banned parental corporal punishment of children. Norway, Finland, Austria, Denmark, Cyprus, and Italy also prohibit parental infliction of corporal punishment on children (Bitensky, 1996).

Children are also vulnerable to sexual abuse by adults, including sexual behavior brought about by force or deceit (Lamanna and Riedmann, 1997). Western culture tends to view childhood as a period of innocence, but sadly this is not always the case. Most sexual abuse of children is perpetrated by members of their own families. Because incest is considered scandalous, there are great pressures to keep it hidden. It is difficult to obtain the actual rate of sexual abuse occurrences from the relatively few cases that are reported. We do know, however, that incest is more likely to be perpetrated by stepfathers than biological fathers, and that often grandparents, siblings, and even mothers are the perpetrators. Although the vast majority of sexual abuse is perpetrated by heterosexuals, there is also a small percentage of homosexual sexual abuse of children, sometimes by a family member but often by a trusted teacher, pastor, or family friend (Collins and Coltrane, 1991). People who were sexually abused as children are more likely to sexually abuse their own children, indicating that a cycle of violence exists. An extensive survey in the 1980s of violence in American families concluded that a child's statistical chances of being kidnapped or molested by a stranger are minuscule compared to that same child's statistical chances of being physically or sexually abused by a family member or friend of the family (Gelles and Straus, 1988).

Child neglect, another social problem, includes acts of omission—failing to provide adequate physical or emotional care (Lamanna and Riedmann, 1997). Although sometimes caused by economic stress, it can be willful. Child neglect also seems to be passed down from one generation to the next. Without a model of what a good parent should be, most adults involved in child neglect perpetuate the neglect they experienced as youngsters.

Education

The United States was the first nation to adopt the idea of universal free education for all its citizens, boys and girls alike. That education was defined as the ability to read and write and do simple arithmetic (the old "three Rs"). Initially, the idea that women should be allowed to pursue higher education was not readily accepted. As some women began to demand the opportunity to receive a college education, reasons were advanced why it was impractical and undesirable. For instance, it was suggested that intellectual pursuits would wreck havoc on women's naturally weak temperament and, in an era when women's long hair was considered her "crowning glory," it was said that if a woman insisted on using her brains, as men do, she was likely to become bald. How many women were persuaded by those arguments is not known, but defining college as "unfeminine" and "masculine" dissuaded many young women from pursing higher education.

In the early days of our nation, women were specifically barred from attending college. It was not until 1833 that Ohio's Oberlin College became the first college to admit women. But not until the late nineteenth century was it generally accepted that privileged, relatively affluent women in this country had the right to higher education. However, the emphasis of that training was to prepare women for homemaking and motherhood, not for careers (Matthaei, 1982). Some university-trained women prepared for the professions from 1870 to 1900 but were consistently shut out from entry into fields like law and medicine. Despite this focus, for some women higher education opened doors to professions like teaching, social work, nursing, and librarianship (occupations that came to be known as *female professions*). In the three decades between 1890 and 1920, women's participation in the paid professions increased by 22.6 percent. During that same time, men's participation in paid professions increased by 78 percent (Matthaei, 1982).

It took a long time for the percentage of educated women to increase to anywhere near their representation in the population, but by the 1990s, women outnumbered men in graduation rates at every level in the United States, except at the doctorate or professional level (Ries and Stone, 1992). College enrollment for both women and men has more than doubled in the past 30 years, but it has gone up much more for women. This is true for Canadians as well (Wills, 1998).

Education is a key element in the ability of women to earn a decent salary in the paid labor force. Other factors being equal, there is a bigger pay-off for college and professional education for women. It is not that women with degrees earn more than men with degrees, but they earn substantially more than women with only a high school education. Proportionately, the income gain of female college graduates is more than it is for male graduates when each group is compared with high school graduates of the same gender.

Unlike years ago, when women were confined to female professions, by 1989, more than one-fourth of all dentistry degrees, one-third of all medical degrees, one-half of all veterinary degrees, and two-fifths of all law degrees were awarded to women. But the classroom climate can still be chilly for many women. Bernice Sandler, a noted professor of education, has extensively researched the equity of women in academia. She found many subtle barriers to women, including that female students are often treated quite differently than male students (even by women teachers). Because of this, women (as a group) tend to participate less than men in class discussion, some women lower their academic aspirations during their college years, and women are still encouraged to major in the traditionally female fields, which perpetuates the occupational ghetto whereby women earn less money than men (Sandler, 1987). As an example, in 1989, only 15 percent of bachelor's degrees in engineering were awarded to women (Ries and Stone, 1992).

Violence against Women

When we think of "family," we like to think of kindness and happiness, as what historian Christopher Lash (1977) calls a "haven in a heartless world." But obviously not all families live in love and harmony. The all-loving, all-nurturing family is an American myth. There is another side of families, one of tension and discord. The intensity that characterizes intimate relationships sometimes gives way to conflict. Some families resolve the inevitable tensions that arise in the course of daily living, but in other families, conflict gives way to violence.

In the United States, we hear a lot about stranger danger, the harm that might come from an unknown attacker in a dark alley or in a parking lot. But statistics show that in this country a person is in greater danger of being attacked, raped, or murdered by a family member (or someone from the immediate friendship group) than by someone unknown (Fingerhut and Kleinman, 1990). Data are hard to come by, as crimes such as acquaintance rape, assault, and spousal abuse often go unreported. In the United States, we have a norm of privacy that protects what happens within the family or in close relationships. We tend, therefore, to typically learn of these activities only when someone is seriously harmed or killed.

There is no evidence that family violence has increased in recent years. What has happened is that it has become far more visible. Because of increased media attention, we are more aware of it. What used to be considered "private" is now far more open to public scrutiny.

Domestic Violence and Abuse against Women

Historically, wife beating was condoned in Western societies. English common law (upon which U.S. law is based) permitted husbands to discipline their wives. The prescribed method was to use a stick no thicker than the husband's thumb; that is, in fact, how the phrase, "rule of thumb" originated (Browne, 1987).

Until well into the nineteenth century in England and the United States, a husband could legally physically abuse his wife (or children), short of serious injury or murder. In many parts of the world, as we have previously seen, such behavior is still legal. In Western industrial nations, although women now have more legal protection from violence, domestic violence remains widespread. The attitude of the police is sometimes unhelpful. Often police have at least an unofficial policy of nonintervention in domestic disputes.

During the last 30 years or so, Western social scientists have begun paying attention to the problem of **domestic violence,** or violence among family members. Originally, this research centered on the abuse of children. Later, the work was expanded to include battered wives, and finally it encompassed all family members, including sibling and elder abuse. We now know domestic violence is a widespread problem, not confined to any country, religion, socioeconomic class, or ethnic group. It is estimated that in the United States as many as 2 million women are abused by their husbands each year (Strauss, Gelles, and Steinmetz, 1980). Thirty percent of women who are murdered are killed by their husbands or boyfriends (Federal Bureau of Investigation, 1993).

When we speak of family violence, it is important to acknowledge that women and children are not the only victims. Research indicates that in this country 12 out of every 100 husbands attack their wives each year, but the rate is almost identical for wives attacking their husbands (Strauss, Gelles, and Steinmetz, 1980). What this figure masks is that even though women may be just as violent as their husbands (or boyfriends), women are still the most harmed victims. Overwhelmingly, women end up the ones most

Domestic violence is a widespread problem, not confined to any country, religion, socioeconomic class, or ethnic group.

seriously hurt—physically, financially, and psychologically. Because, on average, women are smaller and weaker than the men in their lives, they are often seriously hurt physically. Women are also the main economic victims of family violence. If the marriage breaks up because of the abuse, women and their children suffer financially much more than do the men.

International Sexual Enslavement. According to research, some American women are victims of this practice. Recruited mainly from the West Coast, they are promised nonexistent entertainer jobs in countries like Japan and Brunei. These women are promised a specific salary, told where and when they will be performing, and are provided prepaid plane tickets. However, when they arrive, their passports and identification papers are taken away and they are forced to work as prostitutes (Yoon, 1996).

Rape and Sexual Assault. The romantic intimacies of women and men are the subject of novels, love songs, and poetry. But relationships may have a darker side, one that may involve extremes of exploitation and violence. Rape is one of those types of violence, in which power and domination of another person are the goals. In rape, sex is the weapon of choice, not the motive for the crime. Rape is an act of hate and aggression that is designed to humiliate and dominate another.

The definition of what constitutes rape is changing. In times past, the term was used to describe forcible sexual intercourse against the will of the woman. At that time, it was inconceivable in the eyes of the law that men could be raped, too. In the United States, most states are expanding that definition. Frequently the charge is not rape, but sexual assault. Many states now include under the category of sexual assault acts like **date and acquaintance rape** (in which someone known to the victim forces him or her to have sex) and **marital rape** (in which the husband forces the wife to have sex against her will).

However you define it, rape is a major problem in the United States; it is the fastest-growing violent crime (Wood, 1997). However, the actual occurrence of rape is difficult to assess. In 1990, the U.S. Uniform Crime Statistics reported more than 100,000 cases of forcible rape, but the FBI estimates that official figures represent only about a fourth of the actual cases. Moreover, the Uniform Crime Statistics do not include rapes that end in death; those are classified as homicides and, depending on the nature of the incident, some rapes are categorized as some other form of assault.

As rapes have become more publicized in the United States, we have begun to accumulate valuable research evidence about them. The statistics are often given that an American woman has a one in four chance of being sexually assaulted or raped in her lifetime. Those are distressing odds, but the statistic is misleading. Not all women are equally vulnerable. There is a clear connection between rape and social class. Poorer females are the most at risk. Thus, the rape rate is lower for females whose incomes are more than $10,000 a year. You might ask why this is so. Consider: If you are a poor woman, you probably do not own a car, and you are dependent on walking or using public transportation. In addition, you may not qualify for a nine-to-five job, so you work late hours, when relatively few people are about. As you walk the deserted streets or wait for a bus or subway, you are vulnerable to the attack of a stranger. Having said that, we must also point out that stranger rapes account for only about 16 percent of rapes. Like other women, many poor women are also victimized by men they know.

The United States has the unfortunate distinction of being a rape-prone society. According to research cited by Ian Robertson (1987), only 17 percent of societies are rape-prone; the United States is in that category. The extent of rape in a society seems to depend on cultural factors. Rape-prone societies have ideologies of male supremacy and dominance and a disrespect for women and nature.

Rape is rare in cultures that value women and feminine qualities and that have ideologies that promote harmonious interdependence between people and the natural world (Wood, 1997). What is particularly disturbing is the number of boys in the United States who indicate that under some circumstances it is acceptable for a male to have sex with a female, even without her consent:

> Recent research indicates that one reason for the prevalence of rape is that a substantial number of men regard forced sex as acceptable. A shocking 50% of college men reported that they have coerced, manipulated, or pressured a woman to have sex or have had sex with a woman after getting her drunk. As many as 1 out of 12 men at some colleges admitted engaging in behaviors

that met the legal definition of rape or attempted rape. (Wood, 1997:314)

Female Genital Mutilation. You might not think that female genital mutilation, which we previously discussed in a global context, could apply to the United States. You would be wrong. As people emigrate to North America, Great Britain, and Western Europe, they bring their traditional practices with them (see Map 9–2). Some Western physicians comply when asked to perform this practice. Some physicians, although they refuse to perform female genital mutilation themselves, do not report anything to authorities, seeing it as a "quaint" Old World practice. But because the medical complications of female genital mutilation are widespread and serious, the practice has come increasingly under criticism in Western nations, and laws are being drafted to end it there. This, of course, may not prevent it from being performed by mothers or female relatives.

The widespread incidence of genital mutilation reflects that the world is, indeed, "a global village." People are migrating throughout the globe, often carrying the practice with them. In December 1979, the United Nations General Assembly adopted the Convention for the Elimination of All Forms of Discrimination against Women. This convention calls for equal rights for women, regardless of their marital status, in all areas: political, economic, social, and civil (Dorkenoo, 1994). Female genital mutilation is covered in this convention.

One thing to keep in mind when learning of these acts of violence toward women is that there are costs involved. These costs—physical, psychological, mental, and financial—are to the individual women, to their families, to their society, and to their country (see the box "FYI: The Hidden Costs of Violence").

In 1996, the media reported that a 19-year-old woman from Toga (in Africa) was detained in an American jail. Her parents were well educated and decided that she would not be subject to the traditional practice. But when she was 16, her parents were killed in an automobile accident. She became the ward of an uncle who insisted that she must have the procedure. One morning she woke up to learn that it was her wedding day. (The groom was 45 and had three other wives.) Tradition dictated that two days after the wedding, all her external genitalia be removed. Terrified and determined not to have that done, the young woman fled her country to seek asylum in the United States. American laws protect people against human rights persecution, but the Immigration Service decided that she did not qualify for such protection. She spent almost two years in a York, Pennsylvania, jail awaiting a hearing and possible deportation. Her case became a cause célèbre, and support for the young woman came from organizations such as Equality Now (an international feminist organization). Finally it was ruled that her situation did constitute a human rights violation, and she was allowed to remain in this country and avoid having the procedure (Shapiro, 1998; Pollitt, 1996). Because of this case, in 1997, U.S. law was changed to allow situations like this to qualify a person for political asylum. Because of this law, then, immigration policy changed. For the first time in the United States, female genital mutilation was no longer defined as a cultural practice but as a human rights violation that permitted females escaping from it the legal right to asylum in this country.

Women, Government, and Politics

Twenty years ago, female politicians in the United States were rare. In 1971, only 1 percent of elected mayors were females; in 1991, women made up 17 percent of all elected mayors. That trend is true for other officials as well, but considering that females comprise more than half of the U.S. population, they are still vastly underrepresented as both elected officials and as high-level political appointees. For instance, in 1996, the House of Representatives broke a record with 51 women members (which amounts to less than 12 percent of the House). That year there were 9 female senators (another record) out of 100. Americans have never had a woman president or vice president.

In the United States, women were granted the right to vote in 1920, but when women's suffrage was new, some women still believed that voting was inappropriate for women and women's participation lagged behind men's. Not until 1980 did the proportion of women voters edge past that of men. There are a number of possible explanations why women have had minimal participation in the American political process. The long history of not being able to vote or hold office may partly explain this. In addition, perhaps the effects of female roles and gender stereotypes have played a role.

ASSESSING THE SITUATION

Some processes associated with modernization and globalization have profoundly changed families. Even changes in technology have contributed and continue to contribute to the subjugation of women in various and subtle ways. For most of human history, people lived in small groups in rural areas, where they depended on one another and knew one another personally. These tribal equilibrium regimes, discussed in Chapter 5, were held together by strong commitments to groups (such as the tribe, the village, and the family). Individual rights or desires were seldom of concern; it was crucial that the group survive. The move to industrial, urbanized societies (industrial consumptive regimes) undermined the traditional foundations of the family. The changes unleashed a myriad of issues and caused great concern for the future of the family. Pressures are now building that point to the emergence of yet another type of society, variously called "postindustrial," or "postmodern," or the "knowledge society." This latest evolution of society is placing stress on the family structure, which still has not adequately adjusted to the demands of industrialization. Furthermore, as the notion of the universality of human rights becomes widely accepted, there is more grassroots pressure to ensure that everyone—including women and children—be granted basic human rights.

Male Perspectives on Social Problems

Most men, when asked how to solve social problems, typically tend to emphasize the need for more money and training. Many men have great confidence that expensive technology and massive amounts of money will solve social problems.

The loans and technology transfers to developing nations have been tried for more than a quarter of a century with, many argue, little to show for the expenditures. One key reason is that much of the development in the Third World has been directed to helping males. When development emerged in the second half of the twentieth century, Western administrators assumed that the males in developing nations had similar roles to those of males in the developed world. Thus administrators believed that money given to male breadwinners or farmers would not only help agriculture or business in the developing countries, it would help the families of men who received development aid. But in many instances, this did not happen. Limited by their ethnocentric thinking, the administrators were unaware that in much of the Third World women are the farmers and marketers. It is the women's duty to feed the family, particularly the children. When the men received development aid, they continued in the old tradition of defining what they made or had as theirs alone. Thus little if any development money was spent on women and children.

In addition, in many Third World nations, men are lured from rural areas by jobs and opportunities in distant cities. Because transportation is difficult and expensive, they may seldom see the wives and children left at home. The saying "out of sight, out of mind" has sociological relevance, as it is often too true. All this contributes to the trend toward the feminization of poverty.

Female Perspectives on Social Problems

When most women are asked to solve social problems, they focus more on family and health issues: They try to figure out how to provide enough food for everyone, to live in a comfortable and safe dwelling, to be able to secure needed medical care for their children and family, to be educated, to educate their children, to be able to seek challenging, rewarding work. They do not ask for affluent lifestyles, just enough to provide the necessities.

In some countries, such as Bangladesh, banks are beginning to loan women small sums of money to start businesses. By Western standards, the amount is not large, usually the equivalent of under a hundred dollars. The women use the money in a variety of ways—they buy supplies to weave baskets, they purchase fabric to sew blouses or other clothing, they buy a cow to sell milk to the neighborhood, or they purchase a bicycle to rent out to other vendors. These small-scale loans frequently work well. The women tend to pay the money back with interest, and with the added revenue the business provides, they enrich their lives and the lives of their children. In most of the world, if you help women, you also help their families. The money women earn tends to be spent on the family—on additional food, necessary medical care, and the provision of educational opportunities for children.

Increasingly, people are beginning to appreciate that the problems we have discussed in this chapter are not just issues for individuals but are universal human rights issues that need to be addressed on a number of fronts throughout the world. Identifying the problems is a first step. For example, redefining violence against women as a human rights issue gained momentum in 1993, when the media in the United States and Europe reported on the systematic rape, sexual enslavement, torture, and murder of Bosnian Muslim women and children by Serbian military forces in the former Yugoslavia. A European Community team of investigators calculates that in 1993 alone, 20,000 Muslim women and girls were raped by Serbs. The Bosnian government claims that as many as 50,000 Muslim women have been raped. Amnesty International maintains there is evidence that in some cases the rape of women was carried out in an organized or systematic way, with the deliberate detention of women for the purpose of rape and sexual abuse (Morrow, 1993).

SUMMARY

1. People who are poor, female, or young are especially vulnerable to mistreatment.
2. The first typical form of family in European and other Western countries (around the sixteenth to eighteenth centuries) was a nuclear family enmeshed with other kin in the community. In the second family form (around the nineteenth century), the nuclear family became a separate entity. The third type of family (around the mid-nineteenth century) had expectations of close emotional bonds, a norm of privacy, and a major preoccupation with raising children.
3. Giddens identifies six recent changes occurring worldwide to families: the declining influence of kin; the trend toward a free choice of spouse; increasing recognition of women's rights; a wider segment of society from which to choose a spouse; increased sexual freedom; and the extension of children's rights.
4. There is no known society in which women, as a group, are more powerful than men. **Patriarchy** is the practice of giving males more status, power, and authority, both at home and in the larger society.
5. Gender bias can be found in the many research studies that consider only males in the social division of labor that assigns tasks by sex, and in the use of language.
6. Women do two-thirds of the world's work, earn one-tenth of the world's income, and own one-hundredth of the world's property. The **feminization of poverty,** an increase in the proportion of poor people who are female, is a worldwide trend. Typically, women around the world receive wages 30 to 40 percent lower than those of men doing the same jobs.
7. In the Third World, children are particularly vulnerable to problems of malnutrition and exploitative labor practices. In China and India, a strong preference for male babies has led to unbalanced sex ratios, because female babies are aborted, killed at birth, or allowed to die from malnutrition.
8. When females of Third World nations are educated, they most often end up in occupations such as teaching and nursing, in which pay is lower than in jobs reserved for males, a situation known as **employment segregation.**
9. The unequal power balance legitimized by patriarchy permits wife beating and other forms of **domestic violence** (violence within the family) to go unpunished in most nations. The **international slave trade** involves kidnapping women in one country in order to sell them into prostitution in another. **Rape** (forced sexual relations) involves power and the domination of one person over another and is increasingly viewed as a hate crime, rather than a sex crime. **Female genital mutilation,** the removal of healthy tissue from the female genital region, affects an estimated 100 to 120 million females worldwide but occurs most commonly in Africa.
10. The **glass ceiling** is an invisible barrier that limits advancement of many American women along their career paths. **Sexual harassment** (comments, gestures, or physical contact of a sexual nature that is deliberate, repeated, and unwelcome, creating a hostile work environment) is a form of abuse that has only recently been recognized.

Thinking Critically

1. How does patriarchy (the practice of giving males more status, power, and authority) function through the various social institutions (family, economy, politics, religion, education, medicine, and the military)? How does patriarchy affect women and children?
2. If we decided as a society to rid ourselves of patriarchy, how might we go about it? What would it involve? How could we start?
3. What are some of the ways our society unconsciously sanctions (legitimates) male aggression and violence against women?
4. Why do women and girls around the world receive less than males—less education, less compensation for the work they do, less political clout, and less prestigious positions in organized religious groups?
5. Is there any way we can *unlearn* sexism?

Suggested Readings

Anderson, Margaret L. 1993. *Thinking About Women: Sociological Perspectives on Sex and Gender.* Needham Heights, MA: Allyn & Bacon.

Cyrus, Virginia. 1993. *Experiencing Race, Class, and Gender in the United States.* Mountain View, CA: Mayfield Press.

Dorkenoo, Efua. 1994. *Cutting the Rose: Female Genital Mutilation: The Practice and Its Prevention.* London: Minority Rights Publications.

Lindsey, Linda L. 1990. *Gender Roles: A Sociological Perspective.* Englewood Cliffs, NJ: Prentice Hall.

Stockard, Jean and Mirian M. Johnson. 1992. *Sex and Gender in Society,* 2nd ed. Englewood Cliffs, NJ: Prentice Hall.

Web Sites

World's Women On-Line
http://www.asu.edu/wwol
This site provides timely information on women's issues.

Women's Online Media Project
http://wom.vcom.or.jp
This is an excellent source of up-to-date data for and about women.

WomensNet
http://www.igc.org/womensnet
This site is another good source, offering information on a wide variety of issues of concern to women today.

Future of Children
http://www.futureofchildren.org
This site offers information on issues dealing with children.

Children's Rights
http://www.igc.apc.org/igc/issues/educat/ childrights
This site is an excellent source of the latest information on issues relating to the evolving field of children's rights.

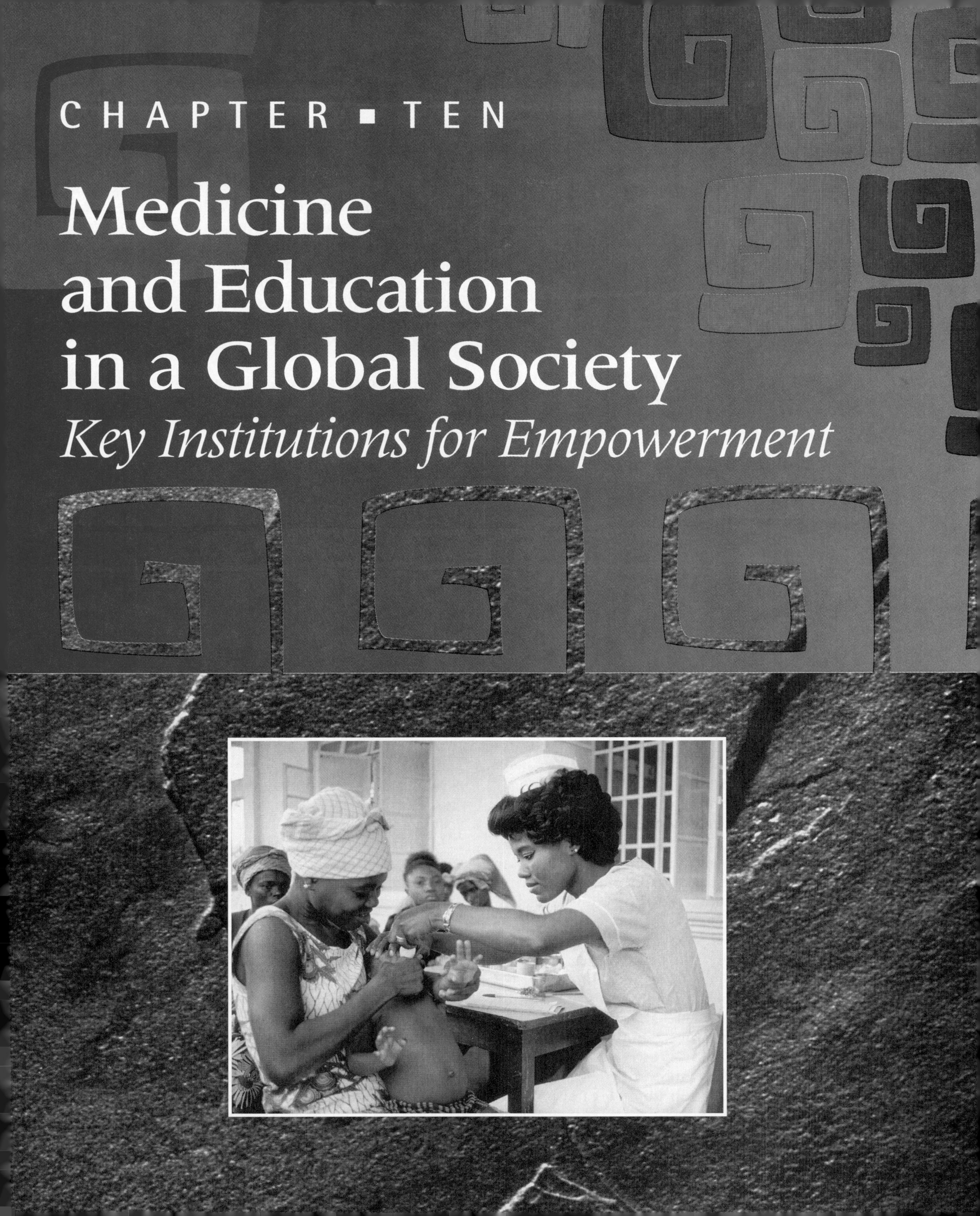

CHAPTER ■ TEN

Medicine and Education in a Global Society

Key Institutions for Empowerment

Case One. According to the UN *World Economic Survey 1990,* although maternal mortality has been virtually eliminated in the industrialized world, in south Asia one out of every two deaths among women of childbearing years is pregnancy related, bringing the total number of maternal deaths to just under one-third of a million each year (United Nations, 1991).

Case Two. In Africa, a woman of childbearing age has a 1 in 20 chance of dying in childbirth. In industrialized countries, the risk of dying in childbirth is 1 in 2,000 (United Nations, 1991).

Case Three. In 1990, it was estimated that 100 million school-age children were not in school. During the 1990s, another 100 million will be added to the school-age cohort. By the year 2000, six out of every ten school-age children will reside in the lower-income countries (Claffey, 1990).

Case Four. In the African nation of Malawi, the pupil-teacher ratio in primary schools has climbed from 41 to 1 in 1970 to 63 to 1 in 1990. In real terms, per-pupil spending has declined 4.1 percent each year. Only 50 cents is now spent annually per pupil on textbooks, writing pads, and other instructional supplies (Fuller, 1990).

Source: Joan M. Claffey, "The Donor Role in Instructional Improvement." In *Improving Educational Quality: A Global Perspective,* ed. David W. Chapman and Carol A. Carrier (New York: Greenwood, 1990), pp. 87–107; Bruce Fuller, "What Investments Raise Achievement in the Third World?" In *Improving Educational Quality: A Global Perspective,* ed. David W. Chapman and Carol A. Carrier (New York: Greenwood, 1990), pp. 17–43; United Nations, *Women: Challenges to the Year 2000* (New York: United Nations, 1991).

A **social institution** is an organized sphere of social life designed to meet important social needs. Social institutions help individuals meet basic needs to survive and provide a satisfying life. In this chapter we focus on two core social institutions—medicine and education. They are core institutions because they touch on almost every aspect of people's lives. That is, in every society, people are conceived, born, taught the culture's key skills and values, get sick, and die. In addition, medicine and education are vital to the empowerment of individuals, they influence and are influenced by global problems, and they have the capacity to improve the quality of life for countless people worldwide.

Medicine is potentially empowering because as the health status of a population improves not only do individuals feel better but they also have more physical and psychological energy to be more productive. Enhanced individual productivity has a ripple effect that enhances the quality of life for the entire family unit. The same process occurs when the educational status of the populations rises. In addition to increasing productivity, education also gives relatively powerless people a measure of control over their own lives. Moreover, as we discuss later in this chapter, quality of health and years of education are closely related.

Globalization and Health

The World Health Organization (WHO) defines **health** as "a state of complete physical, mental, and social well-being" (1946:3). Although most people think of health in terms of physical well-being, this definition helps us to see that good health involves far more than the physical aspects of our bodies. It also has psychological and social aspects.

The sole focus on the physical has led to many misguided efforts to improve the quality of health. The U.S. medical establishment has tended to view health problems as matters of physical changes in the human body. For example, if a patient complains to a doctor of having constant colds, the doctor may see the problem as entirely caused by germs that bring undesirable changes in the body and may prescribe antibiotics to control the physical changes (or symptoms) the patient describes. But in doing so, the doctor may be ignoring other possible contributing factors, such as depression over a job loss or stress induced by family problems. It is not only physicians who have not been taught to look at patients' psychological well-being or the quality of their social life, which also affects health. Neglect of such key elements in health care is fairly common in modern scientific medicine worldwide.

Despite this omission, health has been improving across the globe for some time. The average life span has been increasing, while **infant mortality** (the death of a child in the first year of life) has been decreasing. At the same time, there is considerable variation in health both among the nations of the world and among various groups such as the rich and the poor within individual societies.

In this section, we first look at instances of inequity of health worldwide. Next, we describe factors that physicians, health care officials, and the general public frequently associate with health differences. Finally, we discuss some alternative explanations for global health status. These explanations have significant implications for the improvement of health worldwide.

Global Inequity in Health

In affluent societies, most people take good health and a long life somewhat for granted, but in much of the world, these cannot be assumed. Even today, there are striking health differences between the populations of wealthy, industrialized societies and those of the poorer, less developed countries. Table 10–1 illustrates this problem by showing two key indicators of the overall health of a society—life expectancy and infant mortality rates.

The correlation between level of economic development and money spent on health is not perfect, but per capita income is a strong predictor of the overall health status of a country (Lassey, Lassey, and Jinks, 1997). Figure 10–1 demonstrates that those nations with the highest per capita income also have high per capita expenditures on health care. Expenditure is not, however, always directly correlated with the quality of health care. For example, the United States spends the most on health care of any nation in the world, but it does not lead the world in any major indicator of health status (such as life expectancy, infant mortality rate, immunization rate, and so on). Nevertheless, higher expenditures on health usually mean better quality of overall health in societies.

Wide disparities in health show up not only when we compare industrialized and developing nations. Within any given society, the same types of disparity in terms of health and access to medical care exist. In general, the higher a person's socioeconomic status, the more likely it is that that individual will have good mental and physical health. Gender and race also have a significant impact on whether or not the person will be healthy and have access to good medical treatment.

Between 1950 and 1980, the health of most people throughout the world dramatically improved. This improvement was largely due to great advances in providing basic sanitation, improving

TABLE 10–1 Global Inequity in Health Status

NATION GROUPING	COUNTRY	LIFE EXPECTANCY AT BIRTH	INFANT MORTALITY RATE[a]
Developed Countries	Australia	76.5	6.2
	Canada	79.1	6.1
	Denmark	77.3	4.8
	France	78.4	6.2
	Japan	79.6	4.4
	United States	76	6.7
Developing Countries	Colombia	72.8	25.8
	El Salvador	68.9	72.8
	Indonesia	61.6	63.1
	Philippines	65.9	33.2
	Turkey	71.9	43.2
Least Developed Countries	Chad	47.6	120.4
	Ethiopia	46.8	122.8
	Ghana	56.2	80.3
	Uganda	40.3	99.4
	Zambia	36.3	96.1

[a] Infant Mortality Rate = number of deaths per 1,000 live births within the first year of life.

Source: U.S. Bureau of the Census. 1996. *Statistical Abstract of the United States, 1996*, 116th ed. Washington, DC: U.S. Government Printing Office; Table 1327.

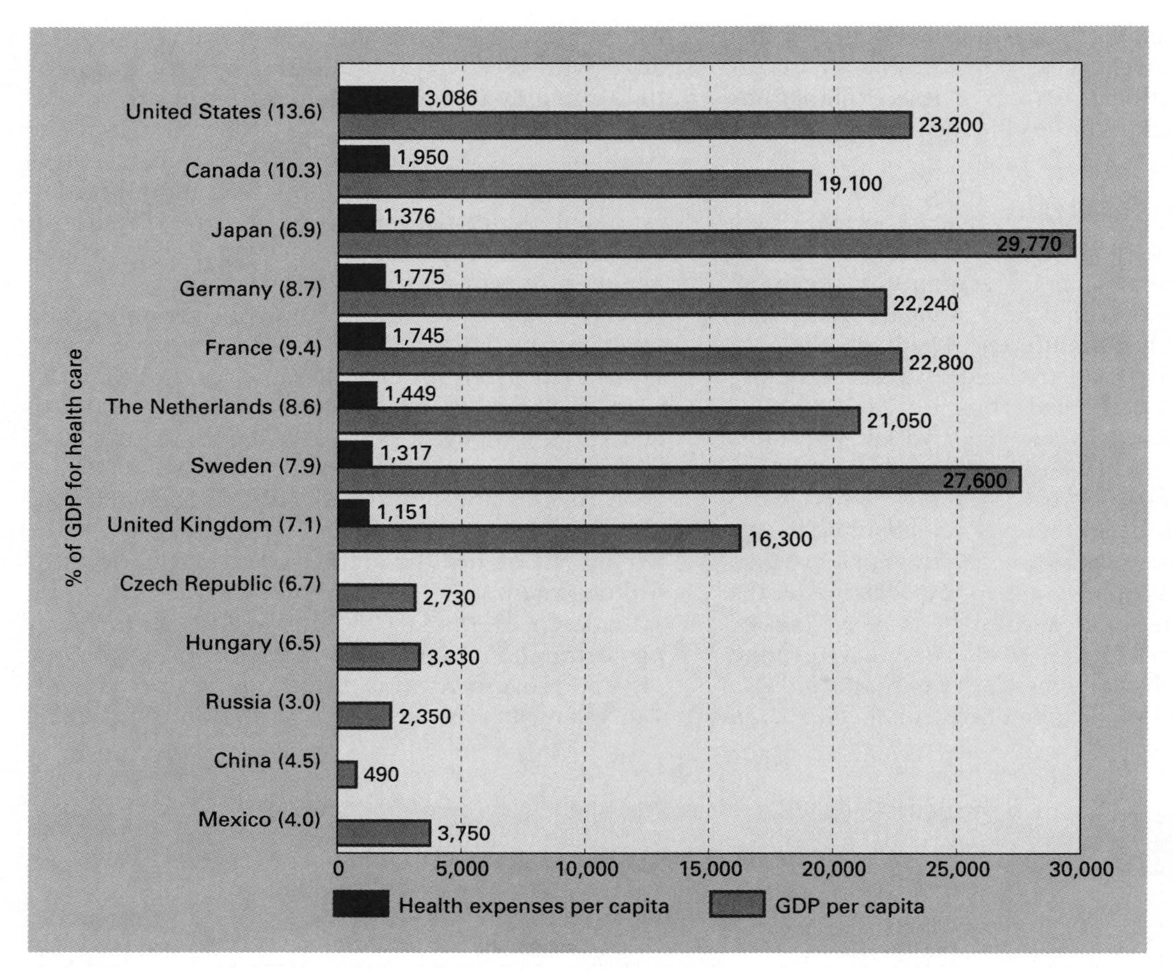

FIGURE 10–1 Percentage of Gross Domestic Product (GDP) for Health Care
Countries spend varying amounts of their gross domestic product on health care. The industrialized nations spend far more on health care and have a higher quality of health than do nonindustrialized nations.

Source: From *Health Care Systems Around the World: Characteristics, Issues, Reforms* by Lassey, Lassey, and Jinks.

nutrition, making primary health care available, and supplying safe, potable water. In 1978, to help augment these gains, the World Health Organization launched a global campaign: "Health for All by the Year 2000." The campaign focused on four areas experts believed would improve health: (1) the improvement of water and sanitation, (2) the improvement of basic nutrition for everyone, (3) the provision of immunization to all children, and (4) the training of primary health care workers (United Nations, 1991).

Clean Water and Sanitation. An estimated 80 percent of all disease is attributed to the lack of clean drinking water and sanitation. In the industrialized West, safe water and sanitation are available to most people, but that is not true in the developing world. There, it is estimated that at least 25 percent of urban dwellers and 71 percent of rural dwellers (excluding China, where the situation is better) do not have access to clean drinking water. The World Health Organization estimates that 47 percent of all urban dwellers and 87 percent of all people living in

Throughout the world, one in four people is malnourished. A famine in Africa left this mother and child emaciated and vulnerable to deadly diseases.

rural areas are without safe sanitation (UN, 1991). The situation is not improving; rapid population growth has led to an increase in the numbers of people living under these conditions. In addition, in the developing nations, the economic crisis of the 1980s and the resulting stabilization programs imposed by international financial institutions have slowed efforts to supply clean drinking water and sanitation.

The lack of availability of clean water and proper sanitation affects health in several ways. First, naturally occurring organisms that cause diseases (e.g., cholera and dysentery) that take a huge toll in human life can spread easily, especially in Third World countries. Second, water sources may become contaminated with humanmade elements, such as cancer-causing pesticides, that detrimentally affect adults and children alike. Finally, water supplies may become contaminated with heavy metals such as lead and mercury that cause life-threatening diseases (e.g., sickle-cell anemia), reproductive anomalies, and retardation.

Improving Basic Nutrition. Malnutrition is a fact of life worldwide. One in four people is malnourished, but women and girls are particularly affected. In many developing nations men and boys are fed first when food is scarce; women and girls who have less social value are left to eat whatever, if anything, remains. Such deeply ingrained societal values may have disastrous health effects, some of which we also discussed in Chapter 9. Here we cite one example, nutritional anemia, which is particularly dangerous to pregnant women. In industrialized countries, 11 percent of women suffer from nutritional anemia, but in Africa and Asia, up to 66 percent of pregnant women are anemic (UN, 1991).

During the 1980s, a combination of factors made the problem of the adequate feeding of citizens in developing countries even more difficult than before. Because of economic problems, many governments ended food subsidies, causing subsequent increases in the price of basic foodstuffs such as grains. This price rise, coupled with a decrease in real wages and soaring unemployment, increased malnutrition in much of the developing world. For example, in Zaire, deaths related to malnutrition rose 10 percent between 1981 and 1987. In Ghana and Peru, malnutrition rates rose by 50 percent in the first half of the 1980s (UN, 1991). In such circumstances, even when deaths are not directly related to malnutrition, undernourished people do not have the energy to work hard and be productive. Malnutrition also may weaken the immune system, which leaves people more vulnerable to diseases that may even kill them, such as influenza and tuberculosis.

Providing Immunization. In the decades after World War II, the incidence of infectious and parasitic diseases dropped sharply in much of the world. Most experts have attributed this decline to the widespread use of inexpensive vaccinations against common childhood diseases and the widespread use of pesticides to decrease mosquito-borne diseases like malaria. Immunization for diphtheria/whooping cough/ tetanus (DPT) and measles is not necessarily a valid measure of overall public health, but it is an indicator of health service resources. Nations such as

Hungary, the Czech Republic, the Netherlands, and Sweden have good records for childhood immunization. But nations that one would expect to have good records, such as the United States and Japan, have much poorer records (Lassey, Lassey, and Jinks, 1997). Health care officials are now warning physicians and parents in the United States of the possibility of epidemics of diseases like whooping cough and measles as a result of the failure to immunize large numbers of children.

Childhood immunization also influences life expectancy. The immunization of children in the developing world is associated with an overall increase in life expectancy in these nations. Fewer die in childhood, thus extending the average life expectancy of the nation. For these reasons, life expectancy at birth is a good indicator of the general health and medical care of a society. During the last three decades, the life expectancy of people in developing countries rose dramatically, particularly in Asia (United Nations, 1991). But a great gap in life expectancy continues to exist between developed and developing countries. In the United States, the average life expectancy is 76 years, but in eastern Africa, it is 48. In Sierra Leone in western Africa, the average life expectancy is even lower—34 years (Population Reference Bureau, 1997).

Training of Primary Health Care Workers. The World Health Organization campaign, "Health for All by the Year 2000," recognizes women as the foremost providers of primary health care. In the developing world, three-quarters of all care for the sick is provided by the family, particularly women. It is women who care for infants and sick family members, look after the disabled, take their children to the health center, or purchase medicine.

Only in the last two or three centuries has illness been studied in a modern scientific way. In preindustrial societies, the family was (and is) the main institution that coped with sickness or affliction. Many of these traditional systems of healing are still practiced today. For 2,000 years, Ayurvedic medicine (traditional healing) has been practiced in India.

Increasingly, though, even in non-Western countries modern scientific medicine is being practiced. Self-taught healers exist side by side with practitioners who have had modern medical training. On the community level, women make up the majority of professional health workers. In developing countries, traditional midwives and village healers are still common. In Honduras, 80 percent of children are delivered by midwives; in Sierra Leone, the figure is 75 percent (United Nations, 1991).

Folk medicine that combines the use of herbs with acupuncture is still practiced in the People's Republic of China. Traditional medicine dates back to the Chou dynasty (1100 B.C.E.) and acupuncture and massage therapy to 200 B.C.E. Traditional nursing developed very early in China, partly because of the strict segregation of the sexes. Women had to be treated by women practitioners. Western medicine was introduced to China in the seventeenth century by Jesuit priests who were missionary physicians.

Making Health Care Accessible

The accessibility of health services is another factor that influences the health of a population. People in the industrialized world have much better access to hospitals, clinics, physicians, and other medical personnel than do people in developing countries. In Third World nations there are about 6 physicians for every 100,000 people, while First World countries average 160 physicians for every 100,000 people (Union of International Associations, 1996). Great variability also exists within nations of the First World regarding access to health care and the quality of health care that is provided. Nowhere is this variability more pronounced than in the United States, where more than 34 million Americans have no health insurance. Most of those without insurance are the working poor and their children. Without such coverage, workers and their children usually have to forgo most medical and dental treatment.

Global economic trends and events also affect health care services. For example, the worldwide economic recession in the 1980s had a great impact on health care services in developing countries. By the mid-1980s, at least 37 of the world's poorest countries had cut their health budgets by half. Africa was the region most affected. In 1982, Ghana's per capita health care expenditure was only one-fifth of its 1975–1976 level (UN, 1991). At least one-third of Asian and Latin American countries also reduced their public health budgets during this period. Doctors and nurses often quit after not having received their salaries for months. Some governments introduced patient fees, which meant that health care became even more inaccessible for poor families in the developing world (UN, 1991).

All of these elements combined to produce a notable decline in health care for people in developing countries, particularly for those most at risk—women and their dependent children. Moreover, cutbacks in health care budgets coincided with new threats to health such as Acquired Immune Deficiency Syndrome (AIDS). In sub-Saharan Africa, it is estimated that AIDS will affect 1 in 20 people by the year 2000. At present, AIDs is an incurable disease that results in premature death. In Africa alone, the World Heath Organization estimates there will be 10 million AIDS orphans by the year 2000 (UN, 1991).

AIDS is only one of many health problems developing nations face. Parasitic diseases take a tremendous toll in less developed nations—a fact that draws scant attention in the First World (see the box "FYI: The Guinea Worm—a Difficult Scourge").

Problems in Providing Health Care

Making good health care accessible at a reasonable cost is a challenge to every nation in today's world. Access to quality care is at the center of quality of life issues, no matter where a person lives, whether in the industrialized world or the developing world. But for people to gain such access, the world's nations must deal with several thorny issues.

First, every government must understand that health care is an important economic activity that is affected by other economic and social factors even as it also affects these factors. In industrialized countries, health care already consumes between 6 to 15 percent of the national income. Yet the health care industry does not only spend money, it is also a significant source of employment; many of these jobs in industrialized countries fall in the medium- to high-paying categories. For a large part of the indus-

The Guinea Worm—a Difficult Scourge

Former American president Jimmy Carter (1977–1981) recently journeyed to Africa for a conference on eliminating the guinea worm—a parasite that disables and disfigures thousands of Africans each year. The worm is spread by contaminated drinking water. Despite a 12-year campaign to eliminate the parasite around the world, 150,000 known cases still exist.

The terrible sores of Scovia Lamunu attest to the damage caused by guinea worms. When she moved into one of Kampala, Uganda's shantytowns, Scovia had no idea that she already carried within her one of the insidious worms she had fled from her rural village to escape. Shortly after her arrival in Kampala, a painful blister appeared on her leg. When it burst, a spaghetti-shaped creature stuck its head out and retreated within her flesh before she had an opportunity to pull it out.

The worm enters a person's body when a villager drinks water that contains fleas that are infested with the worm's larvae. Inside the human body, the larvae hatch, and the worms develop and move into the abdominal cavity, where they mate. The male dies after mating, but the female continues to grow. About a year later, the female, now up to three feet long, bores downward to a leg or foot, where it seeks an exit in order to lay her eggs.

A swelling of the skin that quickly turns into a painful sore is the first sign that the worm is about to emerge. The worm can take three days to a month to show itself. Typically, villagers gently pull at the worm or prod it with a stick, hoping to hasten its exit. Breaking the worm can cause serious infection in its human host. The exit wound is so painful that villagers who have experienced the worm's exit are unable to walk, children who have experienced it cannot attend school, and farmers who have experienced it cannot tend their fields. Among other things, the worm often leaves disfiguring scars.

Source: Adapted from Hugh Dellios. 1998. "Guinea Worm Still Challenges Africa's Top Health Experts." *Chicago Tribune,* April 2, 1998.

trialized world, the health care industry represents about 10 percent of national employment (Lassey, Lassey, and Jinks, 1997).

Health care is of broad international concern because all nations increasingly compete in the same market. Since health care in industrial nations is financed primarily through payroll deductions and employer contributions, the cost of health care raises the cost of products because that is one way companies can pay for their health care contributions. But the company also receives direct financial benefits from its contributions, as good health makes for a productive workforce. A healthy workforce, in other words, helps companies compete effectively in the global marketplace.

Another issue involves the rising numbers of older people in the world's societies. The proportion of older people in any population is a major indicator of general health conditions but is also a significant factor in health care cost. Aging populations, a fact of life in industrialized nations, are now also becoming a major concern in less developed countries as life expectancies there are increasing. How will governments meet the needs of growing elderly populations and continue to provide adequate service to low-income citizens? In several European nations, 15 percent (or more) of the population is over 65 and an increasing proportion is over 85. Chronic and expensive health conditions are more predominant in older people and presently consume 30 to 40 percent of health care resources in these nations (Lassey, Lassey, and Jinks, 1997). As populations age, finding adequate resources for meeting their medical needs will become more and more of a problem around the world.

Another problem most nations now face is a demand for advanced medical technology that is greater than available resources can supply. While it is true that high-technology procedures become more accessible as the per capita wealth of a country increases, there is still a limit to how many of these procedures will be implemented. Philosophies vary from country to country about what procedures should be implemented. For example, although the United States pioneered transplant technology, it gives lower priority to transplants than do France or Sweden. The problem of financing these high-tech procedures is universal. For this reason deliberate rationing is underway or under consideration in some countries (Lassey, Lassey, and Jinks, 1997).

In point of fact, most nations already ration health care in one way or another officially or unofficially. The Canadian system provides universal access to health care, but employs fewer high-tech procedures than does the U.S. system. Part of decreasing the use of high-tech procedures involves making fewer high-tech machines available and authorizing fewer costly procedures. In Canada, the city of Toronto has only two magnetic resonance imaging (MRI) machines. The Canadian government also will pay for fewer open-heart surgeries than are commonly performed in the United States.

The results of such restricted access to high-tech and costly procedures is that physicians who wish (or need) to use MRIs or perform open-heart surgeries either have to forgo these tests and treatments or put their patients on long waiting lists prioritized on a most-needed basis. Wealthy Canadians who need (or think they need) expensive high-tech procedures frequently cross the border into the United States, where they pay for tests and therapies themselves.

Health Care and Its Rationing in the United States

The United States relies heavily on high-tech expensive medicine, which presents a paradox. The American health care system is the most costly in the world, but a substantial segment of the population has little access to the system. Health care absorbed nearly 14 percent of the gross national product in 1995, which is far more than in any other nation. High expenditures mean that people with good health insurance probably secure the best health care in the world (Lassey, Lassey, and Jinks, 1997).

Despite these high health care costs, the United States ranks far behind other nations on many basic measures of health outcomes. For instance, in 1990, we ranked twenty-first in infant mortality, seventeenth in male life expectancy at birth, and sixteenth in female life expectancy (Lassey, Lassey, and Jinks, 1997). These statistics indicate that the high costs do not ensure that everyone gets top-notch medical care. In particular, lower-income mothers and children in large urban centers and in poor rural areas are slighted. Huge variations also exist among racial and ethnic groups in health status and available health care services. For example, African Americans, Mexican Americans, and Native Americans generally have much less access to quality health care than do European Americans.

In brief, the American system rations health care by limiting the access of lower-status and lower-income

THE HUMAN FACE OF MEDICAL COSTS

Too Poor to Treat

"Ninety-six-point-three is the frequency of Justus Upton's favorite radio station in Jackson, Miss. It is also, by macabre coincidence, exactly how low his body temperature fell in 1995 until he took a drug called Zovirax. Upton, 29 and HIV-positive [he has AIDS], switched to 14 medicines a day in January to beat back his dread disease. The good news: that so-called 'cocktail' took the viral levels in his blood down to almost undetectable lows—like tens of thousands of other infected people who have suddenly dared to hope again. The bad news for Upton came from the state of Mississippi a few weeks ago. It told him, and 656 other low-income HIV sufferers, that the money from Washington had run out. They would no longer receive payments for many of the drugs in their cocktail treatments. 'I'd spend everything I have to keep him alive,' frets Justus's mother, Frances. 'I just don't have enough.'

"Neither, it seems, do many state governments. So far, only Mississippi has taken the draconian step of evicting HIV sufferers from the new $12,000-per-year treatment. But 35 of 52 state-administered AIDS programs . . . have had to make some kind of emergency move or another in the past year—such as often curbing access to potent new drugs called protease inhibitors or limiting enrollment to a lucky few patients. Such moves have AIDS workers asking: Are we all, in effect, Mississippi?"

Source: Daniel Pedersen and Eric Larson. 1997. "Too Poor to Treat." *Newsweek*, July 28: 60.

groups (see the box "The Human Face of Medical Costs: Too Poor to Treat"). If the United States concentrated more on making sure that all Americans had access to quality basic services and relied less on high-tech medicine, it would have a more efficient health care system that would provide admirably for all or most of its citizens.

The Global Crisis of Infectious Disease

It is becoming clear that infectious diseases are rapidly becoming a world problem. Diseases once thought to be eliminated or under control are making a comeback, such as tuberculosis, malaria, and measles. In addition, researchers are discovering or identifying new and virulent viruses, with names like Hanta, Lassa fever, and Ebola, whose origins are often in tropical rain forests. Whole new types of diseases such as AIDS are appearing. The renewed threat from infectious diseases that scientists believed they had eliminated has many causes, all directly or indirectly originating from human practices. Ultimately, it is the disruption of social and ecological systems that leads to the spread and outbreak of infectious diseases.

Disease-Causing Factors

Two broad classes of factors affect the occurrence and spread of infectious diseases. On the one hand, various biological organisms cause these diseases, principally bacteria and viruses (which we sometimes refer to as microbes). Bacteria are microscopic single-cell organisms that carry on basic life processes and are able to replicate their own genetic material (DNA) and reproduce themselves. In contrast, viruses cannot reproduce and require a host cell to copy their genetic material. Viruses are very little more than packets of genetic material (DNA or RNA) looking for suitable hosts. They do not carry on life processes themselves but invade other cells to cause these cells to make copies of the viruses before the viruses die.

We can kill bacteria by interrupting their cellular processes. Antibiotics are chemicals designed to do just that; they kill living bacterial cells, although they also kill other cells in the process. In contrast, antibiotics are unable to kill viruses, which do not

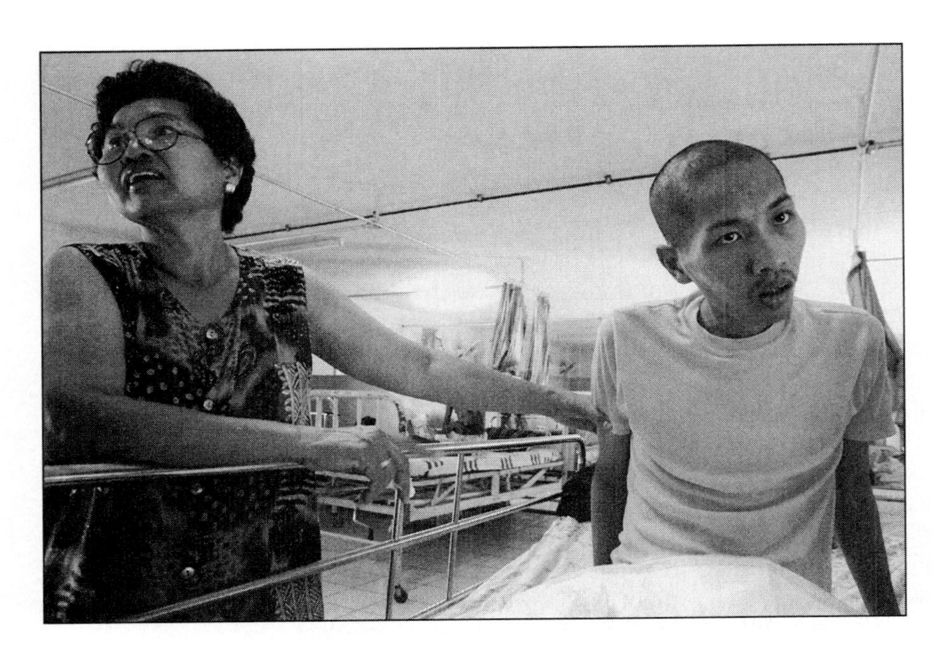

The sexual exploitation of women and children in the form of prostitution is rapidly spreading HIV/AIDS in many parts of the world, often in nations that do not have the ability to deal with such large-scale medical problems.

carry on their own life processes. Therefore, prescribing antibiotics for viral diseases is worse than useless, as antibiotics can weaken the immune system of the human being or animal receiving them or have other unwanted effects that we describe later in the chapter.

The human body also can resist infection from bacteria. Moreover, it can effectively combat viruses. We are only now coming to understand the immune system, which consists of all those processes and structures in the body that enable it to remain healthy or to recover from disease. This system is immensely complex. Later we examine some very important ways in which social, cultural, and psychological factors make key contributions to the immune system and, therefore, to health, resistance to disease, and a prolonged life span.

Disruption and Disease. In a stable human community, the human population establishes a degree of balance with local varieties of microbes. The same is true for stable ecosystems, as populations of animals, plants, fungi, bacteria, and viruses keep one another in check. Many social changes directly or indirectly linked with globalization are encouraging an intensification of threat from infectious diseases in both the underdeveloped and the developed world. For example, the expansion of agriculture and irrigation can alter the breeding habits of species that carry microbes or it may cause increases in the number of microbes available. Killing off natural species may cause bacterial or viral entities to seek new hosts in the form of human beings or the animals we use for food. Destruction of rain forests can release and spread viruses that once lived far from human habitation. The sexual exploitation of women and children in the form of prostitution is rapidly spreading HIV/AIDS and other sexually transmitted diseases in many parts of the world, especially in Africa and Asia. In Africa, the spread of HIV/AIDS is facilitated by the practice of female genital mutilation (see also Chapters 5 and 9). War and economic collapse lead to the breakdown of human community patterns, which causes diseases to spread. Thousands of people flee their homes and diverse populations cluster in refugee camps. Such camps seldom have adequate food or uncontaminated water. The people living in these camps also experience extreme psychological stress, and there is little if any medical care. All of these conditions set the stage for epidemic diseases.

Poverty and malnutrition, prostitution, and community and family breakdown are prevalent in the many slums throughout the world and create a constant disease-breeding medium. Today's extreme weather patterns and climatic change brought about by global warming threaten the natural control mechanisms of many of the world's ecosystems. We cannot foresee all the consequences of continued change of the global life-support system. But we can perceive that the rapid transportation of human beings, animals, agricultural products, and manufactured goods throughout the world can spread a potentially dangerous microbe across the globe in a matter of days or maybe even hours (Platt, 1996). All these changes are occurring at the same time that governments are cutting their budgets for the health care personnel who can monitor these diseases and distribute immunization (Platt, 1996; Garrett, 1994). Even the United States is ill-prepared for an outbreak of any proportion, lacking as we do the facilities for quarantine and treatment in the event of such an emergency (Garrett, 1994).

Infectious disease is the number one killer of human beings in the world. In 1993, 16.5 million people died of infectious disease, as compared to deaths caused by cancer (6.1 million), heart disease (5 million), cardiovascular diseases such as stroke (4 million), and respiratory diseases (3 million) (Platt, 1996). The actual number of deaths from infectious disease is actually higher than these figures because of misdiagnosis, underreporting, and the fact that many deaths from infectious disease are reported in other categories such as maternal or perinatal deaths—those of mothers and newborns (Platt, 1996). The majority of deaths from infectious disease occur in poor and less developed countries. Yet, as we will see, the threat of these diseases is rapidly escalating in the most advanced and wealthiest of societies. A new age of potent killer bacteria and viruses capable of resisting our most powerful treatments may be upon us.

Antibiotics and Superbugs. One technology practice implicated in these world health problems is the overuse and misuse of antibiotics. It has been said that the use of antibiotics is one medical treatment that does not only treat the individual patient but the whole community as well (Garrett, 1993; Levy, 1992). The microbes affected by the antibiotic do not stay within the individual but depart into the air, the sewer system, and the bodies of others, thus affecting the microbial environment of an entire community (Levy, 1992). Our bodies, our waste disposal facilities, and especially our hospitals are breeders of microbes that are increasingly immune to our medicines. Because of high-speed modern transportation, such a microbe-enhancing environment could extend from Chicago to Prague or Bangkok in a matter of hours.

Antibiotics are chemicals produced by one life form that kill other life forms, specifically bacteria. This fact was discovered in the late 1800s but it was not until 1928 that British scientist Alexander Fleming developed the first usable antibiotic. This antibiotic, penicillin, was first used in 1942 to treat victims of a fire in the Coconut Grove restaurant in Boston. Thus began a new age of human control over bacterial infections. But scientists began to gradually realize that bacteria are often able to adapt to the presence of antibiotics and become resistant to them. Studies of bacteria show that they have remarkable abilities not only to develop resistance but to share it with other bacteria, even with bacteria of other species (Garrett, 1994; Levy, 1992).

For humans the result is that many strains of bacteria, including new and more deadly strains of tuberculosis, venereal diseases, and staphylococcus are immune to our most prized magic bullets, the antibiotics. These so-called superbugs have partly been created through the overuse of antibiotics (Drugger, 1997). At times doctors have indiscriminately prescribed antibiotics without adequate testing of the cause of infection. Or doctors have prescribed antibiotics when they did not know what else to do or have even given them to patients with viral infections. Patients have also contributed to the problem by expecting doctors to do something for them immediately, although the same patients may not follow the prescribed usage of the antibiotic, which may lead to even greater bacterial resistance. Pharmaceutical companies have also been at fault because it is more profitable to develop new antibiotics than to develop new vaccines for immunization.

As we can see, mutually reinforcing social patterns are at work, and the situation is even more severe in some less developed countries. For example, in Brazil, the wealthier classes can buy antibiotics without a doctor's prescription or supervision. In many less developed countries, antibiotics are also often sold on the black market. Meanwhile, Third World governments, because of small health budgets, often import older antibiotics that have proven to be less effective. In these nations, the poor rarely receive antibiotic treatment, but when they do, it may be as little as one dose. Such low doses can strengthen the resistance mechanisms of disease entities and help them spread through the population (Levy, 1992).

The World Health Organization published a global plan in 1996 to address the problems associated with antibiotics. This plan involves educating patients not to ask for unnecessary antibiotic treatments and encouraging physicians to be more conservative in prescribing them (LeDuc, 1996). In the United States, the Centers for Disease Control (CDC) and the Institute of Medicine have issued warnings about antibiotic abuse and its relation to the increase in resistant bacteria. As recently as 1997, both the *Journal of the American Medical Association* and the *New England Journal of Medicine,* two of the most prestigious and conservative medical journals in this country, published articles that described the seriousness of the present situation. In the last decade, the rate of resistance of bacteria to antibiotics has been growing, according to a number of studies (Peterson and Kelly, 1997).

In many cases, patients contract a disease in the hospital itself. Each year some 2 million people contract diseases in hospitals in the United States, resulting in 60,000 to 80,000 deaths a year, according to the CDC. Hospitals are prime breeding grounds for resistant bacteria because the environment includes so many antibiotics, and bacteria travel readily throughout the ventilation system. The good news is that a study conducted in Finland showed that reducing the use of a particular antibiotic in a population (in this case, the commonly used antibiotic erythromycin) could cause bacterial resistance to decrease after a period of a few years (Seppala, Klaukka, and Vuopio-Varkiula, 1997). Such a change in policy requires a stringent national effort, however, which may not be forthcoming. Patients (who demand something for their illness), physicians (who want their patients to be satisfied that something is being done), and pharmaceutical companies (who reap large profits from sales of antibiotics) may resist limiting the use of these drugs (Levy, 1992).

The Interaction of Human Community and Microbes. The interactions between the social patterns and practices of the human communities (the hosts) and the communities of viruses and bacteria who live with us are many and varied. Let us use as an example the matter of virulence. *Virulence* refers to the power of a microbe to cause disease (or death). Highly virulent bacteria may cause their hosts to die so quickly that the bacteria are not able to reproduce themselves and spread to new hosts. It was thought that because of this effect, all disease-causing microbes should tend to become only moderately virulent, but the situation turns out to be more complex. Several factors can cause microbes to evolve in the direction of greater virulence. High population density is one such factor. High population density makes it more likely for a disease to spread from host to host quickly, allowing the disease to be quite deadly to its host as it reproduces itself. In cases of sexually transmitted diseases (STDs), high rates of multiple-partner sex allow the disease to spread rapidly among partners and to become highly virulent. Factors that suppress the human host's immune systems also allow rapid spread of disease and encourage high virulence. However, local human populations can develop such strong immunities to a particular disease that the disease can virtually die out and become extinct in the area. This response is called *herd immunity.* Today's rapid transportation systems and extensive travel, however, make it highly unlikely that there will be any areas in the world where such herd immunity will develop in the future.

It is advantageous to a population to be genetically diverse. When all people living in a certain area are genetically similar, they share the same susceptibility to diseases. An epidemic could decimate the entire population in such circumstances. For example, Native American populations were reduced when exposed to the diseases of Europeans after Europeans started to migrate to North and South America in the sixteenth century. At the time, approximately 15 million Native Americans were living around the Caribbean basin. Ten years later, only about 1 million Native Americans survived in the region. Much of this loss of population likely resulted from exposure to European diseases to which the natives had no immunity.

A study of a measles epidemic in Senegal (Africa) showed that when a population lacks genetic diversity a disease microbe may adapt rapidly as it moves from one genetically similar host to another, acquiring increasing virulence (Garenne and Aaby, 1990). The disease microbe becomes, in effect, a more and more specialized killer of that particular population. This finding is a good argument for interracial marriage, migration, and travel because these activities add to the biodiversity of the human population. Contrary to some people's fear that these practices will weaken their race, they may actually be conducive to the long-term survival of human groups and the entire human species.

Many other practices today contribute to the human population's susceptibility to infectious diseases and to the evolution of resistant and virulent disease microbes. Among these is the increasing intensity of interethnic guerilla warfare. This type of war causes disruption of social patterns, dislocation, the orphaning of children, the spread of disease by multiple rape, and a rise in despair and hopelessness (which we will see later as factors in illness). Poverty and homelessness, especially of children who use drugs and sell sexual favors, are additional factors conducive to the widespread transmission and evolution of dangerous bacterial and viral foes of humankind.

In developed and more stable societies, we also face the renewed threat of deadly infectious disease. The data showing that human resistance to disease is to a large extent a function of our relationships with others may, however, provide one source of hope. Strong human relationships, positive attitudes, and supportive social environments are important lines of defense against disease. Yet we have either completely or partially ignored these factors and their bearing on health and illness.

Modernism and Health Reexamined

Modernism and postmodernism play significant and sometimes contradictory roles in our lives. The sense of personal efficacy, the hope for a better future, and the attention we give to intimate communication and strong family relationships are attitudes deeply rooted in modernism that have enormously benefited society. But the individualism and personal freedom associated with modernism may also be undermining marriages, families, and communities. The despair and cynicism that accompany some developments in advanced modernism (also called postmodernism) may contribute to the weakening of social ties and the loss of hope. Along with the disintegration of communities in many societies and the spread of hopelessness rooted in poverty and exploitation in much of the world, these attitudes may turn out to be a greater threat to our overall health than the malnutrition and lack of sanitation that also accompany these conditions.

In order to properly understand the affect of modernism on health, we need to develop a comprehensive and critical perspective. In Chapter 4 we saw how scientific knowledge generally proceeds from assumptions that direct research and guide interpretations of results. The same is true for medical sciences and health issues. In the area of health and illness, the models used have tended to be either health-oriented, with the emphasis on behavioral aspects, or disease-oriented, with the emphasis on environmental factors (Sagan, 1987).

The triumph of mechanistic thinking (see Chapter 4) brought with it a search for the environmental causes of illness. For scientists and the public alike, the discovery of disease "germs" in the form of microorganisms (bacteria, viruses) found in the tissues of sick persons strongly reinforced the rightness of this approach. Today every Western schoolchild learns sooner or later about the danger of germs. The disease model is dominant in our thinking about infection, health, and life expectancy. Only recently have we begun to rediscover the importance of health practices, fitness, and immunity (which are aspects of the health model).

Yet the disease model may not be as useful as we think, according to physician and epidemiologist Leonard A. Sagan. In his study *The Health of Nations: True Causes of Sickness and Well-Being* (1987), he takes a closer look at the social history of disease and life expectancy and comes to some rather startling conclusions. The causes of health and longevity do not seem to be those factors that we usually assume to be most responsible. Sagan rules out many of the modern medical advances as significant factors in bringing about increased life expectancy and the decline in disease-related deaths. Some of what he says has been recognized for years. Demographers, for example, have noted that most of the major gains in longevity (and hence population growth) came too early in history to be accounted for by medical advances, such as the availability of private physicians or by public health benefits such as immunizations and antibiotics.

Demographers have assumed the disease model, however, and therefore have attributed gains in health and life expectancy to material causes such as improved sanitation. But Sagan argues persuasively that the dominant factors in health and illness are largely psychosocial rather than physical. We have not created a more germ-free or healthier environment; rather health gains are caused by improved resistance to disease. This resistance has had a great deal to do with social and cultural conditions apart from sanitation, nutrition, and medical technology. It is due more to the general attitude toward life and sense of personal empowerment that result from modernization. As we see next, a growing body of scientific research supports Sagan's conclusions.

The Health Benefits of Modernization. The single most significant correlation in the history of human longevity and well-being is the association between modernization and longer (healthier) lives. Archaeological evidence shows that our Stone Age ancestors lived on average no more than 30 years (most even less). Contemporary hunter-gatherers can expect to live a comparably short life. Figure 10–2 shows that the average length of life increased by only a few years from the Neolithic (New Stone Age) and Bronze Ages to the time of the Roman Empire, when it reached an average of 35 or 36 years before declining once again in medieval times (Hassan, 1981). Studies of contemporary nonindustrial societies show much the same pattern; the average length of life in such societies is 35 or fewer years. The seventeenth and eighteenth centuries saw the beginning of a rapid rise in life expectancy that has continued to the present (Hassan, 1981; Sagan, 1987).

Although we have often criticized the culture of modernity in this book, it has also brought many benefits in its wake, not the least of which has been the general improvement in health and longevity. Many of the evils attributed to modern life—too much animal fat in the diet, too little exercise and fresh air, artificial pressures and stresses caused by the hectic pace of life—seem not to have a significant negative impact on health and longevity. Life in preindustrial societies involved eating very little meat or fat, plenty of rigorous exercise, lots of fresh air, and none of the time pressures and stresses of modernity. Yet people lived, on the average, no more than 35 years, whereas people in modernized societies live on the average well into their seventies.

How Modernization Changed Life Expectancy. Several explanations have been offered for the increasing length of life that results from modernism. One argument is that the most important effects of modernization are improved nutrition and sanitation, especially the provision of clean water for drinking, cooking, and washing. These explanations, although widely accepted, are not well supported by the data, some of which we examine later in the chapter. The factor that Sagan says is most important is the type of personality or set of attitudes that develop as a result of modernization. This conclusion is supported by the work of sociologist Alex Inkeles, who studied the effects of modernization in six developing countries (Inkeles and Smith, 1974).

Inkeles found that wherever modernization occurred, it produced a particular personality pattern. A modern person is an informed and participating citizen, has a strong sense of personal competence (empowerment), is ready for new experiences and ideas, is mentally open-minded and flexible, and has a highly independent and autonomous attitude toward traditional ideas and practices, especially when making personally important decisions. These attitudes and psychological characteristics, according to the researchers, are produced mostly by one factor—the influence of education (Inkeles and Smith, 1974).

The effects of modernization have not been evenly distributed. The greatest gain in life expectancy has been that of infants. The first year of life is beyond doubt the most difficult period to survive. Childhood up to about the age of five years old is also a challenge. After that, chances of survival improve until the later period of adulthood. Modernization universally means that more infants and children survive to reach adulthood. We explain later in the chapter how the young benefit from the education and changing attitudes of their parents and families. People who are 50, 60, 70, and beyond also benefit from modernization, though not as much as do younger people. In recent years those 50 or older have achieved more of the gains in life expectancy, while the gains of the very young have tended to level off in the most developed countries.

Women have made bigger gains compared to men. Some of the longevity of women is no doubt caused by biological differences. Biologically speaking, women are the stronger, not the weaker, sex. In every age category from infancy to old age, more girls and women survive than boys and men—at least in industrialized countries. But these differences did not manifest themselves until modern times, largely because of the poor treatment of women and girls in many earlier societies (Sagan, 1987).

Most telling as a factor in longevity is social class differential, that is, the tendency of those of higher social class to live longer and healthier lives. In fact, according to Sagan, there was no social class difference in health and longevity in traditional societies. Yet that very difference is one of the most persistent and important health differences in modern societies. The higher one's social class, the more one benefits from the effects of modernization.

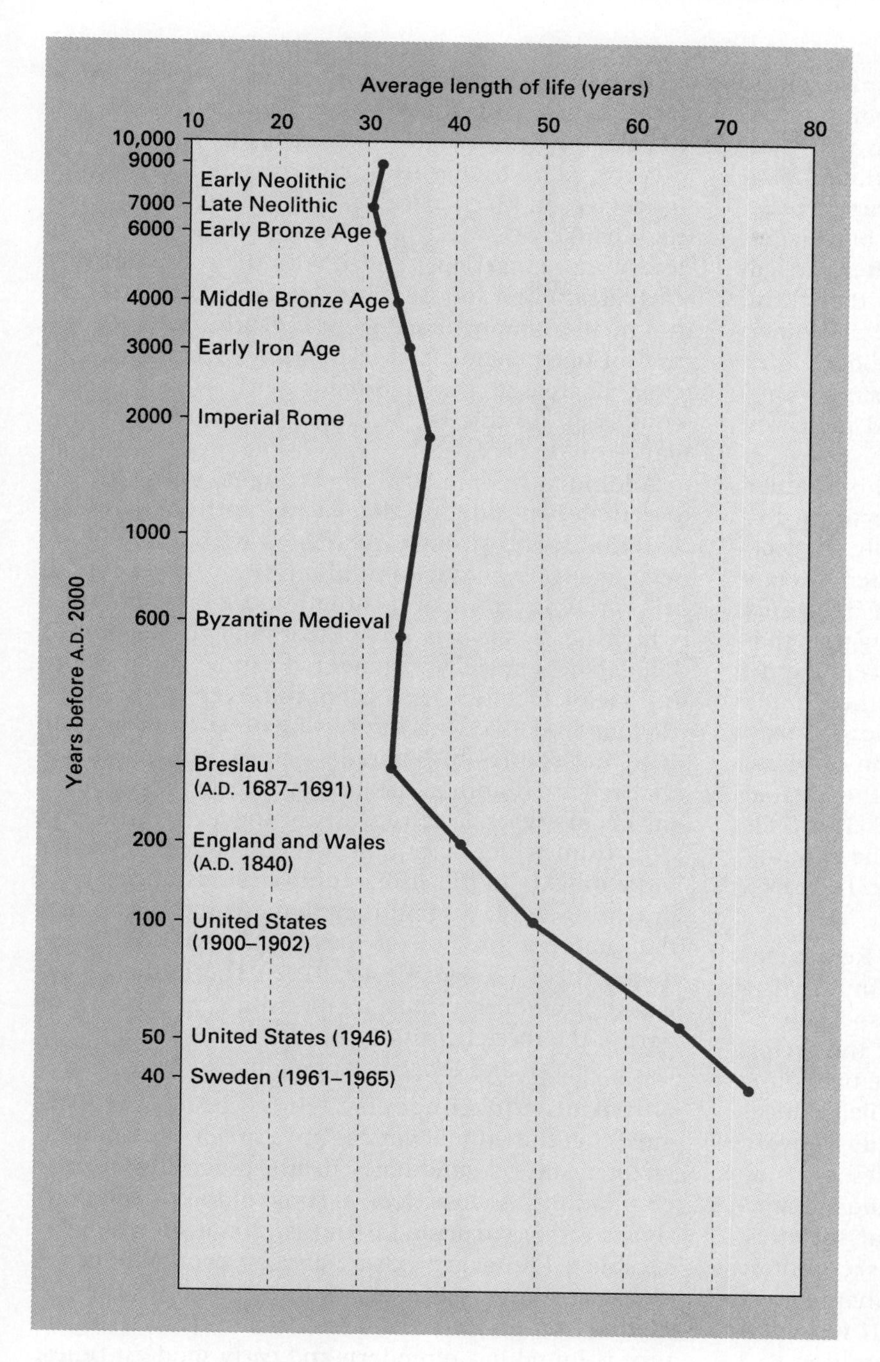

FIGURE 10–2 Prehistoric Mortality
A review of historical data indicates that increased life expectancy began toward the start of the modern period. This was long before the supposed sources of increased longevity, such as modern medicine and improved sanitation, emerged.

Source: *The Modern Rise of Population* by T. McKeown. Copyright © 1976 by Academic Press. Reprinted by permission of Academic Press, Inc.

Sanitation, Nutrition, and Longevity. One explanation for the health benefits of modernization is that it has led to improved sanitation, a condition that has provided a healthier environment. It is true that sanitation has improved with modernization. Open sewers, human and animal feces, and rotting garbage were typical contaminants of the streets of villages and towns in premodern times. This filth often seeped into the drinking water. There is no doubt that clean water and the effective disposal of sewage and other wastes greatly improve the quality of modern life, aesthetically and in terms of health. Yet a simple correlation between improved sanitation and increases in life expectancy cannot be found.

The actual picture presented by the data is a rather different one. For one thing, not all infectious diseases are transmitted via the water supply. In fact, many diseases are airborne or are transmitted by contact with infected persons. Both types of infectious diseases declined at the same time. This suggests that people were simply becoming less susceptible to death from infectious diseases, whatever their mode of transmission (Sagan, 1987). Furthermore, Sagan points out that the actual rate of infection by these diseases has not declined so much as the rate at which people survived them has increased. This finding suggests that the critical factor is not the elimination of the bacteria involved but rather increased immunity.

Changes in Family and Longevity. Remember that Sagan is saying that the increased immunity is a psychological effect of modernization, especially of education. Why then should children be the recipients of the greatest benefits when they are too young to receive education? Our insistence on their education is the result of the changing attitudes toward children, improvements in parenting styles and attitudes, and changes in the relationships among members of the nuclear family. In traditional societies, children were viewed predominantly as economic assets. Families tended to be large and invested less emotionally in each child. Marriage itself was typically arranged and was an economic proposition that was not based on romantic love. Modernism brought major changes in marriage and the family. One of these changes was that the family shifted from being a mainly economic institution based on arranged marriage and duty to one based more and more on affection. For example, romantic love increasingly became the favored reason for getting married. The long-term consequences of this change, however, have been rising expectations concerning the emotional satisfactions to be gained from marriage, and these expectations have been a factor in the rising divorce rate. Modernism also resulted in greater longevity, another factor that contributed to the rising divorce rate. That is, when life expectancy was lower, more marriages ended with the comparatively early death of a spouse. Thus for some at least a way out of an unhappy marriage was death (one's own or that of one's mate). Increased life expectancy, however, decreased the frequency with which people could rely on this factor, thereby increasing the reliance on divorce.

Additionally, modernism brought with it less parental loss due to the early death of parents. Parental loss is strongly correlated with many ill effects, both psychological and physical. For example, it represents a painful situation for a child over which he or she has no control, and the feeling of helplessness thereby engendered can be a contributing factor to later depression and even early death (Seligman, 1975). It is interesting to note in this context that studies of laboratory animals have shown that when an animal has been made to feel helpless (as occurs when it is repeatedly shocked while in a cage from which it cannot escape), it will succumb more quickly to life-threatening circumstances (e.g., drowning while swimming) than would an animal that has not previously been made to experience helplessness (Seligman, 1975). In short, the emergence of modern family relationships, an important part of the modernization process, is itself conducive to the health and longevity of children.

Nutrition and Longevity. It has been widely argued that nutritional deficits are a major contributing factor in disease and early death, especially in poor populations. A closer look at some of the correlations shows rather surprising patterns. A statistically measurable relationship exists between economic crises and death rates, an association usually attributed to higher food prices and underconsumption. This pattern is found in premodern and early modern times, but also more recently, in which case it is probably not due to lack of food but to stress generated by the economic conditions themselves (Brenner, 1984). Even more telling are studies of social conditions in wartime. After World War II, researchers studied European societies such as Belgium, England, and Germany, and Asian societies such as Japan. A surprising finding was that during periods of food deprivation, death rates (taking into account those due to the war itself) declined, as did many diseases (Sagan, 1987).

Studies of animals and human beings have shown that less food is better for health than more food, given that basic nutritional needs are met. Early food deprivation slows the maturation process and thus seems to extend life. (It needs to be pointed out that such deprivation occurs in early childhood and not later in the form of self-starvation as in cases of anorexia nervosa.) Another important piece of data that Sagan cites is that even in poor societies, there are wealthy classes that receive more than enough food. Yet both during times of epidemic disease and normal times, the death rate is not lower for the well-nourished upper classes than it is for the impoverished and malnourished lower classes (Sagan, 1987). These data suggest that nutrition is not the direct cause of longevity or immunity to disease.

Immunization, Medical Care, and Other Modern "Miracles." It is ironic that many of the most highly touted medical achievements of modern times have far less to do with health and longevity than we are taught. Take immunizations, for example. Most of us believe that the introduction of vaccines was very important in bringing infectious diseases under control. The typical image we have from the popular conception of medical treatment is that diseases such as tuberculosis, whooping cough, and polio ran rampant throughout the human population and spread devastation until the discovery of some vaccine. The introduction of the vaccine, we assume, brought the disease under control—another miracle of modern medicine.

But this is not quite the way it works. Look at the data on measles, whooping cough, and tuberculosis in Figure 10–3. What we see is a very different picture. The incidence of these diseases (and others) was rapidly declining for at least a century before the introduction of a vaccine to prevent them. In fact, the diseases had been pretty much conquered before the medical miracle occurred.

When we examine the role played by physicians in increasing longevity, we find another rather surprising correlation. An article entitled "The Anomaly That Won't Go Away" in the British medical journal *The Lancet* shows that the correlation between infant mortality and the number of physicians available is strong and positive, which is just the opposite of what we would expect (St. Leger, Cocrane, and More, 1978). In other words, the more doctors in a population, the greater the number of children who die in infancy. Researchers also conducted a five-year study in North Carolina to find out whether expanded maternal and perinatal care (care provided around the time of birth) reduces infant mortality. The researchers found that infant mortality did indeed decline in the counties receiving the extra medical care. However, they observed that infant mortality fell to a slightly *greater* degree in those areas that *did not* receive the additional care (Siegal et al., 1978). Without involving ourselves in a long discussion of modern medical practices and their relationship to health, we suggest that the evidence does not support many assumptions that people, both health care professionals and the public, commonly believe to be true.

Literacy, Longevity, and Social Class. Extensive research on health and longevity and their causes suggests that the single most strongly correlated variable is literacy (i.e., education, the most important factor in modernization). Although this has been recognized before, it is generally assumed that the reason for this correlation is that more literate groups are also likely to be wealthier. It is then concluded that the correlation goes something like this—more education equals more income, and more income equals more health care (therefore less disease). To some extent these associations occur. When we compare college-educated people with those who are not college educated, we find that 30 percent more of the college educated than those who are less educated report that they are in good health. But when we compare high-income groups with low-income groups, we find that only 10 percent more of the high-income group report that they are healthy than do those in the low-income group. These data suggest that although both education and income account for increases in good health, education is the more important factor. These data were reported in a survey conducted by the National Center for Health Statistics (1986).

As the data in Table 10–2 show, there is a correlation between infant mortality and literacy in India. But the correlation between women's literacy and infant mortality is stronger and more consistent. This correlation has been found to be only slightly related to knowledge of specific health practices such as smoking. Rather, once again the effects seem to have more to do with general attitudes and the

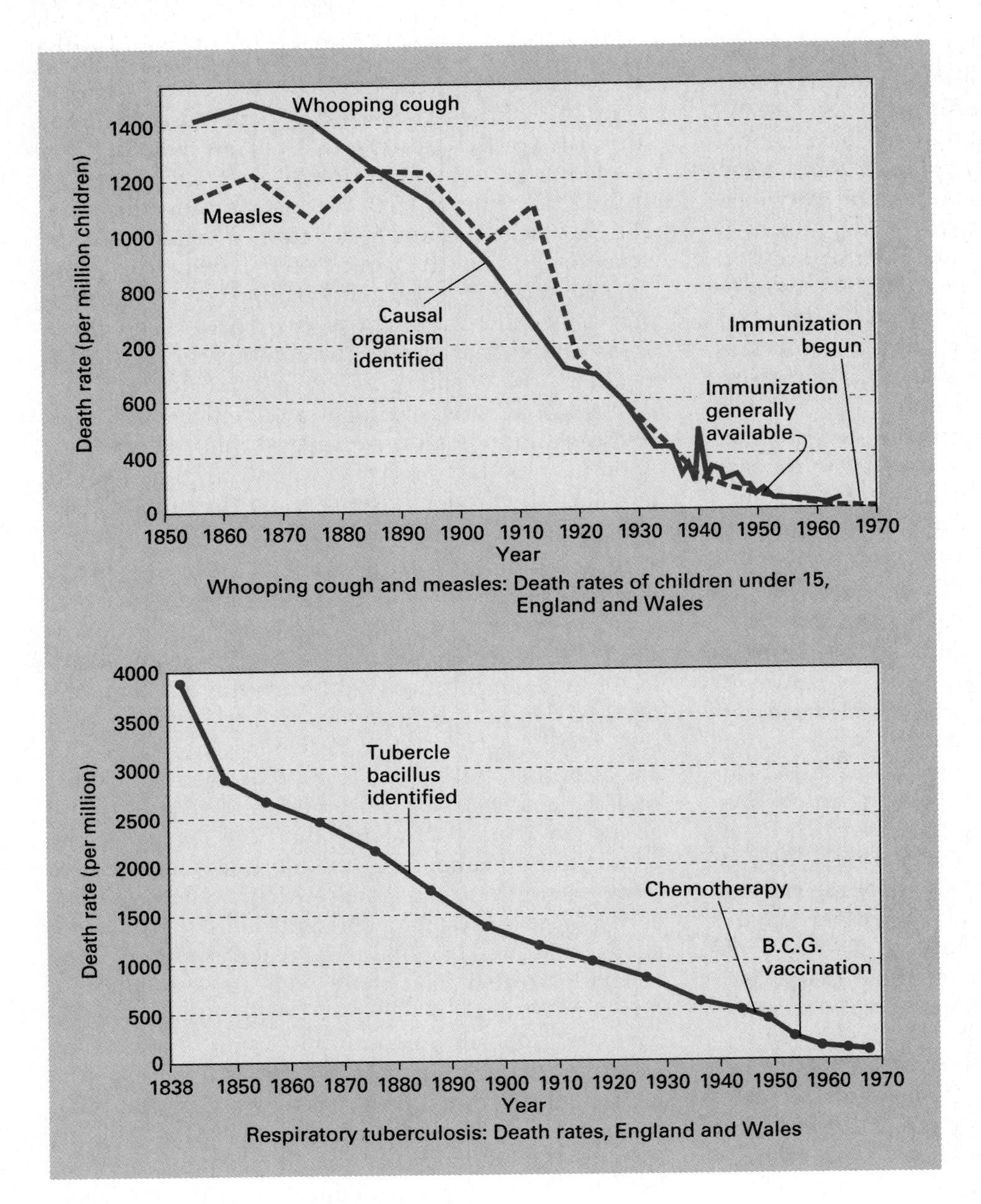

FIGURE 10–3 Immunization and Life Expectancy
Death rates from such common diseases as whooping cough, measles, and tuberculosis were in sharp decline long before the development of vaccines for these diseases.

Source: *The Modern Rise of Population* by T. McKeown. Copyright © 1976 by Academic Press. Reprinted by permission of Academic Press, Inc.

sense of personal competence or efficacy associated with education.

An interesting although troubling correlation that has developed with modernization is that between social class, health, and length of life. On every measure of illness, poor health practices, and serious life problems, social class emerges as a strongly correlated factor. We might guess that in developed countries the health gap is between the poor, who are most deprived, and the rest of society, who have access to basic necessities. But in fact there is a step-by-step gradient; the gap between each higher class and

TABLE 10–2 Infant Mortality Rates, Female Literacy, and Output per Capita in India, Selected States

STATE	INFANT MORTALITY PER 1,000 BIRTHS	FEMALE LITERACY (PERCENT OF POPULATION)	STATE DOMESTIC PRODUCT PER CAPITA (IN U.S. DOLLARS)
Kerala	52	64	96
Kamataka	81	28	99
Maharashtra	94	35	139
Punjab	104	34	162
Tamil Nada	108	34	95
Haryana	113	22	145
Himachal Pradesh	114	31	111
Andhra Pradesh	123	21	86
Assam	128	–	81
Orista	141	21	80
Gujarat	146	32	118
Rajasthan	146	11	83
Madhya Pradesh	146	16	76
Uttar Pradesh	181	14	60

Source: United Nations, *State of the World's Children, 1984*, p. 150. Copyright © 1984 by Oxford University Press. Reprinted by permission of Oxford University Press.

the one immediately below it is of the same magnitude. This pattern appears for mortality (death) rates in the United States and other developed countries.

Many practices related to ill health increase as we descend the social ladder. Smoking, obesity, and problem drinking increase with lower-class status and decrease with higher status. Other problems such as family disintegration, difficulties with the law, and school failure are more frequent among the lower classes. Alcohol consumption is a notable exception. More people drink in the higher classes than in the lower ones, but problem drinking is, however, more frequent in the lower classes.

Mental illness is also more likely among lower-class populations. A sense of helplessness and hopelessness is more likely to exist as we descend the social class ladder. Fewer life options, less effective coping skills, and more family problems accompany lower status. It is these attitudinal and learned personality patterns that Sagan, among others, believes is at the root of this class factor. Remember that this effect of social class does not appear in premodern societies, where presumably all classes share in a general malaise or sense of futility.

Evidence also suggests that some of the health gains of modernization are being lost in contemporary American society. For example, obesity among children has become a serious health problem today (Spradly and Allender, 1996). In addition, although smoking among teenagers has decreased overall, it has risen among female adolescents (U.S. Department of Commerce, 1993). Moreover, during the two decades from 1970 to 1990, the suicide rate for young people aged 10 to 14 tripled (U.S. Department of Commerce, 1993). These negative developments may not be surprising, as many causes of ill health have also been on the rise. Illiteracy has been increasing, as have homelessness and divorce, among other factors, which suggests that the social support and cohesiveness of families and communities are in decline.

Social Relationships and Health: Further Research. Dean Ornish is one of the best-known physicians in the United States. His books have become best-sellers. Ornish has developed a program that combines diet, exercise, meditation, and support groups for the treatment of heart disease that has accomplished goals experts thought were impossible—the reduction of clogging in diseased arteries without surgery. Even in our present era of high-tech medical interventions and soaring costs, his program has attracted the attention of insurance companies and the U.S. government. Over 40 medical insurance companies now pay for patients to participate in the Ornish program, which has proven effective in the treatment of serious heart disease and is far less expensive than surgery and drugs.

In a recent book, *Love and Survival* (1997), Ornish reviews numerous studies that support the role of social factors in health and longevity. Ornish concludes, "The healing power of love and relationships has been documented in an increasing number of well-designed scientific studies involving hundreds of thousands of people throughout the world" (1997:23). He says of love and intimacy, "I am not aware of any other factor in medicine—not diet, not smoking, not exercise, not stress, not genetics, not drugs, not surgery—that has a greater impact on our quality of life, incidence of illness, and premature death from all causes" (1997:3). We suggest that these relationships take form within societies shaped by the values and educational effects of modernism.

The earliest study to show the benefits of social relationships on well-being is the classic 1897 study of suicide by Durkheim (Ornish, 1997). In recent decades there have been many other studies of communities around the world and controlled experimental studies, all of which show the same results—human relationships and caring significantly increase healing and prolongs life. One such study involved a 50-year observation of the Pennsylvania community of Roseto and two neighboring towns, Bangor and Nazareth (Eglof et al., 1992). All three communities were very similar with regard to such health risks as high-fat diet, smoking, and exercise. The communities were also geographically so close that they shared the same health care facilities.

Yet the rate of heart disease was far less in Roseto than in the other two communities for a period of 30 years. Roseto was a close-knit Italian American town with many three-generation families. Its people embraced traditional values (values typical of the earlier period of modernism). In the late 1960s and early 1970s, the town underwent a transformation that led to a more fragmented community life, higher rates of divorce, and less overall cohesion. In brief, Roseto came to resemble the rest of American society. But what is most interesting for our purposes is that during the same period, the town lost its superior health advantages and, in time, its level of wellness became indistinguishable from that of the other two communities in the study.

In Alameda County, California (near San Francisco), Dr. L. F. Berkman and colleagues conducted a study from 1965 to 1974 under the aegis of the California Department of Health Services. In a sample of more than 4,000 people, the researchers found that those who lacked social and community bonds (friends, marriage, church and group memberships) were 1.9 to 3.1 times more likely to die during the period of the study. This correlation between premature death and social support was independent of, and stronger than, other social indicators such as race, gender, age, and socioeconomic status. It was also stronger than, and independent of, related health factors such as smoking, alcoholism, overeating, physical activity, perceived health, and use of health care facilities (Ornish, 1997). In Sweden, a study of 17,000 people showed that lonely and isolated people had four times the risk of dying as more socially integrated people (Ornish, 1997). Interestingly, caring for other living things, even pets and plants, also shows positive effects on health and longevity. Similarly, religious belief has a positive correlation with health and survival rates. Such belief often involves a sense of personal emotional support.

Experimental studies have also been conducted. Figure 10–4 summarizes data from one such study (Oxman et al., 1995). In this study, a sample of persons who had undergone heart surgery (the experimental group) was given social and religious support afterwards, while another group of persons who had undergone heart surgery (the control group) did not receive such support. The individuals who received both social and religious support after heart surgery had significantly lower death rates than those in the control group.

Other findings have shown that social support can make important contributions to recovery from illness and the prevention of the recurrence of illness. David Spiegel, a physician and a professor at Stanford Medical School, was highly skeptical of research findings that showed the benefits of social support in recovery from diseases such as breast cancer. He decided to do his own research for the purpose of *disproving* this relationship. By the time (1989) he and his colleagues published their article in the British journal of medicine *The Lancet,* he had reversed his position and had, in effect, *demonstrated* a strong

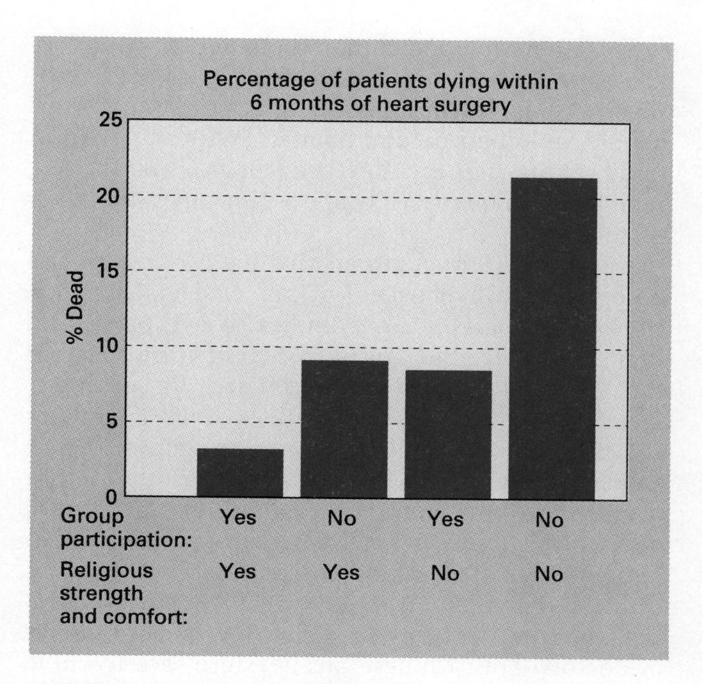

FIGURE 10–4 Intimacy and Healing
The data show that group support and religious belief have a strong correlation with survival after heart surgery. Those people in this study who had neither group support nor religious belief were seven times more likely than those who had group support and religious faith to die in the six months after the surgery.

Source: Dean Ornish. 1997. *Love and Survival*. New York: HarperCollins, p. 51. Reproduced with permission.

connection between psychosocial support and recovery from breast cancer. In this study, women with metastatic breast cancer (that is, cancer that was actively moving to new sites in the body) were randomly assigned to one of two groups. Both groups received standard medical care for cancer—chemotherapy, radiation, surgery, and drugs. In addition, one group (the experimental group) participated in a weekly support session at which they talked about their problems coping with the disease, the reactions of family and friends, fears of dying, and the like.

According to Spiegel, "I finally got around to looking at the data, and I almost fell off my chair. Those women who had the weekly support group lived on the average *twice as long* as did the other group of women who didn't have the support group" (quoted in Ornish, 1997:53, italics in the original). Participation in the support group lasted for only one year, and Spiegel did not review the data until five full years later. The effect had continued for five years or more. No drug or medical intervention by itself has proven this effective in prolonging life in cases of cancer. Were such a drug developed, it would be front-page news. But drugs and other medical interventions have the support of the medical community and the pharmaceutical industry, whereas love and social support have no such powerful interest groups behind them.

Alternative Medicine in the Postmodern World

Several factors operate in the United States today to encourage a shift to forms of healing other than the modern mechanistic system that dominates medical and nursing schools and hospitals. One factor is the extremely high cost of modern health care. As insurance companies and health maintenance organizations (HMOs) increasingly influence medical decisions, the effort to reduce costs in the interest of making a profit will no doubt increase. Both patients and those who provide health insurance and medical care for a profit will seek less expensive methods, such as alternative methods of health care.

Another factor encouraging a shift to alternative forms of healing is the increasing cultural diversity that brings to people's awareness the variety of medical approaches available today, including everything from Chinese acupuncture, which has become almost commonplace in a few short years, to the Indian system of Ayurveda medicine, made popular by the nationally known physician Deepak Chopra, to herbal remedies, many of which have been around for centuries. A third factor, related to the two previous ones, is the emergence of postmodern culture that involves the recognition that there are multiple views of reality; that is, no single theory of health and disease can now be taken as final or definitive. This understanding has led to a proliferation of other medical approaches, and to reactions to them from those who rely on the dominant model and those who profit most from it, such as the pharmaceutical industry.

What are we to call the new and not-so-new methods and models of treatment? *Holistic medicine* refers to a philosophical and practical approach to disease and health that treats all aspects of the person—physical, emotional, social, spiritual—with the goal of promoting optimal well-being and healing. *Alternative medicine* suggests methods and medicines other than those in use by the dominant Cartesian/Newtonian or mechanistic schools of thought, whether these approaches are holistic or not. One example is the use of natural herbal remedies rather than synthetic chemicals supplied by the pharmaceutical industry. The use of these medicinal substances is not actually holistic since they primarily seek to produce physical effects. *Complementary medicine* suggests the use of alternative medicines in conjunction with modern medicine. This is what most patients and practitioners seem to prefer. *Indigenous medicine* refers to alternative medical technology practices embedded in non-Western cultural traditions, which we discuss later. One concern raised about all these forms of medicine that also applies to many modern medical practices is that they need to be tested. People who are ill, especially if the illness is life-threatening or incurable by mainstream methods, are vulnerable to charlatans and cheats.

As of 1990, about a third of all Americans were using one or another form of alternative medicine (Zhang, 1996). A measure of how serious these Americans are about this practice is the fact that almost all of the expense is paid by patients themselves without substantial support from insurance. In 1992 the U.S. Congress, in response to public pressures, mandated that the National Institutes of Health (NIH) establish an Office of Alternative Medicine (OAM). The role of this agency is to promote research into alternative medicine and educate the public about it. As a measure of its increasing significance, the budget of the OAM was $2 million in 1993–1994 but rose to $20 million in 1998. The OAM operates 11 research centers across the country at major universities and clinics. Research at these centers focuses on a variety of areas, including HIV/AIDS, pain, women's health, cancer, and addiction. The OAM collaborates with the World Health Organization in the study of traditional medicine as practiced in a number of countries, including India, China, Vietnam, Japan, the European Union, and Korea.

Every part of the world has indigenous medicine, including Europe and the United States. Human cultures devised medical systems long before modern medicine came into existence. Although there remains a widespread belief in modern society that premodern or "exotic" medical practices (those of other cultures) are little more than superstition and dumb luck, a change of heart has occurred among some medical and pharmacology experts (those who study the health benefits of medical substances).

The medicine people, or shamans, of many tribal groups have extensive knowledge of herbal preparations and of techniques of a more psychological nature. Much of their knowledge has been, or is rapidly being, lost because of the destruction of tribal peoples and their natural habitats. With this crisis in mind, Westerners are now hastening to find the few remaining shamans who are willing to share their secrets.

It is not only tribal groups that have extensive and potentially valuable medical knowledge. The great civilizations of Asia have complex schools of medical thought and technology far different from those of the West. Chinese systems of cure, for example, focus on restoring the proper flow of life energy, or ch'i. Today most people have heard of acupuncture, a Chinese therapy that involves the insertion of thin needles into various energy points in the human body to rebalance ch'i. Chinese herbal knowledge is immense and takes many years to master, as does the Chinese system of diagnosis, which is entirely different from the Western one. Today a growing number of doctors, both Chinese and Western, are learning both systems. The culture of India is no less complex than that of China and possesses a variety of schools of medicine. One school of Indian medicine that has become known in the United States is the Ayurvedic school. Like homeopaths (those who practice one of the alternative Western forms of medicine), the Ayurvedic practitioners of India adjust their remedies to the basic character structure of the person. Practitioners of this form of medicine hold that people's personality differences are linked to their biochemistry, so disease processes and treatments will differ accordingly.

Increasingly, well-educated citizens of the United States and other Western countries are becoming interested in alternative medicine, as it has come to be called in this country. Some insurance programs are beginning to recognize these methods as legitimate forms of health care that may be covered. Such alternatives empower individuals by giving them choices, enlisting their minds in the healing process, reducing the cost of treatment, and offering treatments for conditions (especially chronic ones) that mainstream medicine does not effectively treat. These alternatives are apparently here to stay; rates of usage are growing in the developed countries of the world (Zhang, 1996). About 80 percent of the world's people rely on some form of health care that we in the West would call "alternative." In Ghana, for example, there is one traditional (alternative) health practitioner for every 200 people, but only one medical doctor for every 20,000 people, a typical ratio in the Third World (Zhang, 1996). As the World Health Organization and many Western nations show more interest in these non-Western medicines, a sort of reverse technology transfer may be occurring (Micozzi, 1996). That means that the developed world may continue to adopt techniques and medications invented in tribal and other premodern societies.

Educating for the Global Society

In its broadest sense, education is almost synonymous with socialization. That is, education includes not only formal schooling but all the various informal ways by which society ensures that each new generation gains the relevant knowledge, skills, and values necessary to survive.

Historical Background

If we go back in history several hundred years, we find that most people were not able to read or write, nor was possessing these skills viewed as necessary for ordinary folk. Because people in preindustrial societies had relatively few specialized roles, it was not essential for them to be literate (able to read and write at a basic level). Only those fortunate few (mostly male) who had the time and money to obtain books and pursue learning had the opportunity to become educated. A few others, such as religious leaders, needed to know how to read to interpret sacred writings, but for most people, formal learning was a luxury. (It is interesting to note in this context that the Greek root for the word "school" is leisure or recreation, neither of which implies the necessity for learning.) What most people needed to do was simply to learn the skills that would earn them a living (usually that followed in the footsteps of their parents). In those early preindustrial societies (and today in similar societies), family members and other adults informally taught children in the home the skills they needed to make a living and to perform necessary tasks.

Prior to the invention of the printing press in about 1436, books were copied by hand, which made them very expensive. Only the affluent could afford books and the time and expense of learning to read. Today books are relatively inexpensive, but in the developing world even modest prices still put them out of reach of many. Only after industrialization became widespread did education in its modern form come to be seen as desirable and only then did it become commonplace in the West. By the late nineteenth century, industrialized nations had begun to make elementary education widely available to students of both sexes. But for most young people, formal education ended by the eighth grade. In 1900, only about 7 percent of Americans graduated from high school (Robertson, 1987). At that time, this proportion was higher than that of most of the rest of the world.

Contemporary Education

At the turn of the millennium, it is almost a cliché to say that the way for an individual, or a nation (i.e., its people), to be successful is to obtain a good education. Increasingly throughout the world, education is defined as the institutionalized, formal learning activity that occurs in schools. A formal education is generally viewed as a panacea for what ails an individual and a society. In the industrialized nations of the West, much time and energy, consequently, is spent on trying to improve the quality of education; whereas in the developing world, providing access to school for more children is often the goal.

We live in a world that is more and more industrialized, and now people everywhere want to be able to read and write. Without those skills, they understand that they are excluded from the more specialized, better-paying jobs, and are condemned to a traditional life of poverty and dismal prospects.

Between 1950 and 1980, there was a huge global increase in school enrollments, and every country adopted the goal of universal primary education for its citizens. Not all countries have attained that goal; in developing countries, for example, 45 percent of women are unable to read and write.

Almost universally, formal schooling is considered essential to succeed in the world of work. But besides the teaching of reading and writing, schools have a hidden, or informal, curriculum that teaches youngsters punctuality, discipline, and obedience—traits valued in the modern workplace.

Formal education opens doors and changes a person's perspective about possible life choices. Not only does it increase opportunities by providing specific professional skills, but in many cases, education is the key to financial independence. Certainly many individuals view education that way.

Demand, Quality, and Resource Constraints

In the three decades between 1950 and 1980, a huge global increase in school enrollments in both industrial and developing countries occurred. To meet this challenge, there were massive investments in education budgets—they increased sevenfold in developing nations and fourfold in industrialized countries. Every country adopted the goal of universal primary education for its citizens, although not all countries attained that goal. Near-universal primary school enrollment has been achieved in Latin America and much of Asia (UN, 1991), but there are still several nations where that is not the case, including the kingdom of Bhutan in the eastern Himalayan Mountains, where only one-fourth of school-age children attend school, and Buloma Faso in western Africa, where only 8 percent of school-age children are in school.

Literacy is a baseline of education. Without the ability to read and write, schooling is impossible. The United Nations publication *Women: Challenges to the Year 2000* (1991) calls illiteracy "a lifelong cul-de-sac." In 1990, the last year for which such data are available, UNESCO figures indicated that 26.5 percent of the adult population of the world is illiterate. That is almost 950 million people. Of those, 19.4 percent are male and 33.6 percent are female. In developing countries the illiteracy rate is even higher; 45 percent of women are unable to read or write.

The United Nations Educational, Scientific, and Cultural Organization (UNESCO) maintains that there is a direct correlation between illiteracy and other social indicators—health, economic and political power, and the exercise of informed choice. This correlation is especially true for women. Research indicates that women with seven or more years of education tend to marry an average of four years later and have 2.2 fewer children than women with no schooling (United Nations, 1991). See Chapter 9 for more about this topic.

Many countries have instituted literacy programs. In addition to formal schools (where they are available), television, radio, and other electronic media convey education to the citizens in these countries. Increasingly, around the world there is a demand for at least primary education in formal schools. As this demand continues to rise, concerns about the quality of that education are also becoming more widespread. But throughout the world, resource constraints are a cause for concern. Experts agree that resources for education are not likely to expand in proportion to need. The twin tasks of improving educational quality while serving increasing numbers of students require new resources, especially in the rural areas of developing nations.

Demand for schooling continues to grow, not only for those who currently have no access to education but also for the rising numbers of school-age children. Rapid population growth in the developing world means that more children need to be educated with less money to do so. For example, in Pakistan 70 percent (11 million) of six- to eleven-year-olds are not in school (Claffey, 1990). How can a poor nation such as Pakistan build the schools, train the teachers, and publish the textbooks to educate all those children? For such nations, these represent formidable tasks.

In the 1980s, much of the world experienced economic crisis. In response, international financial institutions slowed aid to developing countries, including funds earmarked for education. The governments of developing nations are still eager to expand schooling, but the money set aside to build more schools, train more teachers, and produce more books has leveled off or declined, especially in Africa, South Asia, and much of Latin America (Fuller, 1990). According to UNICEF, the least developed countries decreased their education budgets by 25 percent during the 1980s. The governments of these nations cut funding for education largely as part of a strategy to help them deal with their debt crisis. Latin America and the Caribbean suffered the largest cuts: Bolivia decreased its education funds by more than 45 percent, Costa Rica by 41 percent, and Jamaica by about 33 percent (United Nations, 1991).

The part of the world hardest hit by budget slashes to education programs is Africa. Some African nations virtually eliminated education from their national budgets. For example, Zaire, one of the world's poorest nations and one with the highest illiteracy rate, slashed its education budget from 15.2 percent of total government expenditure in 1972 to 0.8 percent in 1986 (United Nations, 1991).

Throughout the developing world, school buildings and equipment have deteriorated and spiraling inflation has devalued teachers' salaries up to ten times. To help combat these trends, governments in many countries introduced school fees for the first time, but the poor economy meant that parents could not afford the increased costs. Dropout rates rose in several countries after the introduction of the fees. These trends contributed to the gender gap in education. Education for females is hardly a priority for families, local communities, and national governments in the developing world. When a family has to choose which child will be educated, boys invariably have preference. (Recently, the economic crisis in southeast Asia has caused many poor families to withdraw their female children from school so they can work to help their household to survive.) See Chapter 9 for more on this topic.

The 1980s economic recession also affected education in the industrialized world. Cutbacks harmed the entire educational system, from primary schools to universities. In England, educational grants (considered the right of every citizen) were restricted; in the United States, the cost of a college education became prohibitively high for increasing numbers of middle-class families.

In most of the developing world, educators and policymakers perceive the quality of primary education to be alarmingly low. There is widespread agreement that the fastest way to bring about improvement is to recruit and train more teachers (Thiagarajan, 1990), but in the developing world, college-trained teachers are rare. For example, in Nepal, one-third of all teachers have no more than a primary school education. In northeast Brazil, one-third of all teachers have completed just four years of schooling (through the fourth grade), or less (Fuller, 1990).

The Issue of Language

In many parts of the world (including the United States), the issue of which language to use for school instruction is a lightning rod for dissent. Most experts agree that language differences between home and school, between parents and teachers, and among students is a major barrier to academic achievement (Messec, 1990). The language policy of a country is a central issue; educators sometimes must appease political forces or parental and community demands that the schools reflect a group's heritage or identity.

Africa provides an example of the difficulty posed by the problem of language. An accurate figure of the number of languages in use on the African continent is unknown, but in West Africa alone (Cameroon to Senegal), there are an estimated 500 to 1,000 languages or dialects spoken (Messec, 1990). In some African countries, school authorities have chosen to teach the language of the colonial power that previously controlled that area. In many areas, this has been a way to avoid any potential conflict involved in choosing among the competing local languages. In the French (e.g., Gambia and Zaire) and English (e.g., Union of South Africa) colonies in Africa, the colonial governments established educational systems that employed the mother nation's language for instruction. In most, but not all, of these countries, these languages were still taught as the instructional language even after the achievement of political independence.

Linguistic competition is not limited to postcolonial Africa. It is a near-universal occurrence. We see this conflict in the United States (over the teaching of Spanish), in Canada (over the teaching of French), and India (over the teaching of English). Research indicates that the use of a number of languages is the least efficient way to educate students (Messec, 1990); many never become fluent in the dominant language of the culture. Later in this chapter we discuss language issues in the United States.

Education in the United States

Americans take for granted that everyone has the right to at least a basic formal education. Therefore, we expect each state and community to provide free, or public, elementary and high school education for its children. In fact, the United States was the first nation in the world to provide free, mandatory education. By the beginning of the Civil War (1861), most states offered free education to white children. At the end of the nineteenth century, elementary education was widely available in the industrialized nations. By the 1930s, secondary education was becoming common and even compulsory in industrialized countries. European nations introduced free education much later.

Educating for the Twenty-First Century

Almost from its beginning as a nation, the United States has experienced confusion about the goals of its educational system. Both educators and the public generally agree that the three Rs (reading, 'riting, and 'rithmetic) should be taught, but there is no such consensus concerning what other skills, knowledge, and values children should learn in school. The question of what kind of education we want our children to have is made more difficult by our confusion about how to educate them. This section explores some of these issues.

Americans place a great deal of faith in education as a tool of democratization and upward mobility. In this context, education is supposed to serve two key functions: prepare young people for the rights and duties of citizenship and provide them with vocational preparation. Americans also view education as the great equalizer, in that it enables anyone with drive and discipline to get some share of the American dream. Although the nation's founders believed an educated citizenry was essential to maintain democracy, it was the industrial revolution that served as the great impetus for extending education to all citizens.

Commitment to Mass Education. The industrial revolution not only highlighted the need for all workers to be educated, it also required increasingly high levels of education for them. In the United States, by the early part of the twentieth century, every state provided tax-supported education for citizens and made it mandatory for young people to attend schools for a certain number of years. The number of required years has increased over time.

The United States has long held that no other nation has equaled our goal of educating every citizen. The figures bear this out. In 1900, 7 percent of Americans graduated from high school; by 1990, 71.2 percent did (World Almanac, 1993). The proportion of high school graduates attending colleges has also risen sharply, from 4 percent in 1900 to a record 62 percent in 1991 (World Almanac, 1993). In Canada and Europe, the comparable figures are much lower.

This nation's commitment to mass education has come with a price. Chief among those costs is a lowering of educational standards. Other industrial nations have generally insisted on high standards, even though that decision means denying educational opportunities for the less academically able. In England and Germany, less academically inclined children are tracked into vocational education, which typically ends after ten years. But the United States continues to stand behind its pledge that everyone is entitled to a basic academic (nonvocational) education.

It has been argued, and is widely believed, that education helps reduce disparities of wealth and power. But whether or not formal schooling accomplishes that goal is a matter of debate. A great deal of research has been done on the subject. In the United States, educator James Coleman (1966) and writer Christopher Jencks (1972) concluded that nonschool factors, especially family background, influence the educational and occupational status attained. On their own, educational reforms had a minimal effect on existing class and racial inequalities (Giddens, 1991).

Education as "Cure-All." The American pledge that every child is entitled to an education derives partly from the belief that education is valuable and desirable in itself. But this notion is associated with another idea, namely that education can also serve a wide variety of utilitarian purposes, including the amelioration of social problems. Many Americans believe that public education is the cure-all for social ills. As a result, we frequently tend to advance education as a quick fix for almost any identifiable problem. One such problem was (and continues to be) how to integrate immigrants into American life. In the latter half of the nineteenth century and well into the twentieth century, schools were geared to Americanize immigrant children. Not only did they learn in the public school system how to read and write English, they also learned the values that business and industry considered essential: promptness, reliability, adherence to rules and directions, and so forth.

More recently, education has been called on to help compensate for the demise of social welfare programs to help various segments of the population. Today many conservatives have advocated increased charity work by volunteers to compensate for recent cutbacks in funding for social welfare programs. This approach ignores the fact that volunteerism has been on the decline in recent decades. Several state legislatures have responded to this problem by passing laws to install a community service component as one of the graduation requirements for high schools. Some colleges also have made volunteer service a graduation requirement.

Despite the belief that schools can fix any social problem, American education has fallen short of its high expectations in this regard, partly because the goal is impossible. It is both unfair and unrealistic to expect education alone to solve society's ills. Social problems occur in a complex context (e.g., economic disparities, poor housing, decline of inner cities, the changing nature of work, and the composition of the workforce) and are the result of the interaction of a multitude of forces (e.g., the homeless population is partly made up of the mentally ill, who are without housing largely because of changes that shut down many mental health residential treatment centers during the 1970s and 1980s). The educational system has no control over most of these forces and, indeed, may be as subject to them as the problems it seeks to address. For example, education is often touted as the solution to poverty. Yet the education of many poor students occurs in inner-city neighborhoods where most of the adult residents are poorly educated. Many of them are parents who feel inadequate to assist their children or to deal with authority figures such as teachers and administrators. Such parents or caregivers may consequently appear (often mistakenly) uninterested in their children's education and unsupportive of educators' efforts to improve students' performances. In addition, students in these neighborhoods may feel pressure to quit school as soon as possible to help provide financial support for their households. Drugs, gang violence, and health problems may also spill over into the school from the surrounding environment. As the more affluent residents leave inner cities, tax bases decrease at the same time as problems multiply. Schools then must deal with more needy and problematic students, just as the resources available for them to do so become less and less. Under such circumstances, education may become as much a part of the problem as a part of the solution.

More and more stress has been placed on schools to solve even more of society's social problems. When youngsters were thought to be physically unfit, the school system responded by adding mandatory physical education classes; when young drivers had too many accidents, the schools added driver's education; when society increasingly viewed racism and intolerance as a problem, the government mandated multicultural programs in the schools; when out-of-wedlock births skyrocketed and AIDS became a problem, schools added sex education to the curriculum. But in most of the nation's school districts, the school day and school year did not increase, so less time was available for the so-called basics such as reading and math.

Educating for What and by Whom? Numerous controversies center on the nature of the educational curriculum and who controls it. One set of controversial issues revolves around the type of education necessary for the twenty-first century. There is little disagreement that our society will need a more educated workforce. Nations with a poorly or indifferently educated labor force will obviously be at an extreme competitive disadvantage in the global marketplace. Underprepared workers will be excluded from satisfying and adequately compensated employment. Hard physical labor, the basis for work in preindustrial societies, does not provide the basis for economic security in advanced industrial societies like that of the United States.

But what will be the shape of this education for the next century? On one side, there are those who advocate a return to the basics, emphasizing the three Rs. Others stress the need for various types of technical training. Still others argue that educational content is not as important as the development of skills necessary for people to be good citizens and effective workers in the new information age.

Certainly there will still be a need for good skills in the three Rs. People will have to be able to read, write, and do basic math. In addition to the three Rs, many experts stress that people should possess a basic knowledge of the sciences and basic principles of government, history, and oral communication. They will also need a foundation in such disciplines as geography, anthropology, sociology, or other international studies that acquaint them with people and cultures dissimilar to their own. An understanding of the globalization process, including the changes it produces, will also be more and more essential.

Technical training may be useful for some. Engineers, computer experts, and other highly trained technicians obviously will be in demand. Even when dealing with technical areas, those workers with the ability to create and adapt new knowledge or to find creative uses for existing knowledge are likely to fare well. People educated for such jobs as computer technicians, health care professionals (nurses and nursing assistants, inhalation therapists, physical therapists), and the like also probably will be able to find employment. But those who do not have these abilities will generally find themselves in a precarious economic situation. Finally, skills in gathering, organizing, critically evaluating, and presenting information, along with fundamental competency in reading, writing, and math, will probably be even more essential for good citizens and productive workers in the twenty-first century than ever before.

Community Control. Other curriculum-related issues center on who will, or should, control the content of what is taught in schools. The United States is the only industrialized nation without some form of a national curriculum, standards, and/or tests for its educational system. Throughout the world, most nations regard education as a national enterprise. Many countries have uniform national curriculums, teaching salaries, funding policies, and examinations. That national perspective has never existed in the United States. From the beginning, Americans have regarded schools as the concern of the community; most public school decisions are in the hands of local, elected school boards. The local school board has a great deal of influence in determining the content and direction of local school curriculums. This situation has allowed parents and others to be assured that what is taught in the public schools is consistent with their values and way of life. The community thus shapes the content of education.

Another key outcome of community control is that schools in wealthy districts have far more funding than those in poorer areas. Community control of local schools has many advantages, but a major drawback is that because the federal government provides only a small percentage of educational funding, the educational experience depends so heavily on the neighborhood where the student happens to live.

The lack of a federal standard has led to the extraordinary diversity in what is taught in American schools, but it also has caused inconsistency within the American education system. Part of the reluctance to create national educational standards stems from the powerful tradition of local control of education. Such a local emphasis is progressively dysfunctional in an interconnected globe. Look at the situation this way: For which world should we be educating young people? In which world will they be functioning? Is it the local world of town, neighborhood, or ethnic group? Or is it the national world of the United States? Maybe it is neither but rather the larger world of global society. It seems obvious to the authors of this book that educators must now prepare young people to participate in the larger world, to be citizens of the globe. It is our belief that those people whose education is focused solely on the local or national levels will be increasingly marginalized in global society.

It is possible that this global focus in education may find some opponents, including those parents who believe that it undermines their values and their control over their children. For example, global education stresses acceptance of diversity. But some parents believe that we should not accept or even tolerate certain kinds of other people or their lifestyles, nor should our educational system teach such tolerance and understanding. The kind of "other people" may vary, from religious, racial, or ethnic groups to homosexuals, secular humanists, or modernists. For many adults with school-age children, these "other people" constitute a threat to cherished religious teachings, values, or ways of life.

Diversity within local communities also causes conflicts over school curriculums. Different religious, class, or ethnic groups may have divergent interpretations of what should, or should not, be taught in local schools. To further complicate the situation, a variety of professional groups such as the American Academy of Science and the American Historical Association, teachers' unions, individual teachers themselves, and educational administrators also often seek to influence curriculum.

Declining Performance. There is widespread concern that students who attend American schools are receiving substandard education. Several factors cause this concern. Functional illiteracy is one area of misgiving. *Functional illiteracy* means that people cannot read or use math well enough to adequately conduct their day-to-day business.

Almost all adult Americans have education beyond the primary grades. Ideally, then, all adults should be literate enough to conduct their own affairs. Yet education critic Jonathan Kozol estimates that 25 million Americans are functionally illiterate. Another 25 million perform at just the eighth grade level. Twenty-two percent of adult Americans cannot properly address a piece of mail, and 25 million are unable to understand the writing on a bottle of aspirin. The United States has suffered more than $100 billion in lost productivity and accidents caused by inability to understand written instructions (Kozol, 1980, 1985a, 1985b). Many who are functionally illiterate may be forced onto the welfare rolls to support themselves and their families, another huge cost to the nation.

U.S. students' performance on standardized testing is another cause for concern. The performance of primary and secondary school students in the United States is well below that of their counterparts around the globe. U.S. students trail most Asian and European students on almost every type of test and at practically all grade levels. Americans fare especially poorly in math and science. Meanwhile, in the United States itself, students' accomplishments have declined on most nationwide standardized tests. However, as Table 10–3 shows, this blanket statement hides the complexity of the real-life situation. When compared to scores in the 1960s, SAT scores have declined, but starting in the early 1980s, they either stabilized or began to improve. The ACT scores follow a similar path. By 1994, ACT scores were higher than they were in 1967 (U.S. Bureau of the Census, 1995a).

The interpretation of these scores is controversial. For instance, what should we make of the comparison of U.S. students with students from Asia and Europe? There can be little doubt that geography, math, and science are necessary skills for students to develop. We certainly need to improve our teaching in these areas. Still, the U.S. system has some positive focuses that do not appear in other countries' educational plans. Critical thinking is a good example. From very early on in their education, U.S. students are encouraged to look at options, assess relevant information, and make judgments about issues. American educators generally argue that critical thinking is essential for good citizenship, work productivity, and ethical living. Yet Asian educational systems scarcely address the critical thinking process.

The debates over what abilities tests such as the SAT and ACT measure and how well they measure them spark a number of controversies. These types of tests produce instruments that measure skills possessed by all people who receive a basic education in the United States. However, factors well beyond the classroom powerfully influence test performance. Tests generally designed by white educators probably have at least some bias toward white middle-class test takers. As a result, lower-class and minority students do not do as well on these instruments because the tests do not reflect the subculture in which they are reared.

Another set of questions focuses on whether standardized tests measure skills necessary for success. The predictive ability of these test scores seems questionable, as a student's SAT or ACT scores have very little to do with how well he or she will do in college. For this reason some colleges have abandoned standardized test scores for admissions screening altogether, while others have expanded their admissions process to include a number of other factors besides test scores (e.g., leadership qualities or special gifts like artistic talents).

TABLE 10–3 SAT and ACT Scores 1967–1994

TEST	1967	1980	1990	1994
Scholastic Assessment Test (SAT)				
Verbal	466	424	424	423
Math	492	466	476	479
American College Testing (ACT)				
Composite	19.9	18.5	20.6	20.8
English	18.5	17.8	20.5	19.8
Math	20.0	17.3	19.9	20.2
Reading	19.7	17.2	(NA)	21.2
Science Reasoning	20.8	21.0	(NA)	20.9

Source: U.S. Bureau of the Census, 1995A. *Statistical Abstract of the United States, 1995*, 115th ed. Washington, DC: U.S. Government Printing Office, Tables 272 and 273.

Do standardized tests such as the SAT or ACT measure skills needed for success? Evidence indicates that how a student scores on the SAT or ACT has very little to do with how well he or she will do in college. For this reason colleges now look at other factors besides test scores in their admissions process.

Assuming that standardized test scores say something meaningful about U.S. education, we are left with the question: Why have many types of standardized test scores declined since the 1960s? One reason is that we may not be teaching these subjects as well. Indeed, the 1970s saw a marked retreat from an emphasis on basic academics. This retreat is said to have many sources. According to conservative critics, the liberal emphasis on the necessity for students to feel good about themselves replaced the traditional stress on performance as a measure of quality education. One effect has been an increase in social passing, meaning that students are passed because their self-concept might be negatively affected by failing a course or grade. Others argue that the curriculum's emphasis on academic performance has been diluted by a host of requirements for soft courses, such as consumer education, sex education, parenting, and communication courses, which take time away from serious academic courses.

Other factors that influence student achievement include the academic quality of people attracted to primary and secondary education. Education majors' ACT/SAT scores are among the worst for any academic discipline. Moreover, teaching certification in the United States generally requires that college students major in education and receive, at best, a minor in the discipline they expect to teach. In other industrialized nations, teacher candidates are expected to major in an academic discipline and minor in education. Germany even requires prospective teachers to complete two academic majors before they can begin to pursue education course work.

There also is some indication that a wider range of people have been taking ACT/SAT tests in recent decades, which may partly explain the decline in scores on the standardized tests. But why did this change occur? Young people did not consider college a normative choice until after World War II. Previously, college was for the elite. Most people could obtain relatively good jobs with a high school education. When college became a necessity to ensure a high-paying job, a wider range of people started taking college entrance tests. As a result, we now have more students who are marginally qualified for college taking the tests. Another factor explaining the declining scores for standardized tests may be educational funding decreases, especially in poor areas. These have caused cutbacks in extracurricular activities, reliance on older instructional equipment, and high student-to-teacher ratios—all of which may negatively influence the quality of education.

Education, Social Class, and Funding. Ideally, the U.S. education system serves as the primary vehicle for upward mobility. To some extent, it has functioned in this fashion. Multitudes of immigrants and their children have begun their climb to success by pursuing higher levels of education. Additionally, many poor people still successfully use the educational system as a ladder out of poverty. Nevertheless, it is undeniable that the American educational system, like that of many other countries, is closely aligned with social class. In fact, some critics hold that the main purpose of the U.S. system is to perpetuate the existing class structure by keeping working class and poor people "in their places" (Weis, 1988; Oakes, 1985; Collins, 1979; Bowles and Gintis, 1976). Earlier in this section, we noted how the problems of poor neighborhoods spill over into schools, where they handicap the quality of education. These are hardly the only set of difficulties that hamper the achievement of poor students in the educational system. A number of other factors are related to educational funding.

There is not a direct one-to-one correspondence between the amount of money spent and the overall quality of education. But a good education does cost money. Conversely, most of the schools with markedly inferior educational quality are located in poor areas, which have comparatively little to spend on their pupils. A substantial portion of educational spending comes from local government. Property taxes are the source of almost all of the local funds for education. This means that the moneys available for education vary widely from state to state and among school districts within states. Rural regions and impoverished inner cities usually have much less to spend on education than do affluent suburban areas. Wealthy districts may spend as much as nine times more on each pupil than do poor districts (Curarn and Renzetti, 1996). The irony is that those districts who have students with the fewest academic, social, and personal problems have more money to spend than do districts with needier students. Additionally, voters have become less ready to vote for tax increases or pass other forms of supplemental revenue for educational purposes. Clearly, we must develop new ways to fund public education. Methods other than simply increasing funding to public education have gained popularity. One debatable alternative for improving public education is discussed in the box "Contemporary Discussion: Vouchers for Private Education."

Finally, we need to mention the issue of rising college costs in an era of declining public resources. The United States has more college graduates than any other industrialized nation. As of 1994, 22.2 percent of adult Americans had four or more years of college. The number of Americans with a college education is up dramatically from 7.7 percent in 1960 (U.S. Bureau of the Census, 1995). We have indicated that college is increasingly seen as necessary in order to obtain well-paying positions, ones that provide a measure of financial stability. But as college education has become more important to individual and national futures, its costs have rapidly escalated. Students and their families bear much of these expenses. For school year 1996–1997, tuition alone averaged $2,966 at public institutions and $12,823 at four-year private colleges and universities. These expenses do not include the cost of other fees, books, room and board, incidentals, or travel. When these sums are included, the annual cost of attending college in the United States rises dramatically. For example, at the public University of Illinois–Chicago, the total cost to a student for one year of education is $9,336. The cost of attending the private Northwestern University, another Chicago-area school, is more than $25,000 a year.

The more liberal 1960s and 1970s saw the creation of a number of government programs to make college available to a larger segment of the U.S. population. Their goal was to help low- and moderate-income families finance college. In the 1980s and 1990s, conservatives have eliminated many of these programs. This trend means that the gap in educational opportunities between the affluent and the poor will likely widen. Many middle-income families will have a progressively more difficult time funding advanced education for their children. We seem to be reverting to the system we had at the beginning of the twentieth century, by which only the wealthy received a quality education and could afford to send their children for advanced education.

Competitiveness. Schools in the United States encourage competition. Most schools use a grading system that encourages students to compete with one another for the high grades. Students who do not get high grades are gradually eliminated from the system and sent to labor in the workforce. Competition at school is an important part of the socialization process in the United States. Because they are taught to compete with one another for the scarce rewards of money, power, and prestige, American children are prepared, in effect, for the economic roles they will play as adults. When there were well-paying blue-collar jobs in industry, this was less of a sacrifice than in the current economic situation, in which those jobs are increasingly being transferred overseas.

This competition for good grades and status can become so intense that it undermines the academic goals of education. Some students concentrate on achieving good grades rather than on learning for its own sake. Many take easy courses or seek out teachers known to be nondemanding and easy graders. Many avoid reading that seems irrelevant to tests. These factors leave many American children underprepared for the economic, social, and citizenship demands of adult life.

Assessing the Situation

This chapter has dealt with issues centering on what may seem to be an odd combination—medicine and education. Yet worldwide these two institutions are key mechanisms for improving the quality of human

CONTEMPORARY DISCUSSION

Vouchers for Private Education

By and large, private schools are able to turn out students who are better prepared for college at less cost than public schools. This is the case even when these private schools are located in or near poor areas. Some wealthy sections of American cities and suburbs also have public schools that do a more than adequate job of preparing their students for jobs or advanced education. But it is not possible for poor students to move into more affluent school districts, and many programs to improve schools in poor areas have not been successful. One proposed solution to this problem has been to offer parents of poor children vouchers paid for out of school taxes that parents could then use to pay tuition and other expenses for their children to attend private schools.

People who support the use of vouchers say that they would allow poor parents the same options as wealthier parents. That is, wealthier parents often pay to send their children to expensive private schools even when they have access to good public schools. Poorer parents do not have this choice. Parents at private schools often get more involved with their children's education than do parents in public schools. Vouchers may encourage poor parents to get involved as well. Private schools provide a better education because they are not burdened by sometimes stifling regulations imposed by government officials and are, therefore, more free to innovate in developing programs tailored to individual students' needs.

Supporters of vouchers also contend that discipline problems are fewer in private schools because the private schools can be more selective about which students they accept. Even students with spotty academic performance do better when they are placed in schools in which high academic performance is the expectation. Competition with private schools for students will also force public schools to improve the quality of education for their students. Many private schools are run by religious organizations. However, supporters claim that

life. Good health is one of the factors that is most important in living a happy and productive life. Education also is important in that it widens people's perspective and provides them with the tools needed to care for themselves and their families. As a result, both good health and education are tools of empowerment, giving people an ability to take control of their lives and improve their life situations.

However, more than this, we have shown that health and education are intimately linked. As a society's level of education increases, the overall health of the society also improves. Within some limits this applies to individuals also, since better-educated people generally are healthier and are more likely to believe they are healthier than those with less education. These effects are part of the social and cultural factors associated with the improvement of health that are attributable to modernism. Increasing education gives people a sense of efficacy, meaning that they believe that they have some control over their lives and are not just victims of circumstance.

Human Rights, Health, and Education

The Universal Declaration of Human Rights directly addresses both health concerns and education (see Appendix A). Article 25 states that everyone has a right to a standard of living that provides adequately for his or her health and well-being. As part of ensuring that standard of living, Article 25 indicates that each person must have access to medical care and necessary social services.

Article 26 addresses the issue of education. It holds that everyone has a right to free elementary and fundamental education and that technical, professional, and other forms of higher education should be readily available on the basis of merit. The education provided should be oriented toward the development of using public funds to pay for these religious schools does not violate the First Amendment's mandate for separation of church and state (see Chapter 3), as these funds are used to provide the same type of secular courses that students would take in public schools and are not specifically earmarked for religious education.

Opponents of school vouchers use several different arguments. They note that because of limited funding and limited space in private schools, vouchers can help only a small portion of the students who need help. There is also no evidence that poor schools who are losing students to private schools are then driven by competition to improve their own educational standards. In fact, since the best students in the poor schools will likely be the ones to take advantage of vouchers, opponents argue, the best students will be the ones to leave public schools. This leaves behind only students who are not academically gifted and/or who may have discipline problems. Consequently, the public schools will be even worse off than they were before the vouchers.

Moreover, opponents say, the public school system has been the primary method for assuring that Americans, rich and poor, majority and minority alike, share in a common heritage. To remove significant numbers of students from the common educational environment would lead to increasing divisions among the various segments of our society. In addition, providing funds for religious schools does in effect use public funds to support religious institutions. As more students leave public schools, the commitment of taxpayers to the educational system decreases, making them even less likely to approve tax increases to support education. In sum, rather than improving the public school system, vouchers undermine public education.

◇ **For Critical Thought:** (1) What are the assumptions of each side in this discussion? (2) How does each position relate to major theoretical themes of this book? (3) What are the human rights implications in each side of this discussion? (4) What additional problems might be caused if either of these positions are implemented? (5) Are there other possibilities for improving education that are not addressed by these options?

Source: Joan Beck. 1998. "Skimming Off the Best Students Harms the Rest." *Chicago Tribune,* June 14:1.21; Steve Chapman. 1998. "School Vouchers and the Salvation of Education." *Chicago Tribune,* June 14:1.21.

the full personality. It should support respect for human rights and freedom and should promote tolerance and friendship toward nations, religions, and ethnic groups.

Clearly, from the very beginning of the human rights movement, medical care and education were seen as fundamental to a dignified existence and, therefore, as basic human rights. These are rights that governments have an obligation to protect and promote. It is abundantly clear that governments have the obligation to provide access to essential educational and medical services for all of their citizens, not just majority group members, the wealthy, or favored religious or ethnic groups. Adequate access to services should be available to all citizens, including the poor, children, and women, as well as men. Any government, including that of the United States, that denies access to basic health care and education to some of its citizens on the basis of sex, ethnicity, religion, or wealth is violating human rights. Education that teaches prejudice, hate, or discrimination is also violating basic human rights.

Theoretical Concerns: Medicine as Science and Technology

We have spoken in this chapter about a number of social issues related to the delivery of health care both nationally and globally. In this section we examine the issue of health and disease from the perspective of basic cultural assumptions of modern medicine, that is, medical ideas and practices rooted in the assumptions of modernism. Medicine is both science and technology; some would say it is an art. In this use of the word "art" (or craft), people commonly mean a practice that involves subtle judgments and skills based on intuitions that can be acquired by experience and training but cannot be specified on paper. This knowledge is the most intimate aspect of the *technology practice* (see Chapter 4) of medicine. A less personal, but also deeply ingrained, aspect of this technology practice are the fundamental assumptions of modernism and some of the related scientific paradigms (see Chapter 4). Our tendency to view disease as the product of specific localized causes (bacteria, smoking) rather than to see it as the property of a complex system comprised of social relationships, cultural beliefs, individual practices, and the interpretations and actions of health care itself, reflects the materialistic and mechanistic assumptions of modernism. Another assumption of modernism is visible in the way antibiotics have been used.

Limited and restricted uses of antibiotics could still be a powerful means of dealing with infectious disease. But in using antibiotics, the medical profession has based its practices on the assumption of linearity coupled with an attitude that nature could be conquered. *Linearity* in this case means the idea that each application of a solution will give the same result as the preceding application. In this instance, it means that a little bit of antibiotic is a good thing; therefore, more antibiotic is even better. Because some antibiotic use eliminates a certain amount of infectious disease bacteria, we can continue to use more antibiotics until we have eliminated this type of disease altogether. But natural systems do not follow this linear progression. Rather, natural systems change and adapt. In the case of bacteria, we call this change antibiotic resistance.

There are some other interesting scientific questions involved here. It has long been the assumption of genetic and evolutionary theories that changes in genes occurred according to an entirely random and haphazard process. Contemporary research is bringing about a revolution in our knowledge with regards to this process. As it turns out, bacteria contain bits of DNA (the molecule responsible for storing genetic information) called plasmids. These plasmids in turn often contain the information that enables a bacterium (a single bacterial cell) to resist an antibiotic. Bacteria can literally give their plasmids to other bacteria, not only to those of their own species but to those of other species (types) of bacteria (Garrett, 1994; Levy, 1992). Furthermore, bacteria scan the DNA that is released from other destroyed bacteria and pick up bits of DNA that provide them useful resistance. In her book *The Coming Plague* (1994), Laurie Garrett describes a series of new studies that show that when bacteria are stressed by harmful elements in their environment, whether antibiotics, heat, or lack of nutrients, their DNA undergoes rapid changes that often lead to exactly those modifications that enable them to adjust to the stress. This is not supposed to happen, according to prevailing assumptions. Some researchers are trying to develop new models to account for this occurrence. One researcher, John Cairns of the Harvard School of Public Health, observes, "That such events ever occur seems almost unbelievable, but we have also to realize that what we are seeing probably gives us only a minimum estimate of the efficiency of the process" (cited in Garrett, 1994:583). It seems that bacteria comprise a system of great complexity, and we are only beginning to get a glimpse of the capabilities of this system. We may be on the brink of a scientific revolution in our understanding of the world of bacteria and their interactions with us.

SUMMARY

1. A **social institution** is an organized sphere of social life that is designed to meet important social needs necessary for survival and a satisfying life. Medicine and education are two core social institutions.
2. The World Health Organization (WHO) defines **health** as a state of complete physical, mental, and social well-being. The WHO launched a global campaign: "Health for All by the Year 2000" that focused on three areas experts believe will improve health: (1) improvement of water and sanitation, (2) improvement of basic nutrition for everyone and provision of immunization to all children, and (3) the training of primary health care workers.
3. Health has been improving across the globe for some time. The average lifespan has been increasing, while **infant mortality** (the death of a child in the first year of life) has been decreasing. Several explanations for the increased length of life that results from modernism include improved nutrition and sanitation,

especially the provision of clean water for drinking, cooking, and washing. Some suggest that the type of personality or set of attitudes that develop as a result of modernism is *the* most important factor.

4. The accessibility of health services influences the health of a population. A greater demand for advanced technology than available resources can supply and efforts to meet the needs of a growing elderly population are problems that face most nations. Even though the United States spends more than any other nation on health care, we rank far behind other nations on basic measures of health outcomes such as infant mortality and life expectancy. This may be because Americans of lower status and lower-income groups often have limited access to health care.

5. Various biological organisms—principally bacteria and viruses—cause diseases. *Bacteria* are microscopic single-cell organisms that carry on basic life processes and are able to replicate their own genetic material and reproduce themselves. *Viruses* cannot reproduce, and require a host cell to copy their genetic material. *Antibiotics* are chemicals designed to kill living bacterial cells, although they kill other cells in the process. Overuse and misuse of antibiotics cause microbes affected by the antibiotic to escape into the air, the sewer system, and the bodies of others, affecting the microbial environment of an entire community. Overuse of antibiotics may also result in the formation of superbugs—new and more deadly strains of bacteria that are immune to antibiotics.

6. Social changes linked to globalization are encouraging an intensification of threat from infectious diseases. One example is irrigation, which can alter breeding habits of species that carry microbes or increase the number of microbes available. Poverty, malnutrition, prostitution, and community and family breakdown also create a disease-breeding medium.

7. *Virulence* refers to the power of a microbe to cause disease or death. Highly virulent bacteria may cause their hosts to die so quickly that the bacteria will not be able to reproduce themselves and spread to new hosts. Local human populations can develop such strong immunities to a particular disease that the disease can virtually die out and become extinct in the area. This response is called *herd immunity.* However, travel and high population density make it more likely that a disease will spread from host to host quickly; the disease can be quite deadly to its host as it survives and reproduces.

8. The high cost of modern health care, an increasing cultural diversity, and the recognition that there are multiple views of reality has led to the use of nontraditional healing methods. *Holistic medicine,* for example, is a philosophical and practical approach to disease and health that treats all aspects of the person—physical, emotional, social, and spiritual—with the goal of promoting optimal well-being and healing. *Alternative medicine* suggests methods and medicines other than those in use by the dominant Cartesian/Newtonian, or mechanistic, schools of thought. *Complementary medicine* suggests using alternative medicines in conjunction with modern medicine. *Indigenous medicine* refers to alternative medical technology practices embedded in non-Western cultural traditions.

9. Education is a tool of empowerment that gives people an ability to take control of their lives and improve their life situations. As a society's level of education increases, the overall health of the society also improves. Nations with a poorly or indifferently educated labor force will be at an extreme competitive disadvantage in the global marketplace.

10. Traditionally, Americans have regarded public schools as the concern of the community. Curriculum-related issues center on who will or should control the content of what is taught in schools. Most public school decisions are in the hands of local elected school boards. This lack of a federal standard has led to an extraordinary diversity in what is taught in American schools and causes inconsistency within the American education system. Although every American is entitled to a free elementary and fundamental education, there is a widespread concern that students who attend American public schools are receiving substandard educations. The number of functionally illiterate (incapable of reading or using math well enough to adequately conduct their day-to-day business) graduates and poor performance on standardized tests are among the factors that cause this concern.

Thinking Critically

1. The text presents evidence that shows how modernization has improved life expectancy. Explain in your own words why the evidence suggests that it was more a matter of changing attitudes and social relationships than one of improved physical conditions that led to these changes. Given all social and cultural factors you have learned about in this textbook, what do you think the prospects of health and longevity are for the next century? Defend your answer.
2. The culture of modernism included the belief that science would provide the answers in medicine and that these answers would involve physical remedies for illness. Contemporary culture has been called postmodern. Postmodern thinkers tend to be suspicious of anyone or any professional group that claims to have the one definitive answer. In what ways is the growth of alternative medicine a reflection of postmodern culture?
3. Postmodernism claims that modernism has failed in important ways. For example, our efforts to control nature through science and technology have failed in a number of important cases. Discuss how the use of antibiotics is such a case.

Suggested Readings

Chapman, David W. and Carol A. Carrier, ed. 1990. *Improving Educational Quality: A Global Perspective.* New York: Greenwood Press.

Feagin, Joe R., Hernan Vera, and Nikitah Imani. 1996. *The Agony of Education: Black Students at White Colleges and Universities.* New York: Routledge.

Fisher, Jeffrey A. 1994. *The Plague Makers: How We Are Creating Catastrophic New Epidemics—And What We Must Do to Avert Them.* New York: Simon & Schuster.

Garrett, Laurie. 1994. *The Coming Plague: Newly Emerging Diseases in a World Out of Balance.* New York: Penguin Books.

Lassey, Marie L., William R. Lassey, and Martin J. Jinks. 1997. *Health Care Systems Around the World: Characteristics, Issues, Reforms.* Upper Saddle River, NJ: Prentice Hall.

Levy, Stuart B., M.D. 1992. *The Antibiotic Paradox: How Miracle Drugs Are Destroying the Miracle.* New York: Plenum.

Ornish, Dean. 1997. *Love and Survival: The Scientific Basis for the Healing Power of Intimacy.* New York: HarperCollins.

Matthews, Dale A. with Connie Clark. 1998. *The Faith Factor.* New York: Viking.

Sagan, Leonard A. 1987. *The Health of Nations: True Causes of Sickness and Well-Being.* New York: Basic Books.

Spiegel, D. 1993. *Living Beyond Limits: New Hope and Help for Facing Life-Threatening Illness.* New York: Times Books.

Tye, Barbara Benham and Kenneth A. Tye. 1992. *Global Education: A Study of School Change.* Albany: State University of New York Press.

WEB SITES

Office of Alternative Medicine/National Institute of Health

http://altmed.od.nih.gov/

This is the official site of the Office of Alternative Medicine (OAM). It provides all you ever wanted to know about how the OAM is organized, what it does, how it got started, what sorts of research it is financing, whom it works with, what its budget is like, and what other projects it is involved in. This site is sponsored by the National Institute of Health, a government office.

MedWeb

http://www.gen.emory.edu/MEDWEB/alphakey/alternativemedicine.html

This site is provided by Emory University Health Services Center Library. It is an absolute treasure trove for anyone interested in alternative medicine. Its many listings include access to alternative medicine databases (as complete as they can be at present) and an alphabetical listing of all alternative medicine web sites.

National Center for Infectious Disease Home Page

http://www.cdc.gov/ncidod/ncid.htm

This site is provided by the NCID in association with Centers for Disease Control (CDC), whose purpose is to prevent and control the spread of traditional, new, and emerging infectious diseases in the United States and around the world. Among the useful information it provides is online access to current and back issues of the journal Emerging Infectious Diseases.

World Health Organization

http://www.who.org

This site is a link to the World Health Organization, which among other things produces reports and gathers statistics on health problems worldwide. It also provides links to other similar sites.

Cyber School Bus

http://www.un.org/Pubs/CyberSchoolBus/special/health/units/

As strange as it may seem, this site is not about educational issues. Instead it contains materials on global health issues, including information on infectious diseases.

Educational Resources

http://www.smsu.edu/contrib/library/resource/teached.html

This site allows searches of the U.S. government's ERIC databases, which are extremely valuable sources of information on topics and issues concerning education.

CHAPTER ▪ ELEVEN

Minority Group Tensions

Issues of Race and Ethnicity

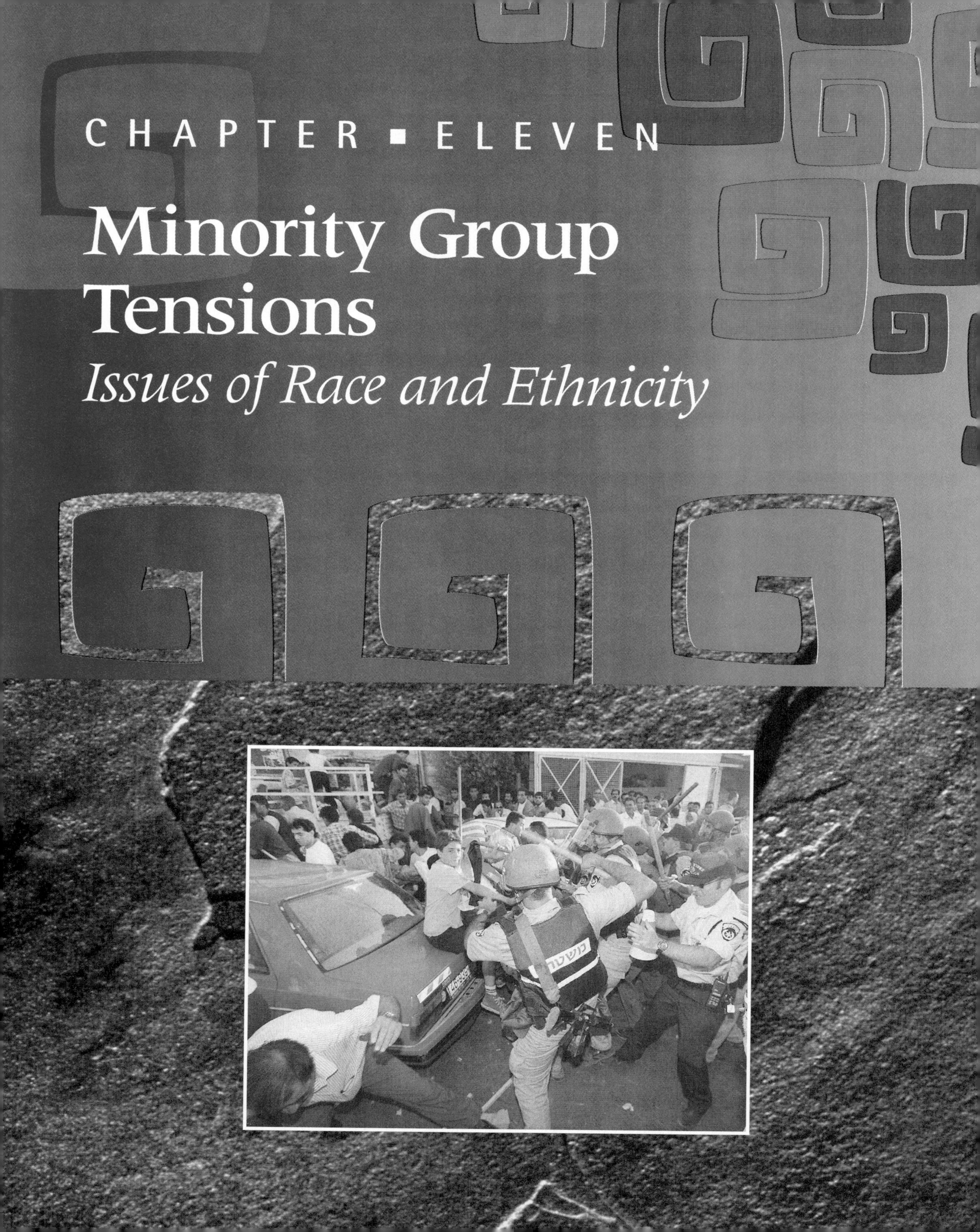

Case One—Tasmania, Early Part of the Nineteenth Century. Tasmania, the large island directly south of Australia, was once part of England's overseas settlements. The island was inhabited by *indigenous people* (groups whose ancestors were the original inhabitants). The English colonists regarded the Tasmanians not as human beings but as wild beasts to be exterminated. Armed with guns, the colonists drove the islanders steadily into the less desirable lands, killed them for meat to feed their dogs, stole their women, and finally decided to simply kill off the survivors. Rewards were offered for the completion of this job, and, in October 1830, nearly 5,000 soldiers, police, and civilians, armed with guns and handcuffs, formed a cordon that literally stretched across the island. They moved southward, drove all remaining natives into the Tasmania Peninsula, and penned them there. Seventy-three years after the British started colonizing the island, there were no indigenous people alive (Berry and Tischler, 1978).

Case Two—Western Hemisphere, Mid-Fifteenth to Mid-Nineteenth Centuries. For more than four centuries, the continent of Africa was raided to satisfy the demand for laborers in both North and South America. The peak period of the slave trade was from 1721 to 1820 (the era often called the "Age of Enlightenment"). Scholars disagree about how many Africans were kidnapped for the trade; the figures range from 10 to 20 million people. Many of the millions of Africans who started the journey to slavery did not survive. An accurate account of the deaths will never be possible, but most experts agree that between 13 and 33 percent died on the ocean voyage. Unknowable numbers were also lost in Africa on the way to the coast and in holding pens awaiting shipment. In the United States, the beginnings of slavery date from 1619, when a Dutch ship unloaded "twenty Negars" at Jamestown. It then took a bloody civil war in the mid-nineteenth century (1861–1865) to end slavery and the civil rights revolution of the mid–twentieth century to make significant advances in ending racial exclusion in the United States (Pedraza and Rumbaut, 1996; Daniels, 1990; Berry and Tischler, 1978).

Case Three—United States, Early Nineteenth Century. Until 1830, the U.S. government dealt with Native American tribes as sovereign nations, entering into treaties with many tribal groups. But in 1830, the federal government passed the Indian Removal Act, which called for the relocation of all tribes living east of the Mississippi River. The rationale for forcing the tribes to move from their ancestral territory was that they were not using the land "as God has intended." The most infamous example of this policy, the Cherokee Removal, has come to be known as the "Trail of Tears." The Cherokees lived in a region where Georgia meets Tennessee and North Carolina. They owned 7 million acres of these lands, but when gold was discovered in the Georgia hills, laws were passed to ensure that whites got the gold and the land. In 1838, 7,000 federal troops rounded up Cherokee men, women, and children. Their homes and barns were burned, and mobs were allowed to seize their cattle and household goods. More than 16,000 Cherokees were forced under guard to march 1,000 miles to what is now Oklahoma. It is estimated that 4,000 died on the journey from starvation and disease (Marger, 1997).

Minority Group Problems in the World

Few issues have a more powerful impact on the world and its people than race and ethnicity. Sociologists reserve the word **race** to mean a category of people who are regarded as socially distinct because they share genetically transmitted physical characteristics, such as skin color, hair texture, or shape of the nose and eyes. **Ethnicity** refers to a category of people who are regarded as socially distinct because of their shared cultural heritage, which includes things such as language, customs, dress, religion, and food preferences.

All societies differentiate among their members. Divisions among people along racial or ethnic lines are a central feature of contemporary life. Often, distinctions are made with regard to people who share similar physical characteristics. Groups are easily identified by inherited physical characteristics, such as skin color, facial features, hair texture, or stature.

Race and ethnicity have profoundly influenced twentieth-century politics and international diplomacy. Both race and ethnicity touch us all, directly and indirectly, on many levels—personal, regional, national, and global. The issue of race in particular has profoundly influenced most major contemporary issues: international politics, diplomacy, the search for peace, national liberation movements, challenges to state sovereignty, and the global concern for human rights.

The extraordinary physical and cultural diversity of humanity has been a source of conflict and inequality throughout human history, and that is still true today. Throughout the world, people are killing one another over differences of color, facial features, language, dress, food habits, and religious faith. Consider the bloodletting in recent decades in the Middle East between Arabs and Jews, in Northern Ireland between Protestants and Catholics, in the former Yugoslavia between Christians and Moslems, and in Central Africa between the Hutu and the Tutsi tribes.

Race and ethnic relations continually change. Periods of relative peace and quiet alternate with times of conflict and problems. These changes depend on a number of factors—economic, political, psychological, and sociological. On the brink of the twenty-first century, there is a global expansion of **racism,** the belief that one racial or ethnic group is inferior or superior to another and, because of that, the belief that unequal treatment is justified. Racism is an ideology that has been responsible for untold misery, including wars, slavery, economic inequality, and inadequate opportunities for whole groups of people. A characteristic feature of racist ideologies is to try to make political, social, and economic injustices among groups of people seem "natural" or "right."

In the West in the nineteenth century, these ideologies of race tended to focus on one major theme—the inequality of human races. The prejudices were not new, but science began to be used to "prove" the superiority of white Europeans and the inferiority of the various nonwhite peoples. According to this view, scientific evidence proved the existence of organic, inherited, biological differences of race. We now use the term "scientific racism" to describe any scientific or pseudoscientific view of race that equates racial differences with racial inferiority or superiority.

One such piece of scientific "evidence" was Charles Darwin's *On the Origin of Species* (1859) and his later book, *The Descent of Man, and Selection in Relation to Sex* (1872), which revolutionized scientific thinking. Darwin's scientific theory described a physical world ruled by "natural selection" in a competition among species that led to the "survival of the fittest." By the end of the nineteenth century, Darwin's ideas provided many European and American thinkers a way of looking not only at the physical world but also at social relations, in which here too "only the fittest survived." Others, such as Houston Stewart Chamberlain and Count Arthur de Gobineau in Europe and Lothrop Stoddard and Madison Grant in the United States, were particularly influential in promoting this application of Darwin's theory of evolution to human affairs, which came to be known as *social Darwinism* (Marger, 1997). Chamberlain's persuasive arguments for the racial inferiority of Jews and "Negroes" and the racial superiority of white Aryans helped perfect the ideology of racism in Europe through the use of pseudoscientific evidence. Soon this ideology was put into practice. Anti-Semitic sentiment, always present in Europe, grew. In Russia, violent pogroms and repressive legislation forced an estimated 300,000 Jews to leave the country in one year alone (1891). Other parts of Europe and the West (as well as nations influenced by the West) sanctioned or countenanced anti-Semitism, too, and an intense consciousness of racial differences developed. Immigration quotas or exclusions were put into place. This was not the first time quotas and exclusions were used, but they now became far more prevalent and widespread. For example, Australia initiated a White Australia policy in the 1920s, designed to keep out the native inhabitants of Africa, Asia, and the Pacific Islands. At the same time, racism escalated throughout much of the world (Berry and Tischler, 1978).

Colonization and Its Effects

All too often, economic inequality is closely linked with racism. **Colonialism** (the formal political and economic domination of one nation by a more powerful one) is the classic example of this connection. European colonialism (which lasted from the fifteenth century to the mid-twentieth century) involved the exploitation of raw materials and indigenous labor, the seizure of land, and the imposition of a system of rigid social stratification. All these measures were designed to secure the colonizing country's economic and political interests.

Before European nations started building their colonial empires, there was relatively little overt racism in Europe. When people from non-Western societies traveled in Europe, they were usually treated with some respect. Not until European countries came to rely on these countries for raw materials, cheap labor, and markets for manufactured goods did racism develop and thrive.

The era of colonial expansion (although colonial expansion began in the sixteenth century, most of the present Third World was colonized in the nineteenth century) was marked by intense racism in Europe. The colonial powers needed an ideology that could justify their treatment of indigenous peoples. When Europeans explored and conquered Africa, the Americas, and Asia, the status of indigenous peoples there plummeted. Western history books, in describing this process, tend to use Western rhetoric, which is racist in its implications. For example, these books typically say that Columbus, and other European explorers, "discovered" the New World. Even though many of the indigenous peoples (called "Indians" by the Europeans, who thought they had discovered a new trade route to India) had sophisticated social and cultural systems, they lacked military technology and sophisticated weapons. Because of this, they were conquered. The conquerors then looked upon indigenous peoples as culturally inferior. Hundreds of thousands of indigenous peoples died of exposure to new (to them) European diseases. Others were killed in warfare with colonizers or by the colonizers' deliberate policies of annihilation. Almost all lost their traditional lands and territories. The result was mass impoverishment and, frequently, death. This treatment of indigenous peoples was clearly at odds with the colonial powers' avowed Christian beliefs. How could they justify the inhuman treatment of these subject peoples? The solution was to classify them as other than human. As subhumans, they could be bought and sold as chattel, exploited, and otherwise treated badly.

In Western tradition, race, particularly as defined by the color of skin, became especially relevant. Black came to represent evil or wickedness—think of the terms "black magic," "black heart," "Black Death" (a popular term for the bubonic plague that swept Europe in the fourteenth century). In contrast, white denoted purity, beauty, cleanliness. When Europeans embarked on their exploration and eventual domination of much of the world, they applied the connotations of color to human races (Lauren, 1988). The result was devastating for people of color. Racism was rampant.

A dramatic expression of this racism was the unprecedented "scramble for Africa" that occurred between 1890 and the outbreak of World War I. European imperialism reached its peak during this period. The colonization of blacks in Africa was accompanied by attacks on nonwhites in Asia and the Pacific. The opportunities for enhanced economic gain, national prestige, and international power were simply too great for the Western imperialist powers to pass up. Even the United States entered the contest (although late in the game), annexing Hawaii (1898) and going to war with Spain (1898) to gain the remaining remnants of the Spanish empire in the Caribbean and the South China Sea. Most of these enterprises were accompanied by a self-serving rhetoric summed up in the term the "white man's burden," coined by English writer and staunch imperialist Rudyard Kipling (1865–1936), which implied that it was a duty for the imperialist powers to civilize peoples who were "less advanced" or "civilized" than whites.

It is important to note that the deplorable treatment of indigenous peoples is not limited to earlier centuries. For the most part, overt colonization has disappeared during the twentieth century, but political independence has not translated into economic autonomy or equality. There have been some gains, but throughout the world the plight of native peoples is still apparent. It is in response to this fact that indigenous peoples all over the globe have begun to demand economic, social, and political rights; they want full equality and justice. Early in this century, African American sociologist and civil rights activist W. E. B. DuBois (1868–1963) wrote, "THE PROBLEM OF THE TWENTIETH CENTURY [will be] the problem of the color line—the relation of the darker to the lighter races of men in Asia and Africa, in America and the islands of the sea" (quoted in Lauren, 1988). In the view of many experts, this prediction has proved accurate.

The open and systematic racism of the kind that led to the wholesale enslavement of blacks in the United States or the extermination of Jews in Nazi Germany is rare today, but racism in other forms is still commonplace. However, slowly but surely, the situation is beginning to change.

Dynamics of Racial and Ethnic Tensions

Minority Groups

Increasingly in sociology, and in the larger society, we are beginning to substitute the term "minority" or "minority groups" for race and ethnicity. This change is occurring because of the recognition that all race and ethnic groups tend to have the same problems. The distinguishing feature of a **minority group** is that its members suffer various disadvantages at the hands of another, more dominant, group.

Minorities around the world are hindered in a variety of ways. They enjoy less of the rewards of society—wealth, power, and status—which means they have fewer privileges, less economic resources, and fewer life chances, and they are frequently the object of discrimination, segregation, and even violent attacks.

A characteristic of a minority group is that its members are identifiable by visible social or physical characteristics. (A physical characteristic would be skin color, shape of the eyes, or hair texture; a social characteristic could be dress, language, or religion.) Minority group members possess some quality that distinguishes them and makes them objects of disapproval, ridicule, suspicion, or hate within their society. Usually the dominant group holds in low regard those characteristics that distinguish the minority, and the dominant group has the power to translate its preferences of behavior, norms, values, and morality into the standards of the society.

Minorities are also self-conscious social units: They are characterized by a consciousness of kind, a strong sense of "oneness." The individuals composing a minority group recognize the fact of their membership, and this recognition affects their behavior. For example, disabled people in the United States have been traditionally denied access to jobs, education, and opportunities, but until they realized they were all in the same boat, they didn't have this sense of oneness. It was only after a consciousness of shared experience developed that members of the group mobilized and petitioned for changes in the laws. The Americans with Disabilities Act (1990) came out of such efforts. The common traits that minority group members share form the basis of an in-group feeling, a sense of belonging to a group distinct from the dominant one. The consciousness of kind is intensified by the members' common status and suffering.

Generally speaking, no one becomes a member of a minority voluntarily; one is born into it. In sociological terms, it is an ascribed status. By choice or necessity, members of a minority group who choose to marry tend to do so within their own group. In-group marriage is enforced sometimes by the dominant group, sometimes by the minority, and frequently by both. For example, until the 1970s, marriage between whites and blacks was not only barred by whites through miscegenation laws in many areas of the United States, it was also informally discouraged by many African Americans. The pattern of mating within one's own group, supported formally and informally, as this example shows, functions to perpetuate both the physical and cultural differences and inequalities of status between the dominant and minority groups.

Notice that the term "minority group" refers to a social relationship with the dominant group, *not* a numerical relationship. To be a member of a minority means to share less of society's money, power, and status. Who you are as an individual makes little difference; you are treated by others both inside and outside your group on the basis of your group identification.

Nature of Prejudice and Discrimination

Prejudice (an irrational, inflexible attitude toward an entire category of people or things) and **discrimination** (the unequal treatment of people on grounds of their group membership) are found in any situation of hostility and inequality between racial and ethnic groups. In ordinary speech, the two words are often used interchangeably, but in fact, they refer to two distinctly different, though related, phenomena—attitudes and behavior.

Prejudice is usually thought of as a negative attitude, but we can be positively prejudiced, too. (For example, some minorities prefer friends from within their own group; thus, they are prejudiced in favor of that group.) The central feature of prejudice is that it is grounded in generalizations and ignores differences among individuals who are members of a group. Anyone who is prejudiced against Asians, for instance, will likely have a negative attitude toward all Asian individuals because "all Asians are alike."

Exposure to cultural norms may even cause minority group members to become prejudiced against themselves. Prejudicial norms develop just like other norms in the society. In some cases, it is possible to trace the specific moment of invention. In other instances, they seem to have been borrowed from other societies. Sometimes the origins are obscure.

Today's world, in which people with different racial, ethnic, and religious identities compete with one another for scarce resources, obviously offers a fertile site for the development of prejudices. In fact, some social scientists maintain that groups "invent" prejudices explicitly for the purpose of gaining or maintaining economic or political dominance. Over time, such prejudices tend to become institutionalized as part of the general culture and begin to play a role in the socialization of the next generation.

Norms of prejudice are sometimes rooted in historical conflicts that go back many centuries. And often they are carried from country to country as part of the immigrants' "baggage." When successive waves of Europeans came to settle in this country, they brought with them the cultures of prejudice that they had shared in the Old Country. The same is true of Europe today, where "guest workers" live and work.

Prejudice must be distinguished from discrimination. Prejudice refers to subjective feelings, whereas discrimination refers to overt behavior. Although it is possible to discriminate in favor of a particular group, "discrimination" usually implies negative actions. Discrimination typically involves refusing to give members of a group the opportunities that would be granted to similarly qualified members of the dominant group. For example, discrimination occurs if an employer refuses to hire or promote individuals on the basis of their race, ethnic background, or gender. Job discrimination (or other types of discrimination, such as in housing) could also be based on age, sexual preference, and physical disability.

Discrimination is an old tradition. Ethnocentrism is a common characteristic; we typically attempt to discriminate against those we see as different or inferior. If we see them as inferior, it is easy to justify unequal treatment, or to try to maintain our group's power, prestige, or wealth at their expense. Discrimination can be based on any one of a number of factors, but among the most common is physical appearance. We find it easy to identify others on the basis of their skin color, hair texture, shape of the nose or skull, or the skin fold of the eye.

People acquire attitudes of prejudice and habits of discrimination in much the same way that they acquire other things such as tastes in literature or music and habits of eating or dressing. All prejudices are learned. As the products of socialization, they reflect cultural and subcultural norms. No one is "born prejudiced," and no one is prejudiced "in general." We learn the particular patterns of prejudice that are present in our own social environment. Understanding individual prejudice as a reflection of cultural and subcultural norms helps us understand how people can become prejudiced against members of a given minority group, even in cases in which they have had little or no direct contact. Seeing prejudice as a product of socialization also helps us understand how members of different minority groups become prejudiced against each other. As participants in American society, Asians may, for example, learn prejudice against African Americans, African Americans may learn prejudice against Jews, and Jews may learn prejudice against Mexicans.

Prejudice and discrimination are not perfectly correlated. Nor can we say that one is the cause and the other the effect. Our attitudes and our overt behavior are obviously closely related, but they are not identical. It is possible to have feelings of antipathy without expressing them overtly or even giving the slightest indication of their presence.

Patterns of Minority-Majority Interaction

The inequality between dominant and minority groups within a society may appear in one of six basic patterns of interaction. To help understand each pattern, we will give examples.

1. In some cases, minority-majority differences are eliminated because minorities are *assimilated,* or absorbed, into the dominant culture. In time, they take on new cultural and/or physical traits. Once assimilated, they tend to have similar values and ideas as the larger society. A recent example of assimilation comes from Bulgaria, where the government attempted to eliminate the ethnic identity of the Turks (who make up 12 percent of their population) by forcing them to change their Islamic names to Slavic ones. The most extreme form of assimilationist thought would see one nation, one language, one culture, one value system, as desirable goals. Sometimes the group voluntarily assimilates, but that is not always the case.

2. Some societies show a pattern of *pluralism,* in which minorities maintain their distinctive cultural and physical traits and coexist with the dominant group. In Switzerland, four ethnic groups, whose members speak French, German, Italian, and Romansch, retain their sense of identity but live and work together with few, if any, problems. Pluralism is also the pattern in Northern Ireland, but there the outcome is the opposite—the region is subject to many problems relative to ethnicity. The logical conclusion of pluralism would be one nation with many languages, diverse cultures, and multiple value systems, all living in relative harmony.

3. In some societies, minorities are *protected by law.* For example, Great Britain passed the Race Relations Act of 1965, which made it illegal to discriminate on racial grounds in employment and housing. Other nations (such as the United States) have similarly tried to protect minorities by making it illegal to discriminate against them.

4. In situations of intense hostility between groups, *population transfers* remove the minority group to other locations on a forced or voluntary basis. When India gained its freedom from Great Britain (1947), the hostility between Hindus and Muslims was so intense that the conflict was resolved only by the division in 1947 of the subcontinent into Pakistan (primarily Muslim) and India (primarily Hindu). The decision anticipated that individual people would move to the state that followed their religion and most did, although some did not.

5. In some cases, the dominant group fully intends to maintain its advantage, and openly exercises its privileged position at the expense of the minority groups. Such *continued subjugation* is a common policy that is illustrated by the treatment of nonwhites in South Africa. *Apartheid* (a legally mandated system of racial classification, segregation, and discrimination) allowed the 15 percent who were white to maintain their advantages over the rest of the population until only recently. Continued subjugation exists when there is unequal power, and the subordinate group possesses little money, power, or prestige.

6. The most extreme form majority-minority relations may take is *extermination.* After World War II, we invented a new word, *genocide,* to describe the murder of an entire group of people, in this case, Jews. Generally, extermination occurs when a crisis situation, such as war or revolution, triggers the felt need for a drastic response.

Contemporary Cleavages

For those of us living in the United States, race and ethnicity problems are long-standing and most Americans are aware of them. But sometimes we fail to see that they are not singularly American problems, but that they occur throughout the world. In this section, we discuss four other nations that experience serious minority group problems.

Territorial Ethnic Conflicts

Frequently, ethnic groups occupy a distinct territory within the larger society. In Europe, most of the multiethnic societies include regionally concentrated minority groups. The Welch and the Scots in Great Britain are two examples. They live in a definable area within the larger society.

When ethnic groups occupy a definable territory, they usually maintain (or wish to maintain) a degree of political autonomy. Sometimes they want full independence from the national state—the Spanish Basques are such a group; in North America, the French-speaking people of Quebec are another.

An example of territorial conflicts imposed by the more powerful on the minority occurred in South Africa. Under apartheid, in 1950, "homelands" or "reserves" were established for the various tribal groups. This policy was a way for the white government to maintain separate living areas for whites and nonwhites. Each racial group was assigned specifically demarcated living areas. Depending on skin color, people might be arbitrarily moved to the land "reserved" for them. Restricting the movement into and residence of blacks within white areas was referred to by whites as "influx control." Residents of the homelands had to have a pass to work or travel elsewhere in the country.

From their inception, the homelands were creations designed to provide South Africa with a cheap labor supply while ensuring that the black majority would remain politically powerless. The areas set aside for Africans were less than 14 percent of the land area, even though the Africans made up more than 70 percent of the population of South Africa. Four of the 10 homelands were granted "independence" by the South African government, but this was a sham designed to cover up the real purpose for their establishment. In 1990, the government unofficially conceded that the homelands policy of separate territories was unworkable (Marger, 1997).

Language as a Focus of Antagonism

In a sense, Canada is not one nation, but two. French Canadians have been a cultural minority since Canada became part of the British colonial empire. Although Quebec was politically British, French inhabitants were granted several cultural rights and privileges. These included the right to continue speaking French, the retention of French civil law in the province, and the right to practice Catholicism.

Canada was settled by two groups, the British and the French. Since the eighteenth century, the language and culture of both groups have been protected by law. Language is a foundation of culture throughout the world; it serves as a symbolic marker, setting the speakers off from other groups. Today French-speaking Canadians make up 27 percent of the population, but most live in the province of Quebec, whereas the English-speaking population is dispersed throughout the country.

In 1867, all the Canadian provinces became linked in a federal system; this system further isolated Quebec from the rest of the country and heightened the minority status of the French-speaking group. Disparities in wealth, power, and social position increased. In time, industrialization and urbanization accelerated the relative powerlessness of French-speaking Canadians. The industrialization of Quebec was sparked by outside capitalists. The skilled jobs went to English-speaking people, and the unskilled, menial jobs went to the French-speaking majority. By the 1960s, French Canadians were the lowest paid group in the country, earning even less than newly arrived immigrants from Europe (Marger, 1997).

By the late 1960s, a new nationalism arose in Quebec that focused on the desire to separate from Canada and become an independent French-speaking nation. The new nationalists formed a political party, demanded a national referendum on sovereignty, and attempted to pave the way for a social and political transformation for Quebec. To this date, their efforts have not been successful, for a variety of reasons. The issues of language and the rights of the French-speaking minority have, however, been increasingly acknowledged by many other Canadians.

Contemporary Canada is a multicultural, pluralistic society. The French-speaking population represents only one of many minorities, albeit the largest one. Together the various ethnic groups, whose origins are neither French nor British, make up almost one-third of the nation's population. The indigenous peoples such as the Inuits are also part of Canadian society. Canada today is a more pluralistic society than the United States and much of the rest of the world.

Religion as a Cause of Strain

Most Americans have heard about the ethnic strife in Northern Ireland, a conflict based not on race (as in South Africa) but on religion. The antagonism there is nominally between Protestants and Catholics. But that is an oversimplification because the true problems are not about religious doctrine but concern religious affiliation, which determines one's place in a society and one's relations with others. In this sense, religion, not color, has become the most important social characteristic. In Northern Ireland, religious affiliation strongly influences all other aspects of social life—education, place of residence, occupation, politics, and even leisure-time activities. Northern Ireland is a classic example of a society exhibiting ethnic pluralism; separate institutional structures exist for each group.

The origin of the conflict in Northern Ireland can be traced to the early seventeenth century when England colonized Ireland. To the British, the native Irish were uncivilized; this ideology was used to rationalize the use of brutal tactics against them. But late in the nineteenth century, for a variety of reasons, England decided to establish "home rule" for Ireland.

The core of the ethnic conflict in Northern Ireland, however, dates back to 1920 when Ireland was partitioned into two states, the Irish Free State (later renamed the Republic of Ireland), which was predominantly Catholic, and Northern Ireland, predominantly Protestant. The Protestant majority in the six northernmost counties feared that if they were incorporated into a Catholic Ireland, they would be the disadvantaged minority. This division also left a substantial Catholic minority in Northern Ireland, which was outnumbered by the Protestants by approximately two to one. For almost 30 years, Catholics have continued to be underrepresented in high-status, high-skill occupations and overrepresented in low-status jobs and joblessness (see Table 11–1). Today unemployment of Catholics is at least twice that of Protestants even though discrimination against Catholics is neither officially legitimized nor enforced through coercive power. For their part, Protestants fear anything that threatens the current political status. For example, they are afraid that if they were reunified into the Republic of Ireland, they would become a minority within a Catholic-majority state (Marger, 1997).

From the late 1920s until 1969, relatively calm relations existed between the two groups in Northern Ireland. The situation changed when Irish Catholics started a civil rights movement to end discrimination in voting, housing, and employment. Protestant extremists began a militant countermovement. Desirous

TABLE 11–1 Religion and Employment in Northern Ireland

OCCUPATION	PROTESTANT	CATHOLIC
Professional (doctor, lawyer)	3.2%	2.1%
Intermediate (manager, teacher)	21.8	19.7
Skilled nonmanual (clerk, shop assistant)	20.6	13.2
Skilled manual (miner, bricklayer)	20.8	18.5
Partly skilled (postman, bus conductor)	16.5	15.0
Unskilled (cleaner, laborer)	5.2	5.2
Unemployed	11.9	26.4

Source: From "Religion and the Labour Market: Patterns and Profiles" in *Discrimination and Public Policy*, edited by Robert J. Cormack and Robert D. Osborne. Copyright © by the authors. Reprinted by permission of Clarendon Press, a division of Oxford University Press.

of maintaining their power, they were willing to use any tactic they could to keep control of the government and the economy. Since 1969, "the troubles," as they came to be known, have escalated between the two groups (Marger, 1997).

From a disinterested outsider's point of view, it is difficult to understand why prejudice and discrimination against Catholics still exists. People of both sides look very much the same, they speak the same language, and they are both Christian. But residential segregation continues, Protestant and Catholic children attend separate school systems taught by teachers from different training colleges, people marry almost exclusively within their religion, and each group tends to hold different types of jobs. The result is that Northern Ireland is one of the most polarized societies today.

Other examples of religion as a source of racial and ethnic tensions may be found in the Middle East between Moslems and Jews, in the former Yugoslavia between Christians and Moslems, and in India between Hindus and Sikhs. The list goes on.

Race as a Source of Hostility

South Africa is the classic example of the ways in which race can become a source of tension and conflict. A unique feature of South Africa is that for more than 150 years, it has contained a relatively large white group that made the country its homeland and still seeks to maintain its position of dominance and privilege. The white minority ensured that South Africa followed an official policy of apartheid. This rigid system of ethnic separation persisted for more than 40 years and only recently has been dismantled.

For four decades, whites received most of the societal rewards (money, power, and prestige), while the black majority received very few. Today South Africa appears to be moving toward a more egalitarian

Throughout the world, people are killing one another over differences of color, facial features, language, dress, food habits, and religious faith. Religion is a source of tensions in Bosnia, with fighting between Christians and Moslems. Here three Bosnian Muslims run for their lives from snipers in Sarajevo.

system, although whites, who constitute fewer than 15 percent of the population, retain their hold over most of the economic and political power. An interesting aspect of South African life is that neither the white nor black populations are themselves unified. Two major white subgroups differ in language, culture, social class, and political power. They are Afrikaners (descendants of the seventeenth-century Dutch who settled there) and descendants of the British (who came at the beginning of the nineteenth century). Blacks are also divided, first on the basis of different backgrounds, then subdivided along ethnic and class lines. The largest number of blacks are the Africans, who derive from several Bantu tribes. They are at the bottom of the social, political, and economic hierarchy. Above them are the Coloureds, the descendants of sexual and marital unions of whites and blacks during the early settlement of the region. In every way except their physical appearance, the Coloureds are thoroughly Europeanized. Highest in the nonwhite hierarchy are the Asians, primarily descendants of people from India, who came in the late nineteenth century as indentured workers.

Under the policy of apartheid, whites lived at a level of comfort they could not have enjoyed without this policy of segregation. In recent years apartheid has ended, but the gap in income and level of education continues (see Table 11–2).

Note in Table 11–2 that whites, who comprise only 15 percent of the population, received more than half the nation's income. South Africa has experienced a series of reforms since 1988, but it is difficult to predict if, or when, full equality will be realized by all its citizens.

TABLE 11–2 Share of Personal Income Received by Each Racial Category in South Africa

YEAR	AFRICAN	ASIAN	COLOURED	WHITE
1985	29%	4%	8%	59%
1990	33	4	9	54

Source: South African Institute of Race Relations, 1992.

International Pressures on Racial and Ethnic Animosity

After World War II, as Western Europe experienced a postwar industrial expansion, workers from southern European countries (Greece, Turkey, Yugoslavia, Italy, Portugal, and Spain) or from newly independent former colonies, such as Algeria or Indonesia, migrated to West Germany, France, Switzerland, the Netherlands, and Scandinavia. England experienced a similar pattern, as thousands of people from the newly independent countries of the British Commonwealth (India, Pakistan, and Jamaica) went there to work. These migrations all illustrate voluntary population transfers.

During the huge task of rebuilding and industrial expansion after the war, workers were in short supply, and companies actively recruited immigrants. The trend continued into the 1950s and 1960s, leaving previously homogeneous Western European countries with substantial ethnic communities comprised of immigrants with vastly different cultures and values from the societies they entered. When the immigrants began to arrive in the 1950s and 1960s, they were seen by Western Europeans as temporary residents who would serve as a supplementary labor force. Their labor was appreciated, but little effort was made to integrate them or their children into the larger society. As time went on, many Western European nations became reluctant hosts to these guest workers and their families (Marger, 1997).

Increasingly, immigration has diminished as new quotas and standards have been adopted, but today most of Western Europe remains ethnically diverse. Large and distinct ethnic minorities have been created, and serious problems often exist between these groups and the host country.

Refugees. Involuntary population transfer also occurs. In the world today, there are more than 16 million refugees. Half the total number, some 8.5 million people, originate from only four countries: Palestine, Afghanistan, Rwanda, and Bosnia-Herzegovina. The refugee problem is confined neither to the Third World nor to the contemporary world. In the twentieth century, the number of refugees has outstripped all earlier population transfers. Increasingly, the concern for human rights—both in the minds of men and women and at international conventions—has been accompanied by the appearance of new forms of oppression, social control, and destruction.

In many parts of the world, civil strife has set in motion a flood of refugees. Around the globe, governments are becoming more reluctant to accept refugees. Even humanitarian intervention is lessening. During the Cold War, refugees were praised for "voting with their feet," but since its end, refugees have come to be seen as a burden or security risk (see the box "FYI: The Refugee Crisis").

International Efforts to Cool Tensions

All major international efforts to reduce racial and ethnic discrimination and promote human rights have come in the wake of wars and revolutions. When there is chaos and upheaval, there are often significant shifts in power, and this change provides the opportunity to reassess and bring about social change.

World War II greatly increased racial consciousness and antagonisms. Prior to the war, many African Americans saw Japan as a key standard-bearer in the struggle against racial discrimination. That ended, of course, with the Japanese attack on American ships in the Pacific naval base of Pearl Harbor (1941). Soon the Western allies portrayed the Japanese as scheming, savage, subhuman creatures. Japan depicted the white enemies as decadent, selfish, and hypocritical people who practiced cruelties on racial minorities.

During World War II, race became a powerful and crucial factor both nationally and internationally. The combat focused attention on our own racial policies as well as those of other nations. In January 1942, 26 nations signed the Atlantic Charter (the basis for the United Nations). The charter proclaimed a commitment to preserve human rights and justice throughout the world. This declaration of principle raised fundamental questions. Would the charter apply to racial discrimination in Asia, Africa, and Latin America? Would it prohibit immigration quotas based on race? Would it apply to racial minorities within Western nations? What about imperialism and the colonial empires? Even today these remain difficult and thorny issues.

Without a doubt, World War II weakened the colonial empires and hastened Asian and African nationalism. In those colonial societies, the war generated important discussions about racial discrimination, immigration restrictions, racial segregation, and anti-Semitism. In particular, discussion centered on the International Declaration of Human Rights. The problem was that guarantees of human rights, by their very nature, impinge upon domestic jurisdiction. Could international law take precedence over national law? These tensions between national and international law continue.

Provisions dealing with human rights had not been a part of the original plans for the United Nations. Non-Western governments and private NGOs wanted to end racial discrimination, and they put pressure on the UN to address these issues. In 1946, the secretary general of the UN established a Division of Human Rights within the Secretariat. The United States wanted a general declaration of principle on human rights, but not a binding international convention that had legal force. That was also the view of some other Western nations. After considerable debate, the Universal Declaration of Human Rights was adopted in 1948. The declaration began with a preamble recognizing "the equal and inalienable rights of all members of the human family." Article 2 asserted this equality must be maintained "without distinction of any kind, such as race, color, sex, language, religion, political, or other opinion, national or social origin, property, birth, or other status" (see Chapter 2 for more information on the issue of human rights).

Much to the surprise of many, the Universal Declaration of Human Rights quickly assumed unprecedented status and influence. It rapidly took on a life of its own. Governments' endorsement of the declaration established the criteria for judging their relations with individuals in their nations. Governments and private citizens began to invoke the Universal Declaration to challenge existing practices and to create new laws. Over time, it inspired a whole series of additional resolutions, binding covenants, and international treaties.

In 1945, when the UN was established, only 3 of the 51 original member states came from Africa and only 3 from Asia. Twenty years later, there were 66 new states, many of them former colonies. After World War II, about 1 billion people had been liberated from colonial rule in Africa and Asia. These people wanted to control their own destinies, free from outside control. The end of imperialism in Africa and Asia brought about the end of white, Western dominance in the world. When they obtained a majority within the UN, non-Western nations began to challenge racial discrimination throughout the world. The goal was to promote human rights and fundamental freedom for all, without distinction on grounds of race, color, descent, or national or ethnic

The Refugee Crisis

Whether at sea in frail craft in the Caribbean, trapped in misnamed "safe havens" in Bosnia or dying of disease and dehydration in overcrowded camps in Central Africa, refugees are the leading indicator of chaos that failed states are leaving in their wake.

Since the mid-1970s, the number of people driven from their homes by war or famine has increased nearly tenfold. In addition to 23 million people uprooted into exile, the United Nations reports that another 26 million are "internally displaced" within their own countries.

New refugee-related crises can be expected to crop up at any time. "To know that the number of rural poor has doubled since 1950, that per capita incomes have fallen steadily in a number of regions and that malnutrition has risen is to know that the stage is set for continuing floods of refugees," says Kathleen Newland, author of a UN report on refugees.

What separates refugees from other migrants is their vulnerability to ill treatment at the hands of their own governments. Under international conventions established after the end of World War II, refugee tides have flowed through two channels—one orderly and one much less so, as when refugees are forced to flee their countries because of violence or repression.

Refugee groups selected for resettlement by willing host nations are carefully processed in advance—usually in so-called countries of first asylum—and then admitted in accordance with preset annual quotas.

But individuals who flee independently are entitled, under international law, to apply for political asylum upon arrival in a foreign land. If such refugees can prove a legitimate threat of persecution in their home country, the receiving nation is obliged to ensure that they are not sent back to face the peril from which they fled.

Today there is a climate of anti-immigrant sentiment. Refugees no longer are neatly tagged with East-Bloc and West-Bloc labels. Even if they were, it might not matter much because in an era of exponential population increases and rising international migration, traditional host countries are rolling *in* their welcome mats.

Nor does it help that racially tinged *xenophobia* (fear and hatred of strangers or foreigners) is on the rise in predominantly white Western industrial nations, most notably France, Germany, and the United States. According to a 1994 survey, more than four of every five refugees are people of color from Africa, Asia, or the Near East. According to a recent review by the U.S. Committee on Refugees, "We have witnessed a major shift in the world's approach toward persons who are forced out of their homes because of potential ethnic violence and the threat of persecution. The international community is now generally committed to keeping would-be refugees at home."

A prime example is the treatment of the estimated 1.3 million Bosnians who have been displaced in the "ethnic cleansing" campaign carried out by Serb militia units. Despite a death toll of close to a quarter-million, the West declined to take sides in the bloodletting that followed the splintering of Yugoslavia.

Western European governments and that of the United States are in the process of tightening their political asylum laws to prevent perceived abuses. For example, in the United States, Bosnian citizens attempting to flee the carnage in their homeland were not recognized as victims of persecution who were entitled to protection as refugees.

Support for the concept of political asylum is on the wane around the world. In Germany, where hate crimes against Turks and other immigrant workers were creating embarrassing headlines, parliament enacted in May 1993 sweeping restrictions to replace what previously had been an unqualified right to apply for asylum in that country.

Western industrialized nations such as Germany, Australia, Canada, and the United States are not the only countries erecting barriers against the rising flood of refugees. Pakistan, which for more than a decade harbored hundreds of thousands of Afghans uprooted by the Soviet invasion of their country, has closed its borders to prevent a new flood of Afghan refugees threatened by internecine warfare among the Muslim factions that ousted the Soviets.

Source: Excerpted from Dick Kirschten, "No Refuge," in *National Journal,* September 10, 1994.

origin. The policy of apartheid in South Africa was one of the issues that many of these nations (and others too) were concerned about. (An interesting aside: The United States remained one of the only countries that, because of domestic policy considerations, consistently refused to ratify the major international agreements on human rights and racial equality.)

The end to racism and discrimination is still not at hand, but work continues that will make this goal possible. We are now beginning to worry about the rights of the least powerful of people, the indigenous tribes throughout the world. The United Nations declared 1993 to be the International Year of the World's Indigenous People, signaling that the injustices and atrocities they experience are beginning to gain worldwide publicity.

Minority Group Issues in the United States

As the twenty-first century approaches, the United States is not the world's only multiracial and multicultural nation. People all over the globe are on the move, seeking economic, political, or social advantages. But when unlike groups meet, there is often conflict (Pedraza and Rumbaut, 1996).

Patterns of Minority-Majority Interaction in the United States

In a very real sense, the history of racial/ethnic relationships in the United States is the history of immigrant groups. Every hour about 500 people are added to our population. Of these, nearly 440 are born here and 60 immigrate from other parts of the world. Over the years, the United States has experienced all the dominant patterns of interaction we mentioned earlier in this chapter.

1. Some minorities have been *assimilated,* or absorbed, into the larger culture. A prime example of voluntary assimilation are the Irish. When they first came to the United States in the nineteenth century, most were poor, Catholic, and illiterate. There was extreme prejudice and discrimination against them, not on the part of the government, but gradually the Irish were absorbed into the dominant culture. Two of our presidents came from Irish backgrounds—John F. Kennedy and Ronald Reagan.

2. In recent decades, the United States has followed a pattern of *pluralism.* Here, minorities maintain their distinctive cultural and physical traits and coexist with the dominant group. (We often call this *multiculturalism.*) As an example, most large American cities have weekend festivals and parades celebrating the various ethnic or national backgrounds of the residents. Customs, dress, and ethnic foods are part of this celebration.

3. Minorities are increasingly *protected by law.* In the United States, the civil rights movement has contributed to this trend. No longer can persons be legally denied access to education, employment, or housing because they are African American, or a member of any other minority group. Specific laws protect the rights of many groups, including all racial/ethnic groups, all religions, women, older citizens, and the disabled.

4. The United States has also experienced *population transfers.* In situations of extreme hostility, a minority group is moved to other locations on a forced or voluntary basis. An example of forced population transfers would be the nineteenth-century transfer of Native Americans from their own lands to reservations. Voluntary population transfers are illus-

In the United States, minorities exist inside the dominant society. Some may be assimilated or absorbed into the larger culture; some maintain their cultural and physical traits and coexist with the dominant group.

trated by the movement of African Americans from the rural south to the urban north in this century.

5. In some cases, the dominant group fully intends to maintain its advantage and openly exercises its privileged position at the expense of the minority groups. Historically, *continued subjugation* has been a common policy and is illustrated by the treatment of African Americans in the century following the Civil War.

6. The most extreme pattern is *extermination* of the unlike group. In the nineteenth century, a policy of extermination was at least the informal policy of the U.S. government toward Native American peoples. The oft-quoted statement of president Theodore Roosevelt (president 1901–1909), "The only good Indian is a dead Indian," illuminates the mentality behind this pattern.

We mentioned earlier in this chapter the rise of racism. The ideology of racism was present in the United States. The target was not only Jews, but anyone other than what we now call a WASP (white, Anglo-Saxon Protestant). Racism legitimated the unequal treatment of Native Americans, African Americans (the first were brought to Jamestown, Virginia, in 1619), Jews, Catholics, Asians, and anyone else whose ancestors did not come from northern Europe.

After centuries of white-Indian warfare, which had begun during colonial times, by the end of the nineteenth century, most tribes had been pushed off their lands by white settlers. The 1890s also saw the passage of rigorous Jim Crow ("for whites only") laws in the South, the loss of the vote for most southern blacks, and a record number of lynchings and race riots throughout the country. The United States excluded Chinese immigration starting in 1872. Early in the twentieth century, a "gentlemen's agreement" was made with Japan, in which the Japanese government agreed to stop emigration at its source in return for better treatment of Japanese already in the United States.

Immigration to the United States

This section of the chapter explores several problems associated with the changing face of America. It reviews enigmas produced by recent immigration trends. This overview is confined to discussion of the identity of the new immigrants, their impact on American culture, and issues raised by this impact. We do not treat intergroup tensions extensively here, nor do we study the relationship of new immigrants to older immigrants. Likewise, the present section looks at changes in U.S. society produced by internal migration but does not review alterations in the U.S. economy that caused population shifts. These transformations are detailed in Chapter 8.

History of U.S. Immigration

Immigration is at the very core of U.S. society. The United States has been the destination of hundreds of thousands of peoples from virtually every country in the world. With the possible exception of Native Americans and some Mexican Americans in the Southwest, every American is a newcomer. Indeed, the United States prides itself on being a nation of immigrants. Throughout our history, successive waves of new arrivals have reshaped this country, sometimes for better and sometimes for worse. Almost inevitably each set of newcomers has met with hostility and generated fears on the part of "natives," but eventually, most have assimilated into the larger culture.

For a century after the American Revolution, few restrictions were placed on who could enter the country. If one could afford the fare, one was welcome to come. This open door policy lasted until the middle of the nineteenth century. Then, in the decade before the Civil War, the federal government began to restrict and regulate entry into the country. The reason? Because the newest immigrants (from southern and eastern Europe and later from Asia) were viewed as unwelcome competitors for increasingly scarce jobs and land. Prejudice against these newcomers was strong, primarily because they were not Protestant Christians.

In the years between 1865 and 1890 (the period following the Civil War), new arrivals came mainly from northwestern Europe (England, Wales, Ireland, Scandinavia, and Germany). All but the Irish were primarily Protestants (although some Germans were Catholic). The Protestants fit into the new culture relatively easily. The Catholic Irish, as indicated, found assimilation more difficult. Then, between 1890 and 1914 (the year of the outbreak of World War I), a wave of immigration from eastern and southern Europe arrived. Because these groups were not Protestant, but were primarily Catholics or Jews, they were the targets of prejudice and discrimination from the larger society.

The great period of immigration reached a peak about the beginning of this century. Immigration then declined as a series of laws reflecting isolationist and nativist sentiments virtually closed the borders of the United States to foreigners. In 1882, Ellis Island, in New York harbor, was designated as the processing center for European immigrants. (Angel Island, in San Francisco harbor, provided the same function for immigrants coming from Asia.) Ellis Island, especially, became the symbol of America's new, tougher immigration policy. Approximately one-third of all new arrivals were sent back to the Old Country.

In the same year that Ellis Island became a processing center for immigrants, Congress passed the Chinese Exclusion Act, denying Chinese people the right to enter for 10 years. The act, which was renewed each decade until 1943 (when China was one of the World War II Allies), set the precedent not only for excluding Chinese, but also for exclusion in general. By the end of the nineteenth century, the federal government imposed strict immigrant policies regarding health standards and some forms of contract labor. Within the United States, strong public sentiment favoring restrictive immigration continued to rise. In 1924, Congress passed the National Origins Act, which established a quota system that strongly favored western European immigrants.

Nevertheless, early in the twentieth century, the term "melting pot" came into general usage. The phrase was a metaphor. America was depicted as a vast crucible in which cultural and genetic blending, it was generally assumed, would inevitably occur. Something new, Americans, would be the alloy that would emerge from that melting pot. But many worried that immigrants from places other than northern Europe would somehow "debase" this new alloy and so weaken the American "character." Immigrants from southern and eastern Europe, from Latin America and Asia, were now seen as potential problems—the "Polish problem," the "Italian problem," the "Chinese or Japanese problem."

The New Immigrants

As the twentieth century comes to a close, the United States is experiencing another major wave of immigration that is transforming the nature of American society. For most of the nation's history, immigrants came mainly from Europe. However, in the 1960s, a basic change in immigration policy occurred, which shifted the bias in American immigration laws away from favoring Europe toward favoring people from other parts of the globe, especially the Third World ("America's Immigrant Challenge," 1993).

The effects of this shift in immigration policy are already being felt throughout society simply because of the sheer numbers. In 1940, only 30 percent of immigrants were non-European. By 1992, 85 percent came from somewhere other than Europe ("Numbers Game," 1993). Spanish-speaking people from Central and South America are now the fastest-growing immigrant group. Unlike past immigrants who came from Europe, these newcomers are relatively close physically to their homelands. (Possible effects of this proximity to native lands are that assimilation may be hindered and that pressures for bilingualism may increase.) Most Spanish-speaking immigrants come from Mexico, Central America, and South America. About 90 percent settle in New Mexico, California, and Texas. South Florida has a large Hispanic population, many of whom are refugees from Cuba. Several large metropolitan areas such as Los Angeles, Chicago, and New York City also serve as magnets for substantial numbers of other immigrants in addition to Spanish-speaking newcomers.

During the last three decades, four countries—the Philippines, Korea, India, and China—have contributed the vast majority of Asian newcomers. Significant numbers have also arrived from Japan and Southeast Asia, particularly Vietnam. Asian immigrants reside mostly in the western states; more live in Hawaii and California than in other states.

Although the level of immigration is not as high today as it was during the peak of the great migrations during the nineteenth century, it is very high when compared with the early decades of this century. This new extensive immigration has touched off a renewed immigration debate, centering not only on the rate of migration but also on the ethnic composition of the newcomers.

This influx of people from non-European countries, combined with low rates of *natural population increase* (growth in a country's population resulting from the fertility rates of those who are its citizens), is radically altering the face of America. Reasonable projections indicate that by the year 2050, white non-Hispanics will compose a mere 52 percent of the population; Hispanic Americans will account for 21 percent, African Americans for 16 percent, and Asian/Pacific Islanders for 11 percent (U.S. Bureau of the Census, 1993). Not only will such changes seriously threaten the dominance of Americans of European origin, but African Americans will be replaced by Hispanics as America's largest minority group.

The Impact of Newcomers on the United States. Analyzing the impact of newcomers on America is made more difficult by the false notion that all immigrants are alike. They are not. Contemporary immigrants to the United States are hardly a homogeneous group. The socioeconomic status of the newcomers often divides them into three categories: highly educated professionals, entrepreneurs, and manual laborers. The professionals are often among the first waves of refugees because of the occupational preferences of U.S. law. Once established as permanent residents or citizens, they can sponsor the immigration of their immediate family members (Pedraza and Rumbaut, 1996). Many of these family members are also well-educated and relatively affluent. They are professionals, businesspeople, or technicians in their own countries. They bring their knowledge, skills, wealth, and energy to the United States. Their out-migration represents a "brain" and economic drain from their country of origin but is an asset to this nation. Likewise, the energetic entrepreneurs and manual laborers bring their skills and talents. These entrepreneurs opened steel mills, built railroads, and created steamship lines, while manual laborers literally built the nation's railroads and canals.

Another distinction is the legal and political status of the immigrants. There are three basic types: regular immigrants (increasingly "regular immigrants" are professionals), undocumented immigrants (those who enter the country illegally by crossing the border or overstaying a temporary visa and who often have no relatives in the United States or are without special skills), and refugees (who are often fleeing political oppression) (Pedraza and Rumbaut, 1996). The common stereotype of newcomers is of hoards of low-skilled poor people who become a drain on this society. Although some immigrants fit that image, large numbers do not.

Some people object because the new immigrants "are not like us," meaning that the newcomers are perceived as nonwhite, non-European, non-English speaking, and non-Christian. The fear is that traditional American culture will be overwhelmed by minorities, given the fact that the immigrants and their descendants (who are now a numerical minority) will likely rival in numbers the current majority of European descent by the middle of the twenty-first century.

Illegal Immigration. Undocumented immigrants are the focus of much attention in the United States. Issues concerning illegal immigration stir up great controversy. Even deciding how many illegal immigrants are actually in this country is difficult. For obvious reasons, undocumented residents do not want to be counted and so the estimates of how many there are vary widely. In the late 1980s, the number of illegal aliens in the United States was estimated from as low as 3 million to as high as 12 million (Marden, Meyer, and Engel, 1992). In 1986, Congress passed the Immigration Reform and Control Act, allowing illegals who entered the United States prior to January 1, 1982, to become legal residents and eventually to apply for citizenship. This act reduced the number of illegal aliens by about 3 million (Pedraza and Rumbaut, 1996).

Sociologist John E. Farley (1995) maintains that the estimates of undocumented immigrants are much too high, even after those who were granted amnesty in the 1986 bill are deducted from the total estimate. Farley maintains that there are no more than 2 million illegal immigrants in the United States, which is less than 1 percent of the U.S. population. Undocumented immigrants come from many countries, including Ireland, the Caribbean, China, and Colombia, but Mexicans and Central Americans constitute the largest proportion of the undocumented population (Pedraza and Rumbaut, 1996). By far the great majority of illegal immigrants from all countries are fleeing grinding poverty.

Illegal immigrants may arrive at any port or international airport, but many enter by simply crossing the borders from Canada or Mexico. The Mexican border is especially porous. About half of all illegal immigrants come from that country, although Central and South American countries contribute a large share, especially El Salvador, Guatemala, and Haiti.

Illegal immigrants do not distribute themselves evenly across this country, preferring to go to states or cities with a sizable community of their ethnic heritage. Nearly half of all illegal immigrants from

Central and South America live in California; considerable portions of the rest are concentrated in New York, Illinois, Florida, and Texas (Glastris, 1997; Garza, 1994).

Whatever their place of origin or their eventual place of residence, undocumented immigrants have one thing in common—their status before the law leaves them open to exploitation with little recourse to authorities and without access to many needed services. Undocumented workers often are hired for difficult jobs that may pay less than the minimum wage. They are frequently exploited by both native-born Americans and legal immigrants of their own nationalities. Even when illegal immigrants are grossly exploited, they usually will not report injustices to authorities for fear of being arrested and deported.

The status of undocumented immigrants before the law is murky at best. They have few rights and do not enjoy the same protections as full citizens or legal immigrants. As an example, California's Proposition 187 (1994) requires schools, hospitals, and other public agencies to report to the Immigration and Naturalization Service (INS) any persons suspected of being in the country illegally. They may be detained, deported, and denied basic public services, such as free education for their children (Pedraza and Rumbaut, 1996).

Many of the services provided to citizens and documented immigrants are not available to illegal immigrants. Moreover, there seems to be little inclination to extend further benefits to illegal immigrants in the current economic and political climate. For example, President Bill Clinton's much-touted 1993 health care reform plan sought to extend basic medical coverage to all Americans, but it ignored entirely undocumented immigrants (Garza, 1994).

Although most Americans have been inclined to take a "live and let live" attitude toward illegal immigrants, this disposition is changing. The 1986 amnesty act also made hiring undocumented immigrants a crime; employers of such workers became subject to fines and even imprisonment. The purpose of this law was to cut down on additional illegal immigration while preventing remaining illegal immigrants from taking jobs supposedly wanted by American citizens.

More recently, politicians have launched a number of attacks on "privileges" supposedly available to illegal immigrants. For example, attempts have been made to deny driver's licenses to undocumented residents because the possession of a driver's license listing an address is the key to obtaining other documents that then establish de facto citizenship, thus allowing illegal immigrants access to government services intended only for citizens. Similarly, a bill has been proposed in Congress to deny citizenship to children born to illegal immigrants in the United States. (At present, anyone born in the United States is automatically considered a citizen. The justification used for denying these children citizenship is that many pregnant Mexican women cross the border to have their children, thus making the newborns U.S. citizens.) Another attack on undocumented workers occurred in 1994, when several states with large undocumented populations (including California, Florida, Texas, Arizona, New Jersey, and New York) filed lawsuits against the federal government seeking to recover billions of dollars in expenses purportedly incurred in providing services to illegal aliens (Wilson, 1994). Whatever the actual merit (or lack thereof) of these assaults on illegal immigrants, they often boost politicians' chances for reelection by appealing to the public's tendency toward *scapegoating* (the process of picking out a group or groups to blame for one's troubles).

Impact of Recent Immigration. Both legal and illegal immigration, then, has sparked spirited debates centered on whether immigration is costly or beneficial to the country. Some critics of high immigration rates assume that a high concentration of immigrants is costly and lowers the standard of living of everyone. However, in 1997, a federal report concluded that the impact of immigration on the economy was insignificant. The costs are small and so are the benefits. The study found that immigrants have no negative effects on the wages of most Americans, with one exception. Workers with less than a high school diploma represent about 15 percent of the American workforce, and these individuals are typically harmed by immigrants who work for low wages. These immigrants may reduce wages for those low-skilled workers by about 5 percent (Glastris, 1997).

According to this study, the country as a whole benefits from immigrants, but the taxpayers in California, Florida, and Texas (where most of the immigrants live) pay more in taxes. In California, the average household pays an extra $1,178 a year in taxes because of the immigrants (Glastris, 1997). Sociologist Vincent Schodolski (1994) indicates that the flow of Mexicans into southern California is beneficial in that it provides a cheap, dependable labor supply. He further shows that the free flow of persons back and forth between Tijuana, Mexico, and San Diego, California, is beneficial to both sides of the border. But the American side benefits most. Tijuana, for example, reaps approximately $2 billion per year from sales to Americans, but San Diego receives about $2.8 billion in sales to Mexicans.

On the East Coast, Florida recently filed suit against the federal government to recover the $1.5 billion it claims to have spent in a two-year period on services to illegal immigrants (Wilson, 1994). In Florida, undocumented immigrants are perceived as a constant drain; few native Floridians see the benefits that even legal newcomers bring to the area. Even so, Miami is increasingly being facetiously referred to as the "capital of Latin America" because of its large number of Spanish-speaking inhabitants (Booth, 1993). Investors from the Caribbean and Central and South America are moving into the city, drawn by its large Spanish-speaking population, its easy access to Hispanic regions, and its firmly established Hispanic business and banking communities. Far from being a drain on native resources, the Hispanics of Florida effectively position that state to take advantage of increasing trade with Spanish-speaking nations to the south.

Not all immigrant groups have the same experience in America. Although some Asians do better than most newcomers from other parts of the world, the achievements of Asian Americans are part myth and part reality (Wood, 1989). It is true that a highly visible group of Asian Americans are college educated, with relatively high-paying occupations, but the myth of Asian American success perpetuates the notion that hard work always reaps commensurate rewards. In fact there is often a gap between the level of education and the subsequent occupational or income gains for Asian Americans (Wood, 1989). In addition, the large Asian immigrant population and the language barriers these newcomers face restrict many of them to menial or entry-level jobs (Wood, 1989). Moreover, not all nationalities within the broad Asian category fare equally well here. For example, in 1980, Japanese immigrant annual family incomes averaged $27,354, whereas Vietnamese immigrant families averaged only $12,840 annually (U.S. Bureau of the Census, 1991). Moreover, the 1990 Census reported that 70 percent of our Asian immigrants depending on welfare were from Southeast Asia, mostly from Laos, Cambodia, and Vietnam.

At least three factors seem to work against the possibility that current immigrants will overwhelm American culture. First, despite increased immigration, the actual rate of immigration relative to the size of our population is lower than in many past decades, and the proportion of foreign-born residents is actually lower now than it was in earlier periods in our history (Salins, 1993). Second,

Despite increased immigration to the United States, the proportion of foreign-born residents is lower now than it was in earlier periods in our history. Nearly 10,000 people participated in this naturalization ceremony in Miami in 1984, the largest naturalization event in American history.

though some recent immigrants are found throughout the country, the majority are concentrated in limited regions along the coasts and borders. Most sections of the country are likely to remain solidly European in ancestry for some time to come. Third, despite an emphasis on multiculturalism, immigrants generally do not wish to remain distinct but plan to assimilate (Hacker, 1992). For instance, most Mexican immigrants do learn to speak English, and their children rapidly come to speak English fluently. The continuation of the Spanish language in the United States is due to the continual influx of new immigrants from Hispanic lands rather than by the failure of new immigrants to learn English (Veltman, 1988). Additionally, sociologist Linda Chavez (1991) found in her study of persons of Mexican ancestry living in the United States that most have a strong commitment to assimilation. Indeed, immigrant children are enrolled in bilingual education more at the request of officials who have an interest in maintaining special programs than out of the desire of their parents to preserve their heritage (Pedalino-Porter, 1990).

When we take all factors into consideration, we feel justified in concluding that the current crop of immigrants undoubtedly will be assimilated into American society, as did those who came before them.

Racial and Ethnic Composition of the United States

WASPs (White Anglo-Saxon Protestants)

Before 1830, Americans were relatively homogeneous. Their backgrounds were remarkably similar as far as national origin (mainly northern Europe), religion (mainly Protestant), and physical type (mainly white). English was the native language of the majority. We have come to call this group WASP. As other immigrant groups arrived, the power of this first group diminished somewhat over time. Over many generations, intermarriage has occurred between people of different ethnic groups and, to a lesser extent, between people of different religions and races. Thus, there has been some biological merging of previously distinct ethnic groups, but American society has continued to be dominated by the original WASP culture, particularly by its requirement that everyone speak English.

As the twentieth century draws to a close, WASPs make up about one-fourth of the population of the United States, but this fourth has a disproportional influence politically, economically, and socially. The values and standards set by WASPs, in other words, continue. Sometimes we refer to it as "Anglo conformity." WASP cultural values have molded our public policies, our religion, our system of education, our laws, our welfare system, and, particularly, our language. This molding represented assimilation to WASP values.

Today ethnicity has no special significance for white Protestants of various national origins except to distinguish them from the rest of the racial/ethnic hierarchy. There are still social, class, and cultural differences among various groups of WASPs, but mostly these people still receive more than their fair share of our society's resources of money, power, and prestige.

White Ethnics

Not all the white people in this country come from a WASP background. Some are non-Protestant immigrants from other parts of Europe. Most white ethnics were Catholics and Jews who came from southern and eastern Europe, but white ethnics also include Catholics from Ireland and France. When they first arrived Irish Catholics were not readily accepted. There were anti-Catholic riots and a lot of other hostile if not violent sentiment against them. In the cities along the eastern seaboard, signs greeted many of the Catholic Irish that said, "No Catholics or Irish." They were excluded from housing and jobs.

For the long run, white ethnics proved the notion that immigrants would conform to the dominant American culture. For generations it was assumed that cultural differences among the various immigrant groups would disappear in time, and that the newcomers, or certainly their children, would conform to the dominant WASP culture. The pattern of interaction was assumed to be assimilation, the so-called "melting pot" notion. The idea was that all the groups would eventually become one and that although physical or racial differences might persist, they should not be the basis for prejudice and discrimination.

Eventually another ideology gained favor, that of pluralism, or amalgamation. Some people call this the "salad bowl" approach. Rather than different groups having to "melt" into one, the idea is that differences should be tolerated and accepted. The belief is that all the diverse peoples will blend their biological and cultural differences into a new group, called Americans.

Native Americans

Many people usually speak of "Native Americans" as if they are all alike. This is not true. There were, and are, literally hundreds of tribal groups, each different from the others. Although estimates vary, historians generally believe that the Indian population of America north of Mexico in the early sixteenth century (before the coming of Europeans) numbered between 7 and 12 million. By 1800, the estimate is that the population declined to about a million (Faragher, Buhle, Czitrom, and Armitage, 1994). After the arrival of the Europeans, the death rate of Native Americans was very high, from a variety of causes. European diseases for which the indigenous people had no immunity, such as smallpox, measles, diphtheria, and syphillis, were one cause of death. When the buffalo and other animals they fed on were decimated by white settlers during the nineteenth century, thousands of Native Americans began to suffer from malnutrition or starvation. In the United States, warfare and policies of genocide initiated by whites killed hundreds of thousands more Native Americans by the late nineteenth century. By 1890, the Indian population had been reduced to its lowest number—228,000 (Faragher et al., 1994).

Today the social and economic position of Native Americans is probably the worst of any minority group in this country. Almost half still live on reservations, where there are few job opportunities and a shortage of amenities, even such basics as potable water. As a group, they have a high alcoholism rate, they have a high suicide rate, they suffer many diseases (such as tuberculosis) that are under control in most other parts of the United States, and they have a markedly lower life expectancy than the general population. They continue to have the lowest median income and larger families than the national average. In 1987, reservation unemployment varied from as low as 25 percent to as high as 87 percent (Marger, 1997).

Data on urban Native Americans are sketchy and inconsistent. Small numbers of Native Americans have lived in towns since colonial times. Beginning in the late nineteenth century, they slowly became more urbanized (Snipp, 1996). Because of discrimination and their lower economic status, those who reside in cities often live in slums and ghettos. Typical apartments are crowded. For many, city life is alienating and may be at least partly responsible for problem drinking among urban Native Americans (Snipp, 1996). Yet because cities offer more economic opportunities than are available on the reservations, for those who can withstand the culture shock of migration, some opportunities exist. Indeed a small middle class is developing among urban Native Americans. Another positive development has been the spread of an ideology of Pan-Indianism; with a few exceptions, community events and social gatherings for urban Native Americans are open to members of all tribes (Snipp, 1996).

Native Americans have a life expectancy markedly below the general population. Despite a sharp increase in the birthrate and size of the population, Native Americans are still more likely to be ill than other Americans and still die younger than other Americans. Inadequate housing, nutrition, and sanitation contribute to their health problems, as have cutbacks in federal health programs. Alcoholism remains an acute problem; Native Americans are five times more likely to die of complications from alcoholism than other groups (Kivisto, 1995).

African Americans

It may seem hard to believe, but after Nigeria, Ethiopia, and Zaire, the United States has the largest black population in the world. African Americans are unique in that they were unwilling immigrants, part of a forced population transfer. That is, they did not make the decision to come to this country; they came as slaves. Most experts maintain that slavery was such a factor in the black experience that it continues to make African Americans a special group in the nation's racial/ethnic hierarchy. The Civil War ended in 1865 and the slaves were freed, but it took another hundred years before they achieved basic civil rights. During that century of so-called "freedom," they were denied the opportunity to compete on an equal basis with white Americans.

At the close of the twentieth century, African Americans make up about 12 percent of the U.S. population, but they are not equally distributed throughout the country or the economy (Marger, 1997). (Traditionally, blacks were a people of the rural South; they began to migrate to large cities,

THE HUMAN FACE OF A CIVIL RIGHTS HERO

James Meredith

On Oct. 1 I will give a speech at Shepherd College at Shepherdstown, W. Va. It will be for me a commemoration of an important event: the 35th anniversary of the week that I became the first black student at the University of Mississippi.

As I write the speech, I can't help reflecting on that week 35 years ago. My admission and enrollment at Ole Miss caused a riot. It resulted in President Kennedy's sending federal troops to the university for the second time in history. It was dangerous, and most of my friends told me, "Don't do it." But by challenging the system, I opened doors for generations to come. I made history. I don't mind taking some pride in that.

At the time, when I walked to the steps of the admissions building at Ole Miss, the struggle of black Americans was a basic one. We wanted our equal rights as Americans, including the right to vote and the right to full access to tax-supported facilities. We wanted the same things white folks wanted: a job, a home in a safe neighborhood, a decent education for our kids, and a shot at the American Dream. And most of all we wanted to participate. We still do.

However, somewhere along the line, someone in power decided that the proud black race, a people who built cultures in Africa and built many of the physical structures of this nation, could not survive without a host of federal programs and giveaways. Thus the "participatory" goals, which united blacks and whites behind black Americans, were abandoned and replaced by programs that divided us. A "dependency mentality" was created and fostered by black and white liberals looking to buy power.

The political "Southern Strategy" that Nixon used in his re-election in 1972 was a reaction to this mentality. The architects of the strategy figured that if the liberals were going to buy support with public programs, conservatives should go after the votes of those who have to pay for them. It worked.

This "dependency mentality" is one of the key dynamics of the black underclass today. Another is a "doomed to fail" attitude—that, try as you may, you can't succeed, mostly because of white racism. It is the predominant rationalization of the black underclass and is somewhat prevalent even in the black working class and middle class. Worst of all, we instill it in our youth at an early age. This way of thinking is self-perpetuating and comes more from a negative self-image than it does with any insurmountable racial roadblock.

No one today inspires me more than Tiger Woods. He impresses me more than anyone else since Joe Louis when I was a boy. He is the confident, proud success that I hoped by now would be commonplace in the black community if only we could participate. However, all of his accomplishments would not have been possible if he had adopted the "doomed to fail" attitude.

In the same way that blacks must reject that minority of whites who are incurable racists, we must also turn away from the small minority of black "leaders" and their white manipulators who perpetuate these negative attitudes.

I have come to realize that while white racism exists, our main roadblocks in the '90s are ones that have been created by our own so-called leadership. My speaking out about this has left me shunned by the prominent black leadership elite and white allies. These are the people who have a vested interest in the failed status quo.

Because I feel that I'm right (in the sense of correct), I will push forward. As I look ahead to what I as a pioneer of the past can do to shape a better future for black Americans, I see three big areas where my voice and work can help bring about positive change:

1. I want to be vocal and confrontational in addressing the issues that are tearing apart the black family and fostering the black underclass. Why are children having children? Why is generation after generation on welfare? Why is black-on-black crime a growing phenomenon? Someone has to openly and aggressively ask questions and demand real answers.
2. I want to lead black people to the library. If you want to develop a young man into a Tiger Woods, you take him to the golf course. If you want to make him a Michael Jordan, you take him to the basketball court. If you want to develop black Americans into intellectual giants, you take them

(continued)

to the library. There can be only so many Tiger Woodses and Michael Jordans. However, every black American can learn to read and can develop intellectually in a way that will help him or her no matter what he or she does.

3. I want to lead a significant percentage of black Americans toward the Republican Party. The Southern Strategy worked only because black Americans crowded into one party, the Democrats. Although the Republicans have a long way to go, I feel they are open to all Americans. We as blacks are ill-served by being part of only one political party. We're taken for granted. I want to change this.

Things do change and for the better. In 1962 Ole Miss refused to acknowledge that I was a person, that I existed. Last year, on March 21, the University of Mississippi honored me by becoming the home for the James H. Meredith papers. Those who attended the ceremony included blacks, whites, and one of the school's first-year graduate students—my son, Kip, who enrolled and entered the university with none of the fanfare that accompanied his father's arrival 35 years ago.

Source: James Meredith, "A Challenge to Change," *Newsweek*, October 6, 1997, p. 18.

mostly in the North, only a generation or two ago.) After the Civil War, they were isolated from the economic mainstream. For a century, African Americans were shut out of the higher-skilled, more prestigious, better-paying jobs. In a very real sense they were unskilled immigrants to industrialized areas, but they arrived when the manufacturing base of cities was disappearing. Not until after the civil rights movement of the 1960s did a significant number of African Americans move out of lower-level jobs. The 1960s was a decade of progress for African Americans, as measured by income, occupation, and education, but the 1970s was a decade of retrenchment. Progress on these fronts during this decade was curtailed or slowed significantly. As the new millennium approaches, the gap between blacks and whites remains great (see the box "The Human Face of a Civil Rights Hero: James Meredith"). In fact, the pay differential between African Americans and whites actually increased during the 1980s (Marger, 1997).

Experts agree that the economic progress of middle-class blacks, who are usually well-educated and well-trained, has had little effect on African Americans at the bottom of the economic scale. About one-third of blacks are now in the middle class in terms of occupation, income, and lifestyle. But despite the civil rights movement, African American families are still 3.5 times more likely than white families to be classified as poor (World Almanac, 1993). Approximately a third of all African American families are classified as living below the official poverty level. In 1990, the poverty level of a family of four was $13,359. For one person in 1990, this meant $6652 a year, or $118 a week (World Almanac, 1993). Poverty among African Americans is related to large family size, lack of education, and lower occupational status, among other factors.

Asian Americans

Today Asian Americans make up only about 2 percent of the American population. The migration from China and Japan began more than a century ago. Chinese immigration first occurred between 1850 and 1880; immigrants came primarily to work in West Coast mines and to build the transcontinental railroads. In 1882, as previously indicated, Chinese immigration was first restricted. Between 1900 and 1943, no Chinese were admitted to the United States. The Japanese originally came around the turn of the twentieth century, mainly as laborers, primarily for agricultural work (see the box "The Human Face of Immigration: Ronald T. Takaki") . They were treated somewhat better than the Chinese because their government was strong enough to look after their interests. But the situation changed during World War II, when, due to anti-Japanese sentiment, about 120,000 Japanese American men, women, and children were sent—most for the duration of the war—to 10 internment camps within the United States. (In 1988, the U.S. Congress voted reparations of $20,000 each and publicly apologized to the surviving 60,000 victims.) Recently, there has been a lot of immigration from other Asian countries such as

THE HUMAN FACE OF IMMIGRATION

Ronald T. Takaki

I had flown from San Francisco to Norfolk and was riding in a taxi to my hotel to attend a conference on multiculturalism. Hundreds of educators from across the country were meeting to discuss the need for greater cultural diversity in the curriculum. My driver and I chatted about the weather and the tourists. The sky was cloudy and Virginia Beach was twenty minutes away. The rearview mirror reflected a white man in his forties. "How long have you been in this country?" he asked. "All my life," I replied, wincing. "I was born in the United States." With a strong southern drawl, he remarked: "I was wondering because your English is excellent!" Then, as I had many times before, I explained: "My grandfather came here from Japan in the 1880s. My family has been here, in America, for over a hundred years." He glanced at me in the mirror. Somehow I did not look "American" to him; my eyes and complexion looked foreign.

Questions like the one my taxi driver asked me are always jarring, but I can understand why he could not see me as American. He had a narrow but widely shared sense of the past—a history that has viewed American as European in ancestry.

Source: Ronald T. Takaki. 1993. *A Different Mirror: A History of Multicultural America.* Boston: Little, Brown.

the Philippines, Indonesia, Korea, and Vietnam. On the whole, Asian immigrants have tended to be remarkably successful, particularly in their achievements in education.

Hispanics

For much of the twentieth century, a significant portion of Spanish-speaking people in this country were "undocumented aliens." This situation began to change with the civil rights movement of the 1960s and changed still more in 1986, with the new immigration amnesty law. Over time, a new emphasis on pride in one's ethnic heritage emerged (see the box "FYI: Arturo Madrid"). Numerous ethnic groups undertook efforts to recover their own traditions and to demand recognition of their nationality's unique contribution to American society. Such efforts have evolved over the last three decades into a stress on **multiculturalism** (sometimes referred to simply as "cultural diversity"). Multiculturalism, with its celebration of diversity, has been embraced by many Hispanics. Increasingly, there is a desire to hold on to their native customs and Spanish language. Some see the retention of the native language as key to the ability to maintain their ethnic culture. To destroy the language is to obliterate the traditional culture. In many large U.S. cities, there are festivals and educational activities about the Mexican culture (or other Hispanic cultures). These are designed not only for Hispanics but for outsiders as well.

Techniques to Reduce Tensions

Responses to subordinate group status can range widely, from deference or withdrawal, to verbal or physical confrontation, to legal action. In the past, governments (on all levels) were the agencies most likely to bring about social change and to try to reduce tensions among minority groups. Increasingly, the global civil society is a major player in minority relations, but others are involved as well.

Certainly one way to reduce tensions and problems among groups is to bring about social change through human action. Two types of human action are particularly relevant: the acts of powerful leaders and other crucially placed individuals, and the collective actions of large numbers of people. Both types of human action have worked to reduce racial/ethnic tensions in the United States.

Actions of American Presidents. We start with Franklin D. Roosevelt (president 1933–1945), because during the last 60 years much had been done

Arturo Madrid

I am a citizen of the United States, as are my parents and as were their parents, grandparents, and great-grandparents. My ancestors' presence in what is now the United States antedates Plymouth Rock, even without taking into account any American Indian heritage I might have.

I do not, however, fit those mental sets that define America and Americans. My physical appearance, my speech patterns, my name, my profession (a professor of Spanish) create a text that confuses the reader. My normal experience is to be asked, "And where are *you* from?"

My response depends on my mood. Passive-aggressive, I answer "From here." Aggressive-passive, I ask, "Do you mean where am I originally from?" But ultimately my answer to those follow-up questions that ask about origins will be that we have always been here.

Overcoming my resentment I will try to educate, knowing that nine times out of ten my words fall on inattentive ears. I have spent most of my adult life explaining who I am not. I am exotic, but—as Richard Rodriguez of *Hunger of Memory* fame so painfully found out—not exotic enough . . . not Peruvian, or Pakistani, or Persian, or whatever.

I grew up in an isolated and historically marginal part of the United States, a small mountain village in the state of New Mexico, the eldest child of parents native to that region and whose ancestors had always lived there. In those vast and empty spaces, people who look like me, speak as I do, and have names like mine predominate.

Despite the operating myth of the day, school did not erase my otherness. It did try to deny it, and in doing so only accentuated it. To this day, school is more socialization than education, but when I was in elementary school—and given where I was—socialization was everything. School was where one became an American. Because there was a pervasive and systematic denial by the society that surrounded us that we were Americans. That denial was both explicit and implicit.

Source: Arturo Madrid. 1988. "Missing People and Others: Joining Together to Expand the Circle," *Change 20,* May/June, pp. 55–59.

in the area of race relations. On matters of race and ethnicity, Roosevelt's record is mixed. On the plus side, he signed Executive Order 8802 (1943), establishing the Fair Employment Practices Committee, which opened defense plant jobs to blacks during World War II. The executive order was significant because not only did some African Americans have their grievances heard at the highest level but they also succeeded in getting well-paying jobs in the defense industry. On the minus side, Roosevelt signed the infamous Executive Order 9066 (1942) that forcibly evacuated 120,000 persons of Japanese ancestry (two-thirds of whom were American citizens by virtue of having been born in the United States) from Washington, Oregon, California, and parts of Arizona. These people were sent to guarded relocation camps in various parts of the West, where they remained for almost four years (Daniels, 1990; Berry and Tischler, 1978).

Roosevelt's successor, Harry S. Truman (president 1945–1953) expanded federal policy requiring equal employment opportunities. In 1948, Truman desegregated the armed forces, opening the doors of the military for black soldiers and sailors. (African Americans had fought in separate units from white Americans during the war.) That same year, Truman recognized that he could not be reelected president without the support of African American voters. As a result, the Democratic Party adopted a civil rights plank in the party platform. President John F. Kennedy (president 1961–1963) also signed an executive order prohibiting racial discrimination by contractors doing business with the federal government (1963). These measures by three Democratic presidents brought real and symbolic gains to minority workers.

The next president, Lyndon B. Johnson (president 1963–1969), also a Democrat, was successful in urging Congress to pass the Civil Rights Act (1964) banning discrimination on the grounds of race, color, religion, national origin, or gender. The law applied to publicly owned facilities such as municipal swimming pools, parks, businesses, and other facilities open to the public. In addition, under Johnson's urging, Congress passed the Voting Rights Act (1965), which required that the same standards be used in registering all citizens in federal, state, and local elections. The act banned literacy tests, whites-only primaries, and other discriminatory practices.

In 1970, Republican president Richard M. Nixon (president 1969–1974) affirmed the federal government's commitment to fulfill treaty obligations with various Native American tribes and to give the right of self-determination to the tribes. But even with these responses by government, much needed to be done in the area of minority rights.

Civil Rights Movement. What came to be known as the civil rights movement was a multifaceted campaign to end legal segregation and discrimination. The campaign lasted from the late 1950s to the mid-1960s. Originally, it was a movement to eliminate inequalities for African Americans, but eventually many minority groups, including women, benefited from the laws and changes it sparked. The civil rights movement was led by powerful African Americans like Martin Luther King Jr. (1929–1968), but in a very real way, it empowered many others, making them realize that their actions could help bring about change.

During this period, nonviolent protest and civil disobedience became a policy of the civil rights movement. The idea behind these forms of action was that individual citizens had a moral duty to disobey unjust laws. (Nonviolent protest was the policy in the 1940s in India, where Mahatma Gandhi [1869–1948] led the movement for independence from British rule.) In the United States, nonviolent demonstrations were frequently met with hostile white retaliation, particularly in the South. Churches were firebombed, citizens' groups tried to prevent the desegregation of southern universities, and activists—black and white—were killed. But despite the protests of reactionary whites, in 1964 laws were passed prohibiting discrimination in voting, public facilities, schools, courts, and employment. These laws ended official segregation and discrimination but not de facto inequalities. (De facto segregation results from apparently voluntary choices. Theoretically, no one is responsible; it "just happens.")

The civil rights movement succeeded for a number of reasons, including the fact that the mass media, particularly television, provided sympathetic coverage of many of the nonviolent protests. Americans who saw these protests on television (and read about them in the print media) were outraged at the

The civil rights movement succeeded for a number of reasons, one of which was the sympathetic coverage of many of the nonviolent protests the mass media provided, which helped create widespread goodwill. Here the Reverend Martin Luther King addresses the crowd at the March on Washington in 1963.

brutality of some southern police and officials. In addition, the members of the movement formed alliances with many other groups (white liberals, college students, and other minorities). The nonviolent activities of the movement created widespread favorable goodwill. Probably most important, the members of the movement demanded nothing more for African Americans than the civil, legal, and political rights available to white Americans. This goal was seen as legitimate and nonthreatening to many in the larger community.

Affirmative Action. *Affirmative action* dates from 1967, when President Johnson issued an executive order concerning enforcement of antidiscrimination requirements for agencies and businesses under contract with the federal government. The order required contractors to make special efforts to ensure that they did not discriminate. Contractors not only had to avoid discrimination but also had to make an active effort to increase the number of women and minority employees. Over time, affirmative action was applied to colleges and universities, unions, and other businesses. The fundamental argument was that preferential treatment seemed the only way to undo the harmful effects of past and present discrimination.

Affirmative action programs in both hiring and college admissions were widespread during the 1970s, but they have become increasingly controversial. Republican presidents such as Ronald Reagan (president 1981–1989) and George Bush (president 1989–1993) sought to portray affirmative action as nothing but the use of quotas. The Clinton administration is more sympathetic to affirmative action, but the policy remains controversial. Many people regard any preference for minority or female applications as reverse discrimination, which they regard as unfair to white and male candidates. The question of qualifications has become central.

As for the practical consequences of affirmative action, comparisons among recent college graduates continue to show that white males earn more than any other group. The pay gap between women and minorities has, however, narrowed (Daniels, 1990). Among less educated minorities, there have also been some benefits of affirmative action. In particular, more minority people have found positions as police officers and firefighters. Minority hiring has also increased in the building trades. But recent data show that affirmative action has had almost no effect on low-income, poorly educated minorities. They continue to be unemployed or underemployed (Daniels, 1990).

Role of the Media. Members of minority groups tend to be excluded from the powerful and desirable jobs. This is true of jobs in the mass media, too. The number of minority members who have been able to enter white-owned print media has traditionally been small. Minorities are usually underrepresented in the broadcast and cable television industry, as well. Throughout all the mass media, minority members have low representation in leadership positions as editors, managers, or owners. There may be a token representative of the minority, but once that position is filled, there is usually no room for any others at that particular station or paper. Perhaps even more significant is the fact that the mass media stereotypes minorities in its movies and television programs. Until recently, cowboy and Indian films were a staple of Hollywood and television programming; Indians were usually the villains who massacred innocent homesteaders. African Americans and other minorities have also been traditionally stereotyped in the media, confined to roles as servants, entertainers, or other small roles.

Assessing the Situation

Race and Ethnic Problems as Human Rights Issues

Throughout history, people have migrated to other countries to avoid the ravages of war and natural disasters. The UN High Commissioner on Refugees estimates that today there are 19 million refugees worldwide (Kane, 1994). Of these, some are classified as *political refugees* (those fleeing persecution or warfare), while others are called *economic refugees* (people who emigrate from their native land because of poor economic conditions). Unfortunately, declining resources, environmental decay, and increasing Third World poverty are predicted to produce greater numbers of economic refugees in the future. Additionally, these factors likely will combine to significantly increase religious, ethnic, and nationalist warfare, along with persecutions of "undesirable" groups (Homer-Dixon, 1994). The number of political refugees fleeing these conflicts also is likely to swell dramatically.

Many refugees live in squatter refugee camps in host nations, where they may lack basic food, clothing, shelter, medicine, and sanitation facilities. Those in camps may be preyed upon by the military, police, or criminal elements in the host countries and may be victimized as well by ruffians in their own company. Other refugees may successfully enter a host society, but then find that they remain on the fringes of that society and are vulnerable to exploitation.

A major problem with refugees is that their sheer numbers threaten to overwhelm the resources of international relief agencies as well as those of host countries. Many, though not all, emigrants move if they can from Third World to First World countries, where they find themselves in a paradoxical situation. On the one hand, they contribute to their new country, often serving as a source of cheap labor. On the other hand, they are seen as a drain on its resources as well as a threat to its workforce. The perceived threat of immigrants has facilitated a swing to the right in most First World countries. At the extreme, this is manifested in an increasing number of right-wing hate groups. Fascism is on the rise in all industrialized nations, including Germany, which is experiencing a sharp escalation in neo-Nazi activities. Physical attacks on "foreigners" also are increasing in most Western nations. Further, many governments are taking only limited action to curb the growth of fascism and racism (Paul, 1991).

The backlash against immigrants in First World nations also is manifesting itself in the form of legislation designed to deny social benefits, such as education and health care, to immigrants and their children. In addition, legislatures are passing increasingly tough laws intended to limit legal immigration, as well as to stifle illegal entry. Some experts see a conspiracy in all this, in that Western Europe is joined by the United States and Japan in implementing almost identical restrictive practices (Paul, 1991). Moreover, though industrialized nations are required by international covenants, such as the 1951 Convention on the Status of Refugees, to offer asylum to any people experiencing persecution in their homelands, political refugees are finding First World nations increasingly cool to their plight. Political asylum is becoming more difficult to obtain. Often those seeking it are arrested and detained while their requests are being considered. Others are deported without any consideration of the validity of their requests for asylum or of the almost certain retribution that awaits them in their country of origin.

One way host nations are avoiding the requirement to take in and protect political refugees is to declare persons fleeing civil repression "economic refugees," whom they are not then obligated to receive. For example, in 1994, the fear of politically motivated violence sparked a wave of Haitians bound for U.S. shores. President Clinton declared most of these to be economic refugees drawn to the United States for financial betterment, not for political protection. Ironically, this declaration was presented at the same moment that the United States was seeking international support for intervening militarily in Haiti to stop political genocide.

This ambivalence over issues of race is not new. Two decades ago in the United States, the Kerner Commission (1968) warned: "Our nation is moving toward two societies, one black and one white—separate and unequal." Since then, some progress has been made, but mostly for middle-class African Americans. The problems of inner city blacks continue to mount. Chronically high unemployment in black neighborhoods (particularly among the youth) has raised fears that the United States may have acquired a permanent underclass. Hardly anyone disagrees that American society is badly divided.

Much the same holds true with respect to ethnicity. The United States is now experiencing an enormous influx of immigrants, many of them illegal. Large numbers of immigrants from Latin America arrive in poverty, poorly educated, and knowing only a few simple phrases of English. Bilingualism has become a fact of life in the Southwest, New York City, and Miami. Some social scientists say that in the decades ahead, we can come to experience some of the same forces of disunity that Canada has experienced between its French-speaking and English-speaking populations.

One of the primary theories in sociology is called the *power-conflict perspective.* This view looks at the world through the eyes of the less powerful; it is concerned with who wins and who loses in any particular situation. The power-conflict perspective is helpful in identifying *why* racial and ethnic inequalities develop.

A Power-Conflict View of Intergroup Relations. According to power-conflict theorist Donald Noel (1968), the following three conditions must be met for discrimination and conflict to occur. First, two or more identifiable racial or ethnic groups must come into contact and feel ethnocentric about their own group. Second, there must be competition between the groups for scarce valued resources. The more the groups compete, the more negatively they view one another. The third condition is that the groups must be unequal in power, enabling one of them to secure scarce resources at the expense of the other(s). The dominant group in the process develops a set of beliefs about the supposed inferiority of the minority group and thereby justifies its own supremacy. Conflict theorists emphasize competition for valuable scarce resources, not the racial and ethnic differences themselves, as the basis for racial and ethnic inequality. They argue that the conflict is reduced only when the minority group gains greater equality with the dominant group.

Summary

1. **Race** refers to a category of people who are regarded as socially distinct because they share genetically transmitted physical characteristics, such as skin color, hair texture, or shape of the nose and eyes. **Ethnicity** refers to a category of people who are regarded as socially distinct because of their shared cultural heritage, including language, customs, dress, religion, and food preferences. **Racism** is a belief that one racial or ethnic group is inferior or superior to another that is used to justify unequal treatment.
2. Social Darwinism is a pseudoscientific argument that seems to justify racism and helped to promote violent pogroms in Russia, anti-Semitic policies in Europe, and immigration quotas in many countries. European colonialism between the fifteenth and twentieth centuries also contributed to the increase in racism. In the West, skin color was the basis for racism and led to the enslavement of blacks in the United States.
3. A **minority group,** identifiable by visible social or physical characteristics, suffers disadvantages at the hands of another, more dominant group.
4. **Prejudice** is an irrational, inflexible attitude toward an entire category of people or things. **Discrimination** is the unequal treatment of people based on their group membership. *Ethnocentrism* is the tendency to judge other cultures by the standards of one's own.
5. There are six basic patterns of minority interaction. *Assimilation* occurs when minorities are absorbed into the dominant culture; *pluralism* occurs when minorities maintain their distinctive cultural and physical traits and coexist with the dominant group; in some societies, minorities are *protected by law,* so that it is illegal to discriminate against minorities; *population transfers* remove minority groups to other locations on a forced or voluntary basis; *continued subjugation* is the open exercise of privilege by the dominant group at the expense of the minority group, such as the practice of *apartheid* in South Africa; *extermination,* or *genocide,* is the murder of an entire group of people.
6. In 1882, Congress passed the Chinese Exclusion Act, denying Chinese the right to immigrate. In 1924, Congress passed the National Origins Act, which established a quota system, strongly favoring European immigrants. In the 1960s, the bias in American immigration laws shifted away from Europe toward favoring people from the Third World.
7. There are three basic types of immigrants: regular immigrants, including professionals and their families; undocumented immigrants, who enter the country illegally; and refugees, who are often fleeing political repression.
8. Some immigrant Asian families have an average income that is even higher than native-born Americans of European descent. White Anglo-Saxon Protestants (WASPs), who make up about one-fourth of the U.S. population, have disproportionate political, economic, and social influence. The social and economic position of Native Americans is probably the worst of that of any minority group in this country.
9. Efforts to improve race relations in the United States have included President Roosevelt's Fair Employment Practices Committee (1943), President Truman's desegregation of the armed forces (1948), and the Civil Rights Act (1964), which banned discrimination on the grounds of race, color, religion, national origin, or gender.

Thinking Critically

1. Why does James Meredith believe that African Americans should join and support the Republican Party? What can African Americans and other concerned citizens do to help resolve the "issues that are tearing apart the black family and fostering the black underclass"?
2. Using Donald Noel's thesis, how are the experiences of some specific minority group (e.g., African American, Native American, Hispanic) shaped by ethnocentrism, competition, and differentials in power?
3. Using material from this chapter and your general knowledge, on balance, do you think immigration is harmful or helpful to the United States? Why do you think so? Are recent immigrants taking a different role in the economy than earlier waves of immigrants did?

Suggested Readings

Feagin, Joe R. and Clairece Booher Feagin. 1996. *Racial and Ethnic Relations.* 5th ed. Upper Saddle River, NJ: Prentice Hall.

Marger, Martin N. 1997. *Race and Ethnic Relations: American and Global Perspective.* 4th ed. Belmont, CA: Wadsworth.

Parillo, Vincent N. 1996. *Diversity in America.* Thousand Oaks, CA: Pine Forge.

Pedraza, Silvia and Ruben G. Rumbaut. 1996. *Origins and Destinies: Immigration, Race, and Ethnicity in America.* Belmont, CA: Wadsworth.

Web Sites

CLNet Diversity Page
http://latino.sscnet.ucla.edu/diversity1.html
This is an excellent source for Hispanic/Latino information.

Latino Issues Forum
http//www.lif.org/
This is another good source for Latino issues.

European Research Center on Migration and Ethnic Relations
http://www.ruu.nl.ercomer/index.html
This site contains comprehensive and up-to-date information on European migration.

Race and ethnicity
http://ethics.acusd.edu/race.html
This site contains listings of recent literature on race and ethnicity.

Asian Americans
http://www.mit.edu:8001/afs/athena.mit.edu/user/i/r/irie/www/aar.html
Try this site for resources on Asian Americans.

Native Americans
http://hanksville.phast.umass.edu/misc/NAresources.html
This site is an informative index of Native American resources.

African American Workers

http://www.ilr.cornell.edu/library/lmdc/afen.html

This site offers primary sources on African American workers, including material on southern tenant farmers, African American railroad unions, and African American involvement in the International Ladies' Garment Workers' Union.

Race Relations Institute

http://www.fiskrri.organ/frames16.htn

This site contains material from the university's race relations institute, including 21 action items.

CHAPTER ■ TWELVE

Terrorism, Crime, Repression, and Warfare

Violence in Global Society

America: The Land of the Free? The concrete-and-steel barricades are up in the streets surrounding the Republican National Convention center, and the delegates, visitors and news reporters line up to be funneled through checkpoints; the purses, bags and briefcases are ordered opened so they can be searched, the men and women carrying them are sent one-by-one through metal-detection sheds, and all of this is done in the name of liberty. Perhaps the most extraordinary thing is that we have now reached the point where this seems ordinary—even good. . . . Authoritarianism, when it comes to any nation, often arrives to welcoming words from the citizens. At first. Authoritarianism, when it is new, is never called that. It goes by other names: "Security." "Defense." "Protection."

In the United States, this has been a gradual process. What began in airports in the early 1970s—those first checkpoints—has now mutated into the texture of the land. The three biggest events of the summer [of 1996]—the Olympic Games, the Republican Convention, the Democratic National Convention—were designed as symbols of freedom and fellowship. And all—willingly, with the gratitude of those in attendance—turned themselves over to armed and uniformed forces with the authority to do just about anything they pleased.

There is nervous joking. A photographer who came directly from the Olympics to the Republican Convention, on his impressions of the two weeks in Atlanta: "I don't much enjoy living in a police state." An attendee at the convention . . . as she watched a squad of highway patrolmen, in their light brown uniforms and black boots, sweep through the aisles of the convention hall: "They look a little too much like [Nazi] storm troopers for me." Both things said with slight smiles—the photographer wasn't really complaining about the atmosphere in Atlanta, just using dark humor to try to process it; the woman . . . wasn't afraid of the patrolmen, just taking note of her visceral reaction.

Once a country has chosen to submit itself to this—once it has concluded that to assure a free way of life, personal freedom must be constrained, amended—there is seldom any going back. . . .

Source: From Bob Greene. 1996. "Land of the Free? Not America, Not in 1996." *Chicago Tribune*, August 14: 5.1.

This vignette illustrates a growing concern around the world as we approach the twenty-first century. The quest for security, whether economic, environmental, or political, has become a feature of the contemporary landscape. That this has occurred stems partly from the general uneasiness and problems that have resulted from the globalization process. However, as newspaper columnist Bob Greene points out in this vignette, such a quest can produce a marked decline in personal liberty that may come to threaten democracy itself.

In this chapter we review some of the most significant contemporary threats to personal, national, and global security. Although we are especially interested in those threats that result in violence against people, we also discuss other types of threats, such as property crimes and drug abuse. Much of the violence committed by people against other people originates in the drive to maintain power or to demand empowerment. The powerful, whether in governments or in criminal organizations, often use violence as a means to intimidate opponents. Conversely, those who are deprived in a political or economic system often resort to violence to force the power structure to include them. Both these forms of violence appear to operate on any number of social levels, from the local community to the global village.

It is within this context of empowerment that we view a range of issues from terrorism to crime to warfare. However, we must introduce several other sociological concepts in order to properly assess the issues in this chapter. We start with a discussion of deviance and social structure.

Deviance and Social Structure

When most of us learn of conduct we do not like, we tend to blame the personal faults or individual pathologies of others. When our government launches a propaganda campaign against a foreign leader such as the late Ayatollah Khomeini of Iran or Iraqi leader Saddam Hussein, we call such leaders "crazy." Similarly, we describe corporate leaders who ruthlessly exploit others and rape the environment as "greedy," or say they lack "empathy" for others. At one level of analysis, it may be appropriate to examine the character defects of others. But from a sociological perspective, blaming others is hardly scientific; it is little more than name-calling and is mostly self-serving. Thus, "they" exploit others because of their greed, whereas "we" are not exploitative. Presumably, when we talk like this, we mean that "we" are more virtuous than "they" are. But probably the truth is that we (as opposed to they) have not yet been given the incentive or the power to exploit others, except in small ways.

Sociologists are interested in such questions as, "Would ordinary people act virtuously if they had the opportunity to take advantage of others and get away with it?" Plenty of evidence in sociological studies shows that many, if not most, ordinary decent people will, in fact, hurt others under social conditions that favor harming others (Milgram, 1974; Zimbardo, 1972). The other side of the coin is that people often act virtuously, even heroically, when the situation favors that kind of action. The specific social situation we are in, especially when it is very compelling (e.g., the same people in a riot situation may act differently if they were simply the audience in a theater), exerts far more influence over our conduct than we would like to think.

Our concern in this chapter is with **deviance,** the socially perceived violation of social norms. Sociologically speaking, we are more interested in explaining large-scale patterns, rates, or trends in deviant conduct rather than in focusing on individual cases of deviance. Rates, social patterns, and trends are facts in their own right and require explanation. Sociologists know, for instance, that violent crime rates in Japan are extremely low when compared to those in other industrialized societies, whereas those in the United States are extremely high. We know too that certain neighborhoods in our country have experienced high rates of crime for decades, even though their ethnic composition has changed several times during this timespan. In addition, we know that large-scale social change such as the shift to modernization dramatically alters the rates and types of crimes committed. Sociologists also know that certain age and gender categories are most prone to certain patterns of crime. None of these very important and very practical bits of knowledge can be rationally explained by reference to personal defects or to individual abnormalities.

Sociologist Robert K. Merton (1957) developed a model of deviant behavior based on the recognition that the social structure itself generates pressures toward deviance. Pressures to deviate from socially approved courses of action, or norms, are channeled by other elements of the social structure (such as available criminal opportunities or learned rationalizations for deviance) into a variety of short- or long-term patterns of deviant conduct. The aspect of social structure most directly implicated in generating deviant reactions is the integration of a society's success goals with patterns of approved behavior that people expect to lead to those goals or ends. A society's institutionalized goals are many and various, ranging from material success (measurable by money), social recognition (fame), and intellectual accomplishment (degrees, academic honors), to name a few. Other less tangible goals include the good life, the greatest good for the greatest number, or personal salvation. A well-integrated and stable society exhibits few problems and little deviance. In such a society, if people use socially approved means (norms), they achieve socially approved goals (ends). These means themselves are (1) valued, (2) accessible to the members of society, and (3) actually lead, step by step, to the valued goals. For example, when people follow the prescribed means of staying in school and studying hard, it usually leads to their obtaining higher degrees and some measure of financial success.

The measures of success in a society (wealth, good grades, fame, political power) may, however, often be achieved more efficiently by not obeying the rules (and not getting caught). Yet, as long as the approved means are themselves valued, as long as the members of society believe them to constitute a ladder to success, and as long as they are reasonably available to people, the tendency toward serious deviation is weak. When a society's goals and socially approved means are effectively integrated in this way, its members are empowered. They are able to achieve valued goals through their own efforts because they have access to socially approved means, including knowledge, education, and income.

Pressures to deviate are generated by a *lack of integration or lack of consistency between a society's goals and approved means.* You may recall that the process of interaction by which persons undergo psychological and social development as they internalize their culture is called socialization. Sometimes pressures to deviate are created, Merton suggests, when socialization leads to a strong emotional commitment to achieve certain ends but *fails to provide the person with an equally strong commitment to behave in socially approved ways.* Or such pressures stem from the *lack of real and effective opportunities (means) to achieve success by large numbers of people.* Thus, a strong emphasis on success goals and either weak commitment to social norms and/or actual (or perceived) lack of opportunity generate pressures to deviate.

Table 12–1 illustrates how Merton understands the origins of deviance. He describes five adaptations that emerge in response to a society's pattern of goals and means. The most common adaptation is **conformity,** or actively seeking socially approved goals by socially approved means. Conformists thus are the bulwark of social order, without whom a society cannot continue to exist. Another response is **innovation,** or the active pursuit of socially approved goals while rejecting socially approved means. The term "innovation" is somewhat misleading. It does not mean that people have invented the deviant actions they perform. In most cases they have learned their deviance from others. Most criminals, from shoplifters to members of organized crime to people who cheat on their taxes, fall into this category. They are motivated by power, prestige, or economic gain but eschew the approved channels of education, honesty, and hard work.

Some political leaders, even though they may occupy positions of legitimate power, are examples of innovation. This occurs when, in order to maintain their power or to secure the compliance of their citizens, they resort to forms of force and deception that are considered deviant by international law. Political leaders who have gained their power by the use of force may literally not have learned how to use noncoercive (i.e., democratic) means of ruling or may hold such means in contempt. Others who achieve political power by more peaceful (usually democratic) means may find that they are unable to maintain loyalty, achieve consensus, or meet the conflicting needs of their people (all of which are approved political goals) and resort to deviant political means to preserve their power. Thus, innovation is not, according to Merton, limited to economically motivated crime.

TABLE 12–1 Merton's Typology of Deviance

	MEANS	ENDS
Conformity	+	+
Innovation	–	+
Ritualism	+	–
Retreatism	–	–
Rebellion	–	–
	(+)	(+)

+ = Accepts; – = Rejects

Source: "Merton's Typology of Deviance" from *Social Theory, Social Structure*, revised edition by Robert K. Merton. Copyright © 1957 by The Free Press; copyright renewed 1985 by Robert K. Merton. Reprinted with the permission of The Free Press, a division of Simon & Schuster.

A second form of deviant reaction is **ritualism,** or the pursuit of socially approved courses of action while surrendering any commitment to achieving socially approved goals. At first glance, ritualism does not seem like deviance at all because persons who fall into this category conform outwardly to social norms. However, they are motivationally deviant. Socially approved ends no longer motivate ritualists, as they have given up on attaining socially approved goals. In this sense we may say that ritualists lead lives of quiet desperation. But ritualism can also cause people to have an exaggerated concern with the rules by which they lead their lives while they simultaneously ignore the purposes those rules are designed to serve. Ritualism then may lead to a kind of hyperconformity that can be found in some bureaucratic and totalitarian settings. As such, ritualism can be seen to be a sort of political deviance on the part of the disempowered and hopeless or as a kind of pathology. For example, it is common for persons in businesses to rise to a certain level in an organization and then realize they are not moving any higher. Moreover, they realize that they can have no impact on changing the organization. Most of these individuals simply accept their fate. They do their job, shuffle their paperwork, and wait for retirement.

The third mode of deviant reaction described by Merton (1957) is **retreatism,** or the rejection of institutionalized means and goals. Merton lists vagrants, outcasts, psychotics, drug addicts, vagabonds, chronic alcoholics, and the like as examples of this form of deviance. These are people who have abandoned the quest for success altogether. They reject society and are rejected by it. Motivationally and behaviorally they have withdrawn from participation in legitimate society and, in some cases, from all social participation. For social and/or individual reasons, they have been totally disempowered.

The fourth mode of deviance is **rebellion,** or the rejection of both the approved goals and the approved means of the existing social order while actively attempting to replace them with an alternative social order. People involved in rebellion withdraw their allegiance from the prevailing social order, which they no longer view as having a legitimate claim over their conduct. They then give their allegiance to new groups possessed of a new myth (Merton, 1957). Political revolution, including withdrawal from the offending society to create a new and independent social order somewhere else, is what this form of deviance entails. Like retreatism, rebellion represents a total rejection of society, but unlike retreatism, it does not involve disempowerment. Rather, people who are rebelling reject society's disempowering social structure as arbitrary and illegitimate and seek to substitute a new and restructured social order. Ethnic conflict aimed at creating or recreating a social order that legitimates one's own culture and empowers one's own people falls under this heading. The "new groups possessed of new myths" that Merton refers to can, in the contemporary context, easily be ethnically, racially, and religiously constituted groups. Their myths, rooted in a real or imagined past, are reconstituted to meet today's global setting.

Merton's typology of deviant reactions is useful to classify and explain the patterns of behavior, including the uses and abuses of power, discussed in this chapter. By itself, however, this typology is not sufficient to account for the timing and location of deviance or for what social and cultural forms such deviance takes, nor does it describe who participates. Other factors such as the availability of deviant opportunities, the effectiveness of socialization and psychosocial development, preexisting groups and their myths, and power struggles and their outcomes (including who has command of the symbolic means of defining what is or is not deviant) are all significant factors that account for patterns of deviant conduct.

TERRORISM

Terrorism is a particularly troubling form of assault often directed against innocents. **Terrorism** is the use of violence or the threat of violence as a means of combat or to achieve some strategic goal by striking fear in victims through ruthless actions. Although we usually associate terrorism with bombings and shootings, terrorists also use chemical attacks, firebombings, arson, kidnappings, and vandalism. Terrorist activities often are conducted by organized groups, but individual malcontents also may carry on terrorist campaigns, such as the infamous Unibomber did in the United States. The type of terrorism we generally identify is called political terrorism. **Political terrorism** uses harsh tactics of intimidation to achieve some type of political goal.

Types of Political Terrorism

James Henslin (1996) notes three categories of political terrorism: revolutionary terrorism, repressive terrorism, and state-sponsored terrorism. **Revolutionary terrorism** occurs when internal enemies of the state rely on terrorist tactics to produce change in the political system. Revolutionary terrorists are a

Terrorism is the use of violence or the threat of violence to achieve a strategic goal. It is often directed against the civilian population, those most likely to have no defense against the violence and thus most fearful of it. Here a terrorist bombing was directed against homes in Northern Ireland.

self-aware religious, ethnic, cultural, or class minority who believe that the political system is unresponsive to their grievances. Their actions may seek to demonstrate the vulnerability of the government but may also have the goal of making known their cause. Revolutionary terrorists, consequently, often rely on publicity via the mass media to enhance their activities. That is, they depend on publicity to multiply the effect of an action far beyond its implications for immediate victims. At times, terrorists even commit violent acts simply to gain public attention for their cause (Metz, 1995). For instance, during 1997 and 1998, Egyptian Islamic fundamentalist terrorists orchestrated a series of attacks on foreign tourists. Their goal was to make other tourists afraid to come to Egypt, thereby depriving the Egyptian government of a valuable source of income. While many others condemn acts of destruction against innocents, the terrorists themselves believe that such acts are virtuous. Terrorists thus assume a position of moral superiority toward both the existing system and their victims to justify their conduct.

The actions and goals of revolutionary terrorists are similar to those of nation-states when they engage in repressive terrorism. **Repressive terrorism** occurs when a government employs harsh tactics to intimidate its own civilian population. The main difference between revolutionary terrorism and repressive terrorism is that revolutionary terrorism represents the actions of the powerless against the powerful. In contrast, terrorism as practiced by nation-states usually consists of actions of the powerful against the powerless (see "The Human Face of Repression: Afghan Orphans Suffer"). For example, in the spring of 1998, the Serb-dominated government of Yugoslavia launched a military offensive in

THE HUMAN FACE OF REPRESSION

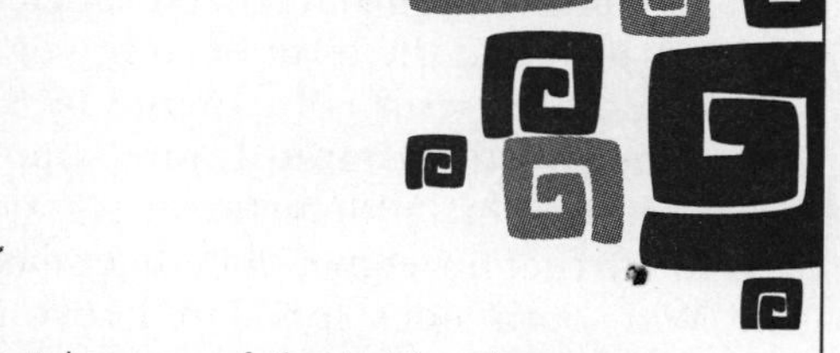

Afghan Orphans Suffer

In the fall of 1996, Taliban Muslim rebels seized control of Kabul, the capital of Afghanistan. One of their first acts was to issue an edict declaring that women must follow traditional Islamic law. Among other things, obedience required that women not hold jobs. Those who did had to retire from public life. Journalist Anwar Faruqi reported that the edict hit war orphans especially hard, as shown in the following excerpt from his newspaper article:

> Parwaneh is barely 7 years old, but she has a lot of grownup chores to do at the orphanage in the beleaguered Afghan capital. . . . Since the arrival of the Taliban religious army in Kabul more than two weeks ago, the older of the 500 children left at the orphanage have had to take care of the younger ones. The women who once cared for them are being kept away by the new rulers, whose strict version of Islam won't let women work outside of the home.
>
> With a chubby 2-year-old propped on her tiny hip, Parwaneh carefully descended the dirty cement stairs to a communal bathing area, where she scrubbed her new charge.
>
> "I have to take care of the babies, because we have no one to take care of them," she said.
>
> Life in Kabul has changed drastically since the Taliban took over Sept. 27. In addition to being kept from working, women have been forced to cover themselves from head to toe. Schools for girls have been closed, and men have been dragged off the streets for prayers. . . .
>
> "Everything is in disarray," said Mirza Mir Bhaluli, deputy director of the orphanage, which was home to about 900 children before the Taliban arrived.
>
> "I don't know what to do. We need women to take care of these children," he said. Women made up about 85 percent of his staff. . . . Moreover, the Taliban don't seem to realize that education for boys also will suffer in Kabul, where 70 percent of the teachers were women.

Source: Anwar Faruqi. 1996. "Edict Hits Afghan Orphans Hard." *Chicago Tribune,* October 15: 1.3.

the state of Kosovo. The ostensible purpose was to control Albanian rebels in the region. However, it soon became obvious that government forces were more interested in ethnic cleansing, as they engaged in extensive shelling of villages where there was no military resistance. Upon taking these villages, the troops burned and destroyed the houses in them. Terrified residents got the message and fled into Albania and other surrounding regions (McMahon, 1998).

One caution is in order. The definition of who are terrorists frequently is a matter of perspective. When, for instance, governments are targeted for violent action, they usually label the perpetrators "terrorists," whereas the perpetrators see themselves as liberators. Conversely, governments may describe their violence against the opposition as "justified acts to ensure national security," while the victims of such violence may see these activities as terrorist actions. Undoubtedly, the "patriots" who fostered the American Revolution that won our independence from England would have been labeled "terrorists" by the British had the term been in vogue then.

At times, terrorism is furthered by **state terrorism,** when nation-states train, support, finance, and protect international terrorists, who they employ to further foreign policy agendas. During the Cold War, both sides sponsored revolutionary and repressive terrorist activities against the other's surrogate states. For example, in response to the former Soviet Union's invasion of Afghanistan (1979), the United States funded and trained Islamic "freedom fighters," who later turned to international terrorism and drug dealing (Weiner, 1994). Such types of activity have declined sharply since the end of the Cold War. However, several nations that had their own terrorist agendas during the Cold War remain active. The U.S. State Department suspects that Libya, Syria, Iraq, and Iran continue to support terrorist activities against the United States and other Western countries.

Terrorism has been used for centuries. However, it emerged as a significant international problem in the 1960s (Kidder, 1990). Acts of international terrorism increased steadily through the 1970s and 1980s, reached their peak in 1987, declined until 1990, and have shown a pattern of ups and downs subsequently (Figure 12–1). Between 1990 and 1994, there were 28 incidents of terrorism in the United States. Of these, two such incidents were identified as the work of international terrorists. Homegrown malcontents engineered the rest. An additional 99 attacks in 1995 were conducted against U.S. interests abroad (Madigan, 1996).

The End of the Cold War and Terrorism

The Cold War fostered global terrorism, as both sides used revolutionary and repressive terrorism to further their political agendas. The end of the Cold War has meant that the United States and Russia are less likely to encourage terrorist turmoil. Fewer nations are now willing to protect terrorists. International cooperation against significant terrorist threats has increased.

These factors combine to make it more difficult for international terrorism to operate. But the end of the Cold War also has unleashed ethnic, religious, and nationalist hatred in many parts of the globe

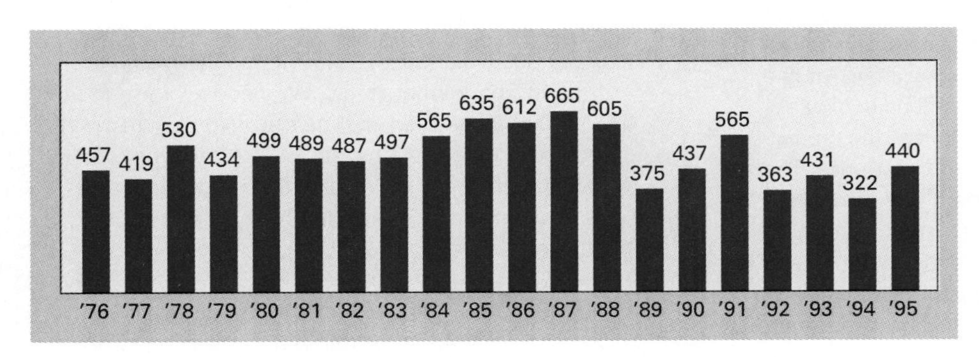

FIGURE 12–1 Global Terrorism

Source: Charles M. Madigan. 1996. "The Global Scourge of Terrorism." *Chicago Tribune*, August 1: 13.

(McColm, 1992). It is likely that we will see an increased use of terrorism by individuals and groups that subscribe to these values. Formerly, outside groups perpetuated much of the terrorism against Western nations. Although that danger has not disappeared, the likelihood of homegrown terrorist attacks is escalating. For instance, in Spain, the government fights terrorism by Basque separatists, and in the United States, the 1995 bombing of the Federal Building in Oklahoma City was carried out by citizens with grievances against the federal government.

Nationalist, separatist, or antigovernment movements have gained added impetus because they are fanned by the flames of religious zeal, as we discussed at greater length in Chapter 3. Further, the trend toward more terrorist activity will likely increase with the worldwide tendency to elect conservative governments that emphasize getting tough with terrorists rather than negotiating with them to solve grievances. For example, the 1996 election of Benjamin Netanyahu as prime minister of Israel signaled the beginning of a new get-tough policy toward negotiating peace with the Palestinians. Already, Netanyahu's government has made a number of policy changes that many experts agree have undermined the peace process begun by the previous government. These changes have invigorated extremists on both sides who want to reignite terrorist warfare between Israelis and Palestinians.

Although homegrown terrorism is likely to increase, this does not mean that the threat of international terrorism has disappeared altogether. In fact, being the object of terrorist incidents is part of the price that the United States and other nations pay for international involvement (Metz, 1995). Significantly, one of the legacies of the Cold War is that the United States now faces the prospect of being the target of terrorists that our operatives formerly trained to inflict damage on allies of the former Soviet Union.

Superterrorism

The threat of superterrorism is another increasing concern. **Superterrorism** is the enhancement of the terrorist threat by using or threatening to use weapons of mass destruction (Jerold, 1990). **Weapons of mass destruction** are those weapons capable of inflicting widespread death and injury in a single attack. Weapons of mass destruction may be chemical, biological, or nuclear. They may come in a form that is small in size and easily concealable. For instance, a terrorist may now conceal a nuclear device capable of destroying a large city in a suitcase. Determined terrorists willing to use such devices are practically unstoppable. Instances of the use of weapons of mass destruction have already occurred. Japan was shaken in 1995 when a terrorist released nerve gas in the Tokyo subway system, killing 11 people and injuring more than 5,500. Japanese society was paralyzed by fear when it learned that the leader of Aum Shinri Kyo, a doomsday cult linked to the gas attack, had predicted that a catastrophe would occur soon (Goozner, 1995). The fear that the attack induced in the populace became more significant than the number killed.

The end of the Cold War has increased the availability of weapons of mass destruction. Both the United States and the former Soviet Union had sizable caches of chemical weapons and possibly also of biological weapons. In addition, thousands of nuclear weapons were in the arsenals of the adversaries. The safety of this ordnance is questionable, especially in the former Soviet Union, where the Russian military now lacks the discipline it had during the Cold War. Many weapons of mass destruction have also fallen under control of the republics that made up the former Soviet Union. Security in both Russia and the republics is unsophisticated and notoriously lax. For instance, U.S. experts contend that none of the nearly 90 facilities where nearly 700 tons of weapons-grade nuclear material is stored have adequate security (Barry, 1995). Economic chaos in Russia and some of its neighboring republics provides additional incentive for persons to sell weapons from the Soviet arsenal on the international black market.

To make matters worse, other nations have accused several rogue, or outlaw, states such as Iran, Iraq, and Libya of developing or attempting to develop biological, chemical, and nuclear weapons. Not only may these nations use such armaments in direct warfare, but they also find their way into the hands of international terrorists. The possibility of the latter scenario is enhanced by the fact that these nations view the United States and Western democracies as their enemies. Regardless of whether or not they support the particular terrorist cause, the governments of some of the former Soviet republics may decide to sell weapons of mass destruction from their nuclear arsenal to terrorists simply because of the possibility that the terrorists may use them against the republics' former enemies—the Western nations (toward whom they may have some lingering feelings of hostility).

Criminal Terrorism and International Crime

Henslin (1996) identifies two other types of terrorism that deserve mention—criminal terrorism and narcoterrorism. In addition, there is growing concern about international crime that may or may not involve terrorist activities but that may cause considerable problems, including a substantial financial drain on individual countries and the global community. Furthermore, dealing with this criminal activity raises significant questions regarding human rights.

Criminal and Narcoterrorism

Criminal terrorism, which involves criminals who use terrorist tactics to achieve their goals, is nothing new. Historically, criminal organizations such as the American Mafia and Chinese Triads have resorted to kidnappings, beatings, torture, bombings, and murder to intimidate innocent victims, competitors, and law enforcement officials. These types of organizations have operated on the international scene for some time. However, the spread of the global trading system, along with ideas associated with human rights and democracy, seem to be giving new life to criminal terrorism.

For example, while Russia was part of the totalitarian Soviet Union, there was little respect for political and civil rights, and citizens frequently became the targets of repressive terrorism. Still, there was relatively little street crime, much less criminal terrorism. The demise of the Soviet Union, the development of actions based on democratic principles (including curbs on the ruthlessness of the police), and the emergence of a tumultuous economic situation have spawned a powerful Russian Mafia. Drive-by shootings, intimidation, and extortion directed at ordinary citizens, government officials, and foreign businesspeople have become commonplace events. For example, Russian gangsters recently murdered a nationally known television reporter who undertook an investigative report on their activities (Grasy, 1995).

Narcoterrorism is another type of violent behavior that seems to be growing, both within nation-states and internationally. **Narcoterrorism** is the use of violent intimidation centering on illegal drug dealing. Some of this activity is aimed at gaining political influence, but much of it is endemic to the drug trade itself. A great deal of the violent behavior in U.S. society, for example, results from turf battles between rival gangs who vie for territory, efforts to control drug dealing, or drug deals gone bad. In southeast Asia and countries such as Colombia, powerful international drug dealers routinely target public officials for intimidation or death to prevent government interference with their operations.

International Crime

It is extremely difficult to obtain accurate statistics on crime, even when we limit our study to crime within individual nations. Because so much of criminal activity is hidden, it never gets reported to officials and so never appears in official reports. Moreover, the national statistics that do appear always underestimate the amount of crime. If it is difficult to obtain data on crime within nation-states, it is obviously almost impossible to obtain accurate estimates on the amount and role of international crime. Much of the data we now have comes in the form of anecdotal reports or studies of specific criminal organizations. Yet the preponderance of such data leads us to assume a rise in international criminal activities. Some examples of increased international criminal undertakings are noted next.

Organized Crime. We have already described the rapid growth of organized crime in Russia. The Russian Ministry of Internal Affairs (MVD) estimated that there are 5,600 criminal groups in Russia. Their activities are so extensive that 25 percent of Russia's gross national income is derived from organized criminal activities (Shabalin, Albini, and Rogers, 1995). The FBI now believes that at least 24 of these groups have gone international, establishing bases of operation in a number of countries, including the United States. In fact, as early as 1992, the California Department of Justice/Bureau of Investigation recognized a "discernible threat" coming from the presence of Russian gangs in certain communities (Lungren, 1996). So far, these California gangs have been involved mainly in fraud, but they now appear to be expanding into more common organized crime activities such as extortion, loan sharking, drug trafficking, auto theft, and prostitution.

Another area of concern is the expansion of traditional Chinese organized criminal fraternities known as Triads (Booth, 1991). Triads were originally formed to oppose corrupt imperial governments. However, they have long since spread their activities into criminal actions. Many Triads now operate out of Hong Kong but have expanded worldwide, particularly among Chinese emigrant communities. Their presence will probably be enhanced in the West as they move their base of operations from Hong Kong, which the Chinese government legally took control of from the British in 1997. Triads are likely to move because they believe that their organizations can operate with less interference from free, democratic governments than from the more repressive, quasi-socialistic Chinese government. Indeed, Western law enforcement officers have made little effort to understand the Triads and consider them to be part of the incomprehensible mysteries of the East (Booth, 1991). This failure is a great mistake because Triads already control widespread racketeering and extortion operations, have corrupted numerous government and police officials, and have extensively infiltrated legitimate businesses in Hong Kong and in many Asian cities. Now their influence may be spreading in Western countries. However, the greatest danger Triads pose is based on their control of expanding poppy crops in the Golden Triangle in southeast Asia, from which a large portion of the world's heroin is derived.

The international drug trade is not limited to activities of Triads. A number of other drug rings operate globally. For instance, Colombian drug organizations supply huge amounts of drugs to markets in the United States. It is estimated that 20 percent of the people in Colombia depend on growing cocaine for a living. The reason is simple: It is far more profitable to produce cocaine for the international drug trade than to grow legal crops.

Smuggling Aliens and Economic Terrorism. We need to note here two other less recognized problems with international organized crime. The first problem concerns the smuggling of illegal aliens into First World nations, especially into the United States. Robert Perito, director of the State Department's Office of International Criminal Justice, recently contended that criminal organizations are warehousing abroad hundreds of thousands, perhaps millions, of immigrants who are waiting to be smuggled into this country. According to his estimates, 500,000 are in Moscow, 20,000 in Prague, 30,000 in Austria, and 100,000 more in France (quoted in the *Washington Times*, 1995). Many of these immigrants are ethnic Chinese who are willing to pay up to $40,000 each for an opportunity to enter the United States, where they hope to obtain forged documents and blend in with Chinese Americans in Chinatowns across the country. The Chinese Triads are smuggling many of these immigrants into the country. In addition, organized gangs operating out of Mexico smuggle numerous immigrants into the United States.

These operations raise questions about the security of national boarders, but there are also concerns for

A number of drug rings operate globally; Colombian drug organizations, for example, supply huge amounts of drugs to markets in the United States. This U.S. customs officer is unloading 1,000 pounds of smuggled cocaine seized in Miami.

the safety and welfare of the immigrants themselves. Instances of Mexican immigrants smuggled into the United States in locked, hot railroad boxcars or of hundreds of Chinese smuggled here on crowded, rusting freighters have been uncovered and reported. We can only speculate about the extent of death and suffering these and similar methods of transport may cause or have already caused.

The problems of illegal immigrants do not necessarily end when they make it safely to the United States. Many simply do not find the freedom they anticipate. Typically, they are forced to work in sweatshops, where they are held as virtual slaves by people from their own country or by the Americans to whom they have been turned over. Immigrants in such situations cannot complain or escape because of fear of being imprisoned or deported by U.S. officials or because of anxiety that their families back home will be harmed by the smuggling gangs.

Counterfeiting of U.S. currency by international organized crime presents another growing problem. Nearly $135 million in counterfeit bills were confiscated outside the United States in 1994. This sum represents a sharp rise from the $30 million confiscated just two years earlier (DeVoss and Gluckman, 1995). A major obstacle to the prevention of this type of criminal activity is that computer technology and new high-quality duplicating processes make the detection of bogus bills, even by experts, far more difficult. Asian gangs from the Pacific Rim account for a large part of such counterfeiting activities. However, the U.S. Congress suspects that Iran, using American equipment and American-trained engravers and printers, is behind much of the global counterfeiting of our currency (DeVoss and Gluckman, 1995). The fear of counterfeiting led the Treasury Department to start issuing new currency in 1996 that is more difficult to counterfeit.

If this is the case, the goal of this activity is more than the obvious one of gaining wealth. The intent then would be to undermine trust in the U.S. currency by the circulation of enough bogus bills to make people fear taking American money for payment. If such fears spread, they could paralyze the global economic system, since the entire system is linked to faith in the U.S. dollar. In fact, the dollar is used as the scale for determining the worth of every currency in the world. That is, the relative value of a Mexican pesos and a French franc can be determined because the international financial community is able to calculate their worth in U.S. dollars. Losing faith in the dollar could bring chaos to the world trading system. This type of counterfeiting and similar techniques intended to destroy or threaten disruption of the global financial system are examples of what is called **economic terrorism** (see the box "FYI: Computer Terrorism: Prevent a High-Tech Pearl Harbor").

Terrorism, Crime, and Civil Rights

Currently, widespread concern exists about terrorism and crime on both the national and international levels, with pressure on politicians to do something about perceived threats from terrorist or criminal bedlam. In discussing this issue, we note that the fear of terrorism or crime is more important in determining the public reaction than is the objective reality of the danger. In most places, including the United States, people are relatively safe against terrorist or criminal attacks. We are not arguing that no threat exists, but that both the public and the government overestimate this menace. To some degree, the actual degree of peril is immaterial. What counts is that people construct a social reality of crime or terrorism as a great hazard. In this context, we need also to understand that it is this magnification of the extent of danger that terrorists depend on to heighten the effectiveness of their deeds. This social perception is often fed by the media, which sensationalizes criminal or terrorist offenses.

Often, the public's fear translates into a demand that politicians get tough with perpetrators. It *is* necessary to have strong national and international laws against both crime and terrorism. In addition, the world's nations need to cooperate to present a united front against crime and terrorism. They must collaborate to formulate laws, arrest and extradite those suspected of crime, share intelligence information about illicit conspiracies, and band together to enforce sanctions against nations that harbor criminals and terrorists or support their activities. Nevertheless, no matter how tough the international response to crime and terrorism might be, these activities will never completely disappear.

One other word of caution is necessary. Politicians often exploit the fear of crime and terrorism to gather additional political and financial support or to gain more power for themselves. The typical result is a serious erosion of the civil and political rights of innocent citizens and those accused of felonious deeds. For example, in 1994, Russian President

FYI

Computer Terrorism: Prevent a High-Tech Pearl Harbor

"In December 1941, a Japanese imperial strike force steamed into American waters under cover of Pacific darkness and sank or severely damaged 18 major warships, destroyed 200 aircraft and killed and wounded about 3,700 U.S. troops. America awoke, already at war. Pearl Harbor became a synonym for devastating sneak attack.

In June 1996, John Deutch, director of the Central Intelligence Agency, went up to Capitol Hill and warned legislators that America is again vulnerable to an enemy sneak attack that could devastate our national defenses and the ability of any citizen to conduct the most simple acts of everyday life.

The world has entered a new age of information warfare, said Deutch, one in which 'cyberwar' could be declared by mischievous teenage hackers, techno-literate terrorists or enemy states with sophisticated supercomputers.

Such a computer-age Pearl Harbor could smash the machines that operate the Pentagon's radars, communications system, and battle-management programs. Civilian power grids and telephone webs also would be at risk. Nationwide air traffic would be limited to essential services only if computers went down and controllers were reduced to pencil-and-paper tracking. A financial crash brought about by a premeditated computer crash? Of course. Personal banking and international monetary transactions would be impossible. Years of recordkeeping could be erased.

'The electron is the ultimate precision-guided weapon,' Deutch declared last week in testimony before the Senate Governmental Affairs subcommittee.

It is time to recognize that planting a computer virus or frying a computer system with a powerful electromagnetic pulse might become a more effective tool of warfare than the gravity bomb."

Source: "Prevent a High-Tech Pearl Harbor." 1996. *Chicago Tribune,* June 30: 1.18.

Boris Yeltsin issued a decree that permitted "urgent measures" to defend the population against "gangsterism" (Shabalin, Albini, and Rogers, 1995). This decree gave Russian police a wide latitude in their behavior, even though the decree violated the Russian constitution and its measures were viewed as overly severe by many. Similarly, after some devastating terrorist acts, antiterrorism legislation was introduced in Congress in 1995. Through a bipartisan effort, both houses of Congress passed the Antiterrorism and Effective Death Penalty Act of 1996, which extended the government's powers in dealing with terrorism. In the view of groups concerned with protecting civil rights, this legislation significantly increased police powers, took power traditionally reserved for the courts and placed it in the hands of the executive branch of government, and seriously imperiled the rights of citizens, such as the rights to presumed innocence, free speech, freedom of assembly, and privacy (ACLU, 1996; Center for National Security Studies, 1995). In this case, public fears, whether based in reality or not, encouraged the introduction of such governmental initiatives. Driven by their fears, citizens are sometimes prone to relinquish hard-won civil and political rights in the hope of gaining greater safety and security. However, people and their leaders must learn to carefully weigh security concerns against the necessity to maintain the liberties and rights that are the lifeblood of democracies.

War and Weapons of Mass Destruction

Human warfare is not a new phenomenon. It has been so prevalent that we may easily conclude that human history is a tale of continuous warfare punctuated by brief periods of peace. However, even if we were to adopt such a view it does not mean that war is inevitable or that it is human nature to make war. Rather, a considerable body of research suggests that war is a learned activity and may potentially be unlearned. For example, sociologist Nicholas Timasheff (1965) argues in a classic work that one of the conditions necessary for war is that groups involved in a conflict must have a cultural tradition of war. Other support for the view that warfare is learned behavior is the existence of cultures in which peace, not war, is the norm. The Mission Indians of North America, the Arunta of Australia, the Andaman Islanders of the South Pacific, and the Inuits of the Arctic possess ritualized ways of handling conflict without resorting to violence. Still, whether it is learned or innate behavior, waging war is not simply a thing of the past. At any given moment today there are approximately 25 wars being waged somewhere in the world (Henslin, 1996).

Technology, Warfare, and Global Arms Trade

What has characterized war in the twentieth century are the massive numbers of people involved and the adaptation of progressively more sophisticated technology that has significantly enhanced the destructiveness of weapons. War has become a modern, scientific, industrial production. Advanced technology greatly multiplies the power of a nation possessing it. The United States, with less than 5 percent of the world's population, is by far the most powerful nation on earth because of the sophisticated technology employed largely by its military.

The acquisition of this technology is not cheap. President Reagan spent more than $2.5 trillion dollars in a huge military buildup during the 1980s. This buildup sped the demise of the Soviet Union because it bankrupted its economy as the Soviets tried to compete in the arms race with the United States. The military buildup during the Cold War crippled the American economy to a lesser degree because it was financed by a budget deficit. A **budget deficit** means that the federal government spends more than it receives in revenues. A country with a budget deficit must borrow the additional money needed to finance government operations from private sources. Because of this budget deficit, the **national debt** (the money owed by the federal government) amounted to more than $2 trillion at the end of Reagan's term in office. Subsequent American administrations have continued to run an escalating deficit. By 1995, the national debt stood at more than $4.6 trillion, which equals almost 71 percent of the GDP (U.S. Bureau of the Census, 1995). Such a burden of debt seriously hampers spending on social programs and environmental protection, business stimulation, tax breaks, or other programs that may directly benefit the American people.

The former Soviet Union and the United States were not the only nations engaged in an arms buildup. During the 1970s and 1980s, two-thirds of the global arms sales went to Third World nations, which provided them with approximately 20,000 tanks and self-propelled howitzers, 28,000 artillery pieces, 37,000 armed personnel carriers, 1,100 warships and submarines, 8,000 military aircraft, 3,600 helicopters, and more than 50,000 missiles. The total transnational shipment of arms is estimated at $1.2 trillion for the past three decades (Renner, 1994). In addition, a great deal of foreign aid to Third World nations has been in the form of military assistance.

Despite these data, total expenditures for arms and other military purposes has declined globally (Table 12–2). The end of the Cold War has meant that the major consumers of arms—the United States and Russia—are no longer buying arms at the same rate that they formerly did. Market competition, consequently, has driven down the price of arms. Therefore, the world's nations can now purchase more arms for less money. This situation is made even more dangerous because a considerable market has also arisen for secondhand arms that are no longer needed by First and Second World countries. In the post–Cold War era, the United States has emerged as the leading supplier of arms to developing countries. Its sales accounted for 60 percent of the arms sold to Third World nations in 1992 (Renner, 1994). Russia, China, and the countries of the European Union also are major suppliers.

Proliferation of Weapons of Mass Destruction

The proliferation of weapons of mass destruction represents another substantial threat to world security. In the early 1950s, the United States and the Soviet Union were the only nations to possess nuclear weapons. But the situation soon changed as more nations developed their own nuclear weaponry. The global accumulation of nuclear warheads peaked in 1986 at 68,480; it has since declined to less than 49,000 (Renner, 1994). Some of this decline is due to the destruction of obsolete weapons; however, much

TABLE 12–2 International Military Expenditures, 1985–1993 (in billions of dollars)

COUNTRY GROUP	1985	1989	1993
Current $, total	$ 943	$1,059	$869
United States	258	304	298
Percent of total U.S. expenditures	27.4%	28.7%	34.2%
Developed countries (United States included)	989	866	648
Developing countries	188	192	221
Total expenditures, 1985–1994 (billions of dollars, in constant 1993 dollars)	1,234	1,204	868

Source: U. S. Bureau of the Census, *Statistical Abstract of the United States, 1995,* 115th ed. (Washington, DC: U.S. Government Printing Office, 1995). Table 555.

of the decrease resulted from international arms reduction treaties.

The United States, Russia, Great Britain, France, and China are declared members of the nuclear club. India and Pakistan joined the nuclear club when each exploded nuclear weapons in 1998. Other nations such as South Africa and Israel have developed nuclear weapons without officially admitting it. Several countries started to develop nuclear weapons but have subsequently stopped development and have renounced the goal of becoming nuclear powers. All but 12 nations of the world are signatories to the Nuclear Nonproliferation Treaty. A treaty that bans testing of new nuclear weapons is now being negotiated.

Iran, Iraq, Libya, and North Korea are suspected of having ongoing nuclear weapons programs but are hampered by the unavailability of weapons-grade nuclear materials, a lack of technical experts, and the low level of sophistication of their technology. Some Third World nations, such as India and Pakistan, nations that are historical enemies, have developed nuclear weapons as a deterrence against each other. (In addition, India fears its larger and more powerful neighbor China and now feels more secure because it possesses nuclear weaponry.) Other nations such as Libya, Iraq, and Iran seem to want nuclear weapons because they will give them a big stick with which to enter the arena of international politics (Map 12–1).

The demise of the Soviet Union has greatly increased the possibility of the spread of nuclear weapons. Thousands of Soviet nuclear experts have found themselves without jobs now that Russia has ceased its nuclear program. It is highly likely that at least some will sell their skills on the global arms market if suitable productive employment is not found for them. We mentioned earlier in this chapter that the low level of security for nuclear materials in Russia could lead to black market sales abroad. In fact, as of 1995, the U.S. Central Intelligence Agency (CIA) had recorded 31 arrests and seizures of nuclear materials from the former Soviet Union. One 1994 case is especially chilling. Police in Prague, Czechoslovakia, found almost six pounds of highly enriched (weapons-grade) uranium in a car occupied by a Czech nuclear scientist and two other Eastern European scientists from Belarus and Ukraine (Barry, 1995).

Many nations of the world also possess chemical and biological weapons of mass destruction. Both Iran and Iraq used these weapons against each other during the 1980s. Iraq also used biological weapons against Kurdish rebels in northern Iraq in 1988. The possibility that other rogue nations, such as Libya, could obtain chemical and biological weapons remains high. The spread of weapons of mass destruction continues to be a major threat to global security.

America's Crime Wave?

A recent *Newsweek* poll found that the primary concern of Americans was the state of the economy; concern about crime and the related topic of illegal drugs followed closely (Fineman, 1996). Most Americans

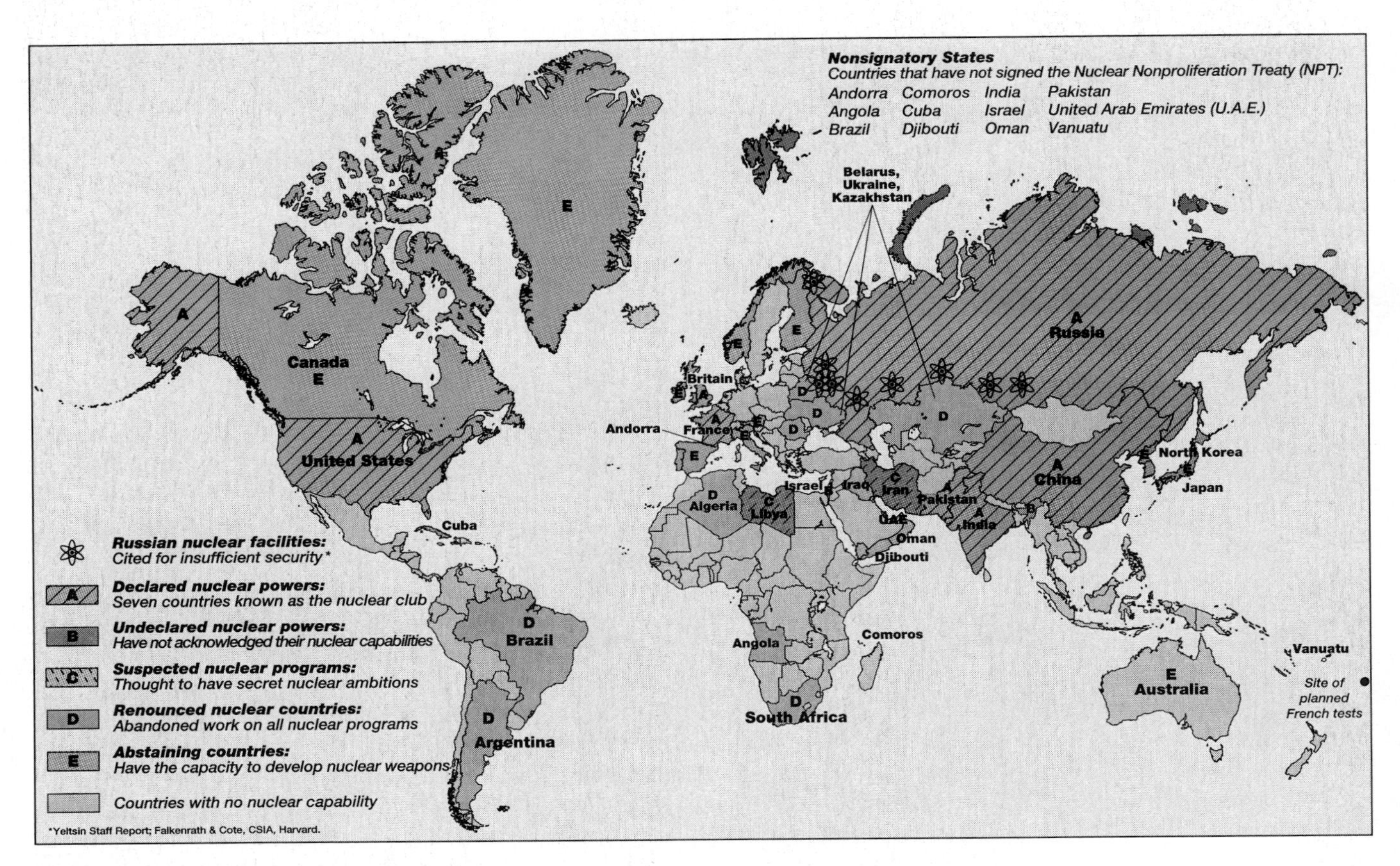

MAP 12–1 Nuclear Nations of the World

Source: Adapted from John Barry. 1995. "Future Shock." *Newsweek*, July 24: 32–33, 36–37.

seem convinced that their country is gripped by an escalating crime wave and is awash in drugs. Since for some time there has been wide consensus that crime and drugs are a problem, politicians have seized on these issues in their campaigns. Democrats and Republicans alike have sought to convince voters that the opposition is soft on crime and that only they have the wherewithal to get tough on criminals, which will relieve our crime and drug crises. In this section, we provide a research-based perspective on crime and illegal drugs and an assessment of some commonly proposed solutions to these problems.

Crime in America

One way to develop some perspective on America's "crime wave" is to review what is considered crime. Technically, **crime** is any law-violating activity. However, some types of crimes are more significant than others in feeding the perception that crime is out of control. For instance, although statistics on it are difficult to obtain, white-collar crime is probably extensive and very costly to our society. One estimate places the annual cost to the American public of all forms of white-collar crime at $174 to $231 billion (Curran and Renzetti, 1990). Despite the damage such crimes do to the economy, most Americans still do not believe that white-collar offenses amount to real crime; and very few convicted white-collar criminals actually spend time in jail.

When Americans express anxiety about crime, they are usually referring to street crimes. **Street crimes** are violations against the person (such as murder, forcible rape, assault, and robbery) and crimes against property (such as burglary, larceny, and motor vehicle theft). If we limit our discussion strictly to street crime, how would we answer the question of whether or not America is experiencing a crime wave? The answer is yes and no. It is yes because this type of crime is farily widespread in our society. In 1992, roughly one household in four was touched by this type of crime (U.S. Bureau of the Census, 1995). Moreover, the United States has a significantly higher rate of crimes against persons than Western European countries, although rates of crime against property are comparable (Myers, 1995).

But if we look at historical evidence, we probably would have to say, "No, we are not experiencing an especially strong crime wave." We are hesitant to draw such a conclusion because even current data on the extent of crime are generally unreliable. Moreover, if we look at the more distant past, it becomes even more difficult to determine how much crime occurred. Much historical data are anecdotal. The frontiers of nineteenth-century America were renowned for their violence and lawlessness. Most people on the frontier armed themselves because they could not depend on the law to protect them. In that environment the Colt .45 pistol was called the "peacemaker" and the Winchester repeating rifle was known as the "gun that won the West." More recently, we can cite numerous times and places when crime was rampant. The Hell's Kitchen section of New York City at the end of the nineteenth century and the early years of this century was known for despair, poverty, violence, crime, and gang activity among its newly arrived immigrant population. Later, during the 1920s and early 1930s, some killers such as the pair Clyde Barrow and Bonnie Parker (notorious for their four-year bank-robbing spree in the southwestern United States, until they were gunned down by the law in 1934) achieved the status of folkloric "heroes."

If we look at the recent past for which data are more reliable, we see cause for concern, but not panic, about crime. A rise in street crime began in the 1960s. However, property crimes reached their peak around 1980 and subsequently have declined steadily. In addition, since the early 1990s, all categories of street crime have declined (see Table 12–3).

Youth Crime. The rise in street crimes among youth under the age of 17 is a notable exception to this trend. Between 1970 and 1993, for example, arrests of youth for murder increased 257 percent, forcible rape increased 170 percent, and robbery increased 152 percent (U.S. Bureau of the Census, 1995). Much of this criminal activity is spurred on by the resurgence of street gangs, which have spread from their traditional base among inner city ethnic youth to suburban, small city, and rural areas. Other disturbing trends are that crimes committed by youths have also become more violent and that members of younger age groups commit more serious offenses than older youths. This trend is occurring not only in this country, but also worldwide (Goozner, 1996; UN Commission for Social Development, 1995). One obvious factor in the rapid escalation in the deadliness of the violence perpetuated by

TABLE 12–3 Street Crime Trends in the United States, 1995 (for selected categories)

REGION	TOTAL FOR ALL INDEX CRIMES[a]	VIOLENT CRIMES	PROPERTY CRIMES	MURDER	FORCIBLE RAPE	ROBBERY	BURGLARY	VEHICLE THEFT
Totals	−2	−4	−1	−8	−6	−7	−5	−6
Northeast	−4	−8	−3	−15	−4	−11	−6	−14
Midwest	−2	−6	−1	−8	−8	−9	−5	−2
South	−1	−3	−1	−9	−6	−4	−6	−3
West	−1	−1	0	−2	−4	−6	−4	−4

[a] % decline from previous year in crimes reported to the police.

Source: Federal Bureau of Investigation. 1996. "Uniform Crime Reports 1995: Preliminary Annual Release." Table 2—Crime Index by Geographic Region. May 5. Electronic transmission: http://www.fbi.gov/ucr/

There is a disturbing trend toward more violent crimes by youths, occurring not only in this country, but also worldwide. This trend, as well as the widespread availability of handguns in the United States, has led to the use of metal detectors in schools in this country.

young people in this country is the ready availability of handguns.

All of these factors have helped create a public image of out-of-control youth. Also contributing to this perception is the fact that since the 1960s, the media, politicians, religious leaders, and concerned citizens have bombarded the public with this image (Goozner, 1996). Advocates of this view have used a variety of sources to support it. In this decade, for example, they have cited high profile cases like that of the affluent Menendez brothers convicted of shooting their parents to death, the gang-related drive-by shootings that occur daily in cities across the country, and the spate of school killings of classmates and teachers by other teens during the school year 1997–1998.

However, a closer examination of the data presents a different picture. For one thing, serious crime by youths started to decrease in 1995 ("Youth Crime on the Decline," 1996). Moreover, although crime by youths has significantly increased, the rates are actually relatively small. In that year, 14 percent of murders, 7 percent of robberies, and 5 percent of forcible rapes were committed by persons under 17 (U.S. Bureau of the Census, 1995).

Another reason to challenge the perception of widespread lawlessness among young people emerges when we examine who actually commits most serious crimes. In the United States, as in other countries, marginalized young people commit the vast majority of serious street crime (Goozner, 1996; UN Commission for Social Development, 1995). By **marginalized youth,** we mean those young people who exist on the fringes of society because of poverty, ethnic minority status, and/or other factors. Marginalized youth have less commitment to existing systems such as education and the economy, are more susceptible to the lure of gang membership, are more likely to live in unstable families, are more exposed to violence themselves either as victims or observers, have less access to positive role models or constructive secular and religious programs than other young people, and live in a socioeconomic environment shaped by poverty.

Although there has been a substantial decline in arrests of youth for violent crime since 1993, the picture for crime among marginalized youth is not quite as rosy. As a nation, we have cut funding for programs that seek to provide positive experiences to marginalized youth, and we have lessened our commitment to public education at a time when the number of marginalized youth entering the most violence-prone years is increasing. Criminologist James Fox holds that this "wholesale divestment" in youth will likely result in 5,000 more teen killers per year after the turn of the new century (in Gest and Pope, 1996).

Illegal Drugs. Many cultures, including our own, have long histories of using drugs for medical, religious, social, and recreational purposes. Perhaps this partly explains why ordinary people generally do not view the use of socially approved drugs as a problem, although many of these drugs are personally injurious and costly to society. It is only when groups define the use of certain substances as undesirable that their use emerges as a social problem.

This observation certainly fits circumstances in our own society. The twentieth century has witnessed the gradual criminalization of widely used drugs that were legal only a century before. For instance, in the nineteenth century, opium, cocaine, and heroin were legal drugs sold over the counter. Used recreationally, they also formed the active ingredients in patent medicines extensively used by respectable citizens to treat a variety of illnesses. In fact, the coke in the original Coca-Cola was cocaine. But in this century, Americans cannot legally use these or a number of other once-legal drugs.

Even though a number of persons continued to use illegal substances and many became addicted, Americans generally were not concerned with the "drug problem" for most of this century. One explanation for this attitude is that such drug use was confined largely to minorities and other marginalized groups. This situation changed in the 1960s, however, when recreational drug use spread to the middle class, especially middle-class young persons. Suddenly middle America became alarmed about what came to be seen as a growing drug problem. Ever since, drug abuse has remained a significant political and social problem.

Table 12–4 illustrates that illegal drug use in the United States climaxed in 1979, after which the level of use declined sharply. But the figures for first-time use of illegal drugs are much higher. For example, in 1979, 30.9 percent of 12- to 17-year-olds, 68.2 percent of 18- to 25-year-olds, and 26.6 percent of persons 26 and older used marijuana at least once. However, the pattern of decline seen in current users (people who have used an illegal drug within the last month) also applies to those who had used drugs at some previous time but who are not current users. Thus, in 1993, 11.7 percent of 12- to 17-year-olds, 47.4 percent of 18- to 25-year-olds, and 34.3 percent of persons 26 and older had smoked marijuana at least once (U.S. Bureau of the Census, 1995). The discrepancy between "previous users" and "current users" should dispel the popular misconception that experimentation with illegal drugs automatically signals a slide into a life of drug abuse. Apparently, many teens and young adults experiment, but relatively few get hooked.

Any viable solution to the drug problem demands a reasoned approach that takes into account some often overlooked facts. One fact is that illegal drugs are not as deadly as is commonly believed. Of course, if a person does become addicted, his or her life can be destroyed. However, only about 3,600 people annually

TABLE 12–4 Current Users of Selected Drugs, 1974–1993[a]

DRUG AND AGE	1974	1979	1985	1988	1993
12–17 years					
Marijuana	12.0%	16.7%	11.9%	6.4%	4.9%
Cocaine	1.0	1.4	1.4	1.1	0.4
Heroin	B[b]	B[b]	0.1	B[b]	0.2
18–25 years					
Marijuana	25.2	35.4	21.9	15.5	11.1
Cocaine	3.1	9.3	7.5	4.5	1.5
Heroin	B[b]	B[b]	0.3	B[b]	0.4
26 years+					
Marijuana	2.0	6.0	6.0	3.9	3.0
Cocaine	B[b]	0.9	1.9	0.9	0.5
Heroin	B[b]	B[b]	B[b]	B[b]	B[b]

[a] Based on national household survey. Figures represent the percentage of the survey population who had used an illegal drug at least once in the past month and so constitute current users.

[b] Sample base too small to count.

Source: U.S. Bureau of the Census, *Statistical Abstract of the United States, 1995.* 115th ed. (Washington, DC: U.S. Government Printing Office, 1995).

die from taking illegal drugs. Many of these deaths occur because illegal drugs are prepared in unregulated laboratories, where the probability rises that one type of dangerous drug will be combined with others, which can result in fatal overdoses. The unsanitary conditions (dirty needles) in which much drug use occurs also leads to death because of the transmission of infections or fatal diseases.

In dealing with the drug problem, we need perhaps to look at our own attitudes as well. What do we define as a problem? For example, an estimated 200,000 deaths per year are related to alcohol, and another 320,000 succumb to diseases associated with tobacco (Kappeler, Blumberg, and Potter, 1996). Yet in our society neither of these highly destructive substances is illegal, and Americans generally do not view them with the same degree of alarm as they do less deadly drugs such as heroin and cocaine.

Although the extent of their use tends to be overestimated, illegal drugs have had a detrimental impact on our society. We have diverted billions of dollars from constructive areas such as education and improving health standards to the war on drugs. Most of the efforts to curb illegal drugs have focused on controlling the available supply of drugs, and relatively little effort has been focused on programs to reduce the demand for drugs or to treat addicted persons. Nevertheless, every American president since the 1970s has declared a war on drugs, and the government has spent billions on interdiction. But the war on drugs has not seriously cut into the supply: Illegal drugs are as available as they were in the 1970s. Apparently, the prospect of severe punishment has deterred relatively few people from experimenting with or dealing in illegal drugs. (Otherwise conservative Americans, in fact, are now engaged in growing illegal drugs, especially marijuana, for the same reason that persons abroad grow illegal drugs—it is highly profitable. This practice makes these drugs still more difficult to control.)

From the evidence, then, it is arguable that the war on drugs has had the net effect of keeping the street price of drugs high and fanning the flames of drug-related violence. This situation has led a number of noteworthy Americans, including former Secretary of State George Schultz, conservative economist Milton Freeman, conservative commentator William F. Buckley, organized crime expert Ralph Salerno, and former New York City Police Commissioner Patrick Murphy to promote the legalization of now illegal drugs like marijuana and cocaine. Advocates of this approach suggest that we should redirect our efforts to deal with drug problems toward preventative measures and rehabilitation of addicts.

The use of the drug problem as a political football deserves more attention. A good example of how this works is the reaction to the National Household Survey on Drug Abuse released in 1996 by the Substance Abuse and Mental Health Services Administration. This study reported an "alarming" 78 percent increase between 1992 and 1995 in drug use among 12- to 17-year-olds. Marijuana use for youths in this age range increased 105 percent over the three-year period, and cocaine use rose 183 percent between 1994 and 1995. Politicians quickly seized on these data to argue that young Americans were at risk and that we were losing the war on drugs. But a somewhat different image emerges when we look at the broader context. The Household Survey found that current use among teenagers was actually low—10.9 percent for all drugs, 8.2 percent for marijuana, and only 0.8 percent for cocaine (Kaplan, 1996).

Still, soon after the release of the Household Survey, Republicans latched on to the idea of a dramatic increase in youth drug use. They accused Democratic President Clinton of being "soft on drugs" and urged an increase in funds for the war on drugs. The Democrats retaliated with figures that indicated that the Republican-controlled Congress had consistently cut funds that the president had requested for drug control efforts. For instance, in 1994, the president had proposed and guided through Congress the Safe and Drug-Free Schools Act. The administration requested $2.4 billion to fund programs in the act, but the Congress appropriated only $1.9 billion. Similarly, the Clinton-backed Crime Act of 1994 contained numerous programs intended to prevent young persons from becoming involved with crime and drugs. Although the Republican-controlled Congress approved the Crime Act, it failed to appropriate any money to implement the preventative programs ("Reno Chides Congress' Drug Effort," 1996).

Many Americans have become cynical about politicians because of their realization of the extent to which partisan politics propels issues for which finding viable solutions—as is the case with illegal drugs—should take precedence. Furthermore, the public also understands to some degree that focusing solely on the use of drugs such as marijuana and cocaine takes attention from two other drugs that are extensively used by young people but are more socially acceptable—tobacco and alcohol.

Punishment and Curbing America's Crime

The perception that the American nation is overwhelmed by a crime wave has fueled a flurry of political activities intended to control crime over the last two decades. Politicians of both parties have generally accused their opponents of being soft on crime, and each side has outdone the other to show that it is the one that really advocates a tough approach. Someone who is soft on crime, politicians generally agree, would support preventative programs and efforts to attack conditions associated with street crime, such as low educational levels and poverty. Other policies that those soft on crime would support, according to their critics, would include rehabilitating prisoners, using probation and other approaches that offer alternatives to imprisonment, giving judges latitude to take circumstances into consideration in determining sentences, and observing the constitutional rights of the accused and the convicted alike.

Conversely, being tough on crime, according to politicians, means strongly advocating greater punishment of criminals and dealing with crime solely as a problem of individual responsibility rather than of social pathology. Toughness includes trimming rehabilitative programs, using imprisonment (and also longer prison terms) for more offenders and more types of offenses (including relatively minor ones), curtailing the latitude judges have to sentence through mechanisms such as mandatory prison sentences for convictions, and increasing police power while showing less concern for the constitutional protections of the accused and the convicted.

Increasing the Punishment. The emphasis on increasing punishment as the major method of curbing crime has had a number of significant results. We now have 1.6 million persons in prison, more than twice as many as a decade ago ("Prison Population Doubles," 1996). Figure 12–2 demonstrates that we have by far the highest rates of incarceration in the industrialized world.

Keeping this many people in prison costs the American public $26 billion annually. This amounts to a yearly cost of more than $17 thousand per prisoner. We can send a person to some private colleges more cheaply than we can keep him or her in prison.

The increased incarceration rate has made prison construction one of the fastest growing industries in

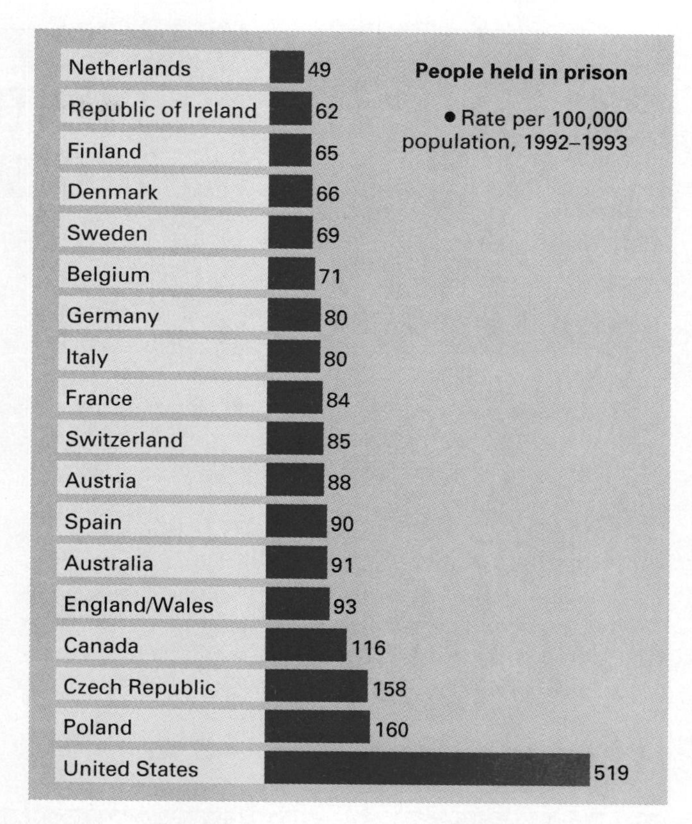

FIGURE 12–2 International Incarceration Rates, 1992–1993

Source: Linnet Myers. 1995. "Cultural Divide over Crime and Punishment," *Chicago Tribune*, October 13: 1.1. Copyright © 1995 by Chicago Tribune Company. All rights reserved. Used with permission.

the country. Prison construction is very costly. For instance, in 1995, Texas alone had more than 75,000 new prison beds under construction at a cost of $1.5 billion. Despite the expense, politicians and voters alike are more willing to build more prisons than to approve funds for school construction. Yet even with all the new prisons, facilities from county jails to federal prisons are becoming so seriously overcrowded that states and localities are often forced to release existing prisoners before they can take in new ones.

Increasing the number of offenses that require mandatory sentences has also meant that more persons must now stand trial. This situation has led to a serious overload for prosecutors and courts alike. Both prosecutors and public defenders have scant time to devote to individual cases, including ones in which the charges are more serious, such as murder. Serious cases as well as minor ones wait for extended periods for trial. This delay imperils the constitutional

CONTEMPORARY DISCUSSION

Three Strikes and You're Out

One of the new get-tough weapons in the legal system is a series of state and federal laws that have come to be known as "Three Strikes and You're Out" laws. These laws mandate that persons convicted of committing a felony (no matter how minor) for the third time will be sentenced to life in prison without possibility of parole.

Advocates of these laws believe that judges are frequently too soft on repeat offenders, sentencing them to probation or light sentences when these criminals have demonstrated time and again how they pose a threat to the community. Supporters of three-strike laws also point out that even when a judge sentences felons to a long sentence, they are eligible for parole in a fraction of the time they were supposed to serve. The remedy is to ensure that criminals convicted under these laws will spend the rest of their lives in prison. Because of these laws, the argument continues, liberal judges do not have the latitude to not sentence felons to prison or to sentence them for a short time before letting them out. Prison officials also do not have the option of letting prisoners out before they have served their lengthy sentences. No-parole sentences serve to make criminals pay for their crimes while protecting the community from proven predators. In addition, such laws are strong deterrents to crime, for criminals already convicted of two felonies will think long and hard before committing a third offense that will land them in prison for life.

People who oppose these laws do so for several reasons. They suggest that if the criminal justice system is

guarantee of speedy trials. Even strong cases may be threatened because during such a prolonged wait authorities may accidentally misplace or contaminate evidence. The memories of witnesses may fade, or they may move or die. The suffering of the accused, the victims, and their families may also be prolonged as they wait for trials to bring some measure of closure in their lives. For these reasons, there is some accuracy to the statement, "Justice delayed is justice denied."

The chief culprit in such overloading has been the tremendous increase in minor drug offenses that now go to trial. Moreover, convictions for drug offenses are swelling the prison population. In 1983, only 8.3 percent of admissions to prison were for drug offenses. But the get-tough policies of the 1980s allowed judges less latitude to use corrective measures other than imprisonment, such as probation, court supervision, counseling, or remitting to substance abuse programs. By 1992, drug offenses accounted for 30.4 percent of prison admissions (Myers, 1995). See the box "Contemporary Discussion: Three Strikes and You're Out" for another crime-fighting policy that is having dubious effects on crime and the criminal justice system.

The Death Penalty. Thirty-eight states have now reinstituted the death penalty as part of the get-tough-on-crime trend. This is at a time when most industrial nations have either eliminated the death penalty or have restricted its application to the most dastardly cases. As of 1993, there were 2,580 prisoners on death row across the nation; 4,089 have been executed since 1930 (U.S. Bureau of the Census, 1995). Opponents of the death penalty note that it is disproportionately applied to minorities and the poor. There also is the possibility of executing an innocent person. At least 150 innocent persons were executed in the United States between 1900 and 1972. Moreover, between 1977 and 1996, sixty-one innocent persons were released from death row (Page, 1996). Many human rights groups believe that using the death penalty is a clear violation of human rights.

to be fair (and perceived as fair), the punishment must fit the crime. Imposing life sentences for minor felonies undermines the idea that the criminal justice system is really just. Opponents of get-tough laws believe that there are good reasons to allow judges to do what they are paid to do—make judgments. Probation and other forms of sentencing that do not involve imprisonment were created to allow judges the latitude to decide when a specific crime by a specific person merits long imprisonment and when other punishments are more appropriate. In addition, "Three Strikes and You're Out" laws continue the trends in criminal justice that are already overloading the courts and prison systems. For instance, prosecutors cannot plea-bargain cases (negotiate an agreement in which the defendant pleads guilty to a crime and an agreement is reached between the defendant and the prosecution about the exact nature of the punishment, say, seven to twelve years for manslaughter, with the possibility of parole in five years), which means that more cases will come to full trial. When people are sent to prison for minor crimes, prison overcrowding is further aggravated. Prisoners in for more serious crimes may have to be released to make room for those convicted of less serious offenses.

In addition, these laws, critics contend, may actually work against their intended purposes. Juries may be less inclined to convict a person if they know that person will spend the rest of his or her life in prison. And criminals may actually be forced into more serious crime. For instance, they may kill witnesses to ensure there is no one to testify against them or they may shoot it out with arresting police in an effort to escape rather than be sent to prison with no possibility of parole.

◇ **For Critical Thought:** (1) What are the assumptions of each side in this discussion? (2) What are the political, economic, and cultural implications of the arguments each side makes? (3) What are the practical problems created by each position? (4) Are there other possibilities than the ones presented?

Thirty-eight states in this country have now reinstituted the death penalty. Some groups continue to protest against the use of the death penalty, saying that it is a clear violation of human rights. Here Ellen Burns leads a demonstration against the execution of a prisoner in Texas.

A recent trend, derived from the get-tough mentality, is the move to try to sentence convicted people under 18 as adults. This process has extended to the death penalty; younger and younger persons are on trial for crimes that could result in their execution if they are convicted. Massachusetts has lowered the minimum age for trying youths as adults, opening the possibility of the execution of 14-year-olds. Oregon has lowered the minimum age for trial as an adult to 12, while in Wisconsin, 10-year-olds may be tried as adults. Tennessee has even eliminated age barriers altogether when it comes to trying those accused (Gest and Pope, 1996). But executing persons younger that 18 is a violation of the UN Safeguards Guaranteeing Protection of the Rights of Those Facing the Death Penalty. Moreover, the trend to try young people as adults reverses a century-old practice of putting persons younger than 18 through a separate juvenile court system that emphasizes reforming young persons rather than punishing them.

Punishment's Effectiveness. Hard-liners point to declining crime rates as indicators of the effectiveness of punishment-oriented programs even as they call for yet stiffer penalties for law violators. However, a more balanced perspective is attained when we assess the four main justifications for punishing criminals—retribution, rehabilitation, societal protection, and deterrence.

Retribution involves exacting the same level of suffering from the criminal as was caused by the offense. Retribution resembles the Old Testament teaching of "an eye for an eye and a tooth for a tooth." *Rehabilitation* involves reforming offenders so that they will not commit offenses in the future. Supporters of rehabilitation assume that criminals can change their ways and will not return to a life of crime. Traditionally, rehabilitation has not only included punishment but also positive programs that assist convicts to alter the attitudes that caused them to become criminals. Such programs may include psychotherapy to change patterns of thought and behavior or the teaching of learning skills to enable prisoners to more effectively participate in society on their release.

Proponents of *societal protection* hold that punishment in the form of imprisonment or execution renders offenders temporarily or permanently incapable of harming society. Advocates of *deterrence* believe that crime is lowered by severe punishment, as criminals will come to see their crime as too costly. When enough pain is associated with the offense, the criminal will see the error of his or her ways. Punishment may also serve a general deterrence function by demonstrating the costs of crime, thereby preventing people from turning to criminal activities.

When critically evaluating the functions of punishment, we see that punishment may have some positive effects, but by and large it fails to live up to its promises as a deterrent to crime. Like retribution, punishment may well maintain the moral balance of society by demonstrating that criminal acts do cause criminals to suffer. This may help victims and their families to come to closure and contribute to the general societal feeling that justice has been done. Punishment may also be somewhat effective in protecting society at least in the short term. When criminals are executed, they can no longer threaten society; when locked up, they cannot harm other citizens. However, most prisoners eventually return to society, and their time in prison provides the basis for further deviance. Indeed, considerable evidence exists to indicate that prisons serve as crime schools. Many former prisoners return to society to commit not only more crimes, but more serious ones.

A similar pattern emerges when we look at rehabilitation and deterrence. Punishment may work to rehabilitate some criminals. Still, punishment per se does not appear to be especially effective to either rehabilitate or deter further crime. For instance, **criminal recidivism,** or subsequent offenses by persons previously imprisoned, remains very high in the United States. In 1991, almost 81 percent of persons in prison had at least one prior conviction (U.S. Bureau of the Census, 1995). Many of these prisoners were repeat offenders with multiple previous convictions.

Additionally, if severe punishment did serve as an effective deterrent, then the death penalty would be the most influential weapon in lowering the crime rate. The United States relies more heavily on the death penalty in contrast to other industrialized societies that have banned it, but it does not have the lowest crime rates, especially for violent crimes (Bohm, 1991; Bailey, 1990; Bailey and Peterson, 1989; van den Haag and Conrad, 1983). In addition, if the death penalty is an effective deterrent for violent crime, then Texas, which has executed more convicts over the last two decades than any other state, should have the lowest rates of violent crime in the country. However, Texas by no means has the lowest rate of violent crimes, including murder. Conversely, New Hampshire has never carried out an execution but has one of the lowest violent crime rates in the nation (U.S. Bureau of the Census, 1995). If severe punishment has not been a key factor in curbing crime, what then does account for declining crime rates? Most criminologists believe that the aging of the American population is the primary catalyst. They point to the fact that rates for serious crimes begin to rise dramatically in the later teen years; the vast majority of such offenses are committed by persons 18 to 44 years old. As the median age of population has passed middle age, the crime rate has gone down.

Crime and Drugs in Western Europe. We have already noted that Western European nations have similar rates of property crime but far lower rates of violent crime than does the United States. This development is relatively recent. Prior to the industrial revolution, Europe had much higher rates of robbery, assault, and murder than those in modern-day America. It is difficult to know exactly why this change has occurred. One line of reasoning holds that the move to industrial societies in Western Europe led the way to a decrease in violent crime rates. With more people making a comfortable living and less people desperately poor, with more highly educated people, with the professionalization of police forces, along with more reliable criminal justice systems that accompanied industrialization, crime rates dropped dramatically.

The United States went through similar transitions, but although its crime rates declined considerably after the repeal of Prohibition, they started to rise dramatically in the 1960s. Most commentators explain the contrast between Western Europe and the United States by cultural differences. Once that is granted, however, it becomes difficult to pinpoint exactly which differences are the crucial ones. Explanations include that U.S. society is more diverse, the gap between the rich and poor is increasing in this country, and the American middle class feels more economic pressure and greater alienation from the political and social system. Explanations even include differences in child-rearing practices between Americans and Western Europeans. For instance, some argue that because most Americans spank their children, they are teaching the use of violence to solve problems. Western Europeans, so this argument goes, are less likely to use physical discipline on their children and, therefore, have lower levels of violence in their nations.

Another possible factor to explain the lower crime rates in Western Europe is that people there look at crime much differently than do Americans. Europeans rely much less on severe punishment to curb crime than do Americans. For example, Europeans favor applying the death penalty for murder but not for more minor offenses. Several European nations, such as England and France, have eliminated the death penalty without a huge surge in violent activity. In Western Europe, people are also more likely to develop programs to rehabilitate criminals and to attack the root causes of crime than we are in the United States. Perhaps because greater class, racial, religious, and ethnic differences exist in the United States than in Western Europe, Americans are more likely to see criminals as "one of them" who are threatening "us." The industrialized nations of Western Europe, with less diverse populations, have more of a tendency to treat criminals as "one of us."

These elements show up in the way Western European governments have reacted to increased drug usage. Their overall approach has been to decriminalize soft drugs such as marijuana and to try to rehabilitate addicts rather than make them pay for their "crime." Comparatively little government money is spent to prevent drugs from coming into society, though there is some effort to interdict hard drugs such as heroin and cocaine. Drugs of all kinds are available in most European countries at low prices. Soft drugs are sold legally and openly in some cases. However, these policies have not led to a tidal wave of increased use or addiction. European addicts are more likely to have government help to break their addiction than are their American counterparts.

Conversely, the United States has concentrated most of its efforts on interdiction and the punishment of dealers and users alike, and comparatively few funds are earmarked for rehabilitation and for decreasing the demand for drugs. The net result of almost 20 years of the war to take drugs off the streets is that there are more drugs available. Moreover, these drugs are of higher quality and are more potent than those sold on the streets 20 years ago. Typically, the price for illegal drugs is lower (in constant dollars) than it was 20 years ago. The drug trade in this country remains highly lucrative and violent. Perhaps it is worth remembering that the prohibition against the manufacture and sale of alcohol (1920–1933) had similar results. Demand remained high, illegal fortunes were made, organized crime prospered, drive-by shootings and turf wars were common, gangsters out-gunned police on the streets, and officials were intimidated or corrupted. This orgy of crime, violence, and greed ended only after the repeal of Prohibition.

Assessing the Situation

In this chapter we have examined some of the more pressing concerns of many citizens in the industrialized world. We have argued that it is difficult to demonstrate that there is more crime or violence in the modern world than there was in times past. However, modern weapons of mass destruction have significantly increased the potential destructiveness of terrorism or warfare. Large numbers of people around the world are without significant personal power and have little access to power for themselves or the groups to which they belong. A major difficulty is how to deal with the results of this disempowerment. We next examine this issue by looking at some of the ways to assess proposed solutions.

Terrorism and Legitimacy

The availability of weapons of mass destruction undermines the power of the nation-state, especially that of the United States, by undermining its ability to prevent violence. The high-tech weaponry of the United States and other established military powers has proved overwhelmingly effective against traditional military threats, as the armies of Saddam Hussein discovered in the 1991 Persian Gulf War. But high-tech weaponry is ineffective against terrorism. The lesson learned from this by those who would oppose the dominant powers and the world order they support, is that traditional militaries are useful in the political suppression of their own people, but terrorism is the means of exerting political influence in the new world order.

Should such threats continue into the future, the political stability of the global system will be in serious jeopardy. Two dimensions are involved in the stability of a government or regime (Lipset, 1960). *Legitimacy* refers to the ability of a government to attain and maintain the loyal commitments of its people on the basis of their belief in the rightness or appropriateness of the government or regime. *Effectiveness* refers to the ability of a government to carry out its policies, satisfy its constituencies, and balance the interests of diverse groups. A fundamental requirement for a government to be effective is its ability to constrain unauthorized violence. Terrorism works to undermine this effectiveness. Once a government has lost its effectiveness, it may also lose its legitimacy in the eyes of its people.

The Role of the Media

In Chapter 1, we discussed the role of powerful groups in defining social problems. We noted that how we define problems implies certain solutions to them. The communications media are key players in forming those definitions. Especially powerful in this context are the visual media, particularly television. The visual media not only bring news into our home but also convey to us striking graphic images that can be used to manipulate our emotions and change our opinions. Additionally, we are dependent on all the media for information about issues that affect our daily lives. In preindustrial societies, people learned most of the news they needed to plan their daily activities by word of mouth. However, in modern societies, the growing interdependence of large populations and the geographic size of modern nations mean that we cannot receive the data we need by word of mouth. As globalization has progressed, we now are in need of news about occurrences all over the world. We are dependent on the media for these data.

The media have an especially significant role in democracies. Ideally, they not only provide information but are also the purveyors of political debate and the guardians of public interest. All of this assumes a free and responsible media. However, the media also are businesses that have to attract readers and viewers. Because of this factor, there is a tendency for the media to both concentrate on the startling or shocking and to sensationalize more mundane news as a way to attract both a larger segment of the public and more business support in the form of advertising.

Many in the media assume that bad news is more appealing to audiences than is good news. The negative, therefore, is often reported while more positive news receives less attention. Murders, rapes, random violence, and child abuse are the daily stuff of the media in large cities. Especially shocking cases are reported from all over the world. This kind of reportage presents a distorted image to the public. Crime is an example. Earlier in this chapter, we described how most Americans believe that crime is running amok, even though there has actually been a steady decline in property crimes since the 1970s, accompanied in recent years by a drop in rates for crimes against individuals.

Unfortunately, sensational bad news may, in fact, attract viewers. Much of the power of television to rivet attention is based on the use of techniques like fast cuts and images that seem to rush toward the viewer and thus stimulate the vigilance response of the nervous systems. Thus, by stimulating mild and even unconscious anxiety, television maintains the attention of its audience. Bad news invokes the same response process.

Ben Bagdikian (1983) and Michael Parenti (1986), among others, have argued that the major reason why the networks rely on disaster and crime news is that they are essentially noncontroversial and lack political content. Financial and legal control of the media is highly concentrated in the hands of ever fewer corporations. These corporations and the power concentration they foster are themselves often implicated in the social and political issues of our day. Serious or significant news (racial tensions, the widened gap between the rich and the poor) might actually cast a negative light on the owners of the media themselves. By avoiding dealing with these issues and by focusing on noncontroversial, sensational, and largely apolitical events such as bad weather (tornadoes, floods) and violent crimes, the media provide the appearance of reporting the news but actually steer public attention away from a deeper understanding of society.

Distorted images in the media make it difficult to conduct rational debate on key problems and also become the basis for manipulation by political leaders. Terrorists depend on the media to magnify the results of their activities (e.g., the Unabomber insisted that the press publish a manifesto to forestall further terrorism on his part). Dramatic and deadly actions intimidate potential victims and bring the causes of malcontents to the attention of society. In either instance, the media may become unwitting partners in advancing terrorists' causes. These issues point to the need for the media to be especially cautious about what and how they report and suggest the necessity for the public to critically evaluate the information we receive.

Security and Human Rights

We began this chapter with a vignette that depicted a gradual loss of American civil rights that stemmed from fear of terrorism. We also noted that globalization has produced a great deal of uncertainty that may eventually cause people to turn to authoritarian leadership to relieve anxiety. Additionally, governments tend to resort to repressive measures as internal dissent grows or scarce resources decline. All these responses share something in common: Those involved rationalize them by referring to the need for increasing security. None of these responses bodes well for human rights.

But can we afford to compromise human rights? For one thing, the global community views these rights as absolute; that is, we cannot afford to compromise a single one of our human rights. Rather, we must make every effort to actualize each right. Sometimes, however, this is not always practical. In real life, rights may contradict one another. For instance, the Universal Declaration of Human Rights calls for the security of the individual, presumption of innocence, protection of privacy, and freedom of association. The right to individual security is based on the assumption that people are living in a society that is reasonably orderly and safe. But it is impossible to have personal security in a society racked by terrorism, crime, and violence. To secure personal safety in such a society may involve using the coercive power of the state and the limiting of certain rights, such as the rights to privacy and freedom of association.

But we must exercise caution when we trade other rights for promises of security. The whole concept of political and civil rights assumes that citizens must be protected from the unwarranted intrusions by their own governments. Even in democratic societies, government officials are tempted to tread on rights for political gain. For example, in 1996, two presumed terrorist attacks occurred in rapid succession in the United States. One involved the explosion of a pipe bomb at the Summer Olympic games in Atlanta, Georgia. The other was the explosion of a TWA flight that had just departed from New York. President Clinton responded with new proposals for getting tough on terrorists. One proposal involved making credit histories, payment records, and other personal information available to airlines, which would then use these data to screen each ticket buyer. Although this has not happened, it raises the question: Should we trade the right to personal privacy so easily for a vague promise of greater security?

Theoretical Concerns

In this chapter we have used Merton's concepts of how structural strain contributes to various forms of deviance, including crime and terrorism. Merton maintained that every society establishes socially approved goals, or ends, that citizens are to pursue, as well as legitimate means to obtain them. Deviance is likely to occur when the means established do not lead to the ends society deems desirable. A second, and perhaps more pervasive, cause for crime in Merton's model is the weak commitment that many have to the social norms, or legitimate means.

These observations are potent when we look at terrorism, crime, and violence. The usual reaction by officials to these forms of deviance is to fight fire with fire. That is, they respond strongly and frequently with violence. However, Merton's constructs suggest another possible response, namely that deviance will lessen if we open the social system to as many as possible. Disempowered individuals are not likely to engage in deviance if legitimate means to achieve socially approved ends are available. Moreover, when extremist groups are made part of the system, they tend to become more moderate and less threatening. They now have a vested interest in the existing political, economic, and social arrangements. If current trends in employment and underemployment continue as predicted by experts such as Jeremy Rifkin (1996), this sort of empowerment and access to legitimate means may continue to erode. As we discussed in Chapter 8, Rifkin predicts the end of work as we have traditionally known it. Neither the public nor the private sector will be able (or willing) to provide full-time, well-paying jobs for large portions of the world's population. Rifkin places hope in innovative arrangements in the social sector to take up the slack, furnishing legitimate ways to provide for persons unable to make a living by traditional means. The alternative is indeed grim if legitimate means are not provided. More and more people will find themselves marginalized and are likely to resort to illegitimate means such as crime, violence, dropping out, and even revolution to have their needs fulfilled.

Finally, Merton suggests that if people are properly socialized, they are more likely to conform to society's expectations. One element that we may possibly include in such socialization is the importance of commitment to the means as ends in themselves. For example, as part of the socialization process, we might emphasize that work is valuable and rewarding in and of itself or that education is a mechanism for living a more gratifying life. From this perspective, education is not simply a way of receiving access to higher-paying jobs, but an end in itself.

Summary

1. **Deviance** is the socially perceived violation of social norms. Sociologists are interested in explaining large-scale patterns, rates, or trends in deviant conduct rather than in focusing on individual cases of deviance. Pressures to deviate are generated by a lack of integration or lack of consistency between a society's goals and approved means.

2. There are five adaptations to a society's pattern of goals and means. **Conformity,** the most common, is the active seeking of socially approved goals by socially approved means. **Innovation** is the active pursuing of socially approved goals while rejecting socially approved means. **Ritualism** is the pursuit of socially approved courses of action while surrendering any commitment to achieving socially approved goals. **Retreatism** is the rejection of institutionalized means and goals. **Rebellion** is the rejection of both the approved goals and the approved means of the existing social order while actively attempting to replace them with an alternative social order.

3. **Terrorism** is the use of violence or the threat of violence as a means of combat or to achieve some strategic goal by striking fear in victims through ruthless actions.

4. **Political terrorism** uses harsh tactics of intimidation to achieve some type of political goal. The three categories of political terrorism are **revo-**

lutionary terrorism—when internal enemies of the state rely on terrorist tactics to produce change in the political system; **repressive terrorism**—when a government employs harsh tactics to intimidate its own civilian population; and **state terrorism**—when nation-states train, support, finance, and protect international terrorists whom they employ to further foreign policy agendas.

5. An increasing concern is the threat of **superterrorism**—when terrorists enhance their threat by using or threatening to use weapons of mass destruction. **Weapons of mass destruction** may be chemical, biological, or nuclear weapons capable of inflicting widespread death and injury in a single attack.

6. Both within nation-states and internationally, criminal terrorism and narcoterrorism are growing. **Criminal terrorism** involves criminals who use terroristic tactics to gain their goals. **Narcoterrorism** is the use of violent intimidation centering on illegal drug dealing. Two less recognized problems with international crime include the smuggling of illegal aliens into First World nations and counterfeiting currency. Counterfeiting and similar techniques that destroy or threaten to disrupt the global financial system are also referred to as **economic terrorism.**

7. **Street crimes** are violations against the person, such as murder, rape, assault, and robbery, and crimes against property, such as burglary, larceny, and motor vehicle theft.

8. **Youth crime,** street crime committed by those under the age of 17, is on the rise. Youth crime has been spurred on by the resurgence of street gangs, which have spread from their traditional base in the inner city to suburban and rural areas. The move to try to sentence convicted people under 18 as adults is derived from the get-tough mentality. This process has extended to the death penalty in some states.

9. The legal system has implemented *get-tough policies* in the form of state and federal laws that have become known as the "Three Strikes and You're Out" laws. These laws mandate that persons convicted of committing a felony for the third time will be sentenced to life in prison without possibility of parole. Even so, **criminal recidivism,** or subsequent offenses by persons previously imprisoned, remains very high in the United States.

10. Justifications for punishing criminals can be categorized in four ways: retribution, rehabilitation, societal protection, and deterrence. *Retribution* involves extracting the same level of suffering from the criminal as was caused by the offense. *Rehabilitation* involves reforming offenders so that they will not commit offenses in the future. Proponents of *societal protection* hold that punishment in the form of imprisonment or execution renders offenders temporarily or permanently incapable of harming society. Punishment may also serve a general *deterrence* function by demonstrating the costs of crime, thereby preventing people from even turning to criminal activities.

THINKING CRITICALLY

1. Discuss how both repressive and revolutionary terrorism represent forms of deviance found in Merton's typology of deviance. What does Merton's typology suggest that governments should do to deal with dissident citizens?

2. We have discussed how conventional weapons and tactics used by governments are ineffective against terrorist threats. What other techniques might prove more effective? Suggest ideas to use on the local, national, or international levels.

3. The influx of illegal drugs has caused a number of major social problems in our country. In what sense is the war on drugs driven by irrational fears? How has it been more destructive than beneficial? In what ways can sociological research contribute to a more effective use of resources to combat drug-related problems?

Suggested Readings

Abadinsky, Howard. 1990. *Organized Crime.* 3d ed. Chicago: Nelson-Hall.

Booth, Martin. 1991. *The Triads: The Chinese Criminal Fraternity.* New York: St. Martin's.

Jankowski, Martin. 1991. *Islands in the Street: Gangs and American Urban Society.* Berkeley, CA: University of California Press.

Kappeler, Victor E., Mark Blumberg, and Gary W. Potter. 1996. *The Mythology of Crime and Criminal Justice.* 2d ed. Prospect Heights, IL: Waveland.

Kegley, Charles, Jr., ed. 1990. *International Terrorism: Characteristics, Causes, and Controls.* New York: St. Martin's.

Reiman, J. 1995. *The Rich Get Richer and the Poor Get Prison.* 4th ed. Boston: Allyn & Bacon.

Web Sites

Crime Statistics Site

http://www.crime.org

This site offers visitors two important services. First, it provides a Crime Statistics Tutorial that explains what crime rates are, where they come from, and how accurate they are. Second, the site provides a Crime Statistics Link Guide that includes historical crime statistics, college and university links, county and city links, and international links. The international links include the Bureau of Justice Statistics International Crime Statistics, the United Nations Crime and Justice Information Network, and crime profiles of places from the United States to Ireland to Zimbabwe.

International Criminal Justice Online

http://www.acsp.uic.edu/index.htm

At this site, the Office of International Criminal Justice presents many paths of information from which to choose, including international crime and justice, terrorist groups, patterns of global terrorism, extremist groups, and the International Association for the Study of Organized Crime.

National Criminal Justice Reference Center (NCJRC)

http://www.ncjrc.org/

This site contains access to thousands of links on courts, crime prevention, criminal justice statistics, drugs and crime, juvenile justice, law enforcement, and victims. It also has articles and abstracts on crimes and criminal justice. Of the many links located at this site, various bureaus and organizations that deal with crime and criminal justice are included, in addition to searchable indexes.

Perilous Times—Terrorist Page

http://www.teleport.com/~jstar/terror.html

This web page provides many links to sites that contain information on terrorism, from travel warnings to terrorist groups to weaponry to countering terrorism. This site functions mostly as a brief informative directory for information about terrorism.

Statistical Abstract Frequently Requested Tables

http://www.census.gov/stat_abstract/

This site allows you to search for relevant statistics from various government agencies. Table topics include a wide range of subjects, including a number related to crime.

The Terrorism Research Center

http://www.terrorism.com/

The Terrorism Research Center is dedicated to providing information about terrorism and information warfare. The two sections featured at this site, terrorism and information warfare, contain the most current issues and links to other terrorism and information warfare–related web sites. New links are added weekly.

Uniform Crime Reports

http://www.fbi.gov/ucrpre97.htm

The FBI has prepared the Uniform Crime Reports *since the 1930s. This site makes the more recent statistics on crime and crime trends available electronically.*

United Nations Crime and Justice Information Network

http://www.ifs.univie.ac.at/~uncjin.html

This site contains a great deal of information regarding international law and criminal and legal issues. Links include UN documents, information on crime and justice in various countries, international statistics and research sources, constitutions, treaties, laws, court decisions related to crime and justice, and other organizations that share the goals of the UN relative to these issues.

Epilogue

Reimaging the Future

"The [current] quest [for human rights, peace and protection of our lands] is a renewal of what we enjoyed before the coming of our white brothers from across the sea. We lived contentedly under the Great Law of Peace. We were instructed to create societies based upon the principles of peace, equality, justice, and the power of the 'good mind.'

"Our societies are based upon great democratic principles of authority in the people and of equal responsibilities of men and women. This was a great way of life across the great Turtle Island [North America]; and freedom, with respect, was everywhere. Our leaders were instructed to be men with vision and to make every decision on behalf of the seventh generation to come, to have compassion and love for those generations yet unborn. We were instructed to give thanks for all that sustains us. . . .

"We were instructed to be generous and to share equally with our brothers and sisters, so that all may be content. We were instructed to respect and love our elders, to serve them in their declining years, to cherish one another. We were instructed to love our children—indeed to love all children. . . .

"The catastrophes that we have suffered at the hands of our brothers from across the sea have been unremitting and inexcusable. They have crushed our peoples and our nations down through the centuries. You brought us disease and death and the idea of Christian dominion over 'heathens,' 'pagans,' 'savages.' Our lands were declared vacant by papal bulls [decrees issued in the form of letters by the pope]. You created laws to justify the pillaging of our lands. We were systematically stripped of our resources, religions, and dignity. Indeed, we became resources of labor for gold mines and in [sugar] cane fields. Life for us was unspeakably cruel. Our black and dark-skinned brothers and sisters were brought here from distant lands to share our misery, suffering, and death. Yet we survive. I stand before you as a manifestation of the spirit of our people and our will to survive. The wolf, our spiritual brother, stands beside us, and we are alike in the Western mind: hated, admired, and still a mystery to you. And still undefeated. . . .

"Five hundred years ago, you came to our pristine lands of great forests, rolling plains, and crystal clear lakes, streams, and waters. Since then we have suffered in your quest for god, for glory, for gold. But we have survived. Can we survive another five hundred years of 'sustainable development'? I don't think so."

Source: From a speech before the United Nations by Oren Lyons—Chief, Faithkeeper of the Onondaga Nation of the Haudenosaunee (North America), December 10, 1992.

These words of Oren Lyons raise what has been a central issue of this book, the issue of progress. Modern people believe that their way of life is more advanced than that of traditional peoples. This belief has too often been used to justify the exploitation and destruction of other people and their cultures. But what is progress? In fact, is there even such a thing as progress? Is "progress" simply an illusion, an ideology used to justify the dominance of Europeans and their American descendants over all other peoples, all other ways of life, and over nature itself?

When looking at issues of modernization, development, and progress, romantics have assumed incorrectly that the tribal, or traditional, way of life (and the lives of individual members of these societies) was always better than modern ways of life or that nothing has been gained in the last five centuries by the development of European and American culture. But it may be equally naive and false to assume, as many Western modernists have done, that all that is traditional is inferior and therefore can be safely discarded and ignored. The future requires that we reassess our global past and that we engage in open dialogue with all contemporary points of view, including those of tribal and traditional peoples who can offer wisdom that may be of inestimable value for all of us.

Such a reassessment is arguably underway; we are living in a time of crisis produced by the more destructive elements of modernism. This crisis is fitfully generating a new form of world culture through the process of globalization. In this epilogue, we bring together themes that have appeared throughout this book by looking at some of the trends that give clues to the direction of the emerging culture. We do so in part by arguing that a reimaging of the future is not only necessary but is actually occurring.

Problems without Technical Solutions

Modernism has placed a great deal of faith in the ability of technology to solve humankind's most pressing problems. For example, the solution to increasing population is to introduce modern birth control devices into societies with rapidly expanding populations. The solution to shortages of food is to bring genetically altered high-yield grains into areas where these grains are not native. The solution to AIDS is to use modern science and technology to produce an AIDS vaccine. And the solution to poverty is to introduce advanced technology into societies that rely on traditional low-tech methods of production.

There is, however, a growing realization among political leaders, government officials, scientists, and ordinary citizens that technology often is a source of problems and not a solution. Likewise, there is an increasing recognition that technical solutions are not possible for many problems. Technical solutions offer resolutions that involve new scientific or technological methods. For example, in 1992, the American Academy of Sciences and the Royal Society of London, the two most prestigious organizations of scientists in the world, came together for the first time in history to offer a joint statement on the present global dilemma. The statement they released said, "If current predictions of population growth prove accurate and patterns of human activity on the planet remain unchanged, science and technology may not be able to prevent either irreversible degradation of the environment or continued poverty for much of the world" (Brown, 1993:3). As this statement indicates, we are coming to recognize the distinct category of problems without a technical solution.

The Trap of the Global Commons

One most pressing example of a situation in which technological solutions are not possible is found in what biologist Garrett Harding (1968) has called a "tragedy of the commons." A tragedy of the commons involves a social or economic system in which rational self-interest compels people to destroy the foundation of their own well-being. Common but vital resources that were free and shared are destroyed in a futile effort to raise the standard of living of individuals and their families. In the short run, greater exploitation of "free" common resources may seem desirable. In the long run, however, the cost is infinite, since what is involved is the survival of the planet itself. At the point at which the commons is depleted, it is too late. Yet until that fatal point, the incentive to exploit the common resource grows.

Today's global commons include the atmosphere, the water cycle, the oceans, rain forest resources, genetic information, and the reproductive capacity of the human being. What makes these global resources commons is that they are available to all or most of us with no fee or market price attached to them. Although there are very real costs involved in overuse of the common resource, because there has traditionally been no market price (and no imposed fee such as a tax) attached to our use of them, there is individual incentive to overuse the common resource simply because it is considered to be free. In a market economy, pollution or destruction of a free resource (such as the air, rivers, or forests) is simply not calculated as a cost of doing business. Moreover, as these resources are destroyed, they become rarer and more precious and the incentive to exploit what little remains becomes even more compelling. A tragedy is in the making, because persons acting out of rational self-interest to exploit the global commons are dooming all life on this planet to destruction.

Is there any solution? Clearly, technology alone cannot save us from our own folly. Technological development may enable us to make more efficient use of scarce resources or may allow us to shift consumption from scarce resources to more plentiful ones. For example, our supply of oil is being depleted rapidly. Automobiles consume significant portions of the oil extracted from world reserves. Technological advances can make cars more fuel efficient or may allow the use of more plentiful resources such as hydrogen for fuel (see Chapter 3). Nevertheless, the only viable long-range solution involves altering the sociosphere by making changes in behaviors and attitudes that are conducive to the limitation of consumption and the preservation of the biosphere.

The Need for a World Government?

When it comes to preserving the global commons, short-range solutions that can produce significant changes in lifestyles may well include the use of fees to pass the real costs of destruction of common resources along to companies and individuals. These fees must be high enough to discourage people from resorting too readily to using the commons. The imposition of such fees would probably require government action in the form of taxes. As an example, governments can tax families for having more than a certain number of children. They can tax corporations for polluting rivers or for emitting too much carbon. The latter type of taxes are called green taxes. (Worldwide, the agenda of the various so-called green political parties is the protection of the environment.) Since there really is a cost involved in using up the commons, it is reasonable to attach a monetary price or market value to the resources being destroyed.

This is not a solution that arises out of the market itself; it has to be imposed. But it has implications for market behavior. As corporations or families find that it is not profitable to keep exploiting the commons, they are more likely to seek new and more environmentally and socially beneficial solutions. Indeed, creativity and discipline will be enhanced. To avoid paying green taxes, improved technologies and the elimination of wastes will result. This is a reasonable approach, but is it feasible? That is an issue of politics and governance.

It remains unclear whether contemporary politicians and citizens will have the courage and vision shown by Chief Lyons and make decisions "on behalf of the seventh generation yet to come." However, one thing is abundantly clear. Given the interconnectedness of social, political, and economic systems in global society, no one nation or group of nations can undertake all of the changes necessary to save our global commons. Such changes must truly be a worldwide effort. This realization has led many social theorists and politicians to speculate on the need for a world government or global state to deal effectively with contemporary problems.

Global State and Global Governance

What are the prospects of a world government or global state? There have been several attempts to predict when and under what conditions such a One World Government might come about. According to Yale University sociologist and futurist Wendell Bell (1996), the main justification for these predictions is that over the course of human history there has been a trend toward larger territorial social units. For some 99.8 percent of human history, the species was dispersed in nomadic hunting-gathering bands. By 1000 BCE, there were possibly 600,000 separate bands (Bell, 1996). Since that time human beings have become aggregated into ever larger units, first into chiefdoms and later into empires. These larger units subsumed a growing population and came to command larger and larger territories, which they then subjected to centralized political control (Bell, 1996). If these trends continue, at some point there will emerge a global superstate. This state would have all human beings under its jurisdiction and the entire planet as its territory. Yet as Bell points out, the best available predictions do not foresee the advent of such a world government in the near future. Actual predictions have ranged from the year 2750 to the year 3500, which is not soon enough to do us any good if we are to preserve our global commons (Bell, 1996). Obviously, such projections are also at best extremely speculative.

What Bell describes as an "optimistic forecast" was offered by Wildavsky and Singer (1993). They see parts of today's world as regions of wealth, peace, and democracy, with long life expectancies, good health, low birthrates, equality for women, political participation, a growing concern for the environment, and the creation of a global community. But they view other regions of the world as in turmoil. This turmoil we have seen throughout this book in continuing poverty and underdevelopment, interethnic warfare, economic exploitation, environmental collapse, low status of women and high rates of birth, and other social injustices. Because of these realities, even the authors of the optimistic scenario predict a twenty-first century of great misery and suffering before a large-scale unity evolves in which these problems can be resolved.

Governance refers to the directing of collective actions toward certain goals, whereas *government* (the state) in the final analysis uses coercion or threat of force to ensure compliance. Governmental actions, according to this view, must then inevitably generate resistance and evasion. The state rarely, if ever, converts the minds and hearts of the majority of people to do what the government (through its officials) believes they ought to do. Fundamental to the operation and effectiveness of the state itself is the nonstate network of groups and relationships called civil society. Bell's article (1996), which forms the basis of this discussion, is actually about the prospects of global community integration or a global civil society, not about the necessity of a global state.

Global Civil Society and Global Integration

There are many signs of increasing global integration. Bell underscores the subjective aspects of globalization by pointing to the fact that human beings have multiple social identities and thus we can and do identify with large-scale groups, including humanity as a whole. There is nothing absolute about the identification people feel with the nation-state. It is only one of the large-scale groups with which people may identify.

We can see this increasing integration manifested in a variety of ways. INGOs, as we have seen throughout this book, are playing an increasingly significant role. According to Bell, there are currently 2,000 INGOs. In addition, some 62,000 treaties now integrate nation-states, and there are a growing number of agreements among the world's nation-states enacted in national and international law. Some of these agreements include the Outer Space Treaty of 1967, the 1972 Stockholm Conference on the Human Environment, the 1985 Vienna Convention for the Protection of the Ozone Layer, and the 1987 Montreal Protocol. Conferences on environmental and other global issues are also now an almost continuous activity, with increasing participation by governments and industry. Nor can we ignore the role of the United Nations and its many agencies and 50 information services in the global integration process.

In contrast to these forms of integration, which occur mostly at the state level, NGOs have proliferated, as we have noted throughout this book, although political analysts have largely failed to note their increasing significance. NGOs focus on a wide range of interests, including religion, science, culture, and sports. The thousands of NGOs that were active in the 1990s form an international network. These organizations may focus their attention on local (or grassroots) issues, the behavior of states, or the global community itself. Wherever they focus their energies, their very existence forms part of a developing global community whether or not they want this outcome.

Global Civil Society and Core Values

Bell's main interest apparently is the possibility of universal core values. Earlier (see Chapter 2) we discussed how the founders of American anthropology (e.g., Franz Boas and Clyde Kluckhohn) never intended to argue that the values and cultures of different societies were entirely incompatible with one another; in fact, they understood that there are many commonalities among societies. The practice of cultural relativity itself, so highly valued among social scientists, contains implicit values. These values include respect for the worth and dignity of human beings and human cultures (Selznick, 1992).

Bell refers to several efforts to specify the core value system. In one case, a study by Kidder (1994) of 24 prominent men and women found considerable consensus on the following eight values:

1. Love (mutual assistance, caring, compassion)
2. Truthfulness (honesty)
3. Fairness (fair play, justice, the golden rule)
4. Freedom (democracy)
5. Unity (brother/sisterhood, oneness with others, cooperation, community)
6. Tolerance (respect for the dignity of others and their right to have their own ideas and beliefs, but not "tolerance" of evil behaviors such as genocide, for the individual has to consider the morality of others' actions before choosing to tolerate them)
7. Responsibility (taking care of yourself and others, as well as concern for the welfare of the larger community)
8. Respect for life (unquestionable acceptance of "Thou shalt not kill").

Other values mentioned by some, but not the majority of the 24 people interviewed, included knowing right from wrong, obedience, wisdom, and hospitality (Bell, 1996).

Another example of the several cited by Bell is "Toward a Global Ethic," a statement that came out of the 1993 Parliament of the World's Religions held in Chicago that we discussed in Chapter 3. Among the values enunciated in this document are the equality of men and women; the dignity and worth of all human beings without regard to race, gender, language, national or cultural origins, religion, mental or physical abilities, and so on; generosity, compassion, and caring for one another; economic and social justice; nature-friendly ways of life; respect for human rights and fundamental values; truthfulness and honesty; moderation and modesty; sexuality that expresses and reinforces a loving relationship between equal partners; loyalty; freedom as long as one does not impose upon others; and security and safety. As you can see, these values encompass both personal and private values as well as the more public values of social and economic security and justice and full participation by all (Bell, 1996).

With the possibility of a growing recognition of core values there will, however, ironically come the recognition of how far short of these values the present system falls and deep questioning of why that is so, of how we got to where we are, and where it is we are going. These questions bring us to the topic of the future and of hope.

Reimaging the Future

What sort of future do we want? And after we have answered that question, there comes a more troubling one—can we get there from here? It is necessary to believe that we *can* get there, if we are to make collective efforts to change or even to explore possible ways of changing.

The "Image of the Future"

Social philosopher Fred Polak has explored the history of different visions of the future in Western culture. Serious thinking about the future, not mere musing, but the kind of thinking that leads to potent social effects, makes important demands. Among these demands, Polak (1973) includes faith and visionary powers, philosophical detachment, a rich emotional life, and creative imagination. This creative vision that can inspire (or cause despair), that can motivate people to make changes that are sometimes sacrificial (or, alternatively, cause them to give up ways of thinking and living), Polak calls the *image of the future*. Today we are very much in need of an image of the future that will inspire and motivate people. But first of all, it must convince people. Possession of a rich emotional life, philosophical detachment, and creative fantasy (imagination) requires deep familiarity with cultural traditions and knowledge, as well as the freedom and capacity to cause a rethinking of these traditions and the creation of fresh approaches. The commercialized fantasies and prepackaged images of television and the movies will not serve this purpose but may well defeat it.

His study of Western history led Polak to several conclusions. First, he argues that positive images of the future lead to the creative flowering of cultures, whereas weak images lead to cultural decay. Throughout history we may see a "dialectic," in which hopeful views replace pessimistic views and vice versa. Furthermore, a culture's inherent strength can be attributed to the energy and intensity of its images of the future. Analysis of these images leads us from a diagnosis of the causes of cultural strength (or, conversely, its decline) and on to *prognosis,* the projection of the future course of a culture.

Polak's prognosis for Western culture, written in 1973, seemed rather grim for the time. He argued that Western culture has become preoccupied with a futureless present. Since Polak's day, however, many people have come to view the future of humankind with despair. Today our shared images of the future tend to be negative, but the crisis mentality that is so common today narrows our vision to the immediate present and undermines the philosophical detachment that is so needed. According to Polak, Western culture has either turned aside from its own positive images of the future or set out to destroy them and turn them into negative ones. The two most important such images in Western history, Polak asserted, are (1) the *eschatological image* of the Middle Ages that held that the suffering of sinful humankind will come to an end and a perfect age of justice and human perfection will be established by God; and (2) the *utopian image* (which emerged with Enlightenment humanism) that a just and prosperous society will come about from human efforts guided by reason and science. Today there are many within the Christian faith who embrace the eschatological image. The utopian view had both liberal (capitalist market-oriented) and socialist versions. No less an authority about the search for global values than German theologian Hans Küng (who contributed so much to "Toward a Global Ethic") has written recently that both the liberal and the socialist viewpoints are no longer credible in the eyes of educated people as we approach the end of the twentieth century (Küng, 1998). We cannot afford to be complacent and rely on the idea that a hopeful phase will replace today's pessimism. According to Polak, the sort of images of the future necessary to motivate and guide a civilization are difficult to construct; nor is it possible that we can simply revive the previously prevailing images, either eschatological or utopian.

Rediscovery of Values and Reimaging the Future

In Chapter 2, we saw that the United Nations Universal Declaration of Human Rights can serve as a useful guideline for our discussion of global issues. We also mentioned that there are flaws not only with this document, but with the entire concept of human rights. A problem with this concept is that as we bring into the picture actual social membership and other attributes such as race and gender or sexual preference, people begin to lay claim to an ever expanding set of rights. The emphasis on social duty and responsibility has been lacking in many Western formulations of rights and law but is strongly emphasized in many, if not all, non-Western traditions.

We also discussed in Chapter 2 the growing number of social scientists who have come to recognize that cultures are not quite as diverse as we have been led to believe, especially when dealing with basic moral or ethical values. The renewed interest in universal human values has brought the recognition that it is possible to discuss and defend value commitments rationally (Küng, 1998; Bell, 1996; Barbour, 1993; Selznick, 1992). The divorce of value judgments from reason and from questions of truth was part of the rupture that modern thought caused in the tissue of Western culture. Value judgments came to be seen as having no truth value; that is, they were not considered to be a form of knowledge. Rather, intellectuals like the sociologist Max Weber claimed that values were essentially nonrational preferences, more a matter of feeling or taste than of judgment. That is, values were said to be purely subjective. Now, however, we recognize them as having a more objective (shared) basis (Selznick, 1992).

The same charge of subjectivity has been applied to all knowledge. It is true that "all facts are theory laden," "all beliefs are culturally relative," and "all knowledge is socially constructed." But there are degrees of relativity. Not all knowledge is equally relative. The strong claim that all knowledge is socially constructed, and therefore we must distrust it, is a self-defeating one. This notion is also self-contradictory. When we claim that there are core values to be found in most or all human cultures, we do not mean that these values are absolutes or identical. All statements or formulations of value statements are limited expressions of values and are therefore relative to the cultural and social situations of those making them.

What Are Values? It may be helpful at this point to define the term *value* in a way that is not conventionally employed by social scientists. According to Ian Barbour, a value is "a general characteristic of an object or a state of affairs that a person views with favor, believes is beneficial, and is disposed to act toward" (Barbour, 1993:26). As sociologists we are obliged to add that such values are generally shared and have their origins in social life. Barbour goes on to add some important characteristics of values when he says:

> To hold a value is to have a favorable attitude toward its realization: in this respect values resemble preferences or desires. However, subscription to a value also includes beliefs about benefits or moral obligations that can be used to justify or defend it or recommend it to others; such beliefs are open to rational reflection and discussion, as individual preferences are not. When a choice is defended in terms of values, reasons are given and general principles are invoked. Principles of right and wrong in human actions and good and evil in the consequence of action, constitute the domain of ethics. (Barbour, 1993:26–27)

The use of reasons in defense of our actions and the counterarguments that others use in response are not only rational but social. Although norms and laws may be imposed on people by arbitrary social authority or unquestioned tradition, this is not inherent in the nature of values, social norms, or laws. The rightness or goodness of social policies and practices must ultimately stand the test of dialogue (Coles, 1995). Such dialogue must be unfettered by repression, censorship, and manipulation and must include all parties whose well-being might be affected by such policies and practices, including generations yet unborn. This is a tall order, but it is essential to strive for it.

As the globalization process continues, it tends to become more and more inclusive; consciousness and understanding of the issues increases, and a growing awareness of shared values and of shared fate unfolds. At present the forces that would undermine the hope of a just and sustainable future seem extremely powerful. These negative forces range from the power and material greed of corporations to the despair of Western intellectuals over the loss of meaning to fundamentalist Christian fears of a world government headed by the Antichrist. That is, the factors range from failures of universalism in our values and treatment of others to regressions to particularistic worldviews that regard the outside world as threatening, even demonic. But at least within the developed world, there is evidence of change in the value systems of many people.

Evidences of Change in Western Value Systems

In the last two decades, studies of the values and perspectives of Americans and Europeans suggest that a transformation is occurring. One example is offered by Willis Harman, who worked for a major government think tank, SRI International. Harman is a futurist who, along with former astronaut Edgar Mitchell, founded an organization for the study of the many neglected aspects of consciousness, The Institute of Noetic Sciences. In 1976 Harman published *An Incomplete Guide to the Future*, in which he argued that a shift in Western culture was taking place and that a new "dominant social paradigm" or worldview was emerging.

In this book, he called the older view, rooted in modernism and the Enlightenment, the *industrial era paradigm*. This way of thinking is familiar to us all because it is so deeply ingrained in Western culture that it forms the dominant mindset of most people. Or, as Harman argues, it used to. This paradigm involves a belief that the good life is defined by unlimited material progress and increased consumption; faith in the ability of science and technology to solve all our problems; assertion of the goals of efficiency, growth, and productivity; human mastery over nature; and the values of competition and individualism. Harman traces environmental degradation, the decay of community, the loss of meaningful work, and the social injustice of contemporary times to our belief in this paradigm. Although simplistic as a complete explanation of global issues, nevertheless this paradigm underpins much of the present system that creates these problems.

In Harman's view the *postindustrial paradigm*, which he says emerged in the 1970s, contained a different set of values and beliefs about the world and humanity's role in it. These included the ideas that people should be content with meeting basic needs rather than the pursuit of excessive consumption; societies should shift to renewable resources and use them sparingly; individuals and societies should involve themselves with human development; self-realization, growth in awareness, and creativity should be fostered; and community and cooperation should replace competition and individualism (Harman, 1988).

We might ask whether there is empirical evidence of this emergent paradigm, or cultural shift. If there is, we might then ask whether these new attitudes, beliefs, and values are spreading. Several studies of values in developed Western nations suggest that this shift is occurring and that new values and beliefs are diffusing more widely. Ian Barbour reports on several of these studies in his book *Ethics in an Age of Technology* (1993). For example, a survey conducted in West Germany, the United States, and Great Britain by Lester Milbrath (1989) showed that citizens of these nations gave higher priority to environmental protection than to more economic growth by a ratio of three to one. This sampling was in keeping with what Milbrath called the *new environmental paradigm* (see Part Two Introduction). It must be pointed out that the respective governments of these three countries did not honor the views of their citizens. A series of surveys conducted in the United States between 1981 and 1989 asked respondents to agree or disagree with the following statement: "Protecting the environment is *so* important that requirements and standards cannot be too high, and continuing environmental improvements must be made *regardless* of costs." This strong statement was supported by 45 percent of respondents in 1981 and by 80 percent in 1989 (cited in Barbour, 1993).

Ronald Inglehart's *Cultural Shift in Advanced Industrial Society* (1990), based on survey data from 1970 to 1990 in 12 nations, also found evidence of an ongoing shift from materialist goals to postmaterialist goals. Postmaterialist goals had to do with democracy and justice, including greater participation in society's decision-making processes, greater freedom of speech, and increased concern over environmental and long-term quality of life issues. Inglehart traces the beginning of this shift to the 1970s, noting that it continued throughout the 1980s despite several social factors that might have blocked it, such as periods of economic recession and rising conservatism in government. The long period of time covered in the study suggests a deep change in consciousness rather than a fad or intellectual fashion trend. In 1970 materialists outnumbered those with postmaterialist values by four to one, but this difference had declined considerably by 1988, when materialists outnumbered postmaterialists by only four to three. Ingelhart found this value shift in each of the 12 nations he studied, although its magnitude was greatest in the northern European countries and least in southern countries, with the United States and Britain in between the two extremes. But Barbour questions whether values and beliefs that are now widely held are *deeply* held. When push comes to shove and people have to make sacrifices for the new values they claim to have, will they do so?

A more recent study by sociologist Paul H. Ray (1996), published by the Institute of Noetic Sciences, also documents a rapid value shift in the United States (see also Part One Introduction). Ray finds that the U.S. population falls roughly into three subcultural groupings, which he labels as *heartlanders, modernists,* and *cultural creatives.* Heartlanders embrace a largely premodern worldview based on their version of European tradition going back to Roman Catholic and Protestant roots. But it is questionable whether all these traditionalists really embrace traditional views. In fact, many are fundamentalists who reinvent tradition to suit their own purposes (see Chapter 3). This category comprises around 29 percent of the U.S. population. The second category or subculture embraces the modernism that began to emerge about five hundred years ago during the Renaissance. Today's age of technology and its industrial age paradigm express the point of view of the modernist. Some 47 percent of U.S. citizens believe in the modernist worldview (Ray, 1996).

The third category or subculture—the cultural creatives—is of most interest to us, as it is to Ray. In 1970 there was no evidence of this group except for a few isolated individuals or pockets of individuals. By 1996 those who believed in the values of this group had grown to represent 24 percent of the U.S. population. Such a rate of growth is phenomenal. Social and cultural revolutions usually involve a smaller proportion of the total population than 24 percent and occur over longer periods of time. Ray describes this group's culture as *transmodern.* He traces it to the alternative scientific and religious perspectives that have existed since the Renaissance, if not before. In Chapter 4, we briefly referred to these alternative traditions, which in the Renaissance arose in Europe as Romanticism and in America as Transcendentalism, to compete with the mechanistic worldview. Ray suggests that today's cultural creatives are combining the achievements of post-Enlightenment culture, such as science, technology, liberal democracy, and the market, with the insights, perspectives, and concerns of this alternative tradition.

The cultural creative group has two branches. Ray calls one branch the core cultural creatives. Members of this subgroup are person-centered and environmentally concerned. They emphasize psychological growth and spirituality, embrace aspects of other cultures, advocate women's issues, enjoy mastering new ideas, and are leading-edge thinkers and creators. They tend to be upper middle class and are twice as likely to be women as men. They comprise 10.6 percent of the population. The second branch Ray calls the green cultural creatives. Members tend to be concerned with political and social issues relative to the environment and justice but lack the intense interest in personal growth and spirituality of the core. The greens account for 13 percent of Americans. Ray argues that this rapidly emerging cultural transformation spells the end of modernism both as a belief system and a way of life embodied in political, economic, and social institutions. In his view, the core cultural creatives embrace a transmodern culture that can best be described as *integral,* in that it integrates important features of both traditional culture and modernism.

We started this epilogue by referring to problems without technical solutions. The solution to such problems may require nothing less than a revolution in the way we think and act as a culture. A transformation of socially shared perspectives seems to be coming about, and with it a value shift. We may think of these occurrences as the emergence of new values or simply as a change in emphasis or a reinterpretation of values that have been around a long time. Whichever way we view it, some key questions are: Will this new perspective become the dominant one? Will it provide practical and politically feasible solutions and, if so, will it do so in time? We spoke previously of dialogue and of the importance of being inclusive or allowing all points of view to be heard. Will this new perspective allow this to become possible, or will it lead to a stalemate? Or will the new dominant perspective, however environmentally sensitive and committed to justice and social participation it may be, simply drown out any opposition?

What are some of the difficulties ahead even if a new belief system does emerge and become influential or even dominant on a global scale? Ray describes three major subcultures, but he ignores the differences that exist within each. For example, he is not concerned about the differences between a Catholic heartlander and a fundamentalist Protestant heartlander. What he sees is simply that these people are committed to worldviews grounded in premodern traditions. What is perhaps even more important to our discussion is that cultural creatives are divided over essential issues, which may hamper the transition to a new cultural model. Moreover, what will become of the other subcultures if and when the integral culture assumes the dominant role in society? They will not simply disappear. After all, we have had five hundred years of modernism, yet we still have heartlander traditionalists. This suggests that even with a new dominant cultural model (or even a transformation of consciousness), conflicting and irreconcilable views will be a constant of social and political dialogue in any foreseeable future. Ultimately, these differences are inherent in the positions or statuses persons occupy in social systems and in the groups and cultural beliefs with which they identify.

Globalization: Identities, Rights, and Choices

An individual's identity and the rights and powers that come with and support it are clearly central to all the processes of globalization. Today globalization is going through a phase that is still strongly influenced by modernism and the European Enlightenment. Modernist or Enlightenment culture attacked traditional identities that were based on hereditary class privilege and the eschatological worldview of the Church, putting a superior value on other identities. We have previously pointed out (see Chapter 11, for example) the tension between *universalistic* identities (open and inclusive) and *particularistic* identities (more closed and restricting). The effects of modernism were actually somewhat contradictory in this regard. On the one hand, modernists emphasized our common identity as human beings (our shared human nature). That is, they defined and underscored human rights and also our individuality and our separateness from the particularistic, or limiting and restricting, ties of local community and ancient custom. In this sense, modernism is highly universalistic and challenges the significance of all identities that are rooted in inherited privilege, including ascribed statuses like race and gender.

Yet, on the other hand, the modernist or Enlightenment trend emphasized the importance of "the people," those who shared a common cultural and linguistic heritage. The people made up the "nation." (The word *nation* refers to having a common birth or origin.) The French and American Revolutions drove home this point. They inaugurated a new form of particularism, a new form of limited or closed identity. In the twentieth century, men like American President Woodrow Wilson (president 1913–1921) announced the right of self-determination of nations. Indeed, to participate in the universalism of the global community often requires membership in a particular national or ethnic subgroup. In addition, the politically organized national or ethnic subgroup, the nation-state, may be necessary to defend and protect the individual's universal human rights.

As we just suggested, in order for a people (or a nation) to have self-determination and to exercise its rights, a degree of mutual recognition and of social organization must be achieved. In modern times the territorial state has been the form of social organization that has been recognized as the appropriate instrument for securing the rights and expressing the common identity of a people or a nation. But there are numerous problems inherent in this form. One is that it is often (or usually) the case that clear-cut traditions and the people who embrace them are not easy to find and have to be created, forming what one commentator calls an "imagined community" (Anderson, 1983). This was true in the formation of nations such as Germany, Italy, Norway, France, and the United States. And it remains true today. Even when this issue is somewhat resolved, the territorial claims of states rarely, if ever, correspond to the geographical distribution of the nations or the cultural/linguistic groups they represent. These claims cause problems—from wars to unite the geographically separated nation (which Germany claimed it sought to do in starting World War II) to the troublesome problems of the rights of national or ethnic minority groups. The struggle over which ethnic or religious or cultural or linguistic "nation" within a territory will control the state leads to deadly internal wars, such as in Bosnia, Chechnya, and Northern Ireland.

Another issue that troubles the global community and its governance today is the right of states to act within their own territories. This is the issue of national sovereignty. How far may a state go in asserting its sovereignty in view of the rights and claims of our common humanity as expressed by the global community? First, consider the issue of the rights of citizens within their own nation, the issue of universal human rights, and the failure of some political authorities in the world even to acknowledge that such rights exist. Such national leaders do not acknowledge that the core values of which we have spoken need to be recognized in the laws and policies of all states. This situation means that there is real room for a nation-state or a culture to have a different interpretation or application of "rights" or "values." It may be true that the Western nations and Western culture have a great deal to learn from the way that the core values are expressed in non-Western cultures. But if there is validity to the existence of global core values, then we must question the motives of some of the world's political leaders and the leaders of political parties who deny those values. There is also the need to have nation-states comply with rules governing the usage of the global commons, as our mutual survival depends on this compliance. Related to this is the issue of sharing and preserving what might be called the universal heritage of humankind. Included in our universal heritage are the earth's natural beauty, rare and endangered species, the genetic information and biological products of living species, and the rich cultural heritage of threatened peoples such as tribal groups in rain forests and of the Tibetan people, to name a few. Many people in the Third World nations also believe that not only modern science but also modern technology are part of this common heritage in which they are entitled to share. But developed nations and corporations still generally prefer to see technology (and also the genetic codes of rain forest species!) as private property.

In *State of the World, 1996,* author Lester Brown of Worldwatch Institute published the article "The Acceleration of History" (Brown, 1996). Brown argues that it is safe to say that positive change is still small in relation to processes leading to negative effects. We seem to have passed a point in history when it would have been possible to prevent the breakdown of natural systems we depend on. As these natural systems begin to fail, the human political and social realities will become more grim and conflict ridden. Increasing conflict and social stress may make it more difficult for nations and groups to agree about what needs to be done and more difficult for them to cooperate in pursuit of common goals. Desperate times may lead to calls for desperate measures, that is, for coercive and even totalitarian governmental controls. All indications lead to the conclusion that even if we were to end all the undesirable human practices that we follow today, the degradation of soils, air, and water; the evolution of dangerous and resistant new diseases; climatic change; and the extinction of species and loss of biological diversity will continue for at least decades. That is the optimistic projection based on the immediate correction of all the hazardous and ill-conceived human actions. But that scenario is not likely to unfold. Realistically, the state of the planet will worsen, although we cannot predict by how much.

Conclusion

Humanity clearly faces a new and unprecedented situation. We can no longer rely on the old way of thinking. This conclusion is not just true in some general and abstract sense, it is true in specific cases. There was a time when if you wanted to produce more wheat, you increased your acreage and your agricultural inputs in the form of fertilizers, pesticides, and water. No more. There was a time when if you wanted to catch more fish, you invested in more trawlers. No more. In that time, which passed into history less than a decade ago, shortages in agricultural and fish production, or basic food staples, would lead to rising prices. The higher prices were incentives to invest money in producing more wheat or catching more lobsters. In short, the market worked like a kind of cumbersome clockwork, but it worked predictably. In a fall 1996 appearance on C-SPAN, Lester Brown spoke of how the leaders of three different nations had recently consulted with him because they no longer believed their own economic advisers. The reason, said Brown, is that we have passed certain natural limits. Economic processes work in a world of no limits and an absolute abundance of resources. But today fertilizers are failing to do the job, erosion of cropland is beginning to reduce food production, and 13 of the 15 global fisheries have been fished beyond sustainable capacity. We are in the early stages of the downward phase of a tragedy of the global commons. We are beyond a technical solution. We are beyond the parameters in which past economic reasoning applies. Perhaps, we are also beyond what is politically feasible in terms of present global institutions and the distribution of interests and political ideologies in the world today. But we are not yet beyond hope.

The possibility exists of the continuing transformation of the awareness of enough people, people who are active in the local, national, and global arenas. These people may participate in governmental sectors or, even better, in the nongovernmental civic dialogue that may soon form the context of an effective global community and its emerging culture. Such a culture will not be quite like any that has gone before it. There will be an embrace, we hope, of universalistic standards that are not impersonal or materialistic. One such universalistic standard would be a renewed appreciation for particularism and traditionalism and a respect for traditional wisdom. Such a culture will have to incorporate all that we have learned since the beginning of the modernist era, not only about science and technology, but also about democratic government and the market economy. Yet its leaders will not make absolutes of the market or material values or political structures. They will have to acknowledge what sociologists and philosophers have known for a long time, that markets and governments can thrive and serve us well only in the context of a strong human community and a set of inviolable and transcendent values. The expression of those values and their application is an evolutionary development that is never final, but always subject to the standards of open, free, and inclusive dialogue.

Appendix A Universal Declaration of Human Rights, December 1948

Preamble

Whereas recognition of the inherent dignity and of the equal and inalienable rights of all members of the human family is the foundation of freedom, justice and peace in the world,

Whereas disregard and contempt for human rights have resulted in barbarous acts which have outraged the conscience of mankind, and the advent of a world in which human beings shall enjoy freedom of speech and belief and freedom from any fear and want has been proclaimed as the highest aspiration of the common people,

Whereas it is essential, if man is not to be compelled to have recourse, as a last resort, to rebellion against tyranny and oppression, that human rights should be protected by the rule of law,

Whereas it is essential to promote the development of friendly relations between nations,

Whereas the peoples of the United Nations have in the Charter reaffirmed their faith in fundamental human rights, in the dignity and worth of the human person and in the equal rights of men and women and have determined to promote social progress and better standards of life in larger freedom,

Whereas Member States have pledged themselves to achieve, in co-operation with the United Nations, the promotion of universal respect for and observance of human rights and fundamental freedoms,

Whereas a common understanding of these rights and freedoms is of the greatest importance for the full realization of this pledge,

Now, Therefore,

THE GENERAL ASSEMBLY

proclaims

THIS UNIVERSAL DECLARATION OF HUMAN RIGHTS as a common standard of achievement for all peoples and all nations, to the end that every individual and every organ of society, keeping this Declaration constantly in mind, shall strive by teaching and education to promote respect for these rights and freedoms and by progressive measures, national and international, to secure their universal and effective recognition and observance, both among the peoples of Member States themselves and among the peoples of territories under their jurisdiction.

Article 1. All human beings are born free and equal in dignity and rights. They are endowed with reason and conscience and should act towards one another in a spirit of brotherhood.

Article 2. Everyone is entitled to all the rights and freedoms set forth in this Declaration, without distinction of any kind, such as race, colour, sex, language, religion, political or other opinion, national or social origin, property, birth or other status.

Furthermore, no distinction shall be made on the basis of the political, jurisdictional or international status of the country or territory to which a person belongs, whether it be independent, trust, non-self-governing or under any other limitation of sovereignty.

Article 3. Everyone has the right to life, liberty and security of person.

Article 4. No one shall be held in slavery or servitude; slavery and the slave trade shall be prohibited in all their forms.

Article 5. No one shall be subjected to torture or to cruel, inhuman or degrading treatment or punishment.

Article 6. Everyone has the right to recognition everywhere as a person before the law.

Article 7. All are equal before the law and are entitled without any discrimination to equal protection of the law. All are entitled to equal protection against any discrimination in violation of this

Declaration and against any incitement to such discrimination.

Article 8. Everyone has the right to an effective remedy by the competent national tribunals for acts violating the fundamental rights granted him by the constitution or by law.

Article 9. No one shall be subjected to arbitrary arrest, detention or exile.

Article 10. Everyone is entitled in full equality to a fair and public hearing by an independent and impartial tribunal, in the determination of his rights and obligations and of any criminal charge against him.

Article 11. (1) Everyone charged with a penal offence has the right to be presumed innocent until proved guilty according to law in a public trial at which he has had all the guarantees necessary for his defence.

(2) No one shall be held guilty of any penal offence on account of any act or omission which did not constitute a penal offence, under national or international law, at the time when it was committed. Nor shall a heavier penalty be imposed than the one that was applicable at the time the penal offence was committed.

Article 12. No one shall be subjected to arbitrary interference with his privacy, family, home or correspondence, nor to attacks upon his honour and reputation. Everyone has the right to the protection of the law against such interference or attacks.

Article 13. (1) Everyone has the right to freedom of movement and residence within the borders of each state.

(2) Everyone has the right to leave any country, including his own, and to return to his country.

Article 14. (1) Everyone has the right to seek and to enjoy in other countries asylum from persecution.

(2) This right may not be invoked in the case of prosecutions genuinely arising from non-political crimes or from acts contrary to the purposes and principles of the United Nations.

Article 15. (1) Everyone has the right to a nationality.

(2) No one shall be arbitrarily deprived of his nationality nor denied the right to change his nationality.

Article 16. (1) Men and women of full age, without any limitation due to race, nationality or religion, have the right to marry and to found a family. They are entitled to equal rights as to marriage, during marriage and at its dissolution.

(2) Marriage shall be entered into only with the free and full consent of the intending spouses.

(3) The family is the natural and fundamental group unit of society and is entitled to protection by society and the State.

Article 17. (1) Everyone has the right to own property alone as well as in association with others.

(2) No one shall be arbitrarily deprived of his property.

Article 18. Everyone has the right to freedom of thought, conscience and religion; this right includes freedom to change his religion or belief, and freedom, either alone or in community with others and in public or private, to manifest his religion or belief in teaching, practice, worship and observance.

Article 19. Everyone has the right to freedom of opinion and expression; this right includes freedom to hold opinions without interference and to seek, receive and impart information and ideas through any media and regardless of frontiers.

Article 20. (1) Everyone has the right to freedom of peaceful assembly and association.

(2) No one may be compelled to belong to an association.

Article 21. (1) Everyone has the right to take part in the government of his country, directly or through freely chosen representatives.

(2) Everyone has the right of equal access to public service in his country.

(3) The will of the people shall be the basis of the authority of government; this will shall be expressed in periodic and genuine elections which shall be by universal and equal suffrage and shall be held by secret vote or by equivalent free voting procedures.

Article 22. Everyone, as a member of society, has the right to social security and is entitled to realization, through national effort and international co-operation and in accordance with the organization and resources of each State, of the economic, social and cultural rights indispensable for his dignity and the free development of his personality.

Article 23. (1) Everyone has the right to work, to free choice of employment, to just and favourable conditions of work and to protection against unemployment.

(2) Everyone, without any discrimination, has the right to equal pay for equal work.

(3) Everyone who works has the right to just and favourable remuneration ensuring for himself and his family an existence worthy of human dignity, and supplemented, if necessary, by other means of social protection.

(4) Everyone has the right to form and to join trade unions for the protection of his interest.

Article 24. Everyone has the right to rest and leisure, including reasonable limitation of working hours and periodic holidays with pay.

Article 25. (1) Everyone has the right to a standard of living adequate for the health and well-being of himself and of his family, including food, clothing, housing and medical care and necessary social services, and the right to security in the event of unemployment, sickness, disability, widowhood, old age or other lack of livelihood in circumstances beyond his control.

(2) Motherhood and childhood are entitled to special care and assistance. All children, whether born in or out of wedlock, shall enjoy the same social protection.

Article 26. (1) Everyone has the right to education. Education shall be free, at least in the elementary and fundamental stages. Elementary education shall be compulsory. Technical and professional education shall be made generally available and higher education shall be equally accessible to all on the basis of merit.

(2) Education shall be directed to the full development of the human personality and to the strengthening of respect for human rights and fundamental freedoms. It shall promote understanding, tolerance and friendship among all nations, racial or religious groups, and shall further the activities of the United Nations for the maintenance of peace.

(3) Parents have a prior right to choose the kind of education that shall be given to their children.

Article 27. (1) Everyone has the right freely to participate in the cultural life of the community, to enjoy the arts and to share in scientific advancement and its benefits.

(2) Everyone has the right to the protection of the moral and material interests resulting from any scientific, literary or artistic production of which he is the author.

Article 28. Everyone is entitled to a social and international order in which the rights and freedoms set forth in this Declaration can be fully realized.

Article 29. (1) Everyone has duties to the community in which alone the free and full development of his personality is possible.

(2) In the exercise of his rights and freedoms, everyone shall be subject only to such limitations as are determined by law solely for the purpose of securing due recognition and respect for the rights and freedoms of others and of meeting the just requirements of morality, public order and the general welfare in a democratic society.

(3) These rights and freedoms may in no case be exercised contrary to the purposes and principles of the United Nations.

Article 30. Nothing in this Declaration may be interpreted as implying for any State, group or person any right to engage in any activity or to perform any act aimed at the destruction of any of the rights and freedoms set forth herein.

Glossary

Absolute poverty The condition of being so poor that people have to live in life-threatening conditions.

Acid rain Precipitation generated when carbon dioxide, oxides of nitrogen, or sulfur dioxide interacts with water vapor in the air to form mild levels of acids that then generate snow, ice, or raindrops.

Adaptive regime A society's normatively regulated practices relative to population size and to the consumption of environmental energy.

Advanced industrial nations Those countries that have been industrialized the longest but are shifting the preponderance of their workforces from manufacturing to service and information sectors.

Amnesty International A privately funded organization that works to improve human rights around the world.

Androcentricity (androcentrism) The tendency to view the world from a culturally masculine point of view.

Anti-Semitism Prejudice against Semitic peoples, especially Jews.

Apartheid A policy by which a white numerically minority government rules a heavily black majority, enforcing a system of segregation, as occurred in South Africa.

Appropriate technology Technology designed to fit the needs of the recipient culture.

Beliefs Understandings about the universe and its component parts, including human beings.

Biodiversity The great variety of living systems, from differing ecosystems, to varieties of species within given ecosystems, to genetic variations within species.

Biosphere The delicate set of natural ecological systems necessary to sustain life on this planet.

Bipolar politics Politics driven by the two-sided conflict between capitalist and communist countries.

Boundaries Symbolic limits that separate one person, group, or species from other people, groups, or species.

Budget deficit Condition caused when the federal government spends more than it receives in revenues.

Carrying capacity The largest number of any species that the planet can sustain for an extended period of time.

Centrally planned economies Economies in which the government regulates what goods and services are to be manufactured and how much are to be produced.

Civil society Nonstate network of groups and relationships.

Colonialism The formal political and economic domination of one nation by a more powerful one.

Colonies Geographical regions ruled by an external sovereign power; these regions' politics and economic activities are controlled, not to benefit the indigenous people, but to enhance that power's economic and political strength.

Conformity The active seeking of socially approved goals by socially approved means.

Confucianism Moral and religious system born in China in the sixth century B.C.E. during a period of social unrest and feudal warfare.

Contextual interaction model Model stating that the three forces of society, technology, and science are related in such ways that each can be the cause or effect of the other.

Cosmologies Complex sets of ideas about how the universe was formed and how it functions.

Creation science Belief that the biblical accounts of creation are as scientifically valid as explanations based on evolution.

Crime Any violation of the criminal law.

Criminal recidivism Subsequent offenses by persons previously imprisoned.

Criminal terrorism Acts involving criminals who employ terrorist tactics to gain their goals.

Cultural imperialism The imposition of outside values and practices on a culture or society.

Cultural relativism The practice of judging a culture by its own standards.

Culture The way of life shared by a group of people.

Culture lag The condition in which some aspects of culture (science and technology in particular) change rapidly, whereas other parts of culture (especially values and customs) lag behind, causing considerable social stress.

Date and acquaintance rape The form of rape in which a person known to the victim forces him or her to have sex.

Decolonialization The process by which colonial people achieve freedom from foreign domination.

Deep ecology A profoundly spiritual movement that sees nature and humanity as inseparable from each other, thus challenging the most basic modern notions about the cosmos and about the human person (or self).

Demographers Scientists who study population.

Demographic transition theory A theory that postulates that as nations industrialize, they tend to pass through stages, moving from dramatic population growth at the beginning and ending up with a stable state consisting of a large overall population made up of numerous small families.

Dependency theory A theory that argues that the condition of underdeveloped countries is not the result of internal weaknesses, but the product of a global economic system that favors the wealthy nations while exploiting poorer countries.

Desired state That condition or situation to which a society or the planet should be aspiring.

Development Improvement in the fundamental quality of life of the citizens of a country.

Deviance The socially perceived violation of social norms.

Disappearances The practice, usually employed by totalitarian regimes, of making perceived opponents vanish without ever acknowledging their apprehension or detention.

Discrimination The unequal treatment of people on the grounds of their group membership.

Domestic violence Physical violence among family members.

Dominance hierarchies Centralized, top-down control structures characteristic of androcentric, or patriarchal, culture.

Dowry deaths An all-too-common practice in India, especially in the north of the country, in which husbands and in-laws deliberately set a wife on fire if her parents cannot come up with the large, agreed-upon dowry.

Due process The act of conducting trials according to legal norms designed to protect the accused from abusive governmental practices.

Ecological economics Practice that takes into account the price of environmental destruction and resource depletion when figuring a company's costs of producing goods. Ecological economics encourages limiting environmental damage and recycling and switching to more abundant resources for manufacturing, thereby saving scarce resources.

Ecological niche The function of a particular organism within the community of organisms comprising its habitat.

Ecology The study of systems, including plants, animals, microbes, and people that live *together as interdependent beings.*

Economic terrorism A type of counterfeiting and similar techniques intended to destroy or to threaten disruption of the global financial system.

Ecosystem An identifiable network formed by a community of living organisms interacting with their environment.

Elitist models of power Models that postulate how power is really in the hands of a relatively few people.

Embedded particularism A point of view that seeks to maintain the distinctiveness of groups, but sees these groups as integral to the larger globalization process.

Employment segregation A condition in which female-dominated occupations receive significantly less pay and benefits than male-dominated occupations.

Entitlements Various types of government bequests that people can expect as givens.

Ethnic cleansing A program of genocide and intimidation intended to drive Croatian and Muslim civilians out of sections of the former Yugoslavia that are occupied by Serbian forces.

Ethnic groups People sharing given cultures within contemporary nation-states.

Ethnicity A category of people who are regarded as socially distinct because of their shared cultural heritage, including language, customs, dress, religion, and food preferences.

Ethnocentrism The practice of using the standards of one's own culture to judge other cultures.

Ethnonationalist movements Movements by ethnic groups within multiethnic nation-states whose goal is to establish separate nations or, at least, a measure of political autonomy for themselves.

Eurocentrism The assumption that European culture (also commonly referred to as Western culture, which includes the United States) and European experience are the norm.

Fascism A system of government led by a dictator holding complete power who crushes the opposition, espouses extreme nationalism, and often employs racism in pursuit of state ends.

Female genital mutilation The removal of healthy tissue from the female genital region.

Female infanticide The aborting of female fetuses.

Feminization of poverty Condition involving an increase in the proportion of the poor who are female; also the escalating numbers of females living in poverty.

Fertility rate The number of children the average woman has.

Final solution An extensive, systematic program to kill "undesirables" practiced by Germany in World War II.

First generation of human rights Political and civil rights.

First World Capitalistic, industrialized Western nations.

Fossil fuels Coal, oil, gasoline, and natural gas—found in deposits created by decaying plant and animal remains buried underground for millions of years.

Fourth generation of human rights Intergenerational rights, or those rights presumed to exist between generations.

Fourth World Nations whose economies are in such disarray that they have little hope of participating in the global trading system, let alone dealing with the myriad of social and political problems plaguing them.

Free trade The unrestricted international exchange of goods without protective customs tariffs.

Functional approach An approach that looks at the effects that such things as the sacred and religion in general have on persons, groups, and societies.

Fundamentalism A socioreligious reaction to the perceived threat posed by contemporary society; people responding in this way seek to return society to an imagined past characterized by strict conformity to religious tradition as defined by their unique interpretation of that tradition.

Gender roles Expectations in a society about which behaviors are appropriate for girls and boys and men and women.

Genocide Any act committed with the intent to destroy partly or totally any national, ethnic, racial, or religious group; the deliberate and systematic killing of people from racial, religious, ethnic, or political groups deemed to have common undesirable characteristics.

Glass ceiling An invisible barrier that limits advancement of women and some minorities along their career paths.

Global civil society The collective activity that takes place above the individual and below the state yet across state boundaries.

Global problem An identifiable subset of interrelated conditions resulting from negative effects of relations affecting not only individual countries but the world.

Global warming The rising of the earth's average temperature.

Globalization The growing interconnectedness of the sociosphere on a worldwide scale.

Great American Myth The myth originating in Puritan New England that views the United States as a "righteous nation" endowed by God with the special mission of being a "light in the world."

Greenhouse effect The phenomenon whereby the earth's atmosphere traps solar radiation, caused by the presence in the atmosphere of gases such as carbon dioxide, water vapor, and methane that allow incoming sunlight to pass through but absorb heat radiated back from the earth's surface.

Greenpeace A group that focuses on ways to stop the deterioration of our natural habitat.

Gridlock Condition caused by the inability to deal with key issues resulting from power politics.

Hate crimes Illegal acts directed against persons or property such as physical attacks, defacing or destroying property, or acts of intimidation motivated by hatred against specific categories of people.

Hate groups Organizations that thrive on rhetoric, literature, or actions fostering acrimony and intimidation of religious, ethnic, or national groups.

Health A state of complete physical, mental, and social well-being.

Holocaust The period during World War II of hitherto unknown systematic, business-like slaughter of Jews and other groups by the Nazis.

Homocentrism The practice of placing the interests and well-being of the human species before that of any other species or of the biosphere itself.

Human rights Those individual rights and freedoms that pertain to the human person by reason of his [her] humanity, whether they are civil and political or economic, social, and cultural rights.

Humanism A belief system characterized by an optimistic faith in human creativity and intelligence.

Hydrosphere The earth's surface water and groundwater.

Identities Individuals' sense of what or who they are in relationship to the surrounding world in which they perceive themselves to live.

Ideology An idea used to persuade and convince people to think in a way that promotes the interests of one group over those of other groups, despite the evidence.

Indigenous technologies Technologies developed by local peoples themselves.

Indivisibility of human rights The understanding that in the quest for justice, security, and peace, political and civil rights cannot be separated from economic, social, and cultural rights.

Industrialized nations Countries in which the largest portion of the workforce is engaged in manufacturing some type of goods. Industrializing nations have experienced the movement of their workforces from agricultural and other activities intended to meet the basic needs of their populations to industrial manufacturing.

Industrializing nations Countries that have begun a movement of their workforce from agricultural and other activities intended to meet the basic needs of their populations toward industrial manufacturing.

Infant mortality The death of a child in the first year of life.

Innovation The active pursuit of socially approved goals while rejecting socially approved means.

Insular particularism A view that seeks to insulate a group from outside interference.

International Bill of Human Rights The Universal Declaration and the two Covenants on Human Rights issuing from the United Nations.

International slave trade The practice of kidnapping women in one country to be sold abroad into prostitution.

Islam A religion, like Judaism and Christianity, that originated in the Middle East and sees itself as the fulfillment of these two earlier faiths.

Isolationism A policy of nonparticipation in international political and economic affairs.

Lobbying The process of influencing legislation, usually conducted by professional lobbyists involving contact with lawmakers and their staff, the generation of grassroots support, and the making of contributions to campaign funds.

Male dominance The personal right of males to control women's behavior and act as though women are inherently inferior.

Marginalized youth Young people who exist on the fringes of society because of poverty, ethnic minority status, and/or other factors.

Marital rape Rape in which the husband forces the wife to have sex against her will.

Market-driven economy An economy in which multiple producers of goods and services compete with one another (at least in theory) to make a profit.

Mechanistic worldview The view that all of nature (and ourselves) may be seen as a machine—lifeless, mindless, and pointless, unconnected with human values and goals.

Middle-class slide The erosion of the economic position of middle-income families along with their intensifying financial instability.

Militant particularism The view that a group's uniqueness is superior and should become universal.

Minority group A group whose members suffer various disadvantages at the hands of another, more dominant group.

Mirror image concepts Concepts that lead one to view the other as an exact opposite of oneself.

Modernism A set of assumptions and orientations to the world that holds that progress in all aspects of human life can be achieved by the application of reason to nature and to society.

Modernization theory A theory describing how underdeveloped societies are hindered by their failure to employ advanced technology in production and by traditional modes of thought that stress family and relationships rather than the individual and economic efficiency.

Mortality rate The incidence of death in a society's population.

Multiculturalism The recognition of the cultural diversity within a society.

Narcoterrorism The utilization of violent intimidation centering on the dealing of illegal drugs.

Nation A group of people, often of diverse origins, inhabiting a common territory and (in theory) sharing a common identity.

Nation-state A modern form of political system in which a single governmental body claims to act on behalf of a group of people who share a common identity and territory; the concept of the nation-state is based on the idea that the people who occupy a given territory share a common culture and common identity and should be governed by a unified political system.

National debt The money owed by the federal government.

National sovereignty The idea that a nation-state has absolute control of its own territory, and other nations cannot interfere with its internal affairs.

Nationalism The love for and devotion to one's country.

Nativism A movement that strongly espouses a halt to large-scale immigration within a country.

Nazis Members of the National Socialist German Workers' Party; they were fascists who ruled Germany from 1933 to 1945 under the leadership of Adolf Hitler.

Nested hierarchy A series of graded levels, for example, a number of lower-level ecological systems residing within the next higher level of the biosphere.

Nongovernmental organizations (NGOs) Organizations not representing governments, but speaking for various causes at UN sessions of the General Assembly, the Economic and Social Council, the U.S. Congress, or other governmental meetings.

Nonindustrialized nations Countries that have yet to make any movement from meeting basic needs to manufacturing.

Norms The behavioral expectations within a society.

Objective globalization The notion of the increasing planetary interconnectedness of human social activity and the worldwide effects or repercussions of that activity.

Oligarchy A relatively small cadre of elites within a society.

Overurbanization A situation in which so many people are concentrated in cities that they overwhelm the city's capacity to provide basic services and necessities like housing, safe water, and sufficient jobs.

Ozone layer depletion The destruction of the earth's protective ozone layer.

Particularism A concept that stresses the uniqueness of a given group's ways, practices, and ideas.

Patriarchy The policy of giving males more status, power, and authority than females, both at home and in the larger society.

Peace dividend The money spent for arms worldwide, which now can be diverted to more productive uses such as improving health care, eliminating hunger, and slowing environmental decay.

Per capita [for each person] income An indicator of the wealth of a nation, derived by dividing the *gross national product* (GNP) by the nation's population for a specified time period such as a year.

Personal troubles Private matters that affect mainly individuals and their immediate circle of family, friends, or coworkers.

Phenomenological approach An approach that does not deny sociological, psychological, or physical elements in religion but insists that we must take religion and religious experience at face value.

Pluralism The bringing together of people of different views, religions, nationalities, and/or races.

Pluralist models of power Sociological models operating on the assumption that power exists at a number of different levels and/or is shared by a number of distinct groups in the social structure.

Political action committees Committees that funnel large amounts of money to politicians' election campaigns; they are particularly powerful in the United States.

Population explosion A situation caused by an increase in the birthrate, a decrease in the death rate, or out-migration (individual people or families who emigrate to another part of the world).

Postmodernism The phase of contemporary culture that recognizes the failure of modernism to achieve progress after centuries of effort.

Power elite A group composed of top-ranking business, government, and military officials.

Prejudice An irrational, inflexible attitude toward an entire category of people or things.

Premodern communities Communities based on ascribed statuses, close kinship ties, and, in many, if not most cases, an unquestioned acceptance of patriarchy.

Prisoners of conscience People held for expressing their views usually in opposition to an authoritarian regime.

Private sector The sector, or part, of the economy consisting of all the economic activity based on personal (or corporate) sources of capital and undertaken for personal or family gain.

Privatization of religion The tendency to make religion a private and individual experience.

Progressive tax system A system that compels wealthier taxpayers to pay increasingly higher percentages in taxes as their income rises.

Protestant work ethic The belief that if a person works hard, success will follow.

Public issues Matters that transcend the immediate lives of individuals.

Public sector The sector of the economy consisting of all economic activity and exchanges involving the use of government money and other capital, which originates largely through the collection of taxes.

Race A category of people who are regarded as socially distinct because they share genetically transmitted physical characteristics, such as skin color, hair texture, or shape of the nose and eyes.

Racism The belief that one racial or ethnic group is inferior/superior to another and, because of that, their unequal treatment is justified.

Radical ecology A radical view of environmentalism that does not accept a boundary between nature (environment) and human beings.

Rape The act of forcing sexual relations on someone without his or her consent.

Rebellion The rejection of both the approved goals and approved means of the existing social order while actively attempting to replace them with an alternative social order.

Rehabilitation The process of reforming offenders so that they will not commit offenses in the future.

Relative poverty The condition of being poor compared to the rest of the domestic population.

Religion A system of beliefs and practices by means of which a group of people struggles with the ultimate problems of human life.

Repressive terrorism A form of terrorism that occurs when a government employs harsh tactics to intimidate its own civilian population.

Retreatism The rejection of institutionalized means and goals.

Revolutionary movements Movements that propose sweeping changes in society, often demanding that existing institutions be demolished and replaced with new institutions deemed more desirable by the revolutionaries.

Revolutionary terrorism Terrorism that occurs when internal enemies of the state rely on terrorist tactics to produce change in the political system.

Ritualism The pursuit of socially approved courses of action while surrendering any commitment to achieving socially approved goals.

Science The systematic attempt to understand and explain any realm of human experience, including nature, society, and human mental processes by methods that can be replicated and lead to socially shared knowledge.

Second generation of human rights Economic, social, and cultural rights.

Second World The nations of the Commonwealth of Independent States (the former Soviet Union) and its East European allies.

Sex The physical differences between men and women.

Sex ratio The number of males for every hundred females in a given population.

Sexual harassment Comments, gestures, or physical contact of a sexual nature that is deliberate, repeated, and unwelcome, creating a *hostile work environment.*

Social construction of reality The process of interaction that creates a shared reality.

Social ecology A movement that draws attention to the issues of human suffering and social injustice viewed to be at the root of the ecological crisis of our times.

Social economy The sector of the economy that is based on volunteer activities.

Social indicators Data used for judging where a group ranks in a society.

Social inequality The condition in which some groups or categories of people have unequal access to society's valued resources, goods, and services.

Social institution An organized sphere of social life designed to meet important social needs, such as the family, religion, or the economy.

Social movements Organized collective behavior aimed at producing change in existing social structures. Social movements are relatively large scale, loosely organized forms of social action developing outside of established social institutions in an effort to deal with issues widely perceived to be problems.

Social perspective taking The process of taking into account the point of view of others.

Social problem A condition affecting a significant number of people in an adverse way.

Social web The complex net of social relations stemming from the interlocking relationships among various groups to which we belong—at almost every moment from birth to death.

Sociological imagination The ability to place our personal biographies in the larger social and historical context.

Sociology The disciplined study of patterns of human social interaction and their effects on human thought and conduct.

Sociosphere The social systems, including such elements as the economy and technology, by which humans organize their lives and sustain themselves.

Special interest groups Collectivities organized to promote a political agenda advancing their concerns.

Spiritual ecology An ecological movement based on the view that a transformation of consciousness is necessary if the present ecological crisis is to be averted.

State The governmental apparatus by which decisions are made and enforced on behalf of the group of people living in a nation.

State terrorism The training, supporting, financing, and protecting by nation-states of international terrorists whom the nation-states generally employ to further their foreign policy agenda.

Stewardship The idea that humans are not masters over the universe, but are responsible for the care and maintenance of all of God's other creatures.

Street crimes Violations against the person such as murder, forcible rape, assault, and robbery and crimes against property such as burglary, larceny, and motor vehicle theft.

Subjective globalization The social redefinition of identities and worldviews that emerges from the human confrontation and dialogue occasioned by objective globalization itself.

Superterrorism The enhancing of the terrorist threat through employing or threatening to utilize weapons of mass destruction.

Sustainable development Development that meets the needs of the present without compromising the ability of future generations to meet their own needs.

Sweatshop A factory where workers are forced to work long hours in unsafe conditions for very low wages.

Symbiotic relationship A relationship in which dissimilar organisms live together in mutually beneficial associations.

Symbols Objects, actions, or sounds given specific meanings by social definition.

Technological determinism The idea that technology, while following its own inner tendencies, is an independent cause of social, cultural, and psychological patterns.

Technological imperative The belief that technology will follow a set course because of an inner necessity and, therefore, human beings can do little to alter this course.

Technology The systematic application of ideas to produce some desired outcome by manipulating the material world.

Technology practice The complex set of social and cultural patterns in which a society's technologies are embedded.

Technology transfer The direct sharing of the developed world's technology with the less developed peoples of the world.

Terrorism The use of violence or the threat of violence as a means to achieve some strategic goal by striking fear in victims.

Third generation of human rights The privileges that collectivities—often defined loosely as "peoples"—may claim.

Third World Those nations that are not yet industrialized or are in the process of industrializing.

Transnational corporations Businesses that are headquartered in one country but operate in one or more other countries.

Universal Declaration of Human Rights An extremely significant document for establishing the standards of the "desirable state" in the global community. The Universal Declaration, a response to Nazi atrocities during World War II and the resultant perceived need for acceptable standards of behavior in the world community, was written in 1948 for the United Nations by an international committee chaired by the U.S. delegate to the UN, Eleanor Roosevelt. The declaration, a resolution of the UN, did not bind member states to obey its articles.

Universalism The orientation to those common principles or constructs that apply to all people everywhere.

Urbanization The process referring to the degree to which people are concentrated in cities and to *how* people live, their patterns of behavior, and their social relationships.

Value conflicts Disagreements among groups over which set of values should dominate.

Value judgment An assessment of conditions or situations based on deeply held values.

Values Defensible criteria for determining what is desirable or undesirable, good or bad, and beautiful or ugly in a society.

Vulnerable groups Identifiable categories of people who are especially open to abuse and exploitation.

Wealthfare All those programs, policies, and "breaks" given by government to more affluent members of society.

Weapons of mass destruction Weapons capable of inflicting widespread death and injury in a single attack.

Welfare programs Any of a host of federal, state, and local programs that contribute to the well-being of the American people or specific segments of the population such as the elderly, the young, the poor, the wealthy, the disabled, farmers, businesspeople, and the like.

Wetlands Ground on which standing water can be found for 15 consecutive days in any year, or which was saturated to the surface for at least 21 days a year.

White collar crime Crimes committed by professionals, managers, and businesspeople in the course of their professional lives.

Workfare A program in the United States of public sector jobs created so that welfare recipients can work for their checks.

Zero sum game A process in which the gains of some groups must be subtracted from the assets of other groups.

References

CHAPTER ONE

Barney, G. O. 1980. *The Global 2000 Report to the President,* Vols. 1, 2, and 3. Washington, DC: U.S. Government Printing Office.

Basseches, Michael. 1984. *Dialectical Thinking and Adult Development.* Norwood, NJ: Ablex.

Berger, Peter L. and Thomas Luckman. 1967. *The Social Construction of Reality: A Treatise in the Sociology of Knowledge.* Garden City, NY: Anchor Books.

De Kadt, Emanuel. 1980. "Some Basic Questions on Human Rights and Development." *World Development* 8 (February):97–105.

Durkheim, Emile. 1950. *Rules of the Sociological Method,* 8th ed. Translated by S. A. Solvay and J. H. Mueller. Edited by G. E. G. Catlin. New York: The Free Press.

Erikson, Kai T. 1966. *Wayward Puritans: A Study in the Sociology of Deviance.* New York: John Wiley and Sons.

Ferrante, Joan. 1992. *Sociology: A Global Perspective.* Belmont, CA: Wadsworth Publishing Company.

Fuller, R. C. and R. R. Meyer. 1941a. "Some Aspects of a Theory of Social Problems." *American Sociological Review* 6 (February):24–31.

———. 1941b. "Natural History of a Social Problem." *American Sociological Review* 6 (June):320–27.

Gusfield, Joseph R. 1989. "Constructing the Ownership of Social Problems: Fun and Profit in the Welfare State." *Social Problems* 37 (December):431–41.

Horton, Paul B., Gerald R. Leslie, Richard F. Larson, and Robert L. Horton. 1994. *Sociology of Social Problems,* 11th ed. Englewood Cliffs, NJ: Prentice Hall.

Kitsuse, John I. and Malcolm Spector. 1973. "Toward a Sociology of Social Problems: Social Conditions, Value Judgements, and Social Problems." *Social Problems* 20 (4):407–19.

Kohlberg, Lawrence. 1981. *Essays on Moral Development.* New York: Harper & Row.

Lopata, Helena Z. 1984. "Social Construction of Social Problems over Time." *Social Problems* 31 (February):249–71.

Mauss, Armand L. 1976. *Social Problems as Social Movements.* New York: J. B. Lippincott Company.

Mead, George Herbert. 1934. *Mind, Self, and Society from the Standpoint of a Strict Behaviorist.* Chicago: University of Chicago Press.

Mills, C. Wright. 1959. *The Sociological Imagination.* New York: Oxford University Press.

Milton, Kay. 1996. *Environmentalism and Cultural Theory.* New York: Routledge.

Reich, Robert B. 1988. "Corporation and Nation." *Atlantic Monthly* (May):76–81.

Restivo, Sal. 1991. *The Sociological Worldview.* Cambridge, MA: Basil Blackwell, Inc.

Robertson, Roland. 1992. *Globalization: Social Theory and Global Culture.* Newberry Park, CA: Sage.

Selman, Robert. 1971. "The Relation of Role-Taking to the Development of Moral Judgment in Children." *Child Development* 42:79–91.

Spector, Malcolm and John I. Kitsuse. 1974. "Social Problems: A Reformulation." *Social Problems* 20:145–59.

Tallman, Irvin. 1976. *Passion, Action, and Politics: A Perspective on Social Problems and Social Problem Solving.* San Francisco: W. H. Freeman and Company.

Thomas, W. I. with Dorothy Swaine Thomas. 1928. *The Child in America.* New York: Knopf.

Waller, Willard. 1936. "Social Problems and Mores." *American Sociological Review* 6 (December):922–33.

White, Stephen W. 1995. *The Cambridge Companion to Habermas.* New York: Cambridge University Press.

Woolgar, Steve and Dorothy Pawluch. 1985. "Ontological Gerrymandering: The Anatomy of Social Problems Explanations." *Social Problems* 32 (February):214–27.

PART ONE INTRODUCTION

Berger, Peter. 1979. *The Heretical Imperative: Contemporary Possibilities of Religious Affirmation.* Garden City, NY: Anchor Press.

Milton, Kay. 1996. *Environmentalism and Cultural Theory.* New York: Routledge.

Wapner, Paul. 1996. *Environmental Activism and World Civic Politics.* Albany: State University of New York Press.

CHAPTER TWO

Adler, Jerry. 1995. "The Last Days of Auschwitz." *Newsweek* (January 16):47–55.

Alston, Philip. 1990. "The Fortieth Anniversary of the Universal Declaration of Human Rights: A Time More for Reflection than Celebration." In *Human Rights in a Pluralistic World: Individuals and Collectivities,* ed. Jan Berting et al. London: Meckler.

Baehr, Peter R. and Koo VanderWal. 1990. "Introduction Item: Human Rights as Individual and as Collective Rights." In *Human Rights in a Pluralistic World: Individuals and Collectivities,* ed. Jan Berting. London: Meckler.

Beaubien, Greg. 1995. "Witness to War: Testimony of Bosnian Victims Rattles Observers from Chicago." *Chicago Tribune* (March 22):5.1, 5.2.

Bothwick, Mark. 1992. *Pacific Century: The Emergence of Modern Pacific Asia.* Boulder, CO: Westview Press.

Burns, James MacGregor and Stewart Burns. 1991. *A People's Charter: The Pursuit of Rights in America.* New York: Knopf.

Council for a Parliament of the World's Religions. 1993. *Towards a Global Ethic (An Initial Declaration).* Chicago: Author.

De Kadt, Emanuel. 1980. "Some Basic Questions on Human Rights and Development." *World Development* 8 (February):97–105.

"Democracies Double in 20 Years." 1994. *Chicago Tribune* (December 16):1.9

Eide, Asbjorn. 1986. "The Human Rights Movement and the Transformation of the International Order." *Alternatives* 11:365–402, 535–38.

Forsythe, David P. 1991. *The Internationalization of Human Rights.* Lexington, MA: Lexington.

Frank, Anne. 1952. *The Diary of a Young Girl.* New York: Pocket Books.

Frankel, Marvin E. 1989. *Out of the Shadows of Night: The Struggle for International Human Rights.* New York: Delacorte.

Humphrey, John. 1989. *No Distant Millennium: The International Law of Human Rights.* Paris: United Nations Educational, Scientific, and Cultural Organization.

Jackson, James O. 1995. "The Balkans: No Rush to Judgment." *Time* (June 17). Electronic transmission. Available at: *http://www.pathfinder.com/time/magazine/domestic/1994/940627/balkans.html*

———. 1995. "Remembrance: Return to Auschwitz." *Time* (February 3). Electronic transmission. Available at: *http://www.pathfinder.com/time/magazine/domestic/1995/950203/*

Kegley, Charles W., Jr. and Eugene R. Wittkopf. 1995. *World Politics: Trends and Transformation,* 5th ed. New York: St. Martin's Press.

Luft, Kerry and Laurie Goering. 1995. Confronting Horrors of the Past: Latin America Comes to Terms with Tyranny." *Chicago Tribune* (March 19):1.13.

MacIntyre, Alasdair C. 1988. *Whose Justice? Which Rationality?* Notre Dame, IN: University of Notre Dame Press.

MacKinnon, Catharine. 1993. "Crimes of War, Crimes of Peace." In *On Human Rights: The Oxford Amnesty Lectures 1993,* ed. Stephen Shute and Susan Hurley. New York: Basic Books.

Mayor, Frederico. 1993. Foreword to *Human Rights in a Pluralistic World: Individuals and Collectivities,* ed. Jan Berting. London: Meckler.

Miller, Perry. *Errand into the Wilderness.* Cambridge, MA: Harvard University Press.

Moseley, Ray. 1995. "Dresden Recalls the Allies' Act of 'Terror.'" *Chicago Tribune* (February 12):1.21, 1.24.

Panniker, Raimundo. 1995. *Invisible Harmony: Essays on Contemplation and Responsibility.* Minneapolis, MN: Fortress.

Schmetzer, Uli. 1994. "Rights Lose Out as U.S., China Deal on Trade." *Chicago Tribune* (August 30):1.1 and 1.2.

Selznick, Philip. 1992. *The Moral Commonwealth: Social Theory and the Promise of Community.* Berkeley, CA: University of California Press.

Solzhenitsyn, Aleksandr. 1975. *The Gulag Archipelago.* New York: Harper.

Staunton, Marie, Sally Fenn, and Amnesty International U.S.A., eds. 1991. *The Amnesty International Handbook.* Claremont, CA: Hunter House.

"21 Serbs Indicted for War Crimes." 1995. *Chicago Tribune* (February 14):1.3.

"UN Agency Meets to Study Worst Rights Abuses in '94." 1995. *Boston Globe* (January 30): National/Foreign Section, 6.

"U.S. Halves Pledge for Foreign Food Aid." 1995. *Chicago Tribune* (April 3):1.3.

United Nations. 1995. "Convention Against Genocide." In *A Summary of United Nations Agreements on Human Rights.* Electronic transmission. Available at: *http://www.hrweb.org/legal.undocs.html*

Wapner, Paul. 1996. *Environmental Activism and World Civic Politics.* Albany: State University of New York Press.

Whalen, Lucille. 1989. *Human Rights: A Reference Handbook.* Santa Barbara, CA: ABC-CLIO.

Wronka, Joseph. 1992. *Human Rights and Social Policy in the 21st Century.* Lanham, MD: University Press of America.

Zimmerman, Tim, with Kenneth T. Walsh, Julie Cowin, and Robin Knight. 1995. "The Art of the Deal." *U.S. News and World Report* (February 13):58–60.

CHAPTER THREE

Abdo, Genevive. 1994. "As Algeria Watches, Berber Villagers Hold Islamic Guerrillas at Bay." *Chicago Tribune* (November 3):1A.35

Anderson, Sherry Ruth and Patricia Hopkins. 1991. *The Feminine Face of God: The Unfolding of the Sacred in Women.* New York: Bantam Books.

Barbour, Ian. 1991. *Ethics in an Age of Technology: The Gifford Lectures, 1990–1991,* Vol. II. New York: HarperCollins.

Bawer, Bruce. 1997. *Stealing Jesus: How Fundamentalism Betrays Christianity.* New York: Crown.

Berdyaev, Nicholai. 1992. *The Russian Idea.* Hudson, NY: Lindisfarne.

Berger, Peter. 1967. *The Sacred Canopy: Elements of a Sociological Theory of Religion.* Garden City, NY: Doubleday.

———. 1979. *The Heretical Imperative: Contemporary Possibilities of Religious Affirmation.* Garden City, NY: Doubleday.

———. 1992. *A Far Glory.* New York: Doubleday.

Beversluis, Joel. 1995. *A Sourcebook for the Earth's Community of Religions.* Grand Rapids, MI: CoNexus Press.

Beyer, Peter. 1994. *Religion and Globalization.* Thousand Oaks, CA: Sage.

Bourguignon, Erika. 1973. *Religion, Altered States of Consciousness, and Social Change.* Columbus: Ohio State University Press.

Carter, Stephen L. 1993. *The Culture of Unbelief: How American Law and Politics Trivialize Religious Devotion.* New York: Basic Books.

Coates, James and Mike Dorning. 1995. "On the Internet, Extremists Spread Hate with Every Keystroke." *Chicago Tribune* (April 26):1.14.

Cousins, Ewert. 1992. *Christ of the 21st Century.* Rockport, MA: Element.

Cunningham, Lawrence, John Kelsay (Contributor), R. Maurice Barineau. 1995. *The Sacred Quest: An Invitation to the Study of Religion,* 2nd ed. Englewood Cliffs, NJ: Prentice Hall.

Eisler, Riane. 1987. *The Chalice and the Blade: Our History, Our Future.* San Francisco: Harper & Row.

Engels, Frederich. 1940. *Dialectics of Nature.* New York: International Publishers Company.

———. 1964. *Economic and Philosophic Manuscripts of 1844.* New York: International Publishers Company.

Faruqi, Abwar. 1996. "Edict Hits Afghan Orphans Hard." *Chicago Tribune* (October 15):1.3.

Fenwick, Peter and Elizabeth Fenwick. 1995. *The Truth in the Light.* New York: Berkley Books.

Fowler, James. 1981. *Stages of Faith: The Psychology of Human Development and the Search for Meaning.* San Francisco: Harper & Row.

Frankl, Victor. 1963. *One Man's Search for Meaning.* Boston: Beacon.

Gould, Stephen Jay. 1983. *Hen's Teeth and Horse's Toes.* New York: W. W. Norton and Co.

Hexam, Irving and Karla Poewe. 1997. *New Religions as Global Cultures: Making the Human Sacred.* Boulder, CO: Westview Press.

Hofstadter, Richard. 1965. *The Paranoid Style in American Politics.* New York: Knopf.

Hundley, Tom. 1993. "Moderate Arab States Wary of Militant Islam." *Chicago Tribune* (July 4):1.1, 11.

———. 1998. "Terrorism's Vigor Killing Egypt Tourism." *Chicago Tribune* (April 5):1.3.

James, William. [1902] 1961. *Varieties of Religious Experience.* New York: Collier.

Johnson, Phillip E. 1991. *Darwin on Trial.* Downers Grove, IL: InterVarsity Press.

Kegan, Robert. 1994. *In Over Our Heads: The Mental Demands of Modern Life.* Cambridge: Harvard University Press.

Kenney, Jim. 1996. "The Parliament Experience: 1993 and Beyond." In *The Community of Religions: Voices and Images of the Parliament of the World's Religions,* ed. Wayne Teasdale and George Cairns. New York: Continuum.

Kepel, Gilles. 1994. *The Revenge of God: The Resurgence of Islam, Christianity, and Judaism in the Modern World.* Translated by Alan Braley. University Park: University of Pennsylvania Press.

Kohlberg, Lawrence. 1981. *Essays on Moral Development,* Vol. I. San Francisco: Harper.

Kung, Hans, Joseph van Ess, Heinrich von Streitencron, and Heinz Bechert. 1993. *Christianity and the World's Religions.* Maryknoll, NY: Orbis Books.

Lev, Michael. 1996. "Tyranny of Religion Imperils Rich Culture." *Chicago Tribune* (December 3):1.1, 24.

Lind, Michael. 1996. *Up from Conservatism: Why the Right Is Wrong for America.* New York: Free Press.

Madigan, Charles M. 1996. "The Global Scourge of Terrorism." *Chicago Tribune* (August 1):1.1, 12, 13.

Maslow, Abraham. 1968. *Toward a Psychology of Being.* New York: Van Nostrand Reinhold.

———. 1970. *Religions, Values, and Peak Experiences.* New York: Viking.

———. 1971. *The Farther Reaches of Human Nature.* New York: Viking.

Marty, Martin E. and R. Scott Appleby, eds. 1994. *Accounting for Fundamentalism.* Chicago: University of Chicago Press.

———. 1997. *Religion, Ethnicity, and Self-Identity: Nations in Turmoil.* Hanover, NH: University Press of New England.

Merchant, Carolyn. 1992. *Radical Ecology: The Search for a Livable World.* New York: Routledge.

Milton, Kay. 1996. *Environmentalism and Cultural Theory.* New York: Routledge.

Moore, Dinty. 1997. *The Accidental Buddhist: Mindfulness, Enlightenment, and Sitting Still.* Chapel Hill, NC: Algonquin Books of Chapel Hill.

Moseley, Ray. 1998. "Germany's New Storm Troopers." *Chicago Tribune* (April 5):1.1, 1.11.

———. "Fanatics' War Grips Algeria." *Chicago Tribune* (October 12):1.1, 1.22.

Ray, Paul H. 1996. "The Rise of Integral Culture." *Noetic Sciences Review* (Spring):5–15.

Ring, Kenneth. 1982. *Near Death Studies: A New Area of Consciousness Research.* Storrs, CT: International Association for Near Death Studies.

Rudolph, Susanne H. and James Piscatori, eds. 1997. *Transnational Religion and Fading States.* Boulder, CO: Westview Press.

Sabom, Michael. 1982. *Recollections of Death.* New York: Harper & Row.

Schmidt, Roger. 1988. *Exploring Religion.* Belmont, CA: Wadsworth.

Seager, Richard Hughes. 1996. "In Two Parliaments, the 1893 Original and the Centennial in 1993: A Historian's View." In *The Community of Religions: Voices and Images of the Parliament of the World's Religions,* ed.

Wayne Teasdale and George Cairns. New York: Continuum.

Smart, Ninian. 1995. *Worldviews: Crosscultural Explorations of Human Beliefs.* Englewood Cliffs, NJ: Prentice Hall.

Southern Poverty Law Center. 1998. "What's New." Electronic transmission. Available at: *http://www.splcenter.org*

Tackett, Michael. 1998. "Campaign for Righteousness." *Chicago Tribune* (May 25):1.1, 1.13.

Tribune News Services. 1995. "Europeans Target Immigrants with New Hatred." (November 16). Electronic transmission. Available at: *http://www.chicago.tribune.com/news/nationworld/article/0,1051-art-6426,00.html*

———. 1997. "Taliban Win May Bring Peace to Afghanistan, but Women are Likely to Pay a Steep Price." *Chicago Tribune* (May 26):1.3.

Wapner, Paul. 1996. *Environmental Activism and World Civic Politics.* Albany: State University of New York Press.

Wilber, Ken. 1981. *Up from Eden.* New York: Doubleday/Anchor.

———. 1998. *The Marriage of Sense and Soul: Integrating Science and Religion.* New York: Random House.

Wilson, Bryan. 1973. *Magic and the Millennium: A Sociological Study of Religious Movements of Protest among Tribal and Third World Peoples.* New York: Harper & Row.

Yinger, Milton J. 1970. *The Scientific Study of Religion.* New York: Macmillan.

CHAPTER FOUR

Barbour, Ian. 1990. *Religion in an Age of Science: The Gifford Lectures,* Vol. I. New York: HarperCollins.

Berger, Peter. 1979. *The Heretical Imperative: Contemporary Possibilities of Religious Affirmation.* Garden City, NY: Anchor Press.

Briggs, John and F. David Peat. 1989. *Turbulent Mirror.* New York: Harper & Row.

Capra, Fritjof. 1976. *The Tao of Physics.* Boston: Shambala.

Davidson, John. 1989. *The Secret of the Creative Vacuum: Man and the Energy Dance.* Saffron Walden, England: C. W. Daniel.

Drengson, Alan. 1995. *The Practice of Technology: Exploring Technology, Ecophilosophy, and Spiritual Disciplines for Vital Links.* Albany: State University of New York Press.

Eddington, Arthur. 1929. *The Nature of the Physical World.* New York: Macmillan.

Etzioni, Amitai. 1988. *The Moral Dimension: Toward a New Economics.* New York: Free Press.

Gleick, James. 1987. *Chaos: The Making of a New Science.* New York: Viking Press.

Hayles, N. Katherine. 1990. *Chaos Bound: Orderly Disorder in Contemporary Literature and Science.* Ithaca, NY: Cornell University Press.

Kane, Hal. 1996. "Shifting to Sustainable Industries." In *State of the World 1996: A Worldwatch Institute Report on Progress Toward a Sustainable Society.* New York: W. W. Norton and Co.

Kuhn, Thomas. 1970. *The Structure of Scientific Revolutions.* Chicago: University of Chicago Press.

Macionis, John J. 1996. *Sociology.* Upper Saddle River, NJ: Prentice Hall.

Marx, Leo. 1964. *The Machine in the Garden: Technology and the Pastoral Ideal in America.* New York: Oxford University Press.

Merchant, Carolyn. 1980. *The Death of Nature: Women, Ecology, and the Scientific Revolution.* New York: Harper & Row.

McGinn, Robert E. 1991. *Science, Technology, and Society.* Englewood Cliffs, NJ: Prentice Hall.

Moore, Walter. 1989. *Schrödinger: Life and Thought.* Cambridge: Cambridge University Press.

Noble, David F. 1977. *America by Design: Technology and the Rise of Corporate America.* New York: Knopf.

Ogburn, William F. 1964. *On Culture and Social Change: Selected Papers.* Chicago: University of Chicago Press.

O'Leary, Brian. 1996. *Miracle in the Void: Free Energy, UFOs and Other Scientific Revelations.* Kihei, HI: Kamapua'a Press.

Perrow, Charles. 1984. *Normal Accidents.* New York: Basic Books.

Peters, Thomas J. 1987. *Thriving on Chaos: Handbook for a Management Revolution.* New York: Knopf.

Petersen, John L. 1994. *The Road to 2015: Profiles of the Future.* Corte Maders, CA: The Waite Group Press.

Polanyi, Karl. 1944. *The Great Transformation.* Boston: Beacon Press.

Prigogine, Ilya and Isabelle Stengers. 1984. *Order Out of Man's New Dialogue with Nature.* New York: Bantam Books.

Ravetz, Jerome. 1971. *Scientific Knowledge and Its Social Problems.* Oxford: Clarendon Press.

Ray, Paul H. 1996. "The Rise of Integral Culture." *Noetic Sciences Review* (Spring):5–15.

Roszak, Theodore. 1994. *The Cult of Information: A Neo-Luddite Treatise on High Tech, Artificial Intelligence, and the True Art of Thinking.* Berkeley: University of California Press.

Sahlins, Marshall. 1976. *The Use and Abuse of Biology: An Anthropological Critique of Sociobiology.* Ann Arbor, MI: University of Michigan Press.

Schumacher, E. F. 1973. *Small Is Beautiful: Economics as if People Mattered.* London: Blond and Briggs.

Segal, Howard P. 1994. *Future Imperfect: The Mixed Blessing of Technology in America.* Amherst: University of Massachusetts Press.

Senge, Peter M. 1990. *The Fifth Discipline: The Art and Practice of the Learning Organization.* NY: Doubleday/Currency.

Spretnak, Charlene. 1997. *The Resurgence of the Real.* New York: Addison-Wesley.

Stoll, Clifford. 1995. *Silicon Snake Oil: Second Thoughts on the Information Highway.* New York: Doubleday.

Talbott, Stephen L. 1995. *The Future Does Not Compute: Transcending the Machines in Our Midst.* Sebastopol, CA: O'Reilly and Associates, Inc.

Waldrop, M. Mitchell. 1992. *Complexity: The Emerging Science at the Edge of Order and Chaos.* New York: Simon & Schuster.

PART TWO INTRODUCTION

Catton, William, Jr. and Riley Dunlap. 1980. "A New Ecological Paradigm for Post-Exuberant Sociology." *American Behavioral Scientist* 24 (September/October):15–47.

Lovelock, James. 1979. *Gaia: A New Look at Life on Earth.* New York: Oxford University Press.

Senge, Peter M. 1990. *The Fifth Discipline: The Art of Learning Cooperation.* New York: Bantam Doubleday Dell.

CHAPTER FIVE

Barr, Cameron. 1992. "Female Empowerment Leads to Fewer Births." *The Christian Science Monitor* (July 8):14.

Bodley, John F. 1990. *Victims of Progress.* Mountain View, CA: Mayfield.

Brown, Lester R. 1994. "Facing Food Insecurity." In *State of the World 1994: A Worldwatch Institute Report on Progress Toward a Sustainable Society.* New York: W. W. Norton.

Bryjak, George J. 1997. "Is It Possible to Rescue Sub-Saharan Africa?" *USA Today Magazine* (July):34–36.

Bryjak, George J. and Michael P. Soroka. 1994. *Sociology: Cultural Diversity in a Changing World,* 2nd ed. Boston: Allyn & Bacon.

Daly, Herman E. 1991. "From Empty-World to Full-World Economics: Reorganizing a Historical Turning Point in Economic Development." In *Environmentally Sustainable Development: Building on Brundtland,* ed. Robert J. A. Goodland, Herman E. Daly, Salah El Serafy, and Bernd von Droste. Paris: United Nations Education, Scientific, and Cultural Organization.

DeBlij, H. J. and Peter O. Muller. 1997. *Geography: Realms, Regions, and Concepts,* 8th ed. New York: John Wiley & Sons.

Hardin, Garett J. 1977. *The Limits of Altruism: An Ecologist's View of Survival.* Bloomington, IN: Indiana University Press.

Klare, Michael T. 1992. "We Must Hear the Third World." *The Progressive* (April):19–21.

Linden, Eugene. 1996. "The Exploding Cities of the Developing World." *Foreign Affairs* (January/February):52–65.

Mann, Charles C. 1993. "How Many Is Too Many?" *Atlantic Monthly* (February):47–67.

Marger, Martin N. 1997. *Race and Ethnic Relations: American and Global Perspectives,* 4th ed. Belmont, CA: Wadsworth.

Massignon, Nicole. 1993. "The Urban Explosion in the Third World." *The OECD Observer* (June/July):18–22.

Maybury-Lewis, David. 1992. *Millennium: Tribal Wisdom and the Modern World.* New York: Viking.

Newland, Kathleen. 1994. "Refugees: The Rising Flood." *World Watch* (May/June):10–20.

Palen, J. John. 1987. *The Urban World.* 3rd ed. New York: McGraw-Hill.

Pedraza, Silvia and Ruben G. Rumbaut. 1996. *Origins and Destinies: Immigration, Race, and Ethnicity in America.* Belmont, CA: Wadsworth.

Population Reference Bureau. 1997. *1997 World Population Data Sheet.* Washington, DC: Author.

Postel, Sandra. 1994. "Carrying Capacity: Earth's Bottom Line." In *State of the World 1994: A Worldwatch Institute Report on Progress Toward a Sustainable Society.* New York: W. W. Norton.

Queen, S. A. and R. W. Habenstein. 1974. *The Family in Various Cultures,* 4th ed. Philadelphia: J. B. Lippincott.

Ray, James Lee. 1995. *Global Politics,* 6th ed. Boston: Houghton Mifflin.

Reuters Service. 1994. "Vatican, Family Planning Groups Ready to Square Off in UN Debate." *Chicago Tribune* (April 4):1.1.

Robertson, Ian. 1987. *Sociology,* 3rd ed. New York: Worth Publishers, Inc.

Sadik, Nafis. 1991. "World Population Continues to Rise." *The Futurist* (March/April):9–14.

Simmons, Alan B. 1992. "Sixty Million on the Move." *The UNESCO Courier* (January):30–33.

Sjoberg, Gideon. 1960. *The Preindustrial City.* New York: Free Press.

UN Population Fund. 1990. *The State of World Population, 1990.* New York: Author.

U.S. Immigration and Naturalization Service. 1991. *1990 Statistical Yearbook of the Immigration and Naturalization Service.* Washington, DC: U.S. Government Printing Office.

Wax, Murry L. 1981. *Indian Americans: Unity and Diversity.* Englewood Cliffs, NJ: Prentice Hall.

Weber, Peter. 1994. "Safeguarding Oceans." In *State of the World 1994: A Worldwatch Institute Report on Progress Toward a Sustainable Society.* New York: W. W. Norton.

Wirth, Louis. 1938. "Urbanization as a Way of Life." *American Journal of Sociology* 44:8–20.

Worldwatch Institute. 1994. *State of the World 1994: A Worldwatch Institute Report on Progress Toward a Sustainable Society.* New York: W. W. Norton.

CHAPTER SIX

Brown, Lester, Hal Kane, and David Malin Roodman. 1994. *Vital Signs 1994: The Trends That Are Shaping Our Future.* New York: W. W. Norton.

Bukro, Casey. 1994. "The Debate on Dioxin: Is It the No. 1 Environmental Hazard?" *Chicago Tribune* (September 22):3.1.

Caldicott, Helen. 1992. *Love This Planet: A Plan to Heal the Earth.* New York: W. W. Norton.

Carson, Rachel. 1962. *Silent Spring.* Boston: Houghton Mifflin.

"Centuries-Old Lead Fallout Is Still a Threat." 1994. *Chicago Tribune* (March 24):1.24.

Coleman, James W. and Donald R. Cressey. 1990. *Social Problems,* 4th ed. New York: Harper & Row.

Cowen, Robert C. 1994. "Scientists Question Global Warming Theory." *Christian Science Monitor* (September 14):8.

Cox, Paul A. and Michael J. Balick. 1994. "The Ethnobotanical Approach to Drug Discovery." *Scientific American* 270 (June):82–87.

Cunningham, William P. and Barbra W. Saigo. 1992. *Environmental Science: A Global Concern.* Dubuque, IA: William C. Brown.

Dasmann, Raymond. 1976. "Future Primitive: Ecosystem People versus Biosphere People." *CoEvolution Quarterly* (Fall):26–31.

Ehrlich, Paul R. 1968. *The Population Bomb.* New York: Ballantine Books.

Fox, Warwick. 1990. *Toward a Transpersonal Ecology: Developing New Foundations for Environmentalism.* Boston: Shambala.

Gallagher, James P. 1994. "Russians Suffer Effect of Deadly Environment." *Chicago Tribune* (October 7):7.1, 12.

Ganey, Terry. 1995. "How Waste Spill Wipes Out Fish as Panel Considers Restrictions." *St. Louis Post-Dispatch* (September 13):A.1, A.6.

Gore, Al. 1993. *Earth in the Balance: Ecology and the Human Spirit.* New York: Plume.

Henslin, James M. 1996. *Social Problems,* 4th ed. Upper Saddle River, NJ: Prentice Hall.

Holloway, Marguerite. 1994. "Diversity Blues: Oceanic Biodiversity Wanes as Scientists Ponder Solutions." *Scientific American* 271 (August):16.

Homer-Dixon, Thomas F. 1993. *Environmental Scarcity and Global Security.* Headline Series No. 300. Fall. New York: Foreign Policy Association.

Intergovernmental Panel on Climate Change (IPCC). 1992. *Climate Change 1992: The IPCC Supplementary Report.* Cambridge, UK: Cambridge University Press.

Kemp, David. 1990. *Global Environmental Issues: A Climatological Approach.* New York: Routledge.

Langone, John. 1989. "A Stinking Mess." *Time* (January 2):44–47.

Lean, Geoffrey and Don Hinrichsen. 1994. *Atlas of the Environment,* 2nd ed. New York: Perennial.

McNulty, Timothy J. 1995. "Two Groups Warn of Contaminated Drinking Water." *Chicago Tribune* (June 2):1.3.

Merchant, Carolyn. 1992. *Radical Ecology: The Search for a Livable World.* New York: Routledge.

Odum, Eugene P. 1993. *Ecology and Our Endangered Life-Support Systems,* 2nd ed. Sunderland, MA: Sinauer.

Passmore, John. 1974. *Man's Responsibility to Nature: Ecological Problems and Western Traditions.* New York: Scribners.

Pielke, Roger. 1994. "Don't Rely on Computer Models to Judge Global Warming." *Christian Scientist Monitor* (August 24):19.

Postel, Sandra. 1994. "Carrying Capacity: Earth's Bottom Line." In *State of the World 1994: A Worldwatch Institute Report on Progress Toward a Sustainable Society.* New York: W. W. Norton.

Sahlins, Marshall D. and Elman R. Service. 1960. *Evolution and Culture.* Ann Arbor, MI; University of Michigan Press.

Schmetzer, Uli. 1994. "In China, Pollution Can Turn Snowflakes Black." *Chicago Tribune* (November 2):1.1

Smil, Vaclav. 1994. *Global Ecology: Environmental Change and Social Flexibility.* New York: Routledge.

United Nations Conference on Environment and Development (UNCED). 1991. "PC/58 Ozone Depletion." Report to the Secretary-General of the Conference. New York: United Nations.

U.S. Bureau of the Census. 1993. *Statistical Abstract of the United States, 1993,* 113th ed. Washington, DC: U.S. Government Printing Office.

Wagner, Richard H. 1974. *Environment and Man,* 2nd ed. New York: W. W. Norton.

White, Stephen. 1995. *The Cambridge Companion to Habermas.* New York: Cambridge University Press.

Wilson, Edward O. 1992. *The Diversity of Life.* Cambridge, MA: Harvard University Press.

World Almanac 1993. 1993. New York: World Almanac.

"The Worst Is Yet to Come, Ozone Experts Report." 1994. *Chicago Tribune* (September 7):1.14.

CHAPTER SEVEN

Dahl, Robert A. 1982. *Dilemmas of Pluralistic Democracy: Autonomy vs. Control.* New Haven, CT: Yale University Press.

"Democracies Double in 20 Years." *Chicago Tribune* (16 December 1994):1.9.

Domhoff, G. William. 1990. *The Power Elite and the State: How Policy Is Made in America.* New York: Aldine de-Gruyter.

———. 1983. *Who Rules America Now?* Englewood Cliffs, NJ: Prentice Hall.

Dye, Thomas R. 1990. *Who's Running America: The Bush Era,* 5th ed. Englewood Cliffs, NJ: Prentice Hall.

Fukuyama, Francis. 1992. *The End of History and the Last Man.* New York: Free Press.

Homer-Dixon, Thomas F. 1994. "Environmental Scarcity and Intergroup Conflict." In *World Security: Challenges for a New Century,* ed. Michael T. Klare and Daniel C. Thomas. New York: St. Martin's Press.

———. 1993. *Environmental Scarcity and Global Security.* Headline Series. No. 300. Fall. New York: Foreign Policy Association.

Huntington, Samuel P. 1996. *The Clash of Civilizations and the Remaking of the World Order.* New York: Simon & Schuster.

Jowitt, Kenneth. 1993. "A World Without Leninism." In *Global Transformation and the Third World,* ed. Robert O. Slater, Barney M. Schulta, and Steven R. Door. Boulder, CO: Lynne Rienner.

Kaplan, David A. 1995. "Anger and Ambivalence." *Newsweek* (7 August):24–29.

Kegley, Charles W., Jr. and Eugene R. Wittkopf. 1995. *World Politics: Trends and Transformations,* 5th ed. New York: St. Martin's Press.

Klare, Michael T. 1993. "The New Challenges to Global Security." *Current History* (April):151–61.

Kline, Joe. 1995. "Stalking the Radical Middle." *Newsweek* (25 September):32–36.

Krauss, C. 1994. "U.S. Aware of Killing, Kept Ties to Salvadoran Rightists, Papers Suggest." *New York Times* (9 November):A.9.

McColm, R. Bruce. 1992. "Between Two Worlds." In *Freedom in the World: Political Rights and Civil Liberties 1991–1992,* ed. R. Bruce McColm, Dale Bricker, James Finn, Jonathan D. Karl, Douglas W. Payne, Joseph E. Ryan, and Georgy Zaryky. New York: Freedom House.

McMahon, Colin. 1996. "Guatemalan Village Women Unite." *Chicago Tribune* (10 October):1.20.

Michels, Robert. 1991. *Political Parties.* New York: Free Press.

Mills, C. Wright. 1956. *The Power Elite.* New York: Oxford University Press.

Page, Clarence. 1996. "Being the Butt of Reefer Jokes Has Its High Side." *Chicago Tribune* (21 July):1.19.

Petras, James and Morris Morley. 1991. "Latin America: Poverty of Democracy and the Democracy of Poverty." *Homines* 15/16 (October–December):74–94.

Polsby, Nelson W. 1959. "Three Problems in the Analysis of Community Power." *American Sociological Review* 24 (December):796–803.

Sitarz, Daniel, ed. 1994. *Agenda 21: The Earth Summit Strategy to Save Our Planet.* Boulder, CO: Earth Press.

U.S. Bureau of the Census. 1995. *Statistical Abstract of the United States, 1995,* 115th ed. Washington, DC: U.S. Government Printing Office.

CHAPTER EIGHT

Banfield, Edward C. 1974. *The Unheavenly City Revisited.* Boston: Little, Brown.

Batra, Ravi. 1988. *The Great Depression of 1990.* New York: Dell.

Borthwick, Mark. 1992. *Pacific Century: The Emergence of Modern Pacific Asia.* Boulder, CO: Westview Press.

Braun, Denny. 1997. *The Rich Get Richer: The Rise of Income Inequality in the United States and the World,* 2nd ed. Chicago: Nelson-Hall.

Chapman, Stephen. 1997. "Sugar-Coated Subsidies." *Chicago Tribune* (20 July):1.15.

Epstein, Jack. 1994. "Chile's Economy Still Bustling." *Christian Science Monitor* (8 December):90.

Etzioni, Amitai. 1988. *The Moral Dimension: Toward a New Economics.* New York: Free Press.

French, Hilary F. 1994. "Rebuilding the World Bank." In *The State of the World 1994: A Worldwatch Institute Report on Progress Toward a Sustainable Society.* New York: W. W. Norton.

Goozner, Merril. 1997. "Leaving the Dole: Many Call, Few Chosen." *Chicago Tribune* (20 July):1.4.

Jackson, Robert M., ed. 1995. *Annual Editions: Global Issues 95/96,* 11th ed. Guilford, CT: Dushkin.

Institute on Hunger and Development. 1992. *Hunger 1992: The 2nd Annual Report on the State of World Hunger.* Washington, DC: Author.

Kegley, Charles W., Jr. and Eugene R. Wittkopf. 1995. *World Politics: Trends and Transformation,* 5th ed. New York: St. Martin's Press.

Kerbo, H. R. 1991. *Social Stratification and Inequality.* New York: McGraw-Hill.

Kidder, Rushworth M. 1988. "The North-South Affluence Gap." *The Christian Science Monitor* (25 July):B6–B8.

Kristof, Nicholas D. 1993. "China Sees 'Market-Leninism' as Way to Future." *New York Times* (6 September):1, 5.

Lenski, Gerhard and Jean Lenski. 1987. *Human Societies: An Introduction to Macrosociology,* 5th ed. New York: McGraw-Hill.

Lewis, Oscar. 1961. *The Children of Sanchez.* New York: Random House.

Longworth, R. C. 1996. "Corporate Giants Dwarf Many Nations." *Chicago Tribune* (11 October):1.1, 28.

———. 1997. "Backlash at the Global Economy." *Chicago Tribune* (28 September):1.1, 10.

Macionis, John J. 1997. *Sociology,* 6th ed. Upper Saddle River, NJ: Prentice Hall.

Raymond, Nicholas. 1993. "The 'Lost Decade' of Development: The Role of Debt, Trade, and Structural Adjustment." In *Global Issues 93/94,* 9th ed., ed. Robert M. Jackson. Guilford, CT: Dushkin.

Rich, Bruce. 1994. *Mortgaging the Earth: The World Bank, Environmental Impoverishment, and the Crisis of Development.* Boston: Beacon.

Rifkin, Jeremy. 1996. *The End of Work: The Decline of the Global Labor Force and the Dawn of the Post-Market Era.* New York: Putnam.

Rubin, Beth A. 1996. *Shifts in the Social Contract: Understanding Change in American Society.* Thousand Oaks, CA: Pine Forge.

Sitarz, Daniel, ed. 1994. *Agenda 21: The Earth Summit Strategy to Save Our Planet.* Boulder, CO: Earth Press.

UNCED (United Nations Conference on Environment and Development). 1991. "PC/46 Environment and Development." Report to the Secretary-General of the Conference, August 2, 1991. New York: United Nations.

U.S. Bureau of the Census. 1996a. "Table A. Persons and Families in Poverty by Selected Characteristics: 1996 and 1995." Electronic transmission. Available at: *http://www.census.gov/ftp/pub/hhes/poverty/pov95/povest1.html*

———. 1996b. "Table 1. Weighted Average Poverty Thresholds for Families of Specific Size." Electronic transmission. Available at: *http://www.census.gov/income95/income95hi.html*

Wolff, Edward N. 1995. "The Rich Get Increasingly Richer: Latest Data on Household Wealth During the 1980s." *Research in Politics and Society* 5:32–68.

World Bank. 1990. *World Development Report, 1990.* New York: Oxford University Press.

———. 1991. *World Development Report, 1991: The Challenge of Development.* New York: Oxford University Press.

———. 1994. *World Development Report, 1994: Infrastructure for Development.* New York: Oxford University Press.

World Commission on Environment and Development. 1987. *Our Common Future.* New York: Oxford University Press.

"World's Jobless Hits 1 Billion; Debt Reduction Plans Blamed." 1996. Dupage County, Illinois *Daily Herald.*

PART THREE INTRODUCTION

Hobshawn, Eric J. 1959. *Primitive Rebels.* New York: Norton.

Hofstadter, Richard. 1965. *The Paranoid Style in American Politics.* New York: Knopf.

Kegan, Robert. 1994. *In Over Our Heads: The Mental Demands of Modern Life.* Cambridge, MA: Harvard University Press.

Lipset, Seymour Martin and Earl Raab. 1970. *The Politics of Unreason.* New York: Harper & Row.

Wilson, Bryan R. 1973. *Magic and the Millennium: A Sociological Study of Religious Movements of Protest Among Tribal and Third-World People.* New York: Harper & Row.

Yablonksy, Lewis. 1972. *The Violent Gang.* Baltimore: Penguin.

CHAPTER NINE

Anderson, Margeret L. 1993. *Thinking About Women: Sociological Perspectives on Sex and Gender,* 3rd ed. New York: Macmillan.

Anderson, John Ward and Molly Moore. 1993. "The Burden of Womanhood." *The Washington Post (National Weekly Edition)* (22–28 March):6–7.

Applebaum, Richard and William J. Chambliss. 1995. *Sociology.* New York: HarperCollins.

Barr, Cameron. 1992. "Female Empowerment Leads to Fewer Births." *The Christian Science Monitor* (8 July):14.

Bitensky, Susan. 1996. "Final Straw: To Spank or Not to Spank." *Chicago Tribune* (25 July):1.25.

Bonvillain, Nancy. 1998. *Women and Men: Cultural Constructs of Gender,* 2nd ed. Upper Saddle River, NJ: Prentice Hall.

Browne, Angela. 1987. *When Women Kill.* New York: Free Press.

Collins, Randall and Scott Coltrane. 1995. *Sociology of Marriage and the Family: Gender, Love, and Property,* 4th ed. Chicago: Nelson-Hall.

Cyrus, Virginia. 1993. *Experiencing Race, Class, and Gender in the United States.* Mountain View, CA: Mayfield.

Dorkenoo, Efua. 1994. *Cutting the Rose: Female Genital Mutilation: The Practice and Its Prevention.* London: Minority Rights Group.

Federal Bureau of Investigation. 1992. *Hate Crimes in the U.S.* Washington, DC: U.S. Government Printing Office.

Fingerhut, Louis A. and Joel C. Kleinman. 1990. "International and Interstate Comparison of Homicide Among Young Males." *Journal of the American Medical Association* 263 (17 June):3292–95.

Gelles, Richard J. and Murray A. Strauss. 1988. *Intimate Violence.* New York: Simon & Schuster.

Giddens, Anthony. 1996. *Introduction to Sociology,* 2nd ed. New York: W. W. Norton.

Goodwin, Jan. 1996. "The State of Women in the World." *Cosmopolitan*(June):225–27.

Gordon, Linda. 1988. *Heroes of Their Own Lives: The Politics and History of Family Violence.* New York: Viking Press.

Graham, Patricia Albjerg. 1978. "Expansion and Exclusion: A History of Women in American Higher Education." *Signs* 3 (Summer).

Heise, Lori. 1989. "The Global War Against Women." *The Washington Post* (9 April).

Hochschild, Arlie R. with Anne Machung. 1989. *The Second Shift: Working Parents and the Revolution at Home.* New York: Viking.

Human Rights Watch Women's Rights Project. 1995. *The Human Rights Watch Global Report on Women's Human Rights.* New York: Human Rights Watch.

Kristof, Nicholas D. 1995. "China's Crackdown on Births: A Stunning, and Harsh Success." *New York Times (International)* (25 April):1,6.

Lamanna, Mary Ann and Agnes Riedmann. 1997. *Marriages and Families: Making Choices in a Diverse Society,* 6th ed. Belmont, CA: Wadsworth.

Lindsey, Linda L. 1997. *Gendered Roles: A Sociological Perspective,* 3rd ed. Upper Saddle River, NJ: Prentice Hall.

Matthaei, Julie A. 1982. *An Economic History of Women in America.* New York: Schocken Books.

Morrow, Lance. 1993. "Behavior: Rape and War." *Time Magazine* (22 February):48–50.

Negrey, Cynthia. 1993. *Gender, Time, and Reduced Work.* Albany: State University of New York Press.

Pollitt, Kathe. 1996. "Women's Rights, Human Rights." *Nation* (13 May):9.

Reuters Service. 1994. "Vatican, Family Planning Groups Ready to Square Off in UN Debate." *Chicago Tribune* (4 April):1.1.

Ries, Paula and Anne J. Stone, eds. 1992. *The American Woman, 1992–93: A Status Report.* New York: W. W. Norton.

Rhoodie, Eschel M. 1989. *Discrimination Against Women: A Global Survey of the Economic, Educational, Social, and Political Status of Women.* Jefferson, NC: McFarland.

Robertson, Ian. 1987. *Sociology,* 3rd ed. New York: Worth Publishers.

Rosenblum, Karen E. and Toni-Michelle C. Travis. 1996. *The Meaning of Difference: American Constructions of Race, Sex and Gender, Social Class, and Sexual Orientation.* New York: McGraw-Hill.

Ruth, Sheila. 1998. *Issues in Feminism: An Introduction to Women's Studies,* 4th ed. Mountain View, CA: Mayfield.

Safilos-Rothschild, C. 1974. *Women and Social Policy.* Englewood Cliffs, NJ: Prentice Hall.

Sandler, Bernice Resnick. 1987. "The Classroom Climate: Still a Chilly One for Women." In *Gendered Voices: Readings from an American Experience,* ed. by Karin Bergstrom-Costello. Fort Worth: Harcourt Brace.

Shapiro, Laura. 1998. "A Long Ride to Freedom." *Newsweek* (16 March):57.

Stockard, Jean and Miriam M. Johnson. 1992. *Sex and Gender in Society,* 2nd ed. Englewood Cliffs, NJ: Prentice Hall.

Straus, Murry A., Richard J. Gelles, and Suzanne K. Steinmetz. 1980. *Behind Closed Doors: Violence in the American Family.* Garden City, NY: Anchor Press/Doubleday.

Tannen, Deborah. 1990. *You Just Don't Understand: Women and Men in Conversation.* New York: Ballantine Books.

United Nations. 1995. *The World's Women, 1995: Trends and Statistics.* Social Statistics and Indicators, Series K12. New York: United Nations Publications.

Van der Gagg, Nikki. 1995. "Women: Still Something to Shout About." *The New Internationalist* (August):7–10.

Wills, Terrance. 1998. "Women's Work?" *Montreal Gazette* (4 May).

Wood, Julia T. 1997. *Gendered Lives: Communication, Gender, and Culture,* 2nd ed. Belmont, CA: Wadsworth.

Yoon, Youngik. 1994. "International Sexual Slavery." *Touro International Law Review* 6(1). Electronic transmission. Available at: *http://law.touro.edu/Publications/InternationalLawRev/vol6/PART7.html*

CHAPTER TEN

Black, D., J. Morris, C. Smith, and P. Townsend. 1982. *Inequities in Health: The Black Report.* New York: Penguin Books.

Bowles, Samuel and Herbert Gintis. 1976. *Schooling in Capitalist America: Education Reform and the Contradictions of American Life.* New York: Basic Books.

Brenner, M. 1984. *Estimating the Effects of Economic Change on National Health and Well-Being.* Washington, DC: U.S. Government Printing Office.

Claffey, Joan M. 1990. "The Donor Role in Instructional Improvement." In *Improving Educational Quality: A Global Perspective,* ed. David W. Chapman and Carol A. Carrier. New York: Greenwood.

Coleman, James S., Frederick Mostellerr, and Daniel P. Moynihan. 1966. *Equality of Educational Opportunity.* U.S. Department of Health, Education and Welfare. Washington, DC: U.S. Government Printing Office.

Collins, Randall. 1979. *The Credential Society: An Historical Sociology of the Effect of Family and Schooling in America.* New York: Basic.

Curran, Daniel J. and Claire M. Renzetti. 1990. *Social Problems,* 2nd ed. Needham Heights, MA: Allyn & Bacon.

Drugger, Brenda. 1997. "Antimicrobial Drug Resistance: A Danger to World Health." *Journal of Intravenous Nursing* 20:101–8.

Eglof, B., J. Lasker, S. Wolf, and L. Potvin. 1992. "Featuring Health Risks and Mortality: The Roseto Effect: A 50-Year Comparison of Mortality Rates." *American Journal of Public Health* 82:1089–92.

Fuller, Bruce. 1990. "What Investments Raise Achievement in the Third World?" In *Improving Educational Quality: A Global Perspective,* ed. David W. Chapman and Carol A. Carrier. New York: Greenwood Press.

Garenne, Michael and Peter Aaby. 1990. "Pattern of Exposure and Measles Mortality in Senegal." *Journal of Infectious Diseases* 161:1088–94.

Garrett, Laurie. 1994. *The Coming Plague: Newly Emerging Diseases in a World Out of Balance.* New York: Penguin Books.

Giddens, Anthony. 1991. *Introduction to Sociology.* New York: W. W. Norton.

Hassan, Fekri K. 1981. *Demographical Archaelogy.* New York: Academic Press.

Inkeles, A. and D. Smith. 1974. *Becoming Modern: Individual Change in Six Developing Countries.* Cambridge, MA: Harvard University Press.

Jencks, Christopher, et al. 1972. *Inequality: A Reassessment of the Effect of Family and Schooling in America.* New York: Basic.

Kitagawa, E. M. and P. M. Hauser. 1973. *Differential Mortality in the United States.* Cambridge, MA: Harvard University Press.

Kozol, Jonathan. 1980. *Prisoners of Silence: Breaking the Bonds of Adult Illiteracy in the United States.* New York: Continuum.

———. 1985a. "A Nation's Wealth." *Publisher's Weekly* (24 May):28–30.

———. 1985b. *Illiterate America.* Garden City, NY: Doubleday.

Lassey, Marie L., William R. Lassey, and Martin J. Links. 1997. *Health Care Systems Around the World: Characteristics, Issues, Reforms.* Upper Saddle River, NJ: Prentice Hall.

LeDuc, J. W. 1996. "World Health Organization Strategy for Emerging Infectious Diseases." *JAMA* 275:318–20.

Levy, Stuart B. 1992. *The Antibiotic Paradox: How Miracle Drugs Are Destroying the Miracle.* New York: Plenum.

Messec, Jerry L. 1990. "Language Issues and National Educational Systems: Experiences in African Developing Nations." In *Improving Educational Quality: A Global Perspective,* ed. David W. Chapman and Carol A. Carrier. New York: Greenwood Press.

Micozzi, Marc S. 1996. "Medicine for a Small Planet." *World Health* 49 (March–April):8–9.

National Center for Health Statistics. 1986. "Trends in Smoking, Alcohol Consumption, and Other Health Practices Among U.S. Adults, 1977 and 1983." DHEW Pub. No. (HRA) 86–1232. Washington, DC: U.S. Government Printing Office.

Oakes, Jeannie. 1985. *Keeping Track: How Schools Structure Inequality.* New Haven, CT: Yale University Press.

Ornish, Dean. 1997. *Love and Survival: The Scientific Basis for the Healing Power of Intimacy.* New York: HarperCollins.

Oxman, T. E., D. H. Freeman Jr., and E. D. Manheimer. 1995. "Lack of Social Participation or Religious Strength and Comfort as Risk Factors for Death After Cardiac Surgery in the Elderly." *Psychosomatic Medicine* 57:5–15.

Pedersen, Daniel and Eric Larson. 1997. "Too Poor to Treat." *Newsweek* (28 July):60.

Peterson, Don and Steve Kelly. 1997. "Antibiotic Resistance—Is the Plague Coming?" *Chiropractic News* (17 November):32–33, 42.

Platt, Anne E. 1996. "Confronting Infectious Disease." In *State of the World, 1996.* New York: W. W. Norton.

Population Reference Bureau. 1997. *1997 World Population Data Sheet.* Washington, DC: Author.

Robertson, Ian. 1987. *Sociology,* 3rd ed. New York: Worth.

Sagan, Leonard A. 1987. *The Health of Nations: True Causes of Sickness and Well-Being.* New York: Basic Books.

St. Leger, A., A. Cochrane, and F. Moore. 1978. "The Anomaly That Won't Go Away." *Lancet* 2:1153.

Seppala, H., T. Klaukka, J. Vuopio-Varkila, et al. 1997. "The Effect of Changes in the Consumption of Macrolide Antibiotics on Erythromycin Resistance in Group A Streptococci in Finland." *New England Journal of Medicine* 337:441–46.

Siegal, E., et al. 1985. "A Controlled Evaluation of Rural Regional Perinatal Care: Impact on Mortality and Morbidity." *American Journal of Public Health* 75:243–46.

Spiegel, D., J. R. Bloom, H. C. Kraemer, and E. Gottheil. 1989. "Effect of Psychosocial Treatment on Survival of Patients with Metastatic Breast Cancer." *Lancet* 2:888–91.

Spradley, B. W. and J. A. Alexander. 1996. *Community Health Nursing: Concepts and Practice.* New York: Lippincott.

Thiagarajan, Sivasailam. 1990. "An Integrated Approach to Primary School Teacher Support and Training." In *Improving Educational Quality: A Global Perspective,* ed. David W. Chapman and Carol A. Carrier. New York: Greenwood.

United Nations. 1991. *Women: Challenges to the Year 2000.* New York: United Nations Publications.

U.S. Bureau of the Census. 1995. *Statistical Abstract of the United States, 1995,* 115th ed. Washington, DC: U.S. Government Printing Office.

U.S. Bureau of the Census. 1993. *Statistical Abstract of the United States, 1993,* 113th ed. Washington, DC: U.S. Government Printing Office.

Union of International Associations. 1996. *Encyclopedia of World Problems and Human Potential.* Electronic transmission. Available at: *http://www.uia.org*

World Almanac. 1993. *The World Almanac and Book of Facts, 1993.* New York: St. Martin's Press.

World Health Organization. 1946. *Constitution of the World Health Organization.* New York: World Health Organization Interim Commission.

Zhang, Xiaouri. 1996. "Traditional Medicine and WHO." *World Health* 49 (March–April):4–5.

CHAPTER ELEVEN

"America's Immigrant Challenge." 1993. *Time.* Special Issue: "The New Face of America." (29 December). Electronic transmission. Available at: *http://web2.searchbank.com/infotrac/session/610/174/25365653w3/7!Xrn_1*

Berry, Brewton and Henry L. Tischler. 1978. *Race and Ethnic Relations,* 4th ed. Boston: Houghton Mifflin.

Booth, Cathy. 1993. "Miami: The Capital of Latin America." *Time* (29 December). Electronic transmission. Available at: *http:///web2.searchbank.com/infotrac/session/610/174/25365653w3/sig!4*

Chavez, Linda. 1991. *Out of the Barrio: Toward a New Politics of Assimilation.* New York: Basic Books.

Daniels, Roger. 1990. *Coming to America: A History of Immigration and Ethnicity in American Life.* New York: HarperCollins.

Faragher, John, Mari Jo Buhle, Daniel Czitrom, and Susan Armitage. 1994. *Out of Many: A History of the American People.* Englewood Cliffs, NJ: Prentice Hall.

Farley, John E. 1995. *Minority-Majority Relations,* 3rd ed. Englewood Cliffs, NJ: Prentice Hall.

Garza, Melita Marie. 1994. "Reforms Are Said to Shortchange Illegal Immigrants." *Chicago Tribune* (23 December). Electronic transmission. America Online.

Giddens, Anthony. 1991. *Introduction to Sociology.* New York: W. W. Norton.

Glastris, Paul. 1997. "The Alien Payoff." *U.S. News & World Report* (26 May):20–22.

Hacker, Andrew. 1995. *Two Nations: Black and White, Separate, Hostile, Unequal.* New York: Ballantine.

Homer-Dixon, Thomas F. 1994. "Environmental Scarcity and Intergroup Conflict." In *World Security: Challenges for a New Century,* ed. Michael T. Klare and Daniel C. Thomas. New York: St. Martin's Press.

Kane, Hal. 1994. "Refugee Flows Swelling." In *Vital Signs 1994: The Trends That Are Shaping Our Future,* ed. Lester R. Brown, Hal Hane, and David M. Roodman. New York: W. W. Norton.

Kivisto, Peter. 1995. *Americans All: Race and Ethnic Relations in Historical, Structural, and Comparative Perspectives.* Belmont, CA: Wadsworth.

Lauren, Paul Gordon. 1988. *Power and Prejudice: The Politics and Diplomacy of Racial Discrimination.* Boulder, CO: Westview Press.

Marden, Charles F., Gladys Meyer, and Madeline H. Engel. 1992. *Minorities in American Society,* 6th ed. New York: HarperCollins.

Marger, Martin N. 1997. *Race and Ethnic Relations: American and Global Perspectives,* 4th ed. Belmont, CA: Wadsworth.

Noel, Donald L. 1968. A Theory of Ethnic Stratification." *Social Problems* 16:157–72.

"The Numbers Game." 1993. *Time* (29 December). Electronic transmission. Available at: *http://web2.searchbank.com/infotrac/session/610/174/25365653/27!Xrn.77*

Paul, Ram. 1991. "Black and Third World Peoples' Citizenship and 1992." *Critical Social Policy* 11 (Autumn):52–64.

Pedalino-Porter, Rosalie. 1990. *Forked Tongue: The Politics of Bilingual Education.* New York: Basic Books.

Pedraza, Silvia and Ruben G. Rumbaut. 1996. *Origins and Destinies: Immigration, Race, and Ethnicity in America.* Belmont, CA: Wadsworth.

Robertson, Ian. 1987. *Sociology,* 3rd ed. New York: Worth.

Salins, Peter D. "Take a Ticket." *The New Republic* (13 December). Electronic transmission. Available at: *http://web2.searchbank.com/infotrac/session/610/174/25365653w3/sig!//*

Scholdolski, Vincent J. 1994. "NAFTA Helps Meld San Diego, Tijuana." *Chicago Tribune* (13 May):1.1, 1.8.

Snipp, C. Matthew. 1996. "The First Americans: American Indians." In *Origins and Destinies: Immigration, Race, and Ethnicity in America,* ed. Silvia Pedraza and Ruben G. Rumbaut. Belmont, CA: Wadsworth.

U.S. Bureau of the Census. 1991. *Statistical Abstract of the United States, 1993.* Current Population Reports. Series P23–185. Washington, DC: U.S. Government Printing Office.

Veltman, Calvin. 1988. *The Future of the Spanish Language in the United States.* Washington, DC: Hispanic Policy Development Project.

Vobejda, Barbara. 1991. "The Changing Face of America: Racial and Ethnic Shifts Are Remixing the Pot." *The Washington Post* (National Weekly Edition) (23–29 September):6–7.

Wilson, Bernice. 1994. "California Sues Federal Government for Immigration Money." America Online (29 April). Electronic transmission. America Online.

Wood, Deborah. 1989. "The Gap Between Striving and Achieving: The Case of Asian American Women." In *Making Waves: An Anthology of Writings By and About Asian American Women,* ed. Asia Women United of California. Boston: Beacon Press.

CHAPTER TWELVE

ACLU (American Civil Liberties Union). 1996. "Executive Summary of the House Terrorism Bill, H.R. 2768." February 9. Electronic transmission. Available at: *http://www.aclu.org/congress/hr2768.html*

Bagdikian, Ben. 1983. *The Media Monopoly.* Boston: Beacon.

Bailey, William C. 1990. Murder, Capital Punishment, and Television: Execution Publicity and Homicide Rates." *American Sociological Review* 54 (October):722–43.

Bailey, William C. and Ruth Peterson. 1989. "Murder and Capital Punishment: A Weekly Time-Series Analysis of Execution Publicity." *American Sociological Review* 54 (October):722–43.

Barry, John. 1995. "Future Shock." *Newsweek* (24 July): 32–33, 36–37.

"The Body Sellers: Hundreds of Thousands of Illegal Immigrants in Overseas Pipeline, Says State Dept." 1995. *Washington Times* (4 April). Electronic transmission. Available at: *http://www.fracus.org/member/newslett/smuggler.htm*

Bohm, Robert M. 1991. "American Death Penalty Opinion, 1936–1986: A Critical Examination of the Gallup Polls." In *The Death Penalty in America: Current Research,* ed. Robert M. Bohm. Cincinnati: Anderson.

Booth, Martin. 1991. *The Triads: The Chinese Criminal Fraternity.* New York: St. Martin's Press.

Center for National Security Studies. 1995. "Clinton Terrorism Legislation Threatens Constitutional Rights." (26 April). Electronic transmission. Available at: *http://www.terrorism.com/Index.htm*

Curran, Daniel J. and Claire M. Renzetti. 1990. *Social Problems,* 2nd ed. Needham Heights, MA: Allyn & Bacon.

DeVoss, David and Ron Gluckman. 1995. "Assault on the Dollar: Have Asian Gangs Mastered the Counterfeit $100 Bill?" Asia, Inc. Electronic transmission. Available at: *http://www.asia-inc.com/archive/dollar.html*

Fineman, Howard. 1996. "Bring on the Baby Boomers." *Newsweek* (26 August):18–25.

Gest, Ted and Victoria Pope. 1996. "Crime Time Bomb." *U.S. News & World Report* (26 March). Electronic transmission. Available at: *http://www.usnews.com/usnews/issue/crime/htm*

Goozner, Merril. 1995. "Fear Stalks Japan After Cult Warning." *Chicago Tribune* (15 April):1.1, 1.2.

———. 1996. "Crazed Teens at Large? Facts Don't Fit Image." *Chicago Tribune* (14 July):2.5.

Grasy, Malcom. 1995. "A Nation in Mourning." *McLeans* (13 March):44.

Greene, Bob. 1996. "Land of the Free? Not America, Not in 1996." *Chicago Tribune* (14 August):5.1.

Henslin, James M. 1996. *Social Problems*, 4th ed. Upper Saddle River, NJ: Prentice Hall.

Jerold, M. 1990. "Superterrorism: Biological, Chemical, and Nuclear." *Terrorism* 13:165–68.

Kaplan, Joel. 1996. "Drug Use Rising Among Youths, New Study Says." *Chicago Tribune* (21 August):1.1, 14.

Kappeler, Victor E., Mark Blumberg, and Gary W. Potter. 1996. *The Mythology of Crime and Criminal Justice*, 2nd ed. Prospect Heights, IL: Waveland.

Kidder, Rushworth M. 1990. "Why Modern Terrorism?" In *International Terrorism: Characteristics, Causes, and Controls*, ed. Charles Kegley, Jr. New York: St. Martin's Press.

Lipset, Seymour M. 1960. *The Political Man: The Social Bases of Politics*. Garden City, NY: Doubleday.

Lungren, Daniel E. 1966. "Russian Organized Crime." State of California. Office of the Attorney General. Electronic transmission. Available at: *http://www.laren.ns.net/org/gangs/RUSORCHTM*

Madigan, Charles M. 1996. "The Global Scourge of Terrorism." *Chicago Tribune* (1 August):1.1, 12, 13.

McColm, R. Bruce. 1992. "Between Two Worlds." In *Freedom in the World: Political Rights and Civil Liberties 1991–1992*, ed. R. Bruce McColm, Dale Bricker, James Finn, Jonathan D. Karl, Douglas W. Payne, Joseph E. Ryan, and Georgy Zaryky. New York: Freedom House.

McMahon, Colin. 1998. "NATO Displays Might, Yeltsen to Talk with Milosevic over Kosovo." *Chicago Tribune* (16 June). Electronic transmission. Available at: *http://progwest.umi.com/pgdweb?RQT=395+5htm=901134413*

Merton, Robert K. 1957. *Social Theory and Social Structure*, rev. ed. Glencoe, IL: Free Press.

Metz, Steven. 1995. "To Insure Domestic Tranquility: Terrorism and the Price of Global Engagement." Electronic transmission. Available at: *terrorism.com/Index.htm*

Milgram, Stanley. 1974. *Obedience to Authority: An Experimental View*. New York: Harper & Row.

Myers, Linnet. 1995. "Cultural Divide over Crime and Punishment." *Chicago Tribune* (13 October):1.1, 8.

Page, Clarence. 1996. "Death Undeserved: Innocents Are the Death Penalty's Dirty Little Secret." *Chicago Tribune* (10 July):1.9.

Parenti, Michael. 1986. *Inventing Reality*. New York: St. Martin's Press.

"Prison Population Doubles in Decade." 1996. *Chicago Tribune* (19 August):1.3.

Renner, Michael. 1994. "Nuclear Arsenals Shrinking." In *Vital Signs 1994: The Trends That Are Shaping Our Future*, ed. Lester R. Brown, Hal Hane, and David M. Roodman. New York: W. W. Norton.

"Reno Chides Congress's Drug Effort." *Chicago Tribune* (19 August):1.3.

Rifkin, Jeremy. 1996. *The End of Work: The Decline of the Global Labor Force and the Dawn of the Post-Market Era*. New York: Putnam.

Shabalin, Victor, J. L. Albini, and R. E. Rogers. 1995. "The New Stage of the Fight Against Organized Crime in Russia." The Joint Russia/American Committee for the Promotion of the Study of Comparative Criminal Justice. Electronic transmission. Available at: *http://www.acsp.uic.edu/iasoc/newstage.htm*

Timasheff, Nicholas S. 1965. In *War and Revolution*, ed. Joseph F. Sheuer. New York: Sheed and Ward.

United Nations Commission for Social Development. 1995. *Report on the Thirty-Fourth Session*. New York: United Nations.

U.S. Bureau of the Census. 1995. *Statistical Abstract of the United States, 1995*, 115th ed. Washington, DC: U.S. Government Printing Office.

van den Haag, Ernest and John P. Conrad. 1983. *The Death Penalty: A Debate*. New York: Plenum.

Weiner, Tim. 1994. "CIA-Formed Unit Later Tied to Narcotics Trade." *New York Times* (14 November):1, 12.

"Youth Crime on the Decline, Report Shows." DuPage County, Illinois *Daily Herald*.

EPILOGUE

Anderson, Benedict. 1983. *Imagined Community: Reflections on the Origin and Spread of Nationalism*. New York: Verso.

Barbour, Ian. 1993. *Ethics in an Age of Technology*. San Francisco: Harper.

Bell, Wendell. 1996. "World Order, Human Values, and the Future." *Futures Research Quarterly* 12 (Spring).

Brown, Lester R. 1993. "A New Era Unfolds." In *State of the World, 1993*, ed. Lester R. Brown. New York: W. W. Norton.

———. "The Acceleration of History." In *State of the World, 1996*, ed. Lester R. Brown. New York: W. W. Norton.

Coles, Romand. 1995. "Identity and Difference in the Ethical Positions of Adorno and Habermas." In *The Cambridge Companion to Habermas*, ed. Stephen K. White. Cambridge: Cambridge University Press.

Harman, Willis. 1976. *An Incomplete Guide to the Future*. Stanford, CA: Stanford University Press.

———. 1988. *Global Mind Change: The Promise of the Last Years of the Twentieth Century*. Indianapolis: Knowledge Systems.

Inglehart, Ronald. 1990. *Cultural Shift in Advanced Industrial Society*. Princeton, NJ: Princeton University Press.

Kidder, Rushworth. 1994. *Shared Values for a Troubled World*. San Francisco: Jossey-Bass.

Küng, Hans. 1998. *A Global Ethic for Global Politics and Economics*. New York: Oxford University Press.

Lyons, Oren. 1994. [Speech before the United Nations, 10 December 1992.] In *Voices of Indigenous People,* ed. Alexander Ewen. Sante Fe, NM: Clear Light.

Milbrath, Lester. 1989. *Envisioning a Sustainable Society.* Albany: State University of New York Press.

Polak, Fred. 1973. *The Image of the Future.* New York: Elsevier Scientific Publishing Company.

Ray, Paul H. 1996. "The Rise of Integral Culture." *Noetic Sciences Review* 37 (Spring):5–15.

Selznick, Philip. 1992. *The Moral Commonwealth: Social Theory and the Promise of Community.* Los Angeles: University of California Press.

Wildavsky, A. and M. Singer. 1993. *The Real World Order.* Chatham, NJ: Chatham House.

Photo Credits

Chapter One: Page 2, AP/Wide World Photos; p. 7, Michael Mancuso/Omni-Photo Communications, Inc.; p. 11, Corbis-Bettmann; p. 14, Steve Norgan, Spooner/Liaison Agency, Inc.; p. 19, The Travelers; p. 21, B. K. Bangash/AP/Wide World Photos; p. 26, Charles Gatewood/Simon & Schuster/PH College.

Chapter Two: Page 36, Kaku Kurita/Liaison Agency, Inc.; p. 46, UPI/Corbis-Bettmann; p. 54, Paul Conklin/PhotoEdit; p. 58, David Brauchli/AP/Wide World Photos; p. 64, Alan G. Dejecacion/Liaison Agency, Inc.

Chapter Three: Page 72, Kamran Jebreili/AP/Wide World Photos; p. 82, Barry Jarvinen/AP/Wide World Photos; p. 88, Shahriar Saeedvafa/Corbis-Bettmann; p. 97, Robert Fried/Stock Boston; p. 99, Pat Sullivan/AP/Wide World Photos.

Chapter Four: Page 108, Michael Rosenfeld/Tony Stone Images; p. 111, Bruce Ayres/Tony Stone Images; p. 118, Baldwin H. Ward/Corbis-Bettmann; p. 125, John Chiasson/Liaison Agency, Inc.; p. 131, Kent F. Berg/The Herald/LiaisonAgency, Inc.

Chapter Five: Page 144, Corbis-Bettmann; p. 146, Alain Evrard/Photo Researchers, Inc.; p. 151, Alison Wright/Photo Researchers, Inc.; p. 161, Food and Agriculture Organization of the UN; p. 168, John Littlewood/United Nations.

Chapter Six: Page 177, John McConnico/AP/Wide World Photos; p. 182, NASA Headquarters; p. 187, National Oceanic and Atmospheric Administration/Seattle; p. 195, Brian Parker/Tom Stack & Associates; p. 201,Don Ryan AP/Wide World Photos

Chapter Seven: Page 208, Anthony Suau/Liaison Agency, Inc.; p. 220, AP/Wide World Photos; p. 224, Katsumi Kasahara/AP/Wide World Photos; p. 226, Robert Brenner/PhotoEdit; p. 229, David Woo/Liaison Agency, Inc.

Chapter Eight: Page 238, Richard Laird/FPG International LLC; p. 246, AP/Wide World Photos; p. 248, Peter Menzel/Stock Boston; p. 257, Mark Richards/PhotoEdit; p. 266, Stephen Ferry/Liaison Agency, Inc.

Chapter Nine: Page 282, Mike Fiala/AP/Wide World Photos; p. 285, John Chiasson/Liaison Agency, Inc.; p. 293, George Holton/UNICEF/ICEF 4788/Holton; p. 302, Mark Richards/PhotoEdit; p. 307, Jack Star/PhotoDisc., Inc.

Chapter Ten: Page 313, Bernard Pierre Wolff/Photo Researchers, Inc.; p. 317, Andrew Holbrooke/The Stock Market; p. 322, David Longstreath/AP/Wide World Photos; p. 335, Alan McEvoy/Simon & Schuster/PH College; p. 342, Jeffrey W. Myers/Stock Boston.

Chapter Eleven: Page 350, Zoom 77/AP/Wide World Photos; p. 358, Peter Northall/AP/Wide World Photos; p. 362, Chuck Savage/The Stock Market; p. 367, UPI/Corbis-Bettmann; p. 374, Archive Photos.

Chapter Twelve: Page 380, Defense Nuclear Agency; p. 384, Paul McErlane/AP/Wide World Photos; p. 389, Lynne Sladky/AP/Wide World Photos; p. 396, Michael Newman/PhotoEdit; p. 401, Jack Plunkett/AP/Wide World Photos.

Name Index

Subject Index